Plan of the Book

CONTINUED ON [illegible] →

Plan of the Book

Thirteenth Edition

The Little, Brown Handbook

H. Ramsey Fowler
St. Edward's University

Jane E. Aaron

PEARSON

Boston Columbus Hoboken Indianapolis New York San Francisco
Amsterdam Cape Town Dubai London Madrid Milan
Munich Paris Montréal Toronto Delhi Mexico City São Paulo
Sydney Hong Kong Seoul Singapore Taipei Tokyo

Vice President and Editor in Chief: Joseph Opiela
Program Manager: Eric Jorgensen
Senior Development Editor: Anne Brunell Ehrenworth
Product Marketing Manager: Ali Arnold
Executive Field Marketing Manager: Joyce Nilsen
Executive Digital Producer: Stefanie A. Snajder
Content Specialist: Erin Jenkins
Project Manager: Savoula Amanatidis
Project Coordination, Text Design, and Page Makeup: Cenveo® Publisher Services
Design Lead and Cover Designer: Heather Scott
Cover Images: *Left*: Stack of reading material (Jocic/Shutterstock); *Right*: Laptop (Boule/Shutterstock)
Photo Research: QBS Learning
Senior Manufacturing Buyer: Roy L. Pickering, Jr.
Printer and Binder: R. R. Donnelley and Sons Company–Crawfordsville
Cover Printer: R. R. Donnelley and Sons Company–Crawfordsville

Acknowledgments of third-party content appear on page 847 and constitute an extension of the copyright page.

Library of Congress Cataloging-in-Publication Data
Fowler, H. Ramsey (Henry Ramsey)
The Little, Brown handbook / H. Ramsey Fowler, Jane E. Aaron.—Thirteenth edition.
pages cm
Includes bibliographical references and index.
ISBN 978-0-321-98827-0
1. English language–Grammar–Handbooks, manuals, etc. 2. English language—Rhetoric—Handbooks, manuals, etc. 3. Report writing–Handbooks, manuals, etc. I. Aaron, Jane E. II. Title.
PE1112.F64 2016
808'.042–dc23
2014041651

---

1 16

Student Edition
ISBN-10: 0-13-458633-6
ISBN-13: 978-0-13-458633-5

À La Carte Edition
ISBN-10: 0-13-458263-2
ISBN-13: 978-0-13-458263-4

www.pearsonhighered.com

Preface for Students: Using This Book

The Little, Brown Handbook is a basic resource that will answer almost any question you have about writing. Here you can find how to get ideas, develop paragraphs, punctuate quotations, find sources for research projects, cite sources, or write a résumé. The handbook can help you not only in writing courses but also in other courses and outside of school.

Don't let the size of the handbook put you off. You need not read the whole book to get something out of it, and no one expects you to know everything included. Primarily a reference tool, the handbook is written and arranged to help you find the answers you need when you need them, quickly and easily.

Using this book will not by itself make you a good writer; for that, you need to care about your work at every level, from finding a subject to spelling words. But learning how to use the handbook and its information can give you the means to write *what* you want in the *way* you want.

Reference aids

You have many ways to find what you need in the handbook:

- **Use the directory.** "Plan of the Book," inside the front cover, displays the book's entire contents.
- **Use a glossary.** "Glossary of Usage" (pp. 807–23) clarifies more than 275 words that are commonly confused and misused. "Glossary of Terms" (pp. 824–46) defines more than 350 words used in discussing writing.
- **Use the index.** Beginning on page 849, the extensive index includes every term, concept, and problem word or expression mentioned in the book.
- **Use a list.** Three helpful aids fall inside the book's back cover: (1) "CULTURE LANGUAGE Guide" pulls together all the book's material for students who are using standard American English as a second language or a second dialect. (2) "Editing Symbols" explains abbreviations often used to comment on papers. And (3) "Useful Lists and Summaries" indexes topics that students frequently ask about.
- **Use the elements of the page.** As shown in the illustration on the next page, the handbook constantly tells you where you are and what you can find there.

Content and organization

An overview of the handbook's contents appears inside the front cover. Briefly, the book divides into the following sections.

The handbook's page elements

Running head (header) showing the topic being discussed on this page

325 Adjectives and adverbs

16 Adjectives and Adverbs

Chapter essentials summarizing key concepts and learning objectives

Chapter essentials

- Use adjectives only to modify nouns and pronouns (below).
- After a linking verb, use an adjective to modify the subject (p. 326).
- After a direct object, use an adjective to modify the object and an adverb to modify the verb (p. 327).
- Use comparative and superlative forms appropriately (p. 327).
- Avoid most double negatives (p. 329).
- Use nouns sparingly as modifiers (p. 330).
- Distinguish between present and past participles as adjectives (p. 330).
- Use *a, an, the,* and other determiners appropriately (p. 331).

Link to *MyWritingLab*, with the eText and other resources

Visit MyWritingLab™ for more resources on adjectives and adverbs.

Page tab containing the section code (**16a**) and editing symbol (**ad**)

ad 16a

Adjectives and adverbs are modifiers that describe, restrict, or otherwise qualify the words to which they relate.

Summary or checklist box providing key information in accessible form

Functions of adjectives and adverbs

Adjectives modify nouns:	serious student
pronouns:	ordinary one
Adverbs modify verbs:	warmly greet
adjectives:	only three people
adverbs:	quite seriously
phrases:	nearly to the edge of the cliff
clauses:	just when we arrived
sentences:	Fortunately, she is employed.

Culture-language connection, a pointer for students using standard American English as a second language or a second dialect

CULTURE LANGUAGE In standard American English an adjective does not change along with the noun it modifies to show plural number: *white* [not *whites*] *shoes, square* [not *squares*] *spaces.* Only nouns form plurals.

Section heading, a main convention or topic labeled with the section code, **16a**: chapter number (**16**) and section letter (**a**)

16a Use adjectives only to modify nouns and pronouns.

Adjectives modify only nouns and pronouns. Do not use adjectives instead of adverbs to modify verbs, adverbs, or other adjectives:

Examples, always indented, with underlining and annotations highlighting sentence elements and revisions

Faulty The groups view family values different.

Revised The groups view family values differently.

Exercise providing opportunity for practice

Exercise 16.1 Revising: Adjectives and adverbs

Revise the following sentences so that adjectives and adverbs are used appropriately. If any sentence is already correct as given, mark the number preceding it.

Example:

The announcer warned that traffic was moving very slow.
The announcer warned that traffic was moving very slowly.

1. People who take their health serious often believe that movie-theater popcorn is a healthy snack.
2. Nutrition information about movie popcorn may make these people feel different.
3. One large tub of movie popcorn has twelve hundred calories and sixty grams of saturated fat—both surprisingly high numbers.
4. Once people are aware of the calories and fat, they may feel badly about indulging in this classic snack.

- **Chapters 1–5:** The writing process, writing and revising paragraphs, and presenting your writing in print, online, and orally.
- **Chapters 6–11:** Reading and writing in and out of college, with chapters on academic writing, critical reading and writing, reading arguments, writing arguments, essay exams, and public writing.
- **Chapters 12–26:** Sentence basics, including the conventions of English grammar, errors that affect clarity, and techniques of effective sentences.
- **Chapters 27–36:** Punctuation and mechanics (capital letters, italics, and the like).
- **Chapters 37–40:** Words—how to use them appropriately and precisely, how to edit them for conciseness, how to spell them.
- **Chapters 41–48:** Research writing, from planning through revising, with detailed help on finding and evaluating sources, avoiding plagiarism, and citing sources, along with two annotated sample papers.
- **Chapters 49–52:** Writing in the academic disciplines, including concepts, tools, and source citations in literature, other humanities, the social sciences, and the natural and applied sciences.

Recommended usage

The conventions described and illustrated in this handbook are those of standard American English—the label given the dialect used in higher education, business, and the professions. (See also pp. 141–43.) The handbook stresses written standard English, which is more conservative than the spoken dialect in matters of grammar and usage. A great many words and constructions that are widely spoken remain unaccepted in careful writing.

When clear distinctions exist between the language of conversation and that of careful writing, the handbook provides examples of each and labels them *spoken* and *written*. When usage in writing itself varies with the level of formality intended, the handbook labels examples *formal* and *informal*. When usage is mixed or currently changing, the handbook recommends that you choose the more conservative usage because it will be accepted by all readers.

Preface for Instructors

The Little, Brown Handbook always addresses both the current and the recurrent needs of writing students and teachers. This thirteenth edition is no exception. Writing and its teaching change continuously, and the handbook has changed substantially in content. At the same time, much about writing does not change, and the handbook remains a comprehensive, clear, and accessible guide to a host of writing situations and challenges.

The Little, Brown Handbook is actually many books in one, and each is stronger in this edition. The revisions—highlighted below with New—affect most pages.

A guide to academic writing

The handbook gives students a solid foundation in the goals and requirements of college writing.

- New The chapter on academic writing, now at the start of Part 2, includes a greatly expanded overview of common academic genres, such as responses, critical analyses, arguments, informative and personal writing, and research papers and reports. The discussion highlights key features of each genre and points students to examples in the handbook.
- New Eighteen examples of academic writing in varied genres appear throughout the handbook, among them a new critical analysis of an advertisement and a new social-science research report documented in APA style.
- New With each of the sample papers, a summary box titled "The writing situation" gives an overview of the situation to which the student responded—subject, purpose, audience, genre, and use of sources—thus connecting concepts with actual writing.
- New Emphasizing critical analysis and writing, the expanded chapter on critical reading and writing includes two full-length opinion pieces as exercises in critical reading, a new advertisement with a student's analysis, a revised discussion of writing critically about texts and visuals, and a new critical analysis paper.
- New Pulling together key material on academic integrity, Chapter 6 on academic writing and Chapter 44 on plagiarism discuss developing one's own perspective on a topic, using and managing sources, and avoiding plagiarism. Other chapters throughout the handbook reinforce these important topics.
- Synthesis receives special emphasis wherever students might need help balancing their own and others' views, such as in responding to texts and visuals.

- Parts 9 and 10 give students a solid foundation in research writing and writing in the disciplines (literature, other humanities, social sciences, natural and applied sciences), along with extensive coverage of documentation in MLA, Chicago, APA, and CSE styles.

A guide to research writing

With detailed advice, the handbook always attends closely to research writing. The discussion stresses using the library Web site as the gateway to finding sources, managing information, evaluating and synthesizing sources, integrating source material, and avoiding plagiarism.

- New Coverage of the working bibliography groups sources by type, reflecting a streamlined approach to source material throughout the handbook.
- New The discussion of libraries' Web sites covers various ways students may search for sources—catalog, databases, and research guides.
- New A revised discussion of keywords and subject headings helps students develop and refine their search terms.
- New A streamlined discussion of gathering information from sources stresses keeping accurate records of source material, marking borrowed words and ideas clearly, and using synthesis.
- New A chapter on documenting sources explains key features of source documentation, defines the relationship between in-text citations and a bibliography, and presents pros and cons of bibliography software.
- To help students develop their own perspectives on their research subjects, the text advises asking questions, entering into dialog with sources, and presenting multiple views fairly and responsibly.
- The discussion of evaluating sources—library, Web, and social media—helps students discern purposes and distinguish between reliable and unreliable sources. Case studies show the application of critical criteria to sample articles, Web documents, and a blog.
- The extensive chapter on avoiding plagiarism discusses deliberate and careless plagiarism, shows examples of plagiarized and revised sentences, and gives updated advice about avoiding plagiarism with online sources.
- Two complete research papers illustrate MLA style. One of them is a paper-in-progress, following a student through the research process and culminating in an annotated essay on green consumerism.

An updated guide to documentation

The extensive coverage of four documentation styles—MLA, Chicago, APA, and CSE—reflects each style's latest version.

- New Reorganized chapters for all four styles group sources by type, thus simplifying the process of finding appropriate models and clarifying differences among print, database, Web, and other sources.
- New Updated, annotated samples of key source types illustrate MLA and APA documentation, showing students how to find the bibliographical information needed to cite each type and highlighting the distinctions among different source media.
- New The chapter on MLA documentation reflects the new eighth edition of the *MLA Handbook*. In addition, the sample papers and other examples that show MLA have been updated to reflect the latest MLA guidelines.
- New A complete social-science research report shows APA style in the context of student writing.
- New The chapter on CSE documentation reflects the new eighth edition of *Scientific Style and Format: The CSE Manual for Authors, Editors, and Publishers*.
- For all styles, color highlighting makes authors, titles, dates, and other citation elements easy to grasp.

A guide to writing as a process

The handbook takes a practical approach to assessing the writing situation, generating ideas, developing the thesis statement, revising, and other elements of the writing process.

- New An expanded discussion of thesis covers using the thesis statement to preview organization.
- New A reorganized presentation of drafting, revising, and editing distinguishes revising more clearly as a step separate from editing.
- New A revised discussion of preparing a writing portfolio gives an overview of common formats and requirements.
- New Chapter 4 on paragraphs offers new, relevant examples illustrating important concepts of coherence, organization, and development.
- New A revised and streamlined chapter on presenting writing focuses on essential information related to document design, visuals and other media, writing for online environments, and oral presentations.

A guide to usage, grammar, and punctuation

The handbook's core reference material reliably and concisely explains basic concepts and common errors, provides hundreds of annotated examples from across the curriculum, and offers frequent exercises (including end-of-part exercises that combine several kinds of problems).

- New Throughout the handbook, revised explanations of grammar concepts and rules simplify the presentation and emphasize key material.
- New Dozens of new and revised examples and exercises clarify and test important concepts.
- New Two common trouble spots—sentence fragments and passive voice—are discussed in greater detail and illustrated with new and more examples.
- New Added examples in Part 8 on effective words show common shortcuts of texting and other electronic communication and how to revise them for academic writing.
- Summary and checklist boxes provide quick-reference help with color highlighting to distinguish sentence elements.

A guide to visual and media literacy

The handbook helps students process nonverbal information and use it effectively in their writing.

- New A student work-in-progress illustrates the process of analyzing an advertisement and culminates in a sample critical analysis.
- New Updated and detailed help with preparing or finding illustrations appears in Chapter 5 on presenting writing and Chapter 42 on finding sources.
- Thorough discussions of critically reading advertisements, graphs, and other visuals appear in Chapter 7 on critical reading, Chapter 8 on reading arguments, and Chapter 43 on working with sources.

A guide for writing beyond the classroom

Chapter 11 on public writing extends the handbook's usefulness beyond academic writing.

- New Discussions of writing for social media encourage students to consider their potential audience now and in the future, whether they are writing to express themselves or to represent an organization.
- New Updated coverage of writing a job application discusses cover letters, résumés, and professional online profiles.

A guide for culturally and linguistically diverse writers

At notes and sections labeled CULTURE LANGUAGE, the handbook provides extensive rhetorical and grammatical help, with examples, for writers whose first language or dialect is not standard American English.

- Fully integrated coverage, instead of a separate section, means that students can find what they need without having to know which problems they do and don't share with native SAE speakers.
- "CULTURE LANGUAGE Guide," inside the back cover, orients students with advice on mastering SAE and pulls all the integrated coverage together in one place.

An accessible reference guide

The handbook is designed to be easy to use.

- New Streamlined explanations and new explanatory headings make key information easier to find.
- A clean, uncluttered page design uses color and type clearly to distinguish parts of the book and elements of the pages.
- Color highlighting in boxes and on documentation models distinguishes important elements.
- Annotations on both visual and verbal examples connect principles and illustrations.
- Dictionary-style headers in the index make it easy to find entries.
- Helpful endpapers offer several paths to the book's content.
- More than 160 boxes provide summaries and checklists of key information.
- A preface just for students outlines the book's contents, details reference aids, and explains the page layout.

Writing resources and supplements

Pearson offers a variety of support materials to make teaching easier and to help students improve as writers. The following resources are geared specifically to *The Little, Brown Handbook.* For more information on these and scores of additional supplements, visit *pearsonhighered.com* or contact your local Pearson sales representative.

- MyWritingLab This tutorial, homework, and assessment program provides engaging experiences for teaching and learning. Flexible and easy to customize, *MyWritingLab* helps students improve their writing through context-based learning. Whether through self-study or instructor-led learning, *MyWritingLab* supports and complements course work.

  Writing at the center: In new composing and "Review Plan" spaces, *MyWritingLab* brings together student writing, instructor feedback, and remediation via rich multimedia activities, allowing students to learn through their own writing.

  Student success: *MyWritingLab* identifies the skills needed for success in composition classes and provides personalized remediation for students who need it.

Assessment tools: *MyWritingLab* generates powerful gradebook reports whose visual analytics give insight into student achievement at individual, section, and program levels.

- The *Instructor's Annotated Edition* of *The Little, Brown Handbook* has been thoroughly revised by Cynthia Marshall, Wright State University. It provides a complete teaching system in one book. Integrated with the student text are essays on teaching, updated reading suggestions, specific tips for class discussions and activities, and answers to the handbook's exercises.
- The *Instructor's Resource Manual* includes all the teaching material and exercise answers from the *Instructor's Annotated Edition.*
- *The Little, Brown Handbook Answer Key* provides answers to the handbook's exercises.
- *Diagnostic and Editing Tests and Exercises* are cross-referenced to *The Little, Brown Handbook* and are available online.

Acknowledgments

The Little, Brown Handbook remains relevant and fresh because instructors give feedback: they talk with Pearson's sales representatives and editors, answer questionnaires, write detailed reviews, and send us personal notes. For the thirteenth edition, we wish to thank the following instructors who communicated with us directly or through reviews. Their experiences and their insights into the handbook led to the improvements in this new edition: Monique Leslie Akassi, Bowie State University; Joshua Austin, Cumberland County College; Ken Bishop, Itawamba Community College; LaToya W. Bogard, Mississippi State University; Cheryl Borman, Hillsborough Community College, Ybor City Campus; Sonia Bush, North Lake College; Helen Ceraldi, North Lake College; Michael Dittman, Butler County Community College; Jesse Doiron, Lamar University–Beaumont; Genesis Downey, Owens Community College; Anthony Edgington, University of Toledo; Guy Steven Epley, Samford University; Marilyn Y. Ford, East Mississippi Community College; Jacquelyn Gaiters-Jordan, Pikes Peak Community College; Patricia Gallo, Delaware Technical Community College; Jennifer Hazel, Owens Community College; Sue Henderson, East Central College; Debra Johanyak, University of Akron, Wayne College; Cheryl Johnson, Lamar University; Melisa Jones, Texarkana College; Erin Kramer, Owens Community College; Elizabeth Kuechenmeister, Lindenwood University; Isera Tyson Miller, State College of Florida; Steve Moore, Arizona Western College; Ann C. Spurlock, Mississippi State University; Ishmael Matthew Stabosz, Delaware Technical Community College; Greg Stone, Tulsa Community College, Metro Campus; Alex Tavares, Hillsborough Community College; John Valliere, Saint Petersburg College; Joy Walsh, Butler Community College; Natasha Whitton, Southeastern Louisiana University;

Debbie Williams, Abilene Christian University; L. Ureka Williams, Tulsa Community College, Metro Campus; Sara Yaklin, University of Toledo.

In responding to the ideas of these thoughtful critics, we had the help of several creative people. Valerie Vlahakis, John Wood Community College, prompted us to rethink and reorganize the documentation chapters and graciously allowed us to adapt her guide to finding appropriate models. Sigrid Anderson Cordell, University of Michigan, guided us through the ever-changing contemporary academic library. Sylvan Barnet, Tufts University, continued to lend his expertise in the chapter "Reading and Writing about Literature," which is adapted from his *Short Guide to Writing about Literature* and *Introduction to Literature*. Ellen Kuhl Repetto provided creative, meticulous, and invaluable help with the material on research writing. And Carol Hollar-Zwick, sine qua non, served brilliantly as originator, sounding board, critic, coordinator, researcher, producer, and friend.

A superb publishing team helped us make this book. Our editors at Pearson—Joseph Terry, Joseph Opiela, and Anne Brunell Ehrenworth—offered perceptive insights into instructors' and students' needs. Our project manager, Savoula Amanatidis, and production editor, Kathy Smith, shepherded the manuscript skillfully through the many stages of becoming a book. Vernon Nahrgang copyedited the manuscript with precision and care. Jerilyn Bockorick once again made the book a pleasure to use. We are grateful to all these collaborators.

PART 1

The Process of Writing

1 Assessing the Writing Situation

Chapter essentials

- Understand the writing process (below).
- Analyze the writing situation (p. 4).
- Choose and limit a subject (p. 6).
- Define your purpose (p. 6).
- Consider your audience (p. 11).
- Understand the genre (p. 15).

Visit MyWritingLab™ for more resources on assessing the writing situation.

"Writing is easy," snarled the late sportswriter Red Smith. "All you do is sit down at the typewriter and open a vein." Most writers would smile in agreement, and so might you. Like anything worthwhile, writing well takes hard work. This chapter and the next two will show you some techniques that writers have found helpful for starting, continuing, and completing college assignments.

1a Understanding how writing happens

Every time you sit down to write, you embark on a **writing process**—the term for all the activities, mental and physical, that go into creating what eventually becomes a finished piece of work. Even for experienced writers the process is usually messy, which is one reason that it is sometimes difficult. Though we may get a sense of ease and orderliness from a published magazine article, we can safely assume that the writer had to work hard to achieve those qualities, struggling to express half-formed thoughts, shaping and reshaping paragraphs to make a point convincingly.

There is no *one* writing process; no two writers proceed in the same way, and even an individual writer adapts his or her process to the task at hand. Still, most writers experience writing as a **recursive** process in which the following stages overlap and influence one another:

- **Analyzing the writing situation:** considering subject, purpose, audience, genre (type of writing), and other elements of the project (pp. 4–6).
- **Discovering or planning:** posing a question, gathering information, focusing on a central theme, and organizing material (pp. 17–45).
- **Drafting:** answering the question and expressing and connecting ideas (pp. 47–51).

The process of writing

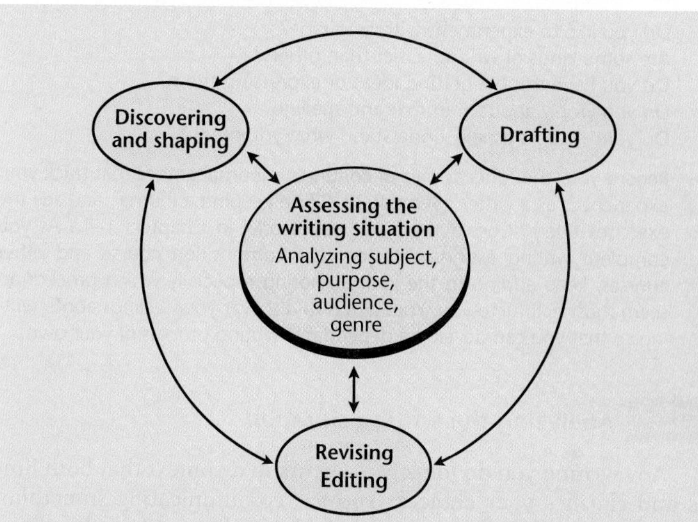

Writing is usually a recursive process: at each stage your work can affect and be affected by every other stage. Assessing the writing situation generally starts the process and then continues in the other stages.

- **Revising:** reconsidering the central question or idea, rethinking and improving content and organization, developing supporting ideas more thoroughly, and deleting tangents (pp. 51–55).
- **Editing:** improving sentences and checking grammar, punctuation, word choice, and presentation (pp. 61–64).

Note Like many others, you may believe that writing is only, or even mainly, a matter of correctness. True, any written message will find a more receptive audience if it is correct in grammar, spelling, and similar matters. But these concerns should come late in the writing process, after you've allowed yourself to discover what you want to say, freeing yourself to make mistakes along the way. As one writer put it, you need to get the clay on the potter's wheel before you can shape it into a bowl, and you need to shape the bowl before you can perfect it. So get your clay on the wheel, and work with it until it looks like a bowl. Then worry about correctness.

Exercise 1.1 Starting a writing journal

Recall several writing experiences that you have had—an e-mail you had difficulty composing, an essay you enjoyed writing, a term paper that involved a happy or miserable all-nighter, a post to a blog that received a surprising response. What do these experiences reveal to you about writing, particularly your successes and problems with it? Consider the following questions:

Do you like to experiment with language?
Are some kinds of writing easier than others?
Do you have trouble getting ideas or expressing them?
Do you worry about grammar and spelling?
Do your readers usually understand what you mean?

Record your thoughts as part of continuing journal entries that track your experiences as a writer. (See pp. 20–22 on keeping a journal, and see the exercises titled "Considering your past work" in Chapters 1–4.) As you complete writing assignments for your composition course and other courses, keep adding to the journal, noting especially which procedures seem most helpful to you. Your aim is to discover your feelings about writing so that you can develop a dependable writing process of your own.

1b Analyzing the writing situation

Any writing you do for others occurs in a context that both limits and clarifies your choices. You are communicating something about a particular subject to a particular audience of readers for a specific reason. You may be required to write in a particular genre. You may need to conduct research. You'll be up against a length requirement and a deadline. And you may be expected to present your work in a certain format and medium.

These are the elements of the **writing situation**, and analyzing them at the very start of a project can tell you much about how to proceed. (For more information about these elements, refer to the page numbers given in parentheses.)

Context

- **What is your writing for?** A course in school? Work? Something else? What do you know of the requirements for writing in this context?
- **What are the basic requirements of the writing task?** Consider requirements for length, deadline, subject, purpose, audience, and genre. What leeway do you have?
- **What medium will you use to present your writing?** Will you deliver it on paper, online, or orally? What does the presentation method require in preparation time, special skills, and use of technology?

Subject (pp. 6–9)

- **What does your writing assignment require you to write about?** If you don't have a specific assignment, what subjects might be appropriate for this situation?
- **What interests you about the subject?** What do you already know about it? What questions do you have about it?
- **What does the assignment require you to do with the subject?**

Purpose (pp. 9–11)

- **What aim does your assignment specify?** For instance, does it ask you to explain something or argue a position?
- **Why are you writing?**
- **What do you want your work to accomplish?** What effect do you intend it to have on readers?
- **How can you best achieve your purpose?**

Audience (pp. 11–14)

- **Who will read your writing?** Why will your readers be interested (or not) in your writing? How can you make your writing interesting to them?
- **What do your readers already know and think about your subject?** What characteristics—such as education or political views—might influence their response?
- **How should you project yourself in your writing?** What role should you play in relation to your readers, and what information should you provide? How informal or formal should your writing be?
- **What do you want readers to do or think after they read your writing?**

Genre (pp. 15–16)

- **What genre, or type of writing, does the assignment call for?** Are you to write an analysis, a report, a proposal, or some other type? Or are you free to choose the genre in which to write?
- **What are the conventions of the genre you are using?** For example, readers might expect a claim supported by evidence, a solution to a defined problem, clear description, or easy-to-find information.

Research (pp. 542–624)

- **What kinds of evidence will best suit your subject, purpose, audience, and genre?** What combination of facts, examples, and expert opinions will support your ideas?
- **Does your assignment require research?** Will you need to consult sources or conduct interviews, surveys, or experiments?
- **Even if research is not required, what information do you need to develop your subject?** How will you obtain it?
- **What documentation style should you use to cite your sources?** (See pp. 623–24 on source documentation in the academic disciplines.)

Deadline and length

- **When is the assignment due?** How will you apportion the work you have to do in the time available?
- **How long should your writing be?** If no length is assigned, what seems appropriate for your subject, purpose, and audience?

Presentation

- **What format or method of presentation does the assignment specify or imply?** (See pp. 108–21 on academic writing, pp. 125–29 on oral presentations, and pp. 232–44 on business and other public writing.)
- **How might you use illustrations, video, and other elements to achieve your purpose?** (See pp. 108–16.)

Exercise 1.2 Analyzing a writing situation

The following assignment was given in a survey course in psychology. What does the assignment specify about the elements of the writing situation? What does it imply? Given this assignment, how would you answer the preceding questions about the writing situation?

> When is psychotherapy most likely to work? That is, what combinations of client, therapist, and theory tend to achieve good results? In your paper, cite studies supporting your conclusions. Length: 1500 to 1800 words. Post your paper online to me and to your discussion group by March 30.

1c Discovering and limiting a subject

For most college writing, you will write in response to an assignment. The assignment may specify your subject, or it may leave the choice to you. (If you're stuck, use the discovery techniques on pp. 17–27 to think of subjects.) Whether the subject is assigned or not, it will probably need thought if it is to achieve these aims:

- **The subject should be suitable for the assignment.**
- **It should be neither too general nor too limited** for the length of the project and the deadline assigned.
- **It should be something that interests you and that you are willing to learn more about.**

1 Responding to a specific assignment

Many assignments will set boundaries for your subject. For instance, you might be asked to discuss what makes psychotherapy effective, to prepare a lab report on a physics experiment, or to analyze a character in a short story.

Such assignments may seem to leave little room for you to move around, but in fact you'll have several questions to answer:

- **What's wanted from you?** Writing assignments often contain words such as *discuss, describe, analyze, report, interpret, explain, define, argue,* and *evaluate.* These words specify your approach to your subject, the kind of thinking expected, your general purpose, and even the form your writing should take. (See pp. 9–11 for more on purpose.)

- **For whom are you writing?** Many assignments will specify or imply your readers, but sometimes you will have to figure out for yourself who your audience is and what it expects from you. (For more on analyzing audience, see pp. 11–14.)
- **What kind of research is required, if any?** Sometimes an assignment specifies the kinds of sources you are expected to consult, and you can use such information to choose your subject. (If you are unsure whether research is required, check with your instructor.)
- **How can you narrow the assigned subject to do it justice in the length and time required?** (See below.)

2 Responding to a general assignment

Some assignments specify features such as length and amount of research, but they leave the choice of subject entirely to you. Others are somewhat more focused—for instance, "Respond to a reading assigned in this course" or "Discuss a proposal for solving a local social problem"—but still give you much leeway in choosing a particular reading or a particular proposal. To find your approach, consider your own experiences or interests:

- **What subject do you already know something about or have you been wondering about?** Athletic scholarships? Unemployment in your town?
- **Have you recently disagreed with someone over a substantial issue?** The change in relations between men and women? The cost of health insurance?
- **What have you read or seen lately?** A shocking book? A violent or funny movie? An effective Web advertisement or television commercial?
- **What topic in the reading or class discussion for a course has intrigued you?** An economic issue such as taxes? A psychological problem such as depression?
- **What makes you especially happy or especially angry?** A volunteer activity? The behavior of your neighbors?
- **Which of your own or others' dislikes and preferences would you like to understand better?** The demand for hybrid cars? The decision to become a vegetarian?

Once you have a subject, you'll also need to answer the questions in the bulleted list on specific assignments (opposite and above).

3 Narrowing a subject to a question

Let's say you've decided to write about social-networking Web sites or about a character in a short story. You've got a subject, but it's still broad, worthy of a lengthy article if not a whole book. For a relatively brief paper, you'll need a narrow focus in order to provide the specific details that make writing significant and interesting—all within the required length and deadline.

One helpful technique for narrowing a subject is to ask focused questions about it, seeking one that seems appropriate for your assignment and that promises to sustain your interest through the writing process. The following examples illustrate how questioning can scale down broad subjects to specific subjects that are limited and manageable:

Broad subjects	**Specific subjects**
Social-networking sites	What draws people to these sites? How do the sites alter the ways people interact? What privacy protections should the sites provide for users?
Mrs. Mallard in Kate Chopin's "The Story of an Hour"	What changes does Mrs. Mallard undergo? Why does Mrs. Mallard respond as she does to news of her husband's death? What does the story's irony contribute to the character of Mrs. Mallard?
Lincoln's weaknesses as President	What was Lincoln's most significant error as commander-in-chief of the Union army? Why did Lincoln delay emancipating the slaves? Why did Lincoln have difficulties controlling his cabinet?
Federal aid to college students	Which students should be entitled to federal aid? How adequate are the kinds of federal aid available to college students? Why should the federal government aid college students?

As these examples illustrate, your questions should not lend themselves to yes-or-no answers but should require further thinking.

Here are some guidelines for posing questions:

- **Reread the assignment.** Consider what it tells you about purpose, audience, genre, sources, length, and deadline.
- **Pursue your interests.** If questions don't come easily, try free-writing or brainstorming (pp. 22–24) or use a tree diagram (pp. 36–37).
- **Ask as many questions as you can think of.**
- **Test the question that seems most interesting and appropriate by roughly sketching out the main ideas.** Consider how many paragraphs or pages of specific facts, examples, and other details you would need to pin those ideas down. This thinking should give you at least a vague idea of how much work you'd have to do and how long the resulting paper might be.
- **Break a too-broad question down further, and repeat the previous step.**

Don't be discouraged if the perfect question does not come easily or early. You may find that you need to do some planning and writing, exploring different facets of the general subject and pursuing your specific interests, before you hit on the best question. And the question you select may require further narrowing or may shift subtly or even dramatically as you move through the writing process.

Exercise 1.3 Narrowing subjects

Following are some general writing assignments. Use the given information and your own interests to pose specific questions for three of these assignments.

1. For a writing course, consider how Web sites such as *YouTube* are altering the experience of popular culture. Length: three pages. Deadline: one week.
2. For a course in sociology, research and analyze the dynamics of a particular group of people. Length: unspecified. Deadline: four weeks.
3. For a writing course, read and respond to an essay in a text you are using. Length: three pages. Deadline: two weeks.
4. For a government course, consider possible restrictions on legislators. Length: five pages. Deadline: two weeks.
5. For a letter to the editor of the town newspaper, describe the effects of immigration on your community. Length: two pages. Deadline: unspecified.

Exercise 1.4 Considering your past work: Discovering and limiting a subject

Think of something you've recently written—perhaps an application essay, a business report, or a term paper. How did your subject evolve from beginning to end? In retrospect, was it appropriate for your writing situation? How, if at all, might it have been modified?

Exercise 1.5 Finding and narrowing a subject for your essay

As the first step in developing a three- to four-page essay for the instructor and the other students in your writing course, choose a subject and narrow it. Use the guidelines in the previous section to come up with a question that is suitably interesting, appropriate, and specific.

1d Defining a purpose

When you write, your **purpose** is your chief reason for communicating something about a topic to a particular audience. Purpose thus links both the specific situation in which you are working and the goal you hope to achieve. It is your answer to a potential reader's question, "So what?"

The general purposes for writing

- To entertain readers
- To express your feelings or ideas
- To explain something to readers (exposition)
- To persuade readers to accept or act on your opinion (argument)

1 Defining a general purpose

Your purpose may fall into one of four general categories: entertainment, self-expression, explanation, or persuasion. These purposes may overlap in a single piece of writing, but usually one predominates. And the dominant purpose will influence your particular slant on your topic, the supporting details you choose, even the words you use.

In college or public writing, by far the most common purposes are explanation and persuasion:

- **Writing that is mainly explanatory and informative is often called *exposition*** (from a Latin word meaning "to explain or set forth"). Using examples, facts, and other evidence, you present an idea about your subject so that readers understand it as you do. Almost any subject is suitable for exposition: how to pitch a knuckleball, why you want to major in business, the implications of a new discovery in genetics, the interpretation of a short story, the causes of an economic slump. Exposition is the kind of writing encountered most often in newspapers, magazines, and textbooks.
- **Writing that is primarily persuasive is often called *argument*.** Using examples, facts, and other evidence, you support your position on a debatable subject so that readers will at least consider your view and perhaps agree with it or act on it. A newspaper editorial favoring more bike lanes, a business proposal for a new hiring policy, a student paper recommending more foreign language courses or defending a theory about human psychological development—all these are arguments. (Chapters 8–9 discuss argument in some detail and provide examples.)

2 Defining a specific purpose

A writing assignment will often specify or imply both a general and a specific purpose. Say, for instance, that a psychology teacher assigns a review of the research on infants' perception of color. You know that the purpose is generally to explain, more specifically to summarize and analyze the established findings on the subject. You want readers to come away understanding the current state of the investigation into the subject. In addition, you want your instructor to see that you can competently read and write about others' work. (See pp. 132–33 for more on purpose in academic writing.)

Here are more examples of specific purposes:

To explain the methods and results of an engineering experiment so that readers understand and accept your conclusions

To explain the reasons for a new policy on technology use in dorm rooms so that students understand why the guidelines are needed

To analyze how Annie Dillard's "Total Eclipse" builds to its climax so that readers appreciate the author's skill

To persuade readers to support the college administration's plan for more required courses

To argue against additional regulation of guns so that readers perceive the disadvantages for themselves

To argue that gun deaths would be reduced through a new program of background checks.

With any writing assignment, try to define your specific purpose as soon as you have formed a question about your subject. Don't worry, though, if you feel uncertain of your purpose at the start. Sometimes you may not discover your purpose until you begin drafting, or you may find that your initial sense of purpose changes as you move through the writing process.

Exercise 1.6 Finding purpose in assignments

For each of your questions from Exercise 1.3 (p. 9), suggest a likely general purpose (entertainment, self-expression, explanation, persuasion) and try to define a specific purpose as well.

Exercise 1.7 Considering your past work: Defining a purpose

Look over two or three things you've written in the past year or so. What was your specific purpose in each one? How did the purpose influence your writing? Did you achieve your purpose?

Exercise 1.8 Defining a purpose for your essay

For your essay-in-progress, use your thinking so far about your subject (Exercise 1.5, p. 9) to define a general and specific purpose for your writing.

1e Considering the audience

- **Who are my readers?**
- **Why will they read my writing?**
- **What will they expect from my writing?**
- **What can I do to interest them in my writing?**
- **How do I want them to perceive me?**
- **What do I want them to think or do after they read my writing?**

The preceding questions are central to any writing project, and they will crop up again and again. Except in writing meant only for yourself, you are always trying to communicate with readers—something about a particular subject, for a particular purpose.

Your audience will often be specified or implied in a writing assignment. When you write an editorial for the student newspaper, your audience consists of other students at your school. When you write a report on a physics experiment, your audience consists of your physics instructor and perhaps other physicists or your classmates. Considering the needs and expectations of your readers can help you form or focus a question about your subject, gather answers to the question, and ultimately decide what to say and how to say it.

1 Knowing what readers expect

As a reader yourself, you know what readers expect from writing:

- **Context:** a link between what they read and their own knowledge and experiences.
- **Predictability:** an understanding of the writer's purpose and how it is being achieved.
- **Information:** the specific facts, examples, and other details that make the subject clear, interesting, and convincing.
- **Respect:** a sense that the writer respects their values and beliefs, their backgrounds, and their intelligence.
- **Voice:** a sense that the writer is a real person whose mind and values are expressed in the writing (see opposite).
- **Readability, clarity, and correctness:** writing that is organized, focused, and free of unnecessary stumbling blocks and mistakes.

For much academic and public writing, readers have definite needs and expectations. Thus Chapter 6 discusses academic writing in general, Chapters 49–52 discuss writing in various disciplines, and Chapter 11 discusses public writing. Even in these areas, you must make many choices based on audience. In other areas where the conventions of structure and presentation are less well defined, the choices are even more numerous. The following box contains questions that can help you define and make these choices.

Questions about audience

Identity and expectations

- **Who *are* my readers?**
- **What are my readers' expectations for the genre of my writing?** Do readers expect features such as a particular organization and format, distinctive kinds of evidence, or a certain style of documenting sources?

- **What do I want readers to know or do after reading my work?** How should I make that clear to them?
- **How should I project myself to readers?** How formal or informal will they expect me to be? What role and tone should I assume?

Characteristics, knowledge, and attitudes

- **What characteristics of readers are relevant for my subject and purpose?** For instance:

  Age and sex
  Occupation: students, professional colleagues, etc.
  Social or economic role: subject-matter experts, voters, car buyers, potential employers, etc.
  Economic or educational background
  Ethnic background
  Political, religious, or moral beliefs and values
  Hobbies or activities

- **How will the characteristics of readers influence their attitudes toward my subject?**
- **What do readers already know and *not* know about my subject?** How much do I have to tell them? What aspects of my subject will be interesting and relevant to them?
- **How should I handle any specialized terms?** Will readers know them? If not, should I define them or avoid them?
- **What ideas, arguments, or information might surprise, excite, or offend readers?** How should I handle these points?
- **What misconceptions might readers have of my subject and/or my approach to it?** How can I dispel these misconceptions?

Uses and format

- **What will readers do with my writing?** Should I expect them to read every word from the top, to scan for information, to look for conclusions? Can I help readers by providing a summary, headings, illustrations, or other aids? (See pp. 108–29 on presenting writing.)

2 Expressing your voice

Your sense of your audience will influence three key elements of what you write:

- **The specific information you use to gain and keep the attention of readers and to guide them to accept your conclusions.** This information may consist of concrete details, facts, examples, or other evidence that makes your ideas clear, supports your assertions, and suits your readers' needs. The evidence may come from your experience or from outside sources.
- **The role you choose to play in relation to your readers.** Depending on your purpose and your attitude toward your topic, you will want readers to perceive you in a certain way. The possible

roles are many and varied—for instance, scholar, storyteller, lecturer, guide, reporter, advocate, inspirer.

- **The tone you use. Tone** in writing is like tone of voice in speaking: words and sentence structures on the page convey some of the same information as pitch and volume in the voice. Depending on your aims and what you think your readers will expect and respond to, your tone may be formal or informal. The attitude you convey may be serious or light, forceful or calm, irritated or cheerful.

These three elements contribute to what's often called **voice**: your projection of yourself into the writing. Your voice conveys your sense of the world as it applies to the particular writing situation: this subject, this purpose, this audience. Thus voice can vary quite a bit from one writing situation to another, as the following memos illustrate. Both were written by a student who worked part-time in a small company and wanted to get the company to recycle paper. But the two memos address different readers.

To coworkers

Ever notice how much paper collects in your trash basket every day? Well, most of it can be recycled with little effort, I promise. Basically, all you need to do is set a bag or box near your desk and deposit wastepaper in it. I know, space is cramped in these little cubicles. But can't we all accept a little more crowding when the earth's at stake? . . .

Voice: a peer who is thoughtful, cheerful, and sympathetic

Information: how employees could handle recycling; no mention of costs

Role: colleague

Tone: informal, personal (*Ever notice*; *Well*; *you*; *I know, space is cramped*)

To management

In my four months here, I have observed that all of us throw out baskets of potentially recyclable paper every day. Considering the drain on our forest resources and the pressure on landfills that paper causes, we could make a valuable contribution to the environmental movement by helping to recycle the paper we use. At the company where I worked before, employees separate clean wastepaper from other trash at their desks. The maintenance staff collects trash in two receptacles, and the trash hauler (the same one we use here) makes separate pickups. I do not know what the hauler charges for handling recyclable material. . . .

Voice: a subordinate who is thoughtful, responsible, and serious

Information: specific reasons; view of company as a whole; reference to another company; problem of cost

Role: employee

Tone: formal, serious (*Considering the drain*; *forest resources*; *valuable contribution*; no *you*)

Projecting your writing voice can be challenging when you are responding to a reading or drawing on multiple sources for evidence. Especially if you feel unconfident about your subject, you may be tempted to let the other writers do the talking for you. See pages 172–74 and 593–94 on maintaining your voice by using synthesis.

Exercise 1.9 Considering audience

Choose one of the following subjects and, for each audience specified, ask the questions on pages 12–13. Decide on four points you would make, the role you would assume, and the tone you would adopt for each audience. Then write a paragraph for each based on your decisions.

1. The effects of smoking: for elementary school students and for adult smokers
2. Your opposition to a proposed law requiring adult bicyclists to wear helmets: for cyclists who oppose the law and for people who favor it
3. Why your neighbors should remove the wrecked truck from their front yard: for your neighbors and for your town zoning board

Exercise 1.10 Considering your past work: Writing for a specific audience

How did audience figure in a piece of writing you've done in the recent past—perhaps an essay for an application or a paper for a course? Who were your readers? How did your awareness of them influence your voice? At what point in the writing process did you find it most productive to consider your readers consciously?

Exercise 1.11 Analyzing the audience for your essay

Use the questions on pages 12–13 to determine as much as you can about the probable readers of your essay-in-progress (see Exercises 1.5 and 1.8). What might be an appropriate voice for your writing? What specific information will your readers need? What role do you want to assume? What tone will best convey your attitude toward your topic?

1f Understanding genres

Writers use familiar **genres**, or types of writing, to express their ideas. You can recognize many genres: the poems and novels of literature, the résumé in business writing, the news article about a sports event. In college you will be asked to write in a wide range of genres, such as analyses, lab reports, reviews, proposals, oral presentations, even blog posts.

Most simply, a genre is the conventional form that writing takes in a certain context. In academic writing, genre conventions help to further the aims of the disciplines; for instance, the features of a lab report emphasize the procedures, results, and conclusion that are important in scientific investigation. The conventions also help to improve communication because the writer knows what readers expect and readers can predict what they will encounter in the writing. Suppose your instructor assigns an argument essay and asks classmates to read one another's drafts. As you approach one paper titled "Animal Rights," you expect the essay to contain the conventional elements of argument: an introduction, a main claim or thesis about animal rights, paragraphs that develop that claim with evidence, and a conclusion. When the draft meets your expectations in these respects, you can settle into its substance. However, if instead of an argument you find a funny narrative about the writer's dog, your thwarted expectations will throw off your response. Searching for the argument, you might even miss the humor in the story.

When you receive a writing assignment, be sure to understand any requirements relating to genre:

- **Is a particular genre being assigned?** An assignment that asks you to write an analysis, an argument, or a report has specified the genre for you to use. In contrast, an assignment that asks you to write for the purpose of recruiting new members to a club leaves the choice of genre up to you—perhaps a flyer to post on campus, a brochure to hand out in the cafeteria, an e-mail message, or a *Facebook* page.
- **What are the conventions of the genre?** Your instructor and/or your textbook will probably outline the requirements for you. You can also learn about a genre by reading samples of it. Consult pages 134–38 for descriptions of the sample documents in this handbook.
- **What flexibility do you have?** Within their conventions, most genres still allow room for your own approach and voice. Again, reading samples will show you much about your options.

Exercise 1.12 Thinking about genre

Following is a list of writing genres in no particular order. You should be familiar with most of them even if you haven't studied or written in them.

personal essay	posting on the college Web site
brochure	memoir
oral report	written report
letter to the editor	informative Web site

For each of the following subject-audience pairs, suggest one of the above genres that might be appropriate and explain why you think its features would work.

1. Subject: your memories of learning to read. Audience: your writing class.
2. Subject: state laws against texting while driving. Audience: sixteen-year-olds.
3. Subject: a new cyberbullying policy on your campus. Audience: students on your campus.
4. Subject: the carbon footprint of dogs. Audience: people in your city.
5. Subject: results of a survey on dating behavior on your campus. Audience: a psychology class.

Exercise 1.13 Considering your past work: Analyzing genre

Look over two or three things you've recently written, such as an application essay, a report, an essay for class, or a letter of complaint. Can you identify the genre of each piece? How does what you wrote meet your readers' expectations for the genre? How does your writing change from one genre to another?

Exercise 1.14 Determining the genre for your essay

For your essay-in-progress, use your thinking so far about your subject, purpose, and audience to determine the genre of your essay. List the expectations readers will have for an essay in that genre.

2 Discovering and Shaping Ideas

Chapter essentials

- Use invention techniques to discover ideas: reading, keeping a journal, observing, freewriting, brainstorming, drawing, questioning, and using the patterns of development (below and pp. 18–27).
- Develop a thesis question and a thesis statement (p. 28).
- Use a tool for organizing your ideas (p. 34).
- Choose a structure for your writing (p. 40).

Visit MyWritingLab™ for more resources on discovering and shaping ideas.

Once you have assessed your writing situation, or even while you're assessing it, you'll begin answering the question you posed about your subject (pp. 6–7). As you generate ideas and information, they in turn may cause you to rephrase your lead question, which will open up new areas to explore. Throughout this discovery process, you'll also be bringing order to your thoughts, focusing and organizing them so that readers will respond as you intend.

2a Discovering ideas

Many college writing projects ask you to address a significant question related to your subject. For some projects, you may have little difficulty finding something substantial to say. But when you're stuck for ideas, you'll have to get your mind working to coax out serious and interesting thoughts.

The following pages describe techniques for discovering ideas. These techniques are to be selected from, not followed in sequence: some may help you during early stages of the writing process, even before you're sure of your topic; others may help you later on; and one or two may not help at all. Give yourself ample time with the techniques, experimenting to discover which ones work best for you.

Discovering and shaping ideas

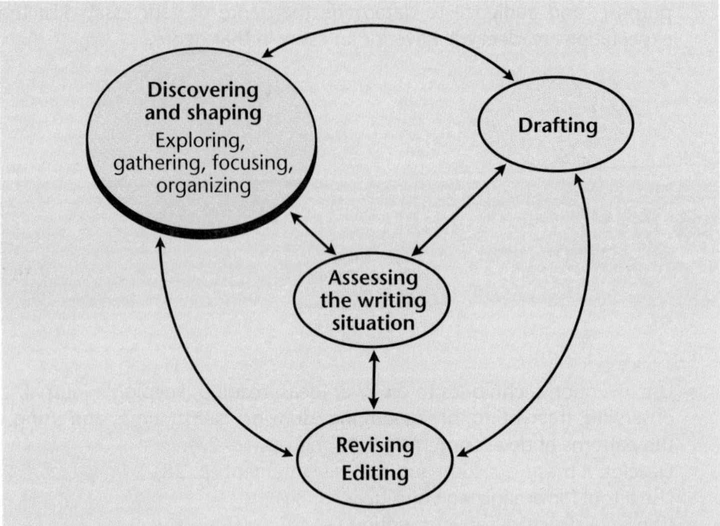

Discovering ideas and shaping them may occur at any point in the writing process, from the initial choice of subject through drafting and revision.

Note **Whatever discovery techniques you use, do your work in writing, not just in your head.** Your work will be retrievable, and the act of writing will help you concentrate and lead you to fresh, sometimes surprising, insights.

CULTURE LANGUAGE The discovery process encouraged here rewards rapid writing without a lot of thinking beforehand about what you will write or how. If your first language is not standard American English, you may find it helpful initially to do this exploratory writing in your native language or dialect and then to translate the worthwhile material for use in your drafts. This process can be productive, but it is extra work. Eventually, you'll want to move to composing in standard American English.

1 Reading

Many assignments require you to respond to reading or to consult texts as sources for your writing. But even when reading is not required, it can help you locate or develop a subject by introducing you to ideas you didn't know or by expanding on what you already know.

For example, say you were writing in favor of amateur athletics, a subject to which you had given a lot of thought. You might

Techniques for discovering a subject

- Read (opposite and below).
- Keep a journal (p. 20).
- Observe your surroundings (p. 22).
- Freewrite (p. 22).
- Brainstorm (p. 23).
- Draw (p. 24).
- Use the journalist's questions (p. 24).
- Use the patterns of development (p. 25).

be inclined to proceed entirely on your own, drawing on facts, examples, and opinions already in your head. But a little digging in sources might open up more ideas. For instance, an article in *Time* magazine could introduce you to an old rule for amateur status, or a comment on a blog could suggest an argument in favor of amateurism that hadn't occurred to you. *Remember: whenever you use the information or ideas of others in your writing, you must acknowledge your sources in order to avoid the serious offense of plagiarism.* (See Chapter 44.)

Often you will be given an assignment that asks you to use a text or texts in your writing. In a composition course, Katy Moreno's instructor distributed "It's a Flat World, after All," an essay by Thomas L. Friedman about globalization and the job market, and gave the following assignment, calling for a response to reading.

Instructor's assignment

In "It's a Flat World, after All," Thomas L. Friedman describes today's global job market, focusing not on manufacturing jobs that have been "outsourced" to overseas workers but on jobs that require a college degree and are no longer immune to outsourcing. Friedman argues that keeping jobs in the United States requires that US students, parents, and educators improve math and science education. As a college student, how do you respond to this analysis of the global market for jobs? What do you think today's college students should be learning?

To respond to Friedman's essay, Moreno had to digest its argument. On first reading the essay, she had found it convincing because Friedman's description of the job market matched her family's experience: her mother had lost her job when it was outsourced to India. After rereading the essay, however, Moreno was not persuaded that more math and science would necessarily improve students' opportunities and preserve their future jobs. She compared Friedman's advice with details she recalled from her mother's experience, and she began to develop her own angle on the topic in her journal.

Student's journal entry

Friedman is certainly right that more jobs than we realize are going overseas—that's what happened to Mom's job and we were shocked! But he gives only one way for students like me to compete—take more math and science. At first I thought he's totally right. But then I thought that what he said didn't really explain what happened to Mom—she had lots of math + science + tons of experience, but it was her salary, not better training, that caused her job to be outsourced. An overseas worker would do her job for less money. So she lost her job because of money + because she wasn't a manager. Caught in the middle. I want to major in computer science, but I don't think it's smart to try for the kind of job Mom had—at least not as long as it's so much cheaper for companies to hire workers overseas.

When you read for ideas, you need to be active, probing the text and illustrations with your mind, nurturing any sparks they set off. Always write while you read, taking notes on content and—just as important—on what the content makes you *think.*

2 Keeping a journal

A **journal** is a place to record your responses, thoughts, and observations about what you read, see, hear, or experience. It can also be a good source of ideas for writing. It is a kind of diary, but one more concerned with ideas than with day-to-day events. *Journal* comes from the Latin for "daily," and many journal keepers do write faithfully every day; others make entries less regularly, when the mood strikes or an insight occurs or they have a problem to work out.

Advantages of a journal

Writing in a journal, you are writing to yourself. That means you don't have to worry about main ideas, organization, correct grammar and spelling, or any of the other requirements of writing for others. You can work out your ideas and feelings without the pressure of an audience "out there" who will evaluate your thinking and expression. The freedom and flexibility of a journal can be liberating. Like many others, you may find writing easier, more fun, and more rewarding than you thought possible.

You can keep a journal either on paper (such as a notebook) or on a computer. If you write in the journal every day, or almost, even just for a few minutes, the routine will loosen up your writing muscles and improve your confidence. Indeed, journal keepers often become dependent on the process for the writing practice it gives them, the concentrated thought it encourages, and the connection it fosters between personal, private experience and public information and events.

CULTURE LANGUAGE A journal can be especially helpful if your first language is not standard American English. You can practice writing to improve your fluency, try out sentence patterns, and experiment with vocabulary words. Equally important, you can experiment with applying what you know from experience to what you read and observe.

Uses of a journal

Two uses of a journal are discussed elsewhere in this book: a reading journal, in which you think critically (in writing) about what you read (pp. 148, 719–20); and a research journal, in which you record your activities and ideas while you pursue a research project (p. 543). But you can use a journal for other purposes as well. Here are just a few:

- **Prepare for or respond to a course you're taking** by puzzling over a reading or a class discussion.
- **Build ideas for specific writing assignments.**
- **Sketch possible designs for a Web composition.**
- **Explore your reactions to events, trends, or the media.**
- **Write about your own history:** an event in your family's past, a troubling incident in your life, a change you've seen.
- **Analyze a relationship that disturbs you.**
- **Practice various forms or styles of writing**—for instance, poems or songs, reviews of movies, or reports for TV news.

The writing you produce in your journal will help you learn and grow. Even the personal and seemingly nonacademic entries can supply ideas when you are seeking a subject to write about or you are developing an essay.

On the facing page you read Katy Moreno's journal response to an essay. The next two student samples give a taste of journal writing for different purposes. In the first, Charlie Gabnes tries to work out a personal problem with his child.

Student's journal entry

Will's tantrums are getting worse—more often, more intense. Beginning to realize it's affecting my feelings for him. I feel resentment sometimes, and it's not as easy for me to cool off afterward as for him. Also I'm afraid of him sometimes for fear a tantrum will start, so treat him with kid gloves. How do we break this cycle?

In the second example Megan Polanyis ponders something she learned from her biology textbook.

Student's journal entry

Ecology and *economics* have the same root—Greek word for house. Economy = managing the house. Ecology = studying the house. In ecology the house is all of nature, ourselves, the other animals, the plants, the earth, the air, the whole environment. Ecology has a lot to do with economy: study the house in order to manage it.

3 Observing your surroundings

Sometimes you can find a good subject or good ideas by looking around you, not in the half-conscious way most of us move from place to place in our daily lives but deliberately, all senses alert. On a bus, for instance, are there certain types of passengers? What seems to be on the driver's mind? On campus, which buildings stand out? Are bicyclists and pedestrians at peace with each other?

To get the most from observation, you should have a device or a notepad and pen handy for taking notes and making sketches. If you have a camera, you may find that the lens sees things your unaided eyes do not notice. (When observing or photographing people, though, keep some distance, take photographs quickly, and avoid staring. Otherwise your subjects will feel uneasy.) Back at your desk, study your notes, sketches, or photographs for oddities or patterns that you'd like to explore further.

In some academic writing, you'll be expected to formalize observation and perhaps combine it with surveys, interviews, or experiments. See pages 576–78.

4 Freewriting

Writing into a subject

Many writers find subjects or discover ideas by **freewriting**: writing without stopping for a certain amount of time (say, ten minutes) or to a certain length (say, one page). The goal of freewriting is to generate ideas and information from *within* yourself by going around the part of your mind that doesn't want to write or can't think of anything to write. The physical act of freewriting may give you access to ideas you were unaware of. You let words themselves suggest other words. *What* you write is not important; that you *keep* writing is. Don't stop, even if that means repeating the same words until new words come. Don't go back to reread, don't censor ideas that seem off-track or repetitious, and above all don't stop to edit: grammar, punctuation, vocabulary, spelling, and the like are irrelevant at this stage.

The following freewriting by Terrence MacDonald drew him into the subject of underpaid college football players.

Student's freewriting

Seems to be a lot of money in college football. Carlos from high school got a full scholarship and expenses. Football is very important at this univ.—huge stadium with skyboxes & everyone knows the coach's name. Games get covered on TV. Team often goes to a bowl game. In the championship series on ESPN, many bowl games are named after corporate sponsors. A lot of money is spent on facilities, salaries, sponsorships, and advertising—and a lot of people are probably getting rich. Not Carlos though. Even his full ride isn't much of a share in that pie.

If you can dim or turn off your computer monitor, you can try invisible writing to keep moving forward while freewriting. As you type to a dark screen, the computer will record what you type but keep it from you and thus prevent you from tinkering with your prose. Invisible writing may feel uncomfortable at first, but it can free the mind for very creative results.

CULTURE LANGUAGE Invisible writing can be especially helpful if you are uneasy writing in standard English and you tend to worry about errors while writing. The blank computer screen leaves you no choice but to explore ideas without giving attention to the way you are expressing them. If you choose to write with the monitor on, concentrate on *what* you want to say, not *how* you are saying it.

Focused freewriting

Focused freewriting is more concentrated: you start with your question about your subject and answer it without stopping for, say, fifteen minutes or one full page. As in all freewriting, you push to bypass mental blocks and self-consciousness, not debating what to say or editing what you've written. With focused freewriting, though, you let the physical act of writing take you into and around your subject.

An example of focused freewriting can be found in Katy Moreno's journal response to Thomas L. Friedman's "It's a Flat World, after All" (p. 20). Since she already had an idea about Friedman's essay, Moreno was able to start there and expand on the idea.

5 Brainstorming

In **brainstorming**, you focus intently on your subject for a fixed amount of time (say, fifteen minutes), pushing yourself to list every idea and detail that comes to mind. Like freewriting, brainstorming requires turning off your internal editor so that you keep moving ahead instead of looping back over what you have already written to correct it. It makes no difference whether the ideas and details are expressed in phrases or complete sentences. It makes no difference if they seem silly or irrelevant. Just keep pushing. If you are working on a computer, the technique of invisible writing, described above, can help you move forward.

Following is an example of brainstorming by a student, Johanna Abrams. She was responding to the question *What can a summer job teach?*

Student's brainstorming

summer work teaches—

how to look busy while doing nothing
how to avoid the sun in summer
seriously: discipline, budgeting money, value of money

which job? Burger King cashier? baby-sitter? mail-room clerk?
mail room: how to sort mail into boxes: this is learning??
how to survive getting fired—humiliation, outrage
Mrs. King! the mail-room queen as learning experience
the shock of getting fired: what to tell parents, friends?
Mrs. K was so rigid—dumb procedures
Mrs. K's anger, resentment: the disadvantages of being smarter than your boss
The odd thing about working in an office: a world with its own rules for how to act
what Mr. D said about the pecking order—big chick (Mrs. K) pecks on little chick (me)
probably lots of Mrs. Ks in offices all over—offices are all barnyards
Mrs. K a sad person, really—just trying to hold on to her job, preserve her self-esteem
a job can beat you down—destroy self-esteem, make you desperate enough to be mean to other people
how to preserve/gain self-esteem from work??
if I'd known about the pecking order, I would have been less arrogant

When you think you've exhausted the ideas on your topic, you can edit and shape the list into a preliminary outline of your paper (see pp. 35–36).

6 Drawing

Like freewriting and list making, the technique of **clustering** or **idea mapping** uses free association to produce rapid, unedited work. But it also emphasizes the *relations* between ideas by combining writing and nonlinear drawing. Start with your topic at a center point and then radiate outward with ideas. Pursue related ideas in a branching structure until they seem exhausted. Then do the same with other ideas, staying open to connections, continuously branching out or drawing arrows.

The example opposite shows how Terrence MacDonald used the technique for ten minutes to expand on the topic of money in college football, an idea he developed through freewriting (see pp. 22–23).

7 Using the journalist's questions

Asking yourself a set of questions about your subject—and writing out the answers—can help you look at the subject objectively

Clustering or idea mapping

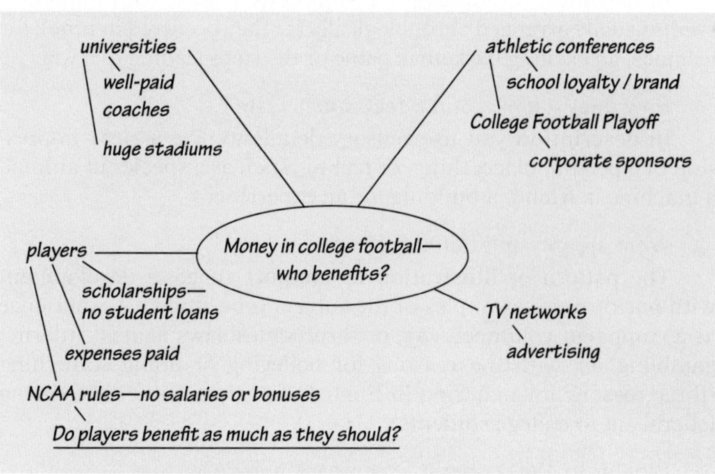

and see fresh possibilities in it. Asking questions can also provide some structure to the development of ideas.

One such set of questions is that posed by a journalist with a story to report:

- **Who was involved?**
- **What happened and what were the results?**
- **When did it happen?**
- **Where did it happen?**
- **Why did it happen?**
- **How did it happen?**

These questions can also be useful in probing an essay subject, especially if you are telling a story or examining causes and effects.

8 Using the patterns of development

The **patterns of development**—such as narration, definition, and classification—are ways we think about and understand a vast range of subjects, from our own daily experiences to the most complex scientific theories. They also serve as strategies and patterns for writing about these subjects, as illustrated by the discussions and paragraph-length examples on pages 90–99. You may want to refer to those pages for more information about each pattern.

To see your subject from many angles and open up ideas about it, you can ask the following questions based on the patterns of development. Not all these questions will be productive, but at least a few should open up new possibilities.

How did it happen?

In **narration** you develop the subject as a story, with important events usually arranged chronologically (as they occurred in time): for instance, an exciting basketball game or the steps leading to a war.

How does it look, sound, feel, smell, taste?

In **description** you use sensory details to give a clear impression of a person, place, thing, or feeling, such as a species of animal, a machine, a friend, a building, or an experience.

What are examples of it or reasons for it?

The pattern of **illustration** or **support** suggests development with one or more examples of the subject (one student's experience as a campaign volunteer, say, or three states' laws against Internet gambling) or with the reasons for believing or doing something (three reasons for majoring in English, four reasons for increasing federal aid to college students).

What is it? What does it encompass, and what does it exclude?

These questions lead to **definition**: specifying what the subject is and is not to give a precise sense of its meaning. Abstract terms—such as *justice, friendship,* and *art*—especially need defining (see pp. 184–85).

What are its parts or characteristics?

Using the pattern of **division** or **analysis**, you separate a subject such as a bicycle or a short story into its elements and examine the relations between elements. The first step in critical thinking, analysis is also discussed on pages 158–59.

What groups or categories can it be sorted into?

Classification involves separating a large group (such as cars) into smaller groups (conventional gas, hybrid, plug-in electric) based on the characteristics of the individual items (the kinds of engines). Another example: academic, business, personal, literary, and other types of writing.

How is it like, or different from, other things?

With **comparison and contrast** you point out the similarities and differences between ideas, objects, people, places, and so on: the differences between two similar computer systems, for instance, or the similarities between two opposing political candidates.

Is it comparable to something that is in a different class but more familiar to readers?

This question leads to **analogy**, an extended comparison of unlike subjects. Analogy is often used to explain a topic that may be unfamiliar to readers (for instance, the relation of atoms in a molecule) by reference to a familiar topic (two people dancing close together).

Why did it happen, or what results did it have?

With **cause-and-effect analysis**, you explain why something happened or what its consequences were or will be, or both: the causes of cerebral palsy, the effects of a Supreme Court decision, the causes and effects of a gradual change in the climate.

How do you do it, or how does it work?

In **process analysis** you explain how the subject happens (how a plant grows, how a robot works) or how to accomplish it (how to write an essay).

Exercise 2.1 Considering your past work: Discovering ideas

In the past how have you generated the ideas for writing? Have you used any of the techniques described on the preceding pages? Have you found the process especially enjoyable or difficult? If some writing tasks were easier than others, what do you think made the difference?

Exercise 2.2 Keeping a journal

If you haven't already started a journal on your own or in response to Exercise 1.1 (pp. 3–4), try to do so now. Every day for at least a week, write for at least fifteen minutes about anything on your mind—or consult the list on page 21 for ideas of what to write about. At the end of the week, write about your experience. What did you like about journal writing? What didn't you like? What did you learn about yourself or the world from the writing? How can you use this knowledge?

Exercise 2.3 Using freewriting, brainstorming, or drawing

If you haven't tried any of them before, experiment with freewriting, brainstorming, or drawing. Continue with the subject you selected in Exercise 1.5 (p. 9), or begin with a new subject. Write or draw for at least ten minutes without stopping to reread and edit. (Try using invisible writing as described on p. 23 if you're freewriting or brainstorming on a computer.) When you finish your experiment, examine what you have written for ideas and relationships that could help you develop the subject. What do you think of the technique you tried? Did you have any difficulties with it? Did it help you loosen up and generate ideas?

Exercise 2.4 Sending an online query

When you have spent some time developing your subject, consider any doubts you may have or any information you still need. Send a message to your classmates posing your questions and asking for their advice and insights.

Exercise 2.5 Developing your subject

Use at least two of the discovery techniques discussed on the preceding pages to develop the subject you selected in Exercise 1.5 (p. 9). (If you completed Exercise 2.3 above, then use one additional technique.) Later exercises for your essay-in-progress will be based on the ideas you generate in this exercise.

2b Developing a thesis

Your readers will expect an essay you write to be focused on a central idea, or **thesis**, to which all the essay's paragraphs, all its general statements and specific information, relate. The thesis is the controlling idea, the main point, the conclusion you draw from your evidence. In answering your question about your subject, the thesis is the intellectual position you are taking.

Often the thesis is expressed in a one- or two-sentence **thesis statement** toward the beginning of an essay. As an expression of the thesis, the thesis statement serves four crucial functions and one optional one:

Functions of the thesis statement

- **The thesis statement narrows your subject to a single, central idea** that you want readers to gain from your essay.
- **It claims something specific and significant about your subject,** a claim that requires support.
- **It conveys your purpose**—usually explanation or argument in college writing.
- **It establishes your voice,** suggesting your attitude toward your subject and the role you assume with readers.
- **It often concisely previews the arrangement of ideas,** in which case it can also help you organize your essay.

1 Starting with a thesis question

A thesis statement probably will not leap fully formed into your head. Many writers begin the process of developing a thesis by turning the assignment into a **thesis question**. If you used questions to narrow your subject (pp. 7–8), the thesis question continues this approach but with a sharper focus. A thesis question can help you figure out your position, organize your ideas, start drafting, and stay on track.

Consider again Katy Moreno's assignment on page 19:

> . . . As a college student, how do you respond to [Friedman's] analysis of the global market for jobs? What do you think today's college students should be learning?

Responding to the assignment, Moreno first rephrased it as two questions:

> To what extent do I agree or disagree with Friedman's argument that students today need better technical training to compete in the global job market?
>
> What should college students be learning?

Then Moreno reread Friedman's essay to clarify the disagreement she first expressed in her journal writing (p. 20) and to begin applying this response to her own experience of her mother's job loss. The result was a single question that would guide her thinking:

> How does my mother's job loss contradict Friedman's argument about technical training as key to success in the global job market?

2 Moving from thesis question to thesis statement

Drafting a thesis statement can occur at almost any time in the process of writing. Some instructors suggest that students develop a thesis statement when they have a good stock of ideas, to give a definite sense of direction. Other instructors suggest that students work with their thesis question at least through drafting, to keep options open. And no matter when it's drafted, a thesis statement can change during the writing process, as the writer discovers ideas and expresses them in sentences.

Katy Moreno chose to try writing her thesis statement before drafting. Working from her thesis question (above), she wrote a sentence that named a topic and made a claim about it:

> The outsourcing of my mother's job proves that Thomas L. Friedman's advice to improve students' technical training is too narrow.

Moreno's topic is the outsourcing of her mother's job, and her claim is that Friedman's advice is too narrow. Although Moreno later revised her thesis statement (p. 30), this draft statement gave her direction, and she used it in the first draft of her paper.

Following are more examples of thesis questions and answering thesis statements. Each statement consists of a topic and a claim. Notice how each statement also expresses purpose. Statements 1–3 are **explanatory**: the writers mainly want to explain something to readers, such as the benefits of military service. Statements 4–6 are **argumentative**: the authors mainly want to convince readers of something, such as the need to outlaw drivers' use of cell phones. Most of the thesis statements you write in college papers will be either explanatory or argumentative.

Thesis question	Explanatory thesis statement
1. What are the advantages of serving in the US military?	Military service teaches teamwork, discipline, and job-related skills that transfer well to civilian life. [**Topic:** military service. **Claim:** teaches skills that transfer to civilian life.]
2. Why did Abraham Lincoln delay in emancipating the slaves?	Lincoln delayed emancipating any slaves until 1863 because his primary goal was to restore and preserve the Union, with or without slavery. [**Topic:** Lincoln's delay. **Claim:** was caused by his goal of preserving the Union.]

Thesis question	Explanatory thesis statement
3. What steps can prevent juvenile crime?	Juveniles can be diverted from crime by active learning programs, full-time sports, frequent contact with positive role models, and intervention by consistent mentors. [**Topic:** juvenile crime. **Claim:** can be prevented in four ways.]

Thesis question	Argumentative thesis statement
4. Why should drivers' use of cell phones be banned?	Drivers' use of cell phones should be outlawed because people who talk and drive at the same time cause accidents. [**Topic:** drivers' use of cell phones. **Claim:** should be outlawed because it causes accidents.]
5. Which college students should be entitled to federal aid?	As an investment in its own economy, the federal government should provide a tuition grant to any college student who qualifies academically. [**Topic:** federal aid. **Claim:** should be provided to any college student who qualifies academically.]
6. Why should strip-mining be controlled?	Strip-mining should be tightly controlled in this region to reduce its pollution of water resources, its destruction of the land, and its devastating effects on people's lives. [**Topic:** strip-mining. **Claim:** should be tightly controlled for three reasons.]

CULTURE LANGUAGE In some cultures it is considered rude or unnecessary for a writer to state his or her main idea outright or to state it near the beginning. When writing in American schools or workplaces, you can assume that your readers expect a clear and early idea of what you think.

3 Using the thesis statement to preview organization

You can write a thesis statement that suggests the organization of your essay. Readers often appreciate such a preview, and students often prefer it because it helps them organize their main points and keep on track during drafting. Several statements in the preceding section preview the organization:

Thesis statement	Organization of essay
Military service teaches teamwork, discipline, and job-related skills that transfer well to civilian life.	Three aspects of military service that transfer well to civilian life.
Juveniles can be diverted from crime by active learning programs, full-time sports, frequent contact with positive role models, and intervention by consistent mentors.	Four ways to reduce juvenile crime.

Strip-mining should be tightly controlled in this region to reduce its pollution of water resources, its destruction of the land, and its devastating effects on people's lives.	Three reasons for controlling strip-mining.

4 Revising a thesis statement

You may have to write and rewrite a thesis statement before you come to a conclusion about your position.

Focusing the claim

Katy Moreno used her draft thesis statement (p. 29) in the first draft of her paper, but it didn't work well at that stage. She saw that it put too little emphasis on her actual topic (*technical training*) and overstated her disagreement with Friedman (*proves . . . is too narrow*). In addition, a reader's comment showed Moreno that her claim wasn't specific: Friedman's advice is *too narrow* for what? In her first revision, Moreno tried to emphasize her intended subject:

> Technical training by itself . . .

Then she worked on her claim:

> . . . can be too narrow to produce the communicators and problem solvers needed by contemporary businesses.

This statement clarified the claim (*can be too narrow to produce . . .*) and said why the subject was significant (*. . . communicators and problem solvers needed by contemporary businesses*). However, Moreno had dropped her mother's experience of losing her job to outsourcing, which was a key point in her response to Friedman's essay. Moreno tried again, adding her mother's experience:

> My mother's experience of having her job outsourced showed that technical training by itself can be too narrow to produce the communicators and problem solvers needed by contemporary businesses.

For her final revision, Moreno responded to another reader's suggestion that she state her point of disagreement with Friedman more clearly:

> My mother's experience of having her job outsourced taught a lesson that Thomas L. Friedman overlooks: technical training by itself can be too narrow to produce the communicators and problem solvers needed by contemporary businesses.

Considering audience

Often you must deliberately consider your audience as you draft a thesis statement. One student, Ben Nelson, was writing an argument for more student parking on campus. He arrived fairly easily at his initial claim:

> Most students who commute to campus must drive to school, and they need more places to park.

However, to persuade school administrators to take action, Nelson realized that he needed to focus on them as his audience and to strengthen his voice:

> The school must provide enough parking spaces to accommodate the many students who drive to school and to protect all students from otherwise dangerous traffic congestion.

Testing the thesis statement

As you draft and revise your thesis statement over the course of the writing process, test it by asking the questions in the following box.

Checklist for revising the thesis statement

- How well does the **subject** of your statement capture the subject of your writing?
- What **claim** does your statement make about your subject?
- What is the **significance** of the claim? How does it answer "So what?" and convey your purpose?
- How can the claim be **limited** or made more **specific**? Does it state a single idea and clarify the boundaries of the idea?
- How **unified** is the statement? How does each word and phrase contribute to a single idea?
- How well does the statement convey your **voice**?
- How well does the statement **preview the organization** of your writing?

Here are other examples of thesis statements revised in answer to the questions in the box:

Original	Revised
Cell phones can be convenient, but they can also be dangerous. [Not unified: how do the two parts of the sentence relate?]	The convenience of cell phones does not justify the risks of driving while talking or texting.
This new product brought in over $300,000 last year. [A statement of fact, not a claim about the product: what is significant about the product's success?]	This new product succeeded because of its innovative marketing campaign, including widespread press coverage, in-store entertainment, and a consumer newsletter.

Original	Revised
People should not go on fad diets. [A vague statement that needs limiting with one or more reasons: what's wrong with fad diets?]	Fad diets can be dangerous when they deprive the body of essential nutrients or rely excessively on potentially harmful foods.
Televised sports are different from live sports. [A general statement: how are they different, and why is the difference significant?]	Although television cannot transmit all the excitement of a live game, its close-ups and slow-motion replays reveal much about the players and the strategy of the game.
Television viewing can reduce loneliness, cause laughter, and teach children. [Previews organization but lacks voice: what is the writer's attitude toward the subject?]	Despite its many faults, television has at least one strong virtue: it provides replacement voices that can ease loneliness, spark healthful laughter, and even educate young children.

Note You may sometimes need more than one sentence for your thesis statement, particularly if it requires some buildup:

> Modern English, especially written English, is full of bad habits that interfere with clear thinking. Getting rid of these habits is a first step to political regeneration.
>
> —Adapted from George Orwell, "Politics and the English Language"

However, don't use this possibility to produce a wordy, general, or disunified statement. The two (or more) sentences must build on each other, and the final sentence must present the key assertion of your paper.

Exercise 2.6 Evaluating thesis statements

Evaluate the following thesis statements, considering whether each one makes a claim that is sufficiently significant, specific, and unified. Rewrite the statements as necessary to meet these goals.

1. Aggression usually leads to violence, injury, and even death, and we should use it constructively.
2. The religion of Islam is widely misunderstood in the United States.
3. Manners are a kind of social glue.
4. One episode of a radio talk show amply illustrates both the appeal of such shows and their silliness.
5. The poem is about motherhood.

Exercise 2.7 Considering your past work: Developing a thesis

Have you been aware in the past of focusing your essays on a central idea, or thesis? Have you found it more efficient to try to pin down your idea early or to let it evolve during drafting? To what extent has a thesis helped or hindered you in shaping your draft?

Exercise 2.8 Drafting and revising your own thesis statement

Continuing from Exercise 2.5 (p. 27), write a thesis statement for your essay-in-progress. As much as possible at this point, your statement should be significant, specific, and unified, and it should convey your attitude toward your subject.

2c Organizing ideas

An effective essay has a recognizable shape—an arrangement of parts that guides readers, helping them see how ideas and details relate to each other and contribute to the whole. You may sometimes let an effective organization emerge over one or more drafts. But many writers find that organizing ideas to some extent before drafting can provide a helpful sense of direction. If you feel uncertain about the course your essay should follow or have a complicated topic with many parts, devising a shape for your material can clarify your options.

Before you begin organizing your material, look over all the writing you've done so far—freewriting, notes from reading, whatever—and pull together a master list of all the ideas and details that you think you might want to include.

1 Distinguishing the general and the specific

To organize material for an essay, you need to distinguish general and specific ideas and see the relations between ideas. **General** and **specific** refer to the number of instances or objects included in a group signified by a word. The "ladder" below illustrates a general-to-specific hierarchy.

Most general

↑ life form
plant
flowering plant
rose
American Beauty rose
↓ Uncle Dan's prize-winning American Beauty rose

Most specific

Here are some tips for arranging the ideas in your preliminary writing:

- **Underline, boldface, or circle the most general ideas.** These are the ideas that offer the main support for your thesis statement. They will be more general than the evidence that supports them.
- **Make connections between each general idea and the more specific details that support it.** On paper, write each general idea down with space beneath it, and add specific information in the

appropriate spaces. On a computer, rearrange supporting information under more general points. You can use the Comment function to add notes about connections.

- **Respect the meanings of ideas.** Think through the implications of ideas as you sort them. Otherwise, your hierarchies could become jumbled, with *rose,* for instance, illogically subordinated to *animal,* or *life form* somehow subordinated to *rose*.
- **Remove information that doesn't fit.** If you worry about losing deleted information, transfer the notes to a separate sheet of paper or word-processing file.
- **Fill holes where support seems skimpy.** If you recognize a hole but don't know what to fill it with, try using a discovery technique such as freewriting or drawing, or go back to your research sources.
- **Experiment with various arrangements of general ideas and supporting information.** Seek an order that presents your material clearly and logically. On paper, you can cut the master list apart and paste or tape each general idea and its support on a separate piece of paper. Then try different orders for the pages. On a computer, save the master list in a new file before you move blocks of text.

2 Choosing an organizing tool

Some writers view outlines as chores and straitjackets, but they need not be dull or confining. There are different kinds of outlines, some more flexible than others. All of them can enlarge and clarify your thinking, showing you patterns of general and specific, suggesting proportions, and highlighting gaps or overlaps in coverage.

Many writers use outlines not only before but also after drafting—to check the underlying structure of the draft when revising it (see p. 53). No matter when it's made, though, an outline can be changed to reflect changes in your thinking. View any outline you make as a tentative sketch, not as a fixed diagram.

A scratch or informal outline

For many essays, especially those with a fairly straightforward structure, a simple listing of ideas and perhaps their support may provide adequate direction for your writing.

A **scratch outline** lists the key points of the paper in the order they will be covered. Here are Katy Moreno's thesis statement and scratch outline for her essay on the global job market:

Thesis statement

My mother's experience of having her job outsourced taught a lesson that Thomas L. Friedman overlooks: technical training by itself can be too narrow to produce the communicators and problem solvers needed by contemporary businesses.

Scratch outline

Mom's outsourcing experience
  Excellent tech skills
  Salary too high compared to overseas tech workers
  Lack of planning + communication skills, unlike managers who kept jobs
Well-rounded education to protect vs. outsourcing
  Tech training, as Friedman says
  Also, experience in communication, problem solving, other management skills

Moreno put more into this outline than its simplicity might imply, not only working out an order for her ideas but also sketching their implications.

An **informal outline** is usually more detailed than a scratch outline, including key general points as well as the specific evidence for them. A student's thesis statement and informal outline appear below.

Thesis statement

After Home Inc.'s hiring practices were exposed in the media, the company avoided a scandal with policy changes and a well-publicized outreach to employees and consumers.

Informal outline

Background on scandal
  Previous hiring practices
  Media exposure and public response (brief)
Policy changes
  Application forms
  Interviewing procedures
  Training of personnel
Outreach to employees
  Signs and letters
  Meetings and workshops
Outreach to consumers
  Press conference
  Store signs
  Advertising—print and radio

A tree diagram

In a **tree diagram**, ideas and details branch out in increasing specificity. Like any outline, the diagram can warn of gaps, overlaps, and digressions. But unlike more linear outlines, it can be supplemented and extended indefinitely, so it is easy to alter for new ideas and arrangements discovered during drafting and revision.

Following are a thesis statement and tree diagram by Johanna Abrams, based on her earlier brainstorming about a summer job (p. 24).

Thesis statement

Two months working in a large government agency taught me that an office's pecking order should be respected.

Tree diagram

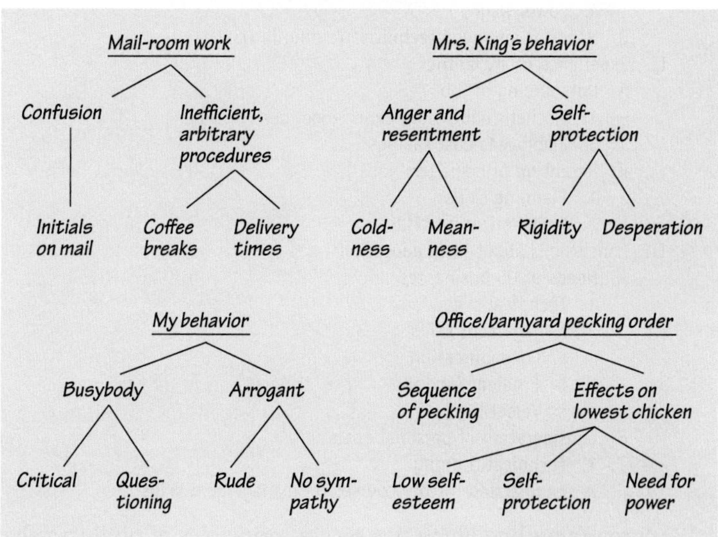

Each main part of the four-part diagram represents a different general idea about the summer-job experience. Within each part, information grows more specific as it branches downward.

A formal outline

For complex topics requiring complex arrangements of ideas and support, you may want or be required to construct a **formal outline**. More rigidly arranged and more detailed than other outlines, a formal outline not only lays out main ideas and their support but also shows the relative importance of all the essay's elements and how they connect with one another.

Note Because of its structure, a formal outline can be an excellent tool for planning a revision. For instance, you might use an outline to check that your organization is logical. Katy Moreno created the formal outline on the next page to plan expansions and other changes that were suggested by readers of her first draft.

Thesis statement

My mother's experience of having her job outsourced taught a lesson that Thomas L. Friedman overlooks: technical training by itself can be too narrow to produce the communicators and problem solvers needed by contemporary businesses.

Formal outline

I. Summary of Friedman's article
   A. Reasons for outsourcing
      1. Improved technology and access
      2. Well-educated workers
      3. Productive workers
      4. Lower wages
   B. Need for improved technical training in US
II. Experience of my mother
   A. Outsourcing of job
      1. Mother's education, experience, performance
      2. Employer's cost savings
   B. Retention of managers' jobs
      1. Planning skills
      2. Communication skills
III. Conclusions about ideal education
   A. Needs of US businesses
      1. Technical skills
      2. Management skills
         a. Communication
         b. Problem solving
         c. Versatility
   B. Consideration of personal goals
      1. Technical training
      2. English and history courses for management skills

Moreno's outline illustrates several principles of outlining that can help ensure completeness, balance, and clear relationships. (These principles largely depend on distinguishing between the general and the specific. See p. 34.)

- **All the outline's parts are systematically indented and labeled.** Roman numerals (I, II) label primary divisions of the essay, followed by capital letters (A, B) for secondary divisions, Arabic numerals (1, 2) for principal supporting points, and small letters (a, b) for details. Each succeeding level contains more specific information than the one before it.
- **The outline divides the material into several groups.** A list like the one following needs tighter, more logical groups to show the relationships between A and B and between C and D. (Compare this example with part III of Moreno's actual outline.)

  III. Conclusions about ideal education
     A. Business needs for technical skills
     B. Needs for management skills such as communication and problem solving
     C. Personal goal of technical training
     D. Additional courses for management skills

- **Within each part of the outline, distinct topics of equal generality appear in parallel headings,** with the same indention and numbering or lettering. In the following example, points 3, 4, and

Principles of the formal outline

- Labels and indentions indicate order and relative importance.
- Sections and subsections reflect logical relationships.
- Topics of equal generality appear in parallel headings.
- Each subdivision has at least two parts.
- Headings are expressed in parallel grammatical form.
- The introduction and conclusion may be omitted (though not, of course, from the essay).

5 are more specific than point 2, not equally general, so they should appear as subheadings a, b, and c under it. (See section III.A of Moreno's outline.)

```
A. Needs of US businesses
   1. Technical skills
   2. Management skills
   3. Communication
   4. Problem solving
   5. Versatility
```

- **All subdivided headings in the outline break into at least two parts** because a topic cannot logically be divided into only one part. The following example violates this principle:

```
B. Consideration of personal goals
   1. Technical training along with other courses for management skills
```

Any single subdivision should be matched with another subdivision (as in section III.B of Moreno's actual outline), combined with the heading above it, or rechecked for its relevance to the heading above it.

- **All headings are expressed in parallel grammatical form** (see pp. 400–04 on parallelism). Moreno's is a **topic outline**, in which the headings consist of a noun (*summary, reasons, technology and access*, and the like) with modifiers (*of Friedman's article, improved, well-educated*, and the like). In a **sentence outline** all headings are expressed as full sentences, as in the following rewrite of part III.A of Moreno's outline.

```
III. Friedman's article and my mother's experience lead me to conclusions
     about the ideal education.
   A. US businesses have dual needs for the jobs they keep here.
      1. They need employees with technical training.
      2. They need employees with management skills.
```

See pages 684–85 for a complete sentence outline.

- **The outline covers only the body of the essay, omitting the introduction and the conclusion**. The beginning and the ending are important in the essay itself, but you need not include them in the outline unless you are required to do so or you anticipate special problems with their organization.

3 Choosing a structure

Introduction, body, and conclusion

Structure is one of the features that distinguish genres of writing. For instance, a social-science research report generally has distinct sections in an established order: abstract, introduction, method, results, and discussion. Many academic genres, particularly those in the humanities, do not come with such a detailed plan, but they still share a basic shape:

- **The *introduction*, usually a paragraph or two, captures and focuses readers' attention.** At a minimum, it announces and clarifies the topic. Often it ends with the thesis statement, making a commitment that the rest of the work delivers on. (See pp. 101–04 for more on introductions.)
- **The *body* of the essay develops the thesis and thus fulfills the commitment of the introduction.** The paragraphs in the body develop the general points that support the thesis—the items that would be labeled with Roman numerals and capital letters in a formal outline like the one on page 38. These general points are like the legs of a table supporting the top, the thesis. Each general point may take a paragraph or more, with the bulk of the content providing the details, examples, and reasons (the wood of each table leg) to support the general point and thus the thesis.
- **The *conclusion* gives readers something to take away from the writing**—a summary of ideas, for instance, or a suggested course of action. (See pp. 105–06 for more on conclusions.)

CULTURE LANGUAGE If you are not used to reading and writing American academic prose, its pattern of introduction-body-conclusion and the particular organizations discussed on the next three pages may seem unfamiliar. For instance, instead of introductions that focus quickly on the topic and thesis, you may be used to openings that establish personal connections with readers or that approach the thesis indirectly. And instead of body paragraphs that first emphasize general points and then support those points with specific evidence, you may be used to general statements without support (because writers can assume that readers will supply the evidence themselves) or to evidence without explanation (because writers can assume that readers will infer the general points themselves). When writing American academic prose, you need to take into account readers' expectations for directness and for the statement and support of general points.

Schemes for organizing ideas in an essay

- **Space**
- **Time**
- **Emphasis:**

General to specific	Increasing importance (climax)
Specific to general	Decreasing familiarity
Problem-solution	Increasing complexity

Organizing the body by space or time

Two organizational schemes—spatial and chronological—grow naturally out of the topic.

Spatial

A **spatial organization** is especially appropriate for essays that describe a place, an object, or a person. Following the way people normally survey something, you move through space from a chosen starting point to other features of the subject. Describing a building, for instance, you might begin with an impression of the whole, then scan exterior details from top to bottom, and then describe interior spaces.

Chronological

A **chronological organization** reports events as they occurred in time, usually from first to last. This pattern, like spatial organization, corresponds to readers' own experiences and expectations. It suits an essay in which you do one of the following:

- **Recount a sequence of events,** such as a championship baseball game or the Battle of Gettysburg.
- **Explain a process from beginning to end**—for instance, how to run a marathon or how a tree converts carbon dioxide to oxygen.
- **Explain the causes that led to an effect,** such as the lobbying that helped to push a bill through the legislature. Alternatively, explain how a cause, such as a flood or a book, had multiple effects.
- **Tell a story about yourself or someone else.**
- **Provide background**—for instance, the making of a film you are analyzing or the procedure used in an experiment you are reporting.

Organizing the body for emphasis

Some organizational schemes must be imposed on ideas and information to aid readers' understanding and achieve a desired emphasis.

General to specific

Two ways of organizing essays depend on the distinction between the general and the specific, discussed on page 34. The **general-to-specific scheme** is common in expository and argumentative essays that start with a general discussion of the main points and then proceed to specific examples, facts, or other evidence. The following thesis statement forecasts a general-to-specific organization:

> As an investment in its own economy, the United States should provide a tuition grant to any college student who qualifies academically.

The body of the essay might first elaborate on the basic argument and then provide the supporting data.

Specific to general

Sometimes you may anticipate that readers will not appreciate or agree with your general ideas before they see the support for them—for instance, in an argumentative essay that takes an unpopular view. In these cases a **specific-to-general scheme** can arouse readers' interest in specific examples or other evidence, and you can let the evidence build to statements of more general ideas. The following thesis statement could be developed in this way:

> Although most of us are unaware of the public relations campaigns directed at us, they can significantly affect the way we think and live.

The writer might introduce the essay with a specific example of a public relations campaign and use it throughout the essay to illustrate the effects of public relations campaigns.

Problem-solution

Many arguments use a **problem-solution scheme**: first outline a problem that needs solving; then propose a solution. (If the solution involves steps toward a goal, it may be arranged chronologically.) The following thesis statement announces a problem-solution paper:

> To protect users' privacy, social-networking sites such as *Facebook* should make removing photographs, videos, and other links a transparent and simple process.

Climax

A common scheme in both explanations and arguments is the **climactic organization**, in which ideas unfold in order of increasing drama or importance to reach a climax. For example, the following thesis statement lists three effects of strip-mining in order of their increasing severity, and the essay would cover them in the same order:

> Strip-mining should be tightly controlled in this region to reduce its pollution of water resources, its destruction of the land, and its devastating effects on people's lives.

As this example suggests, the climactic organization works well in arguments because it leaves readers with the most important point freshest in their minds. In exposition such an arrangement can create suspense and thus hold readers' attention.

Familiarity or complexity

Expository essays can also be arranged to take account of readers' knowledge of the subject. An essay on the effects of air pollution might proceed from **most familiar to least familiar**—from effects readers are likely to know to ones they may not know. Similarly, an explanation of animals' nervous systems might proceed from **simplest to most complex**, so that the explanation of each nervous system provides a basis for readers to understand the more difficult one following.

4 Checking for unity and coherence

In conceiving your organization and writing your essay, you should be aware of two qualities of effective writing that relate to organization: unity and coherence. When you perceive that someone's writing "flows well," you are probably appreciating these two qualities. An essay has **unity** if all its parts relate to and support the thesis statement. Check for unity with these questions:

- **Is each main section relevant to the main idea (thesis) of the essay?**
- **Within main sections, does each example or detail support the principal idea of that section?**

An essay has **coherence** if readers can see the relations among parts and move easily from one thought to the next. Check for coherence with these questions:

- **Do the ideas follow in a clear sequence?**
- **Are the parts of the essay logically connected?**
- **Are the connections clear and smooth?**

A unified and coherent outline will not necessarily guide you to a unified and coherent essay because so much can change during drafting. Thus you shouldn't be too hard on your outline, in case a seemingly wayward idea proves useful. But do cut obvious digressions and rearrange material that clearly needs moving.

Sample essay (informative)

The following essay illustrates some ways of achieving unity and coherence (highlighted in the annotations).

Who Benefits from the Money in College Football?

Anyone who follows Division 1-A college football cannot fail to notice the money that pours into every aspect of the sport—the lavish stadiums, corporate sponsorships, televised games, and long post-season playoff tournament. The money may seem to flow to everyone, but in reality it doesn't. Although college football is a multimillion-dollar industry for the schools, conferences, and television networks, the benefits do not extend to the players.

Introduction establishing subject of essay

Informative thesis statement

The writing situation: Informative essay

- **Subject:** Who benefits from income generated by college football; student's choice for an essay assigned in a first-year writing course
- **Purpose:** To inform readers about money in college football
- **Audience:** Classmates, instructor, others who are interested in collegiate athletics
- **Genre:** Informative essay—writing that seeks to teach readers about a subject (see pp. 135–36)
- **Sources:** Personal knowledge: outside sources not required for this assignment

Paragraph idea, linked to thesis statement

Paragraph developed with evidence supporting its idea

Colleges and universities are major players in the for-profit football industry. A vibrant football program attracts not only skilled coaches and talented players but also wealthy, sports-minded donors who give money for state-of-the art stadiums and facilities. These great facilities in turn attract fans, some of whom are willing to pay high ticket prices to watch games in luxurious sky boxes and thus generate more profits for the schools' athletic departments.

Paragraph idea, linked to thesis statement

Paragraph developed with evidence supporting its idea

The athletic conferences to which the schools belong—such as the Big Ten, the Atlantic Coast Conference, and the Pac-12—reap financial rewards from college football. Each conference maintains a Web site to post schedules and scores, sell tickets and merchandise, and promote interest in its teams. However, the proceeds from ticket and merchandise sales surely pale in comparison to the money generated by the annual College Football Playoff—the three-week-long post-season football extravaganza. Each game is not only televised but also carries the name of a corporate sponsor that pays for the privilege of having its name attached to a bowl game.

Paragraph idea, linked to thesis statement

Paragraph developed with evidence supporting its idea

Like the schools and athletic conferences, the television networks profit from football. Networks sell advertising slots to the highest bidders for every televised game during the regular season and the College Football Playoff, and they work to sustain fans' interest in football by cultivating viewers on the Web. For instance, one network generates interest in up-and-coming high school players through *Scout.com*, a Web site that posts profiles of boys being recruited by colleges and universities and that is supported, at least in part, through advertising and paid subscriptions.

Transition and new paragraph idea, linked to thesis statement

Amid these money-making players are the actual football players, the young men who are bound by NCAA rules to play as amateurs and to receive no direct compensation for their hours of practice and field time.

They may receive scholarships that cover tuition, room and board, uniforms, medical care, and travel. Yet these payments are a small fraction of the millions of dollars spent on and earned from football.

Paragraph developed with evidence supporting its idea

Many critics have pointed out the disparity between players' rewards and the industry's profits. Recent efforts to unionize the players and file lawsuits on their behalf have caused schools, conferences, and the NCAA to make some concessions in scholarship packages and rules. However, these changes do not fundamentally alter a system in which the big benefits go to everyone but the players.

Conclusion echoing thesis statement and summarizing

—Terrence MacDonald (student)

Unity and coherence within paragraphs

The unity and coherence of writing begin in its paragraphs, so the two concepts are treated in greater detail in Chapter 4. Before you begin drafting, you may find it helpful to consult two sections in particular:

- **The topic sentence and unity** (pp. 73–76)
- **Coherence and transitions** (pp. 77–87, 106–07)

Exercise 2.9 Organizing ideas

The following list of ideas was extracted by a student from freewriting he did for a brief paper on soccer in the United States. Using his thesis statement as a guide, pick out the general ideas and arrange the relevant specific points under them. In some cases you may have to infer general ideas to cover specific points in the list.

Thesis statement

Although its growth in the United States has been slow and halting, professional soccer may finally be poised to become a major American sport.

List of ideas

In countries of South and Latin America, soccer is the favorite sport.

In the United States the success of a sport depends largely on its ability to attract huge TV audiences.

Soccer was not often presented on US television.

In 2010 and 2014, the World Cup final was broadcast on ABC and on Spanish-language Univision.

In the past, professional soccer could not get a foothold in the United States because of poor TV coverage and lack of financial backing.

The growing Hispanic population in the United States could help soccer grow as well.

Investors have poured hundreds of millions of dollars into the top US professional league.

Potential fans did not have a chance to see soccer games.

Failures of early start-up leagues made potential backers wary of new ventures.

Recently, the outlook for professional soccer has changed dramatically.

The US television audience for the 2014 US-Ghana match was larger than the average US television audience for baseball's World Series.

Exercise 2.10 Creating a formal outline

Use your arrangement of general ideas and specific points from Exercise 2.9 as the basis for a formal topic or sentence outline. Follow the principles given on pages 38–40.

Exercise 2.11 Considering your past work: Organizing ideas

What has been your experience with organizing your writing? Many writers find it difficult. If you do, too, can you say why? What kinds of outlines or other organizing tools have you used? Which have been helpful and which have not?

Exercise 2.12 Organizing your own essay

Continuing from Exercise 2.8 (p. 34), choose an appropriate organization for your essay-in-progress. Then experiment with organizing tools by preparing a tree diagram or other visual map or a scratch, informal, or formal outline.

3 Drafting, Revising, and Editing

Chapter essentials

- Start writing and maintain momentum (opposite).
- Revise your draft using a revision checklist (pp. 51, 53).
- Collaborate on revisions (p. 56).
- Edit the revised draft using an editing checklist (pp. 61, 62).
- Proofread the final draft (p. 66).
- Prepare a portfolio of your writing (p. 69).

Visit MyWritingLab™ for more resources on drafting, revising, and editing.

The separation of drafting, revising, and editing from the planning and development discussed earlier is somewhat artificial because the stages almost always overlap during the writing process. Indeed, if you compose on a computer, you may not experience any boundaries between stages at all. Still, your primary goal during the writing process will usually shift from gathering and shaping information to forming connected sentences and paragraphs in a draft and then restructuring and rewriting the draft for presentation to an audience.

3a Writing the first draft

The only correct drafting style is the one that works for you. Generally, though, the freer and more fluid you are, the better. Some writers draft and revise at the same time, but most let themselves go during drafting and *especially* do not worry about errors. Drafting is the occasion to find and convey meaning through the act of writing. If you fear making mistakes while drafting, that fear will choke your ideas. You draft only for yourself, so errors do not matter. Write freely until you have worked out what you want to say; *then* focus on any mistakes you may have made.

Starting to draft sometimes takes courage, even for seasoned professionals. Students and pros alike find easy ways to procrastinate—checking messages, meeting for coffee, napping, tweeting about procrastinating. Such delays may actually help you if you let

Drafting

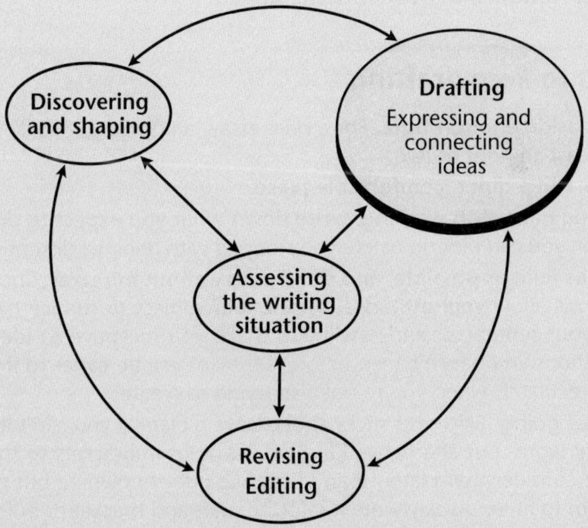

When you draft an essay, you work toward expressing and connecting the ideas you've developed. If you change direction or run out of ideas during drafting, you can always circle back to renew your purpose, discover new ideas, or rethink your thesis.

ideas for writing simmer at the same time. At some point, though, enough is enough: the deadline looms; you've got to get started. If the blankness still stares back at you, then try one of the techniques for unblocking listed in the following box.

Ways to start drafting

- **Read over what you've already written**—notes, outlines, and so on. Immediately start your draft with whatever comes to mind.
- **Freewrite** (see pp. 22–23).
- **Pretend you're talking to a friend about your subject.**
- **Describe an image that represents your subject**—a physical object, a facial expression, two people arguing over something, a giant machine gouging the earth for a mine, whatever.
- **Write a paragraph.** Explain what you think your essay will be about when you finish it.
- **Skip the opening and start in the middle.** Or write the conclusion.
- **Start writing the part that you understand best or feel most strongly about.** Using your outline, divide your work into chunks—say, one for the introduction, another for the first point, and so on. One of these chunks may call out to be written.

You should find some momentum once you've started writing. If not, however, or if your energy flags, try one or more of the following techniques to keep moving ahead.

Ways to *keep* drafting

- **Set aside enough time.** For a brief essay, a first draft is likely to take at least an hour or two.
- **Work in a quiet, comfortable place.**
- **If you must stop working, write down what you expect to do next.** Then you can pick up where you stopped with minimal disruption.
- **Be as fluid as possible, and don't worry about mistakes.** Spontaneity will allow your attitudes toward your subject to surface naturally in your sentences, and it will also make you receptive to ideas and relations you haven't seen before. Mistakes will be easier to find and correct later, when you're not also trying to create.
- **Keep going.** Skip over sticky spots; leave a blank if you can't find the right word; put alternative ideas or phrasings in brackets so that you can consider them later. If an idea pops out of nowhere but doesn't seem to fit in, quickly write it into the draft and bracket or boldface it for later attention. Use an asterisk (*) or some other symbol to mark places where you feel blocked or uncertain.
- **Resist self-criticism.** Don't worry about your style, grammar, spelling, punctuation, and the like. Don't worry about what your readers will

think. These are very important matters, but save them for revision. On a computer, turn off automatic spelling- or grammar-checking functions if they distract you.

- **Use your thesis statement and outline** to remind you of the purpose, organization, and content that you planned.
- **But don't feel constrained by your thesis and outline.** If your writing leads you in a more interesting direction, follow.

If you write on a computer, frequently save the text you're drafting—at least every five or ten minutes and every time you leave the computer.

Whether you compose on paper or on a computer, you may find it difficult to tell whether a first draft is finished. The distinction between drafts can be significant because creating text is different from rethinking it and because your instructor may ask you and your classmates to submit your drafts, either on paper or online, so that others can give you feedback on them. For your own revision or others' feedback, you might consider a draft finished for any number of reasons: perhaps you've run out of ideas; perhaps you find yourself writing the conclusion; perhaps you've stopped adding content and are just tinkering with words.

Sample first draft

Following is Katy Moreno's first-draft response to Thomas L. Friedman's "It's a Flat World, after All." (The first two paragraphs include the page numbers in Friedman's article that Moreno summarized material from.) As part of her assignment, Moreno showed the draft to four classmates, whose suggestions for revision appear in the margin of this draft. They used the Comment function of *Microsoft Word*, which allows users to add comments without inserting words into the document's text. Notice that the classmates ignore errors in grammar and punctuation, concentrating instead on larger issues such as thesis, clarity of ideas, and unity.

Title?

In "It's a Flat World, after All," Thomas L. Friedman argues that, most US students are not preparing themselves as well as they should to compete in today's economy. Not like students in India, China, and other countries are (34-37). The outsourcing of my mother's job proves that Thomas L. Friedman's advice to improve students' technical training is too narrow.

Comment [Jared]: Your mother's job being outsourced is interesting, but your introduction seems rushed.

Comment [Rabia]: The end of your thesis statement is a little unclear—too narrow for what?

Friedman describes a "flat" world where technology like the Internet and wireless communication makes it possible for college graduates all over the globe, in particular in India and China, to get jobs that once were gotten by graduates of US colleges and universities (37). He argues that US students need more math and science in order to compete (37).

Comment [Erin]: Can you include the reasons Friedman gives for overseas students' success?

I came to college with first-hand knowledge of globalization and outsourcing. My mother, who worked for sixteen years in the field of information technology (IT), was laid off six months ago when the company she worked for decided to outsource much of its IT work to a company based in India. My mother majored in computer science, had sixteen years of experience, and her bosses always gave her good reviews. She never expected to be laid off and was surprised when she was. She wasn't laid off because of her background and performance. In fact, my mother had a very strong background in math and science and years of training and job experience. The reason was because her salary and benefits cost the company more than outsourcing her job did. Which hurt my family financially, as you can imagine.

Comment [Nathaniel]: Tighten this paragraph to avoid repetition? Also, how does your mother's experience relate to Friedman and your thesis?

A number of well-paid people in the IT department where my mother worked, namely IT managers, were not laid off. As my mother explained at the time, they kept their jobs because they were better at planning and they communicated better, they were better writers and speakers than my mother.

Comment [Erin]: What were the managers better at planning for?

Like my mother, I am more comfortable in front of a computer than I am in front of a group of people. I planned to major in computer science. Since my mother lost her job, though, I have decided to take courses in English and history too, where the classes will require me to do different kinds of work. When I enter the job market, my well-rounded education will make me a more attractive job candidate, and, will help me to be a versatile, productive employee.

Comment [Nathaniel]: Can you be more specific about the kinds of work you'll need to do?

Comment [Rabia]: Can you work this point into your thesis?

We know from our history that Americans have been innovative, hard-working people. We students have educational opportunities to compete in the global economy, but we must use our time in college wisely. As Thomas L. Friedman says, my classmates and I need to be ready for a rapidly changing future. We will have to work hard each day, which means being prepared for class, getting the best grades we can, and making the most of each class. Our futures depend on the decisions we make today.

Comment [Jared]: Conclusion seems to go off in a new direction. Friedman mentions hard work, but it hasn't been your focus before.

Comment [Rabia]: Don't forget your works cited.

Exercise 3.1 Analyzing a first draft

Compare Moreno's draft with the previous step in her planning (her scratch outline) on page 36. List the places in the draft where the act of drafting led Moreno to rearrange her information, add or delete material, or explore new ideas. Mark Moreno's thesis statement and each key idea developing the thesis. Note places where you think the ideas could be clearer or better supported.

Exercise 3.2 Considering your past work: Drafting

Think back over a recent writing experience. At what point in the writing process did you begin drafting? How did drafting go—smoothly, haltingly, painfully, painlessly? If you had difficulties, what were they? If you didn't, why do you think not?

Exercise 3.3 Drafting your essay

Prepare a draft of the essay you began in Chapters 1 and 2. Use your thesis statement and your outline as guides, but don't be unduly constrained by them. Concentrate on opening up options, not on closing them down. Do not, above all, worry about mistakes.

3b Revising a draft

Revision literally means "re-seeing"—looking anew at ideas and details, their relationships and arrangement, the degree to which they work or don't work for the thesis. While drafting, you focus inwardly, concentrating on pulling your topic out of yourself. In revising, you look out to your readers, trying to anticipate how they will see your work. You adopt a critical perspective toward your work, examining it as an athlete or dancer would examine a video of his or her performance.

1 Revising, then editing

Think of revision and editing as separate stages: in revision you deal with the underlying meaning and structure of your essay; in editing you deal with the surface, with the manner of expression, clarity, and correctness. By making separate drafts beyond the first—a revised one and then an edited one—you'll be less likely to waste time tinkering with sentences that you end up cutting, and you'll avoid the temptation to substitute editing for more substantial revision.

The temptation to edit while revising can be especially attractive on a computer because it's easy to make changes. Indeed, writers sometimes find themselves editing compulsively, spinning their wheels with changes that cease to have any marked effect on meaning or clarity and that may in fact sap the writing of energy. Planning to revise and then to edit encourages you to look beyond

Revising and editing

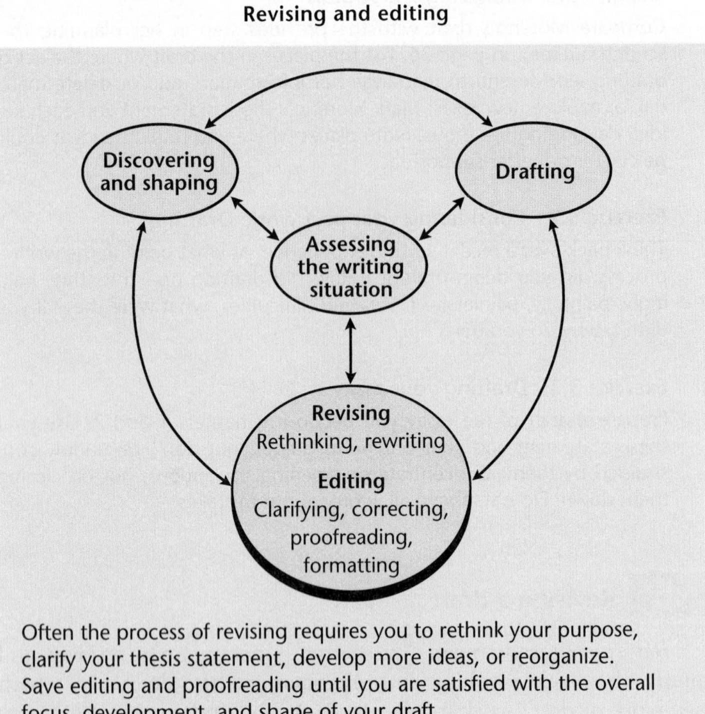

Often the process of revising requires you to rethink your purpose, clarify your thesis statement, develop more ideas, or reorganize. Save editing and proofreading until you are satisfied with the overall focus, development, and shape of your draft.

the confines of the screen so that deeper issues of meaning and structure aren't lost to surface matters such as word choice and sentence arrangement.

2 Gaining distance from your work

Reading your own work critically can be difficult. Changing or even deleting material that you've worked hard to express can be still more difficult. The key is to gain some objectivity toward your writing. The following techniques may help:

- **Take a break after finishing your draft.** A few hours may be enough; a whole night or day is preferable. The break will clear your mind, relax you, and give you some objectivity.
- **Ask someone to respond to your draft.** A roommate, family member, classmate, or tutor in the writing center can call attention to what needs revising.
- **Read your draft in a new medium.** Typing a handwritten draft or printing out a word-processed draft can reveal weaknesses that you didn't see in the original.

- **Outline your draft.** Highlight the main points supporting the thesis, and write these sentences down separately in outline form. Then examine the outline you've made for logical order, gaps, and digressions. A formal outline can be especially illuminating because of its careful structure. (See pp. 37–40.)
- **Listen to your draft.** Read the draft out loud, record and listen to it, or have someone read the draft to you.
- **Use a revision checklist.** Don't try to re-see everything in your draft at once. Use a checklist like the one that follows, making a separate pass through the draft for each item.

Checklist for revision

Assignment

How have you responded to the assignment for this writing? Verify that your genre, subject, and purpose are appropriate for the assignment.

Purpose

What is the purpose of your writing? Is it consistent throughout the paper? (See pp. 9–11.)

Audience and voice

How does the writing address the intended audience? How clearly can readers hear your writer's voice? What role will they see you as playing? What tone will they hear? (See pp. 11–14.)

Genre

How does your writing fit the conventions of the genre you're using—features such as organization, evidence, and format? (See pp. 15–16.)

Thesis

What is the thesis of your writing? Where does it become clear? Does any part of the paper stray from the thesis? Does the paper fulfill the commitment of the thesis? (See pp. 28–33.)

Organization

What are the main points of the paper? (List them.) How well does each support the thesis? How effective is their arrangement for the paper's purpose? (See pp. 34–35, 40–43.)

Development

How well do details, examples, and other evidence support each main point? Where, if at all, might readers find support skimpy or have trouble understanding the content? (See pp. 25–27, 90–99.)

Unity

What does each sentence and paragraph contribute to the thesis? Where, if at all, do digressions occur? Should they be cut, or can they be rewritten to support the thesis? (See pp. 43–45, 73–76.)

(continued)

Checklist for revision
(continued)

Coherence

How clearly and smoothly does the paper flow? Where does it seem rough or awkward? Can any transitions be improved? (See pp. 43–45, 77–79.)

Title, introduction, conclusion

How accurately and interestingly does the title reflect the essay's content? (See below.)

How well does the introduction engage and focus readers' attention? (See pp. 101–04.)

How effective is the conclusion in providing a sense of completion? (See pp. 105–06.)

3 Titling your essay

The revision stage is a good time to consider a title. After drafting, you have a clearer sense of your direction, and the attempt to sum up your essay in a title phrase can help you focus sharply on your topic, purpose, and audience.

Here are suggestions for titling an essay:

- **A *descriptive title* is almost always appropriate and is often expected for academic writing.** It announces the topic clearly, accurately, and as briefly as possible. The final title of Katy Moreno's essay is an example: "Can We Compete? College Education for the Global Economy." Other examples include "Images of Lost Identity in *North by Northwest,*" "An Experiment in Small-Group Dynamics," "Why Lincoln Delayed Emancipating the Slaves," and "Food Poisoning Involving *E. coli* Bacteria: A Review of the Literature."
- **A *suggestive title*—the kind often found in popular magazines—may be appropriate for more informal writing.** Examples include "Making Peace" (for an essay on the Peace Corps) and Thomas L. Friedman's "It's a Flat World, after All" (on the global job market). For a more suggestive title, Moreno might have chosen "Training for the New World" or "Education for a Flat World" (echoing Friedman's title). A suggestive title conveys the writer's attitude and main concerns but not the precise topic, thereby pulling readers into the essay to learn more. A source for such a title may be a familiar phrase, a fresh image, or a significant expression from the essay itself.
- **A title tells readers how big the topic is.** For Moreno's essay, the title "Globalization and Jobs" or "Competing in Today's Job Market" would have been too broad, whereas "Outsourcing Our Jobs" or "The Importance of a Broad Education" would have

been too narrow because each deals with only part of the paper's content.

- **A title should not restate the assignment or the thesis statement,** as in "The Trouble with Thomas L. Friedman's View of the Global Job Market" or "What I Think about Technical Training and Today's Job Market."

More information on essay titles can be found elsewhere in this handbook: see pages 355 (avoiding reference to the title in the opening of the paper), 481 (capitalizing words in a title), and 680–81 (formatting a title in the final paper).

4 Revising on a computer

Word processors have removed the mechanical drudgery of revising by hand, but they have also complicated the process: you must conscientiously save your changes and manage the files you create, both discussed below. At the same time, like the more cumbersome revision methods, word processors allow you to display changes as you make them.

Saving changes and managing files

When you revise on a computer, take a few precautions to keep track of your drafts and to avoid losing your work:

- **Work on a copy of your latest draft.** The original will remain intact until you're truly finished with it, so you won't inadvertently lose anything.
- **Save each draft under its own file name.** You may need to consult an earlier draft for ideas or phrasings.
- **Save your work every five to ten minutes.** Most word processors will save your work automatically as you type, at the interval you specify. Still, get in the habit of saving manually whenever you make major changes.
- **After doing any major work on a project, create a backup version of the file.** Use a removable flash drive, or save files to the Internet with a storage service such as *Dropbox* or *Google Drive.*

Displaying changes

You can keep track of the revisions you make in a document with an option often called Track Changes. The function highlights additions and deletions so they're easy to spot (see Katy Moreno's revised draft on pp. 58–60). Tracking changes may encourage you to revise more freely because you can always revert to your original text. You can weigh the original and revised versions as you view them side by side. You can also evaluate the kinds of changes you are making. For instance, if during revision you see only minor surface alterations (word substitutions, added punctuation, and the like), then you might consider whether and where to read more deeply for more fundamental changes.

3c Collaborating on revisions

In many writing courses students work together, often commenting on each other's writing to help with revision. This collaborative writing provides experience in reading written work critically and in reaching others through writing. The collaboration may occur face to face in small groups, on paper via drafts and comments, or online, either through a course-management system such as *Blackboard* or *Canvas* or through a class blog, e-mail list, or wiki.

Whatever the medium of collaboration, following a few guidelines will help you gain more from others' comments and become a more constructive reader yourself.

CULTURE LANGUAGE In some cultures writers do not expect criticism from readers, or readers do not expect to think critically about what they read. If critical responses are uncommon in your native culture, collaboration may at first be uncomfortable for you. As a writer, consider that readers are responding to your draft or even your final paper more as an exploration of ideas than as the last word on your subject; then you may be more receptive to readers' suggestions. As a reader, know that your tactful questions and suggestions about focus, content, and organization will usually be considered appropriate.

1 Benefiting from comments on your writing

- **Think of your readers as counselors or coaches.** They can help you see the virtues and flaws in your work and sharpen your awareness of readers' needs.
- **Read or listen to comments closely.**
- **Know what the critic is saying.** If you need more information, ask for it, or consult the appropriate section of this handbook.
- **Don't become defensive.** Letting comments offend you will only erect a barrier to improvement in your writing. As one writing teacher advises, "Leave your ego at the door."
- **Revise your work in response to appropriate comments.** You will learn more from the act of revision than from just thinking about changes.
- **Remember that you are the final authority on your work.** You should be open to suggestions, but you are free to decline advice when you think it is inappropriate.
- **Keep track of both the strengths and the weaknesses others identify.** Then in later assignments you can build on your successes and give special attention to problem areas.

As the last item in the preceding list indicates, you'll gain the most from collaboration if you carry your learning from one assignment into the next. To keep track of things to work on, try a chart like the one on page 64.

2 Commenting on others' writing

- **Be sure you know what the writer is saying.** If necessary, summarize the paper to understand its content. (See pp. 155–57.)
- **Address only your most significant concerns with the work.** Focus on the deep issues in other writers' drafts, especially early drafts: thesis, purpose, audience, organization, and support for the thesis. Use the revision checklist on pages 53–54 as a guide to what is significant. Unless you have other instructions, ignore mistakes in grammar, punctuation, spelling, and the like. (The temptation to focus on such errors may be especially strong if the writer is less experienced than you are with standard American English.) Emphasizing mistakes will contribute little to the writer's revision.
- **Remember that you are the reader, not the writer.** Don't edit sentences, add details, or otherwise assume responsibility for the paper.
- **Phrase your comments carefully.** Avoid misunderstandings by making sure comments are both clear and respectful. If you are responding on paper or online, not face to face with the writer, remember that the writer has nothing but your written words to go on. He or she can't ask you for immediate clarification and can't infer your attitudes from gestures, facial expressions, and tone of voice.
- **Be specific.** If something confuses you, say *why*. If you disagree with a conclusion, say *why*.
- **Be supportive as well as honest.** Tell the writer what you like about the paper. Phrase your comments positively: instead of *This paragraph doesn't interest me,* say *You have an interesting detail here that I almost missed.* Question the writer in a way that emphasizes the effect of the work on you, the reader: *This paragraph confuses me because. . . .* And avoid measuring the work against a set of external standards, as in *This essay is poorly organized* or *Your thesis statement is inadequate.*
- **While reading, make your comments in writing.** Even if you will be delivering your comments in person later on, the written record will help you recall what you thought.
- **Link comments to specific parts of a paper.** Especially if you are reading the paper on a computer, be clear about what in the paper each comment relates to. You can use a word processor's Comment function, which annotates documents.

3d Examining a sample revision

Katy Moreno was satisfied with her first draft: she had her ideas down, and the arrangement seemed logical. Still, from the revision checklist she knew the draft needed work, and her classmates' comments (pp. 49–50) highlighted what she needed to focus on. The following revised draft shows Moreno's changes in response to these comments. Moreno used the Track Changes function on her word processor, so that deletions are crossed out and additions are in blue.

Descriptive title names topic and forecasts approach.

Can We Compete?

College Education for the Global Economy

~~Title?~~

Expanded introduction draws readers into Moreno's topic, clarifies her point of agreement with Friedman, and states her revised thesis.

Today's students cannot miss news stories about globalization of the economy and outsourcing of jobs, but are students aware of how these trends are affecting the job market? In "It's a Flat World, after All," Thomas L. Friedman argues that most US students are not preparing themselves as well as ~~they should to compete in today's economy. Not like~~ students in India, China, and other countries ~~are~~ to compete in today's economy, which requires hard-working, productive scientists and engineers (34-37). Friedman's argument speaks to me because my mother recently lost her job when it was outsourced to India. But her experience taught a lesson that Friedman overlooks: technical training by itself can be too narrow to produce the communicators and problem solvers needed by contemporary businesses. ~~The outsourcing of my mother's job proves that Thomas L. Friedman's advice to improve students' technical training is too narrow.~~

Expanded summary of Friedman's article specifies qualities of overseas workers.

Friedman describes a "flat" world where technology like the Internet and wireless communication makes it possible for college graduates all over the globe~~, in particular~~ to compete for high paying jobs that once belonged to graduates of US colleges and universities (34). He focuses on workers in India and China~~,~~ who graduate from college with excellent educations in math and science, who are eager for new opportunities, and who are willing to work exceptionally hard, often harder than their American counterparts and, for less money ~~to get jobs that once were gotten by graduates of US colleges and universities~~ (37). ~~He~~ Friedman argues that US students must be better prepared academically, especially in

~~need more~~ math and science, so that they can get and keep jobs that will otherwise go overseas ~~in order to compete~~ (37).

~~I came to college with first hand knowledge of globalization and outsourcing. My mother, who worked for sixteen years in the field of information technology (IT), was laid off six months ago when the company she worked for decided to outsource much of its IT work to a company based in India. My mother~~ At first glance, my mother's experience of losing her job might seem to support the argument of Friedman that better training in math and science is the key to competing in the global job market. Her experience, however, adds dimensions to the globalization story, which Friedman misses. First my mother had the kind of strong background in math and science that Friedman says, today's workers need. She majored in computer science, rose within the information technology (IT) department of a large company, ~~had sixteen years of experience,~~ and her bosses always gave her good performance reviews. Still, when her employer decided to outsource most of its IT work, my mother lost her job. ~~She never expected to be laid off and was surprised when she was. She wasn't laid off because of her background and performance. In fact, my mother had a very strong background in math and science and years of training and job experience.~~ The reason wasn't because her technical skills were inadequate. Instead, her salary and benefits cost the company more than outsourcing her job did. Until wages rise around the globe, jobs like my mother's will be vulnerable. No matter how well you are trained. ~~Which hurt my family financially, as you can imagine.~~

New opening sentences connect to introduction and thesis statement, restating points of agreement and disagreement with Friedman.

Revisions condense long example of mother's experience.

Concluding sentences reinforce the point of the paragraph and connect to thesis statement.

The second dimension that Friedman misses is that ~~A~~a number of well-paid people in ~~the~~ my mother's IT department ~~where my mother worked~~, namely IT managers, were not laid off. As my mother explained at the time, they kept their jobs because they were experienced at figuring out the company's IT needs, planning for changes and, researching and proposing solutions. They also communicated better and were better at writing and speaking than my mother was. ~~were better at planning and, they communicated better, they were better writers and speakers than my mother.~~ Friedman misses these skills by focusing only on technical training. Without the ability to solve problems creatively and to communicate, people with technical expertise alone may not have enough to save their jobs. It wasn't enough to save my mother's.

Numbered point (*second*) connects this paragraph to the previous one.

New examples support general point.

Concluding sentences connect paragraph to thesis.

Like my mother, I am more comfortable in front of a computer than I am in front of a group of people, and I had planned to major in computer science. Since my mother lost her job, ~~though~~ however, I have decided to take courses in English and history too, where the classes will require me to ~~do different kinds of work~~ read broadly, think critically, research, and communicate ideas in writing—skills that make managers. When I enter the job market, my well-rounded education will make me a more attractive job candidate, and, will help me ~~be a versatile, productive employee~~ become the kind of forward-thinking manager that US companies will always need to employ here in the United States.

New examples add specificity.

Expanded sentence connects to thesis statement.

~~We know from our history that Americans have been innovative, hard working people. We students have educational opportunities to compete in the global economy, but we must use our time in college wisely. As Thomas L. Friedman says,~~ Many jobs that require a college degree are indeed going overseas, as Thomas L. Friedman says, and my classmates and I need to be ready for a rapidly changing future. But rather than focus only on math and science, we need to broaden our academic experiences so that the skills we develop make us not only employable, but also indispensable. ~~We will have to work hard each day, which means being prepared for class, getting the best grades we can, and making the most of each class. Our futures depend on the decisions we make today.~~

New conclusion recaps Friedman's points and Moreno's thesis and points to the future.

Work Cited

Friedman, Thomas L. "It's a Flat World, after All." *The New York Times Magazine,* 3 Apr. 2005, pp. 32-37.

New work-cited entry. (See p. 644 on MLA style.)

Exercise 3.4 Analyzing a revised draft

Can you see the reasons for most of the changes Moreno made in her revised draft? Where would you suggest further revisions, and why?

Exercise 3.5 Considering your past work: Revising

In the past, have you usually revised your drafts extensively? Do you think your writing would benefit from more revision of the sort described in this chapter? Why or why not? Many students who don't revise much explain that they lack the time. Is time a problem for you? Can you think of ways to resolve the problem?

Exercise 3.6 Revising your own draft

Revise your own first draft from Exercise 3.3 (p. 51). Use the checklist for revision on pages 53–54 as a guide. Concentrate on purpose, content, and organization, leaving smaller problems such as sentence structure, word choice, and grammar for the next draft.

3e Editing the revised draft

Editing for style, clarity, and correctness may come second to more fundamental revision, but it is still very important. A carefully developed essay will fall flat with readers if you overlook awkwardness and errors. In the following example of editing, Katy Moreno tightens wording, improves parallelism (with *consistently received*), corrects several comma errors, and repairs the final sentence fragment.

> At first glance, my mother's experience of losing her job might seem to support ~~the~~ Friedman's argument ~~of Friedman~~ that better training in math and science is the key to competing in the global job market. However, ~~H~~her experience~~, however,~~ adds dimensions to the globalization story~~, which~~ that Friedman misses. First, my mother had the kind of strong background in math and science that Friedman says~~,~~ today's workers need. She majored in computer science, rose within the information technology (IT) department of a large company, and consistently received ~~her bosses always gave her~~ good performance reviews. Still, when her employer decided to outsource most of its IT work, my mother lost her job. The reason wasn't ~~because~~ that her technical skills were inadequate. Instead, her salary and benefits cost the company more than outsourcing her job did. Until wages rise around the globe, jobs like my mother's will be vulnerable,~~.~~ ~~N~~no matter how well ~~you are~~ a person is trained.

1 Discovering what needs editing

After you've read and reread a draft to revise it, finding awkwardness and errors can be difficult. Try the following approaches to spot possible flaws in your revised draft:

- **Take a break,** even fifteen or twenty minutes, to clear your head.
- **Read the draft *slowly*, and read what you *actually see*.** Otherwise, you're likely to read what you intended to write but didn't. (If you have trouble slowing down, try reading your draft from back to front, sentence by sentence.)
- **Read as if you are encountering the draft for the first time.** Put yourself in the reader's place.
- **Have a classmate, friend, or relative read your work.** Make sure you understand and consider the reader's suggestions, even if eventually you decide not to take them.
- **Read the draft aloud or, even better, record it.** Listen for awkward rhythms, repetitive sentence patterns, and missing or clumsy transitions.

- **Learn from your own experience.** Keep a record of the problems that others have pointed out in your writing. (See p. 64 for a suggested format.) When editing, check your work against this record.

2 Using an editing checklist

The following checklist emphasizes students' most common editing challenges. In your editing, work first for clear and effective sentences that flow smoothly. Then check your sentences for correct spelling, grammar, and punctuation. Use the checklist's questions to guide your editing, making several passes through your draft. Refer to the page numbers in parentheses as needed.

Checklist for editing

Are my sentences clear?

Do my words and sentences mean what I intend them to mean? Is anything confusing? Check especially for these:

Exact language (pp. 507–18)
Parallelism (pp. 400–04)
Clear modifiers (pp. 363–72)
Clear reference of pronouns (pp. 351–56)
Complete sentences (pp. 338–44)
Sentences separated correctly (pp. 345–49)

Are my sentences effective?

How well do words and sentences engage and hold readers' attention? How appropriate and effective is the voice created by words and sentences? Where does the writing seem wordy, choppy, or dull? Check especially for these:

Expression of voice (pp. 13–14)
Emphasis of main ideas (pp. 382–90)
Smooth and informative transitions (pp. 85–86, 106–07)
Variety in sentence length and structure (pp. 407–13)
Appropriate language (pp. 498–506)
Concise sentences (pp. 519–24)

Do my sentences contain errors?

Where do surface errors interfere with the clarity and effectiveness of my sentences? Check especially for these:

- **Spelling errors** (pp. 526–37)
- **Sentence fragments** (pp. 338–44)
- **Comma splices** (pp. 345–49)

- **Verb errors**

  Verb forms, especially *-s* and *-ed* endings, correct forms of irregular verbs, and appropriate helping verbs (pp. 282–98)

  Verb tenses, especially consistency (pp. 298–304, 300)

  Agreement between subjects and verbs, especially when words come between them or the subject is *each, everyone,* or a similar word (pp. 311–18)

- **Pronoun errors**

  Pronoun forms, especially subjective (*he, she, they, who*) vs. objective (*him, her, them, whom*) (pp. 274–81)

  Agreement between pronouns and antecedents, especially when the antecedent contains *or* or the antecedent is *each, everyone, person,* or a similar word (pp. 319–22)

- **Punctuation errors**

  Commas, especially with comma splices (pp. 345–49), with *and* or *but* (422–24), with introductory elements (425–26), with nonessential elements (427–31), and with series (433)

  Apostrophes in possessives but not plural nouns (*Dave's/witches*) and in contractions but not possessive personal pronouns (*it's/its*) (pp. 451–57)

Note No writer needs every item on this list. As you receive feedback on your writing and grow more experienced with editing, you'll learn which items you need to focus on. To create an individualized editing checklist, see below.

3 Tracking your errors

You won't make every kind of error; instead, you may make the same three or four kinds of errors in each essay you write. The key to correcting such errors is recognizing them, keeping track of them, and checking for them each time you edit your writing.

To track your errors, try making a chart like the one on the next page, with a vertical column for each assignment (or draft) and a horizontal row for each error or weakness that you or others have noted in your writing. Check marks indicate how often the problem occurs in every essay. The chart also provides a convenient place to keep track of words you misspell so that you can master their spellings. When you edit, check your work against the list so that you learn to see—and correct—the errors that you typically make.

4 Editing on a computer

When you write on a word processor, consider the additional approaches to editing given in the list on the next page.

Record of errors

Weaknesses	paper 1	paper 2	paper 3
not enough details for readers	✓	✓	✓
unity—wanders away from thesis	✓		
subject-verb agreement	✓		✓
comma splice	✓✓	✓	✓
misspellings	among deceive	rebel seize	omission cruelty

- **Don't rely on a spelling or grammar/style checker to find what needs editing.** See the discussion of these checkers below.
- **If possible, edit a double-spaced paper copy.** Many people find it much harder to spot errors on a computer screen than on paper.
- **Use the Find command to locate and correct your common problems**—certain misspellings, wordy phrases such as *the fact that,* overuse of *there is,* and so on.
- **Resist overediting.** The ease of editing on a computer can lead to rewriting sentences over and over, stealing the life from your prose. If your grammar/style checker contributes to the temptation, consider turning it off.
- **Take special care with additions and omissions.** Make sure you haven't omitted needed words or left in unneeded words.

5 Working with spelling and grammar/style checkers

A spelling checker and a grammar/style checker can be helpful *if* you work within their limitations. The programs miss many problems and may even flag items that are actually correct. Further, they know nothing of your purpose and your audience, so they cannot make important decisions about your writing. Always use these tools critically:

- **Read your work yourself to ensure that it's clear and error-free.**
- **Consider a checker's proposal corrections carefully, weighing each one against your intentions.** If you aren't sure whether to accept a checker's suggestion, consult a dictionary, writing handbook, or other source. Your version may be fine.

Using a spelling checker

Your word processor's spelling checker can be a great ally: it will flag words that are spelled incorrectly and will usually suggest alternative spellings that resemble what you've typed. However, this ally also has the potential to undermine you because of its limitations:

- **The checker may flag a word that you've spelled correctly** just because the word does not appear in its dictionary.
- **The checker may suggest incorrect alternatives.** In providing a list of alternative spellings for your word, the checker may highlight the one it considers most likely to be correct. For example, if you misspell *definitely* by typing *definately,* your checker may highlight *defiantly* as the correct option. You need to verify that the alternative suggested by the checker is actually what you intend before selecting it. Consult an online or printed dictionary when you aren't sure about the checker's recommendations.
- **Most important, a spelling checker will not flag words that appear in its dictionary but you have misused.** The paragraph in the following screen shot contains eleven errors that a spelling checker overlooked. Can you spot them?

Spelling checker

The whether effects all of us, though it's affects are different for different people. Some people love a fare day with warm temperatures and sunshine. They revel in spending a hole day outside. Other people enjoy dark, rainy daze. They like to slow down and here they're inner thoughts. Most people agree, however, that to much of one kind of weather makes them board.

A spelling checker failed to catch any of the eleven errors in this paragraph.

Using a grammar/style checker

Grammar/style checkers can flag incorrect grammar or punctuation and wordy or awkward sentences. You may be able to customize a checker to suit your needs and habits as a writer—for instance, instructing it to look for problems with subject-verb agreement, passive verbs, or apostrophes in plural nouns.

Like spelling checkers, however, grammar/style checkers are limited:

- **They miss many errors** because they are not yet capable of analyzing language in all its complexity.
- **They often question passages that don't need editing,** such as an appropriate passive verb or a deliberate and emphatic use of repetition.

The screen shot below illustrates these limitations. Each time a grammar/style checker questions something, you must determine whether a change is needed at all and what change will be most effective, and you must read your papers carefully on your own to find any errors the program missed.

Grammar/style checker

Though there was only a light light breeze, I could not light the match so there was no way to light the light.

The checker flagged only one repetition of *light*, not the other three.

These programs are not yet capable of analyzing the language in all its complexity (for instance, they can't accurately distinguish a word's part of speech when there are different possibilities, as *light* can be a noun, a verb, or an adjective).

The checker flagged this sentence because it is long, but it is actually clear and correct.

Exercise 3.7 Considering your past work: Editing

How do you find what needs editing in your drafts? What kinds of changes do you make most often? Have you tried focusing on particular kinds of changes, such as correcting mistakes you made in previous writing? If your readers often comment on editing concerns in your work, what can you do to reduce such comments?

Exercise 3.8 Editing your own draft

Use the checklist for editing (pp. 62–63) and your own sense of your essay's needs to edit the revised draft of your essay-in-progress.

3f Preparing and proofreading the final draft

After editing your essay, format and proofread it before you submit it to your instructor. Follow any required document format, such as MLA (pp. 680–82), Chicago (pp. 757–58), APA (pp. 782–83), or CSE (p. 802). If no format is specified, consult the sample on page 109.

Be sure to proofread the final essay several times to spot and correct errors. To increase the accuracy of your proofreading, you may need to find ways to keep yourself from relaxing into the rhythm and the content of your prose. The following box gives a few tricks, including some used by professional proofreaders:

Techniques for proofreading

- **Read printed copy,** even if you will eventually submit the paper electronically. Most people proofread more accurately when reading type on paper than when reading it on a computer screen. (At the same time, don't view the printed copy as necessarily error-free just because it's clean. Clean-looking copy may still harbor errors.)

- **Read the paper aloud.** Slowly and distinctly pronounce exactly what you see.
- **Place a ruler under each line as you read it.**
- **Read "against copy."** Compare your final draft one sentence at a time against the edited draft you copied it from.
- **Ignore content.** To keep the content of your writing from distracting you while you proofread, read the essay backward, end to beginning, examining each sentence as a separate unit. Or, taking advantage of a computer, isolate each paragraph from its context by printing it on a separate page. (Of course, reassemble the paragraphs before submitting the paper.)

3g Examining a final draft

Katy Moreno's final essay begins below, presented in MLA format except for page breaks and page numbers. Comments in the margins point out key features of the essay's content.

Katy Moreno

Professor Lacourse

English 110

14 February 2014

Can We Compete?

College Education for the Global Economy

Descriptive title

Introduction

Today's students cannot miss news stories about globalization of the economy and outsourcing of jobs, but are students aware of how these trends are affecting the job market? In "It's a Flat World, after All," Thomas L. Friedman argues that most US students are not preparing themselves as well as students in India, China, and other countries to compete in today's economy, which requires hard-working, productive scientists and engineers (34-37). Friedman's argument speaks to me because my mother lost her job when it was outsourced to India. But her experience taught a lesson that Friedman overlooks: technical training by itself can be too narrow to produce the communicators and problem solvers needed by contemporary businesses.

Summaries of Friedman cited with parenthetical page numbers using MLA style (p. 634)

Thesis statement: basic disagreement with Friedman

Summary of Friedman's article

Friedman describes a "flat" world where technology like the Internet and wireless communication makes it possible for college graduates all over the globe to compete for high-paying jobs that once belonged to graduates of US colleges and universities (34). He focuses on workers in India and China who graduate from college with excellent educations in math and science, who are eager for new opportunities, and who are

The writing situation: Personal response to a reading

- **Subject:** Student's reflection on her mother's job experience and the student's own choice of majors; responding to an assigned reading, "It's a Flat World, after All," by Thomas L. Friedman
- **Purpose:** To explain why the writer disagrees with Friedman about the training needed for today's job market
- **Audience:** Classmates and instructor
- **Genre:** Personal response to a reading—an essay involving close reading, summary, and use of personal evidence to agree or disagree (or both) with the author's argument (see p. 134)
- **Sources:** Personal experience and reading (cited in MLA style)

willing to work exceptionally hard, often harder than their American counterparts, and for less money (37). Friedman argues that US students must be better prepared academically, especially in math and science, so that they can get and keep jobs that will otherwise go overseas (37).

Transition to disagreements with Friedman

At first glance, my mother's experience of losing her job might seem to support Friedman's argument that better training in math and science is the key to competing in the global job market. However, her experience adds dimensions to the globalization story that Friedman misses. First, my mother had the kind of strong background in math and science that Friedman says today's workers need. She majored in computer science, rose within the information technology (IT) department of a large company, and consistently received good performance reviews. Still, when her employer decided to outsource most of its IT work, my mother lost her job. The reason wasn't that her technical skills were inadequate; instead, her salary and benefits cost the company more than outsourcing her job did. Until wages rise around the globe, jobs like my mother's will be vulnerable, no matter how well a person is trained.

First disagreement with Friedman

Examples to support first disagreement

Example to qualify first disagreement

Clarification of first disagreement

The second dimension that Friedman misses is that a number of well-paid people in my mother's IT department, namely IT managers, were not laid off. As my mother explained at the time, they kept their jobs because they were experienced at figuring out the company's IT needs, planning for changes, researching and proposing solutions, and communicating in writing and speech—skills that her more narrow training and experience had missed. Friedman misses these skills by focusing only on technical training. Without the ability to solve problems creatively and to communicate, people with technical expertise alone may not have enough to save their jobs, as my mother learned.

Second disagreement with Friedman

Explanation of second disagreement

Conclusion summarizing both disagreements with Friedman

Like my mother, I am more comfortable in front of a computer than I am in front of a group of people, and I had planned to major in computer science. Since my mother lost her job, however, I have decided to take courses in English and history as well. Classes in these subjects will require me to read broadly, think critically, research, and communicate ideas in writing—in short, to develop skills that make managers. When I enter the job market, my well-rounded education will make me a more attractive job candidate and will help me to become the kind of forward-thinking manager that US companies will always need to employ here in the United States.

Final point: business needs and author's personal goals

Explanation of final point

Many jobs that require a college degree are indeed going overseas, as Thomas L. Friedman says, and my classmates and I need to be ready for a rapidly changing future. But rather than focus only on math and science, we need to broaden our academic experiences so that the skills we develop make us not only employable but also indispensable.

Conclusion recapping points of agreement and disagreement with Friedman and summarizing essay

[New page.]

Work Cited

Friedman, Thomas L. "It's a Flat World, after All." *The New York Times Magazine*, 3 Apr. 2005, pp. 32-37.

Work cited in MLA style (see p. 644)

Exercise 3.9 Proofreading

Proofread the following passage, using any of the techniques listed on pages 66–67 to bring errors into the foreground. There are thirteen errors in the passage: missing and misspelled words, typographical errors, and the like. If you are in doubt about any spellings, consult a dictionary.

An envirnmental group, Natural Resources Defense Council, has estimated that 5500 to 6200 children who are preschool today may contract cancer durng there lives becuase of the pesticides they consume in there food In addition, these children will be at greater risk for kidney damage, problems with immunity, and other serious imparments. The government bases it's pesticide-safety standards on adults, but childen consume many more the fruits and fruit products likely too contain pestcides.

Exercise 3.10 Preparing your final draft

Prepare the final draft of the essay you have been working on throughout Chapters 1–3. Proofread carefully and correct all errors before submitting your essay for review.

3h Preparing a writing portfolio

Your instructor may ask you to assemble samples of your writing into a portfolio once or more during the course. A portfolio gives you a chance to consider all your writing over a period and to choose the work that best represents you as a writer.

The purposes and requirements for portfolios vary. As you consider what work to include in your portfolio, answer the following questions:

- **What is the purpose of the portfolio?** A portfolio may be intended to showcase your best work, demonstrate progress you have made, or provide examples of your versatility as a writer.
- **What are the requirements of the portfolio?** You may be asked to submit final drafts of your best work; journal entries, notes, early drafts, and a final draft of one or more essays; or projects representing different types of writing—say, one narrative, one critical analysis, one argument, and so on.
- **Is a reflective essay or letter required as part of the portfolio?** Many teachers require an opening essay or letter in which you discuss the selections in the portfolio, explain why you chose each one, and perhaps evaluate your development as a writer. If a reflective essay is required, be sure you understand its purpose and scope.
- **Should the portfolio be print or electronic, or can you choose the medium?** If you plan to submit your portfolio electronically, be sure you know how to upload your files before the deadline.
- **How will the portfolio be evaluated?** Will it be read by peers, your instructor, or a committee of teachers? Will it be graded?

Unless the guidelines specify otherwise, provide error-free copies of your final drafts and label all your samples with your name before you place them in a folder or upload them as files.

4 Writing and Revising Paragraphs

Chapter essentials

- Relate each paragraph to the essay as a whole (p. 72).
- Maintain the unity of each paragraph, focusing it on a central idea (p. 73).
- Make each paragraph coherent (p. 77).
- Develop the central idea of each paragraph (p. 90).
- Write introductory and concluding paragraphs that set up and finish your writing (pp. 101, 105).

Visit MyWritingLab™ for more resources on writing and revising paragraphs.

Paragraphs develop the main ideas that support the thesis of a piece of writing, and they break these supporting ideas into manageable chunks. For readers, paragraphs signal the movement between ideas and provide breathers from long stretches of text.

In the body of an essay, you may use paragraphs for any of these purposes:

- **To introduce and give evidence for a main point that supports the thesis of your essay.** See pages 28–33 for a discussion of an essay's thesis.
- **Within a group of paragraphs centering on one main point, to develop a key example or other important evidence.**
- **To shift approach**—for instance, from pros to cons, from problem to solution, from questions to answers.
- **To mark movement in a sequence,** such as from one reason or step to another.

In addition, you will use paragraphs for special purposes:

- **To introduce or to conclude an essay.** See pages 101 and 105.
- **To emphasize an important point or to mark a significant transition between points.** See pages 106–07.
- **In dialog, to indicate that a new person has begun speaking.** See page 107.

CULTURE LANGUAGE Not all cultures share the paragraphing conventions of American academic writing. In some other languages, writing moves differently from English on the page—not from left to right, but from right to left or down rows from top to bottom. Even in languages that move as English does on the page, writers may not use paragraphs at all, or they may use paragraphs but not state their central ideas. If your native language

Checklist for revising paragraphs

- **Does each paragraph contribute to the essay as a whole?** Does each support the essay's central idea, or thesis? Does each relate to the paragraphs that come before and after it? (See the next page.)
- **Is each paragraph unified?** Does it adhere to one general idea that is either stated in a topic sentence or otherwise apparent? (See p. 73.)
- **Is each paragraph coherent?** Do the sentences follow a clear sequence? Are the sentences linked as needed by parallelism, repetition or restatement, pronouns, consistency, and transitional expressions? (See p. 77.)
- **Is each paragraph developed?** Is the general idea of each paragraph well supported with specific evidence such as details, facts, examples, and reasons? (See p. 90.)

is not English and you have difficulty writing paragraphs, don't worry about paragraphing during drafting. Instead, during a separate step of revision, divide your text into parts that develop your main points, and mark those parts with indentions. Then you can make sure that each paragraph has a clear central idea supported by evidence such as facts and examples.

4a Relating paragraphs in the essay

Paragraphs do not stand alone: they are key units of a larger piece of writing. Even if you draft a paragraph separately, it needs to connect to your central idea, or thesis—explaining it and deepening it. Together, paragraphs need to flow from one to the other so that readers easily grasp the points you are making and how each point contributes to the whole essay.

To see how effective body paragraphs work to help both writer and reader, look at the third and fourth paragraphs of Katy Moreno's essay "Can We Compete?" from the previous chapter. Responding to an article by Thomas L. Friedman, Moreno is supporting her thesis that Friedman overlooks the need for technical employees to be good communicators and problem solvers.

> At first glance, my mother's experience of losing her job might seem to support Friedman's argument that better training in math and science is the key to competing in the global job market. However, her experience adds dimensions to the globalization story that Friedman misses. [Link to previous paragraph and to thesis] First, my mother had the kind of strong background in math and science that Friedman says today's workers need. [New main point connected to thesis] She majored in computer science, rose within the information technology (IT) department of a large company, and consistently received good performance reviews. Still, when her employer decided to outsource most of its IT work, my mother lost her job. [Details to support new point] The reason wasn't that her technical skills were inadequate; instead, her salary and benefits cost the company more than outsourcing her job did. Until wages rise around the globe, jobs like my mother's will be vulnerable, no matter how well a person is trained. [Concluding sentences summing up paragraph and linking to thesis]
>
> The second dimension that Friedman misses is that a number of well-paid people in my mother's IT department, namely IT managers, were not laid off. [New main point linking to previous paragraph and to thesis] As my mother explained at the time, they kept their jobs because they were experienced at figuring [Details to support new point]

out the company's IT needs, planning for changes, researching and proposing solutions, and communicating in writing and speech—skills that her more narrow training and experience had missed. Friedman misses these skills by focusing only on technical training. Without the ability to solve problems creatively and to communicate, people with technical expertise alone may not have enough to save their jobs, as my mother learned.

Concluding sentence summing up paragraph and linking to previous paragraph and to thesis

Exercise 4.1 Analyzing paragraphs in an essay

Analyze the fifth paragraph in Katy Moreno's essay in Chapter 3, page 69. How does she relate the paragraph to the thesis statement and to other paragraphs?

Exercise 4.2 Considering your past work: Paragraphs in the essay

Examine the final draft of the essay you wrote throughout Chapters 1–3. Do all the paragraphs relate to your thesis? Are they arranged clearly and logically so that your main ideas flow from one paragraph to the next? What improvements can you make?

4b Maintaining paragraph unity

Just as readers expect paragraphs to relate clearly to an essay's central idea, they also generally expect each paragraph to explore a single idea. They will be alert for that idea and will patiently follow its development. In other words, they will seek and appreciate paragraph unity: clear identification and clear elaboration of one idea and of that idea only.

In an essay the thesis statement often asserts the main idea as a commitment to readers (see p. 28). In a paragraph a **topic sentence** often alerts readers to the essence of the paragraph by asserting the central idea and expressing the writer's attitude toward it. In a brief essay each body paragraph will likely treat one main point supporting the essay's thesis statement; the topic sentences simply elaborate on parts of the thesis. In longer essays paragraphs tend to work in groups, each group treating one main point. Then the topic sentences will tie into that main point, and all the points together will support the thesis.

1 Focusing on the central idea

Like the thesis sentence, the topic sentence is a commitment to readers, and the rest of the paragraph delivers on that commitment. Look again at the second paragraph by Katy Moreno on these two pages: the opening statement conveys Moreno's promise that she will explain something lacking in Friedman's argument, and the next sentences keep the promise. But what if Moreno had written this paragraph instead?

> The second dimension that Friedman misses is that a number of well-paid people in my mother's IT department, namely IT managers, were not laid off. As my mother explained at the time, they kept their jobs because they were experienced at figuring out the company's IT needs, planning for changes, researching and proposing solutions, and communicating in writing. Like my mother, these managers had families to support, so they were lucky to keep their jobs. Our family still struggles with the financial and emotional effects of my mother's unemployment.

Topic sentence: general statement

Details supporting topic sentence

Digression

By wandering from the topic of why some managers kept their jobs, the paragraph fails to deliver on the commitment of its topic sentence.

You should expect digressions while you are drafting: if you allow yourself to explore ideas, as you should, then of course every paragraph will not be tightly woven, perfectly unified. But spare your readers the challenge and frustration of repeatedly shifting focus to follow your rough explorations: revise each paragraph so that it develops a single idea. You may want to highlight the central idea of each paragraph to be sure it's stated clearly and then focus on it.

2 Placing the topic sentence

The topic sentence of a paragraph and its supporting details may be arranged variously, depending on how you want to direct readers' attention and how complex your central idea is. In the most common arrangements, the topic sentence comes at the beginning of the paragraph, comes at the end, or is not stated at all but is nonetheless apparent. The advantages of each approach are described here, with examples. If you write on a computer, you can easily experiment with the position of the topic sentence by moving the sentence around (or deleting it) to see the effect. (The sentence will probably take some editing to work smoothly into various positions.)

Topic sentence at the beginning

When you place the topic sentence first in a paragraph, it can help you select the details that follow. For readers, the topic-first model establishes an initial context for understanding all the supporting details. In Moreno's second paragraph on pages 72–73, we easily relate all the content back to the point made in the first sentence.

The topic-first model is common in explanatory writing as well as in argument, as shown in the following paragraph:

> It is a misunderstanding of the American retail store to think we go there necessarily to buy.

Topic sentence: statement of misconception

> Some of us shop. There's a difference. Shopping has many purposes, the least interesting of which is to acquire new articles. We shop to cheer ourselves up. We shop to practice decision-making. We shop to be useful and productive members of our class and society. We shop to remind ourselves how much is available to us. We shop to remind ourselves how much is to be striven for. We shop to assert our superiority to the material objects that spread themselves before us.
>
> —Phyllis Rose, "Shopping and Other Spiritual Adventures"

Correction of misconception

Topic sentence at the end

In some paragraphs the central idea may be stated at the end, after supporting sentences have made a case for the general statement. Since this model leads the reader to a conclusion by presenting all the evidence first, it can prove effective in argument. And because the point of the paragraph is withheld until the end, this model can be dramatic in exposition, too, as illustrated by the following example from an essay about William Tecumseh Sherman, a Union general during the US Civil War:

> Sherman is considered by some to be the inventor of "total war": the first general in human history to carry the logic of war to its ultimate extreme, the first to scorch the earth, the first to consciously demoralize the hostile civilian population in order to subdue its army, the first to wreck an economy in order to starve its soldiers. He has been called our first "merchant of terror" and seen as the spiritual father of our Vietnam War concepts of "search and destroy," "pacification," "strategic hamlets," and "free-fire zones." As such, he remains a cardboard figure of our history: a monstrous arch-villain to unreconstructed Southerners, and an embarrassment to Northerners.
>
> —Adapted from James Reston, Jr., "You Cannot Refine It"

Information supporting and building to topic sentence

Topic sentence

Expressing the central idea at the end of the paragraph does not eliminate the need to unify the paragraph. The idea in the topic sentence must still govern the selection of all the preceding details.

Central idea not stated

Occasionally, a paragraph's central idea will be stated in the previous paragraph or will be so obvious that it need not be stated at all. The following is from an essay on the actor Humphrey Bogart:

> Usually he wore the trench coat unbuttoned, just tied with the belt, and a slouch hat, rarely tilted. Sometimes it was a captain's cap and a

yachting jacket. Almost always his trousers were held up by a cowboy belt. You know the kind: one an Easterner waiting for a plane out of Phoenix buys just as a joke and then takes a liking to. Occasionally, he'd hitch up his slacks with it, and he often jabbed his thumbs behind it, his hands ready for a fight or a dame.

—Peter Bogdanovich,
"Bogie in Excelsis"

Details adding up to the unstated idea that Bogart's character could be seen in his clothing

Paragraphs in descriptive writing (like the one above) and in narrative writing (relating a sequence of events) often lack stated topic sentences. But a paragraph without a topic sentence still should have a central idea, and its details should develop that idea.

Exercise 4.3 Finding the central idea

What is the central idea of each of the following paragraphs? In what sentence or sentences is it expressed?

1. At each step, with every graduation from one level of education to 1
the next, the refrain from bystanders was strangely the same: "Your parents must be so proud of you." I suppose that my parents were proud, 2
although I suspect, too, that they felt more than pride alone as they
watched me advance through my education. They seemed to know that 3
my education was separating us from one another, making it difficult to
resume familiar intimacies. Mixed with the instincts of parental pride, a 4
certain hurt also communicated itself—too private ever to be adequately
expressed in words, but real nonetheless.

—Richard Rodriguez "Going Home Again"

2. Though they do not know why the humpback whale sings, scien- 1
tists do know something about the song itself. They have measured the 2
length of a whale's song: from a few minutes to over half an hour. They 3
have recorded and studied the variety and complex arrangements of low
moans, high squeaks, and sliding squeals that make up the song. And 4
they have learned that each whale sings in its own unique pattern.

—Janet Lieber (student), "Whales' Songs"

Exercise 4.4 Revising a paragraph for unity

The following paragraph contains ideas or details that do not support its central idea. Identify the topic sentence in the paragraph and delete the unrelated material.

In the southern part of the state, some people still live much as they did a century ago. They use coal- or wood-burning stoves for heating and cooking. Their homes do not have electricity or indoor bathrooms or running water. The towns they live in don't receive adequate funding from the state and federal governments, so the schools are poor and in bad shape. Beside most homes there is a garden where fresh vegetables are gathered for canning. Small pastures nearby support livestock, including cattle, pigs, horses, and chickens. Most of the people have cars or trucks, but the vehicles are old and beat-up from traveling on unpaved roads.

Exercise 4.5 Considering your past work: Paragraph unity

For a continuing exercise in this chapter, choose a paper you've written in the past year. Examine the body paragraphs for unity. Do they have clear topic sentences? If not, are the paragraphs' central ideas still clear? Are the paragraphs unified around their central ideas? Should any details be deleted for unity? Should other, more relevant details be added in their stead?

Exercise 4.6 Writing a unified paragraph

Develop the following topic sentence into a unified paragraph by using the relevant information in the supporting statements. Delete each statement that does not relate directly to the topic, and then rewrite and combine sentences as appropriate. Place the topic sentence in the position that seems most effective to you.

Topic sentence

Mozart's accomplishments in music seem remarkable even today.

Supporting information

Wolfgang Amadeus Mozart was born in 1756 in Salzburg, Austria.
He began composing music at the age of five.
He lived most of his life in Salzburg and Vienna.
His first concert tour of Europe was at the age of six.
On his first tour he played harpsichord, organ, and violin.
He published numerous compositions before reaching adolescence.
He married in 1782.
Mozart and his wife were both poor managers of money.
They were plagued by debts.
Mozart composed over six hundred musical compositions.
His most notable works are his operas, symphonies, quartets, and piano concertos.
He died at the age of thirty-five.

Exercise 4.7 Turning topic sentences into unified paragraphs

Develop three of the following topic sentences into detailed and unified paragraphs.

1. Men and women are different in at least one important respect.
2. The best social-media site is [*name*].
3. Fans of ______ music [*country, classical, rock, rap, jazz, or another kind*] come in [*number*] varieties.
4. Professional sports have [*or* have not] been helped by extending the regular season with championship playoffs.
5. Working for good grades can interfere with learning.

4c Achieving paragraph coherence

A paragraph is unified if it holds together—if all its details and examples support the central idea. A paragraph is **coherent** if readers can see *how* the paragraph holds together—how the sentences relate to each other—without having to stop and reread.

Ways to achieve paragraph coherence

- Organize effectively (opposite).
- Repeat or restate key words and word groups (p. 82).
- Use parallel structures (p. 83).
- Use pronouns (p. 83).
- Be consistent in nouns, pronouns, and verbs (p. 84).
- Use transitional expressions (p. 85).

Incoherence gives readers the feeling of being yanked around, as the following example shows.

> The ancient Egyptians were masters of preserving dead people's bodies by making mummies of them. [Topic sentence] Mummies several thousand years old have been discovered nearly intact. The skin, hair, teeth, finger- and toenails, and facial features of the mummies were evident. One can diagnose the diseases they suffered in life, such as smallpox, arthritis, and nutritional deficiencies. The process was remarkably effective. Sometimes apparent were the fatal afflictions of the dead people: a middle-aged king died from a blow on the head, and polio killed a child king. Mummification consisted of removing the internal organs, applying natural preservatives inside and out, and then wrapping the body in layers of bandages. [Sentences related to topic sentence but disconnected from each other]

The paragraph as it was actually written begins below. It is much clearer because the writer arranged information differently and also built links into his sentences so that they would flow smoothly:

- After stating the central idea in a topic sentence, the writer moves to two more specific explanations and illustrates the second with four sentences of examples.
- Words in green repeat or restate key terms or concepts.
- Words in orange link sentences and clarify relationships.
- Underlined phrases are in parallel grammatical form to reflect their parallel content.

> The ancient Egyptians were masters of preserving dead people's bodies by making mummies of them. [Topic sentence] Basically, mummification consisted of removing the internal organs, applying natural preservatives inside and out, and then wrapping [Explanation 1: What mummification is]

the body in layers of bandages. And the process was remarkably effective. Indeed, mummies several thousand years old have been discovered nearly intact. Their skin, hair, teeth, finger- and toenails, and facial features are still evident. Their diseases in life, such as smallpox, arthritis, and nutritional deficiencies, are still diagnosable. Even their fatal afflictions are still apparent: a middle-aged king died from a blow on the head; a child king died from polio.

—Mitchell Rosenbaum (student), "Lost Arts of the Egyptians"

Explanation 2: Why the Egyptians were masters

Specific examples of explanation 2

Though some of the connections in this paragraph were added in revision, the writer attended to them while drafting as well. Not only superficial coherence but also an underlying clarity of relationships can be achieved by tying each sentence to the one before—generalizing from it, clarifying it, qualifying it, adding to it, illustrating it. Each sentence in a paragraph creates an expectation of some sort in the mind of the reader, a question such as "How was a mummy made?" or "How intact are the mummies?" or "What's another example?" When you recognize these expectations and try to fulfill them, readers are likely to understand relationships without struggle.

1 Organizing the paragraph

The paragraphs on mummies illustrate an essential element of coherence: information must be arranged in an order that readers can follow easily and that corresponds to their expectations. The common organizations for paragraphs correspond to those for entire essays: by space, by time, and for emphasis. (In addition, the patterns of development also suggest certain arrangements. See pp. 90–99.)

Note On a computer you can experiment with different paragraph organizations and emphases. Copy a paragraph, paste the copy into your document, and then try moving sentences around. To evaluate the versions, you'll need to edit each one so that sentences flow smoothly, attending to repetition, parallelism, transitions, and the other techniques for achieving coherence.

Organizing by space or time

A paragraph organized **spatially** focuses readers' attention on one point and scans a person, object, or scene from that point. The movement usually parallels the way people look at things, from top to bottom, from side to side, from near to far. Virginia Woolf follows the last pattern in the following paragraph:

Spatial organization

The sun struck straight upon the house, making the white walls glare between the dark windows. Their panes, woven thickly with green branches, held circles of impenetrable darkness. Sharp-edged wedges of light lay upon the window-sill and showed inside the room plates with blue rings, cups with curved handles, the bulge of a great bowl, the criss-cross pattern in the rug, and the formidable corners and lines of cabinets and bookcases. Behind their conglomeration hung a zone of shadow in which might be a further shape to be disencumbered of shadow or still denser depths of darkness.

—Virginia Woolf, *The Waves*

Description moving from outside (closer) to inside (farther)

Unstated central idea: Sunlight barely penetrated the house's secrets.

Another familiar way of organizing the elements of a paragraph is **chronologically**—that is, in order of their occurrence in time. In a chronological paragraph, as in experience, the earliest events come first, followed by more recent ones.

Chronological organization

In early spring, millions of monarch butterflies that have spent the winter months in Mexico begin an annual migration north to the monarch's summer habitats. After covering about fifty miles a day, most make their first stop in Texas, where they lay their eggs on milkweed and die soon after. Their offspring continue the flight to the northern United States and Canada, laying the eggs of the next generation of monarchs along the way. By late spring, these offspring or their offspring reach their summer homes. In August, the third or fourth generation of the original monarchs begins the long return migration south. They do not reproduce in the north but return to where their ancestors wintered and hibernate there. The following spring they start the cycle over by flying north to Texas.

—Ben Kampe (student), "The Monarch Trail"

Topic sentence

Details in order of their occurrence

Organizing for emphasis

Some organizational schemes are imposed on paragraphs to achieve a certain emphasis. The most common is the **general-to-specific** scheme, in which the topic sentence often comes first and then the following sentences become increasingly specific. The paragraph on mummies (pp. 78–79) illustrates this organization: each sentence is either more specific than the one before it or at the same level of generality. Here is another illustration:

General-to-specific organization

Perhaps the simplest fact about sleep is that individual needs for it vary widely. Most adults sleep between seven and nine hours, but occasionally people turn up who need twelve hours or so, while some rare types can get by on three or four. Rarest of all are those legendary types who require almost no sleep at all; respected researchers have recently studied three such people. One of them—a healthy, happy woman in her seventies—sleeps about an hour every two or three days. The other two are men in early middle age, who get by on a few minutes a night. One of them complains about the daily fifteen minutes or so he's forced to "waste" in sleeping.

—Lawrence A. Mayer,
"The Confounding Enemy of Sleep"

Topic sentence

Supporting examples, increasingly specific

In the less common **specific-to-general** organization, the elements of the paragraph build to a general conclusion:

Specific-to-general organization

It's disconcerting that so many college women, when asked how their children will be cared for if they themselves work, refer with vague confidence to "the day care center" as though there were some great amorphous kiddie watcher out there that the state provides. But such places, adequately funded, well run, and available to all, are still scarce in this country, particularly for middle-class women. And figures show that when she takes time off for family-connected reasons (births, child care), a woman's chances for career advancement plummet. In a job market that's steadily tightening and getting more competitive, these obstacles bode the kind of danger ahead that can shatter not only professions, but egos. A hard reality is that there's not much more support for our daughters who have family-plus-career goals than there was for us; there's simply a great deal more self and societal pressure.

—Judith Wax,
Starting in the Middle

Common belief

Actual situation

General conclusion: topic sentence

As its name implies, the **problem-solution** arrangement introduces a problem and then proposes or explains a solution. The next paragraph argues that the legal drinking age causes problems that a lower age would help to solve.

Problem-solution organization

Although designed to keep young adults away from alcohol, the drinking age of twenty-one

¶ coh
4c

actually does the opposite. It attracts youths by making the behavior illegal, and it pushes alcohol consumption underground, thus removing it from the reach of law enforcement and school administrators. The drinking age should be lowered to eighteen. The lower age would not stop drinking on college campuses, but it would weaken the appeal of drinking and help the police and colleges control the behavior and its effects.

Topic sentence and clarification: statement of the problem

Solution to the problem

—Yvonne St. Pierre (student), "Drinking and the Law"

When your details vary in significance, you can arrange them in a **climactic** order, from least to most important or dramatic:

Climactic organization

Nature has put many strange tongues into the heads of her creatures. There is the frog's tongue, rooted at the front of the mouth so it can be protruded an extra distance for nabbing prey. There is the gecko lizard's tongue, so long and agile that the lizard uses it to wash its eyes. But the ultimate lingual whopper has been achieved in the anteater. The anteater's head, long as it is, is not long enough to contain the tremendous tongue which licks deep into ant-hills. Its tongue is not rooted in the mouth or throat: it is fastened to the breastbone.

Topic sentence

Least dramatic example

Most dramatic example

—Alan Devoe, "Nature's Utmost"

In other paragraph organizations, you can arrange details according to how you think readers are likely to understand them. In discussing the virtues of public television, for instance, you might proceed from **most familiar to least familiar**, from a well-known program to less well-known programs. Or in defending the right of government employees to strike, you might arrange your reasons from **simplest to most complex**, from the employees' need to be able to redress grievances to the more subtle consequences for relations between employers and employees.

2 Repeating or restating key words

Repeating or restating the important words in a paragraph binds the sentences together and keeps the paragraph's topic uppermost in readers' minds. In the next example, notice how the shaded words relate the sentences and stress the important ideas of the paragraph:

The proposed "Stop Cyberbullying" program aims to reduce the behavior through a month-long campaign of awareness, prevention, and support modeled on the college's "Alcohol Awareness Month" program. The program can raise awareness of cyberbullying by explaining what cyberbullying is and by informing students about the college's code of conduct, which prohibits cyberbullying but which few people read. The program can work to prevent cyberbullying by appealing to students to treat those around them respectfully. And, with the participation of the counseling department, the program can provide support for victims, their friends, and others involved in the behavior.

—Aimee Lee (student), "Awareness, Prevention, Support: A Proposal to Reduce Cyberbullying"

Note Though planned repetition can be effective, careless or excessive repetition weakens prose (see p. 522).

3 Using parallel structures

Another way to achieve coherence is through **parallelism**, the use of similar grammatical structures for similar elements of meaning within a sentence or among sentences. (See Chapter 25 for a detailed discussion of parallelism.) Parallel structures help tie together the last three sentences in the paragraph on mummies (pp. 78–79). In the following paragraph the underlined parallel structures link all sentences after the first one, and parallelism also appears within many of the sentences (as in *by supporting candidates and making speeches* in sentence 5 and *He served . . . , survived . . . , and earned* in sentence 8). The paragraph comes from a student's profile of President Ronald Reagan.

Ronald Reagan holds a particularly interesting place in American history, combining successful careers in show business and in politics. After graduating from college in 1932, he worked as a radio sports announcer with an affinity for describing game details. He then launched a successful film career, starring in dozens of movies. After a stint in the US Army, he assumed the role of host for *General Electric Theater*, a weekly TV program that ran from 1953 to 1962. He first entered politics by supporting candidates and making speeches in the 1950s and early 1960s. He became governor of California in 1966 and served for eight years. He ran unsuccessfully for the US presidency in 1976 and then won the job in 1980, when he became the fortieth President. He served two terms, survived an assassination attempt, and earned a popularity that most politicians can only envy.

—William Brooks (student), "Ronald Reagan, the Actor President"

4 Using pronouns

Pronouns such as *she, he, it, they,* and *who* refer to and function as nouns (see p. 250). Thus pronouns naturally help relate sentences to one another. In the following paragraph the pronouns and the nouns they refer to are shaded:

> After dark, on the warrenlike streets of Brooklyn where I live, I often see women who fear the worst from me. They seem to have set their faces on neutral, and with their purse straps strung across their chests bandolier-style, they forge ahead as though bracing themselves against being tackled. I understand, of course, that the danger they perceive is not a hallucination. Women are particularly vulnerable to street violence, and young black males are drastically overrepresented among the perpetrators of that violence. Yet these truths are no solace against the kind of alienation that comes of being ever the suspect, a fearsome entity with whom pedestrians avoid making eye contact.
>
> —Brent Staples,
> "Black Men and Public Space"

5 Being consistent

Being consistent is the most subtle way to achieve paragraph coherence because readers are aware of consistency only when it is absent. Consistency (or the lack of it) occurs primarily in the tense of verbs and in the number and person of nouns and pronouns (see Chapter 20). Although some shifts will be necessary to reflect your meaning, inappropriate shifts, as in the following passages, will interfere with a reader's ability to follow the development of ideas.

Shifts in tense

In the Hopi religion, water is the driving force. Since the Hopi lived in the Arizona desert, they needed water urgently for drinking, cooking, and irrigating crops. Their complex beliefs are focused in part on gaining the assistance of supernatural forces in obtaining water. Many of the Hopi kachinas, or spirit essences, were directly concerned with clouds, rain, and snow.

Shifts in number

Kachinas represent the things and events of the real world, such as clouds, mischief, cornmeal, and even death. A kachina is not worshiped as a god but regarded as an interested friend. They visit the Hopi from December through July in the form of men who dress in kachina costumes and perform dances and other rituals.

Shifts in person

Unlike the man, the Hopi woman does not keep contact with kachinas through costumes and dancing. Instead, one receives a small likeness of a kachina, called a *tihu*, from the man impersonating the kachina. You are more likely to receive a tihu as a girl approaching marriage, though a child or older woman sometimes receives one, too.

6 Using transitional expressions

Specific words and word groups, called **transitional expressions**, can connect sentences whose relationships may not be instantly clear to readers. Notice the difference in the following two versions of the same paragraph:

> Medical science has succeeded in identifying the hundreds of viruses that can cause the common cold. It has discovered the most effective means of prevention. One person transmits the cold viruses to another most often by hand. An infected person covers his mouth to cough. He picks up the telephone. His daughter picks up the telephone. She rubs her eyes. She has a cold. It spreads. To avoid colds, people should wash their hands often and keep their hands away from their faces.

Paragraph is choppy and hard to follow

> Medical science has thus succeeded in identifying the hundreds of viruses that can cause the common cold. It has also discovered the most effective means of prevention. One person transmits the cold viruses to another most often by hand. For instance, an infected person covers his mouth to cough. Then he picks up the telephone. Half an hour later, his daughter picks up the same telephone. Immediately afterward, she rubs her eyes. Within a few days, she, too, has a cold. And thus it spreads. To avoid colds, therefore, people should wash their hands often and keep their hands away from their faces.
>
> —Kathleen LaFrank (student), "Colds: Myth and Science"

Transitional expressions (shaded) remove choppiness and spell out relationships

There are scores of transitional expressions on which to draw. The following box shows many common ones, arranged according to the relationships they convey.

Transitional expressions

To add or show sequence

again, also, and, and then, besides, equally important, finally, first, further, furthermore, in addition, in the first place, last, moreover, next, second, still, too

(continued)

Transitional expressions

(continued)

To compare

also, in the same way, likewise, similarly

To contrast

although, and yet, but, but at the same time, despite, even so, even though, for all that, however, in contrast, in spite of, nevertheless, notwithstanding, on the contrary, on the other hand, regardless, still, though, yet

To give examples or intensify

after all, an illustration of, even, for example, for instance, indeed, in fact, it is true, of course, specifically, that is, to illustrate, truly

To indicate place

above, adjacent to, below, elsewhere, farther on, here, near, nearby, on the other side, opposite to, there, to the east, to the left

To indicate time

after a while, afterward, as long as, as soon as, at last, at length, at that time, before, earlier, eventually, formerly, immediately, in the meantime, in the past, lately, later, meanwhile, now, presently, shortly, simultaneously, since, so far, soon, subsequently, suddenly, then, thereafter, until, when

To repeat, summarize, or conclude

all in all, altogether, as has been said, in brief, in conclusion, in other words, in particular, in short, in simpler terms, in summary, on the whole, that is, therefore, to put it differently, to summarize

To show cause or effect

accordingly, as a result, because, consequently, for this purpose, hence, otherwise, since, then, therefore, thereupon, thus, to this end, with this object

Note Draw carefully on the preceding lists because the expressions in each group are not interchangeable. For instance, *besides, finally,* and *second* may all be used to add information, but each has its own distinct meaning.

To see where transitional expressions might be needed in your paragraphs, examine the movement from each sentence to the next. You can highlight the transitional expressions already present and then review the sentences that lack them. Abrupt changes are most likely to need a transition: a shift from cause to effect, a contradiction, a contrast. You can smooth and clarify transitions *between* paragraphs, too. See pages 78, 87–88, and 106–07.

CULTURE LANGUAGE If transitional expressions are not common in your native language, you may be tempted to compensate when writing in English by adding them to the beginnings of most sentences. But such explicit transitions aren't needed everywhere, and in fact too many can be intrusive and awkward. When inserting transitional expressions, consider the reader's need for a signal: often the connection from sentence to sentence is already clear from the context, or it can be made clear by relating the content of sentences more closely (see pp. 82–83). When you do need transitional expressions, try varying their positions in your sentences, as shown in the sample paragraph on page 85.

Punctuating transitional expressions

A transitional expression is usually set off by a comma or commas from the rest of the sentence:

> Immediately afterward, she rubs her eyes. Within a few days, she, too, has a cold.

See pages 429–30 for more on this convention and its exceptions.

7 Combining devices to achieve coherence within and among paragraphs

The devices for achieving coherence rarely appear in isolation in effective paragraphs. As any example in this chapter shows, writers usually combine sensible organization, parallelism, repetition, pronouns, consistency, and transitional expressions to help readers follow the development of ideas.

The following excerpts from Katy Moreno's essay on pages 67–69 illustrate how coherence techniques can bind sentences and paragraphs. The individual paragraphs are clearly organized and are closely linked by transitional sentences (noted in the annotations) and transitional words (shaded in orange). Verb tenses shift only to reflect changes in actual time between the past (*my mother had, She majored*) and the present (*better training . . . is, Friedman says, I am*). The pronouns *she* and *her* (underlined) make it clear when Moreno is discussing her mother. And Moreno uses repetition and restatement (shaded in green) to emphasize important words.

> At first glance, my mother's experience of losing her job might seem to support Friedman's argument that better training in math and science is the key to competing in the global job market. However, her experience adds dimensions to the globalization story that Friedman misses. First, my mother had the kind of strong background in math and science that Friedman says today's workers need. She majored in computer science, rose within the information technology

Transitional sentence connecting to previous paragraph and to thesis

(IT) department of a large company, and consistently received good performance reviews. . . .

The second dimension that Friedman misses is that a number of well-paid people in my mother's IT department, namely IT managers, were not laid off. . . .

Transitional sentence connecting to previous paragraph and to thesis

Like my mother, I am more comfortable in front of a computer than I am in front of a group of people, and I had planned to major in computer science. Since my mother lost her job, however, I have decided to take courses in English and history as well. . . .

Transitional sentence connecting to previous paragraph

Exercise 4.8 Analyzing paragraphs for coherence

Study the paragraphs by Janet Lieber (p. 76), Hillary Begas (p. 91), and Freeman Dyson (pp. 92–93) for the authors' use of various devices to achieve coherence. Look especially for organization, parallel structures and ideas, repetition and restatement, pronouns, and transitional expressions.

Exercise 4.9 Arranging sentences coherently

After the topic sentence (sentence 1), the sentences in the student paragraph below have been deliberately scrambled to make the paragraph incoherent. Using the topic sentence and other clues as guides, rearrange the sentences in the paragraph to form a well-organized, coherent unit.

Although some people argue that television ruins the minds of chil- 1
dren, others point to the benefits of educational programming. Even 2
some cartoons familiarize children with the material of literature. Many 3
programs for school-age children teach worthwhile lessons. Thus it is 4
important to evaluate actual programming rather than dismiss television for children as uniformly unhealthy. For example, some after-school 5
shows, such as *Sid the Science Kid,* stress academic skills, while other
shows, such as *Arthur,* emphasize social skills.

Exercise 4.10 Eliminating inconsistencies

The following paragraph is incoherent because of inconsistencies in person, number, and tense. Identify the inconsistencies and revise the paragraph to give it coherence. For further exercises in eliminating inconsistencies, see pages 359, 361, and 363–64.

The Hopi tihu, or kachina likeness, is often called a "doll," but its owner, usually a girl or woman, does not regard them as a plaything. Instead, you treated them as a valued possession and hung them out of the way on a wall. For its owner the tihu represents a connection with the kachina's spirit. They are considered part of the kachina, carrying a portion of the kachina's power.

Exercise 4.11 Using transitional expressions

Transitional expressions have been removed from the following paragraph at the numbered blanks. Fill in each blank with an appropriate transitional expression (1) to contrast, (2) to intensify, and (3) to show effect. Consult the list on pages 85–86 if necessary.

All over the country, people are swimming, jogging, weightlifting, dancing, walking, playing tennis—doing anything to keep fit. ___(1)___ this school has consistently refused to construct and equip a fitness center. The school has ___(2)___ refused to open existing athletic facilities to all students, not just those playing organized sports. ___(3)___ students have no place to exercise except in their rooms and on dangerous public roads.

Exercise 4.12 Considering your past work: Paragraph coherence

Continuing from Exercise 4.5 (p. 77), examine the body paragraphs of your essay to see how coherent they are and how their coherence could be improved. Do the paragraphs have a clear organization? Do you use repetition and restatement, parallelism, pronouns, and transitional expressions to signal relationships? Are the paragraphs consistent in person, number, and tense? Revise two or three paragraphs in ways you think will improve their coherence.

Exercise 4.13 Writing a coherent paragraph

Write a coherent paragraph from the following information, combining and rewriting sentences as necessary. First, begin the paragraph with the topic sentence given and arrange the supporting sentences in a climactic order. Then combine and rewrite the supporting sentences, helping the reader see connections by introducing repetition and restatement, parallelism, pronouns, consistency, and transitional expressions.

Topic sentence

Hypnosis is far superior to drugs for relieving tension.

Supporting information

Hypnosis has none of the dangerous side effects of the drugs that relieve tension.
Tension-relieving drugs can cause weight loss or gain, illness, or even death.
Hypnosis is nonaddictive.
Most of the drugs that relieve tension do foster addiction.
Tension-relieving drugs are expensive.
Hypnosis is inexpensive even for people who have not mastered self-hypnosis.

Exercise 4.14 Turning topic sentences into coherent paragraphs

Develop the following topic sentences into coherent paragraphs. Organize your information by space, by time, or for emphasis, as seems most appropriate. Use repetition and restatement, parallelism, pronouns, consistency, and transitional expressions to link sentences.

1. The most interesting character in the book [or movie] was ______.
2. Of all my courses, ______ is the one that I think will serve me best throughout life.

3. Although we in the United States face many problems, the one we should concentrate on solving first is ______.
4. The most dramatic building in town is the ______.
5. Children should not have to worry about the future.

4d Developing the paragraph

In an essay that's understandable and interesting to readers, you will provide plenty of solid information to support your general statements. You work that information into the essay through the paragraph, as you build up each point relating to the thesis.

A paragraph may be unified and coherent but still be inadequate if you skimp on details. Take this example:

> Untruths can serve as a kind of social oil when they smooth connections between people. In preventing confrontation and injured feelings, they allow everyone to go on as before.

General statements needing examples to be clear and convincing

This paragraph lacks **development**, completeness. It does not provide enough information for us to evaluate or even care about the writer's assertions.

1 Using specific information

If they are sound, the general statements you make in any writing will be based on what you have experienced, observed, read, and thought. Readers will assume as much and will expect you to provide the evidence for your statements—sensory details, facts, statistics, examples, quotations, reasons. Whatever helps you form your views you need, in turn, to share with readers.

Here is the actual version of the preceding sample paragraph. With examples, the paragraph is more interesting and convincing.

> Untruths can serve as a kind of social oil when they smooth connections between people. Assuring a worried friend that his haircut is flattering, claiming an appointment to avoid an aunt's dinner invitation, pretending interest in an acquaintance's children—these lies may protect the liar, but they also protect the person lied to. In preventing confrontation and injured feelings, the lies allow everyone to go on as before.
>
> —Joan Lar (student), "The Truth of Lies"

Examples specifying kinds of lies and consequences

If your readers often comment that your writing needs more specifics, you should focus on that improvement in your revisions. Try listing the general statements of each paragraph on lines by themselves with space underneath. Then use one of the discovery techniques discussed on pages 17–27 (freewriting, brainstorming, and so on) to find the details to support each sentence. Write these into your draft. If you write on a computer, you can do this revision directly on a copy of your draft by separating the sentences and exploring their support. Rewrite the supporting details into sentences, reassemble the paragraph, and edit it for coherence.

2 Using a pattern of development

If you have difficulty developing an idea or shaping your information, try asking yourself questions derived from the patterns of development. (The same patterns can help with essay development, too. See pp. 25–27.)

How did it happen? (Narration)

Narration retells a significant sequence of events, usually in the order of their occurrence (that is, chronologically):

> Jill's story is typical for "recruits" to religious cults. She was very lonely in college and appreciated the attention of the nice young men and women who lived in a house near campus. They persuaded her to share their meals and then to move in with them. Between intense bombardments of "love," they deprived her of sleep and sometimes threatened to throw her out. Jill became increasingly confused and dependent, losing touch with any reality besides the one in the group. She dropped out of school and refused to see or communicate with her family. Before long she, too, was preying on lonely college students.
>
> —Hillary Begas (student), "The Love Bombers"

Important events in chronological order

As this paragraph illustrates, a narrator is concerned not just with the sequence of events but also with their consequence, their importance to the whole. Thus a narrative rarely corresponds to real time; instead, it collapses transitional or background events and focuses on events of particular interest. In addition, writers sometimes rearrange events, as when they simulate the workings of memory by flashing back to an earlier time.

How does it look, sound, feel, smell, taste? (Description)

Description details the sensory qualities of a person, place, thing, or feeling. You use concrete and specific words to convey a dominant mood, to illustrate an idea, or to achieve some other purpose. Some description is **subjective**: the writer filters the subject through his or her biases and emotions. In the subjective description by Virginia Woolf on page 80, the *glare* of the walls, the *impenetrable darkness*, the *bulge of a great bowl*, and the *formidable* *corners and lines* all indicate the feelings of the author about what she describes.

In contrast to subjective description, journalists and scientists usually strive for description that is **objective**, conveying the subject without bias or emotion:

> The two toddlers, both boys, sat together for half an hour in a ten-foot-square room with yellow walls (one with a two-way mirror for observation) and a brown carpet. The room was unfurnished except for two small chairs and about two dozen toys. The boys' interaction was generally tense. They often struggled physically and verbally over several toys, especially a large red beach ball and a small wooden fire engine. The larger of the two boys often pushed the smaller away or pried his hands from the desired object. This larger boy never spoke, but he did make grunting sounds when he was engaging the other. In turn, the smaller boy twice uttered piercing screams of "No!" and once shouted "Stop that!" When he was left alone, he hummed and muttered to himself.
>
> —Ray Mattison (student), "Case Study: Play Patterns of Toddlers"

Objective description: specific record of sensory data without interpretation

What are examples of it or reasons for it? (Illustration or support)

Some ideas can be developed simply by **illustration or support**—supplying detailed examples or reasons. The writer of the paragraph on lying (p. 90) developed her idea with several specific examples of her general statements. You can also supply a single extended example:

> Teaching teenagers to drive is a nerve-racking job. During his first lesson, one particularly inept student refused to drive faster than ten miles per hour, forcing impatient drivers behind the car to pass on a residential street with a speed limit of twenty-five and cyclists in the bike lanes. Making a left turn at a four-way stop, the student didn't await his turn and nearly collided with an oncoming car. A few moments later, he jumped the curb when turning right and had to slam on the brakes to avoid hitting a concrete barrier. For a driving instructor, every day is an exercise in keeping one's fear and temper in check.
>
> —Jasmine Greer, "Driving School" (student)

Topic sentence

Single detailed example

Sometimes you can develop a paragraph by providing your reasons for stating a general idea:

> There are three reasons, quite apart from scientific considerations, that mankind needs to

Topic sentence

travel in space. The first reason is the need for garbage disposal: we need to transfer industrial processes into space, so that the earth may remain a green and pleasant place for our grandchildren to live in. The second reason is the need to escape material impoverishment: the resources of this planet are finite, and we shall not forgo forever the abundant solar energy and minerals and living space that are spread out all around us. The third reason is our spiritual need for an open frontier: the ultimate purpose of space travel is to bring to humanity not only scientific discoveries and an occasional spectacular show on television but a real expansion of our spirit.

—Freeman Dyson, "Disturbing the Universe"

Three reasons arranged in order of increasing drama and importance

What is it? What does it encompass, and what does it exclude? (Definition)

A **definition** says what something is and is not, specifying the characteristics that distinguish the subject from the other members of its class. You can easily define concrete, noncontroversial terms in a single sentence: *A knife is a cutting instrument* (its class) *with a sharp blade set in a handle* (the characteristics that set it off from, say, scissors or a razor blade). But defining a complicated or controversial topic often requires extended explanation, and you may need to devote a whole paragraph or even an essay to it. Such a definition may provide examples to identify the subject's characteristics. It may also involve other methods of development discussed here, such as classification or comparison and contrast.

The following definition of *professional middle class* comes from a book about changes in the American middle class:

Before this story [of changes in America's middle class] can be told, I must first introduce its central character, the professional middle class. This class can be defined, somewhat abstractly, as all those people whose economic and social status is based on education, rather than on ownership of capital or property. Most professionals are included, and so are white-collar managers, whose positions require at least a college degree, and increasingly also a graduate degree. Not all white-collar people are included, though; some of these are entrepreneurs who are better classified as "workers." But the professional middle class is still extremely broad, and includes such diverse types as schoolteachers, anchorpersons, engineers, professors, government bureaucrats, corporate executives (at least up through the middle levels of management), scientists, advertising people,

General definition

Specific examples of who is and is not included in the definition therapists, financial managers, architects, and, I should add, myself.

—Barbara Ehrenreich, *Fear of Falling: The Inner Life of the Middle Class*

What are its parts or characteristics? (Division or analysis)

Division and **analysis** both involve separating something into its elements, the better to understand it. Here is a simple example:

A typical daily newspaper compresses considerable information into the top of the first page, above the headlines. The most prominent feature of this space, the newspaper's name, is called the *logo* or *nameplate*. Under the logo and set off by rules is a line of small type called the *folio line*, which contains the date of the issue, the volume and issue numbers, copyright information, and the price. To the right of the logo is a block of small type called a *weather ear*, a summary of the day's forecast. And above the logo is a *skyline*, a kind of advertisement in which the paper's editors highlight a special feature of the issue.

—Kansha Stone (student), "Anatomy of a Paper"

The subject being divided

Elements of the subject, arranged spatially

Generally, analysis goes beyond simply identifying elements. Often used as a synonym for *critical thinking*, analysis also involves interpreting the elements' meaning and significance. You identify and interpret elements according to your particular interest in the subject. (See pp. 157–63 for more on critical thinking and analysis.)

The following paragraph comes from an essay about reality TV shows. The analytical focus of the whole essay is the contrived nature of such shows.

Reality TV shows are anything but "real." Participants are selected from thousands of applicants, and they have auditioned to prove themselves to be competent in front of a camera. The settings for the action are often environments created especially for the shows. Scenes that seem unscripted are often planned to capture entertaining footage. The wardrobes of the participants may be designed to enhance participants' "characters" and to improve their looks on camera. And footage is clearly edited to create scenes that seem authentic and tell compelling stories.

—Darrell Carter (student), "(Un)Reality TV"

Topic sentence

Elements:
- Carefully selected participants
- Created environments
- Planned scenes
- Designed wardrobes
- Edited footage

What groups or categories can it be sorted into? (Classification)

Classification involves sorting many things into groups based on their similarities. Using the pattern, we scan a large group composed of many members that share at least one characteristic—workers, say—and we assign the members to smaller groups on the basis of some principle—salary, perhaps, or dependence on computers. Here is an example:

> In my experience, the parents who hire daytime sitters for their school-age children tend to fall into one of three groups. The first group includes parents who work and want someone to be at home when the children return from school. These parents are looking for an extension of themselves, someone who will give the care they would give if they were at home. The second group includes parents who may be home all day themselves but are too disorganized or too frazzled by their children's demands to handle child care alone. They are looking for an organizer and helpmate. The third and final group includes parents who do not want to be bothered by their children, whether they are home all day or not. Unlike the parents in the first two groups, who care for their children whenever and however they can, these parents are looking for a permanent substitute for themselves.
>
> —Nancy Whittle (student), "Modern Parenting"

Topic sentence

Three groups:
Alike in one way (all hire sitters)
No overlap in groups (each has a different attitude)

Classes arranged in order of increasing drama

How is it like, or different from, other things? (Comparison and contrast)

Asking about similarities and differences leads to **comparison and contrast**: comparison focuses on similarities, whereas contrast focuses on differences. The two may be used separately or together to develop an idea or to relate two or more things. Commonly, comparisons are organized in one of two ways. In the first, **subject by subject**, the two subjects are discussed separately, one at a time:

> Consider the differences also in the behavior of rock and classical music audiences. At a rock concert, the audience members yell, whistle, sing along, and stamp their feet. They may even stand during the entire performance. The better the music, the more active they'll be. At a classical concert, in contrast, the better the performance, the more *still* the audience is. Members of the classical audience are so highly disciplined that they refrain from even clearing their throats or coughing. No matter what effect the powerful music has on their intellects and feelings, they sit on their hands.
>
> —Tony Nahm (student), "Rock and Roll Is Here to Stay"

Subjects: rock and classical audiences

Rock audience

Classical audience

In the second comparative organization, **point by point**, the two subjects are discussed side by side and matched feature for feature:

> Arguing is often equated with fighting, but there are key differences between the two. Participants in an argument approach the subject to find common ground, or points on which both sides agree, while people engaged in a fight usually approach the subject with an "us-versus-them" attitude. Participants in an argument are careful to use respectful, polite language, in contrast to the insults and worse that people in a fight use to get the better of their opponents. Finally, participants in an argument commonly have the goal of reaching a new understanding or larger truth about the subject they're debating, while those in a fight have winning as their only goal.
>
> —Erica Ito (student), "Is an Argument Always a Fight?"

Subjects: arguing and fighting

Approach to subject: argument, fight

Language: argument, fight

Goal: argument, fight

The following examples show the two organizing schemes in outline form. The one on the left corresponds to the point-by-point paragraph about the differences between arguing and fighting. The one on the right uses the same information but reorganizes it to cover the two subjects separately: first one, then the other.

Point by Point

I. Approach to subject
   A. Argument
   B. Fight
II. Language
   A. Argument
   B. Fight
III. Goal
   A. Argument
   B. Fight

Subject by Subject

I. Argument
   A. Approach to subject
   B. Language
   C. Goal
II. Fight
   A. Approach to subject
   B. Language
   C. Goal

Is it comparable to something that is in a different class but more familiar to readers? (Analogy)

Whereas we draw comparisons and contrasts between elements in the same general class (audiences, disputes), we link elements in different classes with a special kind of comparison called **analogy**. Most often in analogy we illuminate or explain an unfamiliar, abstract class of things with a familiar and concrete class of things:

> We might eventually obtain some sort of bedrock understanding of cosmic structure, but we will never understand the universe in detail; it is just too big and varied for that. If we possessed

Abstract subject: the universe, specifically the Milky Way

an atlas of our galaxy that devoted but a single page to each star system in the Milky Way (so that the sun and all its planets were crammed on one page), that atlas would run to more than ten million volumes of ten thousand pages each. It would take a library the size of Harvard's to house the atlas, and merely to flip through it, at the rate of a page per second, would require over ten thousand years.

—Timothy Ferris, *Coming of Age in the Milky Way*

Concrete subject: an atlas

Why did it happen, or what results did it have? (Cause-and-effect analysis)

When you use analysis to explain why something happened or what is likely to happen, then you are determining causes and effects. **Cause-and-effect analysis** is especially useful in writing about social, economic, or political events or problems. In the next paragraph the author looks at the causes of Japanese collectivism, which he elsewhere contrasts with American individualism:

The *shinkansen* or "bullet train" speeds across the rural areas of Japan giving a quick view of cluster after cluster of farmhouses surrounded by rice paddies. This particular pattern did not develop purely by chance, but as a consequence of the technology peculiar to the growing of rice, the staple of the Japanese diet. The growing of rice requires the construction and maintenance of an irrigation system, something that takes many hands to build. More importantly, the planting and the harvesting of rice can only be done efficiently with the cooperation of twenty or more people. The "bottom line" is that a single family working alone cannot produce enough rice to survive, but a dozen families working together can produce a surplus. Thus the Japanese have had to develop the capacity to work together in harmony, no matter what the forces of disagreement or social disintegration, in order to survive.

—William Ouchi, *Theory Z*

Effect: pattern of Japanese farming

Causes: Japanese dependence on rice, which requires collective effort

Effect: working in harmony

Cause-and-effect paragraphs tend to focus either on causes, as Ouchi's does, or on effects, as this paragraph does:

The consumerism of the postwar era [since World War II] has not been without its effects on the way we use our time. As people became accustomed to the material rewards of prosperity, desires for leisure time were eroded. They increasingly looked to consumption to give satisfaction,

Cause: consumerism

Effects:

Erosion of leisure time

even meaning, to their lives. In both the workplace and the home, progress has repeatedly translated into more goods and services, rather than more free time. Employers channel productivity increases into additional income; housewives are led to use their labor-saving appliances to produce more goods and services. Consumerism traps us as we become habituated to the good life, emulate our neighbors, or just get caught up in the social pressures created by everyone else's choices. Work-and-spend has become a mutually reinforcing and powerful syndrome—a seamless web we somehow keep choosing, without even meaning to.

—Juliet B. Schor, *The Overworked American*

Emphasis on goods and services

Higher incomes

Labor-saving devices

Habituation to the good life

Work-and-spend syndrome

How does one do it, or how does it work? (Process analysis)

When you analyze how to do something or how something works, you explain the steps in a **process**. Paragraphs developed by process analysis are usually organized chronologically, as the steps in the process occur. Some process analyses tell the reader how to do a task:

As a car owner, you waste money when you pay a mechanic to change the engine oil. The job is not difficult, even if you know little about cars. All you need is a wrench to remove the drain plug, a large, flat pan to collect the draining oil, plastic bottles to dispose of the used oil, and fresh oil. First, warm up the car's engine so that the oil will flow more easily. When the engine is warm, shut it off and remove its oil-filler cap (the owner's manual shows where this cap is). Then locate the drain plug under the engine (again consulting the owner's manual for its location) and place the flat pan under the plug. Remove the plug with the wrench, letting the oil flow into the pan. When the oil stops flowing, replace the plug and, at the engine's filler hole, add the amount and kind of fresh oil specified by the owner's manual. Pour the used oil into the plastic bottles and take it to a waste-oil collector, which any garage mechanic can recommend.

—Anthony Andreas (student), "Do-It-Yourself Car Care"

Process: changing oil

Equipment needed

Steps in process

Other process analyses explain how processes are done or how they work in nature. The paragraph on monarch butterflies (p. 80) is one example. Here is another:

What used to be called "laying on of hands" is now practiced seriously by nurses and doctors.

Process: therapeutic touch

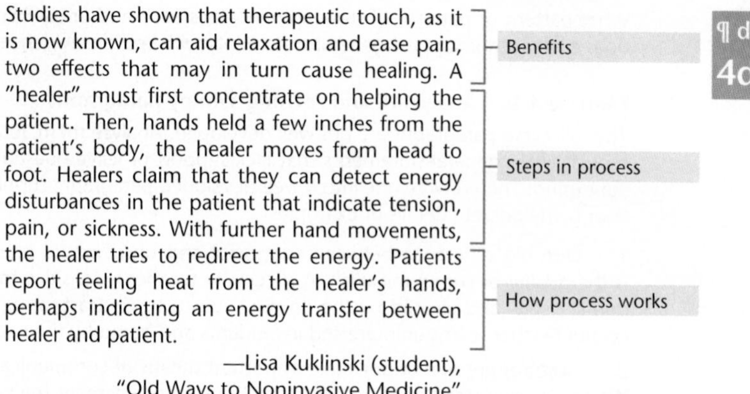

Studies have shown that therapeutic touch, as it is now known, can aid relaxation and ease pain, two effects that may in turn cause healing. A "healer" must first concentrate on helping the patient. Then, hands held a few inches from the patient's body, the healer moves from head to foot. Healers claim that they can detect energy disturbances in the patient that indicate tension, pain, or sickness. With further hand movements, the healer tries to redirect the energy. Patients report feeling heat from the healer's hands, perhaps indicating an energy transfer between healer and patient.
Benefits
Steps in process
How process works
—Lisa Kuklinski (student), "Old Ways to Noninvasive Medicine"

Diagrams, photographs, and other visuals can do much to clarify process analyses. See pages 110–16 for guidelines on creating and clearly labeling visuals.

Combining patterns of development

Whatever pattern you choose as the basis for developing a paragraph, other patterns may also prove helpful. Combined patterns have appeared often in this section: Dyson analyzes causes and effects in presenting reasons (pp. 92–93); Ehrenreich uses examples to define (pp. 93–94); Nahm uses description to compare (p. 95); Ouchi uses process analysis to explain causes (p. 97).

3 Checking length

The average paragraph contains between 100 and 150 words, or between four and eight sentences. The appropriate length of a paragraph depends on the complexity of its topic, its role in developing the thesis of the essay, and its position in the essay. Still, very short paragraphs often lack adequate development; they may leave readers with a sense of incompleteness. And very long paragraphs often contain irrelevant details or develop two or more topics; readers may have difficulty distinguishing or remembering ideas.

When you are revising your essay, reread the paragraphs that seem very long or very short, checking them especially for unity and adequate development. If the paragraph wanders, cut everything from it that does not support your main idea (such as sentences that you might begin with *By the way*). If it is underdeveloped, supply the specific details, examples, or reasons needed, or try one of the methods of development we have discussed here.

Exercise 4.15 Analyzing paragraph development

Examine the paragraphs by Richard Rodriguez (p. 76) and Judith Wax (p. 81) to discover how the authors achieve paragraph development.

What pattern or patterns of development does each author use? Where does each author support general statements with specific evidence?

Exercise 4.16 Analyzing and revising skimpy paragraphs

The following paragraphs are not well developed. Analyze them, looking especially for general statements that lack support or leave questions in your mind. Then rewrite one into a well-developed paragraph, supplying your own concrete details or examples.

1. One big difference between successful and unsuccessful teachers is the quality of communication. A successful teacher is sensitive to students' needs and excited by the course subject. In contrast, an unsuccessful teacher seems uninterested in students and bored by the subject.

2. Gestures are one of our most important means of communication. We use them instead of speech. We use them to supplement the words we speak. And we use them to communicate some feelings or meanings that words cannot adequately express.

3. A computer can do much—but not everything—to help me improve my writing. I can easily make changes and try out different versions of a paper. But I still must do the hard work of revising.

Exercise 4.17 Considering your past work: Paragraph development

Continuing from Exercises 4.5 (p. 77) and 4.12 (p. 89), examine the development of the body paragraphs in your writing. Where does specific information seem adequate to support your general statements? Where does support seem skimpy? Revise the paragraphs as necessary to make your ideas clearer and more interesting. It may help you to pose the questions on pages 91–98.

Exercise 4.18 Writing with the patterns of development

Write at least three unified, coherent, and well-developed paragraphs, each one developed with a different pattern. Draw on the topics provided here, or choose your own topics.

1. **Narration**
   An experience of public speaking
   A disappointment
   Leaving home
   Waking up
2. **Description (objective or subjective)**
   Your room
   A crowded or deserted place
   A food
   An intimidating person
3. **Illustration or support**
   Why study
   Having a headache
   The best sports event
   Usefulness or uselessness of a self-help book
4. **Definition**
   Humor
   An adult
   Fear
   Authority
5. **Division or analysis**
   A television news show
   A barn
   A Web site
   A piece of music
6. **Classification**
   Factions in a dispute
   Styles of playing poker
   Types of Web sites
   Kinds of teachers
7. **Comparison and contrast**
   AM and FM radio DJs

Text messaging and tweeting
High school and college football
Movies on TV and in a theater

8. **Analogy**
   Paying taxes and giving blood
   The US Constitution and a building's foundation
   Graduating from high school and being released from prison
9. **Cause-and-effect analysis**
   Connection between tension and anger
   Causes of failing or acing a course
   Connection between credit cards and debt
   Causes of a serious accident
10. **Process analysis**
    Preparing for a job interview
    Setting up a blog
    Protecting your home from burglars
    Making a jump shot

4e Writing special kinds of paragraphs

Several kinds of paragraphs do not always follow the guidelines for unity, coherence, development, and length because they serve special functions. These are the essay introduction, the essay conclusion, the transitional or emphatic paragraph, and the paragraph of spoken dialog.

1 Opening an essay

Most of your essays will open with a paragraph that draws readers from their world into your world. A good opening paragraph usually satisfies several requirements:

- **It focuses readers' attention on your subject and arouses curiosity about what you have to say.**
- **It specifies what your topic is and implies your attitude.**
- **Often it provides your thesis statement.**
- **It is concise and sincere.**

The box below provides a range of options for achieving these goals.

Some strategies for opening paragraphs

- Ask a question.
- Relate an incident.
- Use a vivid quotation.
- Offer a surprising statistic or other fact.
- State an opinion related to your thesis.
- Outline the argument your thesis refutes.
- Provide background.
- Create a visual image that represents your subject.
- Make a historical comparison or contrast.
- Outline a problem or dilemma.
- Define a word central to your subject.
- In some business or technical writing, summarize your paper.

CULTURE LANGUAGE The requirements and options for essay introductions may not be what you are used to if your native language is not English. In other cultures, readers may seek familiarity or reassurance from an author's introduction, or they may prefer an indirect approach to the subject. In academic and business English, however, writers and readers prefer concise, direct expression.

The funnel introduction

One reliably effective introduction forms a kind of funnel, moving from broad to narrow:

Funnel introduction

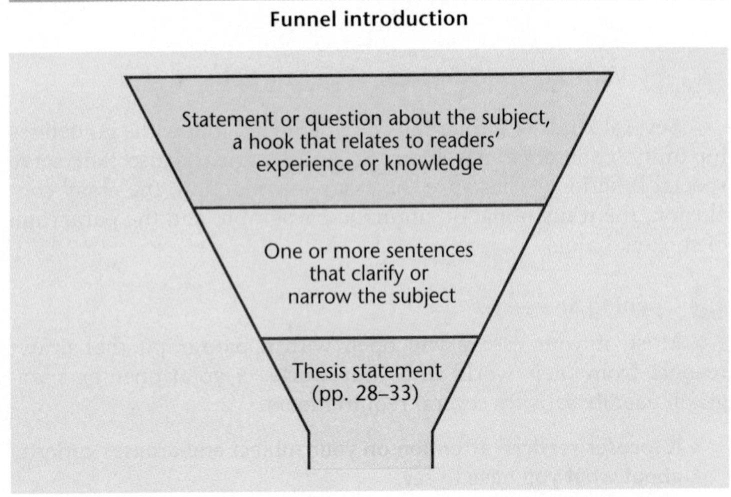
Statement or question about the subject, a hook that relates to readers' experience or knowledge
One or more sentences that clarify or narrow the subject
Thesis statement (pp. 28–33)

Here are two examples of the funnel introduction:

Watching television wastes time, destroys brain cells, contributes to obesity, and can even	Statement about subject
turn viewers violent. These attitudes are supported by serious research as well as popular belief. However, television watching can actually	Clarification of subject: bridge to thesis statement
benefit some people. It provides replacement voices that can ease the loneliness of viewers, spark their healthful laughter, and even teach young children.	Thesis statement

—Craig Holbrook (student), "TV Can Be Good for You"

The Declaration of Independence is so widely regarded as a statement of American ideals that its origins in practical politics tend to	Statement about subject

be forgotten. Thomas Jefferson's draft was intensely debated and then revised in the Continental Congress. Jefferson was disappointed with the result. However, a close reading of both the historical context and the revisions themselves indicates that the Congress improved the document for its intended purpose.

—Ann Weiss (student), "The Editing of the Declaration of Independence"

Clarification of subject: bridge to thesis statement

Thesis statement

Other effective introductions

Several other types of introduction can be equally effective, though they are sometimes harder to invent and control.

Quotation leading into the thesis statement

"It is difficult to speak adequately or justly of London," wrote Henry James in 1881. "It is not a pleasant place; it is not agreeable, or cheerful, or easy, or exempt from reproach. It is only magnificent." Were he alive today, James, a connoisseur of cities, might easily say the same thing about New York or Paris or Tokyo, for the great city is one of the paradoxes of history. In countless different ways, it has almost always been an unpleasant, disagreeable, cheerless, uneasy and reproachful place; in the end, it can only be described as magnificent.

—*Time*

Quotation

Bridge to thesis statement

Thesis statement

Incident or image setting up the thesis statement

Canada is pink. I knew that from the map I owned when I was six. On it, New York was green and brown, which was true as far as I could see, so there was no reason to distrust the map maker's portrayal of Canada. When my parents took me across the border and we entered the immigration booth, I looked excitedly for the pink earth. Slowly it dawned on me: this foreign, "different" place was not so different. I discovered that the world in my head and the world at my feet were not the same.

—Robert Ornstein, *Human Nature*

Incident from writer's experience

Thesis statement

Startling opinion or question

Caesar was right. Thin people need watching. I've been watching them for most of my adult life, and I don't like what I see. When these narrow fellows spring at me, I quiver to my toes. Thin people come in all personalities, most of them menacing. You've got your "together" thin person, your mechanical thin person, your

Opinion

condescending thin person, your tsk-tsk thin person. All of them are dangerous. — Thesis statement

—Suzanne Britt,
"That Lean and Hungry Look"

Background, such as a historical comparison

Throughout the first half of [the twentieth] century, the American Medical Association, the largest and most powerful medical organization in the world, battled relentlessly to rid the country of quack potions and cure-alls; and it is the AMA that is generally credited with being the single most powerful force behind the enactment of the early pure food and drug laws. [Historical background] Today, however, medicine's guardian seems to have done a complete about-face and become one of the pharmaceutical industry's staunchest allies—often at the public's peril and expense. [Thesis statement]

—Mac Jeffery,
"Does Rx Spell Rip-off?"

An effective introductory paragraph need not be long, as the following opener shows:

> I've often wondered what goes into a hot dog. Now I know and I wish I didn't.
> —William Zinsser, *The Lunacy Boom*

Ineffective introductions

When writing and revising an introductory paragraph, avoid the following approaches that are likely to bore readers or make them question your sincerity or control:

Openings to avoid

- **A vague generality or truth.** Don't extend your reach too wide with a line such as *Throughout human history . . .* or *In today's world. . . .* Readers can do without the warm-up.
- **A flat announcement.** Don't start with *The purpose of this essay is . . .*, *In this essay I will . . .*, or any similar presentation of your intention or topic.
- **A reference to the essay's title.** Don't refer to the title of the essay in the first sentence—for example, *This is a big problem* or *This book is about the history of the guitar.*
- ***According to Webster. . . .*** Don't start by citing a dictionary definition. A definition can be an effective springboard to an essay, but this kind of lead-in has become dull with overuse.
- **An apology.** Don't fault your opinion or your knowledge with *I'm not sure if I'm right, but . . .*; *I don't know much about this, but . . .*; or a similar line.

2 Closing an essay

Most of your compositions will end with a closing statement or conclusion, a signal to readers that you have not simply stopped writing but have actually finished. The conclusion completes an essay, bringing it to a climax while assuring readers that they have understood your intention.

Effective conclusions

An essay conclusion may consist of a single sentence or a group of sentences, usually set off in a separate paragraph. The conclusion may take one or more of the following approaches:

Some strategies for closing paragraphs

- Recommend a course of action.
- Summarize the paper.
- Echo the approach of the introduction.
- Restate your thesis and reflect on its implications.
- Strike a note of hope or despair.
- Give a symbolic or powerful fact or other detail.
- Give an especially compelling example.
- Create an image that represents your subject.
- Use a quotation.

The following paragraph concludes the essay on the Declaration of Independence (the introduction appears on pp. 102–05):

> The Declaration of Independence has come to be a statement of this nation's political philosophy, but that was not its purpose in 1776. Jefferson's passionate expression had to bow to the goals of the Congress as a whole to forge unity among the colonies and to win the support of foreign nations.
>
> —Ann Weiss (student), "The Editing of the Declaration of Independence"

Echo of introduction: contrast between past and present

Restatement and elaboration of thesis

The next author uses a different technique—a vivid image—to conclude an essay about an aunt who committed suicide by drowning:

> My aunt haunts me—her ghost drawn to me because now, after fifty years of neglect, I alone devote pages of paper to her, though not origamied into houses and clothes. I do not think she always means me well. I am telling on her, and she was a spite suicide, drowning herself in the drinking water. The Chinese are always very frightened of the drowned one, whose weeping ghost, wet hair hanging and skin bloated, waits silently by the water to pull down a substitute.
>
> —Maxine Hong Kingston, "No Name Woman"

Summary

Image

In the following paragraph the author concludes an essay on environmental protection with a call for action:

> Until we get the answers, I think we had better keep on building power plants and growing food with the help of fertilizers and such insect-controlling chemicals as we now have. The risks are well known, thanks to the environmentalists. If they had not created a widespread public awareness of the ecological crisis, we wouldn't stand a chance. But such awareness by itself is not enough. Flaming manifestos and prophecies of doom are no longer much help, and a search for scapegoats can only make matters worse. The time for sensations and manifestos is about over. Now we need rigorous analysis, united effort and very hard work.
>
> —Peter F. Drucker, "How Best to Protect the Environment"

Summary and opinion

Call for action

Ineffective conclusions

The preceding examples illustrate ways of avoiding several pitfalls of conclusions:

Closings to avoid

- **A repeat of the introduction.** Don't simply replay your introduction. The conclusion should capture what the paragraphs of the body have added to the introduction.
- **A new direction.** Don't introduce a subject that is different from the one your essay has been about. If you arrive at a new idea, this may be a signal to start fresh with that idea as your thesis.
- **A sweeping generalization.** Don't conclude more than you reasonably can from the evidence you have given. If your essay is about your frustrating experience trying to clear a parking ticket, you cannot reasonably conclude that *all* local police forces are tied up in red tape.
- **An apology.** Don't cast doubt on your essay. Don't say, *Even though I'm no expert* or *This may not be convincing, but I believe it's true* or anything similar. Rather, to win your readers' confidence, display confidence.

3 Using short emphatic or transitional paragraphs

A short emphatic paragraph can give unusual stress to an important idea, in effect asking the reader to pause and consider before moving on.

> In short, all those who might have taken responsibility ducked it, and catastrophe was inevitable.

A transitional paragraph, because it is set off by itself, moves a discussion from one point to another more slowly or more completely than does a single transitional expression or even a transitional sentence attached to a larger paragraph.

> These, then, are the causes of the current contraction in hospital facilities. But how does this contraction affect the medical costs of the government, private insurers, and individuals?
>
> So the debates were noisy and emotion-packed. But what did they accomplish? Historians have identified at least three direct results.

Use transitional paragraphs only to shift readers' attention when your essay makes a significant turn. A paragraph like the following one betrays a writer who is stalling:

> Now that we have examined these facts, we can look at some others that are equally central to an examination of this important issue.

4 Writing dialog

When recording a conversation between two or more people, start a new paragraph for each person's speech. The paragraphing establishes for the reader the point at which one speaker stops talking and another begins.

> The dark shape was indistinguishable. But once I'd flooded him with light, there he stood, blinking.
>
> "Well," he said eventually, "you're a sight for sore eyes. Should I stand here or are you going to let me in?"
>
> "Come in," I said. And in he came.
>
> —Louise Erdrich, *The Beet Queen*

Though dialog appears most often in fiction writing (the source of the preceding example), it may occasionally freshen or enliven narrative or expository essays. (For the use of quotation marks and other punctuation in passages of dialog, see pp. 436–37 and 461.)

Exercise 4.19 Analyzing an introduction and conclusion

Analyze the introductory and concluding paragraphs in the first and final drafts of the student essay in Chapter 3, pages 49–50 and 67–69. What is wrong with the first-draft paragraphs? Why are the final-draft paragraphs better? Could they be improved still further?

Exercise 4.20 Considering your past work: Introductions and conclusions

Examine the opening and closing paragraphs of the essay you've been analyzing in Exercises 4.5, 4.12, and 4.17. Do the paragraphs fulfill the requirements and avoid the pitfalls outlined on pages 101–06? Revise them as needed for clarity, conciseness, focus, and interest.

5 Presenting Writing

Chapter essentials

- Format academic writing for the discipline in which you are writing (below).
- Use visuals and other media appropriately in multimodal writing and presentations (p. 110).
- Take account of design when writing for the Web (p. 116).
- Consider the distinctive opportunities and challenges of oral presentations (p. 121).

Visit MyWritingLab™ for more resources on presenting writing.

Presenting your writing gives you a chance to display your hard work in the best possible light. Most of the time, presenting writing also involves challenges: to fulfill the requirements of the assignment, the conventions of the genre, and the expectations of your audience.

5a Formatting academic writing

Many of the assignments you receive in college will require you to submit a written text either on paper or electronically—for instance, attached to an e-mail or uploaded to a course Web site. For most print papers and files of papers, the example opposite shows a basic format that will help make your writing attractive and readable.

Many academic style guides recommend specific formats. This book details four common ones:

- **MLA,** used in English, foreign languages, and some other humanities (pp. 680–82).
- **Chicago,** used in history, art history, religion, and some other humanities (pp. 757–58).
- **APA,** used in the social sciences (pp. 782–83).
- **CSE,** used in some natural and applied sciences (p. 802).

Although they do vary, most academic formats share preferences for the design of standard elements:

- **Margins:** minimum one inch on all sides.
- **Line spacing:** double-spaced throughout.
- **Type fonts and sizes:** standard 10- or 12-point fonts such as Times New Roman and Cambria (serif fonts, with small lines finishing the letters) or Arial and Calibri (sans serif fonts, lacking the small

First page of an academic paper (MLA format)

Torres 1

Mia Torres

Mr. O'Donnell

English 131

14 March 2014

Creating the Next Generation of Smokers

Parents warn their children not to smoke. Schools teach kids and teens about the dangers of smoking. States across the country have enacted smoking bans, making it illegal for adults to smoke in restaurants, bars, workplaces, and public buildings. Yet despite these efforts, smoking among teens and young adults continues, and it does so in part because the film industry creates movies that promote smoking.

According to the organization Smoke Free Movies, a group based in the School of Medicine at the University of California, San Francisco, tobacco companies and filmmakers collaborate to promote smoking: tobacco companies pay filmmakers to feature their products, and filmmakers show celebrity actors smoking in movies and portray smoking as glamorous and socially acceptable (4-5). Stopping young people's exposure to images of smoking in movies requires stopping each of these activities.

Despite proof that showing smoking in movies encourages young people to start smoking, more than half of movies feature well-known stars smoking (Fox). As fig. 1 shows, cigarettes often figure prominently, with the cigarette held close to the celebrity's head so that it is an integral part of the shot.

Fig. 1. The actress Scarlett Johansson in *Black Dahlia*, one of many movies released each year in which characters smoke. From *Daily Mail*, 18 Sept. 2006, www.dailymail.co.uk/article-1602474.html.

Writer's last name and page number.

Identification: writer's name, instructor's name, course title, date.

Title centered.

Double-spaced throughout.

1" margins on top, bottom, and sides.

Indentions marking paragraph breaks.

Source citation in MLA style (see p. 634).

Photograph introduced to indicate its meaning and purpose.

Caption allowing photograph to be read independently from the text.

lines). Serif fonts are generally easier to read on paper, while sans serif fonts are easier to read on a screen.

- **Highlighting:** underlining, *italics,* or **boldface** to mark headings and emphasize text elements such as terms being defined.
- **Headings:** one or two levels as needed to direct readers' attention to significant ideas and transitions. Word headings consistently—for instance, all questions (*What Is Sustainability?*) or all phrases with *-ing* words (*Understanding Sustainability*). Indicate the relative importance of headings with highlighting and position—perhaps bold for first-level headings and lightface italic for second-level headings. (Document format in psychology and some other social sciences requires a particular treatment of headings. See p. 783.)

Considering readers with vision loss

If your audience may include readers who have low vision, problems with color perception, or difficulties processing visual information, adapt your design to meet these readers' needs:

- **Use large type fonts.** Most guidelines call for 14 points or larger.
- **Use standard type fonts.** Many people with low vision find it easier to read sans serif fonts such as Arial than serif fonts. Avoid decorative fonts with unusual flourishes, even in headings.
- **Avoid words in all-capital letters.**
- **Avoid relying on color alone to distinguish elements.** Label elements, and distinguish them by position or size.
- **Use red and green selectively.** To readers who are red-green colorblind, these colors will appear in shades of gray, yellow, or blue.
- **Use contrasting colors.** To make colors distinct, choose them from opposite sides of the color spectrum—violet and yellow, for instance, or orange and blue.
- **Use only light colors for tints behind type.** Make the type itself black or a very dark color.

- **Lists:** numbered or bulleted (as in the list you're reading), to show the relationship of like items, such as the elements of a document or the steps in a process or proposal.
- **Color:** mainly for illustrations, occasionally for headings, bullets, and other elements. Always use black for the text of a paper, and make sure that any other colors are dark enough to be legible.

5b Using visuals and other media in multimodal writing

Academic writing is often **multimodal**—that is, it includes more than one medium, whether text, charts, photographs, video, or audio. A simple multimodal paper involves just two media—mainly text with some illustrations embedded in the text. A paper submitted online might add links to audio or video files as well. This section provides guidelines for selecting and using such media in your writing. The next sections treat media in Web compositions and in blogs and wikis.

Caution Any visual or media file you include or link to in your writing requires the same detailed citation as a written source. See pages 621–22 for more on acknowledging sources.

1 Selecting visuals and other media

You can wait until you've drafted a paper before concentrating on what visuals and other media to include. This approach keeps your focus on the research and writing needed to craft what you want to say. But you can also begin thinking visually at the beginning of a project, as you might if your initial interest in the subject was sparked by a compelling image.

Depending on your writing situation, you might use anything from a table to a bar chart to a video to support your writing. The following pages describe and illustrate the options.

Note The Web is an excellent resource for visuals, audio, and video (see pp. 574–76). Your computer may include a program for creating tables, graphs, and other illustrations, or you can work with specialized software such as *Excel* (for graphs and charts) or *Adobe Illustrator* (for diagrams, maps, and the like). Use *PowerPoint*, *Prezi*, or a similar program for visuals in oral presentations (see pp. 127–29).

Selecting visuals

Visuals can be placed in print or electronic documents. They include tables, pie charts, bar charts, line graphs, infographics, diagrams, flowcharts, and images such as photographs, maps, fine art, advertisements, and cartoons. See the box on the next two pages for common types and their uses.

Selecting video and audio

You can use video or audio files to emphasize or support points in digital writing such as Web pages or blogs and in oral presentations with *PowerPoint* slides. For example, you might explain a process with a video of how something works, support an interpretation of a play with a video of a scene from a performance, or illustrate a profile of a person by linking to a podcast interview. The screen shot below shows a passage of text from an online paper that links to video of the poet Rita Dove reading her poem "American Smooth."

Link to video file

Often a reading by the poet reinforces both the sound and the meaning of the poem. In Rita Dove's "American Smooth," two people move self-consciously through an intricate dance, smiling and holding their bodies just so, when suddenly they experience a moment of perfection: they nearly float. When Dove reads the poem aloud, she builds to that moment, allowing listeners to feel the same magic (http://www.poetryfoundation.org/features/video/267).

5b

Selecting visuals

Tables

Tables present raw data to show how variables relate to one another or how two or more groups contrast. Place a descriptive title above the table, and use headings to label rows and columns.

Table 1

Public- and private-school enrollment of US students, 2013

	Number of students (in thousands)	Percentage in public school	Percentage in private school
All students	74,603	85	15
Kindergarten through grade 8	39,179	88	12
Grades 9-12	16,332	92	8

Source: Data from *Digest of Education Statistics: 2013,* National Center for Education Statistics, Apr. 2014, nces.ed.gov/tables/dt13_205.10.asp.

Diagrams and flowcharts

Diagrams show concepts visually, such as the structure of an organization or the way something works or looks.

Fig. 4. *MyPlate,* a graphic representation of daily food portions recommended for a healthy diet. From *ChooseMyPlate.gov,* US Dept. of Agriculture, 2011, www.choosemyplate.gov.

Images

Photographs, maps, paintings, advertisements, and cartoons can be the focus of critical analysis or can support points you make.

Fig. 5. View from the *Cassini* spacecraft, showing Saturn and its rings. From *Cassini-Huygens: Mission to Saturn and Titan*, NASA, Jet Propulsion Laboratory, 24 Feb. 2015, nasa.gov/multimedia/imagegallery/137.html.

Pie charts

Pie charts show the relations among the parts of a whole, adding up to 100%. Use a pie chart to show shares of data. Label each pie slice, and make it proportional to its share of the whole.

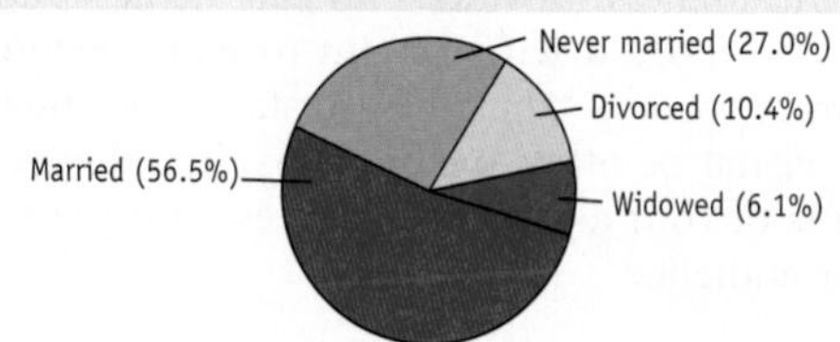

Fig. 1. Marital status in 2013 of adults age eighteen and over. Data from *2013 Statistical Abstract*, US Census Bureau, Jan. 2014, www.census.gov/library/publications/2013/131ed.html.

Bar charts

Bar charts compare groups or time periods. Use a bar chart when relative size is important. On the vertical scale, start with a zero point in the lower left and label the values being measured. On the horizontal scale, label the groups being compared.

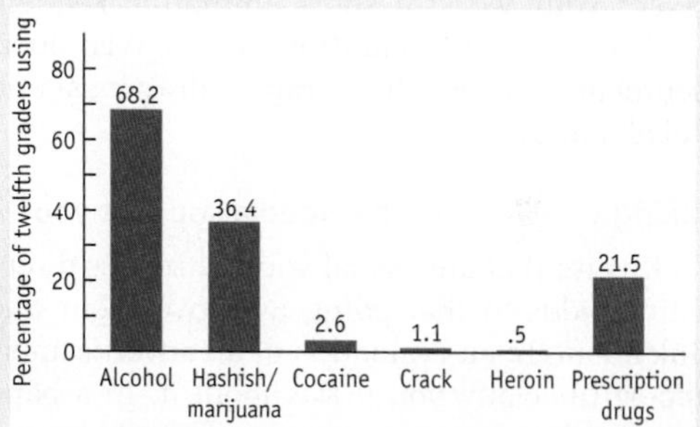

Fig. 2. Lifetime prevalence of use of alcohol, compared with other drugs, among twelfth graders in 2013. Data from *Monitoring the Future: A Continuing Study of American Youth*, U of Michigan, 3 Feb. 2013, www.monitoringthefuture.org/data/data.html.

Line graphs

Line graphs compare many points of data to show change over time. On the vertical scale, start with a zero point in the lower left and label the values being measured. On the horizontal scale, label the range of dates. Label the data lines, and distinguish them with color, dots, or dashes.

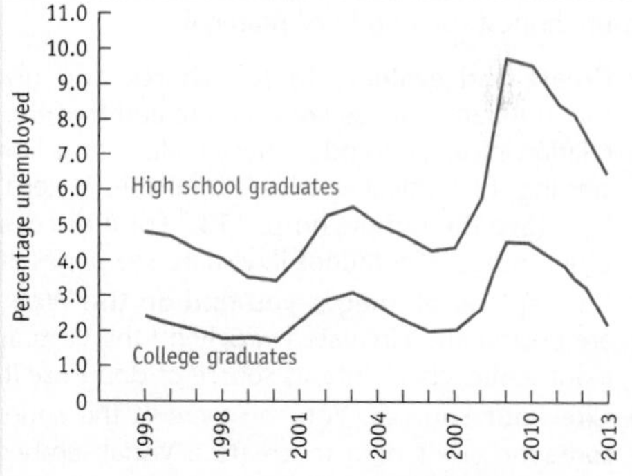

Fig. 3. Unemployment rates of high school graduates and college graduates, 1995-2013. Data from *Economics News Release*, US Dept. of Labor, Bureau of Labor Statistics, 7 Oct. 2013, www.bls.gov/newsrelease/empsit.nr0.htm.

2 Using visuals and other media effectively

An image or a video clip can attract readers' attention, but if it does no more it will amount to mere decoration or, worse, it will distract readers from the substance of your writing. Before using any visual or other media, consider whether it meets the requirements of your assignment, serves a purpose, and is appropriate for your audience.

Considering the requirements and limits of your writing situation

What do the type of writing you're doing and its format allow? Look through examples of similar writing to gauge the kinds of media, if any, that readers will expect. It matters, too, how you will present your work: a short animation sequence might be terrific in a *PowerPoint* presentation or in a Web document, but a printed document requires photographs, drawings, and other static means of explanation.

Making visuals and other media support your writing

Ensure that any visual you use relates directly to a point in your writing, adds to that point, and gives your audience something to think about. In an evaluation of an advertisement, the ad itself would support the claim you make about it. In a paper arguing for earthquake preparedness, a photograph could provide a visual record of

Using visuals and other media responsibly

Visuals and other media require special care to avoid distortion and to ensure honest use of others' material.

- **Create and evaluate tables, charts, and graphs carefully.** Verify that the data you use are accurate and that the highlighted changes, relationships, or trends reflect reality. In a line graph, for instance, starting the vertical and horizontal axes at zero puts the lines in context. (See the sample on p. 113.) For a discussion of distortions and other misrepresentations in visuals, see pages 203–04.
- **Be skeptical of images you find on the Web.** Altered photographs are posted and circulated widely on the Web. If a photograph seems inauthentic, check into its source or don't use it.
- **Cite your sources.** You must credit the source whenever you use someone else's data to create a visual, embed someone else's visual in your document, or link to someone else's media file. See page 116.
- **Obtain permission if it is required.** For projects that will reside on the Web, you may need to clear permission from the copyright holder of a visual or a media file. See pages 621–22 for a discussion of copyright and permission.

earthquake damage and a chart could show levels of current preparedness. The two images below supported a student's paper with this thesis: *By the mid-1960s, depictions of women in advertising reflected changing attitudes toward the traditional role of homemaker.*

Visuals as support

Visual examples support the thesis about changing attitudes toward women as homemakers.

Caption explains the visuals, tying them to the text of the paper and providing source information.

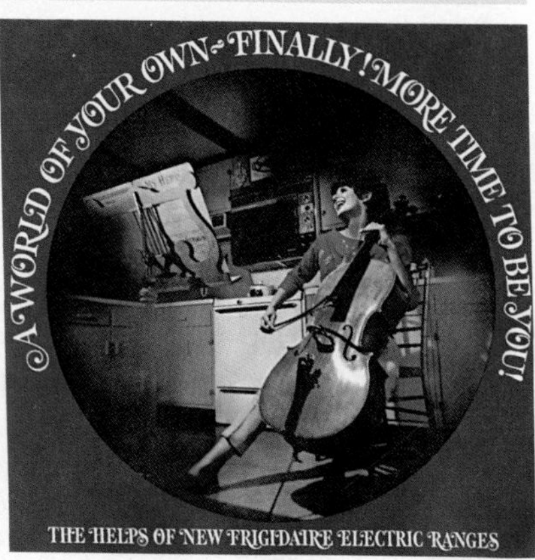

Fig. 1. An advertisement from 1945 (left) and a brochure illustration from 1965 (right) showing a change in the relationship between homemaking women and their appliances. Left: Hoover advertisement, 1945. Right: *Electric Ranges by Frigidaire*, 1965.

Integrating visuals and other media into your writing

Readers should understand why you are including visuals ‹ other media in your writing and how the media relate to the ov‹ project:

- **In projects with embedded visuals, connect the visual**‹ **our** ‹n at **text.** When you include visuals in your writing, refer ‹em— the point(s) where readers will benefit from cons‹ ‹es and for instance, "See fig. 2" or "See table 1." Num‹ ‹2, and tables separately (Fig. 1, Fig. 2, and so on; Ta‹ ‹caption so on). And always include a title above a ‹ under a visual (see the next page).
- **In online projects using audio or video, v**‹ **or links into your text.** Your audience should k‹ ‹intend the media to show, whether you link ‹ ‹a mainly text document or you integrate text, ‹ges, and video into a complex Web project.

5c

Writing captions and source notes

For a figure such as a chart, graph, or diagram, always provide a caption that performs two functions: it ties a visual to your text so that readers don't have to puzzle out your intention; and it cites the source of the data or the entire visual. See the captions below and with the appliance ads on the previous page. Most discipline styles have distinctive formats for captions and source information.

Figure caption (MLA style)

Fig. 1. Marital status in 2013 of adults age eighteen and over. Data from *2013 Statistical Abstract*, US Census Bureau, Jan. 2014, www.census.gov/library/publications/2013/131ed.html.

For a table, provide a title on top that tells readers what the content shows, and then give a note at the bottom that cites the source.

Table title (MLA style)

Public- and private-school enrollment of US students, 2013

Table source note (MLA style)

Source: Data from *Digest of Education Statistics: 2013*, National Center for Education Statistics, Apr. 2014, nces.ed.gov/tables/dt13_205.10.asp.

5c Presenting writing on the Web

You may already be experienced in creating Web-based writing projects—perhaps a *Facebook* page, a *Twitter* account, a blog, a movie, or a digital collage posted on *YouTube*. You know that the purposes and audiences for such multimodal Web writing vary widely, and so do readers' expectations for design.

Many creators of Web-based projects upload files into existing templates that make design fairly easy. Even with such software, ou will still have to make choices about elements such as fonts, lors, and layout. The design guidelines for academic writing on s 108–10 can help you with such decisions, as can the follow- iscussion of academic Web compositions such as a Web site ultimodal project posted on a blog or wiki. For tips on using upport an oral presentation, see pages 127–29.

1 ing a Web composition

comp ou are developing a Web site or preparing a digital lines be posted on the Web, the following general guide- plan your project:

- **Co you esign can reflect your purpose for writing and ence.** Unlike a conventional academic paper, a Web composition often allows considerable design freedom. Think about how type fonts and sizes, headings, visuals and other media, background colors, and other design elements can connect with readers and further the purpose of your writing.

- **Anticipate how readers will move within your composition.** A digital document with links to other pages, posts, Web sites, and media can disorient readers as they scroll up and down and pursue various links. Page length, links, menus, and other cues should work to keep readers oriented.
- **Imagine what readers may see on their screens.** Each reader's screen frames and organizes the experience of reading online. Screen space is limited, and it varies widely. Text and visual elements should be managed for maximum clarity and effectiveness on a variety of screens.
- **Integrate visuals, audio, and video into the text.** Web compositions will likely include visuals such as charts and photographs as well as video (such as animation or film clips) and audio (such as music or excerpts from interviews). Any visual or sound element should add essential information that can't be provided otherwise, and it should be well integrated with the rest of your composition. Avoid using visuals and sound merely as attention grabbers. See pages 110–15 for tips on using media effectively and pages 574–76 for sources of images, audio, and video.
- **Acknowledge your sources.** It's easy to incorporate text, visuals, audio, and video from other sources into a Web composition, but you have the same obligation to cite your sources as you do in a printed document. (See pp. 623–24 on citing sources.) Your Web composition is a form of publication, like a magazine or a book. Unless the material you are using explicitly allows copying without permission, you may need to seek the copyright holder's permission, just as print publishers do. (See pp. 621–22 for more on copyright.)

Note If you anticipate that some of your readers may have visual, hearing, or reading disabilities, you'll need to consider their needs while designing writing that will appear on a screen. Some of these considerations are covered on page 110, and others are fundamental to any effective Web-based design, as discussed in this section. In addition, avoid any content that relies exclusively on visuals or sound, instead supplementing such elements with text descriptions. At the same time, try to provide key concepts in words as well as in visuals and sound. For more on Web design for readers with disabilities, visit the World Wide Web Consortium at *www.w3.org*.

2 Creating a Web site

Traditional printed documents are intended to be read page by page in sequence. In contrast, Web sites are intended to be examined in whatever order readers choose as they follow links to pages within a site and to other sites. The diagram below shows a schematic Web site, with pages at different levels (orange and then blue squares) interconnecting with the home page and with one another.

Web site organization

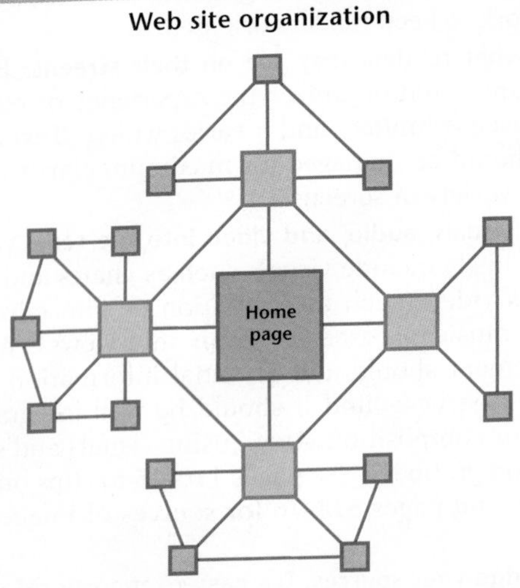

While reading Web sites, readers generally alternate between skimming pages for highlights and focusing intently on one section of text. To facilitate this kind of reading, you'll want to consider the guidelines on the previous two pages and also those following.

Structure and content

Organize a Web site so that it efficiently arranges your content and also orients readers:

- **Sketch possible site plans before getting started.** A diagram like the one above can help you develop the major components of your project and create a logical space for each component.
- **Consider how menus can provide overviews of the organization as well as direct access to the linked content.** The Web site on the facing page includes a menu near the top of the page.
- **Treat the first few sentences of any page as a get-acquainted space for you and your readers.** In the sample Web site, the text hooks readers with questions and orients them with general information.

Web site home page

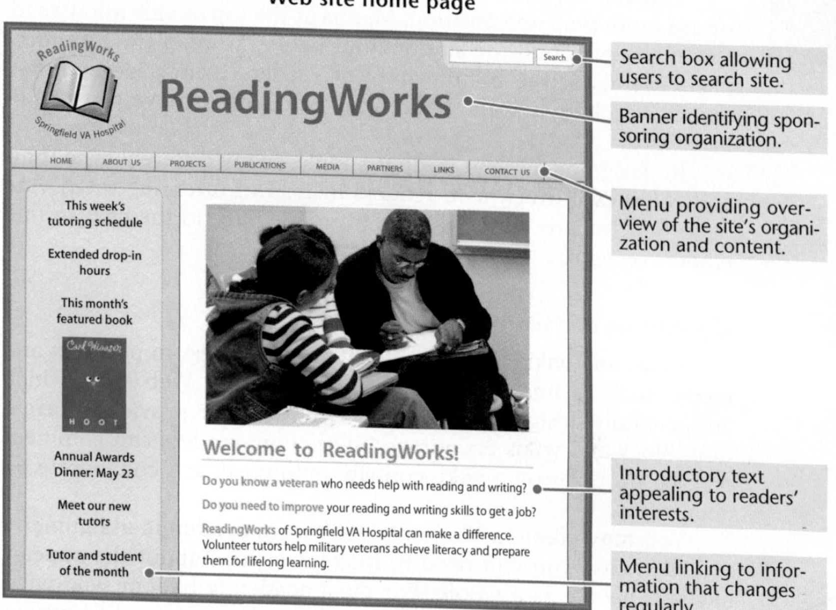

- **Distill your text so that it includes only essential information.** Concise prose is essential in any writing situation, of course, but readers of Web sites expect to scan text quickly.

Flow

Take advantage of the Web's visual nature by thinking about how information will flow on each page:

- **Standardize elements of your design to create and fulfill expectations in readers.** For instance, develop a uniform style for the main headings of pages, for headings within pages, and for menus.
- **Make scanning easy for readers.** Focus readers on crucial text by adding space around it. Add headings to break up text and to highlight content. Use lists to reinforce the parallel importance of items. (See pp. 108–10 for more on all these design elements.)

Navigation

Provide a menu so that readers can navigate your Web site. Like the table of contents in a book, a menu lists the features of a site, giving its plan at a glance.

5c

You can embed a menu at the top, side, or bottom of a page—or use more than one position. Menus at the top or side allow readers to move around the site without having to read the full home page. Menus at the bottom prevent readers from dead-ending—that is, reaching a point where they can't easily move forward or backward.

In designing a menu, keep it simple: many different type fonts and colors will overwhelm readers instead of orienting them. And make your menus look the same from one page to the next so that readers recognize them easily.

3 Posting to a blog or a wiki

Blogs and wikis are Web sites that allow users to post text and media such as images and video. Unlike other Web sites, which are generally designed to advocate a position or provide information, blogs and wikis encourage interaction: readers can comment on blog posts or, on a wiki, contribute to posts and collaborate on documents.

You may create a blog or a wiki as an academic assignment, in which case you will need to make decisions about the appearance of the site as a whole. For most academic blog or wiki writing, however, you will post drafts of your projects and comment on your classmates' work. You can compose and edit your text in your word processor and paste the text into the blog or wiki. At that point, you'll have the opportunity to write a descriptive title for your post, upload images and other media, and add links to other Web sites. You can also preview the post before making it public.

The following illustration shows a student's draft of a personal essay, which he posted to his class blog.

Literacy narrative posted to a blog

FRIDAY, FEBRUARY 21, 2014

Literacy narrative draft

Descriptive title.

Comics: Telling Stories in Words and Art

Anecdote opening the essay.

Standard font for readability.

For my seventh birthday, I received a Calvin and Hobbes comic book. I devoured the book, reading it cover to cover countless times, and was instantly attracted to how drawings and words worked together to tell very funny stories about the characters. I didn't always understand the vocabulary, the jokes, and references to the 1980s, but I laughed at what I did get: the funny arguments, crazy games, and hilarious schemes.

The writing situation: Literacy narrative

- **Subject:** Creating comics; student's choice for an assignment in a first-year writing course
- **Purpose:** To tell a story that explains the significance of reading, writing, and drawing comics in the writer's childhood
- **Audience:** Classmates, instructor, and readers of the student's blog
- **Genre:** Literacy narrative—a personal essay about the writer's experience with learning to read and/or write (see p. 136)
- **Sources:** Personal experience and writer's comics

The summer after my birthday I began drawing my own comics. I created two characters modeled on Calvin and Hobbes—a boy named Timmy and his dog Snuffy. Over the next five years, I drew hundreds of comics about Timmy, Snuffy, and Timmy's family and friends. I drew the strip shown here, about one of Timmy's many mishaps, when I was ten. I have this strip and some of my other favorites posted on my personal blog: johnsdoodles@blogger.com.

Paragraph connecting introductory anecdote to writer's life.

Illustration supporting a point in the post.

Embedded link to another Web site.

Timmy experienced much of what I did over the next several years. He went on vacation to places I visited with my family, like New York and San Francisco. He visited aunts, uncles, and grandparents. He exasperated his parents, learned to play an instrument, and dreamed of being a pilot. He also did things I had not experienced: he once trained for the school marathon and came in third, dreamed of going to the prom like his sister, and slid down what seemed like a mile-long hill on a sled. Through Timmy, I used language and drawing to explore ideas, dreams, and experiences, all the time trying to make them funny.

Paragraph expanding previous paragraph with vivid, concrete details.

Although I still draw and write, I left Timmy behind the summer I turned twelve. However, occasionally I look back at my Timmy comics and find it interesting to see how I used words and images to develop and display my sense of place in the world.

Conclusion pointing out significance of story.

Posted by John Heywood at 4:23 PM.

5d Making oral presentations

Speaking to a group can be anxiety producing, even for those who are experienced at it. This section shows you how to present

Checklist for an oral presentation

- **Purpose:** What do you want your audience to know or do as a result of your presentation? How can you achieve your purpose in the time and the setting you've been given? (See opposite.)
- **Audience:** What do you know about the characteristics and opinions of your audience? How can this information help you adapt your presentation to your audience's interests, needs, and opinions? (See opposite.)
- **Organization and content:** How are your ideas arranged? Where might listeners have difficulty following you? What functions do your introduction and conclusion perform? How relevant and interesting is your supporting material for your topic and your audience? (See opposite.)
- **Method of delivery:** What method of delivery do you plan: extemporaneous? reading from a text? memorized? a mixture? How does your method suit the purpose, setting, and occasion of your presentation? (See pp. 125–26.)
- **Vocal and physical delivery:** In rehearsing your presentation, what do you perceive as your strengths and weaknesses? Is your voice suitably loud for the setting? Are you speaking clearly? Are you able to move your eyes around the room so that you'll be making eye contact during the presentation? Is your posture straight but not stiff? Do your gestures reinforce your ideas? Do you use visual aids appropriately? (See pp. 126–29.)
- **Confidence and credibility:** What techniques will you use to overcome the inevitable anxiety about speaking? How will you project your confidence and competence? (See p. 129.)

your writing to a listening audience, and it offers techniques that are uniquely appropriate for effective oral presentations.

1 Writing and speaking

Writing and speechmaking have much in common: both require careful consideration of your subject, purpose, and audience. Thus the mental and physical activities that go into the writing process can also help you prepare and deliver a successful oral presentation.

Despite many similarities, however, writing for readers is not the same as speaking to listeners. Whereas a reader can go back and reread a written message, a listener cannot stop a speech to rehear a section. Several studies have reported that immediately after hearing a short talk, most listeners cannot recall half of what was said.

Effective speakers adapt to their audience's listening ability by reinforcing their ideas through repetition and restatement. They use simple words, short sentences, personal pronouns, contractions, and colloquial expressions. In formal writing, these strategies might seem redundant and too informal; but in speaking, they improve listeners' comprehension.

2 Considering purpose and audience

The most important step in developing an oral presentation is to identify your purpose: what do you want your audience to know or do as a result of your speech? Topic and purpose are *not* the same thing. Asking *What am I talking about?* is not the same as asking *Why am I speaking?*

An oral presentation may be anything from an informal report before a few peers to a formal address to your class. Whatever the situation, you're likely to be speaking for the same reasons that you write in school or at work: to explain something to listeners or to persuade listeners to accept your opinion or take an action. See pages 9–11 for more on these purposes.

Adapting to your audience is a critical task in public speaking as well as in writing. You'll want to consider the questions about audience on pages 12–13. But a listening audience requires additional considerations as well:

- **Why is your audience assembled?** Listeners who attend because they want to hear you and your ideas may be easier to interest and motivate than listeners who are required to attend.
- **How large is your audience?** With a small group you can be informal. If you are speaking to a hundred or more people, you may need a public address system, a lectern, special lighting, and audiovisual equipment.
- **Where will you speak?** Your approach should match the setting —more casual for a small classroom, more formal for an auditorium.
- **How long are you scheduled to speak?** Whatever the time limit, stick to it. Audiences lose patience with someone who speaks longer than expected.

When speaking, unlike when writing, you can see and hear your audience's responses during your presentation. If you sense that an audience is bored, try to interest listeners in what you are saying. If an audience is restless, check whether you have gone over your time. If you sense resistance, try to make midspeech adjustments to respond to that resistance.

3 Organizing the presentation

An effective oral presentation, like an effective essay, has a recognizable shape. The advice in Chapter 2 for organizing and outlining an essay serves the speechmaker as well as the writer (see pp. 34–43). Here are additional considerations for the introduction, conclusion, and supporting material.

The introduction

First impressions count. A strong beginning establishes an important relationship among three elements in an oral presentation: you, your topic, and your audience. More specifically, the beginning of an oral presentation should try to accomplish three goals:

- **Gain the audience's attention and interest.** Begin with a question, an unusual example or statistic, or a relevant anecdote.
- **Put yourself in the speech.** If you demonstrate your expertise, experience, or concern, your audience will be more interested in what you say and more trusting of you.
- **Introduce and preview your topic and purpose.** By the time your introduction is over, listeners should know what your topic is and the direction you'll take them in as you develop your ideas.

In addition to these principles for beginning a speech, there are pitfalls to avoid:

- **Don't try to cram too much into your introduction.** Focus on engaging the audience and quickly previewing your talk.
- **Don't begin with an apology.** A statement such as *I wish I'd been given more time to get ready for this presentation* will only undermine your listeners' confidence in you.
- **Don't begin with *My speech is about.* . . .** The statement is dull, and it does little to clarify your purpose.

Supporting material

Just as you do when writing, you can and should support your main points with examples, facts, and other evidence. In addition, as a speaker you can draw on other kinds of supporting material:

- **Use vivid description.** Paint a mental image of a scene, a concept, an event, or a person.
- **Use well-chosen quotations.** They can add an emotional or humorous moment to your speech.
- **Use true or fictional stories.** A memorable narrative can rivet the audience's attention and illustrate your point.
- **Use analogies.** Comparisons between essentially unlike things, such as a politician and a tightrope walker, link concepts memorably. (For more on analogy, see p. 96.)
- **Use visuals and other media.** A chart or graph can show data; audio or video can provide an effective example. See the discussion of media on pages 110–15 and tips for using presentation software such as *PowerPoint* or *Prezi* on pages 127–29.

Use a variety of supporting materials in your speech. A presentation that consists of nothing but statistics can bore an audience. Nonstop storytelling may interest listeners but fail to achieve your purpose.

The conclusion

Last impressions count as much as first impressions. You may hope that listeners will remember every detail of your speech, but they are more likely to leave with a general impression and a few ideas about you and your message. You want your conclusion to be clear, of course, but you also want it to be memorable. Remind listeners of how your topic and main idea connect to their needs and interests.

4 Delivering the presentation

Writing and speaking differ most obviously in the form of delivery: the writer is represented in print, the speaker is represented in person. This section describes the methods and techniques of oral presentation as well as some ways of coping with stage fright.

Methods of delivery

An oral presentation may be delivered impromptu, extemporaneously, from a text, or from memory. No one technique is best for all speeches; indeed, a single speech may include two or more forms or even all four—perhaps a memorized introduction, an extemporaneous body in which quotations are read from a text, and impromptu responses to audience questions during or after the speech.

- **Speaking impromptu** is presenting with no planning or practice. You may be called on in a class to express your opinion or to summarize something you've written. An audience member may ask you a question at the end of an oral presentation. The only way to prepare for such occasions is to be well prepared in general—to be caught up on course reading, for instance, or to know the facts in a debate.
- **Speaking extemporaneously,** which is typical of class lectures and many oral presentations, involves speaking from notes that guide you through the presentation. You prepare and practice, but you don't memorize the presentation or read it word for word from a text.
- **Speaking from a text** involves writing the text out in advance and then reading aloud from it. With a text in front of you, you're unlikely to lose your way, but you run the risk of being dull. To enliven reading from a text, write less formally so that the text sounds spoken: for instance, the sentence *Although*

costs rose, profits remained steady reads well in writing but would sound stiff in speech. In addition, rehearse thoroughly so that you can read with expression and can look up frequently to make eye contact with listeners (see below).

- **Speaking from memory** offers the advantage of complete freedom from notes or a text, so that you can look at your audience every minute and can move away from a lectern and even into the audience. However, like most speakers you may seem less relaxed, not more relaxed, when presenting from memory, and you risk forgetting your place or a whole passage. At least reserve this method for just a part or two where you want to make a strong impression—perhaps the introduction and conclusion. And rehearse not only to memorize the words but to deliver the words fresh, as if for the first time.

Vocal delivery

The sound of your voice will influence how your listeners receive you. When rehearsing, consider volume, speed, and articulation.

- **Speak loudly.** In a meeting with five other people, you can speak at normal volume. As your audience grows in size, so should your volume. Most speakers can project to as many as a hundred people, but a larger audience may require a microphone.
- **Speak slowly enough to be understandable.**
- **Speak clearly and correctly.** To avoid mumbling or slurring your words, practice articulating. Sometimes it helps to open your mouth a little wider than usual.

Physical delivery

You are more than your spoken words when you make an oral presentation. Your face and body also play a role in how your speech is received.

- **Stand up.** Always stand for a presentation, unless it takes place in a small room where standing would be inappropriate. You can see more audience members when you stand, and they in turn can hear your voice and see your gestures more clearly.
- **Stand straight and move around.** Turn your body toward one side of the room and then the other, step out from behind any lectern or desk, and gesture appropriately, as you would in conversation.
- **Make eye contact with listeners.** Move your gaze around the entire room, settle on someone, and establish direct eye contact; then move on to someone else.

Eye contact is customary in the United States, both in conversation and in oral presentation.

Listeners expect it and may perceive a speaker who doesn't make eye contact as evasive or insincere.

Visual aids

You can supplement an oral presentation with visual aids such as posters, models, slides, videos, or presentation software such as *PowerPoint* or *Prezi*. Visual aids can emphasize key points, show the organization of your presentation, and illustrate concepts and procedures. They can gain the attention of listeners and improve their understanding and memory.

The following guidelines can help you create effective and appropriate visual aids:

- **Use visual aids to underscore your points.** Short lists of key ideas, illustrations such as graphs or photographs, and objects such as models can make your presentation more interesting and memorable. But use visual aids judiciously: a constant flow of illustrations or objects will bury your message.
- **Match visual aids and setting.** An audience of five people may be able to see a photograph and share a chart; the students in a classroom or an audience of a hundred will need projected images.
- **Coordinate visual aids with your message.** Time each visual aid to reinforce a point you're making. Tell listeners what they're looking at—what they should be getting from the aid. Give them enough viewing time so that they don't mind turning their attention back to you.
- **Show visual aids only while they're needed.** To regain your audience's attention, remove or turn off any aid as soon as you have finished with it.

Many speakers use *PowerPoint*, *Prezi*, or other software to project main points, key images, video, or other elements. To use such software effectively, follow the guidelines in the samples on the next page and also these tips:

- **Don't put your whole presentation on screen.** Select key points and distill them to as few words as possible. Use slides as quick, easy-to-remember summaries or ways to present examples. For a twenty-minute presentation, plan to use approximately ten slides.
- **Use a simple design.** Avoid turning your presentation into a show about the software's many capabilities and special effects.
- **Make text readable.** The type should be easy to see for viewers in the back of the room, whether the lights are on or not.
- **Use a consistent design.** For optimal flow through the presentation, each slide should be formatted similarly.

Presentation Slides

First slide, introducing the project and presentation.

Simple, consistent slide design focusing viewers' attention on information, not software features.

Making a Difference?

A Service-Learning Project at ReadingWorks

Springfield Veterans Administration Hospital

Jessica Cho
Nathan Hall
Alex Ramirez
Spring 2014

Second slide, including a title and brief, bulleted points to be explained by the speaker.

Semester goals

- Research adult literacy.
- Tutor veterans.
- Keep a journal.
- Collaborate on documents for ReadingWorks.
- Report experiences and findings.

Later slide, expanding on earlier "Semester goals" slide.

Link to video about the project's activities.

Photograph reinforcing the project's activities.

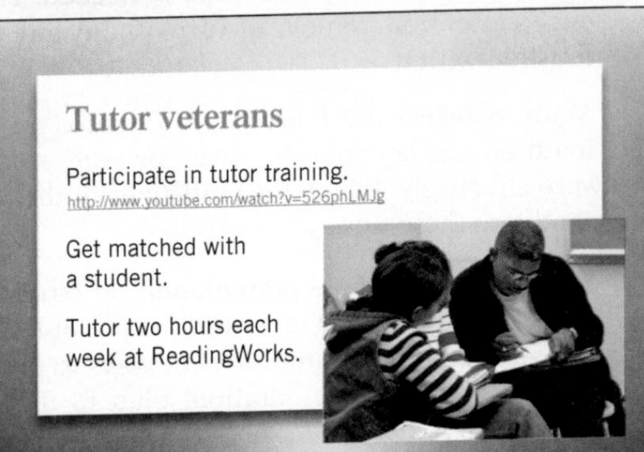

Tutor veterans
Participate in tutor training.
http://www.youtube.com/watch?v=526phLMJg
Get matched with a student.
Tutor two hours each week at ReadingWorks.

- **Add relevant images and other media.** Presentation software allows you to play images, audio, and video as part of your speech. Before you add them, however, be sure each has a point so that you don't overload the presentation. Use the guidelines on pages 110–15 for choosing and using visuals and other media.

- **Review all your slides before the presentation.** Go through the slides to be sure they are complete, consistent, and easy to read. Proofread each slide.
- **Don't talk to the computer or the projection during the presentation.** Move away from both and face the audience.
- **Pace your presentation and your slides.** Keep your presentation in step with your slides. If a section of your presentation has no slide keyed to it, insert a blank slide in the presentation.

Practice

Practicing an oral presentation is the equivalent of editing and proofreading a written text. You won't gain much by practicing silently in your head; instead, you need to rehearse out loud, with the notes you will be using. For your initial rehearsals, you can gauge your performance by making an audio- or videotape of yourself or by practicing in front of a mirror. A recording will let you hear mumbling, too-rapid delivery, grammatical errors, mispronounced words, and unclear concepts. A mirror or video will reveal your stance, your gestures, and your eye contact. Any of these practice techniques will tell you if your presentation is running too long or too short.

If you plan to use visual aids, you'll need to practice with them, too, preferably in the room where you'll make the presentation and certainly with the help of anyone who will be assisting you. Your goal is to eliminate hitches (slides in the wrong order, missing charts) and to weave the visuals seamlessly into your presentation.

Stage fright

Many people report that speaking in front of an audience is their number-one fear. Even many experienced and polished speakers have some anxiety about delivering an oral presentation, but they use this nervous energy to their advantage, letting it propel them into working hard on each presentation and rehearsing until they're satisfied with their delivery. They know that the symptoms of anxiety are usually imperceptible to listeners, who cannot see or hear a racing heart, an upset stomach, cold hands, and worried thoughts.

Several techniques can help you reduce your level of anxiety:

- **Use simple relaxation exercises.** Deep breathing or tensing and relaxing your stomach muscles can ease some of the physical symptoms of speech anxiety.
- **Think positively.** Instead of worrying about the mistakes you might make, concentrate on how well you've prepared and practiced your presentation and how significant your ideas are.
- **Don't avoid opportunities to speak in public.** Practice and experience build speaking skills and offer the best insurance for success.

PART 2

Reading and Writing in and out of College

6 Writing in Academic Situations

Chapter essentials

- Analyze the purpose and audience in each writing situation (below).
- Use an appropriate academic genre (p. 134).
- Choose appropriate structure and content (p. 138).
- Use sources with integrity (p. 139).
- Use academic language (p. 141).
- Communicate effectively with instructors and classmates (p. 144).

Visit MyWritingLab™ for more resources on writing in academic situations.

When you take college courses, you enter a community of teachers and students whose basic goal is to share and build knowledge about a subject, whether it is English, history, engineering, or something else. You participate in this community by studying each subject, by asking questions, and by communicating your answers in writing. This chapter gives you ways to approach academic writing situations and make a contribution to knowledge building.

6a Determining purpose and audience

Like any writing, academic writing occurs in a particular situation created by your assignment and by your subject, purpose, audience, and genre. The assignment and subject will be different for each project, but some generalizations can be made about the other elements. (If you haven't already done so, read Chapter 1 of this book for discussion of writing situations and their elements.)

1 Purpose

For most academic writing, your general purpose will be mainly explanatory or mainly argumentative. That is, you will aim to explain your subject by analyzing, describing, or reporting on it so that readers understand it as you do; or you will aim to gain readers' agreement with a debatable idea about the subject. (See pp. 9–11 for more on general and specific purposes and Chapters 8–9 for more on argument.) Although the general purpose for writing may not be stated outright in an assignment, it will probably be implied, as you can see in these two abbreviated assignments:

Explanation

Compare the depiction of war in two films viewed this semester, considering plots, characters, dialog, battle scenes, production designs, and other elements of the films.

Argument

What ideology do you see informing the movies of director Steven Spielberg? What beliefs about the world do his choices convey, whether explicitly or implicitly, intentionally or unintentionally? Support your claim with evidence from at least four of Spielberg's movies, considering plots, characters, dialog, production designs, and other elements.

Your specific purpose—including your subject and how you hope readers will respond—depends on the genre, the kind of writing that you're doing. (See the next page.) For instance, in a literature review for a biology class, you want readers to understand the research area you're covering, the recent contributions made by researchers, the issues needing further research, and the sources you consulted. Not coincidentally, these topics correspond to the major sections of a literature review. In following the standard format, you both help to define your purpose and begin to meet the discipline's (and thus your instructor's) expectations.

Your specific purpose will be more complex as well. You take a course to learn about a subject and the ways experts think about it. Your writing, in turn, contributes to the discipline through the knowledge you uncover and the lens of your perspective. At the same time, as a student you want to demonstrate your competence with research, evidence, format, and other requirements of the discipline.

2 Audience

Many academic writing assignments will specify or assume an educated audience or an academic audience. Such readers look for writing that is clear, balanced, well organized, and well reasoned. Other assignments will specify or assume an audience of experts on your subject, readers who look in addition for writing that meets the subject's requirements for claims and evidence, organization, language, source citation, and other features discussed in Chapters 49–52.

Much of your academic writing will have only one reader besides you: the instructor of the course for which you are writing. Instructors fill two main roles as readers:

- **They represent the audience you are addressing.** They may actually be members of the audience, as when you address academic readers or subject experts. Or they may imagine themselves as members of your audience—reading, for instance, as if they sat on the city council. In either case, they're interested in how effectively you write for the audience.
- **They serve as coaches,** guiding you toward achieving the goals of the course and, more broadly, toward the academic aims of building and communicating knowledge.

Like everyone else, instructors have preferences and peeves, but you'll waste time and energy trying to anticipate them. Do attend to written and spoken directions for assignments, of course. But otherwise view your instructors as representatives of the community you are writing for. Their responses will be guided by the community's aims and expectations and by a desire to teach you about them.

6b Using an academic genre

Many academic writing assignments will suggest the genre in which you are to write—that is, the kind of writing and/or the format. Sometimes the genre is prescribed, such as the literature review mentioned earlier, with its standard content and format. Often genre is implied, as in the two assignments about movies on the previous two pages: both require analysis and comparison, but the first asks for explanation and the second asks for argument. In these cases, responses would most likely be conventional academic essays—introduction, thesis statement, supporting paragraphs, conclusion—that analyze and compare in order to explain or argue.

Whether genre is specified or implied in your assignment, you are being asked to demonstrate your ability to write competently in that genre. The following sections describe genres commonly assigned in college courses and point out examples that appear elsewhere in this book. You can get a good sense of how other writers work with genre conventions by studying the descriptions here and the samples with their surrounding explanations and annotations.

In addition, Chapter 11 contains examples of genres used in public writing: complaint letter, application letter and résumé, memo, report, proposal, social-networking post, and newsletter.

1 Responses to texts or visuals

Responses to texts or visuals involve close reading, summary, and analysis. For more on analyzing and responding to texts and visuals, see Chapter 7.

- **Personal response to a reading:** Use your own experiences, observations, and opinions to explain how and why you agree or disagree (or both) with the author's argument. A personal-response essay usually includes a thesis statement that conveys the essence of your response, a brief summary of the author's main points, and your own main points of agreement or disagreement. See pages 67–69 for a reading response by Katy Moreno, who draws on her mother's job loss as evidence.
- **Critical analysis (critique) of a text or a visual:** Closely examine a text or visual, identifying and describing important elements of the work and analyzing how the elements contribute to the

whole. Often a critical analysis, or critique, also includes evaluation of the quality and significance of the work. The genre gives an arguable thesis stating your interpretation, a brief summary or description of the work, and examples from the text or visual as support for your thesis and main points. See pages 175–77 for Charlene Robinson's critique of an essay and pages 178–79 for Richard Oliva's critique of an advertisement. (Another type of critical analysis is literary analysis, described on p. 137.)

2 Argument

Argument seeks to persuade readers, moving them to action or convincing them to think as you do. Written arguments contain an arguable thesis statement—a claim reasonable people can disagree over—usually with support for its main points and acknowledgment of opposing views. Arguments often, but not always, involve research. For a detailed discussion of writing arguments, see Chapter 9.

- **Proposal argument:** Define a problem, give a solution, explain how the solution can be implemented, and respond to possible objections to the solution. See pages 221–24 and 686–708 for two proposal arguments that involve research: Aimee Lee's essay on a program to prevent cyberbullying and Justin Malik's research paper on green consumerism.
- **Position argument:** Seek to convince readers to agree with your position on a debatable issue such as lowering the drinking age or requiring military service. A position argument introduces the issue, conveys your position in a thesis statement, makes claims and gives evidence to support your position, and responds to views different from your own. Depending on the assignment, your evidence may be personal or gathered from research or both. (A type of position argument is literary analysis, described on p. 137, in which you make a case for your interpretation of a work of literature.)
- **Evaluation argument:** Judge whether something is good or effective. A common type of evaluation argument is a critical analysis of a text or visual, described opposite and above and illustrated in the essays by Charlene Robinson and Richard Oliva on pages 175–77 and 178–79. Reviews of books, movies, and so on are also evaluation arguments. (For more on reviews, see p. 727.)

3 Informative writing

In college courses or for the public, informative writir to teach readers about a subject. When you write to inf explore a subject in depth and provide information reade know. Informative writing often, but not always, invol In the social, natural, and applied sciences, informat include summaries and case studies in addition to research-based writing (see pp. 760 and 794).

- **Informative essay:** Explain a subject such as a situation or a process. Typically, an informative essay begins with an introduction and a thesis statement that previews your major points and then supports the thesis in the body paragraphs with evidence to clarify the subject. Depending on the assignment, an informative essay may focus on a nonpersonal subject, like Terrence MacDonald's essay on money in college football (pp. 43–45), or it may arise from personal experience and thus overlap the personal essay (see below).
- **Informative research paper or report:** Draw on research to explain a subject, answer a question, or describe the results of a survey or an experiment. This genre includes research papers, research reports, and laboratory reports, all described below and opposite. See pages 784–92 for a sample research report and pages 803–06 for a sample laboratory report.

4 Personal writing

A personal essay often narrates the writer's experience or describes a person or place, usually in vivid detail. What makes a personal essay interesting is the insight the writer provides, showing why the subject is significant to the writer and to readers.

A literacy narrative is a particular kind of personal story: the writer's experience with learning to read and/or write. See pages 120–21 for a student's literacy narrative on creating comics.

5 Research papers and reports

Most research projects involve reporting information or results, interpreting a range of views on a topic, or analyzing a problem and arguing for a solution. Research is discussed in detail in Chapters 41–46. Research and writing in literature courses and in the humanities, social sciences, and natural and applied sciences are discussed in Chapters 49–52.

- **Annotated bibliography:** Give full publication information for sources on a research topic, summarize each source, and evaluate each source for its relevance to your project. See page 554 for an example. You may also be asked to write a short opening essay giving an overview of the sources.
- **Research paper:** Develop an informative or argumentative thesis statement, draw on and cite multiple sources to support the thesis, and emphasize synthesis of your sources' views and data from your own perspective. Justin Malik's research paper on pages 686–708 proposes actions to reduce humans' effects on the environment.

- **Literary research paper:** Combine analysis of a literary work with research about the work. (See below.)
- **Research report:** Explain your own original research or your attempt to replicate someone else's research. A research report generally includes an abstract (or summary), an introduction describing your research and reviewing prior research on the subject, a description of methods, the results, discussion of the results, and a list of any sources you have cited. See pages 784–92 for a research report on violence in dating relationships.
- **Laboratory report:** Explain the procedure and results of an experiment you conducted. A laboratory report generally includes an abstract, an introduction (or objective) describing your experiment and reviewing prior research on the subject, a description of the experimental procedure, the results, discussion of the results, and a list of any sources you have cited. See pages 803–06 for a sample laboratory report on blood pressure and exercise.

6 Literary analyses

Writing about literature involves close reading, analysis, and interpretation.

- **Literary analysis:** Argue for an interpretation of a work based on careful reading, giving particular attention to the work's language, structure, meaning, and themes. You may examine an author's techniques and literary devices, or you may read a work through the lens of a particular literary theory, such as historical, cultural, or feminist. Such an essay gives an arguable thesis stating your interpretation and then examples from the work supporting your thesis and main points. See Janet Vong's analysis of a Kate Chopin story on pages 732–33 and Michael Spinter's analysis of Shakespeare's character Macbeth on pages 739–41.
- **Literary research paper:** Combine your analysis of a literary work, described above, with others' views and information—perhaps a scholar's interpretation of the work or information about the author's life or the historical context in which the author wrote the work. Two samples of literary research papers are Vanessa Haley's essay on a book by Annie Dillard (pp. 710–15) and Jessie Glenn's essay on a poem by Agha Shahid Ali (pp. 736–37). For more on reading and writing about literature, see Chapter 49.

7 Essay exams

In writing an essay exam, you respond directly to a specific assignment, usually in several paragraphs or more, and usually within a time limit. Most essay exams contain key words such as *define* or *evaluate* that tell you whether your response should be informative or argumentative and how to shape your response. You may also be given two or more sides of an issue or interpretations of a text and asked to argue for a position. See pages 229–30 for a sample essay-exam response in an anthropology course.

6c Choosing structure and content

Academic writing assignments vary widely, of course, but they tend to share the following key goals. Each goal is discussed in more detail on the pages cited.

- **Develop a main point for your writing.** Most academic papers center on a main point, or thesis, and support that thesis with evidence. Depending on the genre you are writing in, the main point may be an opinion, a summary of findings, or a conclusion based on primary research you have conducted, such as an experiment or a survey. For more on thesis statements, see pages 28–33.
- **Support the main point with evidence, drawn usually from your reading, personal experience, or primary research.** The kinds of evidence will depend on the discipline you're writing in and the type of paper you're doing. For more on evidence in the disciplines, see pages 726 (literature), 742 (other humanities), 759 (social sciences), and 793 (natural and applied sciences).
- **Synthesize your own and others' ideas.** College writing often involves researching and interacting with the works of other writers—being open to their ideas, responding to them, questioning them, comparing them, and using them to answer questions. Such interaction requires you to read critically (the subject of the next chapter) and to synthesize, or integrate, others' ideas into your own. For more on synthesis in academic writing, see pages 173–74 and 593–95.
- **Use academic language.** Unless your instructor specifies otherwise, choose formal, standard English. For more on academic language, see pages 141–43 in this chapter and also pages 498–500.
- **Acknowledge sources fully, including online sources.** Academic writers build on the work of others by citing borrowed ideas and information. Always record the publication information for your sources, put other writers' words in quotation marks, and cite the source of every quotation, paraphrase, and summary. *Not* acknowledging sources is plagiarism. See the facing page and Chapters 44 and 45 for more on using and acknowledging sources.
- **Organize clearly within the framework of the type of writing you're doing.** Develop your ideas as simply and directly as your

purpose and content allow. Relate sentences, paragraphs, and sections clearly so that readers always know where they are in the paper's development.

CULTURE LANGUAGE These features of academic writing are not universal. In some cultures academic writing may be indirect, may assume that readers will discover the thesis, or may be expected to consult only well-known sources and to adhere to the sources' ideas. In US colleges and universities, students are expected to look for relevant and reliable sources, well known or not, and to use sources mainly to support their own ideas.

6d Using sources with integrity

Academic integrity is the foundation of academic knowledge building. Trusting in one another's honesty allows students and scholars to examine and extend the work of other scholars, and it allows teachers to guide and assess the progress of their students.

You can build your integrity as a writer by working to develop your own ideas and by handling sources responsibly. The following tips can help. Note that Chapters 42–45 contain extensive discussions of researching and citing sources.

1 Avoiding plagiarism

Many writing assignments will require you to consult sources such as journal articles, Web sites, and books. These works belong to their creators; you are free to borrow from them *if* you do so with integrity. That means representing the sources accurately—not misinterpreting or distorting what they say. It also means crediting the sources—not plagiarizing, or presenting sources' ideas and information as if they were your own. On most campuses, plagiarism is a punishable offense.

Plagiarism can be deliberate or careless:

- **Deliberate plagiarism** is outright cheating: copying another writer's sentence or idea and passing it off as your own, buying a paper from the Web, or getting someone else to write a paper for you.
- **Careless plagiarism** is more common among students, often arising from inattentive or inexperienced handling of sources. For instance, you might cut and paste source information into your own ideas without clarifying who said what, or you might present a summary of a source without recognizing that parts of it are actually quoted. In these cases the plagiarism is unintentional, but it is still plagiarism.

See also Chapter 44 for more on plagiarism.

2 Developing perspective on a subject

Consider your own knowledge and perspective on a subject before you start to research. This forethought will make it easier for you to recognize other authors' perspectives and to treat them fairly in your writing—whether or not you agree with them.

- **Before you consult sources, gauge what you already know and think about your subject.** Give yourself time to know your own mind before rushing to others for information. Then you'll be able to reflect on how the sources reinforce, contradict, or expand what you already know.
- **Evaluate sources carefully.** Authors generally write from particular perspectives, and some are more overt about their biases than others. You needn't reject a source because it is biased; indeed, often you'll want to consider multiple perspectives. But you do need to recognize and weigh the writer's position. See pages 580–93 for a discussion of evaluating sources.
- **Treat sources fairly.** Represent an author's ideas and perspectives as they were originally presented, without misreading or distortion. Be careful when paraphrasing and summarizing not to misrepresent the author's meaning. Be careful in editing quotations not to omit essential words.

3 Managing sources

You can avoid plagiarism by keeping close track of the sources you consult, the ideas that influence your thinking, and the words and sentences you borrow—and by carefully citing the sources in your writing. If these habits are unfamiliar to you, keep the following list handy.

- **Keep track of source information as you read.** Get in the habit of always recording publication information (author, title, date, and so on) of any source you read as well as any ideas you glean from it. The box on page 553 lists what to record.
- **Be careful with quotations.** If you cut and paste a portion of an article, Web site, or other source into your document, put quotation marks around it so that you don't mix your words and the source's words accidentally. Check any quotation that you use in your own writing against the original source. For a more detailed discussion of how to quote sources, see pages 603–05.
- **Use your own words in paraphrases and summaries.** A paraphrase or summary presents the ideas of a source but not in the exact words of the original and not in quotation marks. You will be less likely to use the source author's words (and thus plagiarize) if you look away from the source while you write down what you remember from it. Note, though, that you must still cite the source of a summary or paraphrase, just as you do with a

quotation. For a more detailed discussion of how to summarize and paraphrase sources, see pages 599–603.

- **Cite your sources.** As you draft, be conscious of when you're using source information and be conscientious about clearly marking where the borrowed material came from. In your final draft you'll use a particular style of citation within your text to refer to a detailed list of sources at the end. This book presents four such styles: MLA style for English and some other humanities (pp. 634–79); Chicago style for history, philosophy, and some other humanities (744–57); APA style for the social sciences (761–82); and CSE style for the natural and applied sciences (799–802).

6e Using academic language

American academic writing relies on a dialect called standard American English. The dialect is also used in business, government, the media, and other sites of social and economic power where people of diverse backgrounds must communicate with one another. It is "standard" not because it is better than other forms of English, but because it is accepted as the common language, much as the dollar bill is accepted as the common currency.

In writing, standard English varies a great deal, from the formality of an academic research report to the more relaxed language of this handbook to informal e-mails between coworkers. Even in academic writing, standard English allows much room for the writer's own tone and voice, as these passages on the same topic show:

More formal

Responsibility for the widespread problem of obesity among Americans depends on the person or group describing the problem and proposing a solution. Some people believe the cause lies with individuals who make poor eating choices for themselves and parents who feed unhealthy foods to their children. Others take strong issue with the food industry, citing food manufacturers and fast-food chains that create and advertise food that is high in sugar, fat, and sodium. Still others place responsibility on American society as a whole for preferring a sedentary lifestyle centered on screen-based activities such as watching television and using computers for video games and social interaction.

> Drawn-out phrasing, such as *widespread problem of obesity among Americans.*

> More complicated sentence structures, such as *take strong issue with the food industry, citing food manufacturers and fast-food chains that create and advertise. . . .*

> More formal vocabulary: *responsibility, children, television.*

Less formal

Who or what is to blame for the obesity epidemic depends on who is talking and what they want to do about the problem. Some people blame

> More informal phrasing, such as *obesity epidemic.*

eaters for making bad choices and parents for feeding their kids unhealthy foods. Others demonize food manufacturers and fast-food chains for creating and advertising sugary, fatty, and sodium-loaded food. Still others point to Americans generally for spending too much time in front of screens watching TV, playing video games, or going on *Facebook*.

Less complicated sentence structures, such as *demonize food manufacturers and fast-food chains for creating and advertising. . . .*

More informal vocabulary: *blame, kids, TV.*

As different as they are, both examples illustrate several common features of academic language:

- **Its formality varies depending on the writer's voice and audience.** For instance, the first passage might reflect the writer's preference for more formal language and also an audience of experts in the field who expect a serious, measured approach. Addressing peers instead of experts, the same writer might still sound more formal than the second writer does—perhaps retaining the formal vocabulary—but might also shorten sentences and tighten phrasing.
- **It follows the conventions of standard English for grammar and usage.** These conventions are detailed in guides to the dialect, such as this handbook.
- **It uses a standard vocabulary,** not one that only some groups understand, such as slang, an ethnic or regional dialect, or another language. See pages 498–502 for more on specialized vocabularies.
- **It *does not use* the informalities of everyday speech, texting, and instant messaging.** These informalities include incomplete sentences, slang, no capital letters, and shortened spellings (*u* for *you*, *b4* for *before*, *thru* for *through*, and so on.) (See p. 500 for more on these forms.)
- **It generally uses the third person (*he, she, it, they*).** The first-person *I* is sometimes appropriate to express personal opinions, but academic writers tend to avoid it and make conclusions speak for themselves. The first-person *we* can connect with readers and invite them to think along, but, again, many academic writers avoid it. The second-person *you* is appropriate only in addressing readers directly (as in this handbook), and even then it may seem condescending or too chummy. Definitely avoid using or implying *you* in conversational expressions such as *You know what I mean* and *Don't take this the wrong way*.
- **It is authoritative and neutral.** In the examples about obesity, the writers express themselves confidently, not timidly as in *Explaining the causes of obesity requires the reader's patience because. . . .* The writers also refrain from hostility (*The food industry's callous attitude toward health . . .*) and enthusiasm (*The food industry's clever and appealing advertisements . . .*).

At first, the diverse demands of academic writing may leave you groping for an appropriate voice. In an effort to sound fresh and confident, you may write too casually, as if speaking to friends or family:

Too casual

Getting the truth about the obesity epidemic in the US requires some heavy lifting. It turns out that everyone else is to blame for the problem—big eaters, reckless corporations, and all those Americans who think it's OK to be a couch potato.

In an effort to sound "academic," you may produce wordy and awkward sentences:

Wordy and awkward

The responsibility for the problem of widespread obesity among Americans depends on the manner of defining the problem and the proposals for its solution. In some discussions, the cause of obesity is thought to be individuals who are unable or unwilling to make healthy choices in their own diets and parents who similarly make unhealthy choices for their children. [The passive voice in this example—*cause . . . is thought to be* instead of *people blame*—adds to its wordiness and indirection. See pp. 307–09 for more on verb voice.]

The cure for writing too informally or too stiffly is to read academic writing so that the language and style become familiar and to edit your own writing so that it sounds similar. (See pp. 61–63.) With experience and practice, you will develop a voice that is sufficiently formal but still authentic and natural, as in the obesity examples.

CULTURE LANGUAGE If your first language or dialect is not standard American English, you know well the power of communicating with others who share your language. Learning to write standard English in no way requires you to abandon your first language. Like most multilingual people, you are probably already adept at switching between languages as the situation demands—speaking one way with your relatives, say, and another way with an employer. As you practice academic writing, you'll develop the same flexibility with it.

Exercise 6.1 Using academic language

Revise the following paragraph to make the language more academic while keeping the factual information the same.

If you buy into the stereotype of girls chatting away on their cell phones, you should think again. One of the major wireless companies surveyed 1021 cell phone owners for a period of five years and—surprise!—reported that guys talk on cell phones more than girls do. In fact, guys were way ahead of girls, using an average of 571 minutes a month compared to 424 for girls. That's 35% more time on the phone! The survey also asked about conversations on land lines, and while girls still beat the field, the guys are catching up.

6f Communicating with instructors and classmates

As a member of an academic community, you will not only write papers and projects but also write directly to instructors, classmates, and other people at your school via e-mail, course-management systems such as *Blackboard* and *Canvas*, and other electronic media. Your written communication with instructors and classmates will rarely be as formal as assigned writing, but it will also rarely be as informal as a text to a friend, a tweet, or a comment on *Facebook*.

Even in a short e-mail, your message will receive a better hearing if you present yourself well and show respect for your reader(s). The message below illustrates an appropriate mix of formality and informality when addressing an instructor:

E-mail message

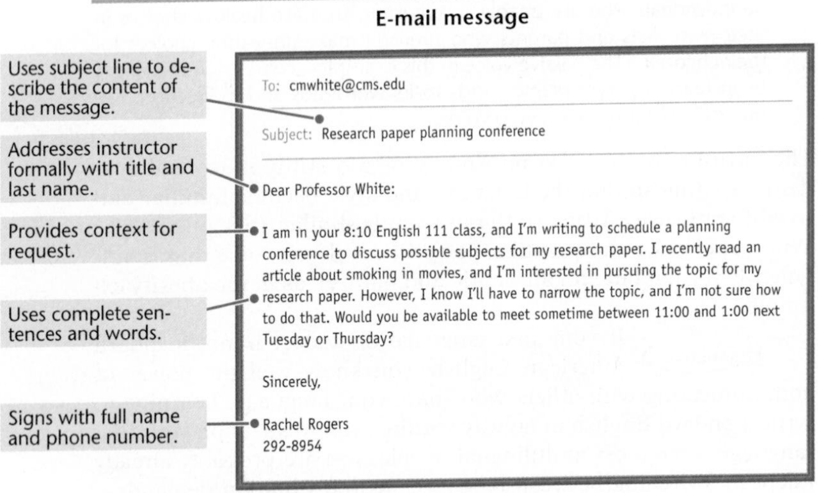
To: cmwhite@cms.edu

Subject: Research paper planning conference

Dear Professor White:

I am in your 8:10 English 111 class, and I'm writing to schedule a planning conference to discuss possible subjects for my research paper. I recently read an article about smoking in movies, and I'm interested in pursuing the topic for my research paper. However, I know I'll have to narrow the topic, and I'm not sure how to do that. Would you be available to meet sometime between 11:00 and 1:00 next Tuesday or Thursday?

Sincerely,

Rachel Rogers
292-8954

Uses subject line to describe the content of the message.
Addresses instructor formally with title and last name.
Provides context for request.
Uses complete sentences and words.
Signs with full name and phone number.

Here are guidelines for such communication:

- **Use the medium your instructor prefers.** Don't text, tweet, or use a social-networking site unless you're invited to do so.
- **Use names.** In the body of your message, address your reader(s) by name if possible. Unless your teachers instruct otherwise, always address them formally, using *Professor, Dr., Ms.,* or *Mr.,* as appropriate, followed by the last name. Sign off with your own name and information on how to contact you.
- **Pay attention to tone.** Don't use all capital letters, which SHOUT. And use irony or sarcasm only cautiously: in the absence of facial expressions, either one can lead to misunderstanding.
- **Pay attention to correctness.** Especially when you write to instructors, avoid the shortcuts of texting and tweeting, such as

incomplete sentences and abbreviations (*u* for *you, r* for *are,* and so on). (See also p. 500.) Proofread for errors in grammar, punctuation, and spelling.

- **Send messages only to the people who need them.** As a general rule, avoid sending messages to many recipients at once—all the students in a course, say—unless what you are writing applies to all of them. Before you hit Reply All in response to a message, ensure that "all" want to see the response.
- **Guard your own and others' privacy.** Online tools allow us to broadcast hurtful information about others—and allow others to do the same to us. Before you post a message about yourself or someone else, consider whether it's worthwhile and who will see it, not only now but in the future. When forwarding messages, make sure not to pass on previous private messages by mistake.
- **Don't write anything that you would not say face to face or would not write in a printed letter.** Electronic messages can be saved and forwarded and can be retrieved in disputes over grades and other matters.

Exercise 6.2 Considering your past work: Writing in academic situations

Look back at a paper you wrote for a course in high school or college. To what extent does it share the features of academic writing discussed in this chapter? How does it differ? Write a revision plan for making the paper more academic.

Exercise 6.3 Considering your native language or dialect

What main similarities do you notice between writing in your native language or dialect and writing for US college courses? What differences do you notice? Consider especially purpose, audience, genre, content, structure, and the expression of ideas. Which aspects of writing for US college courses are easiest for you? Which ones are more difficult? Why?

7 Critical Reading and Writing

Chapter essentials

- Use techniques of critical reading (facing page).
- Summarize (p. 155).
- Form a critical response through analysis, interpretation, synthesis, and sometimes evaluation (p. 157).
- View visuals critically (p. 164).
- Write critical analyses of texts and visuals (p. 172).
- Learn from sample critical analyses (pp. 175 and 177).

Visit MyWritingLab™ for more resources on critical reading and writing.

Throughout college and beyond, you will be expected to think, read, and write critically. **Critical** here means "skeptical," "exacting," "curious." When you operate critically, you question, test, and build on what others say and what you yourself think. The word *critical* does not mean "negative" in this context: you can think critically about something you like, don't like, or just view neutrally.

You already operate critically every day of your life, as when you probe a friendship ("What did she mean by that?") or attempt to solve a problem ("How can I help my study group make progress on our project?"). Such questioning helps you figure out why things happen to you, what your experiences mean, and how you can create a needed change.

This chapter introduces more formal methods of critical thinking that will both engage you in and prepare you for school courses, career, and life in a democratic society:

- **Teachers and employers will expect you to think critically.** In every field, you will need to assess what you read, see, and hear and to make a good case for your own ideas.
- **Critical thinking helps you understand and express yourself.** With it, you gain insight into your actions and ideas, can weigh them against opposing views, and can persuasively articulate your reasoning and motivations.
- **Critical thinking improves your problem-solving skills.** Seeing academic and real-life problems from multiple angles can open your mind to creative solutions.
- **Your very independence and freedom depend on your ability to think, read, and write critically.** An open democracy allows as much play for stupid and false claims as for sound ones, and the claims that seem sound often conflict with each other. Critical thinking empowers you to decide rationally for yourself what's useful, fair, and wise—and what's not.

There's no denying that critical thinking, reading, and writing require discipline and hard work. Besides channeling your curiosity, paying attention, and probing, you will often need to consult experts, interpreting and evaluating their ideas. Such an approach also requires a healthy tolerance for doubt or uncertainty—that feeling you may have when the old rules don't seem to apply or when a change is frightening but still attractive. Out of uncertainty, though, comes creativity—the capacity to organize and generate knowledge, to explain, resolve, illuminate, play. Compared to passive, rote learning, creative work is more involving, more productive, and more enjoyable.

7a Using techniques of critical reading

In college much of your critical thinking will focus on written texts (a short story, a journal article, a blog) or on visual or multimedia texts (a photograph, an advertisement, a film). Like all subjects worthy of critical consideration, such works operate on at least three levels:

1. **What the creator actually says or shows.**
2. **What the creator does not say or show but builds into the work, intentionally or not.**
3. **What you think.**

Discovering each level of the work involves a number of reading techniques that are discussed in this chapter and summarized in the following box.

Techniques of critical reading

For reading a work of literature, which requires a somewhat different approach, see pp. 718–26.

- **Writing:** making notes on your reading throughout the process (next page)
- **Previewing:** getting background; skimming (p. 149)
- **Reading:** interacting with and absorbing the text (pp. 152–54)
- **Summarizing:** distilling and understanding content (pp. 155–57)
- **Forming your critical response** (pp. 157–63):

  Analyzing: separating into parts
  Interpreting: inferring meaning and assumptions
  Synthesizing: reassembling parts; making connections
  Evaluating: judging quality and value

The techniques of critical reading are not steps in a firm sequence. You will not use all of them for all the reading you do. On some occasions, even when a close, critical reading is required, you may simply lack the time to preview, read, and reread. (But if your reading time is continually squeezed by your schedule, you may need to rethink your schedule.) On other occasions your reason for reading (your purpose) will determine which techniques you use.

Even a publication like *People* magazine is open to different methods of reading for different purposes:

Purpose	Learn some gossip while filling time in the dentist's office.
Kind of reading	Quick, uncritical
Purpose	Examine *People* as an artifact of our popular culture that reflects and perhaps even molds contemporary values.
Kind of reading	Close, critical

Course assignments, too, differ in their requirements. A book report may require writing, previewing, reading, and summarizing but not intense critical reading. An evaluation of a journal article, in contrast, requires all the techniques discussed here.

CULTURE LANGUAGE The idea of reading critically may require you to make some adjustments if readers in your native culture tend to seek understanding or agreement more than engagement from what they read. Readers of English use texts for all kinds of reasons, including pleasure, reinforcement, information, and many others. But they also read questioningly, to uncover the author's motives (*What are this author's biases?*), test their own ideas (*Can I support my point of view as well as this author supports hers?*), and arrive at new knowledge (*Why is the author's evidence so persuasive?*).

1 Writing while reading

You will write while you read to record information and ideas for use in a research paper. But writing while reading has another purpose as well: to help you get more from the work.

Critical reading is *active* reading. You interact with the work, bringing to it your experiences, knowledge, and questions. Making notes on what you read helps you construct the text for yourself as you come to understand how it works, why it works that way, and what you think about it.

If the material you're reading belongs to you (for instance, a book, a photocopy, or a PDF or *Word* file), you can make notes in the margins or in the electronic document (see pp. 154 and 165 for examples). If you don't own the material or if your notes won't fit in the margins, make notes separately using pen and paper or your computer.

Many readers keep a **reading journal** in which they regularly work out questions and thoughts about what they read. Such a journal can encourage you to go beyond summarizing what you read to interacting critically with it. See page 154 for an example of this technique.

Note Whenever you photocopy or download a document or take notes separately from the text you're reading, be sure to record the text's publication information so that you can cite it fully if you use it. See page 553 for a list of information to record.

2 Previewing the material

When you're reading a work of literature, such as a story or a poem, it's often best to plunge right in (see pp. 719–20). But for critical reading of other works, it's worthwhile to **skim** before reading word for word, forming expectations and even preliminary questions. The preview will make your reading more informed and fruitful.

Use the questions in the following box as a guide to previewing a text.

Previewing a text

- **Gauge length and level.** Is the material brief and straightforward so that you can read it in one sitting, or does it require more time?
- **Check the facts of publication.** Does the date of publication suggest currency or datedness? Does the publisher or publication specialize in scholarly articles, popular books, news reporting, or something else? For a Web publication, who or what sponsors the site—an individual? a nonprofit organization? a government body? a college or university?
- **Look for content cues.** What do the title, introduction, headings, illustrations, conclusion, and other features tell you about the topic, the author's approach, and the main ideas?
- **Learn about the author.** Does a biography tell you about the author's publications, interests, biases, and reputation in the field? If there is no biography, what can you gather about the author from his or her words? Do a Web search to trace an unfamiliar author.
- **Consider your preliminary response.** What do you already know about the topic? What questions do you have about either the topic or the author's approach to it? What biases of your own—for instance, curiosity, boredom, or an outlook similar or opposed to the author's—might influence your reading of the work?

Exercise 7.1 Previewing an essay

Following is an essay on the US student-loan program by Thomas Sowell, an economist who writes on economics, politics, and education. The essay was first published in the 1990s, but the debate over student loans has hardly subsided. Since Sowell wrote, the number of college graduates with loan debt has increased by a third and the average amount they owe has almost tripled.

Preview the essay using the preceding guidelines, and note your questions and reactions in writing.

Student Loans

The first lesson of economics is scarcity: There is never enough of 1
anything to fully satisfy all those who want it.

The first lesson of politics is to disregard the first lesson of economics. 2
When politicians discover some group that is being vocal about not having as much as they want, the "solution" is to give them more. Where do politicians get this "more"? They rob Peter to pay Paul.

After a while, of course, they discover that Peter doesn't have 3
enough. Bursting with compassion, politicians rush to the rescue. Needless to say, they do not admit that robbing Peter to pay Paul was a dumb idea in the first place. On the contrary, they now rob Tom, Dick, and Harry to help Peter.

The latest chapter in this long-running saga is that politicians have 4
now suddenly discovered that many college students graduate heavily in debt. To politicians it follows, as the night follows the day, that the government should come to their rescue with the taxpayers' money.

How big is this crushing burden of college students' debt that we 5
hear so much about from politicians and media deep thinkers? For those students who graduate from public colleges owing money, the debt averages a little under $7,000. For those who graduate from private colleges owing money, the average debt is a little under $9,000.

Buying a very modestly priced automobile involves more debt than 6
that. And a car loan has to be paid off faster than the ten years that college graduates get to repay their student loans. Moreover, you have to keep buying cars every several years, while one college education lasts a lifetime.

College graduates of course earn higher incomes than other people. 7
Why, then, should we panic at the thought that they have to repay loans for the education which gave them their opportunities? Even graduates with relatively modest incomes pay less than 10 percent of their annual salary on the loan the first year—with declining percentages in future years, as their pay increases.

Political hysteria and media hype may focus on the low-income stu- 8
dent with a huge debt. That is where you get your heart-rending stories—even if they are not at all typical. In reality, the soaring student loans of the past decade have resulted from allowing high-income people to borrow under government programs.

Before 1978, college loans were available through government pro- 9
grams only to students whose family income was below some cut-off level. That cut-off level was about double the national average income, but at least it kept out the Rockefellers and the Vanderbilts. But, in an era of "compassion," Congress took off even those limits.

That opened the floodgates. No matter how rich you were, it still 10
paid to borrow money through the government at low interest rates. The money you had set aside for your children's education could be invested somewhere else, at higher interest rates. Then, when the student loan became due, parents could pay it off with the money they had set aside—pocketing the difference in interest rates.

To politicians and the media, however, the rapidly growing loans 11
showed what a great "need" there was. The fact that many students welshed when time came to repay their loans showed how "crushing" their burden of debt must be. In reality, those who welsh typically have

smaller loans, but have dropped out of college before finishing. People who are irresponsible in one way are often irresponsible in other ways.

No small amount of the deterioration of college standards has been due to the increasingly easy availability of college to people who are not very serious about getting an education. College is not a bad place to hang out for a few years, if you have nothing better to do, and if someone else is paying for it. Its costs are staggering, but the taxpayers carry much of that burden, not only for state universities and city colleges, but also to an increasing extent even for "private" institutions. 12

Numerous government subsidies and loan programs make it possible for many people to use vast amounts of society's resources at low cost to themselves. Whether in money terms or in real terms, federal aid to higher education has increased several hundred percent since 1970. That has enabled colleges to raise their tuition by leaps and bounds and enabled professors to be paid more and more for doing less and less teaching. 13

Naturally all these beneficiaries are going to create hype and hysteria to keep more of the taxpayers' money coming in. But we would be fools to keep on writing blank checks for them. 14

When you weigh the cost of things, in economics that's called "trade-offs." In politics, it's called "mean-spirited." Apparently, if we just took a different attitude, scarcity would go away. 15

—Thomas Sowell

Exercise 7.2 Previewing an essay

The following essay about the drinking age is by John M. McCardell, Jr., the vice-chancellor and president of the University of the South. The essay first appeared in 2012 on the "Room for Debate" page of the online *New York Times*. Preview the essay using the guidelines in the box on page 149. Note your comments, questions, and reactions in writing.

Let Them Drink at 18, with a Learner's Permit

In the United States, as in most of the rest of the world, the age of majority is 18. Unlike most of the rest of the world, however, there is in this country one glaring exception: drinking. Although our laws acknowledge that at age 18 young adults possess sufficient maturity and judgment to operate a motor vehicle, serve in the military, perform jury duty or sign a contract, those same laws deny 18-year-olds the right to purchase, possess or consume alcohol. 1

And yet those against whom this law is directed routinely evade it, and often with life-threatening results. Since the law changed in 1984, fewer young adults are consuming alcohol (of course, under an effective law, none should), but 45% of those who do drink drink excessively. Binge drinking is as widespread now as it was before the age was raised. 2

At the same time, alcohol-related traffic fatalities have declined drastically, but not because of the change in drinking age. Fatalities have dropped in all age groups, and have declined by the same percentage in Canada, where the age is 18. A successful public education campaign pointing out the risks of drinking and driving deserves much of the credit. 3

But what do we do to prepare young adults to make responsible decisions about alcohol? Beyond sometimes hysterical pronouncements about the evils of drink, not much. Suppose, instead of requiring driver 4 education and then issuing a learner's permit and acknowledging that learning to drive safely is a shared obligation of school, state and home, we were simply to allow young people to drive once they reached legal driving age? I suspect we would face a serious "binge driving" problem.

Clearly that would make no sense. Yet that is exactly the conse- 5
quence of the position taken by those who defend the drinking age exception to the age of majority.

We should prepare young adults to make responsible decisions 6
about alcohol in the same way we prepare them to operate a motor vehicle: by first educating and then licensing and permitting them to exercise the full privileges of adulthood so long as they demonstrate their ability to observe the law.

Licensing would work like driver education—it would involve a per- 7
mit, perhaps graduated, allowing the holder the privilege of purchasing, possessing, and consuming alcohol, as each state determined, so long as the holder had passed an alcohol education course and observed the alcohol laws of the issuing state.

Most of the rest of the world has come out in a different place on 8
the drinking age. The United States is one of only four countries—the others are Indonesia, Mongolia and Palau—with an age as high as 21. All others either have no minimum age or have a lower age, generally 18. Some set it at 16.

Young adults know that. And, in their heart of hearts, they also 9
know that a law perceived as unjust, a law routinely violated, can over time breed disrespect for law in general.

The simple solution is not to issue a one-size-fits-all federal mandate. 10
The simple solution is to turn these responsibilities back to the states to be laboratories of experimentation and allow best practices to emerge. That can be accomplished by removing the provision in federal law that reduces highway funding for any state setting its age lower than 21.

If you infantilize someone, do not be surprised when infantile be- 11
havior—like binge drinking—results. Prohibition is not the answer, and never has been. Let us treat young people who turn 18 as the adults who the law, in every other respect, says they are.

—John M. McCardell, Jr.

3 Reading

After previewing a text, you can settle into it to learn what it has to say.

First reading

The first time through new material, read as steadily as possible, trying to get the gist of what the author is saying.

- **Read in a place where you can concentrate.** Choose a quiet environment away from distractions such as music or talking.
- **Give yourself time.** Rushing yourself or worrying about something else you have to do will prevent you from grasping what you read.

- **Try to enjoy the work.** Seek connections between it and what you already know. Appreciate new information, interesting relationships, forceful writing, humor, good examples.
- **Make notes sparingly during this first reading.** Mark major stumbling blocks—such as a paragraph you don't understand—so that you can try to resolve them before rereading.

CULTURE LANGUAGE If English is not your first language and you come across unfamiliar words, don't stop and look up every one. You will be distracted from an overall understanding of the text. Instead, try to guess the meanings of the unfamiliar words by using context clues, such as examples and synonyms of the words. Be sure to circle the words and look them up later. You may want to keep a vocabulary log of the words, their definitions, and the sentences in which they appeared.

Rereading and annotating

After the first reading, plan on at least one other. This time read *slowly*. Your main concern should be to grasp the content and how it is constructed. That means rereading a paragraph if you didn't get the point or using a dictionary to look up words you don't know.

Use the tips in the following box to highlight and annotate a text.

Annotating a text

- **Distinguish main ideas from supporting ideas.** Mark the central idea (the thesis), the main idea of each paragraph or section, and the evidence supporting ideas.
- **Note key terms.** Understand both their meanings and their applications.
- **Identify the connections among ideas.** Be sure you see why the author moves from point A to point B to point C and how those points work together to support the central idea. It often helps to outline the text or summarize it (see p. 155).
- **Distinguish between facts and opinions.** Especially when reading an argument, mark the author's opinions as well as the facts on which the opinions are based. (See pp. 182–83 for more on facts and opinions.)
- **Add your own comments.** In the margins or separately, note links to other readings or to class discussions, questions to explore further, possible topics for your writing, points you find especially strong or weak.

An example of critical reading

The following samples show how a student, Charlene Robinson, approached Thomas Sowell's "Student Loans." After her first reading, Robinson went through Sowell's text more slowly, adding comments and questions in the margin and writing about the essay in her journal. Following are samples of her annotations and her journal entries.

Student's annotations

The first lesson of economics is scarcity: There is never enough of anything to fully satisfy all those who want it.

The first lesson of politics is to disregard the first lesson of economics. When politicians discover some group that is being vocal about not having as much as they want, the "solution" is to give them more. Where do politicians get this "more"? They rob Peter to pay Paul.

After a while, of course, they discover that Peter doesn't have enough. Bursting with compassion, politicians rush to the rescue. Needless to say, they do not admit that robbing Peter to pay Paul was a dumb idea in the first place. On the contrary, they now rob Tom, Dick, and Harry to help Peter.

The latest chapter in this long-running saga is that politicians have now suddenly discovered that many college students graduate heavily in debt. To politicians it follows, as the night follows the day, that the government should come to their rescue with the taxpayers' money.

fact

related opinion—contradiction between economics and politics

biblical reference?

ironic and dismissive language

politicians = fools? or irresponsible

example supporting opinion about economics & politics

For her journal entries, Robinson created a two-column table on her computer. She used the left column to record ideas in Sowell's essay that she found thought provoking; then in the right column she responded to some of those ideas with her own comments and questions.

Student's journal entries

Text	Responses
Economics teaches lessons (1), and politics (politicians) and economics are at odds	Is economics truer or more reliable than politics? More scientific?
Politicians don't accept econ. limits —always trying to satisfy "vocal" voters by giving them what they want (2)	Politicians do spend a lot of our money. Is that what they're elected to do, or do they go too far?
"Robbing Peter to pay Paul" (2)—from the Bible (the Apostles)?	
Politicians support student loan program with taxpayer funds bec. of "vocal" voters (2-4): another ex. of not accepting econ. limits	I support the loan program, too. Are politicians being irresponsible when they do? (Dismissive language underlined on copy.)

You should try to answer the questions about meaning that you raise in your annotations and your journal, and that may take another reading or some digging in other sources, such as dictionaries and encyclopedias. Recording in your journal what you think the author means will help you build an understanding of the text, and a focused attempt to summarize will help even more (see the facing page). Such efforts will resolve any confusion you feel, or they will give you the confidence to say that your confusion is the fault of the author, not the reader.

Exercise 7.3 Reading and annotating

Read Sowell's essay on pages 150–51 at least twice, until you think you understand what the author is saying. Use the guidelines in the box on page 153 to annotate the essay—noting your observations, questions, and reactions—as Charlene Robinson did for the first four paragraphs. Look up any words you don't know, and try to answer your questions. You might want to discuss the essay with your classmates as well.

Exercise 7.4 Reading and annotating

Read "Let Them Drink at 18, with a Learner's Permit" (pp. 151–52) at least twice, until you think you understand what the author is saying. Use the guidelines in the box on page 153 to annotate the essay, noting your observations, questions, and reactions. Look up any words you don't know, and try to answer your questions. You might want to discuss the essay with your classmates as well.

7b Summarizing

A good way to master the content of a text and to see its strengths and weaknesses is to **summarize** it: reduce it to its main points *using your own words*. Assignments sometimes call for brief summaries, as when you summarize the plot in a critical essay about a novel (p. 726). Summary is also an essential tool in research papers and other writing that draws on sources (pp. 599–600). In fact, summarizing is such a useful skill that some instructors give it as a separate assignment. In showing how summary can reveal the meaning of a text, this section will help you learn to summarize for any purpose.

A summary should state in as few words as possible the main ideas of a passage. When you need to summarize a few paragraphs or a brief article, your summary should not exceed one-fifth the length of the original. For longer works, such as chapters of books or whole books, your summary should be quite a bit shorter in proportion to the original. A procedure for drafting a summary appears in the following box.

Writing a summary

- **Understand the meaning.** Look up words or concepts you don't know so that you understand the author's sentences and how they relate to one another.
- **Understand the organization.** Work through the text to identify its sections—single paragraphs or groups of paragraphs focused on a single topic. To understand how parts of a work relate to one another, try drawing a tree diagram or creating an outline (pp. 35–40).
- **Distill each section.** Write a one- or two-sentence summary of each section you identify. Focus on the main point of the section, omitting examples, facts, and other supporting evidence.

(continued)

Writing a summary
(continued)

- **State the main idea.** Write a sentence or two capturing the author's central idea.
- **Support the main idea.** Write a full paragraph (or more, if needed) that begins with the central idea and supports it with the sentences that summarize sections of the work. The paragraph should concisely and accurately state the thrust of the entire work.
- ***Use your own words.*** By writing, you re-create the meaning of the work in a way that makes sense for you. You also avoid plagiarism.
- ***Cite the source.*** If you use a summary in writing that you do for others, always acknowledge the source.

Summarizing even a passage of text can be tricky. Here we'll look at attempts to summarize the following material from an introductory biology textbook:

Original text

As astronomers study newly discovered planets orbiting distant stars, they hope to find evidence of water on these far-off celestial bodies, for water is the substance that makes possible life as we know it here on Earth. All organisms familiar to us are made mostly of water and live in an environment dominated by water. They require water more than any other substance. Human beings, for example, can survive for quite a few weeks without food, but only a week or so without water. Molecules of water participate in many chemical reactions necessary to sustain life. Most cells are surrounded by water, and cells themselves are about 70–95% water. Three-quarters of Earth's surface is submerged in water. Although most of this water is in liquid form, water is also present on Earth as ice and vapor. Water is the only common substance to exist in the natural environment in all three physical states of matter: solid, liquid, and gas.

—Neil A. Campbell and Jane B. Reece, *Biology*

The first attempt to summarize this passage accurately restates ideas in the original, but it does not pare the passage to its essence:

Draft summary

Astronomers look for water in outer space because life depends on it. It is the most common substance on Earth and in living cells, and it can be a liquid, a solid (ice), or a gas (vapor).

The work of astronomers and the three physical states of water add color and texture to the original, but they are asides to the key concept that water sustains life because of its role in life. The following revision narrows the summary to this concept:

Revised summary

Water is the most essential support for life—the dominant substance on Earth and in living cells and a component of life-sustaining chemical processes.

When Charlene Robinson summarized Thomas Sowell's "Student Loans," she first drafted the following sentence about paragraphs 1–4:

Draft summary

As much as politicians would like to satisfy voters by giving them everything they ask for, the government cannot afford a student loan program.

Rereading the sentence and Sowell's paragraphs, Robinson saw that this draft misread the text by asserting that the government cannot afford student loans. She realized that Sowell's point is more complicated than that and rewrote her summary:

Revised summary

As their support of the government's student loan program illustrates, politicians ignore the economic reality that using resources to benefit one group (students in debt) involves taking the resources from another group (taxpayers).

Caution Using your own words when writing a summary not only helps you understand the meaning but also constitutes the first step in avoiding plagiarism, which is discussed on pages 139–40 and 614–20. The second step is to cite the source when you use the summary in something written for others.

Note Do not count on the AutoSummarize function on your word processor for summarizing texts that you may have copied onto your computer. The summaries are rarely accurate, and you will not gain the experience of interacting with the texts on your own.

Exercise 7.5 Summarizing

Start where Robinson's summary of Thomas Sowell's essay ends (at paragraph 5) to summarize the entire essay. Your summary, in your own words, should not exceed one paragraph. For more exercises in summarizing, see page 607.

Exercise 7.6 Summarizing

Use the guidelines in the box on pages 155–56 to summarize "Let Them Drink at 18, with a Learner's Permit" (pp. 151–52). Your summary, in your own words, should not exceed one paragraph. For more exercises in summarizing, see page 607.

7c Developing a critical response

Once you've grasped the content of what you're reading—what the author says—then you can turn to understanding what the author does not say outright but suggests or implies or even lets slip. At this stage you are concerned with the purpose or intention of the author and with how he or she carries it out.

Critical thinking and reading consist of four operations: analyzing, interpreting, synthesizing, and (often) evaluating. Although we'll

Guidelines for analysis, interpretation, and synthesis

- **What is the purpose of your reading?**
- **What questions do you have about the work,** given your purpose?
- **What elements does the most interesting question highlight?** What elements might you ignore as a result?
- **How do you interpret the meaning and significance of the elements?** What are your assumptions about the work? What do you infer about the author's assumptions?
- **What patterns can you see in (or synthesize from) the elements?** How do the elements relate? How does this whole work relate to other works?
- **What do you conclude about the work?** What does this conclusion add to the work?

look at them one by one, these operations interrelate and overlap. Indeed, the first three are often combined under the general label *analysis,* and evaluation is sometimes taken for granted as a result of the process.

In the following pages, two quite different examples—*People* magazine and Sowell's "Student Loans"—show how critical reading can work.

1 Analyzing

Analysis is the separation of something into its parts or elements, the better to understand it. To see these elements in what you are reading, begin with a question that reflects your purpose in analyzing the text: why you're curious about it or what you're trying to make out of it. This question will serve as a kind of lens that highlights some features and not others.

Following are some questions you might ask about *People* magazine—the print version you see at the supermarket checkout. Each question on the left highlights the elements on the right.

Questions for analysis	Elements
Does *People* challenge or perpetuate stereotypes?	Stereotypes: explicit and implicit stereotypes or challenges in the magazine
Does the magazine offer positive role models for its readers?	Role models: text and photographs presenting positive or negative role models
Does the magazine's editorial material (articles and accompanying photographs) encourage readers to consume goods and entertainment?	Encouragement of consumption: references to goods and entertainment, focus on consumers, equation of consumption with happiness or success

As these examples show, a question for analysis concentrates your attention on relevant features and eliminates irrelevant features. To answer the question in the preceding list about *People*'s encouragement of consumption, you would focus on items that feature consumption and the products consumed: photographs of designer clothes and celebrities' well-appointed homes, articles on the authors of best-selling books and the stars of new movies. At the same time, you would skip over items that have little or no relevance to consumption, such as uplifting stories about families or the physically challenged.

Analyzing Thomas Sowell's "Student Loans" (pp. 151–52), you might ask these questions:

Questions for analysis	Elements
What is Sowell's attitude toward politicians?	References to politicians: content, words, tone
How does Sowell support his assertions about the loan program's costs?	Support: evidence, such as statistics and examples

A difference in the kinds of questions asked is a key distinction among academic disciplines. A sociologist neatly outlined three disciplines' approaches to poverty:

> Political science does a wonderful job looking at poverty as a policy issue. Economics does an equally wonderful job looking at it from an income-distribution perspective. But sociology asks how people in poverty live and what they aspire to.

Even within disciplines, approaches may differ. The sociologist quoted above may focus on how people in poverty live, but another may be more interested in the effects of poverty on cities or the changes in the poor population over the last fifty years. (See Chapters 49–52 for more on the disciplines' analytical questions.)

2 Interpreting

Identifying the elements of something is of course only the beginning: you also need to interpret the meaning or significance of the elements and of the whole. Interpretation usually requires you to infer the author's **assumptions**: opinions or beliefs about what is or what could or should be. (*Infer* means to draw a conclusion based on evidence.)

The word *assumption* here has a more specific meaning than it does in everyday usage, where it may stand for expectation (*I assume you'll pay*), speculation (*It was a mere assumption*), or error (*The report was riddled with assumptions*). Defined more strictly as what a person *supposes* to be true, assumptions are unavoidable. We all adhere to certain values and beliefs; we all form opinions. We live our lives by such assumptions.

Though pervasive, assumptions are not always stated outright. Speakers and writers may judge that their audience already understands and accepts their assumptions; they may not even be aware of their assumptions; or they may deliberately refrain from stating their assumptions for fear that the audience will disagree. That is why your job as a critical thinker is to interpret what the assumptions are.

Reasonable inferences

Like an author deciding what to say in an article, the publishers of *People* magazine make assumptions that guide their selection of content for the magazine. One set of assumptions, perhaps the most important, concerns what readers want to see: as a for-profit enterprise, the magazine naturally aims to maintain and even expand its readership (currently about 3.5 million each week). If your analysis of the magazine's editorial material reveals that much of it features consumer products, you might infer the following:

> **Reasonable** The publishers of *People* assume that the magazine's readers are consumers who want to see and hear about goods and entertainment.

Nowhere in *People* will you find a statement of this assumption, but the evidence implies it.

Similarly, Thomas Sowell's "Student Loans" (pp. 150–51) is based on certain assumptions, some obvious, some not so obvious. If you were analyzing Sowell's attitude toward politicians, as suggested earlier, you would focus on his statements about them. Sowell says that they "disregard the first lesson of economics" (paragraph 2), which implies that they ignore important principles (knowing that Sowell is an economist himself makes this a reasonable assumption on your part). Sowell also says that politicians "rob Peter to pay Paul," are "[b]ursting with compassion," "do not admit . . . a dumb idea," are characters in a "long-running saga," and arrive at the solution of spending taxes "as the night follows the day"—that is, inevitably (paragraphs 2–4). From these statements and others, you can infer the following:

> **Reasonable** Sowell assumes that politicians become compassionate when a cause is loud and popular, not necessarily just, and they act irresponsibly by trying to solve the problem with other people's (taxpayers') money.

Unreasonable inferences

Interpreting assumptions gives you greater insight into an author's intentions. But it's crucial that inferences fit the evidence of the text, as do the previous inferences about *People* and Sowell's essay. Sometimes it's tempting to read too much into the text, as in the next examples:

Faulty — *People*'s publishers deliberately skew the magazine's editorial material to promote products on which they receive kickbacks. [The inference is far-fetched. It would be reasonable only if there were hard evidence of kickbacks.]

Faulty — Sowell thinks that politicians should not be entrusted with running the country. [The inference misreads Sowell. Although he does not outline a solution for politicians' irresponsibility, there's no evidence that he would overhaul our democratic political system.]

Faulty inferences like these are often based on the reader's *own* assumptions about the text or its subject. When thinking and reading critically, you need to look hard at *your* ideas, too.

3 Synthesizing

If you stopped at analysis and interpretation, critical thinking and reading might leave you with a pile of elements and possible meanings but no vision of the whole. With **synthesis** you make connections among the parts of the text *or* between the text and other texts. You consider the text through the lens of your knowledge and beliefs, drawing conclusions about how the text works as a whole.

A key component of academic reading and writing, synthesis receives more attention in this chapter (pp. 173–74) and then in the context of research writing (pp. 593–95). Sometimes you'll respond directly to a text, as in the following two conclusions. The first pulls together the earlier analysis of *People* magazine's editorial content and the interpretation of the publisher's assumptions about readers:

Conclusion — *People* magazine appeals to its readers' urge to consume by displaying, discussing, and glamorizing consumer goods.

The next statement, about Thomas Sowell's essay "Student Loans," connects Sowell's assumptions about politicians to a larger idea also implied by the essay:

Conclusion — Sowell's view that politicians are irresponsible with taxpayers' money reflects his overall opinion that the laws of economics, not politics, should drive government.

Often synthesis will take you outside the text to its surroundings. The following questions can help you investigate the context of a work:

- **How does the work compare with similar works?** For instance, how does *People*'s juxtaposition of articles and advertisements compare with that in similar magazines, such as *Us Weekly, Entertainment Weekly,* and *Interview*? Or how have other writers responded to Sowell's views on student loans?
- **How does the work fit into the context of other works by the same author or group?** What distinguishes *People* from the many other magazines published by Time Inc., such as *Time, Sports*

Illustrated, Family Circle, and *Fortune*? How do Sowell's views on student loans typify, or not, the author's other writings on political and economic issues?

- **What cultural, economic, or political forces influence the work?** Why are *People*, other celebrity magazines, and celebrity Web sites increasingly popular with readers? What other examples might Sowell have given to illustrate his view that economics, not politics, should determine government spending?
- **What historical forces influence the work?** How does *People* reflect changes in the ways readers choose magazines? How has the indebtedness of college students changed over the past four decades?

With synthesis, you create something different from what you started with. To the supermarket shopper reading *People* while standing in line, the magazine may be entertaining and inconsequential. To you—after a critical reading in which you analyze, interpret, and synthesize—the magazine can be read (at least in part) as a vehicle of our consumer culture. The difference depends on critical reading, considering how the work's elements and underlying assumptions work together and then developing your own response. For more on how to use synthesis in a written response, see pages 173–74.

4 Evaluating

Many critical reading and writing assignments end at analysis, interpretation, and synthesis: you explain your understanding of what the author says and doesn't say. Only if you are expected to evaluate the work will you state and defend the judgments you've made about its quality and its significance:

- **Collect and test your judgments.** Determine that they are significant and that they apply to the whole work.
- **Turn the judgments into assertions**—for instance, *The poet creates fresh, intensely vivid images* or *The author does not summon the evidence to support his case.*
- **Support these statements with evidence from the text**—mainly quotations and paraphrases.

Evaluation takes a certain amount of confidence. You may think that you lack the expertise to cast judgment on another's work, especially if the text is difficult or the author well known. True, the more informed you are, the better a critical reader you are. But conscientious reading and analysis will give you the internal authority to judge a work *as it stands* and *as it seems to you,* against your own unique experiences, observations, and attitudes.

The following box gives questions that can help you evaluate many kinds of works. There's more on evaluation (including evaluation of online sources) on pages 590–93. For arguments and in academic disciplines, you'll require additional, more specific criteria. See Chapters 8 and 49–52.

Guidelines for evaluation

- **What are your reactions to the work?** What in the work are you responding to?
- **How sound are the work's central idea and evidence?**
- **How well does the author achieve his or her purpose?** How worthwhile is the purpose?
- **How authoritative, trustworthy, and sincere is the author?**
- **How unified and coherent is the work?** Do its parts all support a central idea and clearly relate to one another?
- **What do color, graphics, or (online) sound or video contribute to the work?** Do such elements add meaning or merely decoration?
- **What is the overall quality and significance of the work?**
- **Do you agree or disagree with the work?** Can you support, refute, or extend it?

Exercise 7.7 Thinking critically

Following are three numbered statements about the communications media. Use systematic critical thinking to understand not only what each statement says but also why its author might have said it. As in the example, do your thinking in writing: the act of writing will help you think, and your notes will help you discuss your ideas with your classmates.

Example:

Statement: Every year sees the disappearance of more locally owned hardware stores because big-box stores such as Home Depot and Walmart force them out of business.

Analysis: Why did the author make this statement? Certain words reveal the author's purpose: *disappearance of more locally owned hardware stores; because; big-box stores force them out of business.*

Interpretation: *More locally owned hardware stores* means others have disappeared. *Because* specifies cause. *Force* implies coercion, predator to prey. Author's assumptions: Big-box stores behave like predators. The predatory behavior of big-box stores causes the disappearance of locally owned stores. The more hardware stores there are, the better.

Synthesis: The author objects to the predatory behavior of big-box stores, which he or she holds responsible for eliminating locally owned stores and reducing the total number of hardware stores.

Evaluation: This biased statement against big-box stores holds them responsible for the shrinking number of hardware stores. But are the large companies solely responsible? Do they offer value in return? And why is the shrinking necessarily bad?

1. Newspapers, magazines, and news Web sites are better news sources than television because they demand reading, not just viewing.

2. Radio call-in shows are the true democratic forum, giving voice to people of all persuasions.
3. Participation in online communities threatens to undermine our ability to interact face to face.

Exercise 7.8 Reading an essay critically

Reread Thomas Sowell's "Student Loans" (pp. 150–51) in order to form your own critical response to it. Use the guidelines for analysis, interpretation, synthesis, and evaluation in the boxes on pages 158 and 163. Focus on elements suggested by your questions about the text: perhaps assumptions, evidence, organization, language, tone, authority, vision of education or of students. Be sure to write while reading and thinking; your notes will help your analysis and enhance your creativity, and they will be essential for writing about the selection (Exercise 7.15, p. 180).

Exercise 7.9 Reading an essay critically

Reread "Let Them Drink at 18, with a Learner's Permit" (pp. 151–52) in order to form your own critical response to it. Follow the guidelines for analysis, interpretation, synthesis, and evaluation in the boxes on pages 158 and 163. Focus on any elements suggested by your questions about the text: perhaps assumptions, evidence, organization, use of language, tone, authority, or attitudes toward young adults and alcohol. Be sure to write while reading and thinking; your notes will help your analysis and creative thinking, and they will be useful for writing about the essay (Exercise 7.16, p. 180).

Exercise 7.10 Reading a magazine critically

Do your own critical reading of *People* or another magazine. What do you see beyond the obvious? What questions does your reading raise? Let the guidelines on pages 158 and 163 direct your response, and do your work in writing.

7d Viewing visuals critically

Every day we are bombarded with visuals—pictures on billboards, advertisements on social-networking sites, graphs in textbooks, and charts on Web sites, to name just a few examples. Most visuals slide by without our noticing them, or so we think. But visuals, sometimes even more than text, can influence us covertly. Their creators have purposes, some worthy, some not, and understanding those purposes requires critical reading. The method parallels that in the previous sections for reading text critically: write while reading, preview, read for comprehension, analyze, interpret, synthesize, and (often) evaluate.

1 Writing while reading a visual

Writing as you read a visual helps you view it deliberately and allows you to record your impressions precisely. You can handwrite on a printout of the visual or copy it into a file and annotate it there.

The example below shows how one student annotated an advertisement he saw on the Web. (He copied the ad into a word-processing document and added a text box for his annotations.)

Annotation of an advertisement

Advertisement for *Teach.org*

Guy in photo: Eyes focused ahead (on students?). Caught in mid-speech. Clenched hands = intense, engaged, passionate.

Large, white type highlights message. 1st sentence: what kids hear growing up. 2nd sentence: a challenge to be "someone" important, like a celebrity.

"Join us": direct invitation to be like this guy.

What is Teach.org? Recruits new teachers?

2 Previewing a visual

Your first step in exploring a visual is to form initial impressions of its origin and purpose and to note its distinctive features. This previewing process is like the one for previewing a text (p. 149):

- **What do you see?** What is most striking about the visual? What is its subject? What is the gist of any text or symbols? What is the overall effect of the visual?
- **What are the facts of publication?** Where did you first see the visual? Do you think the visual was created especially for that location or for others as well? What can you tell about when the visual was created?
- **What do you know about the person or group that created the visual?** For instance, was the creator an artist, scholar, or corporation? What seems to have been the creator's purpose?
- **What is your preliminary response?** What about the visual interests, confuses, or disturbs you? Are the form, style, and subject familiar or unfamiliar? How might your knowledge, experiences, and values influence your reception of the visual?

3 Reading a visual

Reading a visual requires the same level of concentration as reading a text. Plan to spend more than one session working with the visual to absorb its meaning and purpose and then to analyze and maybe challenge its message.

Try to answer the following questions about the visual. If some answers aren't clear at this point, skip the question until later.

- **What is the purpose?** Is the visual mainly explanatory, conveying information, or is it argumentative, trying to convince readers of something or to persuade them to act? What information or point of view does it seem to want to get across?
- **Who is the intended audience?** What does the source of the visual, including its publication facts, tell about the visual creator's expectations for readers' knowledge, interests, and attitudes? What do the features of the visual itself add to your impression?
- **What do any words or symbols add?** Whether located on the visual or outside it (such as in a caption), do words or symbols add information, focus your attention, or alter your impression?
- **What action, change, people, places, or things are shown?** Does the visual tell a story? Do its characters or other features tap into your knowledge, or are they unfamiliar?
- **What is the form?** Is the visual a photograph, advertisement, painting, graph, diagram, cartoon, or something else? How do its content and apparent purpose and audience relate to its form?

The following journal entry by a student, Richard Oliva, illustrates the results of asking questions like these about the advertisement on the previous page, which he annotated.

Student's journal entry

Details of the ad	Responses
Guy in the photo: alone, caught in midspeech, hands clenched, eyes looking ahead of him, maybe at students, not at camera	He looks intense, engaged, and even passionate about what he's saying. He makes teaching look lively and rewarding.
Big white text: "You can be anyone. Why not be someone?"	"You can be anyone" addresses the viewer directly with words most kids hear from parents and others. The words give a sense of many options in life.
	"Why not be someone?" seems to say, "Since you have so many options, why not choose a career that will make you important and even famous?"
Below that in orange: "Join us at Teach.org"	Orange color and box around "Join us" stress the invitation to be like the guy in the photo. He likes what he's doing, and now the viewer knows that he's a teacher. Join "us" and you can be "someone" like him.

4 Analyzing a visual

Elements for analysis

As when analyzing a written work, you analyze a visual by identifying its elements. The visual elements you might consider appear in the box below. Few visuals include all the elements, and you can narrow the list further by posing a question about the visual you are reading.

Elements of visuals

- **Emphasis:** Most visuals pull your eyes to certain features: a graph line moving sharply upward, a provocative figure, bright color, thick lines, and so on.
- **Narration:** Most visuals tell stories, whether in a sequence (a TV commercial or a graph showing changes over time) or at a single moment (a photograph, a painting, or a pie chart).
- **Point of view:** The creator of the visual considers both the viewer's physical relation to the subject—for instance, whether it is seen head-on or from above—and the viewer's assumed attitude toward the subject.
- **Arrangement:** Pattern, foreground versus background, and separation can contribute to the visual's meaning and effect.
- **Color:** Color can direct the viewer's attention, convey the creator's attitude, and suggest a mood.
- **Characterization:** The qualities of figures and objects—sympathetic or not, desirable or not—reflect their roles in the visual's story.
- **Context:** The source of a visual affects its meaning, whether it is a graph from a scholarly journal or a car ad on the Web.
- **Tension:** Visuals often communicate a problem or seize attention with features that seem wrong, such as misspelled or misaligned words, distorted figures, or controversial relations between characters.
- **Allusions:** An *allusion* is a reference to something the audience is likely to recognize and respond to. Examples include a cultural symbol such as a dollar sign, a mythological figure such as a unicorn, or a familiar movie character such as Darth Vader from *Star Wars*.

Question for analysis

You can focus your analysis of elements by framing your main interest in the visual as a question. Richard Oliva concentrated his analysis of the *Teach.org* ad by asking the question *Does the ad move viewers to imagine themselves as teachers?* The question led Oliva to focus on some elements of the ad and ignore others:

Student's analysis

Elements of the ad	Responses
Emphasis	The photo grabs the viewer, placing emphasis on the teacher. Then the lines of white text draw the eye away from the photo to the message.

Elements of the ad	Responses
Narration	In just a few words, the ad tells a story about what viewers could become. It appeals to viewers' wish to be known in some way, like a celebrity, but doing important, interesting work, like the guy in the photo. The orange "Join us" then invites viewers to take a step toward that dream.
Point of view	The guy is looking down, probably at his students in front of him, not at the viewer. This might be off-putting, but the man is so engaged in speaking that it's not. Instead, the viewer catches his intensity.
Characterization	The guy's intensity about what he's doing is appealing. He seems to have independence and authority—he's not at a desk and is wearing a casual shirt and bracelets, not a suit. He makes teaching look interesting, rewarding, even cool.

Sample visuals for analysis

The visuals below and on the next two pages give you a chance to analyze selective elements in a line graph, a photograph, and two Web pages. Questions in the annotations can help to open up your thinking.

Elements in a line graph

Color and emphasis: What do the title and labels say you are looking at? How does color focus your attention?

Narration: What story does the graph tell about the changing uses of media?

Context: The graph comes from a reputable research organization, the Pew Research Center for the People and the Press. What does that information contribute to your understanding of the graph?

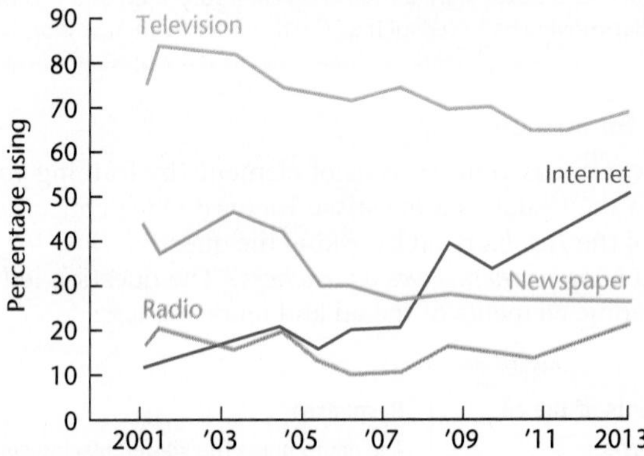

Graph adapted from the Pew Research Center for the People and the Press

Elements in a photograph

Emphasis: What is the focus of the photograph? What are your eyes drawn to?	**Arrangement:** What is interesting about the arrangement of elements?
Characterization: What does the man seem to be feeling? Consider especially his mouth and eyes.	**Color:** What does the black-and-white presentation contribute to the image? How might the image differ in full color?
Narration: What story or stories might the photograph tell?	**Allusion:** What symbol do you see? What meaning does it give to the photograph?

Photograph by Steve Simon

The screen shots on the next page are from *AIDS Clock,* an interactive Web site sponsored by the United Nations Population Fund (*www.unfpa.org/aids_clock*). The top image is the home page, displaying a traditional world map. The bottom image appears when viewers click on "Resize the map": now each country's size reflects the number of its people who live with HIV, the virus that causes AIDS. (For example, South Africa grows while the United States shrinks.) The large blue number at the top changes every twelve seconds.

Note See also pages 199–200 for information on reading visuals that make arguments and on identifying distortions and other misrepresentations in visuals.

5 Interpreting a visual

The strategies for interpreting a visual parallel those for interpreting a written text (pp. 159–61). In this process you look more deeply at the elements, considering them in relation to the likely assumptions and intentions of the visual's creator. You aim to draw

Elements of Web pages

Emphasis and color: What elements on these pages draw your attention? How does color distinguish and emphasize elements?	**Arrangement:** What does the arrangement of elements on the pages contribute to the story being told?
Narration: What story do the two Web pages tell? What does each map contribute to the story? What does the blue number contribute? (Notice that the number changes from the first screen to the second.)	**Tension:** How do you respond to the distorted map in the second image? What does the distortion contribute to your view of the Web site's effectiveness?
	Context: How does knowing the Web site's sponsoring organization, the United Nations Population Fund, affect your response to these images?

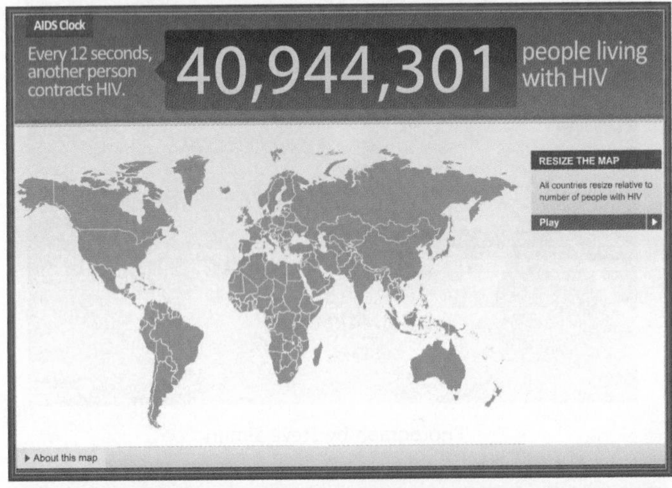

AIDS Clock Web pages, 2014

reasonable inferences about *why* the visual looks as it does. Here's a reasonable inference about the *Teach.org* advertisement on page 165:

Reasonable The creators of the *Teach.org* ad assume that viewers want careers that make them feel important.

This inference is supported by the second sentence of the ad: "Why not be someone?" In contrast, the next inference is *not* reasonable because it leaps to a conclusion that is not supported by the ad:

Faulty The creators of the *Teach.org* ad want readers to help improve the quality of education in the United States.

The ad implies that readers believe education is important, but it does not suggest that readers should take steps to change the educational system.

6 Synthesizing ideas about a visual

As discussed on pages 161–62, with synthesis you take analysis and interpretation a step further to consider how a work's elements and underlying assumptions mesh. You may also want to view the visual in the larger context of similar works or of history and culture.

Placing a visual in its context often requires research. For instance, to learn more about the assumptions underlying the *Teach.org* advertisement and the goals of the larger ad campaign, Richard Oliva visited the *Teach.org* Web site. The following entry from his reading journal synthesizes this research and his own ideas about the ad:

> The *Teach.org* ad is part of a larger campaign designed to attract young people to careers in teaching. Viewers who go to the *Teach.org* Web site can find information about going to college to become a teacher, getting scholarships for college, and preparing for a job search. They can also watch videos of young teachers talking about what inspired them to choose teaching. The ad with the man talking that popped up on my screen is one of several in the campaign, and the elements of the ad are designed to attract viewers by making teaching look exciting and important.

For more on using synthesis in a written response, see pages 173–74.

7 Evaluating a visual

If your critical reading moves on to evaluation, you'll form judgments about the quality and significance of the visual. Questions to ask for evaluation appear in the box on page 163. Briefly: Is the message of the visual accurate and fair, or is it distorted and biased? Can you support, refute, or extend the message? Does the visual achieve its apparent purpose, and is the purpose worthwhile? How does the visual affect you?

See Richard Oliva's paper on pages 178–79 for an evaluation of the *Teach.org* advertisement.

Exercise 7.11 Viewing a visual critically

Review the list of visual elements on page 167 and then take another close look at the *Teach.org* advertisement on page 165. Using the guidelines on the preceding pages, draw your own conclusions about the ad. Write while reading and thinking to help yourself concentrate and develop ideas. A writing suggestion based on this activity appears in Exercise 7.17, page 180.

Exercise 7.12 Viewing a visual critically

Select the graph on page 168, the photograph on page 169, or the Web pages on page 170 to examine in more detail. Using the guidelines on the preceding pages, read the visual(s) methodically and critically. Write down your ideas. A writing suggestion based on this activity appears in Exercise 7.18, page 180.

Exercise 7.13 Comparing visuals critically

Two visuals in this section—the advertisement and the photograph—use people as subjects to reinforce their messages. The other visuals—a line graph and Web pages—center on data and maps. Using the guidelines on the preceding pages, compare these visuals, focusing on each one's emphasis. How effective are these emphases? Write down your responses. A writing suggestion based on this activity appears in Exercise 7.19, page 180.

7e Writing critically

Many academic writing assignments ask for **critical analysis**, or **critique**, in which you write critically about texts or visuals. As you form a response to a work, you integrate its ideas and information with yours to come to your own conclusions (see pp. 157–63). As you write your response, you support your ideas about the work by citing evidence from it.

Note Critical writing is *not* summarizing. You might summarize to clarify a text or a visual for yourself, and you might briefly summarize a work in your larger piece of writing. But in critical writing you go further to bring your own perspective to the work.

1 Deciding how to respond

When an assignment asks you to respond directly to a text or a visual, you might take one of the following approaches to decide on your position.

- **Agree with and extend the ideas expressed in the work, exploring related ideas and providing additional examples.**

- **Agree with some of the ideas but disagree with others.**
- **Disagree with one or more ideas.**
- **Explain how the work achieves a particular effect,** such as balancing opposing views or conveying a mood.
- **Analyze the overall effectiveness of the work**—for example, how well a writer supports a thesis with convincing evidence or whether an advertisement succeeds in its unstated purpose.

2 Shaping a critical analysis

You will likely have an immediate response to at least some of the texts and visuals you analyze: you may agree or disagree strongly with what the author says or shows. But for some other responses, you may need to use the process of critical reading described on pages 147–63 to take notes on the text, summarize it, and develop a view of it. Then, as you write, you can use the tips in the following box to convey your response to readers.

Responding to a text

- **Make sure your writing has a point**—a central idea, or thesis, that focuses your response. (For more on developing a thesis, see pp. 28–33.)
- **Include a very brief summary if readers may be unfamiliar with your subject.** But remember that your job is not just to report what the text says or what a visual shows; it is to *respond* to the work from your own critical perspective. (For more on summary, see pp. 155–57.)
- **Center each paragraph on an idea of your own that supports your thesis.** Generally, state the idea outright, in your own voice.
- **Support the paragraph idea with evidence from the text**—quotations, paraphrases, details, and examples.
- **Conclude each paragraph with your interpretation of the evidence.** As a general rule, avoid ending paragraphs with source evidence; instead, end with at least a sentence that explains what the evidence shows.

3 Emphasizing synthesis in your response

Following the suggestions in the preceding box will lead you to show readers the synthesis you achieved as you developed a critical response to the text or visual. That is, you integrate your perspective on the work with that of the author or creator in order to support a conclusion of your own.

A key to synthesis is deciding how to present evidence from your critical reading or viewing. Especially when you are writing about a relatively unfamiliar subject, you may be tempted to let a text or other source do the talking for you through extensive summary or quotations. However, your voice is crucial in academic writing, where readers expect to see you managing ideas and information to make your points.

A typical paragraph of text-based writing follows the pattern outlined in the preceding box: the writer's own idea, evidence from the text, and the writer's interpretation of the evidence. You can see this pattern in the following paragraph from the essay that begins on the facing page:

> The most fundamental and most debatable assumption underlying Sowell's essay is that higher education is a kind of commodity that not everyone is entitled to. [Writer's idea] In order to diminish the importance of graduates' average debt from education loans, Sowell claims that a car loan will probably be higher (131). [Evidence] This comparison between education and an automobile implies that the two are somehow equal as products and that an affordable higher education is no more a right than a new car is. [Interpretation] Sowell also condemns the "irresponsible" students who drop out of school and "the increasingly easy availability of college to people who are not very serious about getting an education" (132). [Evidence] But he overlooks the value of encouraging education, including the education of those who don't finish college or who aren't scholars. For many in the United States, education has a greater value than that of a mere commodity like a car. [Interpretation] And even from an economic perspective such as Sowell's, the cost to society of an uneducated public needs to be taken into account. By failing to give education its due, Sowell undermines his argument at its core. [Writer's conclusion]
>
> —Charlene Robinson, "Weighing the Costs"

This example meets an important goal of synthesis in academic writing: Robinson finds **balance** in her own and Sowell's claims so that her claims are reasonable and believable. Disagreeing with Sowell, Robinson might simply have dismissed his claims as "ridiculous" and moved on. Instead, she takes a more serious and impartial approach by giving Sowell's claims a fair hearing and detailing the flaws and omissions she sees. Thus she gives readers a chance to evaluate for themselves both Sowell's and her own claims.

Note Effective synthesis requires careful handling of evidence from the text (quotations, paraphrases, and summaries) so that the evidence meshes smoothly into your sentences and yet is clearly distinct from your own ideas. See pages 608–13 on integrating borrowed material.

7f Examining sample critical analyses

Academic disciplines vary in the specifics of critical analysis, but the principles illustrated in the following examples apply across disciplines.

1 Critical analysis of a text

The following essay by the student Charlene Robinson responds to Thomas Sowell's "Student Loans" (pp. 150–51). Robinson arrived at her response through the process of critical reading outlined on pages 147–63 of this chapter and then by gathering and organizing her ideas, developing a thesis about Sowell's text that synthesized his ideas and hers, and supporting her thesis with evidence from her own experience and from Sowell's text.

Robinson did not assume that her readers would see the same things in Sowell's essay or share her views, so her essay offers evidence of Sowell's ideas in the form of direct quotations, summaries, and paraphrases (restatements in her own words). Robinson documents these borrowings from Sowell using the style of the Modern Language Association (MLA): the numbers in parentheses are page numbers in the book containing Sowell's essay, listed at the end as a work cited. (See Chapter 47 for more on MLA style.)

Weighing the Costs

In the essay "Student Loans," the economist Thomas Sowell challenges the US government's student-loan program for three main reasons: a scarce resource (taxpayers' money) goes to many undeserving students, a high number of recipients fail to repay their loans, and the easy availability of money has led to both lower academic standards and higher college tuitions. Sowell wants his readers to "weigh the costs of things" (133) in order to see, as he does, that the loan program should not receive so much government funding. Sowell wrote his essay in the 1990s, but the argument he makes is still heard frequently today and is worth examining. Does Sowell provide the evidence of cost and other problems to lead the reader to agree with his argument? The answer is no, because hard evidence is less common than debatable and unsupported assumptions about students, scarcity, and the value of education.

Introduction

Summary of Sowell's essay

Robinson's critical question

Thesis statement

Sowell's portrait of student-loan recipients is questionable. It is based on averages, some statistical and some not, but averages are often deceptive. For example, Sowell cites college graduates' low average debt of $7,000 to $9,000 (131) without giving the full range of statistics or acknowledging that when he was writing many students' debt was much higher. (Today the average debt itself is much higher.) Similarly, Sowell

First main point

Evidence for first point: paraphrases and quotations from Sowell's text

The writing situation: Critical analysis of a text

- **Subject:** Response to "Student Loans," by Thomas Sowell; student's choice from several readings assigned in a first-year writing course
- **Purpose:** To analyze the essay and evaluate its effectiveness
- **Audience:** Instructor, classmates
- **Genre:** Critical analysis, or critique, of a text—writing that involves close reading, summary, analysis, and often evaluation of a written work
- **Source:** Sowell's essay (cited in MLA style)

dismisses "heart-rending stories" of "the low-income student with a huge debt" as "not at all typical" (132), yet he invents his own exaggerated version of the typical loan recipient: an affluent slacker ("Rockefellers" and "Vanderbilts") for whom college is a "place to hang out for a few years" sponging off the government, while his or her parents clear a profit from making use of the loan program (132). Although such students (and parents) may well exist, are they really typical? Sowell does not offer any data one way or the other—for instance, how many loan recipients come from each income group, what percentage of loan funds go to each group, how many loan recipients receive significant help from their parents, and how many receive none. Together, Sowell's statements and omissions cast doubt on the argument that students don't need or deserve the loans.

Evidence for first point: Sowell's omissions

Conclusion of first point: Robinson's interpretation

Transition to second main point

Another set of assumptions in the essay has to do with "scarcity": "There is never enough of anything to fully satisfy all those who want it," Sowell says (131). This statement appeals to readers' common sense, but the "lesson" of scarcity does not necessarily apply to the student-loan program. Sowell omits many important figures needed to prove that the nation's resources are too scarce to support the program, such as the total cost of the program, its percentage of the total education budget and the total federal budget, and its cost compared to the cost of defense, Medicare, and other expensive programs. Moreover, Sowell does not mention the interest paid by loan recipients, even though the interest must offset some of the costs of running the program and covering unpaid loans. Thus his argument that there isn't enough money to run the student loan program is unconvincing.

Second main point

Evidence for second point: Sowell's omissions

Conclusion of second point: Robinson's interpretation

Third main point

The most fundamental and most debatable assumption underlying Sowell's essay is that higher education is a kind of commodity that not everyone is entitled to. In order to diminish the importance of graduates' average debt from education loans, Sowell claims that a car loan will probably be higher (131). This comparison between education and an

Evidence for third point: paraphrases and quotations from Sowell's text automobile implies that the two are somehow equal as products and that an affordable higher education is no more a right than a new car is. Sowell also condemns the "irresponsible" students who drop out of school and "the increasingly easy availability of college to people who are not very serious about getting an education" (132). But he overlooks the value of encouraging education, including the education of those who don't finish college or who aren't scholars. For many in the United States, education has a greater value than that of a mere commodity like a car. And even from an economic perspective such as Sowell's, the cost to society of an uneducated public needs to be taken into account. By failing to give education its due, Sowell undermines his argument at its core.

Evidence for third point: Sowell's omissions

Conclusion of third point: Robinson's interpretation

Sowell writes with conviction, and his concerns are valid: high taxes, waste, unfairness, declining educational standards, obtrusive government. However, the essay's flaws make it unlikely that Sowell could convince readers who do not already agree with him. He does not support his portrait of the typical loan recipient, he fails to demonstrate a lack of resources for the loan program, and he neglects the special nature of education compared to other services and products. Sowell may have the evidence to back up his assumptions, but by omitting it he himself does not truly weigh the costs of the loan program.

Conclusion

Acknowledgment of Sowell's concerns

Summary of three main points

Return to theme of introduction: weighing costs

[New page.]

Work Cited

Work cited in MLA style (p. 644)

Sowell, Thomas. "Student Loans." *Is Reality Optional? and Other Essays*. Hoover Institution Press, 1993, pp. 131–33.

—Charlene Robinson (student)

2 Writing critically about a visual

The following essay, by the student Richard Oliva, responds to the *Teach.org* advertisement on page 165. Oliva examined the ad over several stages, each time discovering more in it and gradually developing his own ideas. In his paper Oliva takes pains to be sure that readers will see the ad as he does: he reproduces it, captions it, and clearly describes its features. He cites his sources using MLA style (Chapter 47).

Caution A visual is a source just as a written work is, and like a written source it must be acknowledged. Oliva gives full publication information for the *Teach.org* ad in a caption, so he does not cite it again in his list of works cited. (Ask your instructor for his or her preference for citing sources of visuals.) If Oliva published his paper online, he would also need to seek the copyright owner's permission to use the ad. See pages 617–18 for more about acknowledging sources and pages 621–22 for more about permissions for online publication.

Being Someone

Introduction

"You can be anyone." Most children hear it repeatedly from parents, teachers, coaches, and other adults. Now this encouragement is part of an advertising campaign from *Teach.org* aimed at recruiting 100,000 college undergraduates to be teachers by 2021 ("Community"). The Web ad in fig. 1, created by the nonprofit Ad Council, is typical of the campaign in encouraging viewers to consider teaching and to learn more at the *Teach.org* Web site. Through its photography and direct appeals in four lines of text, the ad leads viewers to identify with a teacher and to imagine themselves becoming teachers.

Background information on the ad campaign

Thesis statement

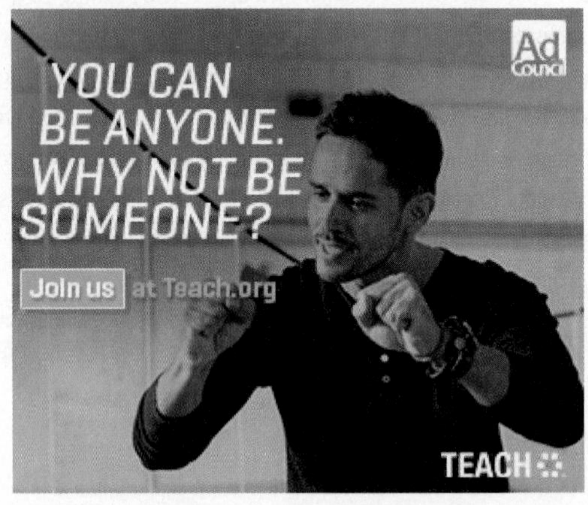

Caption giving the ad's main idea and source

Fig. 1. An advertisement for *Teach.org* encouraging viewers to consider becoming teachers. From "Teacher Recruitment," *Ad Council*, 2014, www.adcouncil.org/Our-Campaigns/Education/Teacher-Recruitment.

First main point

Evidence for first point: analysis of photo

Conclusion of first point: Oliva's interpretation

The main element in the ad is a photograph that fills the frame. The image is of a young-looking man intent on what is in front of him, something he sees but the viewer does not. He is caught in mid-speech, looking down at what viewers eventually assume to be his students, and his clenched hands indicate that he is passionate about what he is saying. He is engaged in what he is doing, which viewers soon learn is teaching. Clearly he finds teaching interesting and fulfilling.

Second main point

Evidence for second point: analysis of message

The next most important element in the ad is four lines of large white type next to the man: "You can be anyone. Why not be someone?" These lines of text explain the photograph and make readers connect to it at an emotional level. "You can be anyone" will resonate with the target audience, college students, particularly those who have been encouraged by the adults in their lives to make the most of their educations. Some viewers will almost hear those familiar words being spoken to them and will be reminded of their dreams of becoming firefighters, doctors, architects, musicians, and, yes, teachers.

The writing situation: Critical analysis of a visual

- **Subject:** Response to a Web advertisement for *Teach.org*; student's choice for an assignment in a first-year writing course
- **Purpose:** To analyze the visual and textual elements of the ad and evaluate its effectiveness
- **Audience:** Instructor, classmates
- **Genre:** Critical analysis, or critique, of a visual—writing that involves close examination, summary, analysis, and often evaluation of a visual work
- **Sources:** Web advertisement, Web site (cited in MLA style)

The following question—"Why not be someone?"—draws the viewer back to the man in the photo. The question could easily read, "Why not be someone like this guy?" Standing alone, he is in charge of a class and is independent—he's not sitting in a cubicle, wearing a suit, or appeasing a boss. "Why not be someone?" also means "Don't be just anyone. Be important." In this way, the ad taps into today's celebrity-obsessed culture, connecting to the desire many people have to become famous or unforgettable in some way.

Evidence for second point: analysis of message

Conclusion of second point: Oliva's interpretation

The final element of the ad that stands out is the orange "Join us at Teach.org." This invitation pulls together the image of the man and the first two sentences, making viewers see that the man is a teacher. Those who haven't yet chosen a career path should see "Join us" as encouragement to explore teaching at the *Teach.org* Web site. The words challenge them to put their desire to be "someone" to good use by pursuing the worthwhile career of teaching.

Third main point

Evidence for third point: analysis of message

Taken together, the elements of the ad make a strong emotional appeal to viewers to identify with the man in the photo—a person who has chosen teaching over other careers, who has a job that is respected and significant, and who enjoys his work. "This can be you," the ad seems to say, effectively appealing to viewers' sense of themselves and their futures.

Conclusion of third point: Oliva's interpretation

Conclusion

[New page.]

Work Cited

"Community." *Teach.org*, 2014, www.teach.org/community.

—Richard Oliva (student)

Work cited in MLA style; no entry for the ad because its caption cites the source

Exercise 7.14 Responding to critiques

Read Charlene Robinson's and Richard Oliva's essays carefully. Do you think the authors' critiques are accurate and fair? Are they perceptive? Do the authors provide enough evidence to convince you of their points? Do they miss anything you would have mentioned? Write your responses to one of the essays in a brief critique of your own.

Exercise 7.15 Writing critically about a text

Write an essay based on your own critical reading of Thomas Sowell's "Student Loans" (Exercise 7.1, p. 149). Your critique may be entirely different from Charlene Robinson's, or you may have developed some of the same points. If there are similarities, they should be expressed and supported in your own way, in the context of your own critical perspective.

Exercise 7.16 Writing critically about a text

Write an essay based on your critical reading of "Let Them Drink at 18, with a Learner's Permit" (Exercise 7.2, p. 151).

Exercise 7.17 Writing critically about a visual

Write an essay based on your own critical reading of the *Teach.org* advertisement (Exercise 7.11, p. 172). Your critique may be entirely different from Richard Oliva's, or you may have developed some of the same points. If there are similarities, they should be expressed and supported in your own way, in the context of your own critical perspective.

Exercise 7.18 Writing critically about a visual

Write an essay based on your critical reading of the graph on page 168, the photograph on page 169, or the Web pages on page 170 (Exercise 7.12, p. 172).

Exercise 7.19 Writing critically about several visuals

Write an essay based on your critical reading and comparison of the visuals on pages 165 and 168–70 (Exercise 7.13, p. 172).

8 Reading Arguments Critically

Chapter essentials

- Analyze the elements of argument: claims, evidence, and assumptions (opposite and pp. 182, 185, and 189).
- Pay attention to an argument's language and tone (p. 190).
- Judge an argument's reasonableness (p. 190).
- Recognize fallacies (p. 193).
- Consider visual arguments (p. 199).

Visit MyWritingLab™ for more resources on reading arguments critically.

Argument is writing that attempts to open readers' minds to an opinion, change readers' own opinions, or move readers to action. A good argument is neither a cold exercise in logic nor an attempt to beat others into submission. It is a work of negotiation and problem solving in which both writer and reader search for the knowledge that will create common ground between them.

Of course, not all arguments are "good." Whether deliberately or not, some are unclear, incomplete, misleading, or downright false. The negotiation fails; the problem remains unsolved. This chapter will help you read written arguments critically, including visual arguments, and the next chapter will help you write effective arguments.

CULTURE LANGUAGE The ways of reading and writing arguments described in this chapter and the next may be uncomfortable to you if your native culture approaches such writing differently. In some cultures, for example, a writer is expected to begin indirectly, to avoid asserting his or her opinion outright, or to establish a compromise rather than argue a position. In American academic and business settings, readers and writers look or aim for a well-articulated opinion, evidence gathered from many sources, and a direct and concise argument for the opinion.

8a Recognizing the elements of argument

Few arguments are an easy read. Most demand the attentive critical reading discussed in Chapter 7. (If you haven't read pp. 147–63, you should do so before continuing.) As a reader of argument, your purpose will almost always be the same: you'll want to know whether you should be convinced by the argument. This purpose focuses your attention on the elements that make an argument convincing, or not.

In a scheme adapted from the work of the British philosopher Stephen Toulmin, an argument has three main elements.

- **Claims:** positive statements that require support. In a written argument the central claim is stated outright in a **thesis statement** (see p. 28). This central claim is what the argument is about. For instance:

  In both its space and its equipment, the college's chemistry laboratory is outdated.

  Several minor claims, such as that the present equipment is inadequate, will contribute to the central assertion.

- **Evidence:** the facts, examples, expert opinions, and other information that support the claims. (Toulmin calls evidence *data* or *grounds,* terms that indicate both its specificity and its work as an argument's foundation.) Evidence to support the preceding claim might include the following:

  The present lab's age and size
  An inventory of equipment
  The testimony of chemistry professors

  Like the claims, the evidence is always stated outright.

Questions for critically reading an argument

- What **claims** does the writer make?
- What kinds and quality of **evidence** does the writer provide to support the claims?
- What **assumptions** underlie the argument, connecting evidence to claims? Are they clear and believable?
- What is the writer's **tone**? How does the writer use **language**?
- Is the writer **reasonable**?
- Is the argument **logical**? Does it contain any **fallacies**?
- Are you convinced? Why or why not?

- **Assumptions:** the writer's underlying (and often unstated) beliefs, opinions, principles, or inferences that tie the evidence to the claims. (Toulmin calls these assumptions *warrants*: they justify making the claims on the basis of the evidence provided.) For instance, the following assumption might connect the evidence of professors' testimony with the claim that a new lab is needed:

  Chemistry professors can reliably evaluate the present lab's quality.

In the following pages, we'll examine each of these elements along with several others: tone and language, reasonableness, and common errors in reasoning. Charlene Robinson's "Weighing the Costs" in the previous chapter (pp. 175–77) provides a good example of critically reading an argument for its claims, evidence, and assumptions.

8b Testing claims

The claims or assertions in an argument will likely state opinions, facts, beliefs, or prejudices. You'll need to distinguish among the kinds of statements and to analyze the definitions of terms.

1 Recognizing opinions

An **opinion** is a judgment based on facts and arguable on the basis of facts. Reasonable people could and probably do disagree over opinions, and they are potentially changeable: with more facts, a writer might change opinions partly or wholly.

The thesis statement of an effective argument is an opinion, often one of the following:

- **A claim about past or present reality:**

  In both its space and its equipment, the college's chemistry laboratory is outdated.

  Academic cheating increases with students' economic insecurity.

- **A claim of value:**

  The new room fees are unjustified given the condition of the dormitories.

  Computer music pirates undermine the system that encourages the very creation of music.

- **A recommendation for a course of action,** often a solution to a perceived problem:

  The college's outdated chemistry laboratory should be replaced incrementally over the next five years.

  Schools and businesses can help to resolve the region's traffic congestion by implementing car pools and rewarding participants.

The backbone of an argument consists of specific claims that support the thesis statement. These may be statements of opinion, too, or they may state facts or beliefs.

Opinions do not make arguments by themselves. As a critical reader, you must satisfy yourself that the writer has specified the evidence for the opinions and that the assumptions linking claims and evidence are clear and believable.

2 Recognizing facts

A **fact** may be a verifiable statement—that is, one that can be proved as true:

> Last year tuition increased by 16%.

Or it may be an inference from verifiable facts:

> Over their lifetimes, four-year-college graduates earn almost twice as much as high-school graduates.

A claim of fact does not work as the thesis of an argument. Although people often dispute facts, they are not fundamentally arguable because ultimately they can be verified. Facts have another important role in argument, providing crucial evidence for other claims (see p. 185).

3 Recognizing beliefs

A **belief** is a conviction based on cultural or personal faith, morality, or values:

> Abortion is legalized murder.
>
> Capital punishment is legalized murder.
>
> The primary goal of government should be to provide equality of opportunity for all.

Such statements are often called opinions because they express viewpoints, but unlike opinions they are not based on facts and other evidence. Since they cannot be disproved by facts or even contested on the basis of facts, they cannot serve as the central or supporting claims of an argument. However, beliefs can play a significant role in argument. Appeals to readers' beliefs can serve as a kind of evidence by tapping into emotions (see pp. 186 and 214–15), and beliefs often form the assumptions that link claims and evidence (see pp. 182 and 189).

4 Recognizing prejudices

One kind of assertion that has no place in argument is a **prejudice**, an opinion based on insufficient or unexamined evidence:

> Women are bad drivers.
> Fat people are jolly.
> Teenagers are irresponsible.
> Athletes are unintelligent.
> People who use wheelchairs have cognitive disabilities.

Unlike a belief, a prejudice is testable: it can be contested and disproved on the basis of facts. Very often, however, we form prejudices or accept them from others—parents, friends, the communications media—without questioning their meaning or testing their truth. Writers who display prejudice do not deserve your confidence and agreement.

When reading arguments that appear online, you should be especially vigilant for claims of belief or prejudice that pose as considered opinions. Anyone with a computer and an Internet connection can post anything online, without passing it through an editorial screening like that undergone by books and by articles in journals and magazines. The filtering of such material is entirely up to the reader.

5 Looking for defined terms

In any argument, but especially in arguments about abstract ideas, the clear and consistent definition of terms is essential. In the following claim, the writer is not clear about what she means by the crucial term *justice*:

> Over the past few decades, justice has deteriorated so badly that it almost does not exist anymore.

The word *justice* is **abstract**: it does not refer to anything specific or concrete and in fact has varied meanings. (The five definitions in *The American Heritage Dictionary* include "the principle of moral rightness" and "the administration and procedure of law.") When the writer specifies her meaning, her assertion is much clearer:

> If by *justice* we mean treating people fairly, punishing those who commit crimes, and protecting the victims of those crimes, then justice has deteriorated badly over the past few decades.

Writers who use highly abstract words such as *justice, equality,* and *success* have a responsibility to define them. If the word is important to the argument, such a definition may take an entire paragraph. As a reader you should evaluate the writer's definitions before you accept his or her assertions. (See p. 93 for more on definition.)

8c Weighing evidence

In argument, evidence demonstrates the validity of the writer's claims. If the evidence is inadequate or questionable, the claims are at best doubtful.

1 Recognizing kinds of evidence

Writers draw on several kinds of evidence to support their claims.

> **Evidence for argument**
>
> - **Facts:** verifiable statements
> - **Statistics:** facts expressed in numbers
> - **Examples:** specific cases
> - **Expert opinions:** the judgments of authorities
> - **Appeals to readers' beliefs or needs**

Facts

Facts are statements whose truth can be verified or inferred (see p. 183). Facts employing numbers are **statistics:**

> Of those polled, 47% stated a preference for a flat tax.
>
> In 2013 there were 1,369,532 men and women on active duty in the US armed forces.
>
> The average American household consists of 2.58 persons.

Numbers may be implied:

> Earth is closer to the sun than Saturn is.
> The cost of medical care is rising.

Or a fact may involve no numbers at all:

> The city council adjourned without taking a vote.
> The President vetoed the bill.

Examples

Examples are specific instances of the point being made, including historical precedents and personal experiences. The passage below uses a personal narrative as partial support for the claim in the first sentence:

> Besides broadening students' knowledge, required courses can also introduce students to possible careers that they otherwise would have known nothing about. Somewhat reluctantly, I enrolled in a psychology course to satisfy the requirement for work in social science. But what I learned in the course about human behavior has led me to consider becoming a clinical psychologist instead of an engineer.

Expert opinions

Expert opinions are the judgments formed by authorities on the basis of their examination of the facts. In the next passage the writer cites the opinion of an expert to support the opening claim:

> Despite the fact that affirmative action places some individuals at a disadvantage, it remains necessary to right the wrongs inflicted historically on whole groups of people. Howard Glickstein, a past director of the US Commission on Civil Rights, maintains that "it simply is not possible to achieve equality and fairness" unless the previous grounds for discrimination (such as sex, race, and national origin) are now considered as grounds for admission to schools and jobs (26).

As this passage illustrates, a citation of expert opinion should always refer you to the source, here indicated by the author's name, Glickstein, and the page number in parentheses, "(26)." Such a citation is also generally accompanied by a reference to the expert's credentials. See pages 611 and 623–24.

CULTURE LANGUAGE In some cultures a person with high standing in government, society, or organized religion may be considered an authority on many different subjects. In American schools and businesses, authority comes from learning and experience: the more knowledge a person demonstrates about a subject, the more authority he or she has. See page 188 on relevant evidence.

Appeals to beliefs or needs

A writer's **appeal to beliefs or needs** asks you to accept an assertion in part because you already accept it as true without evidence or because it coincides with your needs. Each of the following examples combines such an appeal (second sentence) with a summary of factual evidence (first sentence).

> Thus the chemistry laboratory is outdated in its equipment. In addition, its antiquated appearance shames the school, making it seem a second-rate institution. [Appeals to readers' belief that their school is or should be first-rate.]

> That police foot patrollers reduce crime has already been demonstrated. Such officers might also restore our sense that our neighborhoods are orderly, stable places. [Appeals to readers' need for order and stability.]

(For more on beliefs, see pp. 183–84. For more on appeals to emotion, see pp. 214–15.)

2 Judging the reliability of evidence

To be convinced by evidence, you should see it as reliable. The test of reliability for an appeal to beliefs or needs is specific to the situation: whether it is appropriate for the argument and correctly gauges how you, the reader, actually feel (see p. 215). With the other kinds of evidence, the standards are more general and apply to any argument.

Criteria for weighing evidence

- Is it **accurate:** trustworthy, exact, undistorted?
- Is it **relevant:** authoritative, pertinent, current?
- Is it **representative:** true to context?
- Is it **adequate:** plentiful, specific?

Accuracy

Accurate evidence is true:

- **It is drawn from trustworthy sources.**
- **It is quoted exactly.**
- **It is presented with the original meaning undistorted.**

Reading an argument in favor of gun control, you might expect the writer to cite some procontrol sources, which are undoubtedly biased. But you should also look for anticontrol sources (representing the opposite bias) and neutral sources (attempting to be unbiased). If the writer quotes an expert, the quotation should present the expert's true meaning, not just a few words that appear to support the writer's argument. (As a reader you may have difficulty judging the accuracy of quotations if you are not familiar with the expert's opinions.)

Not just opinions but also facts and examples may be misinterpreted or distorted. Suppose you were reading an argument for extending a three-year-old law allowing the police to stop vehicles randomly as a means of apprehending drunk drivers. If the author cited statistics showing that the number of drunk-driving accidents dropped in the first two years of the law but failed to note that the number rose back to the previous level in the third year, then the evidence would be distorted and thus inaccurate. You or any reader would be justified in questioning the entire argument, no matter how accurate the rest seemed.

Relevance

Relevant evidence pertains to the argument:

- **It comes from sources with authority on the subject.**
- **It relates directly to the point the writer is making.**
- **It is current.**

If you are reading an argument against a method of hazardous-waste disposal and the writer offers his church minister's opinion as evidence, you should accept the evidence only if the minister is an authority on the subject and her expertise is up to date. If she is an authority on Method A and not Method B, you should accept her authority only about Method A. If the writer relates his own experience of living near a hazardous-waste site, you should accept the story as relevant only if it pertains to his thesis. His authority in this case is that of a close observer and a citizen. (See also p. 195 on the fallacy of false authority.)

Representativeness

Representative evidence is true to its context:

- **It reflects the full range of the sample from which it is said to be drawn.**
- **It does not overrepresent any element of the sample.**

In an essay arguing that dormitories should stay open during school holidays, a writer might say that "the majority of the school's students favor leaving the dormitories open." But that writer would mislead you and other readers if the claim were based only on a poll of her roommates and dormitory neighbors. A few dormitory residents could not be said to represent the entire student body, particularly the nonresident students. To be representative, the poll would have to take in many more students and the respondents would have to reflect the proportions of resident and nonresident students on campus.

Adequacy

Adequate evidence is sufficient:

- **It is plentiful enough to support the writer's assertions.**
- **It is specific enough to support the writer's assertions.**

A writer arguing against animal abuse should not hope to win you over solely with statements about her personal experiences and claims of her opinions. Her experience may indeed be relevant evidence if, say, she has worked with animals or witnessed animal abuse. And her opinions are indeed important to the argument, so that you know what she thinks. But even together her experiences and opinions are not adequate evidence: they cannot substitute entirely for facts, nonpersonal examples, and the opinions of experts to demonstrate abuse and describe the scope of the problem.

8d Discovering assumptions

Assumptions connect evidence to claims: they are the opinions or beliefs that explain why a particular piece of evidence is relevant to a particular claim. As noted in Chapter 7 on critical thinking, assumptions are not flaws in arguments but necessities: we all acquire beliefs and opinions that shape our view of the world. Here are examples of beliefs that you, or people you know, may hold:

Criminals should be punished.
Hard work is virtuous.
Teachers' salaries are too low.

Assumptions are inevitable in argument, but they aren't neutral. For one thing, an assumption can weaken an argument. Say that a writer claims that real estate development should be prevented in your town. As evidence for this claim, the writer offers facts about past developments that have replaced older buildings. But the evidence is relevant to the claim only if you accept the writer's extreme assumptions that old buildings are always worthy and new development is always bad.

In such a case, the writer's bias may not even be stated. Hence a second problem: in arguments both sound and unsound, assumptions are not always explicit. Following are a claim and evidence forming a reasonable argument. What is the unstated assumption?

Claim

The town should create a plan to manage building preservation and new development.

Evidence

Examples of how such plans work; expert opinions on how and why both preservation and development are needed.

In this instance the assumption is that neither uncontrolled development nor zero development is healthy for the town. If you can accept this assumption, you should be able to accept the writer's claim (though you might still disagree over particulars).

Here are tips for dealing with assumptions:

Guidelines for analyzing assumptions

- **What are the assumptions underlying the argument?** How does the writer connect claims with evidence?
- **Are the assumptions believable?** Do they express your values? Do they seem true in your experience?
- **Are the assumptions consistent with one another?** Is the argument's foundation solid, not slippery?

8e Watching language, hearing tone

Tone is the expression of the writer's attitudes toward himself or herself, toward the subject, and toward the reader (see p. 14 for a discussion). Tone can tell you quite a bit about the writer's intentions, biases, and trustworthiness. For example:

> Some women cite personal growth as a reason for pursuing careers while raising children. Of course, they are equally concerned with the personal growth of the children they relegate to "child-care specialists" while they work.

In the second sentence this writer is being **ironic**, saying one thing while meaning another. The word *relegate* and the quotation marks with *child-care specialists* betray the writer's belief that working mothers may selfishly neglect their children for their own needs. Irony can sometimes be effective in argument, but here it marks the author as insincere in dealing with the complex issues of working parents and child care.

When reading arguments, you should be alert to the author's language. Look for words that **connote,** or suggest, certain attitudes and evoke certain responses in readers. (Notice your own responses to these word pairs with related meanings but different connotations: *daring/foolhardy, dislike/detest, glad/joyous, angry/rabid, freedom/license.*) Connotative language is no failure in argument; indeed, the strongest arguments use it skillfully to appeal to the hearts of readers as well as their minds (see pp. 215–16). But be suspicious if the language runs counter to the substance of the argument.

Look also for evasive words. **Euphemisms**, such as *attack of a sexual nature* for "rape" or *peace-keeping force* for a war-making army, are supposedly inoffensive substitutes for words that may frighten or offend readers (see pp. 502–03). In argument, though, they are sometimes used to hide or twist the truth. An honest, forthright arguer will avoid them.

Finally, watch carefully for sexist, racist, and other biased language that reveals deep ignorance or, worse, entrenched prejudice on the part of the writer. Obvious examples are *broad* for woman and *fag* for homosexual. (See pp. 503–05 for more on such language.)

8f Judging reasonableness

The **reasonableness** of an argument is the sense you get as a reader that the author is being fair and sincere. The reasonable writer does not conceal or distort facts, hide prejudices, mask belief as opinion, manipulate you with language, or resort to any of dozens of devices used unconsciously by those who don't know better and deliberately by those who do.

Reasonableness involves all the elements of argument examined so far: claims, evidence, assumptions, and language. In addition, the fair, sincere argument always avoids so-called fallacies (covered in the next section), and it acknowledges the opposition.

Judging whether a writer deals adequately with his or her opposition is a fairly simple matter for the reader of argument. By definition, an arguable issue has more than one side. Even if you have no preconceptions about a subject, you will know that another side exists. If the writer pretends otherwise or dismisses the opposition too quickly, you are justified in questioning the honesty and fairness of the argument. (For the more complicated business of *writing* an acknowledgment of opposing views, see pp. 216–17.)

Exercise 8.1 Reading arguments critically

Following are two brief arguments. Though not directly opposed, the two arguments do represent different stances on environmental issues. Read each argument critically, following the process outlined in Chapter 7 (pp. 147–63) and answering the questions in the box on page 182 (questions about claims, evidence, assumptions, and the other elements of argument). Develop your responses in writing so that you can refer to them for later exercises and class discussion.

The Environmental Crisis Is Not Our Fault

I am as responsible as most eco-citizens: I bike everywhere; I don't own a car; I recycle newspapers, bottles, cans, and plastics; I have a vegetable garden in the summer; I buy organic products; and I put all vegetable waste into my backyard compost bin, probably the only one in all of Greenwich Village. But I don't at the same time believe that I am saving the planet, or in fact doing anything of much consequence about the various eco-crises around us. What's more, I don't even believe that if "all of us" as individuals started doing the same it would make any but the slightest difference. 1

Leave aside ozone depletion and rain forest destruction—those are patently corporate crimes that no individual actions can remedy to any degree. Take, instead, energy consumption in this country. In the most recent figures, residential consumption was 7.2% of the total, commercial 5.5%, and industrial 23.3%; of the remainder, 27.8% was transportation (about one-third of it by private car) and 36.3% was electric generation (about one-third for residential use). Individual energy use, in sum, was something like 28% of total consumption. Although you and I cutting down on energy consumption would have some small effect (and should be done), it is surely the energy consumption of industry and other large institutions such as government and agribusiness that needs to be addressed first. And it is industry and government that must be forced to explain what their consumption is for, what is produced by it, how necessary it is, and how it can be drastically reduced. 2

The point is that the ecological crisis is essentially beyond "our" control, as citizens or householders or consumers or even voters. It is not something that can be halted by recycling or double-pane insulation. It is the inevitable by-product of our modern industrial civilization, 3 dominated by capitalist production and consumption and serviced and protected by various institutions of government, federal to local. It cannot possibly be altered or reversed by simple individual actions, even by the actions of the millions who take part in Earth Day—even if they all go home and fix their refrigerators and from then on walk to work. Nothing less than a drastic overhaul of this civilization and an abandonment of its ingrained gods—progress, growth, exploitation, technology, materialism, anthropocentricity, and power—will do anything substantial to halt our path to environmental destruction, and it's hard to see how life-style solutions will have an effect on that.

What I find truly pernicious about such solutions is that they get people thinking they are actually making a difference and doing their part to halt the destruction of the earth: "There, I've taken all the bottles to the recycling center and used my string bag at the grocery store; I guess that'll take care of global warming." It is the kind of thing that diverts people from the hard truths and hard choices and hard actions, from the recognition that they have to take on the larger forces of society—corporate and governmental—where true power, and true destructiveness, lie. 4

And to the argument that, well, you have to start somewhere to raise people's consciousness, I would reply that this individualistic approach does not in fact raise consciousness. It does not move people beyond their old familiar liberal perceptions of the world, it does nothing to challenge the belief in technofix or write-your-Congressperson solutions, and it does not begin to provide them with the new vocabulary and modes of thought necessary for a true change of consciousness. We need, for example, to think of recycling centers not as the answer to our waste problems, but as a confession that the system of packaging and production in this society is out of control. Recycling centers are like hospitals; they are the institutions at the end of the cycle that take care of problems that would never exist if ecological criteria had operated at the beginning of the cycle. Until we have those kinds of understandings, we will not do anything with consciousness except reinforce it with the same misguided ideas that created the crisis. 5

—Kirkpatrick Sale

Global Warming Statists Threaten Our Liberty

Life, liberty, and the pursuit of happiness—"unalienable rights" cited by our Founding Fathers in the Declaration of Independence—are now at risk as left-wing activists seek to curtail our liberties and personal choices to save the planet from supposedly man-made global warming. 1

No one is saying global climate change doesn't exist. We all know the hot era of the dinosaurs later gave way to the frigid Ice Age. Throughout recorded human history, with and without the presence of factories and other factors blamed for today's alleged rising temperatures, there have been many warming and cooling trends. 2

What is unresolved is the role man actually plays in climate change. It is easy to be skeptical of the man-made global warming hysterics when the scientific data remain inconclusive and uncontrollable events, such as volcanic eruptions, can do more harm to the atmosphere than man. 3

Despite all the ambiguity, our liberties are at the peril of this dubious theory. 4

Cars and trucks are at the top of the leftist hit list. Special interest groups' attacks, particularly on the SUV, spurred lawmakers to dictate the type of cars and trucks available for consumers in the new energy bill by mandating increased vehicle gas mileage. To meet the proposed increase in the corporate average fuel economy (CAFE) standard of 35 miles per gallon, vehicles will inevitably become smaller and lighter. Consumers who need or prefer bigger and safer vehicles will have fewer choices as manufacturers struggle to meet new government fuel mandates. As a result, the freedom of consumer choice will be greatly diminished. 5

Even lighting your house is now in the crosshairs. Politicians and activists want to invade our homes and empty our wallets when they call for replacing incandescent light bulbs with more costly and energy-efficient compact fluorescent light bulbs (CFLs). To remove any element of consumer choice in the matter, the recent passage of the energy bill will phase out the old bulbs and force consumers to purchase only the federally approved CFLs. While CFLs are said to last longer and reduce power-plant emissions of carbon dioxide, they have a number of drawbacks. Not only is the initial cost of a CFL bulb up to ten times higher, but they emit far less light. CFLs also contain the toxic element mercury, which means they may require special means of disposal and pose a health risk should they break. 6

What you eat is also a target. Animal rights groups want people to adopt a vegan diet because they consider farm animals a significant source of "greenhouse gases." People for the Ethical Treatment of Animals (PETA) is even criticizing Al Gore—who won the Nobel Peace Prize for his global warming activism—for ignoring this alleged connection. The ads show an image of Gore holding a chicken drumstick with a tagline: "Too Chicken to Go Vegetarian? Meat Is the No. 1 Cause of Global Warming." 7

Despite the numerous flaws and ambiguities in trying to link human behavior and global warming, activists and their allies in government use emotion and alarmism to make their case. They are seeking to cut off any reasonable debate and silence their critics by saying these people are motivated by corporate and personal greed and don't care about pollution. That, however, is hardly the case. 8

Critics of the global warming agenda are motivated instead by a love of freedom and civil liberties. They want a discussion based on logic and facts that will address any problems without depriving us of liberty and personal choice. They do not want to sacrifice our way of life based on fears of an unproven theory. 9

After all, the loss of liberty is a greater cause of alarm than global warming. 10

—Deneen Borelli, *The National Center for Public Policy Research*

8g Recognizing fallacies

Fallacies—errors in argument—fall into two groups. Some evade the issue of the argument. Others treat the argument as if it were much simpler than it is.

1 Recognizing evasions

The central claim of an argument defines an issue or answers a question: Should real estate development be controlled? Should drug testing be mandatory in the workplace? An effective argument faces the central issue squarely with relevant opinions, beliefs, and evidence. An ineffective argument dodges the issue.

Begging the question

A writer **begs the question** by treating an opinion that is open to question as if it were already proved or disproved. In essence, the writer begs readers to accept his or her ideas from the start.

> The college library's expenses should be reduced by cutting subscriptions to useless periodicals. [Begged questions: Are some of the library's periodicals useless? Useless to whom?]
>
> The fact is that political campaign financing is too corrupt to be reformed. [Begged questions: How corrupt is campaign financing? Does corruption, even if extensive, put campaign financing beyond reform?]

Non sequitur

In a **non sequitur** a writer asserts or implies a connection between ideas when no logical relation exists. *Non sequitur* means "it does not follow" in Latin: the second idea does not follow from the first. Usually the problem is an unstated assumption that links the ideas but is false, as in these examples:

> She uses a wheelchair, so she must be unhappy. [Unstated assumption: People who use wheelchairs are unhappy.]
>
> Kathleen Newsome has my vote for mayor because she has the best-run campaign organization. [Unstated assumption: A good campaign organization means that the candidate is well qualified for the job.]

Red herring

A **red herring** is literally a kind of fish that might be drawn across a path to distract a bloodhound from a scent it's following. In argument, a red herring is an irrelevant issue intended to distract readers from the relevant issues. The writer changes the subject rather than pursue the argument.

> A campus speech code is essential to protect students, who already have enough problems coping with rising tuition. [Tuition costs and speech codes are different subjects. What protections do students need that a speech code will provide?]
>
> Instead of developing a campus speech code that will infringe on students' First Amendment rights, administrators should be figuring out how to prevent yet another tuition increase. [Again, tuition costs and speech codes are different subjects. How would the code infringe on rights?]

Checklist of fallacies

Evasions

- **Begging the question:** treating an opinion that is open to question as if it were already proved or disproved.
- **Non sequitur** ("it does not follow"): drawing a conclusion based on a false assumption.
- **Red herring:** introducing an irrelevant issue to distract readers.
- **False authority:** citing as expert opinion the views of a person who is not an expert.
- **Inappropriate appeals:**

  Appealing to readers' fear or pity.
  Snob appeal: appealing to readers' wish to be like those who are more intelligent, famous, rich, and so on.
  Bandwagon: appealing to readers' wish to be part of the group.
  Flattery: appealing to readers' intelligence, taste, and so on.
  Argument ad populum ("to the people"): appealing to readers' general values, such as patriotism or love of family.
  Argument ad hominem ("to the man"): attacking the opponent rather than the opponent's argument.

Oversimplifications

- **Hasty generalization (jumping to a conclusion):** asserting an opinion based on too little evidence.
- **Sweeping generalization:** asserting an opinion as applying to all instances when it may apply to some, or to none. **Absolute statements** and **stereotypes** are variations.
- **Reductive fallacy:** generally, oversimplifying causes and effects.
- **Post hoc fallacy:** assuming that *A* caused *B* because *A* preceded *B*.
- **Either/or fallacy (false dilemma):** reducing a complicated question to two alternatives.
- **False analogy:** exaggerating the similarities in an analogy or ignoring key differences.

False authority

Arguments often cite as evidence the opinions of people who are experts on the subject (see p. 186). But writers use **false authority** when they cite as an expert someone whose expertise is doubtful or nonexistent.

> Jason Bing, a recognized expert in corporate finance, maintains that pharmaceutical companies do not test their products thoroughly enough. [Bing's expertise in corporate finance bears no apparent relation to the testing of pharmaceuticals.]

> According to Helen Liebowitz, the Food and Drug Administration has approved sixty dangerous drugs in the last two years alone. [Who is Helen Liebowitz? On what authority does she make this claim?]

Inappropriate appeals

Appeals to readers' emotions are common in effective arguments. But such appeals must be relevant and must supplement rather than substitute for facts, examples, and other evidence. The following appeals do not meet these tests:

- **An appeal to fear or pity** ignores the real issue by stirring up irrelevant emotions in readers.

  By electing Susan Clark to the city council, you will prevent the city's economic collapse. [Trades on people's fears. Can Clark singlehandedly prevent economic collapse? Is collapse even likely?]

  She should not have to pay taxes because she is an aged widow with no friends or relatives. [Appeals to people's pity. Should age and loneliness, rather than income, determine a person's tax obligation?]

- **Snob appeal** sidesteps the real issue by inviting readers to accept an assertion in order to be identified with others they admire.

  As any literate person knows, James Joyce is the best twentieth-century novelist. [But what qualities of Joyce's writing make him a superior novelist?]

  Blake Lively has an account at Big City Bank, and so should you. [A celebrity's endorsement does not guarantee the worth of a product, a service, an idea, or anything else.]

- **The bandwagon approach** tries to persuade readers to accept an assertion because everybody else does.

  As everyone knows, marijuana use leads to heroin addiction. [What is the evidence?]

- **Flattery** compliments readers' intelligence, in a way inviting them to join a conspiracy.

  We all understand campus problems well enough to see the disadvantages of such a policy. [What are the disadvantages of the policy?]

- **Ad populum ("to the people")** asks readers to accept a conclusion based on shared values or even prejudices and nothing else.

  Any truly patriotic American will support the President's action. [But why is the action worth taking?]

- **Ad hominem ("to the man")** addresses *not* the pros and cons of the issue itself but the real or imagined negative qualities of the people who hold the opposing view.

  One of the scientists has been treated for emotional problems, so his pessimism about nuclear waste merits no attention. [Do the scientist's previous emotional problems invalidate his current views?]

2 Recognizing oversimplifications

To **oversimplify** is to conceal or ignore complexities in a vain attempt to create a neater, more convincing argument than reality allows.

Hasty generalization

A **hasty generalization**, also called **jumping to a conclusion**, is a claim based on too little evidence or on evidence that is unrepresentative. (See also p. 188.)

> It is disturbing that several of the school shooters were users of violent video games. Obviously, these games can breed violence, and they should be banned. [A few cases do not establish the relation between the games and violent behavior. Most people who play violent video games do not behave violently.]

> From the way it handled this complaint, we can assume that the consumer protection office has little intention of protecting consumers. [One experience with the office does not demonstrate its intention or overall performance.]

Sweeping generalization

Whereas a hasty generalization comes from inadequate evidence, a **sweeping generalization** probably is not supportable at all. One kind of sweeping generalization is the **absolute statement** involving words such as *all, always, never,* and *no one* that allow no exceptions. Rarely can evidence support such terms. Moderate words such as *some, sometimes, rarely,* and *few* are more reasonable.

Another common sweeping generalization is the **stereotype**, a conventional and oversimplified characterization of a group of people.

> People who live in cities are unfriendly.
> Californians are fad-crazy.
> Women are emotional.
> Men can't express their feelings.

(See also pp. 503–05 on sexist and other biased language.)

Reductive fallacy

The **reductive fallacy** oversimplifies (or reduces) the relation between causes and their effects. The fallacy (sometimes called **oversimplification**) often involves linking two events as if one caused the other directly, whereas the causes may be more complex or the relation may not exist at all. For example:

> Poverty causes crime. [If so, then why do people who are not poor commit crimes? And why aren't all poor people criminals?]

> The better a school's athletic facilities are, the worse its academic programs are. [The sentence assumes a direct cause-and-effect link between athletics and scholarship.]

Post hoc fallacy

Related to the reductive fallacy is the assumption that because *A* preceded *B*, then *A* must have caused *B*. This fallacy is called in Latin *post hoc, ergo propter hoc,* meaning "after this, therefore because of this," or the **post hoc fallacy** for short.

> In the two months since he took office, Mayor Holcomb has allowed crime in the city to increase by 12%. [The increase in crime is probably attributable to conditions existing before Holcomb took office.]
>
> The town council erred in permitting the adult bookstore to open, for shortly afterward two women were assaulted. [It cannot be assumed without evidence that the women's assailants visited or were influenced by the bookstore.]

Either/or fallacy

In the **either/or fallacy** (also called **false dilemma**), the writer assumes that a complicated question has only two answers, one good and one bad, both bad, or both good.

> City police officers are either brutal or corrupt. [Most city police officers are neither.]
>
> Either we permit mandatory drug testing in the workplace or productivity will continue to decline. [Productivity is not necessarily dependent on drug testing.]

False analogy

An **analogy** is a comparison between two essentially unlike things for the purpose of definition or illustration. In arguing by analogy, a writer draws a likeness between things on the basis of a single shared feature and then extends the likeness to other features. For instance, the "war on drugs" equates a battle against a foe with a program to eradicate (or at least reduce) sales and use of illegal drugs. Both involve an enemy, a strategy of overpowering the enemy, a desired goal, officials in uniform, and other similarities.

Analogy can only illustrate a point, never prove it: things that are similar in one respect are not *necessarily* alike in other respects. A **false analogy** assumes such a complete likeness. Here is the analogy of the war on drugs taken to its false extreme:

> To win the war on drugs, we must wage more of a military-style operation. Prisoners of war are locked up without the benefit of a trial by jury, and drug dealers should be, too. Soldiers shoot their enemy on sight, and officials who encounter big drug operators should be allowed to shoot them, too. Military traitors may be executed, and corrupt law enforcers could be, too.

Exercise 8.2 Identifying and revising fallacies

Fallacies tend to appear together, as each of the following sentences illustrates. Identify at least one fallacy in each sentence. Then revise the sentences to make them more reasonable.

1. The American government can sell nuclear technology to nonnuclear nations, so why can't individuals, who after all have a God-given right to earn a living as they see fit?
2. A successful marriage demands a maturity that no one under twenty-five possesses.
3. Students' persistent complaints about the grading system prove that it is unfair.
4. People watch television because they are too lazy to talk or read or because they want mindless escape from their lives.
5. Racial tension is bound to occur when people with different backgrounds are forced to live side by side.

Exercise 8.3 Identifying fallacies in arguments

Analyze the two arguments on pages 191–93 for fallacies. To what extent do any fallacies weaken either argument? Explain.

Exercise 8.4 Identifying fallacies online

At a news Web site such as *Huffington Post* or *Time*, find an article with reader comments about drug testing, environmental pollution, violence in the media, or any other subject that interests you and that is debatable. Read through the arguments made in the article and the comments, noting the fallacies you see. List the fallacious statements as well as the types of fallacies they illustrate, keeping in mind that a given statement may illustrate more than a single type.

8h Reading visual arguments

Arguments can be visual as well as verbal. Advertisements often provide the most vivid and memorable examples of visual argument, but writers in almost every field—from astronomy to music to physiology—support their claims with photographs, charts, graphs, diagrams, and other figures.

Like a written argument, a visual argument has three main elements: claims, evidence, and assumptions. To read visual arguments critically, you analyze all three elements.

1 Testing claims

Claims are positive statements that require support (see pp. 181, 182–85). In a visual argument, claims may be made by composition as well as by content, with or without accompanying words. Here are a few examples of visual claims:

Visual A magnetic sticker shaped like a ribbon and decorated with the colors and symbols of the American flag, positioned prominently on a car.

Claim I support American troops overseas, and you should, too.

Visual A photograph framing hundreds of chickens crammed into small cages, resembling familiar images of World War II concentration camps.

Claim Commercial poultry-raising practices are cruel and unethical.

Visual A chart with dramatically contrasting bars that represent the optimism, stress, and weight reported by people before and after they participated in a program of daily walking.

Claim Daily exercise leads to a healthier and happier life.

Visual A cartoon featuring affluent-looking young adults on an affluent-looking college campus, conversing and frowning sadly as they gaze downhill at rough-looking teens in a dilapidated schoolyard. The caption reads, "Yes, it's sad what's happening to schools today. But everyone knows that throwing money at the problem isn't the solution."

Claim Better funding makes for better schools.

The following advertisement is one in the "Army Strong" series that the United States Army runs for recruitment. As noted in the annotations, the ad makes several claims both in the photograph and in the text.

Claims in a visual

Visual claim: Serving in the US Army requires technical knowledge and skill.

Visual claim: The US Army provides soldiers with technical knowledge and skill.

Text claim: Service in the US Army can give soldiers technical expertise that they may have thought was beyond them.

BELIEVING IN YOURSELF IS STRONG.
ACHIEVING WHAT YOU NEVER
BELIEVED POSSIBLE IS ARMY STRONG.
There's strong. And then there's Army Strong.
There is no limit to the things you can learn from one of over 150 career opportunities available to you in the Army. You can also receive money for college.
Find out more at goarmy.com/strong.
U.S.ARMY
ARMY STRONG.

Advertisement by the United States Army

2 Weighing evidence

The kinds of evidence provided in visuals parallel those found in written arguments (see pp. 185–87):

- **Facts can be verified by observation or research.** In visual arguments facts may be data, as in a graph showing a five-year rise in oil prices or in the text of the US Army advertisement promising "one of over 150 career opportunities." Facts may also be based on or inferred from data, as in the statement that the army provides "money for college."
- **Examples illustrate and reinforce a point.** Visual arguments often focus on an instance of the argument's claims. In the army ad, the soldier using and surrounded by technical equipment is an example supporting the claim that the army gives soldiers technical training.
- **Expert opinions** are the findings of subject-matter authorities based on their research and experience. A visual argument might present a chart from an expert showing a trend in, say, unemployment among high school graduates.
- **Appeals to beliefs or needs** reinforce readers' values or truths. Many visual arguments appeal to beliefs about how things ought to be (for instance, an antidrug ad featuring a teenager refusing to give into peer pressure) or how things should not be (a Web site for an antihunger campaign featuring images of emaciated children).

When you read a visual as an argument, judge the evidence with the same criteria as for a written argument. Use the following questions:

- **Is the evidence accurate?** Analyze a visual for its fairness, precision, and trustworthiness. For example, a graph claiming to show changes in college living expenses between 2004 and 2014 should identify the source and purpose of the research, supply data for all the years, and clarify the definition of *living expenses* (the cost of room and board only, or transportation, recreation, and other expenses as well?).
- **Is the evidence relevant and adequate?** Ask whether the visual pertains to the claims made in the larger argument and sufficiently demonstrates its own claims. In an article on eating disorders, for instance, a relevant and adequate visual might be a graph showing average weights and heights of people who have anorexia. However, a photograph of a skinny celebrity would be merely sensationalistic unless the subject had publicly confirmed that her low weight resulted from an eating disorder.
- **Does the evidence represent the context?** Check whether the visual reflects the full range of the sample it's drawn from and

does not overrepresent or hide important elements of the subject. For example, the US Army ad conveys the soldier's ease and competence with technical equipment, which is presumably the result of his training. At the same time, the photo and text do not address the possible disadvantages of military service, such as rigorous training, separation from family, injury, or even death.

The annotation on the following graph demonstrates one way of analyzing visual evidence for this claim: *After a steady decline since 1990, the teen birthrate has begun to rise again.* The data come from the Centers for Disease Control and Prevention (CDC), a US agency and a reputable source. But the data are incomplete, so the graph is misleading.

Incomplete and unreliable evidence in a visual

The graph shows a decrease in birthrate followed by an increase, as claimed, but the last date, 2007, is not very recent. In fact, later data show continuing *decreases* in the birthrate—facts that undercut the claim about a rise in teen births.

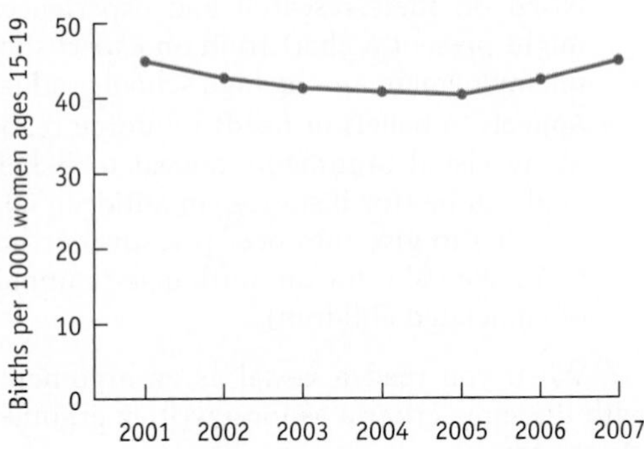

3 Discovering assumptions

Like a written argument, a visual argument is based on **assumptions**—the creator's ideas, often unstated, about why the evidence relates to the claims (see p. 189). In visual arguments many assumptions involve the creator's beliefs about the audience, as detailed below. The examples analyze the ad for the US Army on page 200.

- **Who readers are and where they will see the argument.** The army ad has appeared in magazines with young adult readers who might be interested in the possibility of training, education, and life change.
- **What readers already know about the subject.** Although most readers are familiar with the military, the army presumably considers readers less familiar with its opportunities for training and life change.

- **How familiar readers are with the purpose, format, and style of the argument.** With hundreds of print, TV, and online ads, the "Army Strong" campaign has become a fixture in US culture. Each new ad fits into the framework established by its predecessors.
- **Whether readers are likely to lean toward the argument's claims.** The advertiser clearly assumes that the photograph in the ad will attract the attention of young men and women who are interested in technology. At the same time, it seems to assume that readers need to be persuaded to join the army.
- **What kinds of information, ideas, and images readers will find persuasive.** The advertiser seems to assume that a strictly factual claim about the benefits of joining the army would not be persuasive enough to readers, so it combines a headline and photo that emphasize appealing qualities of competence, strength, and personal development.

4 Recognizing fallacies

Fallacies, or errors in argument, are sometimes accidental, but they are often used deliberately to manipulate readers' responses. All the fallacies of written arguments discussed on pages 193–98 may appear in visual arguments as well. Here we'll focus on examples of the two main categories.

Evasions

Evasions attempt to deflect the reader from the central claim of the argument. One evasion is **snob appeal**, inviting readers to think or be like someone they admire. Look again at the US Army ad on page 200. The soldier is clearly comfortable and competent with the equipment, and the ad appeals to the reader's wish to be someone who is equally as capable and fulfilled. If you join the US Army, the ad says subtly, you too may become strong. The ad does have some substance in its specific and verifiable claim of "over 150 career opportunities" and "money for college," but the soldier in quiet command of his equipment makes a stronger claim.

Oversimplifications

Oversimplifications imply that subjects are less complex than they are. An example is the **hasty generalization**, a claim that is based on too little evidence or that misrepresents the facts. The fallacy appears in the following graph, which is intended to support this claim: *After a sharp rise in 2006 and 2007, the teen birthrate plummeted over the next five years*. At first, the graph appears to demonstrate the claim, but a close look reveals that it—as well as the claim it supports—misrepresents the data.

The vertical axis lacks a zero point and covers a small span, thus misrepresenting and exaggerating the changes in the birthrate.

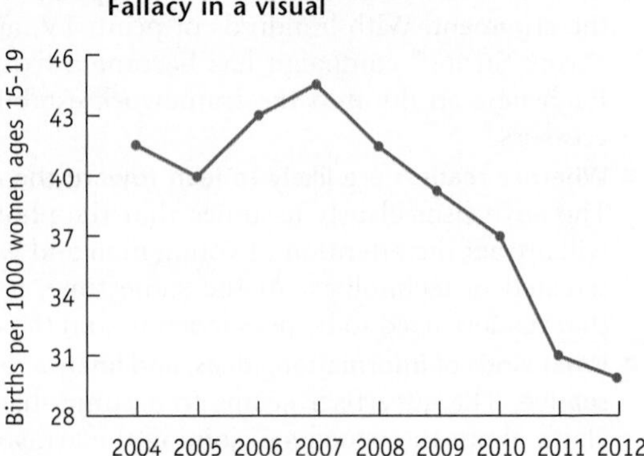

The corrected graph below uses exactly the same data, but presented without manipulation they tell a story of a slight rise and a gradual decrease in the birthrate.

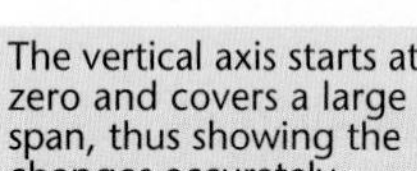
The vertical axis starts at zero and covers a large span, thus showing the changes accurately.

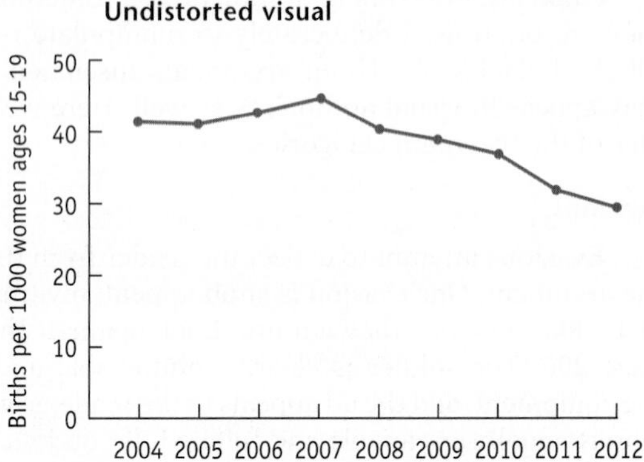

Exercise 8.5 Reading a visual argument

The advertisement on the facing page (a billboard) is from a campaign to discourage drunk driving. Examine the ad closely and jot down your answers to the following questions.

1. Who appears to be the intended audience?
2. What claim does the ad make about language and behavior?
3. What evidence supports the claim? How effective is it?
4. What assumptions underlie the argument, connecting evidence to claims?
5. How does the visual organization (the repetition of the photograph and the placement of the text) make the argument more or less effective?
6. Is the argument persuasive to you? Why or why not?

Exercise 8.6 Identifying fallacies in visual arguments

Locate a current or historical source with extreme views on a subject, such as a sensationalist tabloid newspaper or an example of wartime propaganda (from any nation or era). Photocopy or print a visual that seems especially rife with fallacies and, referring to the complete list of fallacies on page 195, find as many as possible in the visual. The following sites can help you begin your search:

Tabloids

National Enquirer (US): *nationalenquirer.com*
Daily Mail (Great Britain): *www.dailymail.co.uk*

World War II propaganda

Northwestern University (American images): *digital.library.northwestern.edu/wwii-posters*

Calvin College (German images): *www.calvin.edu/academic/cas/gpa*

9 Writing an Argument

Chapter essentials

- Find an appropriate subject for argument (next page).
- Conceive a thesis statement (p. 207).
- Analyze your purpose and audience (p. 207).
- Use inductive and deductive reasoning (p. 208).
- Use evidence responsibly (p. 213).
- Reach readers by making appropriate appeals, acknowledging opposing views, and establishing common ground (p. 214).
- Organize and revise your argument (pp. 218 and 219).
- Learn from a sample argument (p. 220).

Visit MyWritingLab™ for more resources on writing an argument.

In composing an argument, you try to establish common ground with readers so that they will agree with your opinion or accept your solution. Using critical thinking, you develop and test your own ideas. Using a variety of techniques, you engage readers in an attempt to narrow the distance between your views and theirs.

9a Finding a subject

An argument subject must be arguable—that is, reasonable people will disagree over the subject and will be able to support their positions with evidence. This sentence implies a number of *dos* and *don'ts*:

Tests for an argument subject

A good subject:

- **Concerns a matter of opinion**—a conclusion drawn from evidence.
- **Can be disputed:** others might take a different position.
- ***Will* be disputed:** it is controversial.
- **Is something you care about and know about or want to research.**
- **Is narrow enough to argue in the space and time available.**

A bad subject:

- **Cannot be disputed** because it concerns a fact, such as the distance to Saturn or the functions of the human liver.
- **Cannot be disputed** because it concerns a personal preference or belief, such as a liking for a certain vacation spot or a moral commitment to vegetarianism.
- ***Will not* be disputed** because few if any disagree over it—the virtues of a secure home, for instance.

Additional help with subjects for writing appears earlier in this book:

- **Working with a specific assignment,** pages 6–7.
- **Working with a general assignment,** page 7.
- **Narrowing a subject to a question,** pages 7–9.

CULTURE LANGUAGE Choosing a subject for argument may seem difficult if you're not familiar with what people in the United States find debatable. One way to find a subject is to read a newspaper or a news Web site every day for at least a week, looking for issues that involve or interest you. Following the development of the issues in articles, editorials, letters to the editor, and reader comments will give you a sense of how controversial the issues are, what the positions are, and what your position might be.

Exercise 9.1 Finding a subject for argument

Explain why each subject below is or is not appropriate for argument. Refer to the box on the previous page if you need help.

1. Granting of athletic scholarships
2. Care of automobile tires
3. Censoring the Web sites of hate groups
4. History of the town park
5. Housing for the homeless
6. Billboards in urban residential areas or in rural areas
7. Animal testing for cosmetics research
8. Cats versus dogs as pets
9. Ten steps in recycling wastepaper
10. Benefits of being a parent

9b Conceiving a thesis statement

The **thesis** is the main idea of your paper (see pp. 28–33). In an argument the **thesis statement** makes the claim that you want your readers to accept or act on. Here are two thesis statements on the same subject:

> The new room fees are unjustified given the condition of the dormitories.
>
> The administration should postpone the new room fees at least until conditions in the dormitories are improved.

Your thesis statement must satisfy the same requirements as your subject (see the box on the previous page). But it must also specify the basis for your claim. In both thesis statements above, the basis for protesting the room fees is that the dorms are in poor condition.

Note that the writer of either of these arguments must clarify the definition of *condition(s)* if the argument is to be clear and reasonable. Always take pains to define abstract and general terms that are central to your argument, preferably in or just after the thesis statement. (See pp. 184–85.)

Exercise 9.2 Conceiving a thesis statement

For each subject in Exercise 9.1 that you deemed arguable, draft a tentative thesis statement that specifies the basis for an argument. If you prefer, choose five arguable subjects of your own and draft a thesis statement for each one. One thesis statement should interest you enough to develop into a complete argument in later exercises.

9c Analyzing your purpose and your audience

Your purpose in argument is, broadly, to engage readers so that you can convince them of your position or persuade them to act. But arguments have more specific purposes as well, such as the following:

To strengthen the commitment of existing supporters
To win new supporters from the undecided or uninformed
To get the opposition to reconsider
To inspire supporters to act
To deter the undecided from acting

It's no accident that each of these purposes characterizes the audience (*existing supporters, the undecided,* and so on). In argument, even more than in other kinds of writing, achieving your purpose depends on the response of your readers, so you need a sense of who they are and where they stand. The "Questions about audience" on pages 12–13 can help you identify readers' knowledge, beliefs, and other pertinent information. In addition, you need to know how readers stand on your subject—not only whether they agree or disagree generally, but also which specific assertions they will find more or less convincing.

Your purpose can help you fill in this information. If you decide to address supporters or opponents, you essentially select readers with certain inclinations and ignore other readers who may tune in. If you decide to win new supporters from those who are undecided on your topic, you'll have to imagine skeptical readers who will be convinced only by an argument that is detailed, logical, and fair. Like you when you read an argument critically, these skeptical readers seek to be reasoned with, not manipulated into a position or hammered over the head.

Exercise 9.3 Analyzing purpose and audience

Specify a purpose and a likely audience for the thesis statement you chose to develop in Exercise 9.2. What do purpose and audience suggest about the way you should develop the argument?

9d Using reason

As a reader of argument, you seek evidence for the writer's claims and clear reasoning about the relationship of evidence to claims. As a writer of argument, you seek to provide what the reader needs in a way that furthers your case.

The thesis of your argument is a conclusion you reach by reasoning about evidence. Two common processes of reasoning are induction and deduction—methods of thinking that you use all the time even if you don't know their names. You can think of induction and deduction as two different ways of moving among claims, evidence, and assumptions—the elements of argument derived from Stephen Toulmin's work (pp. 181–82).

1 Reasoning inductively

When you're about to buy a car, you consult friends, relatives, and consumer guides before deciding what kind of car to buy. Using **inductive reasoning**, you make specific observations about cars (your evidence) and you induce, or infer, a **generalization** (or claim) that Model X is the most reliable.

Writing a paper on the effectiveness of print advertising, you might also use inductive reasoning:

First analyze statistics on advertising in print, on the Web, and in other media (evidence).

Then read comments by advertisers, publishers, and others who place and sell advertising (more evidence).

Finally, form a conclusion that print remains the most cost-effective advertising medium (generalization).

This reasoning builds from the evidence to the claim, with assumptions connecting evidence to claim. By predicting something about the unknown based on what you know, you create new knowledge out of old.

Inductive reasoning

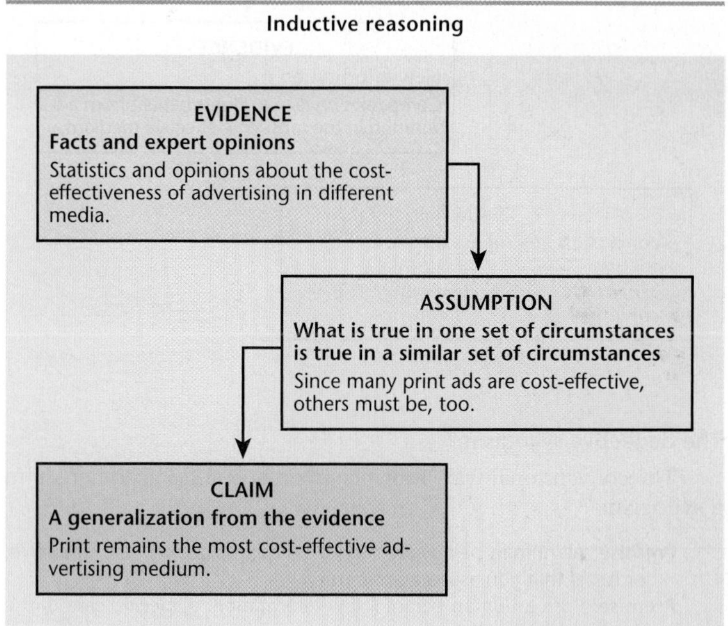

EVIDENCE
Facts and expert opinions
Statistics and opinions about the cost-effectiveness of advertising in different media.
ASSUMPTION
What is true in one set of circumstances is true in a similar set of circumstances
Since many print ads are cost-effective, others must be, too.
CLAIM
A generalization from the evidence
Print remains the most cost-effective advertising medium.

The more evidence you accumulate, the more probable it is that your generalization is true. Note, however, that absolute certainty is not possible. At some point you must *assume* that your evidence justifies your generalization, for yourself and your readers. Most errors in inductive reasoning involve oversimplifying either the evidence or the generalization. See pages 193–98 on fallacies.

2 Reasoning deductively

You use **deductive reasoning** when you proceed from your generalization that Model X is the most reliable car to your own specific circumstances (you want to buy a car) to the conclusion (or claim) that you should buy a Model X car. Like induction, deduction uses the elements of argument—claims, evidence, and assumptions—but with it you apply old information to new.

Deductive reasoning

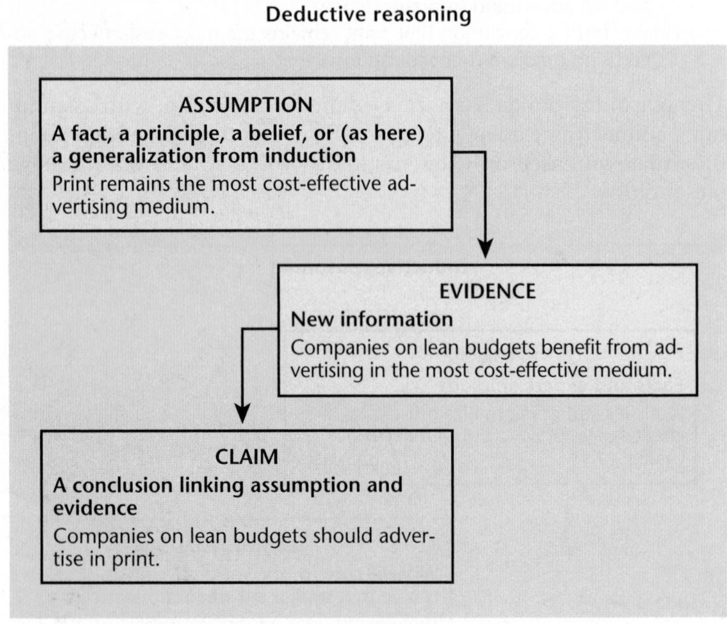

ASSUMPTION
A fact, a principle, a belief, or (as here) a generalization from induction
Print remains the most cost-effective advertising medium.
EVIDENCE
New information
Companies on lean budgets benefit from advertising in the most cost-effective medium.
CLAIM
A conclusion linking assumption and evidence
Companies on lean budgets should advertise in print.

The deductive syllogism

The conventional way of displaying a deductive argument is in a **syllogism**:

> **Premise:** All human beings are mortal. [A generalization, fact, principle, or belief that you assume to be true.]
> **Premise:** I am a human being. [New information: a specific case of the first premise.]
> **Conclusion:** Therefore, I am mortal.

As long as the premises of a syllogism are true, the conclusion derives logically and certainly from them. If you want the school administration to postpone new room fees for one dormitory, your deductive argument might be expressed in this syllogism:

> **Premise:** The administration should not raise fees on dorm rooms in poor condition.
> **Premise:** The rooms in Polk Hall are in poor condition.
> **Conclusion:** Therefore, the administration should not raise fees on the rooms in Polk Hall.

The force of deductive reasoning depends on the reliability of the premises and the care taken to apply them in drawing conclusions. The reasoning process is **valid** if the premises lead logically to the conclusion. It is **true** if the premises are believable.

Problems with syllogisms

Sometimes the reasoning in a deductive argument is true because the premises are believable, but it is *not* valid because the conclusion doesn't derive logically from the premises:

> **Premise:** The administration should not raise fees on dorm rooms in poor condition.
> **Premise:** Tyler Hall is a dormitory.
> **Conclusion:** Therefore, the administration should not raise fees on the rooms in Tyler Hall.

Both premises may be true, but the first does not *necessarily* apply to the second, so the conclusion is invalid.

Sometimes, too, deductive reasoning is valid but *not* true:

> **Premise:** All college administrations are indifferent to students' needs.
> **Premise:** The administration of Central State is a college administration.
> **Conclusion:** Therefore, the administration of Central State is indifferent to students' needs.

This syllogism is valid but useless: the first premise is an untrue assumption, so the entire argument is untrue. Invalid and untrue syllogisms underlie many of the fallacies discussed on pages 193–98.

A particular hazard of deductive reasoning is the **unstated premise**: the basic assumption linking evidence and conclusion is not stated but implied. Here the unstated premise is believable and the argument is reasonable:

> Ms. Stein has worked with drug addicts for fifteen years, so she knows a great deal about their problems. [Unstated premise: Anyone who has worked fifteen years with drug addicts knows about their problems.]

But when the unstated premise is wrong or unfounded, the argument is false. For example:

> As a senator, Jane Lightbow must receive money illegally from lobbyists. [Unstated premise: All senators receive money illegally from lobbyists.]

Tests for inductive and deductive reasoning

Induction

- Have you stated your evidence clearly?
- Is your evidence complete enough and good enough to justify your claim? What is the assumption that connects evidence and claim? Is it believable?
- Have you avoided fallacies?

Deduction

- What are the premises leading to your conclusion? Look especially for unstated premises.
- What does the first premise assume? Is the assumption believable?
- Does the first premise necessarily apply to the second premise?
- Is the second premise believable?
- Have you avoided fallacies?

To avoid such false conclusions, you may be tempted to make your claims sound more reasonable. But even a conclusion that sounds reasonable must be supportable. For instance, changing *must* to *might* modifies the unstated assumption about Senator Lightbow:

> As a senator, Jane Lightbow might receive money illegally from lobbyists. [Unstated premise: *Some* senators receive money illegally from lobbyists.]

But it does not necessarily follow that Senator Lightbow is one of the "some." The sentence, though logical, is not truly reasonable unless evidence demonstrates that Senator Lightbow should be linked with illegal activities.

Exercise 9.4 Reasoning inductively

Study the facts below and then evaluate each of the numbered conclusions that follow. Which of the generalizations are reasonable given the evidence, and which are not? Why?

In 2012 each American household viewed a weekly average of 81 hours of television.

Each individual viewed an average of 34 hours every week.

Those viewing the most television per week (48 hours) were women over age 65.

Those viewing the least television per week (22 hours) were teens ages 12–17.

Households earning under $30,000 a year watched an average of 83 hours a week.

Households earning more than $60,000 a year watched an average of 80 hours a week.

1. Households with incomes under $30,000 tend to watch more television than average.
2. Women watch more television than men.
3. Nonaffluent people watch less television than affluent people.
4. Women over age 65 tend to watch more television than average.
5. Teens watch less television than critics generally assume.

Exercise 9.5 Reasoning deductively

Convert each of the following statements into a syllogism. (You may have to state unstated assumptions.) Use the syllogism to evaluate both the validity and the truth of the statement.

Example:

DiSantis is a banker, so he does not care about the poor.

Premise: Bankers do not care about the poor.
Premise: DiSantis is a banker.
Conclusion: Therefore, DiSantis does not care about the poor.

The statement is untrue because the first premise is untrue.

1. The mayor opposed pollution controls when he was president of a manufacturing company, so he may not support new controls or vigorously enforce existing ones.
2. Information on corporate Web sites is unreliable because the sites are sponsored by for-profit entities.
3. Schroeder is a good artist because she trained at Parsons, like many other good artists.
4. Wealthy athletes who use their resources to help others deserve our particular appreciation.
5. Jimson is clearly a sexist because she has hired only one woman.

9e Using evidence

Whether your argument is reasonable or not depends heavily on the evidence you marshal to support it. The kinds of evidence and the criteria for evaluating evidence are discussed in detail on pages 185–88. Finding evidence is discussed under research writing on pages 556–78. Evaluating sources of evidence, including Web and other online sources, is discussed under research writing on pages 580–93.

The kind and quantity of evidence you use should be determined by your purpose, your subject, and the needs of your audience. Some arguments, such as an appeal for volunteer help in a soup kitchen, will rely most heavily on examples (including perhaps a narrative of your own experience) and on appeals to readers' beliefs. Other arguments, such as a proposal for mandatory side air bags in cars, will rely much more on statistics and expert opinions. Most arguments, including these, will mingle facts, examples, expert opinions, and appeals to readers' beliefs and needs.

In using evidence for argument, you'll need to be especially wary of certain traps that carelessness or zeal can lure you into. These traps are described in the following box.

Responsible use of evidence

- **Don't distort.** You mislead readers when you twist evidence to suit your argument—for instance, when you claim that crime in your city occurs five times more often than it did in 1955, without mentioning that the population is also seven times larger.
- **Don't stack the deck.** Ignoring damning evidence is like cheating at cards. You must deal forthrightly with the opposition. (See pp. 216–17.)
- **Don't exaggerate.** Watch your language. Don't attempt to manipulate readers by characterizing your own evidence as *pure* and *rock-solid* and the opposition's as *ridiculous* and *half-baked.* Make the evidence speak for itself.
- **Don't oversimplify.** Avoid forcing the evidence to support more than it can. (See also pp. 197–98.)
- **Don't misquote.** When you cite experts, quote them accurately and fairly.

Exercise 9.6 Using reason and evidence in your argument

Develop the structure and evidence for the argument you began in Exercises 9.2 and 9.3 (pp. 207 and 208). (You may want to begin drafting at this stage.) Is your argument mainly inductive or mainly deductive? Use the box on page 212 to test the reasoning of the argument. Use the boxes on page 187 and above to test your evidence.

9f Reaching your readers

To reach your readers in argument, you appeal directly to their reason and emotions, you present yourself as someone worth heeding, and you account for views opposing your own.

1 Appealing to readers

In forming convictions about arguable issues, we generally interpret the factual evidence through the filter of our values, beliefs, tastes, desires, and feelings. You may object to placing the new town dump in a particular wooded area because the facts suggest that the site is not large enough and that prevailing winds will blow odors back through the town. But you may also have fond memories of playing in the wooded area as a child, feelings that color your interpretation of the facts and strengthen your conviction that the dump should be placed elsewhere. Your conviction is partly rational, because it is based on evidence, and partly emotional, because it is also based on feelings.

Rational and emotional appeals

In most arguments you will combine **rational appeals** to readers' capacities for reasoning logically between evidence and claims with **emotional appeals** to readers' beliefs and feelings. The following passages, all arguing the same view on the same subject, illustrate how either a primarily rational or a primarily emotional appeal may be weaker than an approach that uses both:

Rational appeal

Advertising should show more people who are physically challenged. The millions of Americans with disabilities have considerable buying power, yet so far advertisers have made no attempt to tap that power. [Appeals to the logic of financial gain.]

Emotional appeal

Advertising should show more people who are physically challenged. By keeping people with disabilities out of the mainstream depicted in ads, advertisers encourage widespread prejudice against disability, prejudice that frightens and demeans those who hold it. [Appeals to a sense of fairness and open-mindedness.]

Rational and emotional appeals

Advertising should show more people who are physically challenged. The millions of Americans with disabilities have considerable buying power, yet so far advertisers have made no attempt to tap that power. Further, by keeping people with disabilities out of the mainstream depicted in ads, advertisers encourage widespread prejudice against disability, prejudice that frightens and demeans those who hold it.

The third passage, in combining both kinds of appeal, gives readers both rational and emotional bases for agreeing with the writer.

For an emotional appeal to be successful, it must be appropriate for the audience and the argument:

- **It must not misjudge readers' actual feelings.**
- **It must not raise emotional issues that are irrelevant to the claims and the evidence.** See page 196 for a discussion of specific inappropriate appeals, such as the bandwagon approach.

One further caution: Visuals and multimedia can reinforce your claims with a strong emotional appeal, but they must be relevant to your claims, and you must explain their relevance in your text and captions.

Ethical appeal

A third kind of approach to readers, the **ethical appeal**, is the sense you give of being a competent, fair, trustworthy person. A sound argument backed by ample evidence—a rational appeal—will convince readers of your knowledge and reasonableness. (So will your acknowledging the opposition. See the following page.)

Appropriate emotional appeals will demonstrate that you share readers' beliefs and needs. An argument that is concisely written and correct in grammar, spelling, and other matters will underscore your competence. In addition, a sincere and even tone will assure readers that you are a balanced person who respects them and wants to reason with them.

A sincere and even tone need not exclude language with emotional appeal—words such as *frightens* and *demeans* at the end of the third example on the previous page. But avoid certain forms of expression that will mark you as unfair:

- **Insulting words,** such as *idiotic* or *fascist.*
- **Biased language,** such as *rednecks* or *fags.* (See pp. 503–04.)
- **Sarcasm**—for instance, using the phrase *What a brilliant idea* to indicate contempt for the idea and its originator.
- **Exclamation points!** They'll make you sound shrill!

See also page 190 on tone.

2 Responding to opposing views

A good test of your fairness in argument is how you handle possible objections. Assuming your thesis is indeed arguable, then others can marshal their own evidence to support a different view or views. By dealing squarely with those opposing views, you show yourself to be honest and fair. You strengthen your ethical appeal and thus your entire argument.

Before or while you draft your essay, list for yourself all the opposing views you can think of. You'll find them in your research, by talking to friends and classmates, and by critically thinking about your own ideas.

Rebutting opposing views

A common way to handle opposing views is to state them, refute those you can, grant the validity of others, and demonstrate why, despite their validity, the opposing views are less compelling than your own. The following paragraph illustrates this approach:

> For Springfield to become a first-rate academic institution, it will need to reduce its funding of intercollegiate sports in favor of academic programs. The athletic director argues against a reduction on the grounds that the team programs more than pay for themselves. It is true that the surpluses from the team programs have gone into the general university fund. However, this argument misses the point that the team programs demand too many resources to begin with for an institution whose main priorities should be

Statement of opposing view

Concession that opposing view is partly valid

Demonstration that opposing view is irrelevant

academic. Some members of the athletic department have acknowledged that intercollegiate sports could manage with budget cuts of 20%. Committing the savings to academic programs would establish a more appropriate balance between the competing goals of athletic power and academic strength.

Evidence for author's claim

Author's claim

Finding common ground

A somewhat different approach to addressing opposing views, developed by the psychologist Carl Rogers, emphasizes the search for common ground. A **Rogerian argument** can be especially helpful when you expect readers to resist your claims. You start by showing that you understand readers' views and by establishing points on which you and readers agree and disagree. Creating a connection in this way can encourage readers to hear you out as you argue your own claims. Recast as a Rogerian argument, the preceding example might read as follows:

The Springfield community seems united in the goal of making the university a first-rate academic institution, but it differs over whether to help pay for the needed improvements by reducing funds for intercollegiate sports. Most of us who support this step do value the sports, and we appreciate the athletic director's point that the team programs more than pay for themselves, contributing surpluses to the general university fund. We certainly do not propose that the university abandon the sports altogether or even dramatically cut their funding. However, some members of the athletic department have acknowledged that intercollegiate sports could manage with budget cuts of 20%. Thus we seek this manageable reduction so that Springfield can continue as a sports power while also putting more resources to work for academic excellence.

Focus on points of agreement

Rejection of more extreme solutions

Evidence for author's claim

Author's claim

Exercise 9.7 Identifying appeals

Identify each passage below as primarily a rational appeal or primarily an emotional appeal. Which passages make a strong ethical appeal as well?

1. Web use may contribute to the global tendency toward breadth rather than depth of knowledge. Relying on those most essential skills—pointing and clicking—our brightest minds may now never encounter, much less read, the works of Plato and Shakespeare.
2. The data collected by these researchers indicate that a mandatory sentence for illegal possession of handguns may lead to a reduction in handgun purchases.
3. Most broadcasters worry that further government regulation of television programming could breed censorship—certainly, an undesirable

outcome. Yet most broadcasters also accept that children's television is a fair target for regulation.

4. Anyone who cherishes life in all its diversity could not help being appalled by the mistreatment of laboratory animals. The so-called scientists who run the labs are misguided.
5. Many experts in constitutional law have warned that the rule violates the right to free speech. Yet other experts have viewed the rule, however regretfully, as necessary for the good of the community as a whole.

Exercise 9.8 Reaching your readers

Continuing your argument-in-progress from Exercise 9.6 (p. 214), analyze whether your claims are rational or emotional and whether the mix is appropriate for your audience and argument. Analyze your ethical appeal, too, considering whether it can be strengthened. Then make a list of possible opposing views. Think freely at first, not stopping to censor views that seem far-fetched or irrational. When your list is complete, decide which views must be taken seriously and why, and develop a response to each one.

9g Organizing your argument

All arguments include the same parts, but depending on the type of argument the organization can vary:

- **Introduction:** Commonly, the introduction establishes the significance of the subject or the scope of the problem, provides the background, and usually includes the thesis statement. However, if you think your readers may have difficulty accepting your thesis statement before they see at least some support for it, then it may come later in the paper. In a Rogerian argument, you might use the introduction to emphasize the common ground between you and readers and delay stating the thesis until the conclusion.
- **Body:** The body paragraphs state and develop the claims supporting the thesis, using clearly relevant evidence. The arrangement of the claims can vary widely, as can their position relative to the response to opposing views. See the box on the next page.
- **Response to opposing views:** The response to opposing views details and addresses those views, finding common ground, demonstrating the arguments' greater strengths, or conceding the opponent's points. For some arguments, readers will be satisfied to see opposing views dealt with at the end. For others, each claim will invite its own objections, and those opposing views will need to be addressed claim by claim. When readers' resistance may be very strong, the Rogerian approach of discussing and conceding opposing views right away can establish a common understanding that opens readers to the argument's claims.

Organizing an argument's body and response to opposing views

A common scheme

Claim 1 and evidence
Claim 2 and evidence
Claim X and evidence
Response to opposing views

A variation

Claim 1 and evidence
Response to opposing views
Claim 2 and evidence
Response to opposing views
Claim X and evidence
Response to opposing views

The Rogerian scheme

Common ground and concession to opposing views
Claim 1 and evidence
Claim 2 and evidence
Claim X and evidence

The problem-solution scheme

The problem: claims and evidence
The solution: claims and evidence
Response to opposing views

- **Conclusion:** The conclusion completes the argument. Often it restates the thesis, summarizes the supporting claims, and makes a final appeal to readers. In a Rogerian argument, the conclusion often states the thesis as a solution, giving ground and inviting the audience to do the same.

For more on introductions and conclusions, see pages 101–06.

You may want to experiment with various organizations—for instance, trying out your strongest claims first or last in the body, stating claims outright or letting the evidence build to them, answering the opposition near the beginning or near the end or claim by claim. Try rearranging your outline as described on page 37. Or try rearranging your draft (work with a copy) by cutting and pasting parts of it for different emphases.

Exercise 9.9 Organizing your argument

Continuing from Exercise 9.8 (facing page), develop a structure for your argument. Consider especially how you will introduce it, how you will arrange your claims, where you will place your responses to opposing views, and how you will conclude.

9h Revising your argument

When you revise your argument, do it in at least two stages—revising underlying meaning and structure, and editing more superficial elements. The checklists on pages 53–54 and 62–63 can be a guide. Supplement them with the following checklist, which encourages you to think critically about your own argument.

Checklist for revising an argument

Thesis

- What is your thesis? Where is it stated?
- In what ways is your thesis statement an arguable claim?

Reasoning

- If your thesis derives from induction, where have you related the evidence to your generalization?
- If your thesis derives from deduction, is your syllogism both true and valid?
- Have you avoided fallacies in reasoning?

Evidence

- Where have you provided the evidence readers need?
- Where might your evidence not be accurate, relevant, representative, or adequate? (Answer this question from the point of view of a neutral or even skeptical reader.)

Appeals

- Where have you considered readers' probable beliefs and values?
- How are your rational appeals and emotional appeals appropriate for your readers?
- What is your ethical appeal? How can you improve it?

Opposing views

- What opposing views have you answered?
- How successfully have you refuted opposing views? (Again, consider the neutral or skeptical reader.)

Organization

- How clearly does your argument move from one point to the next?
- How appropriate is your organization, given the likely views of your readers?

Exercise 9.10 Writing and revising your argument

Draft and revise the argument you have developed in the exercises in this chapter. Use the revision checklists on pages 53–54 and above to review your work.

9i Examining a sample argument

The following essay by the student Aimee Lee is a proposal argument that illustrates the principles discussed in this chapter. As you read the essay, notice especially the organization, the relation of claims and supporting evidence (including illustrations), the kinds of appeals Lee makes, and the ways she responds to opposing views.

Awareness, Prevention, Support:
A Proposal to Reduce Cyberbullying

My roommate and I sat in front of her computer staring at the vicious message under her picture. She quickly removed the tag that identified her, but the comments already posted on the photo proved that the damage was done. While she slept, my roommate had become the victim of a cyberbully. She had joined an increasing number of college students who are targeted in texts, e-mails, social-networking sites, and other Web sites that broadcast photographs, videos, and comments. My roommate's experience alerted me that our campus needs a program aimed at awareness and prevention of cyberbullying and support for its victims.

Introduction: identification of the problem

Thesis statement: proposal for a solution to the problem

Although schoolyard bullying typically ends with high school graduation, cyberbullying continues in college. According to data gathered by researchers at the Massachusetts Aggression Reduction Center (MARC) of Bridgewater State College, cyberbullying behavior decreases when students enter college, but it does not cease. Examining the experiences of first-year students, the researchers found that 8% of college freshmen had been cyberbullied at college and 3% admitted to having cyberbullied another student (Englander et al. 217-18). In a survey of fifty-two freshmen, I found further evidence of cyberbullying on this campus. I asked two questions: (1) Have you been involved in cyberbullying as a victim, a bully, or both? (2) If you answered "no" to the first question, do you know anyone who has been involved in cyberbullying as a victim, a bully, or both? While a large majority of the students I surveyed (74%) have not been touched by cyberbullying, more than one-fourth (26%) have been involved personally or know someone who has, as shown in fig. 1. Taken together, the evidence demonstrates that cyberbullying is significant in colleges and specifically on our campus.

Evidence of the problem: published research

Evidence of the problem: student's own research

The writing situation: Proposal argument

- **Subject:** Proposal for a program to reduce cyberbullying; student's choice for an assignment in a first-year writing course
- **Purpose:** To explain a problem (cyberbullying) and propose a solution to it (a prevention program)
- **Audience:** Classmates, instructor, college administrators
- **Genre:** Proposal argument—writing that defines a problem, proposes a solution, explains how the solution will work, and responds to possible objections to the solution
- **Sources:** Survey results, popular and scholarly articles (cited in MLA style)

Pie chart showing results of student's research

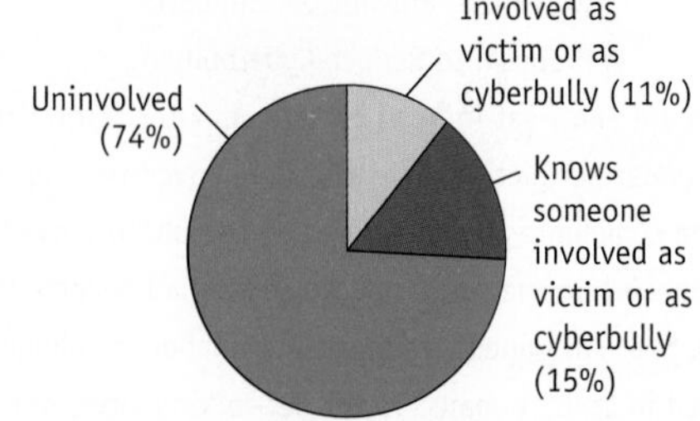

Fig. 1. Involvement in cyberbullying among fifty-two first-year students.

Explanation of proposed solution: goals of the program

The proposed "Stop Cyberbullying" program aims to reduce the behavior through a month-long campaign of awareness, prevention, and support modeled on the college's "Alcohol Awareness Month" program. The program can raise awareness of cyberbullying by explaining what cyberbullying is and by informing students about the college's code of conduct, which prohibits cyberbullying behavior but which few people read. The program can work to prevent cyberbullying by appealing to students to treat those around them respectfully. And, with the participation of the counseling department, the program can provide support for victims, their friends, and others involved in the behavior.

Explanation of proposed solution: specific actions

If adopted, the program can use online and print media to get the message out to the entire college community. For instance, an extensive brochure distributed to first-year students and available through the counseling center can describe cyberbullying and how it violates the college's code of conduct, give strategies for avoiding it, and provide resources for help. During the month-long campaign, flyers posted on campus (see fig. 2) can also raise awareness of the problem, and brief postings to the college's Web site, *Facebook* page, and *Twitter* feed can reach students who take online and hybrid classes as well as those in traditional classes.

Anticipation of objection: code of conduct does enough

Because this college already has a code of conduct in place and because the state has recently enacted anti-bullying legislation that includes cyberbullying, some students and administrators may contend that enough is being done to deal with the problem. To the administration's credit, the code of conduct contains specific language about online behavior, but promises of punishment for proven allegations do not address several aspects of the problem.

Response to objection: anonymity of cyberbullies

First, cyberbullies are sometimes anonymous. To accuse another student of cyberbullying, the victim needs to know the identity of the bully. While postings on *Facebook* are attached to real names, most college gossip

Fig. 2. Sample flyer for proposed "Stop Cyberbullying" program.

Visual evidence of program publicity

sites are anonymous. On such sites, a cyberbully can post photographs, videos, and aggressive messages under the cover of anonymity.

Response to objection: invisibility of the problem

Second, even when the identities of cyberbullies are known, the bullying is often invisible to those in a position to take action against it. According to Ikuko Aoyama and Tony L. Talbert at Baylor University, cyberbullying occurs frequently in groups of people who know each other and who attack and retaliate: students are rarely "pure bullies" or "pure victims" but instead are often part of a "bully-victim group" (qtd. in Laster). Moreover, even if students want to separate from bullying groups, Englander et al. found that they probably will not report cyberbullying incidents to authorities because they generally believe that administrators are unlikely to do anything (221). Thus counselors and administrators who may be interested in helping students to cope are often unaware of the problem.

Response to objection: conduct codes ineffective

Third, conduct codes rarely affect cyberbullying. While some cyberbullying has resulted in tragedy, many aggressive incidents do not rise to the level of punishable offenses ("Cyberbullying"). More often they consist of a humiliating photograph or a mean message—hurtful, to be sure, but not necessarily in violation of the law or the code of conduct. Indeed, the hurdles to getting recourse through official channels are fairly high.

Conclusion

Given its hidden nature and the inability of punitive measures to stop it, cyberbullying needs another approach—namely, a program that teaches students to recognize and regulate their own behavior and provides help when they find themselves in a difficult situation. This program will not heal the wound suffered by my roommate, nor will it prevent all cyberbullying. But if adopted, the program will demonstrate to the college community that the administration is aware of the problem, eager to prevent it, and willing to commit resources to support students who are affected by it.

Works cited in MLA style

Works Cited

"Cyberbullying Goes to College." *Bostonia*, Boston U, Spring 2009, www.bu.edu/bostonia/spring09/bully/.

Englander, Elizabeth, et al. "Cyberbullying and Information Exposure: User-Generated Content in Post-Secondary Education." *International Journal of Contemporary Society*, vol. 46, no. 2, Oct. 2009, pp. 213-20, www.uef.fi/c/document_library/get_file?uuid=113358&p_l_id=144412.

Laster, Jill. "Two Scholars Examine Cyberbullying among College Students." *The Chronicle of Higher Education*, 6 June 2010, chronicle.com/article/2-Scholars-Examine/65766/.

—Aimee Lee (student)

Exercise 9.11 Critically reading an argument

Analyze the construction and effectiveness of the preceding essay by answering the following questions.

1. Where does Aimee Lee make claims related to her thesis statement, and where does she provide evidence to support the claims?
2. Where does Lee appeal primarily to reason, and where does she appeal primarily to emotion? What specific beliefs and values of readers does she appeal to?
3. How would you characterize Lee's ethical appeal?
4. How effective do you find the illustrations as support for Lee's claims? What appeals do they make?
5. What objections to her argument does Lee anticipate? How does she respond to them?
6. How effective do you think this argument is? To what extent does Lee convince you that cyberbullying is a problem and that the program she proposes will be an effective solution? Does Lee respond adequately to objections?
7. Write a critical analysis of "Awareness, Prevention, Support: A Proposal to Reduce Cyberbullying." First summarize Lee's views. Then respond to those views by answering the questions posed in number 6 above.

10 Taking Essay Exams

Chapter essentials

- Prepare in advance for an essay exam (below).
- Take a few minutes to plan your answer before you start to write (below).
- Open an essay exam with a direct response to the question (p. 228).
- Develop your response (p. 228).
- Reread the essay before you turn it in (p. 231).

Visit MyWritingLab™ for more resources on taking essay exams.

In writing an essay for an examination, you summarize or analyze a topic, usually in several paragraphs or more and usually within a time limit. An essay question not only tests your knowledge of a subject (as short-answer and objective questions do) but also tests your ability to think critically about what you have learned. If you have not already done so, read Chapter 7 on critical thinking and reading.

10a Preparing for an essay examination

To do well on an essay exam, you will need to understand the course content, not only the facts but also the interpretation of them and the relations between them.

- **Take careful lecture notes.**
- **Thoughtfully, critically read the assigned texts or articles.**
- **Review regularly.** Give the material time to sink in and stimulate your thinking.
- **Create summaries.** Recast others' ideas in your own words, and extract the meaning from notes and texts. (See pp. 155–57 for instructions on summarizing.)
- **Prepare notes or outlines to reorganize the course material around key topics or issues.** One technique is to create and answer likely essay questions. For instance, in a business course you might focus on the advantages and disadvantages of several approaches to management. In a short-story course you might locate a theme running through all the stories you have read by a certain author or from a certain period.

10b Planning your time and your answer

When you first receive an exam, take a few minutes to get your bearings and plan an approach. The time will not be wasted.

- **Read the exam all the way through at least once.** Don't start answering any questions until you've seen them all.
- **Weigh the questions.** Determine which questions seem most important, which ones are going to be most difficult for you, and approximately how much time you'll need for each question. (Your instructor may help by assigning a point value to each question as a guide to its importance or by suggesting an amount of time for you to spend on each question.)

Planning continues when you turn to an individual essay question. Resist the temptation to rush right into an answer without some planning: a few minutes can save you time later and help you produce a stronger essay.

- **Read the question at least twice.** You will be more likely to stick to the question and answer it fully.
- **Examine the words in the question and consider their implications.** Look especially for words such as *describe, define, explain, summarize, analyze, evaluate,* and *interpret,* each of which requires a different kind of response. Here, for example, is an essay question whose key term is *explain*:

  Question

  Given humans' natural and historical curiosity about themselves, why did a scientific discipline of anthropology not arise until the 20th century? Explain, citing specific details.

  See the box on the facing page and consult earlier discussions of such terms on pages 91–99.
- **Make a brief outline of the main ideas you want to cover.** Use the back of the exam sheet or booklet for scratch paper. In the outline below, a student planned her answer to the question above.

  Outline

  1. Unscientific motivations behind 19th-c anthro.
     Imperialist/colonialist govts.
     Practical goals
     Nonobjective and unscientific (Herodotus, Cushing)
  2. 19th-c ethnocentricity (vs. cultural relativism)
  3. 19th-c anthro. = object collecting
     20th-c shift from museum to univ.
     Anthro. becomes acad. disc. and professional (Boas, Malinowski)

- **Write a thesis statement for your essay that responds directly to the question and represents your view of the topic.** (If you are unsure of how to write a thesis statement, see pp. 28–33.) Include key phrases that you can expand with supporting evidence for your view. The thesis statement of the student writing about

Sample instructions for essay examinations

Sample instructions	Key terms	Strategies for answers	Examples of wrong answers
Define *dyslexia* and compare and contrast it with two other learning disabilities.	Define	Specify the meaning of *dyslexia*—distinctive characteristics, ways the impairment works, etc.	Feelings of children with dyslexia. Causes of dyslexia.
	Compare and contrast	Analyze similarities and differences (severity, causes, treatments, etc.).	Similarities without differences, or vice versa.
Analyze the role of Horatio in *Hamlet.*	Analyze	Break Horatio's role into its elements (speeches, relations with other characters, etc.).	Plot summary of *Hamlet.* Description of Horatio's personality.
Explain the effects of the drug Thorazine.	Explain	Set forth the facts and theories objectively.	Argument for or against Thorazine.
	Effects	Analyze the consequences.	Reasons for prescribing Thorazine.
Discuss term limits for elected officials.	Discuss	Explain and compare the main points of view on the issue.	Analysis of one view. Argument for or against one view.
Summarize the process that resulted in the Grand Canyon.	Summarize	Distill the subject to its main points, elements, or steps.	Detailed description of the Grand Canyon.
How do you evaluate the Laffer curve as a predictor of economic growth?	Evaluate	Provide your opinion of significance or value, supported with evidence.	Explanation of the Laffer curve, without evaluation. Comparison of the Laffer curve and another predictor, without evaluation.

anthropology concisely previews a three-part answer to the sample question:

Thesis statement

Anthropology did not emerge as a scientific discipline until the 20th century because of the practical and political motivations behind 19th-century ethnographic studies, the ethnocentric bias of Western researchers, and a conception of culture that was strictly material.

10c Starting the essay

An essay exam does not require a smooth and inviting opening. Instead, begin by stating your thesis immediately and giving an overview of the rest of your essay. Such a capsule version of your answer tells your reader (and grader) generally how much command you have and also how you plan to develop your answer. It also gets you off to a good start.

The opening statement should address the question directly and exactly, as it does in the successful essay answer beginning on the next page. In contrast, the opening of the unsuccessful essay (p. 230) restates the question but does not answer it, nor does the opening provide any sense of the writer's thesis.

10d Developing the essay

Develop your essay as you would develop any piece of sound academic writing:

- **Observe the methods, terms, or other special requirements of the discipline in which you are writing.**
- **Support your thesis statement with solid generalizations,** each one perhaps the topic sentence of a paragraph.
- **Support each generalization with specific, relevant evidence.**

If you observe a few *don't*s as well, your essay will have more substance:

- **Avoid filling out the essay by repeating yourself.**
- **Avoid other kinds of wordiness that pad and confuse,** whether intentionally or not. (See pp. 519–24.)
- **Avoid resorting to purely subjective feelings.** Keep focused on analysis, or whatever is asked of you. (It may help to abolish the word *I* from the essay.)

The following essays illustrate a successful and an unsuccessful answer to the sample essay question on page 226 about anthropology. Both answers were written in the allotted time of forty minutes. Marginal comments highlight their effective and ineffective elements.

Successful essay answer

Anthropology did not emerge as a scientific discipline until the 20th century because of the practical and political motivations behind 19th-century ethnographic studies, the ethnocentric bias of Western researchers, and a conception of culture that was strictly material.

Introduction stating thesis

Direct answer to question and preview of three-part response

Before the 20th century, ethnographic studies were almost always used for practical goals. The study of human culture can be traced back at least as far as Herodotus's investigations of the Mediterranean peoples. Herodotus was like many pre-20th-century "anthropologists" in that he was employed by a government that needed information about its neighbors, just as the colonial nations in the 19th century needed information about their newly conquered subjects. The early politically motivated ethnographic studies that the colonial nations sponsored tended to be isolated projects, and they aimed less to advance general knowledge than to solve a specific problem. Frank Hamilton Cushing, who was employed by the American government to study the Zuni tribe of New Mexico, and who is considered one of the pioneers of anthropology, didn't even publish his findings. The political and practical aims of anthropologists and the nature of their research prevented their work from being a scholarly discipline in its own right.

First main point: practical aims

Example

Example

Anthropologists of the 19th century also fell short of the standards of objectivity needed for truly scientific study. This partly had to do with anthropologists' close connection to imperialist governments. But even independent researchers were hampered by the prevailing assumption that Western cultures were inherently superior. While the modern anthropologist believes that a culture must be studied in terms of its own values, early ethnographers were ethnocentric: they judged "primitive" cultures by their own "civilized" values. "Primitive" peoples were seen as uninteresting in their own right. The reasons to study them, ultimately, were to satisfy curiosity, to exploit them, or to prove their inferiority. There was even some debate as to whether so-called savage peoples were human.

Second main point: ethnocentricity

The writing situation: Essay exam

- **Subject:** Evolution of the discipline of anthropology; assigned topic
- **Purpose:** To explain why anthropology did not arise as a scientific discipline until the twentieth century
- **Audience:** Instructor
- **Genre:** Essay exam—writing that responds directly to a specific prompt, usually within a time limit

Third main point (with transition *Finally*): focus on objects

Finally, the 19th century tended to conceive of culture in narrow, material terms, often reducing it to a collection of artifacts. When not working for a government, early ethnographers usually worked for a museum. The enormous collections of exotica still found in many museums today are the legacy of this 19th-century object-oriented conception of anthropology, which ignored the myths, symbols, and rituals the objects related to. It was only when the museum tradition was broadened to include all aspects of a culture that anthropology could come into existence as a scientific discipline. When anthropologists like Franz Boas and Bronislaw Malinowski began to publish their findings for others to read and criticize and began to move from the museum to the university, the discipline gained stature and momentum.

Examples

Conclusion, restating thesis supported by essay

In brief, anthropology required a whole series of ideological shifts to become modern. Once it broke free of its purely practical bent, the cultural prejudices of its practitioners, and the narrow conception that limited it to a collection of objects, anthropology could grow into a science.

Unsuccessful essay answer

Introduction, not answering question

No thesis statement or sense of direction

Irrelevant information

The discipline of anthropology, the study of humans and their cultures, actually began in the early 20th century and was strengthened by the Darwinian revolution, but the discipline did not begin to take shape until people like Franz Boas and Alfred Kroeber began doing scientific research among nonindustrialized cultures. (Boas, who was born in Germany but emigrated to the US, is the father of the idea of historical particularism.)

Cliché added to language of question without answering question

Since the dawn of time, humans have always had a natural curiosity about themselves. Art and literature have always reflected this need to understand human emotions, thought, and behavior. Anthropology is yet another reflection of this need. Anthropologists have a different way of looking at human societies than artists or writers. Whereas the latter paint an individualistic, impressionistic portrait of the world they see, anthropologists study cultures systematically, scientifically. They are thus closer to biologists. They are *social scientists*, with the emphasis on both words.

Wheel spinning, positioning contemporary anthropology as a scientific discipline

Not *Another reason* but the first reason given

Assertion without support

Another reason why anthropology did not develop until the 20th century is that people in the past did not travel very much. The expansion of the automobile and the airplane has played a major role in the expansion of the discipline.

Next three paragraphs: discussion of pioneers showing familiarity with their work but not answering question

Cushing's important work among the Zuni Indians in New Mexico is a good example of the transition between 19th-century and 20th-century approaches to anthropology. Cushing was one of the first to develop the method of *participant observation*. Instead of merely coming in as an outsider, taking notes, and leaving, Cushing actually lived among the Zuni, dressing like them and following their customs. In this way, he was able to build a relationship of trust with his informants, learning much more than someone who would have been seen as an outsider.

Franz Boas, as mentioned earlier, was another anthropology pioneer. A German immigrant, Boas proposed the idea of *historical particularism* as a response to the prevailing theory of *cultural evolution*. Cultural evolution is the idea that cultures gradually evolve toward higher levels of efficiency and complexity. Historical particularism is the idea that every culture is unique and develops differently. Boas developed his theory to counter those who believed in cultural evolution. Working with the Kwakiutl Indians, he was also one of the first anthropologists to use a native assistant to help him gain access to the culture under study.

Padding with repetition

Irrelevant information

A third pioneer in anthropology was Malinowski, who developed a theory of *functionalism*—that culture responds to biological, psychological, and other needs. Malinowski's work is extremely important and still influential today.

Vague assertion without support

Anthropologists have made great contributions to society over the course of the past century. One can only hope that they will continue the great strides they have made, building on the past to contribute to a bright new future.

Irrelevant and empty conclusion

10e Rereading the essay

The time limit on an essay examination does not allow for the careful rethinking and revision you would give an essay or research paper. You need to write clearly and concisely the first time. But try to leave yourself a few minutes after finishing the entire exam for rereading the essay (or essays) and doing touch-ups.

- **Correct mistakes:** illegible passages, misspellings, grammatical errors, and accidental omissions.
- **Verify that your thesis is accurate**—that it is, in fact, what you ended up writing about.
- **Ensure that you have supported all your generalizations.** Cross out irrelevant ideas and details, and add any information that now seems important. (Write on another page, if necessary, keying the addition to the page on which it belongs.)

11 Public Writing

Chapter essentials

- Consider how to represent yourself on social media (below).
- Use established formats for business letters and memos (opposite).
- When applying for a job, create a cover letter, a résumé, and an online profile that highlight your strengths (p. 237).
- Write focused reports and proposals (p. 241).
- Create effective documents and other writing for community work (p. 243).

Visit MyWritingLab™ for more resources on public writing.

At some point in your life, you're likely to write for a public audience—outside your instructor, classmates, family, and friends. You have already written publicly if you've posted a comment on a Web news story, blogged, submitted a résumé to a potential employer, or communicated on behalf of an organization.

The conventions of public writing depend on the purpose of the writing, who will read it, and its genre. This chapter discusses several common public-writing situations.

CULTURE LANGUAGE Public writing in the United States, especially in business, favors efficiency. If you are accustomed to public writing in another culture, the US style may seem abrupt or impolite. A business letter elsewhere may be expected to begin with polite questions about the addressee or with compliments for the addressee's company, whereas US business letters are expected to come right to the point. (See the letters in this chapter for examples.)

11a Writing on social media

Public writing on social media varies tremendously. Some is thoughtful and carefully crafted—for example, a personal blog might contain the writer's own poetry or reasoned opinions about politics. Other social-media writing is done quickly, without much craft—for instance, a comment on a Web news story might be dashed off in frustration or anger.

As you make your own writing public—and make yourself public, too—consider these questions:

- **How you are presenting yourself?** How do you want to be viewed by readers—as knowledgeable, reasonable, witty, heartfelt, emotional, ranting, or something else? Consider whether your message comes across in the way you intend.
- **Who might read your post?** Once they are posted, your words potentially have a very large audience consisting of people

whom you do not know and who do not necessarily see things as you do.

- **Are you protecting your own and others' privacy?** Comments, tweets, and photographs that reveal personal information can be hurtful or embarrassing to you and others. Consider who may see your message or photo.
- **How will you feel about the post in the future?** Some online posts, such as comments to news stories, are never truly erased. Think how the message or photo will reflect on you months or years from now.
- **Would you say face to face what you've written?** Imagine saying what you've written to the person your message is about or is addressed to. If you wouldn't say it, don't post it.

11b Writing business letters and memos

When you write in business, you are addressing busy people who want to see quickly why you are writing and how they should respond to you. A wordy letter or a memo with grammatical errors may prevent you from getting what you want, either because the reader cannot understand your wish or because you present yourself poorly.

In all business writing, follow these general guidelines:

- **State your purpose right at the start.**
- **Be straightforward, clear, concise, objective, and courteous.**
- **Observe conventions of grammar and usage,** which make your writing clear and impress your audience with your care.
- **Use a standard format.** Your audience will expect it.

1 Using a standard format for letters

Business letters sent on paper or by e-mail have similar formats, with differences for the different media.

Letters on paper

Use either unlined white paper measuring 8-1/2" × 11" or letterhead stationery with your address preprinted at the top of the sheet. The sample on the next page shows a common format.

Return-address heading Unless you're using letterhead stationery, give your address (but not your name) and the date. If you are using letterhead, add only the date.

Inside address Provide the name, title, and complete address of the person you are writing to.

Salutation Whenever possible, address your letter to a specific person. (Contact the company or department to ask whom to

Business letter on paper

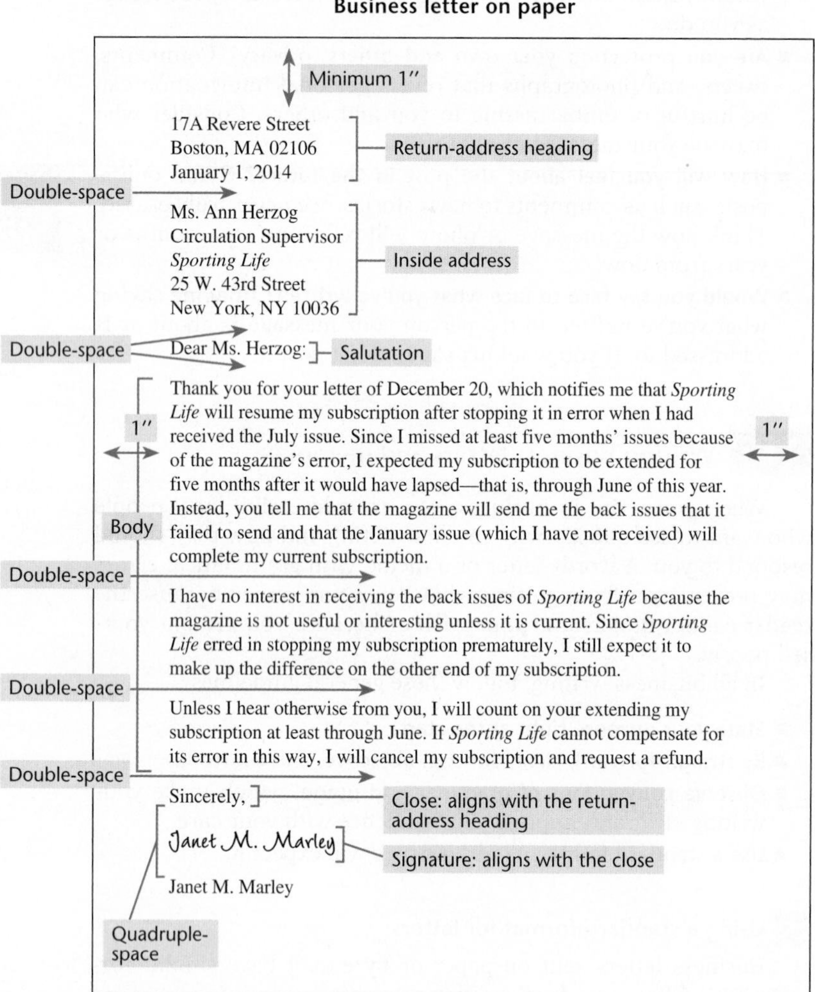
17A Revere Street
Boston, MA 02106
January 1, 2014

Ms. Ann Herzog
Circulation Supervisor
Sporting Life
25 W. 43rd Street
New York, NY 10036

Dear Ms. Herzog:

Thank you for your letter of December 20, which notifies me that *Sporting Life* will resume my subscription after stopping it in error when I had received the July issue. Since I missed at least five months' issues because of the magazine's error, I expected my subscription to be extended for five months after it would have lapsed—that is, through June of this year. Instead, you tell me that the magazine will send me the back issues that it failed to send and that the January issue (which I have not received) will complete my current subscription.

I have no interest in receiving the back issues of *Sporting Life* because the magazine is not useful or interesting unless it is current. Since *Sporting Life* erred in stopping my subscription prematurely, I still expect it to make up the difference on the other end of my subscription.

Unless I hear otherwise from you, I will count on your extending my subscription at least through June. If *Sporting Life* cannot compensate for its error in this way, I will cancel my subscription and request a refund.

Sincerely,

Janet M. Marley

Janet M. Marley

address.) If you can't find a person's name, then use a job title (*Dear Human Resources Manager, Dear Customer Service Manager*) or use a general salutation (*Dear Smythe Shoes*). Use *Ms.* as the title for a woman.

Body The substance of the letter is single-spaced. Instead of indenting the first line of each paragraph, place an extra line of space between paragraphs.

Close Reflect the level of formality in the salutation. For formal letters, *Cordially, Yours truly,* and *Sincerely* are common closes. For less formal letters, you may use *Regards, Best wishes,* or the like.

Only the first word of the close is capitalized, and the close is followed by a comma.

Signature The signature has two parts: your name typed on the fourth line below the close and your handwritten signature in the space above your typed name.

The envelope The envelope should accommodate the letter once it is folded horizontally in thirds. Place your name and address in the upper left and the addressee's in the center. Use common Postal Service abbreviations, which you can find at *usps.com*.

Letters by e-mail

An e-mailed business letter lacks some parts of a paper letter: the return-address heading, handwritten signature, and envelope. (See the sample on p. 238.) Your mailing address falls at the end of the letter rather than the top. Otherwise, it has the same parts listed above: salutation, body, close, and typed signature. And it has two other features that paper letters do not:

E-mail address Use a businesslike address that is a variation on your name, such as *john.doe, johndoe,* or *jdoe.* Do not use an address with an anonymous username.

Subject line Make it short and accurate, reflecting the message of your letter: for instance, *Subscription problem* or *Copy aide position.*

2 Writing requests and complaints

Letters and e-mails in which you request something—for instance, a pamphlet, information about a product, a T-shirt advertised in a magazine—must be specific and accurate about the item you are requesting. Describe the item completely and, if applicable, include a copy or description of the advertisement or other source that prompted your request.

For letters and e-mails in which you complain about a product or a service (such as a wrong billing from the telephone company), see the sample on page 234 and follow these guidelines:

- **Write in a reasonable but firm tone.** Assume that the addressee is willing to resolve the problem when he or she has the relevant information.
- **Say why you are writing in the first sentence.**
- **Describe exactly what you see as the problem.** Stick to facts, and avoid sarcasm or insults, such as your low opinion of the company's management.
- **Specify how you think the problem should be solved.**

Many companies have a specific procedure for complaints about products and services. If you know of such a procedure, be sure to follow it.

3 Writing business memos

Most memos are sent by e-mail, and they may be quite long (such as a regional sales plan) or very brief (such as an answer to a question). The following tips and the sample below and on page 242 can help you draft a memo.

- **Consider whom to address.** Confine the list of recipients to those who need to read your message. In an e-mail memo, avoid sending replies to a large group—look at who will receive your message before you hit Reply All.
- **Make clear your reason for writing.** Use the subject heading and the first sentence to state your topic and purpose.
- **Devote the first paragraph to a succinct presentation of your solution, recommendation, answer, or evaluation.** The first paragraph should be short, and by its end your reader should know precisely what to expect from the rest of the memo.

Memo

Names of addressee and people receiving copies.

Subject description providing context for the memo.

Body paragraphs single-spaced with double spacing between them; paragraphs not indented

Numbered list distilling and emphasizing key points

Writer's electronic signature giving contact information.

Send

From: pphillips@bigelow.com

To: Aileen Rosen

Cc: Larry Mendes; James MacGregor

Subject: 2014 sales of Quick Wax in Territory 12

Since it was introduced in January 2014, Quick Wax has been unsuccessful in Territory 12 and has not affected the sales of our Easy Shine. Discussions with customers and my own analysis of Quick Wax suggest three reasons for its failure to compete with our product.

1. Quick Wax has not received the promotion necessary for a new product. Advertising has been sporadic and has not developed a clear, consistent image for the product. In addition, the Quick Wax representative in Territory 12 is new and inexperienced. He is not known to customers, and his sales pitch (which I once overheard) is weak. As far as I can tell, his efforts are not supported by his home office.

2. When Quick Wax does make it to the store shelves, buyers do not choose it over our product. Though priced competitively with Easy Shine, Quick Wax is poorly packaged. The container seems smaller than ours, though in fact it holds the same eight ounces. The lettering on the package (red on blue) is difficult to read, in contrast to the Easy Shine package.

3. Our special purchase offers and my increased efforts to serve existing customers have had the intended effect of keeping customers satisfied with our product and reducing their inclination to stock something new.

Patricia Phillips
Sales Representative
Bigelow Wax Company
pphillips@bigelow.com
960-556-5565

- **Deliver the support in the body of the memo.** The paragraphs may be numbered or bulleted to highlight the main divisions of your message. A long memo may need headings.
- **Use an appropriate level of formality.** Typically, business correspondence grows more formal as the rank and number of intended readers increase. But even when addressing a few colleagues at your own level, your writing should show respect for the situation and the colleagues.
- **Write concisely.** Say only what readers need to know.
- **Provide contact information.** Give the recipients your e-mail address, phone number, and mailing address.
- **Check your work.** Avoid the shortcuts of texting and tweeting, and proofread for errors in grammar, punctuation, and spelling.

11c Writing a job application

In applying for a job or requesting a job interview, you will submit both a résumé and a cover letter, probably in electronic form. You may also create a social-media profile that prospective employers can consult when considering your application.

1 Writing the cover letter

Use business-letter format for the cover letter, as discussed on pages 233–35. In composing the letter, use the sample on the next page and the following guidelines:

- **Interpret your résumé for the particular job.** Don't detail your entire résumé, reciting your job history. Instead, tailor your cover letter to the job description, highlighting how your qualifications and experience match the job you are applying for.
- **Announce at the outset what job you seek and how you heard about it.**
- **Include any special reason you have for applying,** such as a specific career goal.
- **Summarize your qualifications for this particular job,** including relevant facts about education and employment and emphasizing notable accomplishments. Mention that additional information appears in an accompanying résumé.
- **Describe your availability.** At the end of the letter, mention that you are free for an interview at the convenience of the addressee, or specify when you will be available.

2 Writing and formatting the résumé

The résumé that accompanies your cover letter of application should provide information in table format that allows a potential employer to evaluate your qualifications. The résumé should include your name and address, the position you seek, your education

Job application letter via e-mail

	To: Rchipault@dallnews.com
Subject line describing position sought	Subject: Part-time editorial assistant position
Salutation	Dear Mr. Chipault:
Reason for writing	In response to your posting in the English department of Southern Methodist University, I am applying for the summer job of part-time editorial assistant for the *Dallas News*.
Qualifications Double-space between elements and paragraphs	I am now enrolled at Southern Methodist University as a sophomore, with a dual major in English literature and journalism. My courses so far have included news reporting, copy editing, and electronic publishing. I worked a summer as a copy aide for my hometown newspaper, and for two years I have edited and written sports stories and features for the university newspaper. My feature articles cover subjects as diverse as campus elections, parking regulations, visiting professors, and speech codes.
Description of attachments	As the attached résumé and writing samples indicate, my education and knowledge of newspaper work have prepared me for the posted position.
Availability	I am available for an interview at your convenience and would be happy to show more samples of my writing. Please e-mail me at ianirvine@smu.edu or call me at 214-744-3816.
Close	Sincerely,
Signature and mailing address	Ian M. Irvine 3712 Swiss Avenue Dallas, TX 75204

and employment history, any special skills or awards, and how to obtain your references. All the information should fit on one uncrowded page unless your education and experience are extensive.

Most job seekers prepare two versions of their résumé: a formatted version to print and take to in-person interviews and a plainer version to submit online. See the samples of both formats on the next two pages. Employers may add the electronic version to a computerized database of applicants, so the format and language are important to ensure that your résumé is retrievable:

- **Keep the design simple for accurate scanning or electronic transmittal.** Avoid images, bullets, boldface, italics, underlining, unusual fonts, more than one column, and vertical or horizontal lines.
- **Use concise, specific words to describe your skills and experience.** The employer's computer may use keywords (often nouns) to identify the résumés of suitable job candidates, and you want to ensure that your résumé includes keywords that match the field and the job description. Look for likely keywords in the employer's description of the job you seek, and name your

Résumé (print)

Ian M. Irvine	3712 Swiss Avenue Dallas, TX 75204 214-744-3816 ianirvine@mail.smu.edu	Name and contact information
Position desired	Part-time editorial assistant.	Desired position stated simply and clearly
Education	*Southern Methodist University*, 2012 to present. Current standing: sophomore. Major: English literature and journalism. Journalism courses: news reporting, copy editing, electronic publishing, communication arts, broadcast journalism. *Abilene (Texas) Senior High School*, 2008-12. Graduated with academic, college-preparatory degree.	Education before work experience for most college students
Employment history	2012 to present. Reporter, *Daily Campus*, student newspaper of Southern Methodist University. Write regular coverage of baseball, track, and soccer teams. Write feature stories on campus policies and events. Edit sports news, campus listings, features. Summer 2013. Copy aide, *Abilene Reporter-News*. Assisted reporters with copy routing and research. Summer 2012. Painter, Longhorn Painters, Abilene. Prepared and painted exteriors and interiors of houses.	Headings marking sections, set off with space and highlighting Conventional use of capital letters: yes for proper nouns and after periods; no for job titles, course names, department names, and so on
Special skills	Fluent in Spanish. Proficient in Internet research and word processing.	
References	Available on request: Placement Office Southern Methodist University Dallas, TX 75275	Standard, consistent type font

specific skills. Write concretely with words like *manager* (not *person with responsibility for*) and *reporter* (not *staff member who reports*).

3 Creating an online profile

Many job seekers use social-networking sites such as *LinkedIn* to create online profiles. Like a résumé, an online profile should state the position you seek and use keywords to accurately describe

Résumé (scannable or electronic)

Accurate keywords, allowing the employer to place the résumé into an appropriate database

Simple design, avoiding unusual fonts, bold, italics, multiple columns, decorative lines, and images

Standard font easily read by scanners

Every line aligning at left margin

Ian M. Irvine
3712 Swiss Avenue
Dallas, TX 75204
214-744-3816
ianirvine@mail.smu.edu

KEYWORDS: Editor, editorial assistant, publishing, electronic publishing.

OBJECTIVE
Part-time editorial assistant.

EDUCATION
Southern Methodist University, 2012 to present.
Major: English literature and journalism.
Journalism courses: news reporting, copy editing, electronic publishing, communication arts, broadcast journalism.

Abilene (Texas) Senior High School, 2008-12.
Academic, college preparatory degree.

EMPLOYMENT HISTORY
Reporter, Daily Campus, Southern Methodist University, 2012 to present.
Writer of articles for student newspaper on sports teams, campus policies, and local events. Editor of sports news, campus listings, and features.

Copy aide, Abilene Reporter-News, Abilene, summer 2013.
Assistant to reporters, routing copy and doing research.

Painter, Longhorn Painters, Abilene, summer 2012.
Preparation and painting of exteriors and interiors of houses.

SPECIAL SKILLS
Fluent in Spanish.
Proficient in Internet research and word processing.

REFERENCES
Available on request:
Placement Office
Southern Methodist University
Dallas, TX 75275

your education, skills, and previous work and volunteer experience. In addition, an online profile often contains the following:

- **A summary of your qualifications, goals, and experience,** similar to the opening paragraphs of a cover letter.
- **A portfolio of your best projects that are relevant to the job you seek**—for instance, writing that you completed for classes, internships, or jobs.
- **A current, high-quality headshot of you,** dressed as you would be for a job.

11d Writing business reports and proposals

Reports and proposals are text-heavy documents, sometimes lengthy, that convey information such as the results of research, a plan for action, or a recommendation for change.

Reports and proposals usually divide into sections. The sections vary depending on purpose, but often they include a summary; a statement of the problem or need, which justifies the report or proposal; a statement of the plan or solution, which responds to the problem or need; and a recommendation or evaluation. Consider the following samples and guidelines.

Report

Canada Geese at ABC Institute: An Environmental Problem

Descriptive title conveying report's contents

Summary

The flock of Canada geese on and around ABC Institute's grounds has grown dramatically in recent years to become a nuisance and an environmental problem. This report reviews the problem, considers possible solutions, and proposes that ABC Institute and the US Fish and Wildlife Service cooperate to reduce the flock by humane means.

Standard format: summary, statement of the problem, solutions, and (not shown) recommendations

The Problem

Canada geese began living at Taylor Lake next to ABC Institute when they were relocated there in 1995 by the state game department. As a nonmigratory flock, the geese are present year-round, with the highest population each year occurring in early spring. In recent years the flock has grown dramatically. The Audubon Society's annual Christmas bird census shows a thirty-fold increase from the 37 geese counted in 1996 to the 1125 counted in 2013.

Major sections delineated by headings

The principal environmental problem caused by the geese is pollution of grass and water by defecation. Geese droppings cover the ABC Institute's grounds as well as the park's picnicking areas. The runoff from these droppings into Taylor Lake has substantially affected the quality of the lake's water, so that local authorities have twice (2012 and 2013) issued warnings against swimming.

Formal tone, appropriate to a business-writing situation

Possible Solutions

The goose overpopulation and resulting environmental problems have several possible solutions:

Single spacing with double spacing between paragraphs and around the list

- Harass the geese with dogs and audiovisual effects (light and noise) so that the geese choose to leave. This solution is inhumane to the geese and unpleasant for human neighbors.
- Feed the geese a chemical that will weaken the shells of their eggs and thus reduce growth of the flock. This solution is inhumane to the geese and also impractical, because geese are long-lived.
- Kill adult geese. This solution is, obviously, inhumane to the geese.
- Thin the goose population by trapping and removing many geese (perhaps 600) to areas less populated by humans, such as wildlife preserves.

Bulleted list emphasizing alternative solutions

Though costly (see figures below), the last solution is the most humane. It would be harmless to the geese, provided that sizable netted enclosures are used for traps. [Discussion of solution and "Recommendations" section follow.]

- **Do your research.** To write a successful report or proposal, you must be well informed. Be alert to where you have enough information or where you don't.
- **Focus on the purpose of each section.** Stick to the point of each section, saying only what you need to say, even if you have additional information. Each section should accomplish its purpose and contribute to the whole.
- **Follow an appropriate format.** In many businesses, reports and proposals have specific formatting requirements. If you are unsure about the requirements, ask your supervisor.

Internal proposal

Memo format for internal proposal (pp. 236–37)

"Overview": statement of proposal

"Need": justification for the request

Formal tone appropriate for a proposal

"Plan": explanation of request

"Budget" and "Personnel": details on the proposal's requirements

Single spacing with double spacing between sections

Springfield Veterans Administration Hospital

To: Jefferson Green, Director, Finance and Operations
From: Kate Goodman, Director, ReadingWorks
Date: March 5, 2014
Subject: Budget proposal for ReadingWorks Awards Dinner

OVERVIEW

ReadingWorks requests funding for an awards dinner.

NEED

ReadingWorks, the literacy center operated by Springfield VA Hospital, has for 6 years served between 50 and 70 patients/students a year with a small paid staff and a corps of dedicated volunteers. In the past year the center's paid staff and 20 volunteers provided more than 1260 hours of literacy tutoring to 67 students, an increase of 14 students over last year. I want to recognize the efforts and accomplishments of our students and tutors by holding an awards dinner for them and their families.

PLAN

I propose the following event for Friday, May 23, 7:30 to 10:30 PM: dinner and nonalcoholic beverages for approximately 135 students, tutors, and their guests; entertainment; and certificates for approximately 20 students and tutors. I request the use of Suite 42 because it can accommodate as many as 200 people as well as caterers and a DJ. Hospital staff will need to have the room ready by 6:00 PM on May 23.

BUDGET

Dinner and beverages for about 135 attendees	$2700
Music for two hours	200
Certificates	50
TOTAL	$2950

Bids from local businesses are attached.

PERSONNEL

Five hospital employees will be needed to set up, take down, and clean Suite 42 before and after the dinner.

11e Writing for community work

At some point in your life, you're likely to volunteer for a community organization such as a soup kitchen, a daycare center, or a literacy program. Many college courses involve service learning, in which you do such volunteer work, write about the experience for your course, and write *for* the organization you're helping.

The writing you do for a community group may include creating or updating the group's Web site or *Twitter* account or producing more formal newsletters, flyers, and brochures. The following tips can help you with such writing:

- **Craft your writing for its purpose and audience.** To achieve a specific aim with your readers, use an approach and a tone that will influence their responses. For example, in a letter to local businesses to raise funds for a homeless shelter, you would address the readers formally and focus on the shelter's benefits to them and the community. To recruit volunteers through the shelter's *Facebook* page, you would be more conversational and enthusiastic, emphasizing the rewards of helping out.
- **Remember that your writing represents the organization.** Social media in particular encourage informal communication, but in

Social-media post

Congratulations to ReadingWorks tutors and students, who last year logged more tutoring hours and passed more levels of proficiency than in any prior year. We are proud of you! We will celebrate your accomplishments at the Annual Awards Dinner on May 23. Please mark your calendars and watch for details—at ReadingWorks.

Like • Comment • Share 12

Online post written in a conversational style

Photograph illustrating information in the post

Newsletter

Springfield Veterans Administration Hospital SUMMER 2014

From the director

Can you help? With more and more learners in the ReadingWorks program, we need more and more tutors. You may know people who would be interested in participating in the program, if only they knew about it.

Those of you who have been tutoring VA patients in reading and writing know both the great need you fulfill and the great benefits you bring to the students. New tutors need no special skills—we'll provide the training—only patience and an interest in helping others.

We've scheduled an orientation meeting for Friday, September 12, at 6:30 PM. Please come and bring a friend who is willing to contribute a couple of hours a week to our work.

Thanks,
Kate Goodman

IN THIS ISSUE

First Annual Awards Dinner	1
New Guidelines on PTSD	1
Textbooks	2
Lesson Planning	2
Dyslexia Workshop	2
Support for Tutors	3
Writing by Students	3
Calendar of Events	4

FIRST ANNUAL AWARDS DINNER

A festive night for students and tutors

The first annual ReadingWorks Awards Dinner on May 23 was a great success. Springfield's own Golden Fork provided tasty food and Amber Allen supplied lively music. The students decorated Suite 42 on the theme of books and reading. In all, 127 people attended.

The highlight of the night was the awards ceremony. Nine students, recommended by their tutors, received certificates recognizing their efforts and special accomplishments in learning to read and write:

Ramon Berva
Edward Byar
David Dunbar
Tony Garnier
Chris Guigni
Akili Haynes
Josh Livingston
Alex Obeld
B. J. Resnansky

In addition, nine tutors received certificates commemorating five years of service to ReadingWorks:

Anita Crumpton
Felix Cruz-Rivera
Bette Elgen
Kayleah Bortoluzzi
Harriotte Henderson
Ben Obiso
Meggie Puente
Max Smith
Sara Villante

Congratulations to all!

PTSD: New Guidelines

Most of us are working with veterans who have been diagnosed with post-traumatic stress disorder. Because this disorder is often complicated by alcoholism, depression, anxiety, and other problems, the National Center for PTSD has issued some guidelines for helping PTSD patients in ways that reduce their stress.

- The hospital must know your tutoring schedule, and you need to sign in and out before and after each tutoring session.
- To protect patients' privacy, meet them only in designated visiting and tutoring areas, never in their rooms.
- Treat patients with dignity and respect, even when (as sometimes happens) they grow frustrated and angry. Seek help from a nurse or orderly if you need it.

Multicolumn format allowing room for headings, articles, and other elements on a single page

Two-column heading emphasizing the main article

Elements helping readers skim for highlights: spacing, varied font sizes, lines, and a bulleted list

Color focusing readers' attention on banner, headlines, and table of contents

Lively but uncluttered overall appearance

Box in the first column highlighting table of contents

representing the organization you are obligated to be professional. If you respond to a negative comment on your organization's blog, for example, avoid sounding defensive or angry.

- **Expect input from others.** Much public writing is the work of more than one person. Even if you draft the document on your own, others will review the content, tone, and design. Such collaboration is rewarding, but it sometimes requires patience and goodwill. See pages 56–57 for advice on collaborating.

The illustrations in this section show writing prepared for Reading Works, a literacy program. See also pages 233–37 and 241–42 on business writing and pages 127–29 on visuals for presentations.

PART 3

Grammatical Sentences

12 Understanding Sentence Grammar

Chapter essentials

- Construct sentences with subjects and predicates (opposite).
- Identify nouns, pronouns, and verbs (p. 248).
- Form the basic sentence patterns (p. 251).
- Expand sentences using single words and word groups (pp. 255 and 257).
- Link information in compound sentences (p. 268).
- Construct some sentences without the usual subject-predicate order (p. 270).
- Write varied types of sentences: simple, compound, complex, and compound-complex (p. 272).

Visit MyWritingLab™ for more resources on sentence grammar.

Grammar describes how language works. If you are a native speaker of English, you follow the rules of grammar mostly unconsciously. But when you're trying to improve your communication, making the rules conscious and learning the language for them can help.

Grammar reveals a lot about a sentence, even if you don't know the meanings of all the words:

> The rumfrums prattly biggled the pooba.

You don't know what this sentence means, but you can infer that some things called *rumfrums* did something to a *pooba*. They *biggled* it, whatever that means, in a *prattly* way. Two grammatical cues, especially, make this sentence like *The students easily passed the test*:

- **Word forms.** The ending *-s* means more than one *rumfrum*. The ending *-ed* means that *biggled* is an action that happened in the past. The ending *-ly* means that *prattly* probably describes *how* the rumfrums biggled.
- **Word order.** *Rumfrums biggled pooba* resembles a common sequence in English: something (*rumfrums*) performed some action (*biggled*) to or on something else (*pooba*). Since *prattly* comes right before the action, it probably describes the action.

This chapter explains how such structures work and shows how practicing with them can help you communicate more effectively.

12a Understanding the basic sentence

The **sentence** is the basic unit of thought. Its grammar consists of words with specific forms and functions arranged in specific ways.

1 Identifying subjects and predicates

Most sentences make statements. First the **subject** names something; then the **predicate** makes an assertion about the subject or describes an action by the subject.

Subject	Predicate
Art	thrives.

The **simple subject** consists of one or more nouns or pronouns, whereas the **complete subject** also includes any modifiers. The **simple predicate** consists of one or more verbs, whereas the **complete predicate** adds any words needed to complete the meaning of the verb plus any modifiers.

Sometimes, as in the short example *Art thrives,* the simple and complete subject and predicate are the same. More often, they are different:

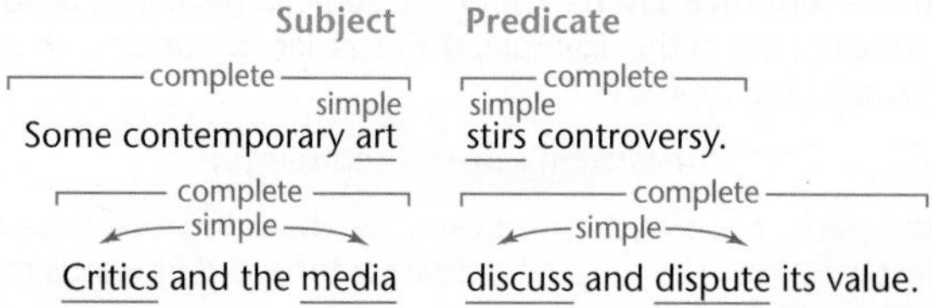

In the second example, the simple subject and simple predicate are both **compound**: in each, two words joined by *and* serve the same function.

Note If a sentence contains a word group such as *that makes it into museums* or *because we dispute its quality,* you may be tempted to mark the subject and verb in the word group as the subject and verb of the sentence. But these word groups are subordinate clauses, made into modifiers by the words they begin with: *that* and *because.* See page 263 for more on subordinate clauses.

CULTURE LANGUAGE The subject of an English sentence may be a noun (*art*) or a pronoun that refers to the noun (*it*), but not both. (See pp. 248–49.)

Faulty Art it can stir controversy.
Revised Art can stir controversy.
Revised It can stir controversy.

When identifying the subject and the predicate of a sentence, be aware that some English words can serve as both nouns and verbs. For example, *visits* in the following sentences functions as a verb and as a noun:

She visits the museum every Saturday. [Verb.]
Her visits are enjoyable. [Noun.]

Tests to find subjects and predicates

The tests below use the following example:

Art that makes it into museums has often survived controversy.

Identify the subject.

- **Ask *who* or *what* is acting or being described in the sentence.**

  Complete subject — art that makes it into museums

- **Isolate the simple subject by deleting modifiers**—words or word groups that don't name the actor of the sentence but give information about it. In the example, the word group *that makes it into museums* does not name the actor but modifies it.

  Simple subject — art

Identify the predicate.

- **Ask what the sentence asserts about the subject:** what is its action, or what state is it in? In the example, the assertion about *art* is that it *has often survived controversy.*

  Complete predicate — has often survived controversy

- **Isolate the verb, the simple predicate, by changing the time of the subject's action.** The simple predicate is the word or words that change as a result.

Example	Art . . . has often survived controversy.
Present	Art . . . often survives controversy.
Future	Art . . . will often survive controversy.
Simple predicate	has survived

2 Identifying the basic words: Nouns, pronouns, verbs

English words fall into eight classes—the **parts of speech** shown in the box opposite. The most common parts of speech are nouns, pronouns, and verbs.

Note In different sentences an English word may serve different functions and take different forms depending on the function. The function of a word always determines its part of speech in the sentence. For example:

The government sent the city aid. [*Aid* functions as a noun.]

Governments aid citizens. [*Aid* functions as a verb.]

Nouns

Meaning

Nouns name. They may name a person (*Angelina Jolie, LeBron James, Jackson, astronaut*), a thing (*chair, book, Mt. Rainier*), a qual-

The parts of speech

Nouns name persons, places, things, ideas, or qualities: *Roosevelt, girl, Kip River, coastline, Koran, table, strife, happiness.* (See opposite and below.)

Pronouns usually substitute for nouns and function as nouns: *I, you, he, she, it, we, they, myself, this, that, who, which, everyone.* (See p. 250.)

Verbs express actions, occurrences, or states of being: *run, bunt, inflate, become, be.* (See p. 250.)

Adjectives describe or modify nouns or pronouns: *gentle, small, helpful.* (See pp. 255–56.)

Adverbs describe or modify verbs, adjectives, other adverbs, or whole groups of words: *gently, helpfully, almost, really, not, someday.* (See pp. 255–56.)

Prepositions relate nouns or pronouns to other words in a sentence: *about, at, down, for, of, with.* (See pp. 257–58.)

Conjunctions link words, phrases, and clauses. **Coordinating conjunctions** and **correlative conjunctions** link words, phrases, or clauses of equal importance: *and, but, or, nor; both . . . and, not only . . . but also, either . . . or.* (See pp. 268–69.) **Subordinating conjunctions** introduce subordinate clauses and link them to main clauses: *although, because, if, whenever.* (See p. 264.)

Interjections express feeling or command attention, either alone or in a sentence: *hey, oh, darn, wow.*

ity (*pain, mystery, simplicity*), a place (*city, Washington, ocean, Red Sea*), or an idea (*reality, peace, success*).

Form

Most nouns form the **possessive** to indicate ownership or source. Singular nouns usually add an apostrophe plus *-s* (*Auden's poems*); plural nouns usually add just an apostrophe (*citizens' rights*).

Nouns also change form to distinguish between singular (one) and plural (more than one). Most nouns add *-s* or *-es* for the plural: *earthquake, earthquakes; city, cities*. Some nouns have irregular plurals: *woman, women; child, children*.

CULTURE LANGUAGE Some useful rules for forming noun plurals appear on pages 532–33. The irregular plurals must be memorized. Note that some English nouns are not considered countable and do not have plural forms. Examples of these **noncount nouns** are *equality, anger, oxygen, bravery*, and *equipment*. (See also p. 332.)

Nouns with *the, a,* and *an*

Nouns are often preceded by *the* or *a* (*an* before a vowel sound: *an apple*). These words are usually called **articles** or **determiners** and always indicate that a noun follows.

See pages 332–34 for the rules governing the use of *the, a/an,* or no article at all before a noun.

Pronouns

Most **pronouns** substitute for nouns and function in sentences as nouns do. In the following sentence all three pronouns—*who, they, their*—refer to *nurses*:

> Some nurses who have families prefer the night shift because they have more time with their children.

The most common pronouns are the **personal pronouns** (*I, you, he, she, it, we, they*) and the **relative pronouns** (*who, whoever, which, that*). Most of them change form to indicate their function in the sentence—for instance, *He called me. I called him back.* (See Chapter 13 for a discussion of these form changes.)

Verbs

Meaning

Verbs express an action (*bring, change, grow*), an occurrence (*become, happen*), or a state of being (*be, seem*).

Form

Most verbs can be recognized by two changes in form:

- **Most verbs add *-d* or *-ed* to indicate a difference between present and past time:** *They play today. They played yesterday.* Some verbs indicate past time irregularly: *eat, ate; begin, began* (see pp. 285–87).
- **Most present-time verbs add *-s* or *-es* with subjects that are singular:** *The bear escapes. It runs. The woman begins. She sings.* The exceptions are *be* and *have,* which change to *is* and *has.*

(See Chapter 14, pp. 282–98, for more on verb forms.)

Helping verbs

Certain forms of all verbs can combine with other words such as *do, have, can, might, will,* and *must.* These other words are called **helping verbs** or **auxiliary verbs.** In phrases such as *could run, will be running,* and *has escaped,* they help to convey time and other attributes. (See Chapter 14, pp. 284, 290–94.)

Exercise 12.1 Identifying subjects and predicates

In the following sentences, insert a vertical line between the complete subject and the complete predicate. Underline each simple subject once and each simple predicate twice. Then use each sentence as a model to create a sentence of your own.

Example:

The pony, the light horse, and the draft horse | are three types of domestic horses.

Sample imitation: Toyota, Honda, and Nissan are three brands of Japanese cars.

1. The leaves fell.
2. October ends soon.
3. The orchard owners made apple cider.
4. They examined each apple carefully for quality.
5. Over a hundred people will buy cider at the roadside stand.

Exercise 12.2 Identifying nouns, pronouns, and verbs

In the following sentences identify all words functioning as nouns with *N*, all pronouns with *P*, and all words functioning as verbs with *V*.

Example:

P V N N
They took the tour through the museum.

1. The trees died.
2. They caught a disease.
3. The disease was a fungus.
4. It ruined a special grove.
5. Our great-grandfather planted the grove ninety years ago.

Exercise 12.3 Using nouns and verbs

Identify each of the following words as a noun, as a verb, or as both. Then create sentences of your own, using each word in each possible function.

Example:
fly
Noun and verb.
The fly sat on the meat loaf. [Noun.] The planes fly low. [Verb.]

1. wish
2. tie
3. swing
4. mail
5. spend
6. label
7. door
8. company
9. whistle
10. glue

3 Forming sentence patterns with nouns and verbs

English builds all sentences on the five basic patterns shown in the box on the next page. As the diagrams indicate, the patterns differ in their predicates because the relation between the verb and the remaining words is different.

CULTURE LANGUAGE Word order in English sentences may not correspond to word order in the sentences of your native language. For instance, some other languages prefer the verb first in the sentence, whereas English strongly prefers the subject first, then the verb, then any other words. The main exceptions to the word patterns discussed here appear on pages 270–71: questions, commands, passive sentences, and sentences with postponed subjects. See also pages 364–69 on positioning modifiers in sentences.

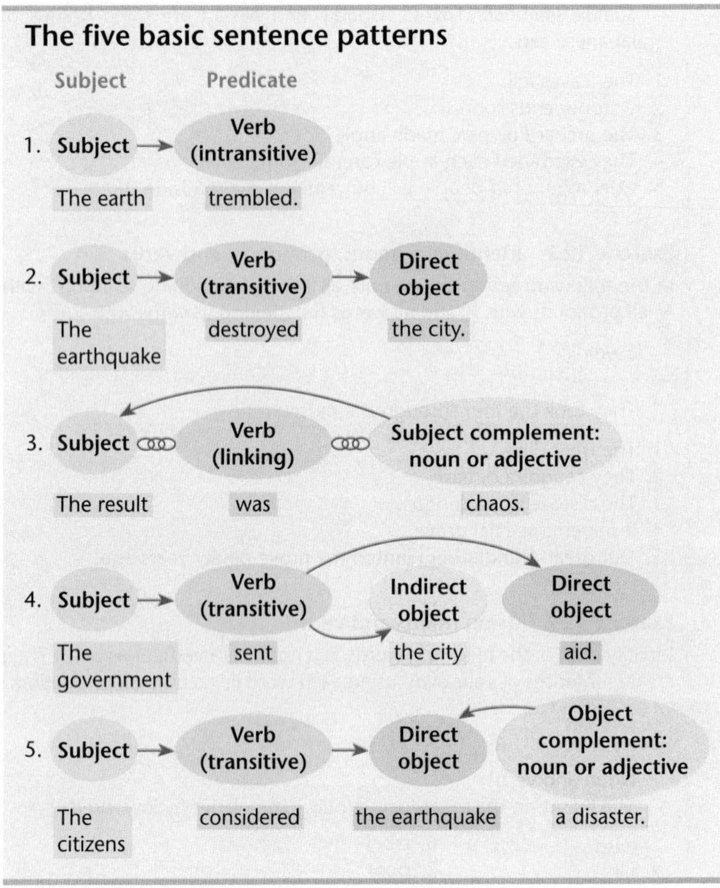

Pattern 1: The earth trembled.

In the simplest pattern the predicate consists only of the verb. Verbs in this pattern do not require following words to complete their meaning and thus are called **intransitive** (from Latin words meaning "not passing over").

Subject	Predicate
	Intransitive verb
The earth	trembled.
The hospital	may close.

Pattern 2: The earthquake destroyed the city.

In pattern 2 the predicate consists of a verb followed by a noun that identifies who or what receives the action of the verb. This noun is a **direct object.** Verbs that require direct objects to complete their meaning are called **transitive** ("passing over"): the verb transfers the action from subject to object.

Subject	Predicate	
	Transitive verb	*Direct object*
The earthquake	destroyed	the city.
Education	opens	doors.

CULTURE LANGUAGE The distinction between transitive verbs (pattern 2) and intransitive verbs (pattern 1) is important because only transitive verbs may be used in the passive voice, when the subject is acted upon: *The city was destroyed by the earthquake.* (See pp. 307–09.) Your dictionary says whether a verb is transitive or intransitive, often with an abbreviation such as *tr.* or *intr.* Some verbs (*begin, learn, read, write,* and others) can be either transitive or intransitive.

Pattern 3: The result was chaos.

In pattern 3 the predicate also consists of a verb followed by a noun, but the noun renames or describes the subject. The sentence could be written *The result = chaos.* The verb is a **linking verb** because it links the subject and the following description. The linking verbs include *be, seem, appear, become, grow, remain, stay, prove, feel, look, smell, sound,* and *taste.* The word that describes the subject is called a **subject complement** (it complements, or completes, the subject).

Subject	Predicate	
	Linking verb	*Subject complement*
The result	was	chaos.
The man	became	an accountant.

Subject complements in this sentence pattern may also be adjectives, words such as *tall* and *hopeful* (see p. 255):

Subject	Predicate	
	Linking verb	*Subject complement*
The result	was	chaotic.
The apartments	seem	expensive.

Pattern 4: The government sent the city aid.

In pattern 4 the predicate consists of a verb followed by two nouns. The second noun, *aid,* is a direct object (see pattern 2). But the first noun, *city,* is an **indirect object,** identifying to or for whom the action of the verb is performed. The direct object and indirect object refer to different things, people, or places.

Subject	Predicate		
	Transitive verb	*Indirect object*	*Direct object*
The government	sent	the city	aid.
One company	offered	its employees	bonuses.

A number of verbs can take indirect objects, including those above and *allow, bring, buy, deny, find, get, leave, make, pay, read, sell, show, teach,* and *write.*

CULTURE LANGUAGE With some verbs that express action done to or for someone, the indirect object must be turned into a phrase beginning with *to* or *for*. In addition, the phrase must come after the direct object. The verbs that require these changes include *admit, announce, demonstrate, explain, introduce, mention, prove, recommend, say,* and *suggest*.

gram 12a

Faulty The manual explains workers [indirect object] the new procedure [direct object].

Revised The manual explains the new procedure [direct object] to workers [*to* phrase].

Pattern 5: The citizens considered the earthquake a disaster.

In pattern 5, as in pattern 4, the predicate consists of a verb followed by two nouns. But in pattern 5 the first noun is a direct object and the second noun renames or describes it. Here the second noun is an **object complement**:

Subject	Predicate		
	Transitive verb	*Direct object*	*Object complement*
The citizens	considered	the earthquake	a disaster.
The class	elected	Kate O'Day	president.

Like a subject complement (pattern 3), an object complement may be a noun or an adjective, as below:

Subject	Predicate		
	Transitive verb	*Direct object*	*Object complement*
The citizens	considered	the earthquake	disastrous.
Success	makes	some people	nervous.

Exercise 12.4 Identifying sentence patterns

In the following sentences, identify each verb as intransitive, transitive, or linking. Then identify each direct object (DO), indirect object (IO), subject complement (SC), and object complement (OC).

Example:

Children give [transitive verb] their parents [IO] both headaches [DO] and pleasures [DO].

1. Many people find New York City exciting.
2. Tourists flock to New York each year.
3. Often they visit Times Square first.
4. The square's lights are astounding.
5. The flashing signs sell visitors everything from TVs to underwear.

Exercise 12.5 Creating sentences

Create sentences by using each of the following verbs in the pattern indicated. (For the meanings of the abbreviations, see the directions for Exercise 12.4.) You may want to change the form of the verb.

Example:
give (S-V-IO-DO)
Sam gave his brother a birthday card.

1. laugh (S-V)
2. elect (S-V-DO-OC)
3. steal (S-V-DO)
4. catch (S-V-DO)
5. bring (S-V-IO-DO)
6. seem (S-V-SC)
7. call (S-V-DO-OC)
8. become (S-V-SC)
9. buy (S-V-IO-DO)
10. study (S-V)

12b Expanding the basic sentence with single words

Most sentences include modifying words that describe or limit nouns and verbs.

1 Using adjectives and adverbs

The most common modifying words are adjectives and adverbs:

- **Adjectives** describe or modify nouns and pronouns. They specify which one, what quality, or how many.

old (adjective) → city (noun)   generous (adjective) → one (pronoun)   two (adjective) → pears (noun)

- **Adverbs** describe or modify verbs, adjectives, other adverbs, and whole groups of words. They specify when, where, how, and to what extent.

nearly (adverb) → destroyed (verb)   too (adverb) → quickly (adverb)

very (adverb) → generous (adjective)   Unfortunately, (adverb) → taxes will rise. (word group)

An *-ly* ending often signals an adverb, but not always: *friendly* is an adjective; *never, not,* and *always* are adverbs. The only way to tell whether a word is an adjective or an adverb is to determine what it modifies.

Adjectives and adverbs appear in three forms:

- **Positive:** The basic form, the one listed in the dictionary: *good, green, angry; badly, quickly, angrily.*
- **Comparative:** The form that indicates a greater degree of the quality named by the word: *better, greener, angrier; worse, more quickly, more angrily.*
- **Superlative:** The form that indicates the greatest degree of the quality named: *best, greenest, angriest; worst, most quickly, most angrily.*

(For further discussion of these forms, see pp. 327–29.)

2 Using other words as modifiers

Nouns and special forms of verbs may sometimes serve as modifiers of other nouns. In combinations such as *office buildings, Thanksgiving dinner,* and *shock hazard,* the first noun modifies the second. In combinations such as *singing birds, corrected papers,* and *broken finger,* the first word is a verb form modifying the following noun.

Exercise 12.6 Identifying and using adjectives and adverbs

Identify the adjectives and adverbs in the following sentences. Then use each sentence as a model for creating a sentence of your own.

Example:

The red (adjective) barn sat uncomfortably (adverb) among modern (adjective) buildings.

Sample imitation: The little girl complained loudly to her busy mother.

1. The blue water glistened in the hot afternoon sunlight.
2. Happily, children dipped their toes in the cool lake.
3. Excitedly, some of the children hopped into the water.
4. Cautious parents watched from their shady porches.
5. The children played contentedly until the day finally ended.

Exercise 12.7 Using verb forms as modifiers

Use each of the following verb forms to modify a noun in a sentence of your own.

Example:

smoking

Only a smoking cigar remained.

1. scrambled
2. twitching
3. rambling
4. typed
5. painted
6. written
7. charging
8. ripened
9. known
10. driven

Exercise 12.8 Sentence combining: Single-word modifiers

To practice expanding the basic sentence patterns with single-word modifiers, combine each group of sentences below into one sentence. You will have to delete and rearrange words.

Example:

Paris offers tourists food. Paris offers food proudly. The food is delicious.

Paris proudly offers tourists delicious food.

1. The turn of the century ushered in technology and materials. The century was the twentieth. The technology was improved. The materials were new.
2. A skeleton made the construction of skyscrapers possible. The skeleton was sturdy. It was made of steel.
3. By 1913 the Woolworth Building, with its ornaments, stood 760 feet (55 stories). The building was towering. The ornaments were Gothic.
4. At 1450 feet the Willis Tower in Chicago doubles the height of the Woolworth Building. The doubling is now. The Woolworth height is puny. The puniness is relative.
5. Skyscrapers became practical in 1857 when Elisha Graves Otis built the elevator. It was the first elevator. The elevator was safe. It served passengers.

12c Expanding the basic sentence with word groups

Most sentences contain phrases and clauses that serve as nouns and modifiers:

- **A *phrase* is a group of related words that lacks either a subject or a predicate or both:** *excited by the results, to enroll more patients.*
- **A *clause* contains both a subject and a predicate:** *When the experiment succeeded* and *the researchers expanded the study* are both clauses, though only the second can stand alone as a sentence.

1 Using prepositional phrases

Prepositions are connecting words. Unlike nouns, verbs, and modifiers, which may change form, prepositions never change form. The box on the next page shows that many prepositions signal relationships of time or space, while others signal relationships such as addition, comparison, opposition, and source. Notice that some prepositions consist of more than one word.

A preposition connects a noun or pronoun to another word in the sentence: *Robins nest in trees.* The noun or pronoun so connected (*trees*) is the **object of the preposition.** The preposition plus its object and any modifiers is a **prepositional phrase:**

Preposition	Object
on	the surface
upon	entering the room
from	where you are standing
except for	ten employees

Prepositional phrases function as adjectives, modifying nouns, or as adverbs, modifying verbs, adjectives, or other adverbs.

Common prepositions

Time or space (position or direction)			Other relationships (addition, comparison, etc.)	
about	by	out of	according to	in spite of
above	down	outside	as	instead of
across	during	over	as for	like
after	for	past	aside from	of
against	from	since	because of	on account of
along	in	through	concerning	regarding
along with	inside	throughout	despite	regardless of
among	inside of	till	except	unlike
around	into	to	except for	with
at	near	toward	excepting	without
before	next to	under	in addition to	
behind	off	underneath		
below	on	until		
beneath	onto	up		
beside	on top of	upon		
between	out	within		
beyond				

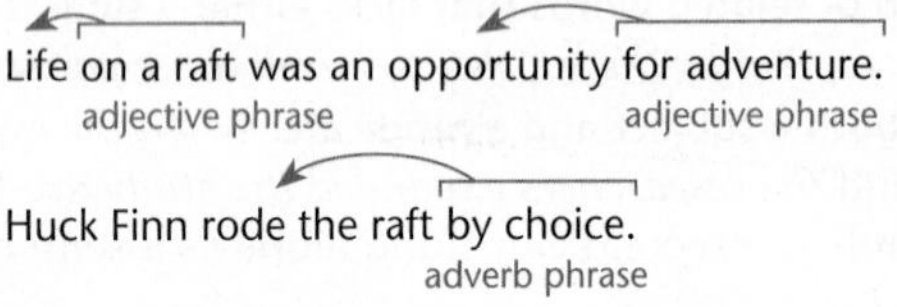

Life on a raft was an opportunity for adventure.
adjective phrase
adjective phrase
Huck Finn rode the raft by choice.
adverb phrase

Note For revising sentence fragments that are prepositional phrases, see pages 342–43. For using commas with prepositional phrases that introduce, interrupt, or conclude sentences, see pages 425–29.

CULTURE LANGUAGE The meanings and idiomatic uses of English prepositions can be difficult to master; most must be memorized or looked up in a dictionary. (A list of dictionaries for English as a second language appears on p. 509.) See pages 297–98 for two-word verbs that include prepositions, such as *look after,* and see pages 513–15 for idioms with prepositions.

Exercise 12.9 Identifying prepositional phrases

Identify the prepositional phrases in the following passage. Indicate whether each phrase functions as an adjective or as an adverb, and underline the word that the phrase modifies.

Example:

After an hour I finally arrived at the home of my professor.

On July 3, 1863, at Gettysburg, Pennsylvania, General Robert E. Lee gambled unsuccessfully for a Confederate victory in the American Civil War. The battle of Pickett's Charge was one of the most disastrous conflicts of the war. Confederate and Union forces faced each other on parallel ridges separated by almost a mile of open fields. After an artillery bombardment of the Union position, nearly 12,000 Confederate infantry marched toward the Union ridge. The Union guns had been silent but suddenly roared against the approaching Confederates. Within an hour, perhaps half of the Confederate soldiers lay wounded or dead.

Exercise 12.10 Sentence combining: Prepositional phrases

To practice writing sentences with prepositional phrases, combine each group of sentences below into one sentence that includes one or two prepositional phrases. You will have to add, delete, and rearrange words. Some items have more than one possible answer.

Example:

I will start working. The new job will pay the minimum wage.
I will start working at a new job for the minimum wage.

1. The slow loris protects itself well. Its habitat is Southeast Asia. It possesses a poisonous chemical.
2. The loris frightens predators when it exudes this chemical. The chemical comes from a gland. The gland is on the loris's upper arm.
3. The loris's chemical is highly toxic. The chemical is not like a skunk's spray. Even small quantities of the chemical are toxic.
4. A tiny dose can affect a human. The dose would get in the mouth. The human would be sent into shock.
5. Predators probably can sense the toxin. They detect it at a distance. They use their nasal organs.

2 Using verbals and verbal phrases

Verbals are special verb forms such as *smoking* or *hidden* or *to win* that can function as nouns (*smoking is dangerous*) or as modifiers (*the hidden money, the urge to win*).

Note A verbal is not a verb: it *cannot* stand alone as the complete verb in the predicate of a sentence. For example, *The man smoking* and *The money hidden* are not sentences but sentence fragments. See page 341 on revising such fragments. And see pp. 425–29 on using commas with verbals that introduce, interrupt, or conclude sentences.

Participles

All verbs have two participle forms: present and past. The **present participle** ends in *-ing*: *beginning, hiding, ending.* The **past participle** usually ends in *-d* or *-ed*: *believed, ended.* Some verbs have an irregular past participle, such as *begun* or *hidden* (see pp. 285–87).

Both present and past participles usually function as adjectives to modify nouns and pronouns:

Shopping malls sometimes frustrate shoppers. [*Shopping* modifies *malls.*]

Shoppers may have a trapped feeling. [*Trapped* modifies *feeling.*]

CULTURE LANGUAGE The present and past participles of verbs that express feelings have different meanings. The present participle modifies the thing that causes the feeling: *It was a boring lecture*. The past participle modifies the thing that experiences the feeling: *The bored students slept*. See pages 330–31.

Gerunds

A **gerund** is the *-ing* form of the verb when it serves as a noun:

subject
Shopping at a mall can be exhausting.

object
Many children learn to hate shopping.

Present participles and gerunds can be distinguished *only* by their function in a sentence. When the *-ing* form functions as an adjective (*a teaching degree*), it is a present participle. When the *-ing* form functions as a noun (*Teaching is difficult*), it is a gerund.

CULTURE LANGUAGE In English, always use a gerund, not any other verb form, as the object of a preposition:

Faulty Diners are prohibited from to smoke.
Revised Diners are prohibited from smoking.

See also the culture-language note below.

Infinitives

The **infinitive** is the dictionary form of a verb preceded by the infinitive marker *to*: *to begin, to hide, to run*. Infinitives may function as adjectives, nouns, or adverbs:

adjective
The question to answer is why shoppers endure mall fatigue.

noun
The solution for mall fatigue is to leave.

adverb
Still, shoppers find it difficult to quit.

CULTURE LANGUAGE Infinitives and gerunds may follow some English verbs and not others and may differ in meaning after a verb:

The cowboy stopped to sing. [He stopped to do the activity.]
The cowboy stopped singing. [He finished the activity.]

(See pp. 295–96.)

Verbal phrases

Participles, gerunds, and infinitives—like other verb forms—may take subjects, objects, or complements, and they may be modified by adverbs. The verbal and all the words immediately related to it make up a **verbal phrase**.

- ***Participial phrases* usually serve as adjectives, modifying nouns or pronouns:**

  Buying things, most shoppers feel themselves in control.

  They make selections determined by personal taste.

- ***Gerund phrases*, like gerunds, always serve as nouns:**

  subject

  Shopping for clothing and other items satisfies personal needs.

  object of preposition

  Malls are good at creating such needs.

- ***Infinitive phrases* may serve as nouns, adverbs, or adjectives:**

  sentence subject — subject complement

  To design a mall is to create an artificial environment.

  noun phrase — noun phrase

  Malls are designed to make shoppers feel safe.

  adverb phrase

  The environment supports the impulse to shop for oneself.

  adjective phrase

When an infinitive or infinitive phrase serves as a noun after verbs such as *hear, help, let, make, see,* and *watch,* the infinitive marker *to* is omitted: *We all heard her tell* [not *to tell*] *the story.*

Exercise 12.11 Identifying verbals and verbal phrases

The following sentences contain participles, gerunds, and infinitives as well as participial, gerund, and infinitive phrases. First underline each verbal or verbal phrase. Then indicate whether it is used as an adjective, an adverb, or a noun.

Example:

adjective — adverb

Laughing, the talk-show host prodded her guest to speak.

1. Written in 1850 by Nathaniel Hawthorne, *The Scarlet Letter* tells the story of Hester Prynne.
2. Shunned by the community, Hester endures her loneliness.
3. Hester is humble enough to withstand her Puritan neighbors' cutting remarks.
4. Enduring the cruel treatment, the determined young woman refuses to leave her home.
5. By living a life of patience and unselfishness, Hester eventually becomes the community's angel.

Exercise 12.12 Sentence combining: Verbals and verbal phrases

To practice writing sentences with verbals and verbal phrases, combine each of the following pairs of sentences into one sentence. You will have to add, delete, change, and rearrange words. Each item has more than one possible answer.

Example:

My father enjoyed mean pranks. For instance, he hid the neighbor's cat.

My father enjoyed mean pranks such as hiding the neighbor's cat.

1. Air pollution is a health problem. It affects millions of Americans.
2. The air has been polluted mainly by industries and automobiles. It contains toxic chemicals.
3. Environmentalists pressure politicians. They think politicians should pass stricter laws.
4. Many politicians waver. They are not necessarily against environmentalism.
5. The problems are too complex. They cannot be solved easily.

3 Using absolute phrases

Absolute phrases consist of a noun or pronoun and a participle, plus any modifiers:

absolute phrase

Many ethnic groups, their own place established, are making way for new arrivals.

absolute phrase

Their native lands left behind, immigrants face many obstacles.

These phrases are called *absolute* (from a Latin word meaning "free") because they have no specific grammatical connection to a noun, verb, or any other word in the rest of the sentence. Instead, they modify the entire rest of the sentence, adding information.

Notice that absolute phrases, unlike participial phrases, always contain a subject. Compare the following sentences:

participial phrase

For many immigrants learning English, the language introduces American culture.

absolute phrase

The immigrants having learned English, their opportunities widen.

Note For using commas to set off absolute phrases, see page 432.

Exercise 12.13 Sentence combining: Absolute phrases

To practice writing sentences with absolute phrases, combine each pair of sentences below into one sentence that contains an absolute phrase. You will have to add, delete, change, and rearrange words.

Example:

The flower's petals wilted. It looked pathetic.

Its petals wilted, the flower looked pathetic.

1. Geraldine Ferraro's face beamed. She enjoyed the crowd's cheers after her nomination for Vice President.
2. A vacancy had occurred. Sandra Day O'Connor was appointed the first female Supreme Court justice.
3. The vote was complete. Madeleine Albright was confirmed as the first female secretary of state.
4. Her appointment was confirmed. Condoleezza Rice became the first female national security adviser.
5. The election was over. Nancy Pelosi became the first female speaker of the House of Representatives.

4 Using subordinate clauses

A **clause** is any group of words that contains both a subject and a predicate. There are two kinds of clauses:

- **A *main* or *independent clause* makes a complete statement and can stand alone as a sentence:**

  [main clause] [main clause]
  The school teaches parents. It is unusual.

- **A *subordinate* or *dependent clause* is just like a main clause except that it begins with a subordinating word:**

  [subordinate clause] [main clause]
  Because the school teaches parents, it is unusual.

The subordinating word reduces the clause to a single part of speech—an adjective, an adverb, or a noun—that supports the idea in the main clause. Because a subordinate clause only modifies or names something, it cannot stand alone as a sentence. (The word *subordinate* means "secondary" or "controlled by another.")

The following examples show the differences between main and subordinate clauses:

[main clause] [main clause]
Some parents avoid their children's schools. They often cannot read.

[main clause]
Often parents who cannot read avoid their children's schools.
[subordinate clause]

Note Because a subordinate clause only modifies or names something, it cannot stand alone as a sentence. See page 342 on revising sentence fragments that are subordinate clauses. And see pages 425–29 on using commas with subordinate clauses that introduce, interrupt, or conclude sentences.

Subordinating conjunctions and relative pronouns

Two kinds of subordinating words introduce subordinate clauses. The first is **subordinating conjunctions,** which are like prepositions in that they never change form. In the following box

gram 12c

they are arranged by the relationships they signal. (Some fit in more than one group.)

Common subordinating conjunctions

Cause or effect	Condition	Comparison or contrast	Space or time
as	even if	as	after
because	if	as if	as long as
in order that	if only	as though	before
since	provided	rather than	now that
so that	since	than	once
Concession	unless	whereas	since
although	when	whether	till
as if	whenever	while	until
even if	whether	**Purpose**	when
even though		in order that	whenever
though		so that	where
		that	wherever
			while

CULTURE LANGUAGE Learning the meanings of subordinating conjunctions can help you to express your ideas clearly. Note that each one conveys its meaning on its own. It does not need help from another function word, such as the coordinating conjunction *and, but, for,* or *so* (see p. 268).

Faulty Even though the parents cannot read, but their children may read well. [*Even though* and *but* have the same meaning, so both are not needed.]

Revised Even though the parents cannot read, their children may read well.

The second kind of subordinating word is **relative pronouns.** They usually act as subjects or objects in their own clauses, and two of them (*who* and *whoever*) change form accordingly (see p. 279).

Relative pronouns

which	what	who (whose, whom)
that	whatever	whoever (whomever)

Subordinate clauses

Subordinate clauses function as adjectives, adverbs, or nouns.

Adjective clauses

Adjective clauses modify nouns and pronouns. They usually begin with the relative pronoun *who, whom, whose, which,* or *that,* although a few adjective clauses begin with *when* or *where* (standing for *in which, on which,* or *at which*). The pronoun is the subject or object of the clause it begins. The clause ordinarily falls immediately after the noun or pronoun it modifies:

Parents who cannot read often have bad memories of school.

Schools that involve parents are more successful with children.

One school, which is open year-round, helps parents learn to read.

The school is in a city where the illiteracy rate is high.

Adverb clauses

Like adverbs, **adverb clauses** modify verbs, adjectives, other adverbs, and whole groups of words. They usually tell how, why, when, where, under what conditions, or with what result. They always begin with subordinating conjunctions.

The school began teaching parents when adult illiteracy gained national attention.

At first the program was not as successful as its founders had hoped.

Because it was directed at people who could not read, advertising had to be inventive.

Noun clauses

Noun clauses function as subjects, objects, and complements in sentences. They begin with *that, what, whatever, who, whom, whoever, whomever, when, where, whether, why,* or *how.* Unlike adjective and adverb clauses, noun clauses *replace* a word (a noun) within a clause; therefore, they can be difficult to identify.

sentence subject
Whether the program would succeed depended on door-to-door advertising.

object of verb
Teachers explained in person how the program would work.

object of preposition
A few parents were anxious about what their children would think.

Elliptical clauses

A subordinate clause that is grammatically incomplete but clear in meaning is an **elliptical clause** (*ellipsis* means "omission"). The meaning of the clause is clear because the missing element can be supplied from the context. Most often the elements omitted are the pronouns *that, which,* and *whom* or the predicate from the second part of a comparison.

Skepticism and fear were among the feelings [that] the parents voiced.
The parents knew their children could read better than they [could read].

Exercise 12.14 Identifying subordinate clauses

Identify the subordinate clauses in the following sentences. Then indicate whether each is used as an adjective, an adverb, or a noun. If the clause is a noun, indicate what function it performs in the sentence.

Example:

noun
The article explained how one could build an underground house. [Object of *explained.*]

1. Scientists who want to catch the slightest signals from space use extremely sensitive receivers.
2. Even though they have had to fight for funding, these scientists have persisted in their research.
3. The research is called SETI, which stands for Search for Extraterrestrial Intelligence.
4. The theory is that intelligent beings in space are trying to get in touch with us.
5. Scientists do not yet know what frequency these beings would use to send signals.

gram 12c

Exercise 12.15 Sentence combining: Subordinate clauses

To practice writing sentences with subordinate clauses, combine each pair of main clauses into one sentence. Use either subordinating conjunctions or relative pronouns as appropriate, referring to the lists on page 264 if necessary. You will have to add, delete, and rearrange words. Each item has more than one possible answer.

Example:

She did not have her tire irons with her. She could not change her bicycle tire.

Because she did not have her tire irons with her, she could not change her bicycle tire.

1. Moviegoers expect something. Movie sequels should be as exciting as the original films.
2. A few sequels are good films. Most sequels are poor imitations of the originals.
3. A sequel to a blockbuster film arrives in the theater. Crowds quickly line up to see it.
4. Viewers pay to see the same villains and heroes. They remember these characters fondly.
5. Afterward, viewers often grumble about filmmakers. The filmmakers rehash tired plots and characters.

5 Using appositives

An **appositive** is usually a noun that renames another noun nearby, most often the noun just before the appositive. (The word derives from Latin meaning "placed near to" or "applied to.") An **appositive phrase** includes modifiers as well.

> Bizen ware, a dark stoneware, has been produced in Japan since the fourteenth century.

> The name Bizen comes from the location of the kilns used to fire the pottery.

All appositives can replace the words they refer to: *A dark stoneware has been produced in Japan.*

Appositives are often introduced by words and phrases such as *or, that is, such as, for example,* and *in other words*:

> Bizen ware is used in the Japanese tea ceremony, that is, the Zen Buddhist observance that links meditation and art.

Appositives are economical alternatives to adjective clauses containing a form of *be*:

> Bizen ware, [which is] a dark stoneware, has been produced in Japan since the fourteenth century.

Although most appositives are nouns that rename other nouns, they may also be and rename other parts of speech, such as the verb *thrown* in the sentence below:

> The pottery is thrown, or formed on a potter's wheel.

Note For revising sentence fragments that are appositives or appositive phrases, see page 343. For how to use punctuation to set off appositives, see pages 429 (commas), 467–68 (the colon), and 469 (dashes).

Exercise 12.16 Sentence combining: Appositives

To practice writing sentences with appositives, combine each pair of sentences into one sentence that contains an appositive. You will have to delete and rearrange words. Some items have more than one possible answer.

Example:

The largest land animal is the elephant. The elephant is also one of the most intelligent animals.

The largest land animal, the elephant, is also one of the most intelligent animals.

1. Some people showed exceptional abilities when they were very young. They were child prodigies.
2. Shirley Temple was an American actress. She received a special Academy Award at age seven.
3. Two great artists began their work at age four. They were Paul Klee and Gustav Mahler.

4. Mahler was a Bohemian composer of intensely emotional works. He was also the child of a brutal father.
5. Paul Klee was a Swiss painter. As a child he was frightened by his own drawings of devils.

12d Compounding words, phrases, and clauses

A **compound construction** combines words that are closely related and equally important.

Diet can affect a person's weight. Exercise can affect a person's weight.

compound subject
Diet and exercise can affect a person's weight.

Diet and exercise can affect weight. They can lower blood pressure. They can relieve stress.

compound predicate
Diet and exercise can affect weight, lower blood pressure, and relieve stress.

1 Using coordinating conjunctions and correlative conjunctions

Two kinds of words create compound constructions: coordinating and correlative conjunctions. **Coordinating conjunctions** do not change form. In the following box the relationship that each conjunction signals appears in parentheses.

Coordinating conjunctions

and (*addition*)	nor (*alternative*)	for (*cause*)	yet (*contrast*)
but (*contrast*)	or (*alternative*)	so (*effect*)	

To remember the coordinating conjunctions, use the word *fanboys: for, and, nor, but, or, yet, so.*

Dieting or exercise alone is not enough for most people to maintain a healthy weight.

Dieting takes discipline, but exercise takes discipline and time.

Exercise takes discipline and time, so some people prefer to work out with others.

Some coordinating conjunctions pair with other words to form **correlative conjunctions**. In the box at the top of the next page, the relationships signaled by the conjunctions appear in parentheses.

Both a balanced diet and regular exercise are necessary to maintain a healthy weight.

Neither diet nor exercise alone will substantially improve a person's health.

Common correlative conjunctions

both . . . and (*addition*)
not only . . . but also (*addition*)
not . . . but (*substitution*)
either . . . or (*alternative*)
neither . . . nor (*negation*)
whether . . . or (*alternative*)
as . . . as (*comparison*)

Note For punctuating compound constructions, see pages 422–24 (main clauses), 433 (items in series), and 440 (words, phrases, or subordinate clauses).

2 Using conjunctive adverbs

One other kind of connecting word, called a **conjunctive adverb,** relates only main clauses, not words, phrases, or subordinate clauses. In the box below, the conjunctive adverbs are arranged by the relationships they signal.

Common conjunctive adverbs

Addition	Emphasis	Comparison or contrast	Cause or effect	Time
also	certainly	however	accordingly	finally
besides	indeed	in comparison	as a result	meanwhile
further	in fact	in contrast	consequently	next
furthermore	still	instead	hence	now
in addition	undoubtedly	likewise	similarly	then
incidentally		nevertheless	therefore	thereafter
moreover		nonetheless	thus	
		otherwise		
		rather		

It's important to distinguish between conjunctive adverbs and conjunctions (coordinating and subordinating) because conjunctive adverbs require distinctive punctuation, as explained on pages 445–46. To tell the difference, try to move the word. A conjunctive adverb is an *adverb*: it describes the relation of ideas in two clauses, and, like most adverbs, it can move around in its clause:

> Relaxation techniques have improved; however, few people know them.
> Relaxation techniques have improved; few people know them, however.

In contrast, coordinating and subordinating conjunctions bind two clauses into a single grammatical unit, and they cannot be moved:

> Although few people know them, relaxation techniques have improved. [The subordinating conjunction can't be moved: *Few people know them although, relaxation techniques have improved.*]

Relaxation techniques have improved, but few people know them. [The coordinating conjunction can't be moved: *Relaxation techniques have improved, few people know them but.*]

Exercise 12.17 Sentence combining: Compound constructions

To practice compounding words, phrases, and clauses, combine each of the following pairs of sentences into one sentence that is as short as possible without altering meaning. Use an appropriate connecting word of the type specified in parentheses, referring to the lists on pages 268 and 269 as necessary. You will have to add and delete words, and you may have to change or add punctuation.

Example:

The encyclopedia had some information. It was not detailed enough. (*Conjunctive adverb.*)

The encyclopedia had some information; however, it was not detailed enough.

1. All too often people assume that old age is not a productive time. Many people in their nineties have had great achievements. (*Conjunctive adverb.*)
2. In his nineties the philosopher Bertrand Russell spoke vigorously for international peace. He spoke for nuclear disarmament. (*Correlative conjunction.*)
3. Grandma Moses did not retire to an easy chair. She began painting at age seventy-six and was still going at one hundred. (*Conjunctive adverb.*)
4. The American dancer and choreographer Martha Graham choreographed works after she was eighty. The American dancer and choreographer Merce Cunningham choreographed works after he was eighty. (*Coordinating conjunction.*)
5. The architect Frank Lloyd Wright designed his first building at age twenty. He designed his last building at age ninety. (*Coordinating conjunction.*)

gram 12e

12e Changing the usual word order

In most English sentences, the subject of the sentence comes first, naming the performer of the predicate's action, and the predicate comes second. Four kinds of sentences change this order.

Questions

In most questions the predicate verb or a part of it precedes the subject:

verb — subject — verb
Have interest rates been rising?

verb subject verb
Why did rates rise today?

subject verb
What is the answer? [Normal subject-verb order.]

Commands

In commands the subject *you* is omitted:

verb — Think of the options. verb — Watch the news.

Passive sentences

In the **active voice** the subject performs the action of the verb. In the **passive voice** the object of the action becomes the subject of the sentence so that the subject is *acted upon*.

Active Kyong [subject] wrote [verb] the paper [object].

Passive The paper [subject] was written [verb] by Kyong.

See pages 307–09 for more on forming the passive voice.

Sentences with postponed subjects

The subject follows the predicate in two sentence patterns. The normal order may be reversed for emphasis:

Henry comes here. [Normal order.]
Here comes Henry. [Reversed order.]

Or the word *there* or *it* may postpone the subject:

There will be [verb] eighteen people [subject] attending the meeting.

It was [verb] surprising that Marinetti was nominated [subject].

There and *it* in such sentences are called **expletives.** Expletive sentences have their uses, but they can also be wordy and unemphatic (see p. 524).

CULTURE LANGUAGE When you use an expletive construction, be careful to include *there* or *it*. Only commands and some questions can begin with verbs.

Faulty No one predicted the nomination. Were no polls showing Marinetti ahead.

Revised No one predicted the nomination. There were no polls showing Marinetti ahead.

Exercise 12.18 Forming questions and commands

Form a question and a command from the following noun and verb pairs.

Example:
wood, split
Did you split all this wood? Split the wood for our fire.

1. water, boil
2. music, stop
3. table, set
4. dice, roll
5. telephone, use

Exercise 12.19 Rewriting passives and expletives

Rewrite each passive sentence below as active, and rewrite each expletive construction to restore normal subject-predicate order. (For additional exercises with the passive voice and with expletives, see pp. 309, 383, and 525.)

Example:

All the trees in the park were planted by the city.
The city planted all the trees in the park.

1. The screenplay for *Monster's Ball* was cowritten by Milo Addica and Will Rokos.
2. The film was directed by Marc Foster.
3. There was only one performance in the movie that received an Academy Award.
4. It was Halle Berry who won the award for best actress.
5. Berry was congratulated by the press for being the first African American to win the award.

12f Classifying sentences

Sentences may be distinguished by their structure: simple, compound, complex, and compound-complex. Each structure gives different emphasis to the sentence's main idea or ideas and to any supporting information.

1 Writing simple sentences

A **simple sentence** consists of a single main clause and no subordinate clause:

main clause
Last summer was unusually hot.

main clause
The summer made many farmers leave the area for good or reduced them to bare existence.

2 Writing compound sentences

A **compound sentence** consists of two or more main clauses and no subordinate clause. The clauses may be joined by a coordinating conjunction and a comma, by a semicolon alone, or by a conjunctive adverb and a semicolon.

main clause — main clause
Last July was hot, but August was even hotter.

main clause — main clause
The hot sun scorched the earth; the lack of rain killed many crops.

main clause — main clause
This summer was also dry; however, it was cooler.

3 Writing complex sentences

A **complex sentence** contains one main clause and one or more subordinate clauses:

main clause | subordinate clause
Rain finally came, although many had left the area by then.

main clause | subordinate clause
Those who remained were able to start anew because the government came to their aid.
(subordinate clause: who remained)

Notice that length does not determine whether a sentence is complex or simple; both kinds can be short or long.

4 Writing compound-complex sentences

A **compound-complex sentence** has the characteristics of both the compound sentence (two or more main clauses) and the complex sentence (at least one subordinate clause):

subordinate clause | main clause | main clause
When government aid finally came, many people had already been reduced to poverty and others had been forced to move.

Exercise 12.20 Identifying sentence structures

Mark the main clauses and subordinate clauses in the following sentences. Identify each sentence as simple, compound, complex, or compound-complex.

Example:

main clause | subordinate clause
The police began patrolling more often when crime in the neighborhood increased. [Complex sentence.]

1. Joseph Pulitzer endowed the Pulitzer Prizes.
2. Pulitzer, incidentally, was the publisher of the New York newspaper *The World.*
3. Although the first prizes were for journalism and letters only, Pulitzers are now awarded in music and other areas.
4. For example, Berke Breathed won for his *Bloom County* comic strip, and Roger Reynolds won for his musical composition *Whispers out of Time.*
5. Although only one prize is usually awarded in each category, in 2010 Sheri Fink's "The Deadly Choices at Memorial" won a prize for investigative journalism, and it shared the honor with "Tainted Justice" by Barbara Laker and Wendy Ruderman.

Exercise 12.21 Sentence combining: Sentence structures

Combine each of the following sets of simple sentences to produce the kind of sentence specified in parentheses. You will have to add, delete, change, and rearrange words.

Example:

The traffic passed the house. It never stopped. (*Complex.*)
The traffic that passed the house never stopped.

1. Recycling takes time. It reduces garbage in landfills. (*Compound.*)
2. People begin to recycle. They generate much less trash. (*Complex.*)
3. White tissues and paper towels biodegrade more easily than dyed ones. People still buy dyed papers. (*Complex.*)
4. The cans are aluminum. They bring recyclers good money. (*Simple.*)
5. Environmentalists have hope. Perhaps more communities will recycle newspaper and glass. Many citizens refuse to participate. (*Compound-complex.*)

13 Case of Nouns and Pronouns

Chapter essentials

- Use the subjective case for subjects and complements: *she and I* (p. 276).
- Use the objective case for objects: *her and me* (p. 277).
- Choose between *we* and *us* (p. 277).
- Choose between *who* or *whom* (p. 279).
- Use the appropriate pronoun case in appositives, after *than* or *as,* and with infinitives and gerunds (pp. 278, 279, 280).

Visit MyWritingLab™ for more resources on case of nouns and pronouns.

Case is the form of a noun or pronoun that shows the reader how it functions in a sentence—that is, whether it functions as a subject, as an object, or in some other way. As shown in the box on the next page, only *I, we, he, she, they,* and *who* change form for each case. Thus these pronouns are the focus of this chapter.

- **The *subjective case* generally indicates that the word is a subject or a subject complement.** (See pp. 247 and 251–53.)

  subject
  She and Novick discussed the proposal.

  subject
  The proposal ignored many who need help.

  subject complement
  The unhappy planners were she and Novick.

Case forms of nouns and pronouns

	Subjective	Objective	Possessive
Nouns	boy	boy	boy's
	Jessie	Jessie	Jessie's
Personal pronouns			
Singular			
1st person	I	me	my, mine
2nd person	you	you	your, yours
3rd person	he	him	his
	she	her	her, hers
	it	it	its
Plural			
1st person	we	us	our, ours
2nd person	you	you	your, yours
3rd person	they	them	their, theirs
Relative and interrogative pronouns			
	who	whom	whose
	whoever	whomever	—
	which, that, what	which, that, what	—
Indefinite pronouns	everybody	everybody	everybody's

case 13

- **The *objective case* generally indicates that the word is the object of a verb or preposition.** (See pp. 252–53 and 257–58.)

  object of verb
  The proposal disappointed her and Novick.

  object of verb / object of verb
  A colleague whom they respected let them down.

  object of preposition
  Their opinion of him suffered.

- **The *possessive case* generally indicates ownership or source:**

  Her counterproposal is in preparation.
  Theirs is the more sensible plan.
  The problem is not his.

Do not use an apostrophe to form the possessive of personal and relative pronouns: *yours* (not *your's*); *whose* (not *who's*). (See p. 455. See also pp. 451–53 for the possessive forms of nouns, which do use apostrophes.)

In standard American English, *-self* pronouns do not change form to show function. Their only forms are *myself, yourself, himself, herself, itself, ourselves, yourselves, themselves.* Avoid nonstandard forms such as *hisself, ourself,* and *theirselves.*

Faulty Novick presented the proposal hisself.
Revised Novick presented the proposal himself.

13a Use the subjective case for compound subjects and for subject complements.

In compound subjects use the same pronoun form you would use if the pronoun stood alone as a subject:

subject
She and Novick will persist.

subject
The others may lend their support when she and Novick get a hearing.

If you are in doubt about the correct form, try the test in the box below.

A test for case forms in compound constructions

1. **Identify a compound construction** (one connected by *and, but, or, nor*).

   [He, Him] and [I, me] won the prize.
   The prize went to [he, him] and [I, me].

2. **Write a separate sentence for each part of the compound.**

   [He, Him] won the prize. [I, Me] won the prize.
   The prize went to [he, him]. The prize went to [I, me].

3. **Choose the pronouns that sound correct.**

   He won the prize. I won the prize. [Subjective.]
   The prize went to him. The prize went to me. [Objective.]

4. **Put the separate sentences back together.**

   He and I won the prize.
   The prize went to him and me.

After a linking verb, such as a form of *be,* a pronoun renaming the subject (a subject complement) should be in the subjective case:

subject complement
The ones who care most are she and Novick.

subject complement
It was they whom the mayor appointed.

If this construction sounds stilted to you, use the more natural order: *She and Novick are the ones who care most. The mayor appointed them.*

Note Avoid using the pronoun *myself* in place of the personal pronoun *I* or *me*: *Stephen and I* [not *myself*] *studied for the test. Everyone went except me* [not *myself*]. For more on the *-self* pronouns, see pages 817–18.

13b Use the objective case for compound objects.

In compound objects use the same pronoun form you would use if the pronoun stood alone as an object:

direct object
The mayor nominated Zhu and him.

indirect object
The mayor gave Zhu and him awards.

object of preposition
Credit goes equally to them and the mayor.

If you are in doubt about the correct form, try the test in the box opposite.

Exercise 13.1 Choosing between subjective and objective pronouns

From the pairs in brackets, select the appropriate subjective or objective pronoun(s) for each of the following sentences.

Example:

"Between you and [I, me]," the seller said, "this deal is a steal."
"Between you and me," the seller said, "this deal is a steal."

1. Kayla and [I, me] were competing for places on the relay team.
2. The fastest runners at our school were [she, her] and [I, me], so [we, us] expected to make the team.
3. [She, Her] and [I, me] were friends but also intense rivals.
4. The time trials went badly, excluding both [she, her] and [I, me] from the team.
5. Next season [she, her] and [I, me] are determined to earn places on the team.

13c Use the appropriate case when the plural pronoun *we* or *us* occurs with a noun.

Whether to use *we* or *us* with a noun depends on the use of the noun:

object of preposition
Freezing weather is welcomed by us skaters.

subject
We skaters welcome freezing weather.

13d In appositives the case of a pronoun depends on the function of the word described or identified.

object of verb — appositive identifies object

The class elected two representatives, DeShawn and me.

subject — appositive identifies subject

Two representatives, DeShawn and I, were elected.

If you are in doubt about case in an appositive, try the sentence without the word the appositive identifies: *The class elected DeShawn and me. DeShawn and I were elected.*

Exercise 13.2 Choosing between subjective and objective pronouns

From the pairs in brackets, select the appropriate subjective or objective pronoun for each of the following sentences.

Example:

Convincing [we, us] veterans to vote yes will be difficult.
Convincing us veterans to vote yes will be difficult.

1. Obtaining enough protein is important to [we, us] vegetarians.
2. Instead of obtaining protein from meat, [we, us] vegetarians get our protein from other sources.
3. Jeff claims to know only two vegetarians, [he, him] and Helena, who avoid all animal products, including milk.
4. Some of [we, us] vegetarians eat fish, which is a good source of protein.
5. [We, Us] vegetarians in my family, my parents and [I, me], drink milk and eat fish.

13e The case of a pronoun after *than* or *as* in a comparison depends on the meaning.

When a pronoun follows *than* or *as* in a comparison, the case of the pronoun indicates what words may have been omitted. When the pronoun is subjective, it must serve as the subject of an omitted verb:

subject

Some critics like Glass more than he [does].

When the pronoun is objective, it must serve as the object of an omitted verb:

object

Some critics like Glass more than [they like] him.

13f Use the objective case for pronouns that are subjects or objects of infinitives.

subject of infinitive
The school asked him to speak.

object of infinitive
Students chose to invite him.

13g Use *who* or *whom* depending on function.

To choose between *who* and *whom, whoever* and *whomever,* you need to figure out whether the word serves as a subject or as an object. Use *who* where you would use *he* or *she*—all ending in vowels. Use *whom* where you would use *him* or *her*—all ending in consonants.

1 At the beginning of a question, use *who* for a subject and *whom* for an object.

subject
Who wrote the policy?

object
Whom does it affect?

A test for *who* versus *whom* in questions

1. **Pose the question.**

   [Who, Whom] makes that decision?
   [Who, Whom] does one ask?

2. **Answer the question, using a personal pronoun.** Choose the pronoun that sounds correct, and note its case.

   [She, Her] makes that decision. She makes that decision. [Subjective.]
   One asks [she, her]. One asks her. [Objective.]

3. **Use the same case (*who* or *whom*) in the question.**

   Who makes that decision? [Subjective.]
   Whom does one ask? [Objective.]

Note In speech the subjective case *who* is commonly used whenever it is the first word of a question, regardless of whether it is a subject or an object. But formal writing requires a distinction between the forms:

Spoken Who should we credit?

object
Written Whom should we credit?

2 In a subordinate clause, use *who* or *whoever* for a subject, *whom* or *whomever* for an object.

The case of a pronoun in a subordinate clause depends on its function in the clause, regardless of whether the clause itself functions as a subject, an object, or a modifier:

subject

Credit whoever wrote the policy.

object

Research should reveal whom to credit.

A test for *who* versus *whom* in subordinate clauses

1. **Locate the subordinate clause.**

   Few people know [who, whom] they should ask.
   They are unsure [who, whom] makes the decision.

2. **Rewrite the subordinate clause as a separate sentence, substituting a personal pronoun for *who, whom*.** Choose the pronoun that sounds correct, and note its case.

   They should ask [she, her]. They should ask her. [Objective.]
   [She, Her] makes the decision. She makes the decision. [Subjective.]

3. **Use the same case (*who* or *whom*) in the subordinate clause.**

   Few people know whom they should ask. [Objective.]
   They are unsure who makes the decision. [Subjective.]

Note Don't let expressions such as *I think* and *she says* confuse you when they come between the subject *who* and its verb:

subject

He is the one who the polls say will win.

To choose between *who* and *whom* in such constructions, delete the interrupting phrase: *He is the one who will win.*

Exercise 13.3 Choosing between *who* and *whom*

From the pairs in brackets, select the appropriate form of the pronoun in each of the following sentences.

Example:

My mother asked me [who, whom] I was going out with.
My mother asked me whom I was going out with.

1. The judges awarded first prize to Inez, [who, whom] they believed gave the best performance.
2. Inez beat the other contestants [who, whom] competed against her.
3. She is a consummate performer, singing to [whoever, whomever] would listen.
4. [Who, Whom] in the school has not heard Inez sing?
5. [Who, Whom] has she not performed for?

Exercise 13.4 Sentence combining: *Who* versus *whom*

Combine each of the following pairs of sentences into one sentence that contains a clause beginning with *who* or *whom*. Be sure to use the appropriate case form. You will have to add, delete, and rearrange words. Each item may have more than one possible answer.

Example:

David is the candidate. We think David deserves to win.
David is the candidate who we think deserves to win.

1. Some children have undetected hearing problems. These children may do poorly in school.
2. They may not hear important instructions and information from teachers. Teachers may speak softly.
3. Classmates may not be audible. The teacher calls on those classmates.
4. Some hearing-impaired children may work harder to overcome their disability. These children get a lot of encouragement at home.
5. Some hearing-impaired children may take refuge in fantasy friends. They can rely on these friends not to criticize or laugh.

13h Ordinarily, use a possessive pronoun or noun immediately before a gerund.

A **gerund** is the *-ing* form of a verb (*running, sleeping*) used as a noun (p. 260). Like nouns, gerunds are commonly preceded by possessive nouns and pronouns: *our vote* (noun), *our voting* (gerund).

The coach disapproved of their lifting weights.

The coach's disapproving was a surprise.

A noun or pronoun before an *-ing* verb form is not always possessive. Sometimes the *-ing* form will be a present participle modifying the preceding word:

Everyone had noticed him weightlifting. [Emphasis on *him*.]
(him: objective pronoun; weightlifting: participle)

Everyone had noticed his weightlifting. [Emphasis on the activity.]
(his: possessive pronoun; weightlifting: gerund)

Note that a gerund usually is not preceded by the possessive when the possessive would create an awkward construction:

Awkward	A rumor spread about everybody's on the team quitting.
Less awkward	A rumor spread about everybody on the team quitting.
Better	A rumor spread that everybody on the team quit.

Exercise 13.5 Revising: Case

Revise all inappropriate case forms in the following paragraph, and explain the function of each case form.

Written four thousand years ago, *The Epic of Gilgamesh* tells of the friendship of Gilgamesh and Enkidu. Gilgamesh was a bored king who his people thought was too harsh. Then he met Enkidu, a wild man whom had lived with the animals in the mountains. Immediately, him and Gilgamesh wrestled to see whom was more powerful. After hours of struggle, Enkidu admitted that Gilgamesh was stronger than him. Now the friends needed adventures worthy of the two strongest men on earth. Gilgamesh said, "Between you and I, mighty deeds will be accomplished, and our fame will be everlasting." Among their acts, Enkidu and him defeated a giant bull, Humbaba, and cut down the bull's cedar forests. Them bringing back cedar logs to Gilgamesh's treeless land won great praise from the people. When Enkidu died, Gilgamesh mourned his death, realizing that no one had been a better friend than him. When Gilgamesh himself died many years later, his people raised a monument praising Enkidu and he for their friendship and their mighty deeds of courage.

Note See page 336 for an exercise involving case along with other aspects of grammar.

14 Verbs

Chapter essentials

- Use correct verb forms, especially with irregular verbs, *-s* and *-ed* endings, and helping verbs (below).
- Use verb tense to show the time of the verb's action (p. 298).
- Use verb mood to show attitude, such as commanding or requesting (p. 305).
- Use verb voice to show whether the sentence subject is acting (active) or is acted upon (passive) (p. 307).

Visit MyWritingLab™ for more resources on verbs.

Verb Forms

All verbs except *be* have five basic forms. The first three are the verb's principal parts.

- **The *plain form* is the dictionary form of the verb.** When the subject is a plural noun or the pronoun *I, we, you,* or *they,* the plain form indicates action that occurs in the present, occurs habitually, or is generally true.

Terms used to describe verbs

Tense

The time of the verb's action—for instance, present (*kick*), past (*kicked*), future (***will** kick*). (See p. 298.)

Mood

The attitude of the verb's speaker or writer—the difference, for example, in *I kick the ball, Kick the ball,* and *I suggested that she kick the ball.* (See p. 305.)

Voice

The distinction between the **active,** in which the subject performs the verb's action (*I kick the ball*), and the **passive,** in which the subject is acted upon (*The ball is kicked by me*). (See p. 307.)

Person

The verb form that reflects whether the subject is speaking (*I/we kick the ball*), spoken to (*You kick the ball*), or spoken about (*She kicks the ball*). (See p. 311.)

Number

The verb form that reflects whether the subject is singular (*The girl kicks the ball*) or plural (*Girls kick the ball*). (See p. 311.)

A few artists live in town today.
They hold classes downtown.

- **The *past-tense form* indicates that the action of the verb occurred before now.** It usually adds *-d* or *-ed* to the plain form, although some irregular verbs create it in other ways, as in *heard* and *taught* (see p. 285).

  Many artists lived in town before this year.
  They held classes downtown. [Irregular verb.]

- **The *past participle* is the same as the past-tense form, except in most irregular verbs.** It combines with forms of *have* or *be* (*has climbed, was created*), or by itself it modifies nouns and pronouns (*the sliced apples*).

  Artists have lived in town for decades.
  They have held classes downtown. [Irregular verb.]

- **The *present participle* adds *-ing* to the verb's plain form.** It combines with forms of *be* (*is buying*), modifies nouns and pronouns (*the boiling water*), or functions as a noun (*Running exhausts me*).

  A few artists are living in town today.
  They are holding classes downtown.

- **The *-s form* ends in *-s* or *-es*.** When the subject is a singular noun, a pronoun such as *everyone,* or the personal pronoun *he, she,* or *it,* the *-s* form indicates action that occurs in the present, occurs habitually, or is generally true.

  The artist lives in town today.
  She holds classes downtown.

The verb *be* has eight forms rather than the five forms of most other verbs:

Plain form	be		
Present participle	being		
Past participle	been		
	I	*he, she, it*	*we, you, they*
Present tense	am	is	are
Past tense	was	was	were

vb 14

CULTURE LANGUAGE If standard American English is not your native language or dialect, you may have difficulty with the *-s* forms of verbs (as in *He skis, and he runs*), with their past-tense forms (*They skied, and they ran*), or with their past participles (*We have skied, and we have run*). See pages 285–87 and 289–90 for more on these forms.

Helping verbs

Helping verbs, also called **auxiliary verbs**, combine with some verb forms to indicate time and other kinds of meaning, as in *can run, was sleeping, had been eaten*. These combinations are **verb phrases**. Since the plain form, present participle, or past participle in any verb phrase always carries the principal meaning, it is sometimes called the **main verb**.

	Verb phrase	
	Helping	*Main*
Artists	can	train others to draw.
The techniques	have	changed little.

These are the most common helping verbs:

Forms of *be*: be, am, is, are, was, were, been, being
Forms of *have*: have, has, had, having
Forms of *do*: do, does, did

be able to	had better	must	used to
be supposed to	have to	ought to	will
can	may	shall	would
could	might	should	

CULTURE LANGUAGE The helping verbs of standard American English may be problematic if you are used to speaking another language or dialect. See pages 290–94 for more on helping verbs.

14a Use the correct forms of regular and irregular verbs.

Most verbs are regular; that is, they form their past tense and past participle by adding *-d* or *-ed* to the plain form.

Plain form	Past tense	Past participle
live	lived	lived
act	acted	acted

Since the past tense and past participle are the same, the forms of regular verbs do not often cause problems (but see pp. 289–90).

About two hundred English verbs are **irregular**; that is, they form their past tense and past participle in some irregular way.

Plain form	Past tense	Past participle
begin	began	begun
break	broke	broken
sleep	slept	slept

You can see the difference between a regular and an irregular verb in these examples:

Plain form	Today the birds twitter. Today the birds sing.
Past tense	Yesterday the birds twittered. Yesterday the birds sang.
Past participle	In the past the birds have twittered. In the past the birds have sung.

The box on the next two pages lists the forms of many irregular verbs. Check this box or a dictionary if you have any doubt about a verb's principal parts. If a dictionary lists only the plain form, the verb is regular: both the past tense and the past participle add *-d* or *-ed* to the plain form. If the verb is irregular, the dictionary will list the plain form, the past tense, and the past participle in that order (*go, went, gone*). If the dictionary gives only two forms (as in *think, thought*), then the past tense and the past participle are the same.

CULTURE LANGUAGE Some English dialects use verb forms that differ from those of standard American English: for instance, *drug* for *dragged, growed* for *grew, come* for *came,* or *went* for *gone.* In situations requiring standard American English, use the forms in the box on the next two pages or in a dictionary.

Faulty They have went to the movies.

Revised They have gone to the movies.

Principal parts of common irregular verbs

Plain form	Past tense	Past participle
arise	arose	arisen
be	was, were	been
become	became	become
begin	began	begun
bid	bid	bid
bite	bit	bitten, bit
blow	blew	blown
break	broke	broken
bring	brought	brought
burst	burst	burst
buy	bought	bought
catch	caught	caught
choose	chose	chosen
come	came	come
cut	cut	cut
dive	dived, dove	dived
do	did	done
draw	drew	drawn
dream	dreamed, dreamt	dreamed, dreamt
drink	drank	drunk
drive	drove	driven
eat	ate	eaten
fall	fell	fallen
find	found	found
flee	fled	fled
fly	flew	flown
forget	forgot	forgotten, forgot
freeze	froze	frozen
get	got	got, gotten
give	gave	given
go	went	gone
grow	grew	grown
hang (suspend)	hung	hung
hang (execute)	hanged	hanged
have	had	had
hear	heard	heard
hide	hid	hidden
hold	held	held
keep	kept	kept
know	knew	known
lay	laid	laid
lead	led	led
leave	left	left
lend	lent	lent
let	let	let
lie	lay	lain

Plain form	Past tense	Past participle
lose	lost	lost
pay	paid	paid
prove	proved	proved, proven
ride	rode	ridden
ring	rang	rung
rise	rose	risen
run	ran	run
say	said	said
see	saw	seen
set	set	set
shake	shook	shaken
shrink	shrank, shrunk	shrunk, shrunken
sing	sang, sung	sung
sink	sank, sunk	sunk
sit	sat	sat
sleep	slept	slept
slide	slid	slid
speak	spoke	spoken
spring	sprang, sprung	sprung
stand	stood	stood
steal	stole	stolen
swim	swam	swum
swing	swung	swung
take	took	taken
teach	taught	taught
tear	tore	torn
throw	threw	thrown
wear	wore	worn
write	wrote	written

Exercise 14.1 Using irregular verbs

For each irregular verb in brackets, give either the past tense or the past participle, as appropriate, and identify the form you used.

Example:

Though we had [hide] the cash box, it was [steal].

Though we had hidden the cash box, it was stolen. [Two past participles.]

1. The world population has [grow] by two-thirds of a billion people in less than a decade.
2. In 2012 it [break] the 7 billion mark.
3. Experts have [draw] pictures of a crowded future.
4. They predict that the world population may have [slide] up to as much as 10 billion by the year 2050.
5. Though the food supply [rise] in the last decade, the share to each person [fall].

14b Distinguish between *sit* and *set*, *lie* and *lay*, and *rise* and *raise*.

The forms of *sit* and *set*, *lie* and *lay*, and *rise* and *raise* are easy to confuse:

Plain form	Past tense	Past participle
sit	sat	sat
set	set	set
lie	lay	lain
lay	laid	laid
rise	rose	risen
raise	raised	raised

In each of these confusing pairs, one verb is **intransitive** (it does not take an object) and one is **transitive** (it does take an object). (See pp. 252–53 for more on this distinction.)

Intransitive

The patients lie in their beds. [*Lie* means "recline" and takes no object.]

Visitors sit with them. [*Sit* means "be seated" or "be located" and takes no object.]

Patients' temperatures rise. [*Rise* means "increase" or "get up" and takes no object.]

Transitive

Nursing aides lay the dinner trays on tables. [*Lay* means "place" and takes an object, here *trays*.]

The aides set the trays down. [*Set* means "place" and takes an object, here *trays*.]

The aides raise the shades. [*Raise* means "lift" or "bring up" and takes an object, here *shades*.]

Note The verb *lie* meaning "to tell an untruth" is a regular verb. Its past tense and past participle forms are *lied*: *Nikki lied to us*. *She has lied to us for many years*.

Exercise 14.2 Distinguishing *sit/set, lie/lay, rise/raise*

Choose the correct verb from the pair given in brackets. Then supply the past tense or past participle, as appropriate.

Example:

After I washed all the windows, I [lie, lay] down the squeegee and then I [sit, set] the table.

After I washed all the windows, I laid down the squeegee and then I set the table.

1. Yesterday afternoon the child [lie, lay] down for a nap.
2. The child has been [rise, raise] by her grandparents.

3. Most days her grandfather has [sit, set] with her, reading her stories.
4. She has [rise, raise] at dawn most mornings.
5. Her toys were [lie, lay] out on the floor.

14c Use the *-s* and *-ed* forms of the verb when they are required.

Speakers of some English dialects and nonnative speakers of English sometimes omit the *-s* and *-ed* verb endings when they are required in standard American English.

Note If you tend to omit these endings in writing, practice pronouncing them when speaking or when reading correct verbs aloud, such as those in the examples here. The spoken practice can help you remember the endings in writing.

Required *-s* ending

Use the *-s* form of a verb when *both* of these situations hold:

- **The subject is a singular noun (*boy*), an indefinite pronoun (*everyone*), or *he, she,* or *it*.** These subjects are third person, used when someone or something is being spoken about.
- **The verb's action occurs in the present.**

The letter asks [not ask] for a quick response.
Delay costs [not cost] money.

Be especially careful with the *-s* forms of *be* (*is*), *have* (*has*), and *do* (*does, doesn't*). These forms should always be used to indicate present time with third-person singular subjects.

The company is [not be] late in responding.
It has [not have] problems.
It doesn't [not don't] have the needed data.
The contract does [not do] depend on the response.

In addition, *be* has the *-s* form *was* in the past tense with *I* and with third-person singular subjects:

The company was [not were] in trouble before.

Except for the past tense *I was*, the pronouns *I* and *you* and all plural subjects do *not* take the *-s* form of verbs:

I am [not is] a student.
You are [not is] also a student.
They are [not is] students, too.

Required *-ed* or *-d* ending

The *-ed* or *-d* verb form is required in *any* of the following situations:

- **The verb's action occurred in the past:**

  Yesterday the company asked [not ask] for more time.

- **The verb form functions as a modifier:**

  The data concerned [not concern] should be retrievable.

- **The verb form combines with a form of *be* or *have*:**

  The company is supposed [not suppose] to be the best.
  It has developed [not develop] an excellent reputation.

Watch especially for a needed *-ed* or *-d* ending when it isn't pronounced clearly in speech, as in *asked, discussed, mixed, supposed, walked,* and *used.*

vb
14d

Exercise 14.3 Using *-s* and *-ed* verb endings 

Supply the correct form of each verb in brackets. Be careful to include *-s* and *-ed* (or *-d*) endings where they are needed for standard English.

A teacher sometimes [ask] too much of a student. In high school I was once [punish] for being sick. I had [miss] some school, and I [realize] that I would fail a test unless I had a chance to make up the classwork. I [discuss] the problem with the teacher, but he said I was [suppose] to make up the work while I was sick. At that I [walk] out of the class. I [receive] a failing grade then, but it did not change my attitude. Today I still balk when a teacher [make] unreasonable demands or [expect] miracles.

14d Use helping verbs with main verbs appropriately.

Helping verbs combine with main verbs to form verb phrases (see p. 284).

Common helping verbs

Forms of *be*: be, am, is, are, was, were, been, being
Forms of *have*: have, has, had, having
Forms of *do*: do, does, did

be able to	had better	must	used to
be supposed to	have to	ought to	will
can	may	shall	would
could	might	should	

1 Use helping verbs when they are required.

Standard American English requires helping verbs in certain situations:

- **The main verb ends in *-ing.***

  Researchers are conducting fieldwork all over the world. [Not Researchers conducting. . . .]

- **The main verb is *been* or *be.***

  Many have been fortunate in their discoveries. [Not Many been. . . .]
  Some could be real-life Indiana Joneses. [Not Some be. . . .]

- **The main verb is a past participle, such as *talked, begun,* or *thrown.***

  Their discoveries were covered in newspapers and magazines. [Not Their discoveries covered. . . .]

  Often the researchers have done TV interviews. [Not the researchers done. . . .]

In every example above, omitting the helping verb would create an incomplete sentence, or **sentence fragment** (see Chapter 17). In a complete sentence, some part of the verb (helping or main) must be capable of changing form to show changes in time: *I run, I ran; you are running, you were running*. But a present participle (*conducting*), an irregular past participle (*been*), and the plain form *be* cannot change form in this way. They need helping verbs to work as sentence verbs.

2 Combine helping verbs and main verbs appropriately.

Helping verbs and main verbs combine into verb phrases in specific ways.

Note The main verb in a verb phrase (the one carrying the main meaning) does not change to show a change in subject or time: *she has studied, you had studied*. Only the helping verb may change.

Form of *be* + present participle

The **progressive tenses** indicate action in progress (see p. 301). Create them with *be, am, is, are, was, were,* or *been* followed by the main verb's present participle, the *-ing* form:

She is working on a new book.

Be and *been* always require additional helping verbs to form the progressive tenses:

can	might	should	} be working	have	} been working
could	must	will		has	
may	shall	would		had	

When forming the progressive tenses, be sure to use the *-ing* form of the main verb:

Faulty Her ideas are grow more complex. She is developed a new approach to ethics.

Revised Her ideas are growing more complex. She is developing a new approach to ethics.

Form of *be* + past participle

The **passive voice** of the verb indicates that the subject *receives* the action of the verb (see pp. 307–09). Create the passive voice with *be, am, is, are, was, were, being,* or *been* followed by the main verb's past participle:

Her latest book was completed in four months.

Be, being, and *been* always require additional helping verbs to form the passive voice:

have / has / had } been completed

am / is / are / was / were } being completed

will be completed

Be sure to use the main verb's past participle for the passive voice:

Faulty Her next book will be publish soon.
Revised Her next book will be published soon.

Only transitive verbs may form the passive voice:

Faulty A philosophy conference will be occurred in the same week. [*Occur* is not a transitive verb.]
Revised A philosophy conference will occur in the same week.

Forms of *have*

Four forms of *have* serve as helping verbs: *have, has, had, having.* One of these forms plus the main verb's past participle creates one of the **perfect tenses**, those expressing action completed before another specific time or action (see pp. 300–01):

Some students have complained about the laboratory.
Others had complained before.

Will and other helping verbs sometimes accompany forms of *have* in the perfect tenses:

Several more students will have complained by the end of the week.

Forms of *do*

Do, does, and *did* have three uses as helping verbs, always with the plain form of the main verb:

- **To pose a question:** *How did the trial end?*
- **To emphasize the main verb:** *It did end eventually.*
- **To negate the main verb, along with *not* or *never*:** The judge *did not withdraw.*

Be sure to use the main verb's plain form with any form of *do*:

Faulty The judge did remained in court.

Revised The judge did remain in court.

Modals

The modal helping verbs include *can, may, should, would,* and several two- and three-word combinations, such as *have to* and *be able to.* Use the plain form of the main verb with a modal unless the modal combines with another helping verb (usually *have*):

Faulty The equipment can detects small vibrations. It should have detect the change.

Revised The equipment can detect small vibrations. It should have detected the change.

Modals convey various meanings. Those following are the most common:

- **Ability:** *can, could, be able to*

  The equipment can detect small vibrations. [Present.]
  The equipment could detect small vibrations. [Past.]
  The equipment is able to detect small vibrations. [Present. Past: was able to. Future: will be able to.]

- **Possibility:** *could, may, might; could/may/might have* + past participle

  The equipment could fail. [Present.]
  The equipment may fail. [Present or future.]
  The equipment might fail. [Present or future.]
  The equipment may have failed. [Past.]

- **Necessity or obligation:** *must, have to, be supposed to*

  The lab must purchase a backup. [Present or future.]
  The lab has to purchase a backup. [Present or future. Past: had to.]
  The lab will have to purchase a backup. [Future.]
  The lab is supposed to purchase a backup. [Present. Past: was supposed to.]

- **Permission:** *may, can, could*

  The lab may spend the money. [Present or future.]
  The lab can spend the money. [Present or future.]
  The lab could spend the money. [Present or future, more tentative.]
  With budget approval, the lab could have spent the money. [Past.]

- **Intention:** *will, shall, would*

  The lab will spend the money. [Future.]
  Shall we offer advice? [Future. Use *shall* for questions requesting opinion or consent.]
  We would have offered advice. [Past.]

- **Request:** *could, can, would*

  Could [or Can or Would] you please obtain a bid? [Present or future.]

- **Advisability:** *should, had better, ought to*; *should have* + past participle

  You should obtain three bids. [Present or future.]
  You had better obtain three bids. [Present or future.]
  You ought to obtain three bids. [Present or future.]
  You should have obtained three bids. [Past.]

- **Past habit:** *would, used to*

  In years past we would obtain five bids.
  We used to obtain five bids.

Exercise 14.4 Using helping verbs CULTURE LANGUAGE

Add helping verbs in the following sentences where they are needed for standard English.

Example:
The story been told for many years.
The story has been told for many years.

1. For as long as I can remember, I been writing stories.
2. While I living with my grandparents one summer, I wrote mystery stories.
3. Nearly every afternoon I sat at the computer and wrote about two brothers who solved mysteries while their mother be working.
4. By the end of the summer, I written four stories.
5. I was very happy when one of my stories published in the school newspaper.

Exercise 14.5 Revising: Helping verbs plus main verbs CULTURE LANGUAGE

Revise the following sentences so that helping verbs and main verbs are used correctly. Mark the number preceding any sentence that is already correct.

Example:
The college testing service has test as many as five hundred students at one time.

The college testing service has tested as many as five hundred students at one time.

1. A report from the Bureau of the Census has confirm a widening gap between rich and poor.
2. As suspected, the percentage of people below the poverty level did increased over the last decade.
3. The richest 1% of the population is make 24% of all the income.
4. These people will keeping an average of $1.3 million after taxes.
5. The other 99% all together will average about $300,000.

14e Use a gerund or an infinitive after a verb as appropriate.

Nonnative speakers of English may find it difficult to see whether a gerund or an infinitive should follow a verb. A **gerund** is the *-ing* form of a verb used as a noun (*opening*). An **infinitive** is the plain form of a verb preceded by *to* (*to open*). (See p. 260 for more on these forms.)

Gerunds and infinitives may follow certain verbs but not others. Sometimes the use of a gerund or an infinitive with the same verb changes the meaning.

Either gerund or infinitive

A gerund or an infinitive may follow these verbs with no significant difference in meaning:

begin	hate	love
can't bear	hesitate	prefer
can't stand	intend	start
continue	like	

The pump began working.
The pump began to work.

Meaning change with gerund or infinitive

With four verbs, a gerund has quite a different meaning from an infinitive:

forget	stop
remember	try

The man stopped eating. [He no longer ate.]
The man stopped to eat. [He stopped in order to eat.]

Gerund, not infinitive

Do not use an infinitive after these verbs:

admit	discuss	mind	recollect
adore	dislike	miss	resent
appreciate	enjoy	postpone	resist
avoid	escape	practice	risk
consider	finish	put off	suggest
deny	imagine	quit	tolerate
detest	keep	recall	understand

Faulty He finished to eat lunch.
Revised He finished eating lunch.

Infinitive, not gerund

Do not use a gerund after these verbs:

agree	decide	mean	refuse
appear	expect	offer	say
ask	have	plan	wait
assent	hope	pretend	want
beg	manage	promise	wish
claim			

Faulty He decided checking the meter.
Revised He decided to check the meter.

Noun or pronoun + infinitive

Some verbs may be followed by an infinitive alone or by a noun or pronoun and an infinitive. The presence of a noun or pronoun changes the meaning.

ask	dare	need	wish
beg	expect	promise	would like
choose	help	want	

He expected to wait.
He expected his friends to wait.

Some verbs *must* be followed by a noun or pronoun before an infinitive:

admonish	convince	invite	teach
advise	encourage	order	tell
allow	forbid	permit	train
cause	force	persuade	urge
challenge	hire	remind	warn
command	instruct	request	

He told his friends to wait.

Do not use *to* before the infinitive when it follows one of these verbs and a noun or pronoun:

feel	make ("force")
have	see
hear	watch
let	

He watched his friends leave without him.

Exercise 14.6 Revising: Verbs plus gerunds or infinitives CULTURE LANGUAGE

Revise the following sentences so that gerunds or infinitives are used correctly with verbs. Mark the number preceding any sentence that is already correct.

Example:

A politician cannot avoid to alienate some voters.
A politician cannot avoid alienating some voters.

1. A program called *Boostup.org* aims to improve students' school attendance.
2. People supporting this program hope that more students will to graduate.
3. Parents who want to help can choose tracking their child's attendance.
4. Because of *Boostup.org*, many students who might have dropped out now plan going to college.
5. The organization persuades parents signing up via its Web site, *Facebook* page, and *Twitter* feed.

14f Use the appropriate particles with two-word verbs.

Standard American English includes some verbs that consist of two words: the verb itself and a **particle**, a preposition or adverb that affects the meaning of the verb. For example:

Look up the answer. [Research the answer.]
Look over the answer. [Examine the answer.]

The meanings of these two-word verbs are often quite different from the meanings of the individual words that make them up. (There are some three-word verbs, too, such as *put up with* and *run out of.*)

A dictionary of English as a second language will define two-word verbs and say whether the verb may be separated in a sentence, as explained below. (See p. 509 for a list of ESL dictionaries.) A grammar checker will rarely recognize misused two-word verbs.

Note Many two-word verbs are more common in speech than in more formal academic or business writing. For formal writing, consider using *research* instead of *look up, examine* or *inspect* instead of *look over.*

Inseparable two-word verbs

Verbs and particles that may not be separated by any other words include the following:

call on	go over	run into	stay up
catch on	grow up	run out of	take care of
come across	keep on	speak up	turn out
get along	look for	speak with	turn up at
get up	look into	stand up	work for
give in	play around	stay away	
go on	run across		

Faulty Children grow quickly up.
Revised Children grow up quickly.

Separable two-word verbs

Most two-word verbs that take direct objects may be separated by the object:

Parents help out their children.
Parents help their children out.

If the direct object is a pronoun, the pronoun *must* separate the verb from the particle:

Faulty Parents help out them.
Revised Parents help them out.

The separable two-word verbs include the following:

bring up	give back	make up	throw out
call off	hand in	point out	try on
call up	hand out	put away	try out
drop off	help out	put back	turn down
fill out	leave out	put off	turn on
fill up	look over	take out	wrap up
give away	look up	take over	

Exercise 14.7 Revising: Verbs plus particles CULTURE LANGUAGE

The two- and three-word verbs in the following sentences are underlined. Some are correct as given, and some are not because they should or should not be separated by other words. Revise the verbs and other words that are incorrect. Consult the lists here or an ESL dictionary if necessary to determine whether verbs are separable.

Example:

Hollywood producers never seem to come up with entirely new plots, but they also never run new ways out of to present old ones.

Hollywood producers never seem to come up with [correct] entirely new plots, but they also never run out of new ways to present old ones.

1. American movies treat everything from going out with someone to making up an ethnic identity, but few people look their significance into.
2. While some viewers stay away from topical films, others turn at the theater up simply because a movie has sparked debate.
3. Some movies attracted rowdy spectators, and the theaters had to throw out them.
4. Filmmakers have always been eager to point their influence out to the public.
5. Everyone agrees that filmmakers will keep creating controversy on, if only because it can fill up theaters.

Tense

Tense shows the time of a verb's action. The box on the next page defines and illustrates the tense forms for a regular verb in the active voice. (See pp. 285 and 307 on regular verbs and voice.)

Tenses of a regular verb (active voice)

Present Action that is occurring now, occurs habitually, or is generally true

Simple present Plain form or *-s* form	**Present progressive** *Am, is,* or *are* plus *-ing* form
I walk. You/we/they walk. He/she/it walks.	I am walking. You/we/they are walking. He/she/it is walking.

Past Action that occurred before now

Simple past Past-tense form (*-d* or *-ed*)	**Past progressive** *Was* or *were* plus *-ing* form
I/he/she/it walked. You/we/they walked.	I/he/she/it was walking. You/we/they were walking.

Future Action that will occur in the future

Simple future *Will* plus plain form	**Future progressive** *Will be* plus *-ing* form
I/you/he/she/it/we/they will walk.	I/you/he/she/it/we/they will be walking.

Present perfect Action that began in the past and is linked to the present

Present perfect *Have* or *has* plus past participle (*-d* or *-ed*)	**Present perfect progressive** *Have been* or *has been* plus *-ing* form
I/you/we/they have walked. He/she/it has walked.	I/you/we/they have been walking. He/she/it has been walking.

Past perfect Action that was completed before another past action

Past perfect *Had* plus past participle (*-d* or *-ed*)	**Past perfect progressive** *Had been* plus *-ing* form
I/you/he/she/it/we/they had walked.	I/you/he/she/it/we/they had been walking.

Future perfect Action that will be completed before another future action

Future perfect *Will have* plus past participle (*-d* or *-ed*)	**Future perfect progressive** *Will have been* plus *-ing* form
I/you/he/she/it/we/they will have walked.	I/you/he/she/it/we/they will have been walking.

CULTURE LANGUAGE In standard American English, a verb conveys time and sequence through its form. In some other languages and English dialects, various markers besides verb form may indicate the time of a verb. For instance, in African American Vernacular English, *I be attending class on Tuesday* means that the speaker attends class every Tuesday. But to someone who doesn't know the dialect, the sentence could mean last Tuesday, this Tuesday, or every Tuesday. In standard English, the intended meaning is indicated by verb tense:

I attended class on Tuesday. [Past tense indicates *last* Tuesday.]

I will attend class on Tuesday. [Future tense indicates *next* Tuesday.]

I attend class on Tuesday. [Present tense indicates habitual action, *every* Tuesday.]

14g Use the appropriate tense to express your meaning.

Many errors in verb tense are actually errors in verb form like those discussed earlier. Still, the present tense, the perfect tenses, and the progressive tenses can cause problems.

1 Observe the special uses of the present tense.

The present tense has several distinctive uses:

Action occurring now

She understands the problem.
We define the problem differently.

Habitual or recurring action

Banks regularly undergo audits.
The audits monitor the banks' activities.

A general truth

The mills of the gods grind slowly.
The earth is round.

Discussion of literature, film, and so on (see also p. 727)

Huckleberry Finn has adventures we all envy.
In one article, the author examines several causes of crime.

Future time

Next week we draft a new budget.
Funding ends in less than a year.

(In the last two examples, time is really indicated by *Next week* and *in less than a year.*)

2 Observe the uses of the perfect tenses.

The perfect tenses generally indicate action completed before another specific time or action. (The term *perfect* derives from the Latin *perfectus*, "completed.") The present perfect tense also indicates action begun in the past and continued into the present. The perfect tenses consist of a form of *have* plus the verb's past participle.

The dancer has performed (present perfect) here only once. [The action is completed at the time of the statement.]

present perfect
Critics have written about the performance ever since. [The action began in the past and continues now.]

past perfect
The dancer had trained in Asia before his performance. [The action was completed before another past action.]

future perfect
He will have danced here again by the end of the year. [The action begins now or in the future and will be completed by a specified time in the future.]

CULTURE LANGUAGE With the present perfect tense, the words *since* and *for* are followed by different information. After *since,* give a specific point in time: *The United States has been a member of the United Nations since 1945.* After *for,* give a span of time: *The United States has been a member of the United Nations for many decades.*

3 Observe the uses of the progressive tenses. 

The progressive tenses indicate continuing (therefore progressive) action. In standard English the progressive tenses consist of a form of *be* plus the verb's *-ing* form (present participle). (The words *be* and *been* must be combined with other helping verbs. See p. 291.)

present progressive
The team is improving.

past progressive
Last year the team was losing.

future progressive
The owners will be watching for signs of improvement.

present perfect progressive
Sports writers have been expecting an upturn.

past perfect progressive
New players had been performing well.

future perfect progressive
If the season goes badly, fans will have been watching their team lose for ten straight years.

Note Verbs that express unchanging conditions (especially mental states) rather than physical actions do not usually appear in the progressive tenses. These verbs include *adore, appear, believe, belong, care, doubt, hate, have, hear, imagine, know, like, love, mean, need, own, prefer, realize, remember, see, sound, taste, think, understand,* and *want.*

Faulty She is wanting to study ethics.
Revised She wants to study ethics.

14h Use the appropriate sequence of verb tenses.

The term **sequence of tenses** refers to the relation between the verb tense in a main clause and the verb tense in a subordinate clause or phrase. The tenses should change when necessary to reflect changes in actual or relative time. (For a discussion of tense shifts—changes *not* required by meaning—see p. 360.)

1 Use the appropriate tense sequence with infinitives.

The **present infinitive** is the verb's plain form preceded by *to*. It indicates action *at the same time* as or *later* than that of the verb:

t seq
14h

verb: present perfect — infinitive: present

She would have liked to see [not to have seen] change before now.

The verb's **perfect infinitive** consists of *to have* followed by the past participle, as in *to have talked, to have won.* It indicates action *earlier* than that of the verb:

verb: present — infinitive: perfect

Other researchers would like [not would have liked] to have seen change as well.

2 Use the appropriate tense sequence with participles.

The present participle shows action occurring *at the same time* as that of the verb:

participle: present — verb: past perfect

Testing a large group, the researcher had posed multiple-choice questions.

The past participle and the present perfect participle show action occurring *earlier* than that of the verb:

participle: past — verb: past

Prepared by earlier failures, she knew not to ask open questions.

participle: present perfect — verb: past

Having tested many people, she understood the process.

3 Use the appropriate tense sequence with the past or past perfect tense.

When the verb in the main clause is in the past or past perfect tense, the verb in the subordinate clause must also be past or past perfect:

main clause: past — subordinate clause: past

The researchers discovered that people varied widely in their knowledge of public events.

main clause: past — subordinate clause: past perfect

The variation occurred because respondents had been born in different decades.

main clause: past perfect — subordinate clause: past

None of them had been born when Warren G. Harding was President.

Exception Always use the present tense for a general truth, such as *The earth is round*:

main clause: past — subordinate clause: present

Most understood that popular Presidents are not necessarily good Presidents.

4 Use the appropriate tense sequence in conditional sentences.

A **conditional sentence** states a factual relation between cause and effect, makes a prediction, or speculates about what might happen. Such a sentence usually contains a subordinate clause beginning with *if, when,* or *unless* along with a main clause stating the result. The three kinds of conditional sentences use distinctive verbs.

Factual relation

Statements linking factual causes and effects use matched tenses in the subordinate and main clauses:

subordinate clause: present — main clause: present

When a voter casts a ballot, he or she has complete privacy.

subordinate clause: past — main clause: past

When voters registered in some states, they had to pay a poll tax.

Prediction

Predictions generally use the present tense in the subordinate clause and the future tense in the main clause:

subordinate clause: present — main clause: future

Unless citizens regain faith in politics, they will not vote.

Sometimes the verb in the main clause consists of *may, can, should,* or *might* plus the verb's plain form: *If citizens regain faith, they may vote*.

Speculation

The verbs in speculations depend on whether the linked events are possible or impossible. For possible events in the present, use the past tense in the subordinate clause and *would, could,* or *might* plus the verb's plain form in the main clause:

subordinate clause: past — main clause: *would* + plain form

If voters had more confidence, they would vote more often.

Use *were* instead of *was* in the subordinate clause, even when the subject is *I, he, she, it* or a singular noun. (See p. 306 for more on this distinctive verb form.)

subordinate clause: past — main clause: *would* + plain form

If the voter were more confident, he or she would vote more often.

For impossible events in the present—events that are contrary to fact—use the same forms as above (including the distinctive *were* when applicable):

subordinate clause: past — main clause: *might* + plain form

If Lincoln were alive, he might inspire confidence.

For impossible events in the past, use the past perfect tense in the subordinate clause and *would, could,* or *might* plus the present perfect tense in the main clause:

subordinate clause: past perfect — main clause: *might* + present perfect

If Lincoln had lived past the Civil War, he might have helped stabilize the country.

Exercise 14.8 Adjusting tense sequence: Past or past perfect tense

The tenses in each sentence below are in correct sequence. Change the tense of one verb as instructed. Then change the tense of infinitives, participles, and other verbs to restore correct sequence. Some items have more than one possible answer.

Example:

Delgado will text us when he reaches his destination. (Change will text to texted.)

Delgado texted us when he reached [or had reached] his destination.

1. Diaries that Adolf Hitler is supposed to have written have surfaced in Germany. (*Change have surfaced to had surfaced.*)
2. Many people believe that the diaries are authentic because a well-known historian has declared them so. (*Change believe to believed.*)
3. However, the historian's evaluation has been questioned by other authorities, who call the diaries forgeries. (*Change has been questioned to was questioned.*)
4. They claim, among other things, that the paper is not old enough to have been used by Hitler. (*Change claim to claimed.*)
5. Eventually, the doubters will win the debate because they have the best evidence. (*Change will win to won.*)

Exercise 14.9 Revising: Tense sequence with conditional sentences

Supply the appropriate tense for each verb in brackets below.

Example:

If Babe Ruth or Jim Thorpe [be] athletes today, they [remind] us that even sports heroes must contend with a harsh reality.

If Babe Ruth or Jim Thorpe were athletes today, they might [or could or would] remind us that even sports heroes must contend with a harsh reality.

1. When an athlete [turn] professional, he or she [commit] to a grueling regimen of mental and physical training.
2. If athletes [be] less committed, they [disappoint] teammates, fans, and themselves.
3. If professional athletes [be] very lucky, they [play] until age forty.
4. Unless an athlete [achieve] celebrity status, he or she [have] few employment choices after retirement.
5. If professional sports [be] less risky, athletes [have] longer careers and more choices after retirement.

Mood

Mood in grammar is a verb form that indicates the writer's or speaker's attitude toward what he or she is saying. The **indicative mood** states a fact or opinion or asks a question:

The theater needs help. [Opinion.]
The ceiling is falling. [Fact.]
Will you contribute to the theater? [Question.]

The **imperative mood** expresses a command or gives a direction. It omits the subject of the sentence, *you*:

Help the theater. [Command.]
Send contributions to the theater. [Direction.]

The **subjunctive mood** expresses a suggestion, a requirement, or a desire, or it states a condition that is contrary to fact (that is, imaginary or hypothetical). The subjunctive mood uses distinctive verb forms.

- **Suggestion or requirement:** plain form with all subjects.

  The manager asked that he donate money. [Suggestion.]
  Rules require that every donation be mailed. [Requirement.]

- **Desire or present condition contrary to fact:** past tense; for *be,* the past tense *were* for all subjects, singular as well as plural.

  We wish that the theater had more money. [Desire.]

  It would be in better shape if it were better funded. [Present condition contrary to fact.]

- **Past condition contrary to fact:** past perfect.

  The theater could have been better funded if it had been better managed.

Note that with conditions contrary to fact, the verb in the main clause also expresses the imaginary or hypothetical with the helping verb *could, would,* or *might*. (See also pp. 303–04.)

For a discussion of keeping mood consistent within and among sentences, see page 360.

14i Use the subjunctive verb forms appropriately.

Contemporary English uses distinctive subjunctive verb forms in only a few constructions and idioms. (For the sequence of tenses in many conditional sentences, see pp. 303–04.)

1 Use the subjunctive in contrary-to-fact clauses beginning with *if* or expressing desire.

If the theater were saved, the town would benefit.
We all wish the theater were not so decrepit.
I wish I were able to donate money.

The indicative form *was* (*We all wish the theater was not so decrepit*) is common in speech and in some informal writing, but the subjunctive *were* is usual in formal English.

Not all clauses beginning with *if* express conditions contrary to fact. In the sentence *If Joe is out of town, he hasn't heard the news,* the verb *is* is correct because the clause refers to a condition presumed to exist.

2 Use *would, could,* or *might* only in the main clause of a conditional statement.

The helping verb *would, could,* or *might* appears in the main clause of a sentence expressing a condition contrary to fact. The helping verb does not appear in the subordinate clause beginning with *if*:

Not Many people would have helped if they would have known.
But Many people would have helped if they had known.

3 Use the subjunctive in *that* clauses following verbs that demand, request, or recommend.

Verbs such as *ask, demand, insist, mandate, recommend, request, require, suggest,* and *urge* indicate demand or suggestion. They often precede subordinate clauses beginning with *that* and containing the substance of the demand or suggestion. The verb in such a *that* clause should be in the subjunctive mood:

The board urged that everyone contribute.
The members insisted that they themselves be donors.
They suggested that each donate both time and money.

Note These constructions have widely used alternative forms that do not require the subjunctive, such as *The board urged everyone to contribute* and *The members insisted on donating.*

Exercise 14.10 Revising: Subjunctive mood

Revise the following sentences with appropriate subjunctive verb forms.

Example:

I would help the old man if I was able to reach him.
I would help the old man if I were able to reach him.

1. If John Hawkins would have known of the dangerous side effects of smoking tobacco, would he have introduced the dried plant to England in 1565?
2. Hawkins noted that if a Florida Indian was to travel for several days, he would have smoked tobacco to satisfy his hunger and thirst.
3. Early tobacco growers feared that their product would not gain acceptance unless it was perceived as healthful.
4. To prevent fires, in 1646 the General Court of Massachusetts passed a law requiring that colonists smoked tobacco only if they were five miles from any town.
5. To prevent decadence, in 1647 Connecticut passed a law mandating that one's smoking of tobacco was limited to once a day in one's own home.

Voice

The voice of a verb tells whether the subject performs the action or is acted upon. In the **active voice** the subject performs the action:

Active voice She wrote the book.
subject verb

In the **passive voice** the subject receives the action. The actual actor may be named in a prepositional phrase or may be omitted.

Passive voice The book was written by her.
subject verb

CULTURE LANGUAGE A passive verb always consists of a form of *be* plus the past participle of the main verb: *Rents are controlled.* Other helping verbs must also be used with *be, being,* and *been*: *Rents will be controlled. Rents are being controlled. Rents have been controlled.* Only a transitive verb (one that takes an object) may be used in the passive voice. (See p. 253.)

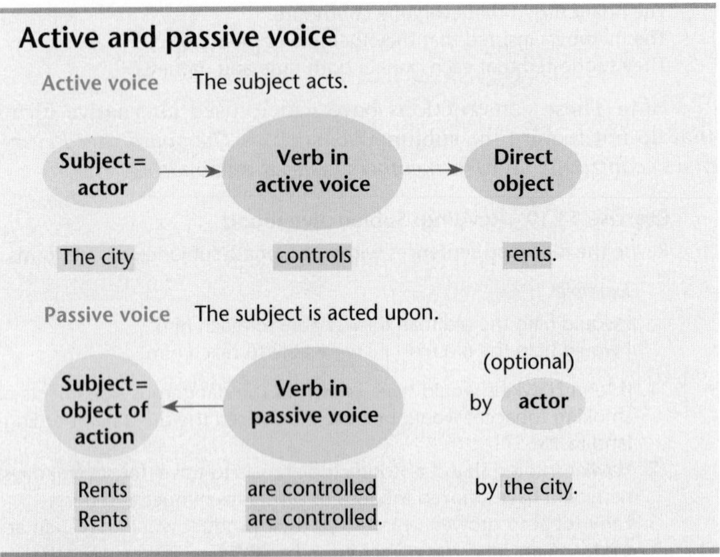

Active and passive voice
Active voice The subject acts.
Subject = actor
Verb in active voice
Direct object
The city
controls
rents.
Passive voice The subject is acted upon.
(optional)
Subject = object of action
Verb in passive voice
by actor
Rents
are controlled
by the city.
Rents
are controlled.

14j Generally, prefer the active voice.

The active voice is usually clearer, more concise, and more forthright than the passive voice.

Weak passive The library is used by both students and teachers for studying and research, and the plan to expand it has been praised by many.

Strong active Both students and teachers use the library for studying and research, and many have praised the plan to expand it.

To change a passive verb to active, name the verb's actor as the subject, use an active verb form, and convert the old subject into an object:

	subject	passive verb	
Passive	Tenants	are protected	by leases.
	new subject	active verb	old subject = object
Active	Leases	protect	tenants.

14k Use the passive voice when the actor is unknown or unimportant or when naming the actor might be offensive.

The passive voice can be useful when naming the actor is not possible or desirable.

- **The actor is unknown, unimportant, or less important than the object of the action.** In the following sentences, the writer wishes to stress the Internet rather than the actors.

  The Internet was established in 1969 by the US Department of Defense. The network has been extended internationally to governments, universities, corporations, and private individuals.

  In the next example the person who performed the experiment, perhaps the writer, is less important than the procedure. Passive sentences are common in scientific writing.

  After the solution had been cooled to 10°C, the acid was added.

- **The actor should be neutral background to the action.** Particularly in sensitive correspondence, this use of the passive can avoid offending readers. In the next example, not naming the person who turned away the shelter residents focuses on the action without accusing anyone specifically.

  The residents of the shelter were turned away from your coffee shop.

To change a transitive verb from active to passive voice, convert either an indirect object or a direct object into the subject of the sentence, and use the passive verb form:

	subject	transitive verb	indirect object	direct object
Active	The city	gives	tenants	leases.
	new subject	passive verb	direct object	
Passive	Tenants	are given	leases.	
	new subject	passive verb	old indirect object	old subject
	Leases	are given	to tenants	by the city.

Make this conversion from active to passive voice only in the situations listed above.

Exercise 14.11 Converting between active and passive voices

To practice using the two voices of the verb, convert the following sentences from active to passive or from passive to active. (In converting from passive to active, you may have to add a subject for the new sentence.) Which version of each sentence seems more effective, and why? For additional exercises with the passive voice, see pages 272 and 383.

Example:

The actor was discovered in a nightclub.
A talent scout discovered the actor in a nightclub.

1. When the Eiffel Tower was built in 1889, it was thought by the French to be ugly.
2. At that time many people still resisted industrial technology.

3. The tower's naked steel construction epitomized this technology.
4. Beautiful ornament was expected to grace fine buildings.
5. Further, the tower could not even be called a building because it had no solid walls.

Exercise 14.12 Revising: Verb forms, tense, mood

In the following paragraph, determine whether each underlined word is in the appropriate form, tense, and mood. Then make corrections as needed.

Over the years the sports of the Winter Olympics have remain the same in many ways, but they also have changed dramatically as new events join the program. Bobsledding was part of the first Winter Games in 1924, but now it is accompany by two other sledding events, luge and skeleton. When alpine skiing became an Olympic sport in 1936, it consists of just two events, but now it includes ten, such as downhill, super G, and giant slalom. The most noticeable changes are the snowboarding and freestyle skiing events, such as ski cross, snowboard cross, aerials, slopestyle, and half-pipe. None of these have been Olympic sports before 1992, and some joined the program as recently as 2014. Many freestylers and boarders insist that the Olympics includes even more of these sports.

Note See page 336 for an exercise involving verbs along with other aspects of grammar.

15 Agreement

Chapter essentials

Make **subjects and verbs** agree in the following situations:

- When other words come between subject and verb (p. 312)
- With subjects joined by *and, or,* or *nor* (p. 314)
- With *everyone* and other indefinite pronouns (p. 315)
- With *group* and other collective nouns (p. 316)
- When the verb precedes the subject or is a linking verb such as *is* or *are* (pp. 316, 317)
- With *who, which,* and *that* (p. 317)
- With *news* and other singular words ending in *-s* (p. 317)
- With titles and words being defined (p. 318)

Make **pronouns and antecedents** agree in the following situations:

- When antecedents are joined by *and, or,* or *nor* (p. 319).
- With *everyone, person,* and other indefinite words (p. 321).
- With *group* and other collective nouns (p. 322).

Visit MyWritingLab™ for more resources on agreement.

Agreement helps readers understand the relations between elements in a sentence.

- **Subjects and verbs agree in number and person:**

  More Japanese Americans (subject) live (verb) in Hawaii and California than elsewhere.

  Daniel Inouye (subject) was (verb) the first Japanese American in Congress.

- **Pronouns and their antecedents—the words they refer to—agree in person, number, and gender:**

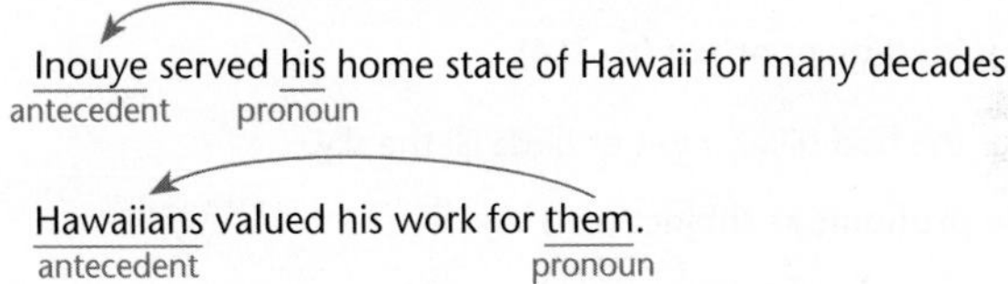

Inouye served his home state of Hawaii for many decades.
antecedent
pronoun
Hawaiians valued his work for them.
antecedent
pronoun

15a Make subjects and verbs agree in number.

Most subject-verb agreement problems arise when endings are omitted from subjects or verbs or when the relation between sentence parts is uncertain.

1 The *-s* and *-es* endings work differently for nouns and verbs.

An *-s* or *-es* ending does opposite things to nouns and verbs: it usually makes a noun *plural,* but it always makes a present-tense verb *singular.* Thus a singular noun as subject will not end in *-s*, but its verb will. A plural noun as subject will end in *-s*, but its verb will not. Between them, subject and verb use only one *-s* ending.

Singular	Plural
The boy plays.	The boys play.
The bird soars.	The birds soar.

Person and number in subject-verb agreement

Person	Number: *Singular*	Number: *Plural*
First	I eat.	We eat.
Second	You eat.	You eat.
Third	He/she/it eats.	They eat.
	The bird eats.	Birds eat.

Summary of subject-verb agreement

- **Basic subject-verb agreement** (previous page):

  singular subject, singular verb: The kite flies. plural subject, plural verb: The kites fly.

- **Words between subject and verb** (p. 312):

  The kite with two tails flies badly. The tails of the kite compete.

- **Subjects joined by *and*** (p. 314):

  The kite and the bird are almost indistinguishable.

- **Subjects joined by *or* or *nor*** (p. 314):

  The kite or the bird dives. Kites or birds fill the sky.

- **Indefinite pronoun as subject** (p. 315):

  No one knows. All the spectators wonder.

- **Collective noun as subject** (p. 316):

  A flock appears. The flock disperse.

- **Verb preceding subject** (p. 316):

  Is the kite or the bird blue? Are the kite and the bird both blue?

- **Linking verb** (p. 317):

  The kite is a flier and a dipper.

- ***Who, which, that* as subject** (p. 317):

  The kite that flies longest wins. Kites that fall lose.

- **Subject with plural form and singular meaning** (p. 317):

  Aeronautics plays a role in kite flying.

- **Title or word named as word** (p. 318):

  Kite Dynamics is one title. *Vectors* is a key word.

The only exception to the single *-s* ending for a subject and its present-tense verb involves the nouns that form irregular plurals, such as *child/children, woman/women*. The irregular plural still requires a plural verb: The *children* play.

CULTURE LANGUAGE If your first language or dialect is not standard American English, subject-verb agreement may be difficult, especially for these reasons:

- **Some English dialects omit the -*s* ending for singular verbs or use the -*s* ending for plural verbs.**

Nonstandard	The voter resist change.
Standard	The voter resists change.
Standard	The voters resist change.

The verb *be* changes spelling for singular and plural in both present and past tenses. (See also p. 284.)

Nonstandard	Taxes is high. They was raised in the last congressional session.
Standard	Taxes are high. They were raised in the last congressional session.

Have also has a distinctive -*s* form, *has*:

Nonstandard	The new tax have little chance of passing.
Standard	The new tax has little chance of passing.

- **Some other languages change all parts of verb phrases to match their subjects.** In English verb phrases, however, only the helping verbs *be, have,* and *do* change for different subjects. The modal helping verbs—*can, may, should, will,* and others—do not change:

Nonstandard	The tax mays pass next year.
Standard	The tax may pass next year.

The main verb in a verb phrase also does not change for different subjects:

Nonstandard	The tax may passes next year.
Standard	The tax may pass next year.

2 Subject and verb should agree even when other words come between them.

When the subject and verb are interrupted by other words, make sure the verb agrees with the subject:

The survival of hibernating frogs in freezing temperatures is [not are] fascinating.

A chemical reaction inside the cells of the frogs stops [not stop] the formation of ice crystals.

Note Phrases beginning with *as well as, together with, along with,* and *in addition to* do not change the number of the subject:

The president, together with the deans, has [not have] agreed to improve the computer labs.

If you really mean *and* in such a sentence, use it. Then the subject is compound, and the verb should be plural: *The president and the deans have agreed to improve the computer labs.*

3 Subjects joined by *and* usually take plural verbs.

Two or more subjects joined by *and* usually take a plural verb, whether one or all of the subjects are singular:

Frost and Roethke were contemporaries.

Frost, Roethke, Stevens, and Pound are among the great American poets.

Exceptions When the parts of the subject form a single idea or refer to a single person or thing, they take a singular verb:

Avocado and bean sprouts is a California sandwich.

When a compound subject is preceded by the adjective *each* or *every*, the verb is usually singular:

Each man, woman, and child has a right to be heard.

But a compound subject *followed* by *each* takes a plural verb:

The man and the woman each have different problems.

4 When parts of a subject are joined by *or* or *nor*, the verb agrees with the nearer part.

When all parts of a subject joined by *or* or *nor* are singular, the verb is singular; when all parts are plural, the verb is plural.

Either the painter or the carpenter knows the cost.

The cabinets or the bookcases are too costly.

When one part of the subject is singular and the other plural, avoid awkwardness by placing the plural part closer to the verb so that the verb is plural:

Awkward Neither the owners nor the contractor agrees.

Revised Neither the contractor nor the owners agree.

When the subject consists of nouns and pronouns of different person requiring different verb forms, the verb agrees with the nearer part of the subject. Reword if this construction is awkward:

Awkward Either Juarez or I am responsible.

Revised Either Juarez is responsible, or I am.

5 With an indefinite pronoun such as *anybody* or *all,* use a singular or plural verb as appropriate.

An **indefinite pronoun** is one that does not refer to a specific person or thing. Most indefinite pronouns take a singular verb, but some take a plural verb and some take a singular *or* a plural verb.

Common indefinite pronouns

Singular			Singular or plural	Plural
anybody	everyone	nothing	all	both
anyone	everything	one	any	few
anything	much	somebody	more	many
each	neither	someone	most	several
either	nobody	something	none	
everybody	no one		some	

The singular indefinite pronouns refer to a single unspecified person or thing, and they take a singular verb:

Something smells. Neither is right.

The plural indefinite pronouns refer to more than one unspecified thing, and they take a plural verb:

Both are correct. Several were invited.

The other indefinite pronouns take a singular or a plural verb depending on whether the word they refer to is singular or plural. The word may be stated in the sentence:

All of the money is reserved for emergencies. [*All* refers to *money.*]

All of the funds are reserved for emergencies. [*All* refers to *funds.*]

The word referred to by the pronoun may also be implied:

All are planning to attend. [*All* implies "all the people."]

All is lost. [*All* implies "everything."]

None may be singular even when referring to a plural word, especially to emphasize the meaning "not one": *None* [*Not one*] *of the animals has a home.*

CULTURE LANGUAGE See pages 334–35 for the distinction between *few* ("not many") and *a few* ("some").

6 Collective nouns such as *group* take singular or plural verbs depending on meaning.

A **collective noun** has singular form but names a group of individuals or things—for example, *army, audience, committee, crowd, family, group, team.* As a subject, a collective noun may take a singular or plural verb, depending on the context. When the group acts as one unit, use a singular verb:

> The team has won five of the last six meets.

But when the group's members act separately, use the plural form of the verb:

> The old team have gone to various colleges.

If a combination such as *team have* seems awkward, reword the sentence: *The members of the old team have gone to various colleges.*

The collective noun *number* may be singular or plural. Preceded by *a,* it is plural; preceded by *the,* it is singular.

> A number of people are in debt.

> The number of people in debt is very large.

CULTURE LANGUAGE In English some noncount nouns (nouns that don't form plurals) are collective nouns because they name groups: for instance, *furniture, clothing, mail.* These noncount nouns usually take singular verbs: *Mail arrives daily.* But some of these nouns take plural verbs, including *clergy, military, people, police,* and any collective noun that comes from an adjective, such as *the poor, the rich, the young, the elderly.* If you mean one representative of the group, use a singular noun such as *police officer* or *poor person.*

7 The verb agrees with the subject even when it precedes the subject.

The verb precedes the subject mainly in questions and in constructions beginning with *there* or *here* and a form of *be*:

> Is voting a right or a privilege?

> Are a right and a privilege the same thing?

> There are differences between them.

In constructions beginning with *there* or *here,* you may use the *-s* form of the verb before a compound subject when the first element in the subject is singular:

> Here lies both the problem and its solution.

Word order may sometimes be reversed for emphasis. The verb still agrees with its subject:

From the mountains comes an eerie, shimmering light.

8 A linking verb agrees with its subject, not the subject complement.

A linking verb such as *is* or *are* should agree with its subject, usually the first element in the sentence, not with the noun or pronoun serving as a subject complement (see p. 253):

The child's sole support is her court-appointed guardians.

Her court-appointed guardians are the child's sole support.

9 *Who, which,* and *that* take verbs that agree with their antecedents.

When used as subjects, *who, which,* and *that* refer to another word in the sentence, called the **antecedent**. The verb agrees with the antecedent:

Mayor Garber ought to listen to the people who work for her.

Bardini is the only aide who has her ear.

Agreement problems often occur with *who, which,* or *that* when the sentence includes *one of the* or *the only one of the*:

Bardini is one of the aides who work unpaid. [Of the aides who work unpaid, Bardini is one.]

Bardini is the only one of the aides who knows the community. [Of the aides, only one, Bardini, knows the community.]

CULTURE LANGUAGE In phrases like those above beginning with *one of the,* be sure the noun is plural: *Bardini is one of the aides* [not *aide*] *who work unpaid.*

10 Nouns with plural form but singular meaning, such as *news,* take singular verbs.

Some nouns with plural form (that is, ending in *-s*) are usually regarded as singular in meaning. They include *athletics, economics, mathematics, measles, mumps, news, physics, politics,* and *statistics,* as well as place names such as *Athens, Wales,* and *United States.*

After so long a wait, the news has to be good.

Statistics is required of psychology majors.

Politics requires compromise.

A few of these words take plural verbs only when they describe individual items rather than whole bodies of activity or knowledge: *The statistics prove him wrong. Her politics make compromise difficult.*

Measurements and figures ending in *-s* may also be singular when the quantity they refer to is a unit:

Three years is a long time to wait.

Three-fourths of the library consists of reference books.

11 Titles and words named as words take singular verbs.

When your sentence subject is the name of a corporation, the title of a work (such as a book), or a word you are defining or describing, the verb should be singular even if the name, title, or word is plural:

Hakada Associates is a new firm.

Dream Days remains a favorite book.

Folks is a down-home word for *people*.

Exercise 15.1 Revising: Subject-verb agreement

Revise the verbs in the following sentences as needed to make subjects and verbs agree in number. If the sentence is already correct as given, mark the number preceding it.

Example:

Each of the job applicants type sixty words per minute.
Each of the job applicants types sixty words per minute.

1. Weinstein & Associates is a consulting firm that tries to make businesspeople laugh.
2. Results from recent research shows that humor relieves stress.
3. Reduced stress in businesses in turn reduce illness and absenteeism.
4. In special conferences held by one consultant, each of the participants practice making the others laugh.
5. One consultant to many companies suggest cultivating office humor with practical jokes such as a rubber fish in the water cooler.
6. When employees or their manager regularly post cartoons on the bulletin board, office spirit usually picks up.
7. When someone who has seemed too easily distracted is entrusted with updating the cartoons, his or her concentration often improves.
8. In the face of levity, the former sourpuss becomes one of those who hides bad temper.
9. Reduced stress can also reduce friction within an employee group, which then work more productively.
10. Every one of the consultants caution, however, that humor has no place in life-affecting corporate situations such as employee layoffs.

15b Make pronouns and their antecedents agree in person, number, and gender.

The **antecedent** of a pronoun is the noun or other pronoun to which the pronoun refers.

> Students fret over their tuition bills.
> (Students = antecedent; their = pronoun)

> Its yearly increases make the tuition bill a dreaded document.
> (Its = pronoun; bill = antecedent)

Since a pronoun derives its meaning from its antecedent, the two must agree in person, number, and gender.

CULTURE LANGUAGE The gender of a pronoun should match its antecedent, not a noun that the pronoun may modify: *Sara Young invited her* [not *his*] *son to join the company's staff.* Also, nouns in English have only neuter gender unless they specifically refer to males or females. Thus nouns such as *book, table, sun,* and *earth* take the pronoun *it*: *I am reading a new book. It is inspiring.*

pn agr 15b

1 Antecedents joined by *and* usually take plural pronouns.

Two or more antecedents joined by *and* usually take a plural pronoun, whether one or all of the antecedents are singular:

> Mr. Bartos and I cannot settle our dispute.

> The dean and my adviser have offered their help.

Exceptions When the compound antecedent refers to a single idea, person, or thing, then the pronoun is singular:

> My friend and adviser offered her help.

Person, number, and gender in pronoun-antecedent agreement

	Number	
Person	*Singular*	*Plural*
First	*I*	*we*
Second	*you*	*you*
Third	*he, she, it,* indefinite pronouns, singular nouns	*they,* plural nouns
Gender		
Masculine	*he,* nouns naming males	
Feminine	*she,* nouns naming females	
Neuter	*it,* all other nouns	

Summary of pronoun-antecedent agreement

- **Basic pronoun-antecedent agreement:**

  antecedent pronoun

  Old Faithful spews its columns of water, each of them over 115 feet high.
- **Antecedents joined by *and*** (previous page):

  Old Faithful and Giant are geysers known for their height.
- **Antecedents joined by *or* or *nor*** (below):

  Either Giant or Giantess ejects its column the highest.
- **Indefinite words as antecedents** (opposite):

  Each of the geysers has its own personality.

  Each person who visits has his or her favorites.

  Some return to their favorites year after year.
- **Collective nouns as antecedents** (p. 322):

  A crowd amuses itself watching Old Faithful.

  Afterward the crowd go their separate ways.

pn agr
15b

When the compound antecedent follows *each* or *every*, the pronoun is singular:

> Every girl and woman took her seat.

2 When parts of an antecedent are joined by *or* or *nor*, the pronoun agrees with the nearer part.

When the parts of an antecedent are connected by *or* or *nor*, the pronoun should agree with the part closer to it:

> Tenants or owners must present their grievances.

> Either the tenant or the owner will have her way.

When one subject is plural and the other singular, the sentence will be awkward unless you put the plural one second:

Awkward Neither the tenants nor the owner has yet made her case.

Revised Neither the owner nor the tenants have yet made their case.

3 With an indefinite word as antecedent, such as *anyone* or *person,* use a singular or plural pronoun as appropriate.

Indefinite words do not refer to any specific person or thing. They include **indefinite pronouns** such as *anyone, everybody,* and *no one* (see p. 315 for a list). They also include **generic nouns**, or singular nouns that refer to typical members of a group, as in *The individual has rights* or *The job requires a person with computer skills.*

Most indefinite pronouns and all generic nouns are singular in meaning. When they serve as antecedents, they take singular pronouns:

> Each of the animal shelters in the region has its population of homeless pets.
> indefinite pronoun

> Every worker in our shelter cares for his or her favorite animal.
> generic noun

Four indefinite pronouns are plural in meaning: *both, few, many, several*. As antecedents, they take plural pronouns:

> Many of the animals show affection for their caretakers.

Six indefinite pronouns may be singular or plural in meaning: *all, any, more, most, none, some*. As antecedents, they take singular pronouns if they refer to singular words, plural pronouns if they refer to plural words:

> Most of the shelter's equipment was donated by its original owner. [*Most* refers to *equipment*.]

> Most of the veterinarians donate their time. [*Most* refers to *veterinarians*.]

None may be singular even when referring to a plural word, especially to emphasize the meaning "not one": *None* [*Not one*] *of the shelters has increased its capacity*.

Most agreement problems arise with the singular indefinite words. We often use these words to mean something like "many" or "all" rather than "one" and then refer to them with plural pronouns, as in *Everyone has their own locker* or *A person can padlock their locker.* Often, too, we mean indefinite words to include both masculine and feminine genders and thus resort to *they* instead of the generic *he*—the masculine pronoun referring to both genders, as in *Everyone deserves his privacy.* (For more on the generic *he,* which many readers view as sexist, see p. 505.)

Although some experts accept *they, them,* and *their* with singular indefinite words, many do not, and many teachers and employers

pn agr 15b

regard the plural as incorrect. To be safe, work for agreement between singular indefinite words and the pronouns that refer to them, using the options in the following box.

Ways to correct agreement with indefinite words

- **Change the indefinite word to a plural, and use a plural pronoun to match:**

  Faulty Every athlete deserves their privacy.

  Revised **Athletes** deserve their privacy.

- **Rewrite the sentence to omit the pronoun:**

  Faulty Everyone is entitled to their own locker.

  Revised Everyone is entitled to **a** locker.

- **Use *he or she* (*him or her, his or her*) to refer to the indefinite word:**

  Faulty Now everyone has their private space.

  Revised Now everyone has **his or her** private space.

  However, used more than once in several sentences, *he or she* quickly becomes awkward. (Some readers do not accept the alternative *he/she.*) Using the plural or omitting the pronoun will usually correct agreement problems and create more readable sentences.

pn agr 15b

4 With a collective noun as antecedent, such as *group* or *team*, use a singular or plural pronoun depending on meaning.

Collective nouns such as *army, committee, family, group,* and *team* have singular form but may be referred to by singular or plural pronouns, depending on the meaning intended. When the group acts as a unit, the pronoun is singular:

The committee voted to disband itself.

When the members of the group act separately, the pronoun is plural:

The old team have gone their separate ways.

In the last example, note that the verb and pronoun are consistent in number (see also p. 359).

Inconsistent The old team has gone their separate ways.

Consistent The old team have gone their separate ways.

If a combination such as *team have . . . their* seems awkward, reword the sentence: *The members of the old team have gone their separate ways*.

CULTURE LANGUAGE In standard American English, collective nouns that are noncount nouns (they don't form plurals) usually take singular pronouns: *The mail sits in its own basket.* A few noncount nouns take plural pronouns, including *clergy, military, people, police, the rich,* and *the poor*: *The police support their unions.* (See also p. 316.)

Exercise 15.2 Revising: Pronoun-antecedent agreement

Revise the following sentences so that pronouns and their antecedents agree in person and number. Some items have more than one possible answer. Try to avoid the generic *he* (see opposite). If you change the subject of a sentence, be sure to change verbs as necessary for agreement. If the sentence is already correct as given, mark the number preceding it.

Example:

Each of the Boudreaus' children brought their laundry home at Thanksgiving.

All of the Boudreaus' children brought their laundry home at Thanksgiving. *Or:* Each of the Boudreaus' children brought laundry home at Thanksgiving. *Or:* Each of the Boudreaus' children brought his or her laundry home at Thanksgiving.

1. Each girl raised in a Mexican American family in the Rio Grande Valley of Texas hopes that one day they will be given a *quinceañera* party for their fifteenth birthday.
2. Such celebrations are very expensive because it entails a religious service followed by a huge party.
3. A girl's immediate family, unless they are wealthy, cannot afford the party by themselves.
4. The parents will ask each close friend or relative if they can help with the preparations.
5. Surrounded by her family and attended by her friends and their escorts, the *quinceañera* is introduced as a young woman eligible for Mexican American society.

Exercise 15.3 Adjusting for agreement

In the sentences below, subjects agree with verbs and pronouns agree with antecedents. Make the change specified in parentheses after each sentence, and then revise the sentence as necessary to maintain agreement. Some items have more than one possible answer.

Example:

The student attends weekly conferences with her teacher. (*Change The student to Students.*)

Students attend weekly conferences with their teacher.

1. The giant panda is endangered. (*Change The giant panda to Giant pandas.*)
2. A conservationist estimates that fewer than two thousand giant pandas live in central China, their natural habitat, because the bamboo forests there are shrinking. (*Change A conservationist to Conservationists.*)

3. The giant panda eats bamboo and gains most of its nutrition from its leaves and stalks. (*Change The giant panda to Giant pandas.*)
4. At the Wolong Wildlife Refuge in China, researchers breed pandas in captivity and release a cub into the wild when it is old enough to survive on its own. (*Change a cub to the cubs.*)
5. A zoo in the United States wishes to raise awareness of the giant panda's plight by breeding a pair of adults and allowing the public to view the adorable cub while it is young. (*Change A zoo to Zoos, a pair to pairs, and cub to cubs.*)

Exercise 15.4 Revising: Agreement

Revise the sentences in the following paragraphs to correct errors in agreement between subjects and verbs or between pronouns and their antecedents. Try to avoid the generic *he*.

The writers Richard Rodriguez and Maxine Hong Kingston, despite their differences, shares one characteristic: their parents was immigrants to California. A frequent theme of their writings are the difficulties of growing up with two languages and two cultures.

A child whose first language is not English is often ridiculed because they cannot communicate "properly." Rodriguez learned Spanish at home, but at school everyone expected him to use their language, English. He remembers his childish embarrassment because of his parents' poor English. College and graduate school, which usually expands one's knowledge, widened the gap between Rodriguez and his Latino culture. His essays suggests that he lost a part of himself, a loss that continue to bother him.

Kingston spoke Chinese at home and also learned her first English at school. She sometimes write of these experiences, but more often she write to recover and preserve her Chinese culture. *The Woman Warrior,* which offer a blend of autobiography, family history, and mythic tales, describe the struggle of Kingston's female relatives. *China Men* focus on Kingston's male ancestors; each one traveled to Hawaii or California to make money for their wife back in China. Kingston's work, like Rodriguez's essays, reflect the tension and confusion that the child of immigrants often feel when they try to blend two cultures.

Note See page 336 for an exercise involving agreement along with other aspects of grammar.

16 Adjectives and Adverbs

Chapter essentials

- Use adjectives only to modify nouns and pronouns (below).
- After a linking verb, use an adjective to modify the subject (p. 326).
- After a direct object, use an adjective to modify the object and an adverb to modify the verb (p. 327).
- Use comparative and superlative forms appropriately (p. 327).
- Avoid most double negatives (p. 329).
- Use nouns sparingly as modifiers (p. 330).
- Distinguish between present and past participles as adjectives (p. 330).
- Use *a, an, the,* and other determiners appropriately (p. 331).

Visit MyWritingLab™ for more resources on adjectives and adverbs.

Adjectives and adverbs are modifiers that describe, restrict, or otherwise qualify the words to which they relate.

Functions of adjectives and adverbs

Adjectives modify nouns:	serious student
pronouns:	ordinary one
Adverbs modify verbs:	warmly greet
adjectives:	only three people
adverbs:	quite seriously
phrases:	nearly to the edge of the cliff
clauses:	just when we arrived
sentences:	Fortunately, she is employed.

CULTURE LANGUAGE In standard American English an adjective does not change along with the noun it modifies to show plural number: white [not whites] *shoes,* square [not squares] *spaces.* Only nouns form plurals.

16a Use adjectives only to modify nouns and pronouns.

Adjectives modify only nouns and pronouns. Do not use adjectives instead of adverbs to modify verbs, adverbs, or other adjectives:

Faulty The groups view family values different.

Revised The groups view family values differently.

Be especially careful not to use *good* and *bad* in place of *well* and *badly*.

Faulty Educating children good is everyone's focus.

Revised Educating children well is everyone's focus.

Faulty Some children suffer bad.

Revised Some children suffer badly.

CULTURE LANGUAGE Choosing between *not* and *no* can be a challenge. Use *not* to make a verb or an adjective negative:

They do not learn. They are not happy. They have not been in class.

(See page 369 for where to place *not* in relation to verbs and adjectives.) Use *no* to make a noun negative:

No child likes to fail. No good school fails children.

Place *no* before the noun or any other modifier.

16b Use an adjective after a linking verb to modify the subject. Use an adverb to modify a verb.

A **linking verb** is one that links, or connects, a subject and its complement, either a noun (*They are golfers*) or an adjective (*He is lucky*). (See also p. 253.) Linking verbs are forms of *be*, the verbs associated with our five senses (*look, sound, smell, feel, taste*), and a few others (*appear, seem, become, grow, turn, prove, remain, stay*).

Some of these verbs may or may not be linking, depending on their meaning in the sentence. When the word after the verb modifies the subject, the verb is linking and the word should be an adjective: *He feels strong*. When the word modifies the verb, however, it should be an adverb: *He feels strongly about that.*

Two word pairs are especially troublesome in this context. One is *bad* and *badly*:

The weather grew bad. (grew: linking verb; bad: adjective)

She felt bad. (felt: linking verb; bad: adjective)

Flowers grow badly in such soil. (grow: verb; badly: adverb)

The other pair is *good* and *well. Good* serves only as an adjective. *Well* may serve as an adverb with a host of meanings or as an adjective meaning only "fit" or "healthy."

Decker trained well. (trained: verb; well: adverb)

She felt well. (felt: linking verb; well: adjective)

Her health was good. (was: linking verb; good: adjective)

16c After a direct object, use an adjective to modify the object and an adverb to modify the verb.

After a direct object, an adjective modifies the object, whereas an adverb modifies the verb of the sentence. (See pp. 252–53 for more on direct objects.)

Campus politics made Mungo angry.
adjective

Mungo repeated the words angrily.
adverb

You can test whether a modifier should be an adjective or an adverb by trying to separate it from the direct object. If you can separate it, it should be an adverb: *Mungo angrily repeated the words.* If you cannot separate it, it is probably an adjective.

The instructor considered the student's work thorough. [The adjective can be moved in front of *work* (*student's thorough work*), but it cannot be separated from *work*.]

The instructor considered the student's work thoroughly. [The adverb can be separated from *work*. Compare *The instructor thoroughly considered the student's work*.]

Exercise 16.1 Revising: Adjectives and adverbs

Revise the following sentences so that adjectives and adverbs are used appropriately. If any sentence is already correct as given, mark the number preceding it.

Example:
The announcer warned that traffic was moving very slow.
The announcer warned that traffic was moving very slowly.

1. People who take their health serious often believe that movie-theater popcorn is a healthy snack.
2. Nutrition information about movie popcorn may make these people feel different.
3. One large tub of movie popcorn has twelve hundred calories and sixty grams of saturated fat—both surprisingly high numbers.
4. Once people are aware of the calories and fat, they may feel badly about indulging in this classic snack.
5. People who want to eat good should think twice before ordering popcorn at the movies.

16d Use the comparative and superlative forms of adjectives and adverbs appropriately.

Adjectives and adverbs can show degrees of quality or amount with the endings *-er* and *-est* or with the words *more* and *most* or *less* and *least*. Most modifiers have three forms:

Positive The basic form listed in the dictionary	**Comparative** A greater or lesser degree of the quality	**Superlative** The greatest or least degree of the quality
Adjectives		
red	redder	reddest
awful	more/less awful	most/least awful
Adverbs		
soon	sooner	soonest
quickly	more/less quickly	most/least quickly

If sound alone does not tell you whether to use *-er/-est* or *more/most,* consult a dictionary. If the endings can be used, the dictionary will list them. Otherwise, use *more* or *most.*

1 Use the correct forms of irregular adjectives and adverbs.

Certain adjectives and adverbs are irregular: they change the spelling of their positive form to show comparative and superlative degrees.

Degrees of irregular adjectives and adverbs

Positive	Comparative	Superlative
Adjectives		
good	better	best
bad	worse	worst
little	littler, less	littlest, least
many some much	more	most
Adverbs		
well	better	best
badly	worse	worst

2 Use either *-er/-est* or *more/most,* not both.

A double comparative or double superlative combines the *-er* or *-est* ending with the word *more* or *most.* It is redundant.

Chang was the wisest [not most wisest] person in town.
He was smarter [not more smarter] than anyone else.

3 Use the comparative for comparing two things and the superlative for comparing three or more things.

It is the shorter of her two books. [Comparative.]
The Yearling is the most popular of the six books. [Superlative.]

In conversation the superlative form is often used to compare only two things: *When two people argue, the angriest one is usually wrong.* But the distinction between the forms should be observed in writing.

4 Use comparative or superlative forms only for modifiers that can logically be compared.

Some adjectives and adverbs cannot logically be compared—for instance, *perfect, unique, dead, impossible, infinite,* and related adverbs such as *perfectly* and *impossibly.* These absolute words can be preceded by adverbs like *nearly* and *almost* that mean "approaching," but they cannot logically be modified by *more* or *most* (as in *most perfect*). This distinction is sometimes ignored in speech, but it should always be made in writing:

Not He was the most unique teacher we had.
But He was a unique teacher.

Exercise 16.2 Revising: Comparatives and superlatives

Revise the sentences below so that the comparative and superlative forms of adjectives and adverbs are appropriate for formal usage. Mark the number preceding any sentence that is already correct.

Example:

Attending classes full time and working at two jobs was the most impossible thing I ever did.

Attending classes full time and working at two jobs was impossible [or the hardest thing I ever did].

1. Charlotte was the older of the three Brontë sisters, all of whom were novelists.
2. Some readers think Emily Brontë's *Wuthering Heights* is the most saddest novel they have ever read.
3. Of the other two sisters, Charlotte and Anne, Charlotte was probably the more talented.
4. Critics still argue about whether Charlotte or Emily wrote more better.
5. Certainly this family of women novelists was the most unique.

16e Watch for double negatives.

In a **double negative** two negative words such as *no, not, none, neither, barely, hardly,* or *scarcely* cancel each other out. Some double negatives are intentional: for instance, *She was not unhappy* indicates with understatement that she was indeed happy. But most double negatives say the opposite of what is intended: *Nadia did not feel nothing* asserts that Nadia felt other than nothing, or something. For the opposite meaning, one of the negatives must be eliminated or changed to a positive: *She felt nothing* or *She did not feel anything.*

Faulty The IRS cannot hardly audit all tax returns. None of its audits never touch many cheaters.

Revised The IRS cannot audit all tax returns. Its audits never touch many cheaters.

Exercise 16.3 Revising: Double negatives

Identify and revise the double negatives in the following paragraph. Each error may have more than one correct revision.

Interest in books about the founding of the United States seems to vary with the national mood. Americans show hardly no interest in books about the founders when things are going well in the United States. However, when Americans can't barely agree on major issues, sales of books about the Revolutionary War era increase. During such periods, one cannot go to no bookstore without seeing several new volumes about John Adams, Thomas Jefferson, and other founders. When Americans feel they don't have nothing in common, their increased interest in the early leaders may reflect a desire for unity.

16f Use nouns sparingly as modifiers.

We often use one noun to modify another. For example:

child care flood control security guard

Such phrases can be both clear and concise, but overuse of noun modifiers can lead to flat, even senseless, writing. To avoid awkwardness or confusion, observe two principles. First, prefer possessives or adjectives as modifiers:

Not A student takes the state medical board exams to become a dentist technician.

But A student takes the state medical board's exams to become a dental technician.

Second, use only short nouns as modifiers and use them only in two- or three-word sequences:

Confusing Minimex maintains a plant employee relations improvement program.

Revised Minimex maintains a program for improving relations among plant employees.

16g Distinguish between present and past participles as adjectives.

Both present participles and past participles may serve as adjectives: *a burning building, a burned building.* As in the examples, the two participles usually differ in the time they indicate.

But some present and past participles—those derived from verbs expressing feeling—can have altogether different meanings. The present participle modifies something that causes the feeling: *That was a frightening storm* (the storm frightens). The past participle modifies something that experiences the feeling: *They quieted the frightened horses* (the horses feel fright).

The following participles are among the ones that are likely to be confused:

amazing/amazed
amusing/amused
annoying/annoyed
astonishing/astonished
boring/bored
confusing/confused
depressing/depressed
embarrassing/embarrassed
exciting/excited
exhausting/exhausted
fascinating/fascinated
frightening/frightened
frustrating/frustrated
interesting/interested
pleasing/pleased
satisfying/satisfied
shocking/shocked
surprising/surprised
tiring/tired
worrying/worried

Exercise 16.4 Revising: Present and past participles CULTURE LANGUAGE

Revise the adjectives in the following sentences as needed to distinguish between present and past participles. If the sentence is already correct as given, mark the number preceding it.

Example:
The subject was embarrassed to many people.
The subject was embarrassing to many people.

1. Several critics found Alice Walker's *The Color Purple* to be a fascinated book.
2. One confused critic wished that Walker had deleted the scenes set in Africa.
3. Another critic argued that although the book contained many depressed episodes, the overall impact was excited.
4. Since other readers found the book annoyed, this critic pointed out its many surprised qualities.
5. In the end most critics agreed that the book was a satisfied novel.

16h Use *a, an, the,* and other determiners appropriately.

Determiners are special kinds of adjectives that mark nouns because they always precede nouns. Some common determiners are *a, an,* and *the* (called **articles**) and *my, their, whose, this, these, those, one, some,* and *any.* They convey information to readers—for instance, by specifying who owns what, which one of two is meant, or whether a subject is familiar or unfamiliar.

Native speakers of standard American English can rely on their intuition when using determiners, but speakers of other languages and dialects often have difficulty with them. In standard English the use of determiners depends on the context they appear in and the kind of noun they precede:

- **Proper noun:** Names a particular person, place, or thing and begins with a capital letter: *February, Joe Allen, Red River.* Most proper nouns are not preceded by determiners.
- **Count noun:** Names something that is countable in English and can form a plural: *girl/girls, apple/apples, child/children.* A singular count noun is always preceded by a determiner; a plural count noun sometimes is.
- **Noncount noun:** Names something not usually considered countable in English and so does not form a plural. A noncount noun is sometimes preceded by a determiner. Here is a sample of noncount nouns, sorted into groups by meaning:

Abstractions: confidence, democracy, education, envy, equality, evidence, health, information, intelligence, knowledge, luxury, peace, pollution, research, success, supervision, truth, wealth, work

Food and drink: bread, candy, cereal, flour, meat, milk, salt, water, wine

Emotions: anger, courage, happiness, hate, joy, love, respect, satisfaction

Natural events and substances: air, blood, dirt, gasoline, gold, hair, heat, ice, oil, oxygen, rain, silver, smoke, weather, wood

Groups: clergy, clothing, equipment, furniture, garbage, jewelry, junk, legislation, machinery, mail, military, money, police, vocabulary

Fields of study: architecture, accounting, biology, business, chemistry, engineering, literature, psychology, science

A dictionary of English as a second language will say whether a noun is a count noun, a noncount noun, or both. (See p. 509 for recommended dictionaries.)

Note Many nouns can be both count and noncount nouns:

The library has a room for readers. [*Room* is a count noun meaning "walled area."]

The library has room for reading. [*Room* is a noncount noun meaning "space."]

1 Use *a, an,* and *the* where they are required.

With singular count nouns

A or *an* precedes a singular count noun when the reader does not already know its identity, usually because you have not mentioned it before:

A scientist in the school's chemistry department developed a process to strengthen metals. [*Scientist* and *process* are being mentioned for the first time.]

The precedes a singular count noun that has a specific identity for the reader, for one of the following reasons:

- **You have mentioned the noun before:**

  A scientist in the school's chemistry department developed a process to strengthen metals. The scientist patented the process. [*Scientist* and *process* were identified in the preceding sentence.]

- **You identify the noun immediately before or after you state it:**

  The most productive laboratory is the research center in the chemistry department. [*Most productive* identifies *laboratory. In the chemistry department* identifies *research center.* And *chemistry department* is a shared facility.]

- **The noun names something unique—the only one in existence:**

  The sun rises in the east. [*Sun* and *east* are unique.]

- **The noun names an institution or facility that is shared by the community of readers:**

  Many men and women aspire to the presidency. [*Presidency* is a shared institution.]

  The cell phone has changed communication. [*Cell phone* is a shared facility.]

The is not used before a singular noun that names a general category:

> Sherman said that war is hell. [*War* names a general category.]
> The war in Iraq left many wounded. [*War* names a specific war.]

ad
16h

With plural count nouns

A or *an* never precedes a plural noun. *The* does not precede a plural noun that names a general category. *The* does precede a plural noun that names specific representatives of a category.

> Men and women are different. [*Men* and *women* name general categories.]
> The women formed a team. [*Women* refers to specific people.]

With noncount nouns

A or *an* never precedes a noncount noun. *The* does precede a noncount noun when it names specific representatives of a general category:

> Vegetation suffers from drought. [*Vegetation* names a general category.]
>
> The vegetation in the park withered or died. [*Vegetation* refers to specific plants.]

With proper nouns

A or *an* never precedes a proper noun. *The* generally does not precede a proper noun:

> Garcia lives in Boulder.

There are exceptions, however. For instance, we generally use *the* before plural proper nouns (*the Murphys, the New England Patriots*) and the names of groups and organizations (*the Department of Justice, the Sierra Club*), ships (*the* Lusitania), oceans (*the Pacific*), mountain ranges (*the Alps*), regions (*the Middle East*), rivers (*the Mississippi*), and some countries (*the United States, the Netherlands*).

2 Use other determiners appropriately.

The uses of English determiners besides articles also depend on context and kind of noun. The following determiners may be used as indicated with singular count nouns, plural count nouns, or non-count nouns.

With any kind of noun (singular count, plural count, noncount)

my, our, your, his, her, its, their
possessive nouns (*boy's, boys'*)
whose, which(ever), what(ever)
some, any, the other
no

Their account is overdrawn. [Singular count.]
Their funds are low. [Plural count.]
Their money is running out. [Noncount.]

Only with singular nouns (count and noncount)

this, that

This account has some money. [Count.]
That information may help. [Noncount.]

Only with noncount nouns and plural count nouns

most, enough, other, such, all, all of the, a lot of

Most money is needed elsewhere. [Noncount.]
Most funds are committed. [Plural count.]

Only with singular count nouns

one, every, each, either, neither, another

One car must be sold. [Singular count.]

Only with plural count nouns

these, those
both, many, few, a few, fewer, fewest, several
two, three, and so forth

Two cars are unnecessary. [Plural count.]

Note *Few* means "not many" or "not enough." *A few* means "some" or "a small but sufficient quantity."

Few committee members came to the meeting.
A few members can keep the committee going.

Do not use *much* with a plural count noun:

Many [not Much] members want to help.

Only with noncount nouns

much, more, little, a little, less, least, a large amount of

Less luxury is in order. [Noncount.]

Note *Little* means "not many" or "not enough." *A little* means "some" or "a small but sufficient quantity."

Little time remains before the conference.
The members need a little help from their colleagues.

Do not use *many* with a noncount noun:

Much [not Many] work remains.

Exercise 16.5 Revising: Articles CULTURE LANGUAGE

For each blank below, indicate whether *a, an, the,* or no article should be inserted.

From _____ native American Indians who migrated from _____ Asia 20,000 years ago to _____ new arrivals who now come by _____ planes, _____ United States is _____ nation of foreigners. It is _____ country of immigrants who are all living under _____ single flag.

Back in _____ seventeenth and eighteenth centuries, at least 75% of the immigrant population came from _____ England. However, between 1820 and 1975 more than 38 million immigrants came to this country from elsewhere in _____ Europe. Many children of _____ immigrants were self-conscious and denied their heritage; many even refused to learn _____ native language of their parents and grandparents. They tried to "Americanize" themselves. The so-called Melting Pot theory of _____ social change stressed _____ importance of blending everyone together into _____ kind of stew. Each nationality would contribute its own flavor, but _____ final stew would be something called "American."

This Melting Pot theory was never completely successful. In the last half of the twentieth century, _____ ethnic revival changed _____ metaphor. Many people now see _____ American society as _____ mosaic. Americans are once again proud of their heritage, and _____ ethnic differences make _____ mosaic colorful and interesting.

Exercise 16.6 Revising: Adjectives and adverbs

Revise the following paragraph so that it conforms to formal usage of adjectives and adverbs.

Americans often argue about which professional sport is better: basketball, football, or baseball. Basketball fans contend that their sport offers more action because the players are constant running and shooting. Because it is played indoors in relative small arenas, basketball allows fans to be more closer to the action than the other sports do. Fans point to how graceful the players fly through the air to the hoop. Football fanatics say they don't hardly stop yelling once the game begins. They cheer when their team executes a real complicated play good. They roar more louder when the defense stops the opponents in a goal-line stand. They yell loudest when a fullback crashes in for a score. In contrast, the supporters of baseball believe that it might be the most perfect sport. It combines the one-on-one duel of pitcher and batter struggling valiant with the tight teamwork of double and triple plays. Because the game is played slow and careful, fans can analyze and discuss the manager's strategy. Besides, they don't never know when they might catch a foul ball as a souvenir. However, no matter what the sport, all fans feel happily only when their team wins.

Exercise on Chapters 13–16 Revising: Grammatical sentences

The following paragraphs contain errors in pronoun case, verb forms, subject-verb agreement, pronoun-antecedent agreement, and the forms of adjectives and adverbs. Revise the paragraphs to correct the errors.

Occasionally, musicians become "crossover artists" whom can perform good in more than one field of music. For example, Wynton and Branford Marsalis was train in jazz by their father, the great pianist Ellis Marsalis. Both of the sons has became successful classical artists. Branford's saxophone captures the richness of pieces by Ravel and Stravinsky. Wynton's albums of classical trumpet music from the Baroque period has brung him many awards. Still, if he was to choose which kind of music he likes best, Wynton would probable choose jazz. In contrast to the Marsalises, violinist Nigel Kennedy growed up studying and performing classical music. In his teens he began playing jazz and even rock music. Today he is known almost as good for his interpretations of Miles Davis and Jimi Hendrix as he is for his classical performances.

Some vocalists sing in several genres. For example, Renée Fleming, one of the great opera sopranos, have recorded popular music. Her technique on the song "In Your Eyes" is nearly perfect, yet she sounded as if she was simply trying to sing proper. Another singer, Bobby McFerrin, been successful singing both pop and classical music. He has won pop Grammy awards, but he is equal able to sing classical pieces *a capella* (without musical accompaniment). His voice's remarkable range and clarity allows him to imitate many musical instruments.

Still other musicians has founded success as crossover composers. The former Beatle Paul McCartney is best known as a pop singer and songwriter, but he has also wrote scores for symphony orchestra, opera, and ballet. Two well-known pop stars, Bono and the Edge from the band U2, had compose music for the Broadway musical *Spider-Man*. Each of these men have showed their ability to adapt to other musical styles.

All of these artists has shown great musicianship in new fields. They are willing to test and stretch their talents, and each of we music fans benefit.

PART 4

Clear Sentences

17 Sentence Fragments

Chapter essentials

- Test sentences for completeness (below).
- Revise sentence fragments (p. 341).
- Understand the types of sentence fragments, such as subordinate clauses, verbal phrases, and prepositional phrases (pp. 342, 343).
- Be aware of the acceptable uses of incomplete sentences (p. 344).

Visit MyWritingLab™ for more resources on sentence fragments.

A **sentence fragment** is part of a sentence that is set off as if it were a whole sentence by an initial capital letter and a final period or other end punctuation. Although writers occasionally use fragments deliberately and effectively, readers perceive most fragments as serious errors because, expecting complete sentences, they find partial sentences distracting or confusing. (Before reading further, you may find it helpful to review pp. 246–48 and 263–65 on sentences and clauses.)

Complete sentence versus sentence fragment

A *complete sentence* or *main clause*

- contains a subject and a predicate verb (*The wind blows*)
- and is not a subordinate clause (beginning with a word such as *because* or *who*).

A *sentence fragment*

- lacks a predicate verb (*The wind blowing*)
- or lacks a subject (*And blows*)
- or is a subordinate clause not attached to a complete sentence (*Because the wind blows*).

17a Test your sentences for completeness, and revise any fragments.

Three tests will help you determine whether a word group punctuated as a sentence is actually a complete sentence. If the word group does not pass *all three* tests, it is a fragment and needs to be revised.

Test 1: Find the predicate verb.

Look for a predicate verb in the group of words. Some fragments lack any verb at all:

Fragment	Millions of sites on the Web.
Revised	Millions of sites make up the Web.

Other sentence fragments contain a verb form, but it is not a predicate verb. Instead, it is often the *-ing* or *to* form (*walking, to walk*):

Fragment	The Web growing with new sites and users every day.
Revised	The Web grows with new sites and users every day.

CULTURE LANGUAGE Some languages allow forms of *be* to be omitted as helping or linking verbs. But English requires stating forms of *be*:

Fragments	The network growing. It much larger than its developers anticipated.
Revised	The network is growing. It is much larger than its developers anticipated.

Test 2: Find the subject.

If you find a predicate verb, look for its subject by asking *who* or *what* performs the action or makes the assertion of the verb. The subject of the sentence will usually come before the verb. If there is no subject, the word group is probably a fragment:

frag 17a

Fragment	The Web continues to grow. And shows no sign of slowing down.
Revised	The Web continues to grow. And it shows no sign of slowing down.

In one kind of complete sentence, a command, the subject *you* is understood: [*You*] *Close the door.*

CULTURE LANGUAGE Some languages allow the omission of the sentence subject, especially when it is a pronoun. But in English, except in commands, the subject is always stated:

Fragment	Web shopping has expanded dramatically. Has hurt traditional stores.
Revised	Web shopping has expanded dramatically. It has hurt traditional stores.

Test 3: Make sure the clause is not subordinate.

A subordinate clause usually begins with a subordinating word:

Subordinating conjunctions			Relative pronouns	
after	once	until	that	who/whom
although	since	when	which	whoever/whomever
as	than	where		whose
because	that	whereas		
if	unless	while		

(See p. 264 for a longer list of subordinating conjunctions.)

Tests for sentence fragments

1. Does the word group have a predicate verb?

Example	Answer	Revision
Millions of devices on cellular networks.	No →	Add a verb.
Millions of devices use cellular networks.	Yes	—

2. Does the word group have a subject?

Example	Answer	Revision
Cell phones are convenient. But annoy many people.	No →	Add a subject.
Cell phones are convenient. But they annoy many people.	Yes	—

3. Is the word group a freestanding subordinate clause?

Example	Answer	Revision
Phones ring everywhere. Because users forget to silence them.	Yes →	Make it a main clause or attach it to a main clause.
Phones ring everywhere. Users forget to silence them.	No (*because* removed)	—
Phones ring everywhere because users forget to silence them.	No (clause attached)	—

frag
17a

Subordinate clauses serve as parts of sentences (as nouns or modifiers), not as whole sentences:

Fragment When the government devised the Internet.

Revised The government devised the Internet.

Revised When the government devised the Internet, no expansive computer network existed.

Fragment The reason that the government devised the Internet.

Revised The reason that the government devised the Internet was to provide secure links among departments and defense contractors.

Note Questions beginning with *how, what, when, where, which, who, whom, whose,* and *why* are not sentence fragments: *Who was responsible? When did it happen?*

Revising sentence fragments

Almost all sentence fragments can be corrected in one of the two ways shown below. The choice depends on the importance of the information in the fragment.

- **Rewrite the fragment as a complete sentence.** Add a predicate verb or a subject as needed, or make a subordinate clause into a complete sentence. This revision gives the information in the fragment the same importance as that in other complete sentences.

  Fragment A major improvement in public health occurred with the widespread use of vaccines. Which protected children against life-threatening diseases.

  Revised A major improvement in public health occurred with the widespread use of vaccines. They protected children against life-threatening diseases.

  Two main clauses may be separated by a semicolon instead of a period (p. 443).

- **Attach the fragment to a main clause.** This revision makes the information in the fragment subordinate to the information in the main clause.

  Fragment The polio vaccine eradicated the disease from most of the globe. The first vaccine to be used widely.

  Revised The polio vaccine, the first to be used widely, eradicated the disease from most of the globe.

Note For adding punctuation to sentences that contain revised fragments, see pages 427 (commas), 467 (the colon), and 469 (dashes).

frag
17a

Exercise 17.1 Identifying and revising sentence fragments

Apply the tests for completeness to each of the following word groups. If a word group is a complete sentence, mark the number preceding it. If it is a sentence fragment, revise it in two ways: by making it a complete sentence, and by combining it with a main clause written from the information given in other items.

Example:

And could not find his money. [The word group has a verb (*could . . . find*) but no subject.]

Revised into a complete sentence: And he could not find his money.

Combined with a new main clause: He was lost and could not find his money.

1. In an interesting article about vandalism against works of art.
2. The motives of the vandals varying widely.
3. Those who harm artwork are usually angry.
4. But not necessarily at the artist or the owner.
5. For instance, a man who hammered at Michelangelo's *Pietà*.

6. And knocked off the Virgin Mary's nose.
7. Because he was angry at the Roman Catholic Church.
8. Which knew nothing of his grievance.
9. Although many damaged works can be repaired.
10. Usually even the most skillful repairs are forever visible.

17b A subordinate clause is not a complete sentence.

Subordinate clauses contain both subjects and verbs, but they always begin with a subordinating conjunction (*although, if,* and so on) or a relative pronoun (*who, which, that,* and so on). (See pp. 263–65.) Subordinate clauses serve as nouns or modifiers, but they cannot stand alone as complete sentences.

To correct a subordinate clause set off as a sentence, combine it with the main clause or remove or change the subordinating word to create a main clause.

Fragment Many pine trees bear large cones. Which appear in August.

Revised Many pine trees bear large cones, which appear in August.

Revised Many pine trees bear large cones. They appear in August.

17c A verbal phrase or a prepositional phrase is not a complete sentence.

Verbal phrases

A **verbal phrase** consists of an infinitive (*to choose*), a past participle (*chosen*), or a present participle or gerund (*choosing*) together with any objects and modifiers it may have (see p. 261). A verbal phrase is a noun or modifier and cannot serve as the verb in a complete sentence:

Fragment For many of the elderly, their house is their only asset. Offering some security but no income.

Revised For many of the elderly, their house is their only asset, offering some security but no income.

Revised For many of the elderly, their house is their only asset. It offers some security but no income.

Prepositional phrases

A **prepositional phrase** is a modifier consisting of a preposition (such as *in, on, to,* or *with*) together with its object and any modifiers (see pp. 257–58). A prepositional phrase cannot stand alone as a complete sentence:

Fragment In a squeeze between a valuable asset and little income. Eventually many elderly people sell their homes.

Revised In a squeeze between a valuable asset and little income, eventually many elderly people sell their homes.

Revised Many elderly people are in a squeeze between a valuable asset and little income. Eventually they may sell their homes.

CULTURE LANGUAGE Some English prepositions consist of two or three words: *as well as, along with, in addition to, on top of,* and others. Don't let prepositions of more than one word mislead you into writing sentence fragments.

Fragment In today's retirement communities, the elderly may have health care, housekeeping, and new friends. As well as financial security.

Revised In today's retirement communities, the elderly may have health care, housekeeping, and new friends as well as financial security.

17d Any word group lacking a subject or a verb or both is not a complete sentence.

frag 17d

Nouns with modifiers

We often follow a noun with a modifier. No matter how long the noun and its modifier are, they cannot stand alone as a sentence:

Fragments People waving flags and cheering. Lined the streets for the parade.

Revised People waving flags and cheering lined the streets for the parade.

Fragment Veterans who fought in Vietnam. They are finally being honored.

Revised Veterans who fought in Vietnam are finally being honored.

Appositives

Appositives are nouns, or nouns and their modifiers, that rename or describe other nouns (see pp. 266–67). They cannot stand alone as sentences:

Fragment When I was a child, my favorite adult was an old uncle. A retired sea captain who always told me long stories of wild adventures in faraway places.

Revised When I was a child, my favorite adult was an old uncle, a retired sea captain who always told me long stories of wild adventures in faraway places.

Compound predicates

Compound predicates are predicates made up of two or more verbs and their objects, if any (see p. 268). A verb or its object cannot stand alone as a sentence:

Fragment	Uncle Marlon drew out his tales. And embellished them.
Revised	Uncle Marlon drew out his tales and embellished them.
Fragment	He described characters he had met. And storms at sea.
Revised	He described characters he had met and storms at sea.

Note Beginning a sentence with a coordinating conjunction such as *and* or *but* can lead to a sentence fragment. Check every sentence you begin with a coordinating conjunction to be sure it is complete.

Exercise 17.2 Revising: Sentence fragments

Correct any sentence fragment below either by combining it with a main clause or by making it a main clause. If an item contains no sentence fragment, mark the number preceding it.

Example:

Jujitsu is good for self-protection. Because it enables one to overcome an opponent without the use of weapons.

Jujitsu is good for self-protection because it enables one to overcome an opponent without the use of weapons.

frag 17e

1. Human beings who perfume themselves. They are not much different from other animals.
2. Animals as varied as insects and dogs release *pheromones*. Chemicals that signal other animals.
3. Human beings have a diminished sense of smell. And do not consciously detect most of their own species' pheromones.
4. The human substitute for pheromones may be perfumes. Especially musk and other fragrances derived from animal oils.
5. Some sources say that humans began using perfume to cover up the smell of burning flesh. During sacrifices to the gods.
6. Perfumes became religious offerings in their own right. Being expensive to make, they were highly prized.
7. The earliest historical documents from the Middle East record the use of fragrances. Not only in religious ceremonies but on the body.
8. In the nineteenth century chemists began synthesizing perfume oils. Which previously could be made only from natural sources.
9. The most popular animal oil for perfume today is musk. Although some people dislike its heavy, sweet odor.
10. Synthetic musk oil would help conserve a certain species of deer. Whose gland is the source of musk.

17e Be aware of the acceptable uses of incomplete sentences.

A few word groups lacking the usual subject-predicate combination are not sentence fragments because they conform to the expectations of most readers. They include commands (*Move along. Shut the window.*); exclamations (*Oh no!*); questions and answers

(*Where next? To Kansas.*); and descriptions in employment résumés (*Weekly volunteer in a soup kitchen.*). Another kind of incomplete sentence, occurring in special situations, is the transitional phrase (*So much for the causes, now for the results. One final point.*).

Experienced writers sometimes use sentence fragments when they want to achieve a special effect. Such fragments appear more in informal than in formal writing. Unless you are experienced and thoroughly secure in your own writing, you should avoid all fragments and concentrate on writing clear, well-formed sentences.

Exercise 17.3 Revising: Sentence fragments

Revise the following paragraph to eliminate sentence fragments by combining them with main clauses or rewriting them as main clauses.

Baby red-eared slider turtles are brightly colored. With bold patterns on their yellowish undershells. Which serve as a warning to predators. The bright colors of skunks and other animals. They signal that the animals will spray nasty chemicals. In contrast, the turtle's colors warn largemouth bass. That the baby turtle will actively defend itself. When a bass gulps down a turtle. The feisty baby claws and bites. Forcing the bass to spit it out. To avoid a similar painful experience. The bass will avoid other baby red-eared slider turtles. The turtle loses its bright colors as it grows too big. For a bass's afternoon snack.

Note See page 380 for an exercise involving sentence fragments along with comma splices, fused sentences, and other sentence errors.

18 Comma Splices and Fused Sentences

Chapter essentials

- Separate main clauses not joined by *and, but,* or another coordinating conjunction (p. 347).
- Separate main clauses related by *however, for example,* or a similar expression (p. 348).

Visit MyWritingLab™ for more resources on comma splices and fused sentences.

When two sentences (main clauses) fall together, readers need a signal that one clause is ending and another is beginning. The following box shows the ways to provide this signal.

Punctuation of two or more main clauses

- **Separate main clauses with periods.**

  Main clause . **Main clause** .

  Hybrid cars are popular with consumers. Automakers are releasing new models.

- **Link main clauses with a comma and a coordinating conjunction.**

  Main clause , *for and or so but nor yet* **main clause** .

  Hybrid cars are popular with consumers, and automakers are releasing new models.

- **Link main clauses with a semicolon.**

  Main clause ; **main clause** .

  Hybrid cars are popular with consumers; automakers are releasing new models.

- **Relate main clauses with a semicolon and a conjunctive adverb or transitional expression.**

  Main clause ; *however, for example,* etc. , **main clause** .

  Hybrid cars are popular with consumers; as a result, automakers are releasing new models.

18

With a comma splice or a fused sentence, two main clauses run together without one of the signals listed in the box, and readers often must reread for sense. A **comma splice** joins (or splices) main clauses *only* with a comma, not with a coordinating conjunction as well:

Comma splice The ship was huge, its mast stood eighty feet high.

A **fused sentence** (or **run-on sentence**) joins main clauses with no punctuation at all:

Fused sentence The ship was huge its mast stood eighty feet high.

CULTURE LANGUAGE An English sentence may not include more than one main clause unless the clauses are separated by a comma and a coordinating conjunction or by a semicolon or colon. If your native language does not have such a rule or has accustomed you to writing long sentences, you may need to edit your English writing especially for comma splices and fused sentences.

18a Separate two main clauses not joined by *and, but,* or another coordinating conjunction.

If your readers point out comma splices or fused sentences in your writing, you're not creating enough separation between main clauses in your sentences. Use one of the following methods to repair the problem.

Make the clauses into separate sentences.

Make the clauses into separate sentences when the ideas expressed are only loosely related:

Comma splice Chemistry has contributed much to our understanding of foods, many foods such as wheat and beans can be produced in the laboratory.

Revised Chemistry has contributed much to our understanding of foods. Many foods such as wheat and beans can be produced in the laboratory.

CULTURE LANGUAGE Making separate sentences may be the best option if you are used to writing very long sentences in your native language and often write comma splices in English.

Revision of comma splices and fused sentences

1. **Underline the main clauses in your draft.**

   Sailors trained on the ship they learned about wind and sails. Trainees who took the course ranged from high school students to Navy officers. The ship was built in 1910, it had sailed ever since. In almost a century, it had circled the globe forty times. It burned in 2001 its cabins and decks were destroyed.

2. **Focus on sentences that contain two or more main clauses.**
3. **If nothing falls between the clauses or only a comma does, revise in one of the following ways.** The choice depends on the relation you want to establish between the clauses, as explained above and on the next page.

   Make the clauses into separate sentences.

   Sailors trained on the ship. They learned about wind and sails.

   Separate the clauses with a comma and a coordinating conjunction.

   The ship was built in 1910, and it had sailed ever since.

   Separate the clauses with a semicolon.

   The ship was built in 1910; it had sailed ever since.

   Make one clause into a subordinate clause when that clause is less important than the other one.

   When it burned in 2001, its cabins and decks were destroyed.

Insert a coordinating conjunction.

Insert a coordinating conjunction in a comma splice when the ideas in the main clauses are closely related and are equally important:

Comma splice	Some laboratory-grown foods taste good, they are nutritious.
Revised	Some laboratory-grown foods taste good, and they are nutritious.

In a fused sentence insert both a comma and a coordinating conjunction:

Fused sentence	Chemists have made much progress they still have a way to go.
Revised	Chemists have made much progress, but they still have a way to go.

Insert a semicolon.

Insert a semicolon between clauses if the relation between the ideas is very close and obvious without a conjunction:

cs / fs 18b

Comma splice	Good taste is rare in laboratory-grown vegetables, they are usually bland.
Revised	Good taste is rare in laboratory-grown vegetables; they are usually bland.

Make one clause into a subordinate clause.

When the idea in one clause is more important than that in the other, express the less important idea in a subordinate clause. Subordination is often more effective than forming separate sentences because it defines the relation between ideas more precisely:

Fused sentence	The vitamins are adequate the flavor is deficient.
Revised	The vitamins are adequate. The flavor is deficient. [Both ideas receive equal weight.]
Improved	Even though the vitamins are adequate, the flavor is deficient. [Emphasis on the second idea.]

18b Separate main clauses related by *however, for example,* or a similar expression.

Two kinds of words that are not conjunctions describe how one main clause relates to another:

- **Conjunctive adverbs,** such as *consequently, finally, hence, however, indeed, therefore,* and *thus*. (See p. 269 for a longer list.)
- **Other transitional expressions,** such as *even so, for example, in fact, of course,* and *to this end*. (See pp. 85–86 for a longer list.)

When two main clauses are related by a conjunctive adverb or a transitional expression, they must be separated by a period or by a semicolon. The adverb or expression is also generally set off by a comma or commas (see p. 445):

Comma splice Healthcare costs are higher in the United States than in many other countries, consequently health insurance is also more costly.

Revised Healthcare costs are higher in the United States than in many other countries. Consequently, health insurance is also more costly.

Revised Healthcare costs are higher in the United States than in many other countries; consequently, health insurance is also more costly.

Conjunctive adverbs and transitional expressions are different from coordinating conjunctions (*and, but,* and so on) and subordinating conjunctions (*although, because,* and so on):

- **Unlike conjunctions, conjunctive adverbs and transitional expressions do not join two clauses into a grammatical unit.** They merely describe the way two clauses relate in meaning.
- **Unlike conjunctions, conjunctive adverbs and transitional expressions can be moved within a clause.** No matter where in the clause an adverb or expression falls, though, the clause must be separated from another main clause by a period or semicolon.

Fused sentence

Increased television watching is not the only cause of the decline in reading ability however it is one of the important causes.

Revised with a period

Increased television watching is not the only cause of the decline in reading ability. However, it is one of the important causes.

Revised with a semicolon

Increased television watching is not the only cause of the decline in reading ability; however, it is one of the important causes.

Increased television watching is not the only cause of the decline in reading ability; it is, however, one of the important causes.

cs / fs

18b

Exercise 18.1 Revising: Comma splices and fused sentences

Correct each of the following comma splices or fused sentences in two ways: (1) make separate sentences of the main clauses; (2) insert a coordinating conjunction or both a comma and a coordinating conjunction between the main clauses; (3) insert a semicolon or both a semicolon and a conjunctive adverb or transitional expression between the main clauses; (4) subordinate one clause to another. If an item contains no comma splice or fused sentence, mark the number preceding it.

1. Money has a long history, it goes back at least as far as the earliest records.

2. Every known society has had a system of money, though the objects serving as money have varied widely.
3. Sometimes the objects have had real value, in modern times their value has been more abstract.
4. Cattle, fermented beverages, and rare shells have served as money each one had actual value for the society.
5. Today money may be made of worthless paper, it may even consist of a bit of data in a computer's memory.
6. We think of money as valuable only our common faith in it makes it valuable.
7. Economic crises often shake the belief in money, indeed, such weakened faith helped cause the Great Depression of the 1930s.
8. Throughout history money and religion were closely linked, there was little distinction between government and religion.
9. Coins were minted of precious metals the religious overtones of money were then strengthened.
10. People already believed the precious metals to be divine, their use in money intensified its allure.

Exercise 18.2 Sentence combining to avoid comma splices and fused sentences

Combine each pair of sentences below into one sentence without creating a comma splice or fused sentence. Combine sentences by (1) supplying a comma and coordinating conjunction, (2) supplying a semicolon, or (3) subordinating one clause to the other. You will have to add, delete, or change words as well as punctuation.

Example:

The sun sank lower in the sky. The colors gradually faded.

As the sun sank lower in the sky, the colors gradually faded. [The first clause is subordinated to the second.]

1. The exact origin of paper money is unknown. It has not survived as coins, shells, and other durable objects have.
2. Perhaps goldsmiths were also bankers. Thus they held the gold of their wealthy customers.
3. The goldsmiths probably gave customers receipts for their gold. These receipts were then used in trade.
4. The goldsmiths were something like modern-day bankers. Their receipts were something like modern-day money.
5. The goldsmiths became even more like modern-day bankers. They began issuing receipts for more gold than they actually held in their vaults.

Exercise 18.3 Revising: Comma splices and fused sentences

Identify and revise the comma splices and fused sentences in the following paragraph.

All those parents who urged their children to eat broccoli were right, the vegetable really is healthful. Broccoli contains sulforaphane, moreover, this mustard oil can be found in kale and Brussels sprouts. Sulforaphane causes the body to make an enzyme that attacks carcinogens, these substances cause cancer. The enzyme speeds up the work of the kidneys then they can flush harmful chemicals out of the body. Other vegetables have similar benefits however, green, leafy vegetables like broccoli are the most efficient. Thus wise people will eat their broccoli it could save their lives.

Note See page 380 for an exercise involving comma splices and fused sentences along with other sentence errors.

19 Pronoun Reference

Chapter essentials

- Make a pronoun refer clearly to one antecedent (below).
- Place a pronoun close enough to its antecedent to ensure clarity (p. 353).
- Make a pronoun refer to a specific antecedent (p. 354).
- Use *you* only to mean "you, the reader" (p. 355).
- Use the pronoun *it* only one way in a sentence (p. 356).
- Use *who, which,* and *that* for appropriate antecedents (p. 356).

Visit MyWritingLab™ for more resources on pronoun reference.

A **pronoun** such as *it* or *they* derives its meaning from its **antecedent,** the noun it substitutes for. Therefore, a pronoun must refer clearly and unmistakably to its antecedent in order for the meaning to be clear. A sentence such as *Jim told Mark he was not invited* is not clear because the reader does not know whether *he* refers to Jim or to Mark.

One way to make pronoun reference clear is to ensure that the pronoun and antecedent agree in person, number, and gender (see pp. 319–23). The other way is to ensure that the pronoun refers unambiguously to a single, close, specific antecedent.

CULTURE LANGUAGE An English pronoun does need a clear antecedent nearby, but don't use both a pronoun and its antecedent as the subject of the same sentence or clause: *Jim* [not *Jim he*] *told Mark to go alone.* (See also p. 374.)

19a Make a pronoun refer clearly to one antecedent.

When either of two nouns can be a pronoun's antecedent, the reference will not be clear:

Principal causes of unclear pronoun reference

- **More than one possible antecedent** (previous page and below):

Confusing	To keep birds from eating seeds, soak them in blue food coloring.
Clear	To keep birds from eating seeds, soak the seeds in blue food coloring.

- **Antecedent too far away** (facing page):

Confusing	Employees should consult with their supervisor who require personal time.
Clear	Employees who require personal time should consult with their supervisor.

- **Antecedent only implied** (p. 354):

Confusing	Many children begin reading on their own by watching television, but this should probably be discounted in government policy.
Clear	Many children begin reading on their own by watching television, but such self-instruction should probably be discounted in government policy.

See also pages 355–56.

Confusing	Emily Dickinson is sometimes compared with Jane Austen, but she led a more reclusive life.

Revise such a sentence in one of two ways:

- **Replace the pronoun with the appropriate noun:**

Clear	Emily Dickinson is sometimes compared with Jane Austen, but Dickinson led a more reclusive life.

- **Avoid repetition by rewriting the sentence.** If you use the pronoun, make sure it has only one possible antecedent:

Clear	Despite occasional comparison of their lives, Emily Dickinson was more reclusive than Jane Austen.
Clear	Though sometimes compared with her, Emily Dickinson was more reclusive than Jane Austen.

Sentences that report what someone said, using verbs such as *said* or *told,* often require direct rather than indirect quotation:

Confusing	Juliet Noble told Ann Torre that she was next in line for the job.
Clear	Juliet Noble told Ann Torre, "I am next in line for the job."
Clear	Juliet Noble told Ann Torre, "You are next in line for the job."

Note Avoid the awkward device of using a pronoun followed by the appropriate noun in parentheses, as in the following example:

Weak Noble and Torre had both hoped for the job, so she (Noble) was disappointed.

Improved Noble was disappointed because she and Torre had both hoped for the job.

19b Place a pronoun close enough to its antecedent to ensure clarity.

A clause beginning *who, which,* or *that* generally should fall immediately after the word to which it refers:

Confusing Jody found a lamp in the attic that her aunt had used.

Clear In the attic Jody found a lamp that her aunt had used.

Even when only one word could possibly serve as the antecedent of a pronoun, the relationship between the two may still be unclear if they are widely separated:

Confusing Jane Austen had little formal education but was well educated at home. Far from living an isolated life in the English countryside, the Austens were a large family with a wide circle of friends who provided entertainment and cultural enrichment. They also provided material for her stories.

Clear Jane Austen had little formal education but was well educated at home. Far from living an isolated life in the English countryside, the Austens were a large family with a wide circle of friends who provided entertainment and cultural enrichment. They also provided material for Jane Austen's stories.

ref 19b

Exercise 19.1 Revising: Ambiguous and remote pronoun reference

Rewrite the following sentences to eliminate unclear pronoun reference. If you use a pronoun in your revision, be sure that it refers to only one antecedent and that it falls close enough to its antecedent to ensure clarity.

Example:

Saul found an old gun in the rotting shed that was just as his grandfather had left it.

In the rotting shed Saul found an old gun that was just as his grandfather had left it.

1. There is a difference between the heroes of today and the heroes of earlier times: they have flaws in their characters.
2. Baseball fans still admire Babe Ruth, Pete Rose, and Mark McGwire even though they could not be perfect.

3. Fans liked Rose for having his young son serve as batboy when he was in Cincinnati.
4. The reputation Rose earned as a gambler and tax evader may overshadow his reputation as a ballplayer, but it will survive.
5. Rose amassed an unequaled record as a hitter, using his bat to do things no one else has ever done. It stands even though Rose was banned from baseball.

19c Make a pronoun refer to a specific antecedent, not an implied one.

A pronoun should refer to a specific noun or other pronoun. The reader can only guess at the meaning of a pronoun when its antecedent is only implied by the context, not stated outright.

1 Use *this, that, which,* and *it* cautiously.

The most common kind of implied reference occurs when the pronoun *this, that, which,* or *it* refers to a whole idea or situation described in the preceding clause, sentence, or even paragraph. Such reference, often called **broad reference,** is acceptable only when the pronoun refers clearly to the entire preceding clause, as in the following sentence:

> I can be kind and civil to people, which is more than you can.
> —George Bernard Shaw

But if a pronoun might confuse a reader, you should avoid using it or provide an appropriate noun:

Confusing The British knew little of the American countryside, and they had no experience with the colonists' guerilla tactics. This gave the colonists an advantage.

Clear The British knew little of the American countryside, and they had no experience with the colonists' guerrilla tactics. This ignorance and inexperience gave the colonists an advantage.

2 *It* and *they* should have definite antecedents.

Although common in speech, using *it* and *they* to refer to indefinite antecedents is inappropriate in writing.

Confusing In Chapter 4 of this book, it describes the early flights of the Wright brothers.

Clear Chapter 4 of this book describes the early flights of the Wright brothers.

Confusing Even in reality TV shows, they present a false picture of life.

Clear	Even reality TV shows present a false picture of life.
Clear	Even in reality TV shows, the producers present a false picture of life.

3 Implied nouns are not clear antecedents.

A noun may be implied in some other word or phrase, as *happiness* is implied in *happy*, *driver* is implied in *drive*, and *mother* is implied in *mother's*. But a pronoun cannot refer clearly to an implied noun, only to a specific, stated one:

Confusing	In Cohen's report she made claims that led to a lawsuit.
Clear	In her report Cohen made claims that led to a lawsuit.
Confusing	Her reports on psychological development generally go unnoticed outside it.
Clear	Her reports on psychological development generally go unnoticed outside the field.

4 Titles of papers are not clear antecedents.

The title of a paper is entirely separate from the paper itself, so a pronoun should not be used in the opening sentence of a paper to refer to the title:

Title	How to Row a Boat
Confusing	This is not as easy as it looks.
Revised	Rowing a boat is not as easy as it looks.

ref 19d

19d Use *you* only to mean "you, the reader."

You should clearly mean "you, the reader." The context must be appropriate for such a meaning:

Inappropriate	In the fourteenth century you had to struggle simply to survive.
Revised	In the fourteenth century one [or a person] had to struggle simply to survive.

Writers sometimes drift into *you* because *one, a person, the individual,* or a similar indefinite word can be difficult to sustain. Sentence after sentence, the indefinite word may sound stuffy, and it requires the sexist *he* or the awkward *he or she* for pronoun-antecedent agreement (see pp. 321–22). To avoid these difficulties, try using plural nouns and pronouns:

Original	In the fourteenth century one had to struggle simply to survive.
Revised	In the fourteenth century people had to struggle simply to survive.

19e Use the pronoun *it* only one way in a sentence.

We use *it* idiomatically in expressions such as *It is raining.* We use *it* to postpone the subject in sentences such as *It is true that jobs are scarce.* And we use *it* as a personal pronoun in sentences such as *Nicole ran the race and won it.* All these uses are standard, but two of them in the same passage can confuse the reader:

Confusing It is true that the Constitution sets limits, but it is also flexible.

Clear The Constitution does set limits, but it is also flexible.

19f Use *who, which,* and *that* for appropriate antecedents.

The relative pronouns *who, which,* and *that* commonly refer to persons, animals, or things. *Who* refers most often to persons but may also refer to animals that have names:

Dorothy is the girl who visits Oz.
Her dog, Toto, who accompanies her, gives her courage.

Which refers to animals and things:

The Orinoco River, which is 1600 miles long, flows through Venezuela into the Atlantic Ocean.

That refers to animals and things and occasionally to persons when they are collective or anonymous:

The rocket that failed cost millions.
Infants that walk need constant tending.

(See also p. 429 for the use of *which* and *that* in nonessential and essential clauses.)

The possessive *whose* generally refers to people but may refer to animals and things to avoid awkward and wordy *of which* constructions:

The book whose binding broke was rare. [Compare *The book of which the binding broke was rare.*]

Exercise 19.2 Revising: Indefinite and inappropriate pronoun reference

Many of the pronouns in the following sentences do not refer to specific, appropriate antecedents. Revise the sentences as necessary to make them clear.

Example:
In Glacier National Park, they have moose, elk, and wolves.
Moose, elk, and wolves live in Glacier National Park.

1. "Life begins at forty" is a cliché many people live by, and this may well be true.

2. When she was forty, Pearl Buck's novel *The Good Earth* won the Pulitzer Prize.
3. Buck was a novelist which wrote primarily about China.
4. In *The Good Earth* you have to struggle, but fortitude is rewarded.
5. Buck received much critical praise and earned over $7 million, but she was very modest about it.
6. Kenneth Kaunda, past president of Zambia, was elected to it in 1964, at age forty.
7. When Catherine I became empress of Russia at age forty, they feared more than loved her.
8. At forty, Paul Revere made his famous ride to warn American revolutionary leaders that the British were going to arrest them. This gave the colonists time to prepare for battle.
9. In the British House of Commons they did not welcome forty-year-old Nancy Astor as the first female member when she entered in 1919.
10. In 610 CE, Muhammad, age forty, began to have a series of visions that became the foundation of the Muslim faith. Since then, millions of people have become one.

Exercise 19.3 Revising: Pronoun reference

Revise the following paragraph so that each pronoun refers clearly to a single specific and appropriate antecedent.

In Charlotte Brontë's *Jane Eyre*, she is a shy young woman that takes a job as governess. Her employer is a rude, brooding man named Rochester. He lives in an eerie mansion on the English moors. Eerier still are the fires and other unexplained happenings in the house, but Rochester refuses to discuss this. Eventually, they fall in love. On the day they are to be married, however, she learns that he has a wife hidden in the house. She is hopelessly insane and violent and is under guard, which explains his strange behavior. Heartbroken, Jane leaves the moors, and many years pass before they are reunited.

Note See page 380 for an exercise involving unclear pronoun reference and other sentence errors.

20 Shifts

Chapter essentials

- Keep nouns and pronouns consistent in person and number (next page).
- Keep verbs consistent in tense and mood (p. 360).
- Keep subject and voice consistent (p. 361).
- Keep quotations and questions consistently direct or indirect (p. 362).

Visit MyWritingLab™ for more resources on shifts.

Shifts are inconsistences in grammatical elements that can confuse your readers and distort your meaning. The box below shows ways to correct these inconsistencies in the use of nouns, pronouns, and verbs.

Shifts are likely to occur while you are trying to piece together meaning during drafting. But during editing you should make the grammatical elements of your sentences consistent.

Ways to correct shifts

First draft

A bank owes more to its customers than is held in reserve. It kept enough assets to meet reasonable withdrawals, but panicked customers may demand all their deposits. Then demands will exceed supplies, and banks will fail. These days, a person's losses are not likely to be great because the government insures your deposits.

Revised

A bank owes more to its customers than **it holds** in reserve. It **keeps** enough assets to meet reasonable withdrawals, but panicked customers may demand all their deposits. Then demands will exceed supplies, and **the bank** will fail. These days, the losses of **customers** are not likely to be great because the government insures **their** deposits.

20a Keep a sentence or related sentences consistent in person and number.

Person in grammar refers to the distinction among the person talking (first person), the person spoken to (second person), and the person, object, or concept being talked about (third person). **Number** refers to the distinction between one (singular) and more than one (plural).

Shifts in person

Most shifts in person occur because we can refer to people in general, including our readers, either in the third person (*a person, one*; *people, they*) or in the second person (*you*):

People should not drive when they have been drinking.
One should not drive when he or she has been drinking.
You should not drive when you have been drinking.

Although any one of these possibilities is acceptable in an appropriate context, a mixture of them is inconsistent:

Shift in person	If a person works hard, you can gain satisfaction.
Revised	If you work hard, you can gain satisfaction.
Revised	If a person works hard, he or she can gain satisfaction.
Better	If people work hard, they can gain satisfaction.

Shifts in number

Inconsistency in number occurs most often between a pronoun and its antecedent (see p. 319):

Shift in number	If a student does not understand a problem, they should consult the instructor.
Revised	If a student does not understand a problem, he or she should consult the instructor.
Better	If students do not understand a problem, they should consult the instructor.
Or	A student who does not understand a problem should consult the instructor.

Note Generic nouns and most indefinite pronouns take singular pronouns with a definite gender: *he, she,* or *it.* When we use a generic noun like *student* or *person* or an indefinite pronoun like *everyone* or *each,* we often mean to include both males and females. To indicate this meaning, use *he or she* rather than *he* (as in the first of the preceding revisions) or, better still, rewrite in the plural or rewrite to avoid the inconsistent pronoun (as in the second and third of the revisions). See pages 321–22 for more discussion and examples.

Inconsistency in number can also occur between other words (usually nouns) that relate to each other in meaning.

Inconsistent	All the boys have a good reputation.
Revised	All the boys have good reputations.

The consistency in the revised sentence is called **logical agreement** because the nouns are consistent (the *boys* have *reputations,* not a single *reputation*).

shift 20a

Exercise 20.1 Revising: Shifts in person and number

Revise the following sentences to make them consistent in person and number.

Example:

A plumber will fix burst pipes, but they won't repair waterlogged appliances.

Plumbers will fix burst pipes, but they won't repair waterlogged appliances.

1. When a taxpayer is waiting to receive a tax refund from the Internal Revenue Service, you begin to notice what time the mail carrier arrives.
2. If the taxpayer does not receive a refund check within six weeks of filing a return, they may not have followed the rules of the IRS.

3. If a taxpayer does not include a Social Security number on a return, you will have to wait for a refund.
4. When taxpayers do not file their return early, they will not get a refund quickly.
5. If one makes errors on the tax form, they might even be audited, thereby delaying a refund even longer.

20b Keep a sentence or related sentences consistent in tense and mood.

Shifts in tense

Within a sentence or from one sentence to another, certain changes in tense may be required to indicate changes in actual or relative time (see pp. 302–03). The following changes are necessary:

> Ramon will graduate from college thirty-one years after his father arrived in the United States.

In speech we often shift tenses even when they don't reflect changes in time. But in writing, changes that are not required by meaning distract readers. Unnecessary shifts between past and present in passages narrating a series of events are particularly confusing:

shift 20b

Shift in tense Immediately after Booth shot Lincoln, Major Rathbone threw himself upon the assassin. But Booth pulls a knife and plunges it into the major's arm.

Revised Immediately after Booth shot Lincoln, Major Rathbone threw himself upon the assassin. But Booth pulled a knife and plunged it into the major's arm.

Use the present tense consistently to describe what an author has written, including the action in literature or a film:

Shift in tense The main character in the novel suffers psychologically because he has a clubfoot, but he eventually triumphed over his disability.

Revised The main character in the novel suffers psychologically because he has a clubfoot, but he eventually triumphs over his disability.

Shifts in mood

Shifts in the mood of verbs occur most frequently in directions when the writer moves between the imperative mood (*Unplug the appliance*) and the indicative mood (*You should unplug the appliance*). (See p. 305.) Directions are usually clearer and more concise in the imperative, as long as its use is consistent:

Shift in mood Cook the mixture slowly, and you should stir it until the sugar is dissolved.

Revised Cook the mixture slowly, and stir it until the sugar is dissolved.

Exercise 20.2 Revising: Shifts in tense and mood

Revise each of the following sentences to make it consistent in tense and mood.

Example:

Jenna tagged the base and keeps running until she slides into second.

Jenna tagged the base and kept running until she slid into second.

1. When your cholesterol count is too high, adjusting your diet and exercise level reduced it.
2. After you lowered your cholesterol rate, you decrease the chances of heart attack and stroke.
3. First eliminate saturated fats from your diet; then you should consume more whole grains and raw vegetables.
4. To avoid saturated fats, substitute turkey and chicken for beef, and you should use cholesterol-free salad dressing and cooking oil.
5. A regular program of aerobic exercise, such as walking or swimming, improves your cholesterol rate and made you feel much healthier.

20c Keep a sentence or related sentences consistent in subject and voice.

When a verb is in the **active voice**, the subject names the actor: *Megan passed the carrots.* When a verb is in the **passive voice**, the subject names the receiver of the action: *The carrots were passed* [*by Megan*]. (See pp. 307–09.)

A shift in voice may sometimes help focus the reader's attention on a single subject, as in *The candidate campaigned vigorously and was nominated on the first ballot.* However, most shifts in voice also involve shifts in subject. They are unnecessary and confusing.

Shift in subject and voice	Blogs cover an enormous range of topics. Opportunities for people to discuss their interests are provided on these sites.
Revised	Blogs cover an enormous range of topics and provide opportunities for people to discuss their interests.

Exercise 20.3 Revising: Shifts in subject and voice

Make the following sentences consistent in subject and voice.

Example:

At the reunion they ate hot dogs and volleyball was played.

At the reunion they ate hot dogs and played volleyball.

1. If students learn how to study efficiently, much better grades will be made on tests.
2. Conscientious students begin to prepare for tests immediately after the first class is attended.
3. Before each class all reading assignments are completed, and the students outline the material and answer any study questions.
4. In class they listen carefully and good notes are taken.

5. Questions are asked by the students when they do not understand the professor.

20d Keep a quotation or a question consistently direct or indirect.

Direct quotations or questions report the exact words of a quotation or question:

"I am the greatest," bragged Muhammad Ali.
In his day few people asked, "Is he right?"

Indirect quotations or questions report that someone said or asked something, but not in the exact words:

Muhammad Ali bragged that he was the greatest.
In his day few people asked whether he was right.

Shifts between direct and indirect quotations or questions are difficult to follow.

Shift in quotation Kapek reports that the rats stayed away from the maze and "none responded to conditioning"(76).

Revised (indirect) Kapek reports that the rats stayed away from the maze and that they did not respond to conditioning (76).

Revised (direct) Kapek reports, "The rats avoided the maze, and none responded to conditioning" (76).

Shift in question The reader wonders whether the experiment failed or did it perhaps succeed?

Revised (indirect) The reader wonders whether the experiment failed or whether it perhaps succeeded.

Revised (direct) Did the experiment fail? Or did it perhaps succeed?

For more on quotations, see pages 436–37 (commas with signal phrases such as *she said*), 458–65 (quotation marks), and 608–13 (integrating quotations into your writing). For more on questions, see pages 419–20.

Exercise 20.4 Revising: Shifts in direct and indirect quotations and questions

Revise each of the following sentences twice, once to make it consistently direct, once to make it consistently indirect. You will have to guess at the exact wording of direct quotations and questions that are now stated indirectly.

Example:

We all wonder what the next decade will bring and will we thrive or not?

Direct: What will the next decade bring? Will we thrive or not?

Indirect: We all wonder what the next decade will bring and whether we will thrive or not.

1. Seaver says that the functions of marriage have changed and "nowhere more dramatically than in industrialized cultures" (88).
2. The question even arises of whether siblings may marry and would the union be immoral?
3. Seaver writes, "Sibling marriage is still illegal everywhere in the United States" and that people are still prosecuted under the law (89).
4. Seaver says that incest could be considered a universal taboo and "the questions asked about the taboo vary widely" (91).
5. Some ask is the taboo a way of protecting the family or whether it may be instinctive.

Exercise 20.5 Revising: Shifts

Revise the following paragraph to eliminate unnecessary shifts in person, number, tense, mood, and voice.

Driving in snow need not be dangerous if you practice a few rules. First, one should avoid fast starts, which may result in the car's getting stuck. Second, drive more slowly than usual, and you should notice the feel of the car: if the steering seemed loose or the wheels were not grabbing the road, slow down. Third, avoid fast stops, which lead to skids. One should be alert for other cars and intersections that may necessitate that the brakes be applied suddenly. If you need to slow down, the car's momentum can be reduced by downshifting as well as by applying the brakes. When braking, press the pedal to the floor only if you have antilock brakes; otherwise, the pedal should be pumped in short bursts. If you feel the car skidding, the brakes should be released and the wheel should be turned toward the skid, and then the brakes should be pressed or pumped again. If one repeated these motions, the skid would be stopped and the speed of the car would be reduced.

Note See page 380 for an exercise involving shifts along with sentence fragments, comma splices, and other sentence errors.

21 Misplaced and Dangling Modifiers

Chapter essentials

- Place modifiers where they will clearly modify the words you intend (next three pages).
- Keep subjects, verbs, and objects together (p. 367).
- Keep parts of infinitives or verb phrases together (p. 368).
- Position adverbs with care (p. 368).
- Arrange adjectives appropriately (p. 370).
- Relate dangling modifiers to their sentences by rewriting (p. 371).

Visit MyWritingLab™ for more resources on misplaced and dangling modifiers.

When reading a sentence in English, we depend principally on the arrangement of the words to tell us how they are related. In writing, we may create confusion if we fail to connect modifiers to the words they modify.

Misplaced Modifiers

A modifier is **misplaced** if readers can't easily relate it to the word it modifies. Misplaced modifiers may be awkward, confusing, or even unintentionally funny.

21a Place modifiers where they will clearly modify the words intended.

Readers tend to link a modifying word, phrase, or clause to the nearest word it could modify: *I saw a man in a green hat*. Thus the writer must place the phrase so that it clearly modifies the intended word and not some other.

Confusing He served steak to the men on paper plates.

Revised He served the men steak on paper plates.

Confusing Many dogs are killed by cars and trucks roaming unleashed.

Revised Many dogs roaming unleashed are killed by cars and trucks.

Confusing This is the only chocolate chip cookie in a bag that tastes like Mom's. [Actual advertisement.]

Revised This is the only bagged [or packaged] chocolate chip cookie that tastes like Mom's.

Exercise 21.1 Revising: Misplaced phrases and clauses

Revise the following sentences so that phrases and clauses clearly modify the appropriate words.

Example:

I came to enjoy flying over time.
Over time I came to enjoy flying.

1. Women have contributed much to knowledge and culture of great value.
2. Emma Willard founded the Troy Female Seminary, the first institution to provide a college-level education for women in 1821.
3. Sixteen years later Mary Lyon founded Mount Holyoke Female Seminary, the first true women's college with directors and a campus who would sustain the college even after Lyon's death.

Ways to revise misplaced modifiers

- **Place modifiers clearly** (facing page).

  Confusing — Listening to music can cause hearing loss at high levels.
  Revised — Listening to music at high levels can cause hearing loss.

- **Place limiting modifiers carefully** (below).

  Confusing — The women only reached the summit on their last climb.
  Revised — The women reached the summit only on their last climb.

- **Make each modifier refer to only one grammatical unit** (next page).

  Confusing — Students who skip class often receive poor grades.
  Revised — Students who often skip class receive poor grades.
  Revised — Students who skip class receive poor grades often.

- **Keep grammatical units together** (next two pages).

  Awkward — The owner ordered the dog to not bark.
  Revised — The owner ordered the dog **not to bark**.

- **Place adverbs and adjectives conventionally** (pp. 368–70).

  Awkward — Once endangered, bald eagles were spotted seldom in the eastern United States.
  Revised — Once endangered, bald eagles were seldom spotted in the eastern United States.

mm 21b

4. *Una* was the first US newspaper, which was founded by Pauline Wright Davis in 1853, that was dedicated to gaining women's rights.
5. Mitchell's Comet was discovered in 1847, which was named for Maria Mitchell.

21b Place limiting modifiers carefully.

Limiting modifiers include *almost, even, exactly, hardly, just, merely, nearly, only, scarcely,* and *simply*. In speech these modifiers often occur before the verb, regardless of the words they are intended to modify. In writing, however, these modifiers should fall immediately before the word or word group they modify to avoid any ambiguity:

Unclear — She only found that fossil on her last dig.

Revised — She found only that fossil on her last dig.

Revised — She found that fossil only on her last dig.

Exercise 21.2 Using limiting modifiers

Use each of the following limiting modifiers in two versions of the same sentence.

Example:
only
He is the only one I like. He is the one only I like.

1. almost
2. even
3. hardly
4. simply
5. nearly

21c Make each modifier refer to only one grammatical element.

A modifier can modify only *one* element in a sentence—the subject, the verb, or some other element. A **squinting modifier** seems confusingly to refer to either of two words:

Squinting Snipers who fired on the soldiers often escaped capture.

Clear Snipers who often fired on the soldiers escaped capture.

Clear Snipers who fired on the soldiers escaped capture often.

When an adverb modifies an entire main clause, as in the last example, it can usually be moved to the beginning of the sentence: *Often, snipers who fired on the soldiers escaped capture.*

Exercise 21.3 Revising: Squinting modifiers

Revise each sentence twice so that the squinting modifier applies clearly first to one element and then to the other.

Example:
The work that he hoped would satisfy him completely frustrated him.
The work that he hoped would completely satisfy him frustrated him.
The work that he hoped would satisfy him frustrated him completely.

1. People who sunbathe often can damage their skin.
2. Sunbathers who apply a sunscreen frequently block some of the sun's harmful ultraviolet rays.
3. Men and women who lie out in the sun often have leathery, dry skin.
4. Doctors tell sunbathers when they are older they risk skin cancer.
5. People who stay out of the sun usually will have better skin and fewer chances of skin cancer.

21d Keep subjects, verbs, and objects together.

English sentences tend to move from subject to verb to object. The movement is so familiar that modifiers between these elements can be awkward.

A subject and verb may be separated by an adjective that modifies the subject: *The hurricane, which hit the city with ferocious winds, damaged many homes and public buildings*. But an adverb of more than a word usually stops the flow of the sentence:

subject — adverb — verb
Awkward The city, after the hurricane, began massive rebuilding.

adverb — subject — verb
Revised After the hurricane, the city began massive rebuilding.

Even a one-word adverb will be awkward between a verb and its object:

verb — adverb — object
Awkward The hurricane had damaged badly many homes in the city.

verb — object
Revised The hurricane had badly damaged many homes in the city.
adverb

21e Keep parts of infinitives or verb phrases together.

An **infinitive** consists of the marker *to* plus the plain form of a verb: *to produce, to enjoy.* The two words in an infinitive are widely regarded as a grammatical unit that should not be split apart by a modifier:

infinitive
Awkward The weather service expected temperatures to not rise.

infinitive
Revised The weather service expected temperatures not to rise.

A split infinitive may sometimes be natural and preferable, though it may still bother some readers:

infinitive
Several US industries expect to more than triple their use of robots.

Here the split infinitive is more economical than the alternatives, such as *Several US industries expect to increase their use of robots by more than three times.*

A **verb phrase** consists of a helping verb plus a main verb, as in *will call, was going, had been writing* (see p. 284). A single-word adverb may be inserted after the helping verb in a verb phrase (or the first helping verb if more than one): *Spacecraft have long been scientific instruments. Scientists have lately been using spacecraft to study the sun.* But when longer adverbs interrupt verb phrases, the result is almost always awkward:

helping verb — adverb
Awkward People who have osteoporosis can, by increasing their daily intake of calcium and vitamin D, improve their bone density.
main verb

adverb
Revised By increasing their daily intake of calcium and vitamin D, people who have osteoporosis can improve their bone density.
verb phrase

In an English question, place a one-word adverb immediately after the subject:

helping verb / subject / adverb / rest of verb phrase

Will spacecraft ever be able to leave the solar system?

Exercise 21.4 Revising: Separated sentence parts

Revise the following sentences to connect separated parts (subject-predicate, verb-object, verb phrase, infinitive).

Example:

Most children have by the time they are seven lost a tooth.

By the time they are seven, most children have lost a tooth.

1. Myra Bradwell founded in 1868 the *Chicago Legal News.*
2. Bradwell was later denied, although she had qualified, admission to the Illinois Bar Association.
3. In an attempt to finally gain admission to the bar, she carried the case to the Supreme Court, but the justices decided against her.
4. Bradwell was determined that no other woman would, if she were qualified, be denied entrance to a profession.
5. The Illinois legislature finally passed, in response to Bradwell's persuasion, a bill ensuring that no one on the basis of gender would be restricted from a profession.

21f Position adverbs with care.

A few adverbs may be difficult for nonnative speakers of English.

Adverbs of frequency

Adverbs of frequency include *always, never, often, rarely, seldom, sometimes,* and *usually.* They appear at the beginning of a sentence, before a one-word verb, or after the helping verb in a verb phrase:

verb phrase / adverb

Awkward Robots have put sometimes humans out of work.

helping verb / adverb / main verb

Revised Robots have sometimes put humans out of work.

adverb / verb phrase

Revised Sometimes robots have put humans out of work.

Adverbs of frequency always follow the verb *be*:

adverb verb

Awkward Robots often are helpful to workers.

verb adverb

Revised Robots are often helpful to workers.

When *rarely, seldom,* and other negative adverbs of frequency begin a sentence, the normal subject-verb order changes. (See also p. 410.)

adverb verb subject

Rarely are robots simple machines.

Adverbs of degree

Adverbs of degree include *absolutely, almost, certainly, completely, especially, extremely, hardly,* and *only*. They fall just before the word modified (an adjective, another adverb, sometimes a verb).

Awkward Robots have been useful [adjective] especially [adverb] in making cars.

Revised Robots have been especially [adverb] useful [adjective] in making cars.

Adverbs of manner

Adverbs of manner include *badly, sweetly, tightly,* and others that describe how something is done. They usually fall after the verb:

Awkward Robots smoothly [adverb] work [verb] on assembly lines.

Revised Robots work [verb] smoothly [adverb] on assembly lines.

The adverb *not*

When the adverb *not* modifies a verb, place it after the helping verb (or the first helping verb if more than one):

Faulty Robots do [helping verb] think [main verb] not.

Revised Robots do [helping verb] not think [main verb].

Place *not* after a form of *be*: *Robots are not thinkers.*

When *not* modifies another adverb or an adjective, place it before the other modifier: *Robots are not sleek machines.*

mm 21g

21g Arrange adjectives appropriately. 

English follows distinctive rules for arranging two or three adjectives before a noun. (A string of more than three adjectives before a noun is rare.) The order depends on the meaning of the adjectives:

Determiner	Opinion	Size or shape	Color	Origin	Material	Noun used as adjective	Noun
many						state	**laws**
	striking		green	Thai			**birds**
a	fine			German			**camera**
this		square			wooden		**table**
all						business	**reports**
the			blue		litmus		**paper**

See pages 433–34 on punctuating adjectives before a noun.

Exercise 21.5 Revising: Placement of adverbs and adjectives

Revise the sentences below to correct the positions of adverbs or adjectives. If a sentence is already correct as given, mark the number preceding it.

Example:

Gasoline high prices affect usually car sales.
High gasoline prices usually affect car sales.

1. Some years ago Detroit cars often were praised.
2. Luxury large cars especially were prized.
3. Then a serious oil shortage led drivers to value small foreign cars that got good mileage.
4. When gasoline ample supplies returned, consumers bought again American large cars and trucks.
5. Consumers not were loyal to the big vehicles when gasoline prices dramatically rose.

Dangling Modifiers

dm 21h

A **dangling modifier** does not sensibly modify anything in its sentence:

Dangling Passing the building, the vandalism became visible.

Dangling modifiers usually introduce sentences, contain a verb form, and imply but do not name a subject. In the preceding example, the implied subject is the someone or something passing the building. Readers assume that this implied subject is the same as the subject of the sentence (*vandalism* in the example), but vandalism does not pass buildings. The modifier "dangles" because it does not connect sensibly to the rest of the sentence.

21h Relate dangling modifiers to their sentences.

Certain kinds of modifiers are the most likely to dangle:

- **Participial phrases:**

  Dangling Passing the building, the vandalism became visible.
  Revised As we passed the building, the vandalism became visible.

- **Infinitive phrases:**

  Dangling To understand the causes, vandalism has been studied.
  Revised To understand the causes, researchers have studied vandalism.

- **Prepositional phrases in which the object of the preposition is a gerund:**

Identifying and revising dangling modifiers

- **Identify the modifier's subject.** If the modifier lacks a stated subject (as *when in diapers* does), identify what the modifier describes.
- **Compare the subject of the modifier and the subject of the sentence.** Verify that what the modifier describes is in fact the subject of the main clause. If it is not, the modifier probably dangles.
- **Revise as needed.** Either (*a*) recast the dangling modifier with a stated subject of its own, or (*b*) change the subject of the main clause to be what the modifier describes.

	modifier subject
Dangling	When in diapers, my mother remarried.
Revision *a*	When I was in diapers, my mother remarried.
Revision *b*	When in diapers, I attended my mother's second wedding.

Dangling	After studying the problem, vandals are now thought to share certain characteristics.
Revised	After studying the problem, researchers think that vandals share certain characteristics.

- **Elliptical clauses in which the subject and perhaps the verb are omitted:**

Dangling	When destructive, researchers have learned that vandals are more likely to be in groups.
Revised	When vandals are destructive, researchers have learned, they are more likely to be in groups.

Dangling modifiers are especially likely when the verb in the main clause is in the **passive voice** instead of the **active voice**, as in *vandalism has been investigated* and *vandals are thought*. (See pp. 307–09 for more on the passive voice.)

Note A modifier may be dangling even when the sentence elsewhere contains a word the modifier might seem to describe, such as *vandals* below:

Dangling	When destructive, researchers have learned that vandals are more likely to be in groups.

In addition, a dangling modifier may fall at the end of a sentence:

Dangling	The vandalism was visible passing the building.

Revising dangling modifiers

Revise most dangling modifiers in one of two ways, depending on what you want to emphasize in the sentence.

- **Change the subject of the main clause to a word the modifier properly describes:**

Dangling To express themselves, graffiti decorate walls.

Revised To express themselves, some youths decorate walls with graffiti.

- **Rewrite the dangling modifier as a complete clause with its own stated subject and verb:**

Revised Because some youths need to express themselves, they decorate walls with graffiti.

Exercise 21.6 Revising: Dangling modifiers

Revise the following sentences to eliminate any dangling modifiers. Each item has more than one possible answer.

Example:

Driving north, the vegetation became increasingly sparse.

Driving north, we noticed that the vegetation became increasingly sparse.

As we drove north, the vegetation became increasingly sparse.

dm 21h

1. Drawing conclusions from several formal studies, pets can improve people's emotional well-being.
2. Suffering from Alzheimer's and unable to recognize her husband, one woman's ability to identify her beloved dog was unaffected.
3. Once subject to violent outbursts, a companion dog calmed an autistic boy.
4. Facing long hospital stays, pet-therapy dogs can cheer up patients.
5. To understand why people with serious illnesses often respond well to animals, pet therapy is being studied.

Exercise 21.7 Sentence combining: Placing modifiers

Combine each pair of sentences below into a single sentence by rewriting one as a modifier. Make sure the modifier applies clearly to the appropriate word. You will have to add, delete, and rearrange words, and you may find that more than one answer is possible in each case.

Example:

Zach demanded a hearing. Zach wanted to appeal the decision.

Wanting to appeal the decision, Zach demanded a hearing.

1. Evening falls in the Central American rain forests. The tungara frogs begin their croaking chorus.
2. Male tungara frogs croak loudly at night. The "songs" they sing are designed to attract female frogs.
3. But predators also hear the croaking. They gather to feast on the frogs.
4. The predators are lured by their croaking dinners. The predators include bullfrogs, snakes, bats, and opossums.
5. The frogs hope to mate. Their nightly chorus can result in death instead.

Exercise 21.8 Revising: Misplaced and dangling modifiers

Revise the following paragraph to eliminate any misplaced or dangling modifiers.

Central American tungara frogs silence several nights a week their mating croaks. When not croaking, the chance that the frogs will be eaten by predators is reduced. The frogs seem to fully believe in "safety in numbers." They more than likely will croak along with a large group rather than by themselves. By forgoing croaking on some nights, the frogs' behavior prevents the species from "croaking."

Note See page 380 for an exercise involving misplaced and dangling modifiers along with other sentence errors.

22 Mixed and Incomplete Sentences

Chapter essentials

- Untangle sentences that are mixed in grammar (below).
- Match subjects and predicates to avoid mixed meaning (p. 375).
- Add needed words to compound constructions (p. 377).
- Make comparisons complete and logical (p. 378).
- Include necessary prepositions, articles, and other words (p. 379).

Visit MyWritingLab™ for more resources on mixed and incomplete sentences.

Mixed Sentences

A **mixed sentence** contains two or more parts that are incompatible—that is, the parts do not fit together. The misfit may be in grammar or in meaning.

22a Untangle sentences that are mixed in grammar.

Sentences mixed in grammar combine two or more incompatible grammatical structures.

1 Make sure subject and verb fit together grammatically.

A mixed sentence may occur when you start a sentence with one plan and end it with another:

modifier (prepositional phrase) — verb

Mixed By paying more attention to impressions than facts leads us to misjudge others.

modifier (prepositional phrase) — subject + verb

Revised By paying more attention to impressions than facts, we misjudge others.

subject (gerund phrase) — verb

Revised Paying more attention to impressions than facts leads us to misjudge others.

Constructions that use *Just because* clauses as subjects are common in speech but should be avoided in writing:

modifier (subordinate clause) — verb

Mixed Just because no one is watching doesn't mean we can break the law.

modifier (subordinate clause) — subject + verb

Revised Even when no one is watching, we cannot break the law.

In some mixed sentences the grammar is so jumbled that the writer has little choice but to start over:

Mixed My long-range goal is through law school and government work I hope to help people deal with those problems we all deal with more effectively.

Revised My long-range goal is to go to law school and then work in government so that I can help people deal more effectively with problems we all face.

A mixed sentence is especially likely when you are working on a computer and connect parts of two sentences or rewrite half a sentence but not the other half. A mixed sentence may also occur when you don't make the subject and the predicate verb carry the principal meaning. (See pp. 382–83.)

2 State parts of sentences, such as subjects, only once.

In some languages other than English, certain parts of sentences may be repeated. These include the subject in any kind of clause and an object or adverb in an adjective clause. In English, however, these parts are stated only once in a clause.

Repetition of subject

You may be tempted to restate a subject as a pronoun before the verb. But the subject needs stating only once in its clause.

Faulty The liquid it reached a temperature of 110°C.

Revised The liquid reached a temperature of 110°C.

Faulty Gases in the liquid they escaped.

Revised Gases in the liquid escaped.

Repetition in an adjective clause

Adjective clauses begin with *who, whom, whose, which, that, where,* and *when* (see pp. 264–65). The beginning word replaces another word: the subject (*He is the person who called*), an object of a verb or preposition (*He is the person whom I mentioned*), or a preposition and pronoun (*He knows the office where [in which] we work*).

Do not state the word that *who, whom,* and so on replace in an adjective clause:

Faulty The technician whom the test depended on her was burned. [*Whom* should replace *her*.]

Revised The technician whom the test depended on was burned.

Adjective clauses beginning with *where* or *when* do not need an adverb such as *there* or *then*:

Faulty Gases escaped at a moment when the technician was unprepared then.

Revised Gases escaped at a moment when the technician was unprepared.

22b Match subjects and predicates in meaning.

In a sentence with mixed meaning, the subject is said to be or do something illogical. Such a mixture is sometimes called **faulty predication** because the predicate conflicts with the subject.

Illogical equation with *be*

When a form of *be* connects a subject and a word that describes the subject (a complement), the subject and complement must be logically related:

Mixed A compromise between the city and the country would be the ideal place to live.

Revised A community that offered the best qualities of both city and country would be the ideal place to live.

Is when, is where

Definitions require nouns on both sides of *be*. Definition clauses beginning with *when* or *where* are common in speech but should be avoided in writing:

Mixed An examination is when you are tested on what you know.

Revised An examination is a test of what you know.

Reason is because

The commonly heard construction *reason is because* is redundant since *because* means "for the reason that":

Mixed The reason the temple requests donations is because the school needs expansion.

Revised The reason the temple requests donations is that the school needs expansion.

Revised The temple requests donations because the school needs expansion.

Other mixed meanings

Mismatched subjects and predicates are not confined to sentences with *be*:

Mixed The use of emission controls was created to reduce air pollution.

Revised Emission controls were created to reduce air pollution.

Exercise 22.1 Revising: Sentences mixed in grammar or meaning

Revise the following sentences so that their parts fit together both in grammar and in meaning. Each item has more than one possible answer.

Example:

When they found out how expensive pianos are is why they were discouraged.

They were discouraged because they found out how expensive pianos are.

When they found out how expensive pianos are, they were discouraged.

1. A hurricane is when the winds in a tropical depression rotate counterclockwise at more than seventy-four miles per hour.
2. Because hurricanes can destroy so many lives and so much property is why people fear them.
3. Through high winds, storm surge, floods, and tornadoes is how a hurricane can kill thousands of people.
4. Many scientists observe that hurricanes in recent years they have become more ferocious and destructive.
5. However, in the last half-century, with improved communications systems and weather satellites have made hurricanes less deadly.

Exercise 22.2 Revising: Repeated sentence parts 

Revise the following sentences to eliminate any unnecessary repetition of sentence parts.

Example:

Over 87 percent of Americans they have heard of global warming.
Over 87 percent of Americans have heard of global warming.

1. Global warming it is caused by the gradual erosion of the ozone layer that protects the earth from the sun.
2. Scientists who study this problem they say that the primary causes of erosion are the use of fossil fuels and the reduction of forests.
3. Many nonscientists they mistakenly believe that aerosol spray cans are the primary cause of erosion.
4. One scientist whom others respect him argues that Americans have effectively reduced their use of aerosol sprays.
5. He argues that we will slow global warming only when the public learns the real causes then.

Incomplete Sentences

The most serious kind of incomplete sentence is the fragment (see Chapter 17). But sentences are also incomplete when they omit one or more words needed for clarity.

22c Omissions from compound constructions should be consistent with grammar and idiom.

In both speech and writing, we commonly omit words not necessary for meaning, such as those bracketed in the examples below. Notice that all the sentences contain compound constructions (see p. 268):

> In this decade, standards for automobile mileage and emissions will be higher, and in the following years [standards for automobile mileage and emissions will be] higher still.
>
> Some cars run on electricity and some [run] on another alternative fuel.
>
> Environmentalists have hopes for alternative fuels and [for] public transportation.

Such omissions are possible only when you omit words that are common to all the parts of a compound construction. When the parts differ in either grammar or idiom, all words must be included in all parts:

> One new car gets eighty miles per gallon of gasoline; some old cars get as little as five miles per gallon. [One verb is singular, the other plural.]
>
> Environmentalists were invited to submit proposals and were eager to do so. [Each *were* has a different grammatical function: the first is a helping verb; the second is a linking verb.]
>
> They believe in and work for fuel conservation. [Idiom requires different prepositions with *believe* and *work*.]

In the sentence *My brother and friend moved to Dallas,* the omission of *my* before *friend* indicates that *brother* and *friend* are the same person. If two different persons are meant, the modifier or article must be repeated: *My brother and my friend moved to Dallas.*

(See p. 514 for a list of English idioms with prepositions and pp. 400–05 for a discussion of grammatical parallelism.)

inc
22d

22d All comparisons should be complete and logical.

Comparisons make statements about the relation between two or more things, as in *Dogs are more intelligent than cats.*

1 State a comparison fully enough to ensure clarity.

Unclear Automakers worry about their industry more than environmentalists.

Clear Automakers worry about their industry more than environmentalists do.

Clear Automakers worry about their industry more than they worry about environmentalists.

2 The items being compared should in fact be comparable.

Illogical The cost of a hybrid car can be greater than a gasoline-powered car. [Illogically compares a cost and a car.]

Revised The cost of a hybrid car can be greater than the cost of [or that of] a gasoline-powered car.

3 Use *any* or *any other* appropriately in comparisons.

Comparing a person or thing with all others in the same group creates two units: (1) the individual person or thing and (2) all *other* persons or things in the group. The two units need to be distinguished:

Illogical Los Angeles is larger than any city in California. [The sentence seems to say that Los Angeles is larger than itself.]

Logical Los Angeles is larger than any other city in California.

Comparing a person or thing with the members of a *different* group assumes separate units to begin with. The two units do not need to be distinguished with *other*:

Illogical Los Angeles is larger than any other city in Canada. [Canadian cities are a group to which Los Angeles does not belong.]

Logical Los Angeles is larger than any city in Canada.

4 Comparisons should state what is being compared.

Brand X gets clothes whiter. [Whiter than what?]
Brand Y is so much better. [Better than what?]

22e Include all needed prepositions, articles, and other words.

In haste or carelessness we sometimes omit small words such as prepositions and articles that are needed for clarity:

Incomplete Regular payroll deductions are a type painless savings. You hardly notice missing amounts, and after period of years the contributions can add a large total.

Revised Regular payroll deductions are a type of painless savings. You hardly notice the missing amounts, and after a period of years the contributions can add up to a large total.

Do not omit *that* when the omission could be confusing:

Incomplete The personnel director expects many employees will benefit from the plan. [*Many employees* seems to be the object of *expects*.]

Revised The personnel director expects that many employees will benefit from the plan.

Attentive proofreading is the best insurance against the kinds of omissions described in this section. *Proofread all your papers carefully.* See pages 66–67 for tips.

CULTURE LANGUAGE If your native language or dialect is not standard American English, you may have difficulty knowing when to use the English articles *a, an,* and *the.* For guidelines on using articles, see pages 332–34.

Exercise 22.3 Revising: Incomplete sentences

Revise the following sentences so that they are complete, logical, and clear. Some items have more than one possible answer.

Example:

Our house is closer to the bank than the subway stop.
Our house is closer to the bank than it is to the subway stop.
Our house is closer to the bank than the subway stop is.

1. The first ice cream, eaten in China in about 2000 BC, was more lumpy than the modern era.
2. The Chinese made their ice cream of milk, spices, and overcooked rice and packed in snow to solidify.
3. In the fourteenth century ice milk and fruit ices appeared in Italy and the tables of the wealthy.
4. At her wedding in 1533 to the king of France, Catherine de Médicis offered more flavors of fruit ices than any hostess offered.
5. Modern sherbets resemble her ices; modern ice cream her soft dessert of thick, sweetened cream.

Exercise 22.4 Revising: Mixed and incomplete sentences

Revise the following paragraph to eliminate mixed or incomplete constructions.

The Hancock Tower in Boston is thin mirror-glass slab that rises almost eight hundred feet. When it was being constructed was when its windows began cracking, and some fell crashing to the ground. In order to minimize risks is why the architects and owners replaced over a third the huge windows with plywood until the problem could be found and solved. With its plywood sheath, the building was homelier than any skyscraper, the butt of many jokes. Eventually, however, it was discovered that the reason the windows cracked was because joint between the double panes of glass was too rigid. The solution of thicker single-pane windows was installed, and the plywood building crystallized into reflective jewel.

Exercise on Chapters 17–22 Revising: Clear sentences

Clarify meaning in the following paragraphs by revising sentence fragments, comma splices, fused sentences, problems with pronoun reference, awkward shifts, misplaced and dangling modifiers, and mixed and incomplete sentences. Most errors can be corrected in more than one way.

Many people who are physically challenged. They have accomplished much. Which proves that they are not "handicapped." Confined to wheelchairs, successful careers were forged by Bob Sampson and Stephen Hawking. Despite Sampson's muscular dystrophy, he earned a law degree he also worked for United Airlines for more than thirty years. Stephen Hawking most famous for his book *A Brief History of Time*. Unable to speak, Hawking's voice synthesizer allows him to dictate his books and conduct public lectures. And teach mathematics classes at Cambridge University.

Franklin D. Roosevelt, Ann Adams, and Itzhak Perlman all refused let polio destroy their lives. Indeed, Roosevelt led the United States during two of the worst periods of its history as President. The Great Depression and World War II. Reassured by his strong, firm voice, Roosevelt inspired hope and determination in the American people. Ann Adams, who was talented in art before polio paralyzed her, knew she had to continue to be one. Having retrained herself to draw with a pencil grasped in her teeth. She produced sketches of children and pets. That were turned into greeting cards. The profits from the cards sustained her. Roosevelt and Adams were stricken with polio when they were adults; Itzhak Perlman when a child. He was unable to play sports, instead he studied the violin, now many think he is greater than any violinist in the world.

Like Perlman, many physically challenged individuals turn to the arts. Perhaps the reason is because the joy of artistic achievement compensates for other pleasures they cannot experience. Stevie Wonder, José Feliciano, and Andrea Bocelli all express, through their music, their souls. Although unable to see physically, their music reveals truly how well they see. Hearing impairment struck Ludwig van Beethoven and Marlee Matlin it did not stop them from developing their talents. Already a successful composer, many of Beethoven's most powerful pieces were written after he became deaf. Similarly, Matlin has had excellent acting roles in movies, plays, and television programs, indeed she won an Oscar for *Children of a Lesser God*. She encourages others to develop their ability, and many hearing-impaired actors have been inspired by her.

PART 5

Effective Sentences

23 Emphasizing Ideas

Chapter essentials

- Use subjects and verbs effectively (below).
- Use sentence beginnings and endings (p. 384).
- Arrange series items in order of increasing importance (p. 386).
- Use an occasional balanced sentence (p. 387).
- Repeat key words and phrases (p. 388).
- Set off important ideas with punctuation (p. 388).
- Write concisely (p. 389).

Visit MyWritingLab™ for more resources on emphasizing ideas.

Emphasis in writing is the use of words and word order to hold and channel readers' attention. When you speak, your tone of voice, facial expressions, and even hand gestures work with your words and sentences to convey your meaning. When you write, your words and sentences alone must do the work of emphasizing your main ideas.

23a Using subjects and verbs effectively

The heart of every sentence is its subject, which usually names the actor, and its predicate verb, which usually specifies the subject's action: *Children* [subject] *grow* [verb]. When these elements do not identify the sentence's key actor and action, readers must find that information elsewhere and the sentence may be wordy and unemphatic.

In the following sentences, the subjects and verbs are underlined:

Unemphatic The intention of the company was to expand its workforce. A proposal was also made to diversify the backgrounds and abilities of employees.

These sentences are unemphatic because their key ideas do not appear in their subjects and verbs. Revised, the sentences are not only clearer but more concise:

Revised The company intended to expand its workforce. It also proposed to diversify the backgrounds and abilities of employees.

The following constructions usually drain meaning from a sentence's subject and verb.

Nouns made from verbs

Nouns made from verbs can obscure the key actions of sentences and add words. These nouns include *intention* (from *intend*), *proposal* (from *propose*), *decision* (from *decide*), *expectation* (from *expect*), *persistence* (from *persist*), *argument* (from *argue*), and *inclusion* (from *include*).

Unemphatic After the company made a decision to hire more workers with disabilities, its next step was the construction of wheelchair ramps and other facilities.

Revised After the company decided to hire more workers with disabilities, it next constructed wheelchair ramps and other facilities.

Weak verbs

Weak verbs, such as *made* and *was* in the unemphatic sentence above, tend to stall sentences just where they should be moving and often bury key actions:

Unemphatic The company is now the leader among businesses in complying with the 1990 Americans with Disabilities Act. Its officers make speeches on the act to business groups.

Revised The company now leads other businesses in complying with the 1990 Americans with Disabilities Act. Its officers speak on the act to business groups.

Passive voice

Verbs in the passive voice state actions received by, not performed by, their subjects. Thus the passive de-emphasizes the true actor of the sentence, sometimes omitting it entirely. Generally, prefer the active voice, in which the subject performs the verb's action. (See also pp. 307–09.)

Unemphatic The 1990 law is seen by most businesses as fair, but the costs of complying have sometimes been objected to.

Revised Most businesses see the 1990 law as fair, but some have objected to the costs of complying.

emph
23a

Exercise 23.1 Revising: Emphasis of subjects and verbs

Rewrite the following sentences so that their subjects and verbs identify their key actors and actions.

Example:

The issue of students making a competition over grades is a reason why their focus on learning may be lost.

Students who compete over grades may lose their focus on learning.

1. The work of many heroes was crucial in helping to emancipate the slaves.
2. The contribution of Harriet Tubman, an escaped slave herself, included the guidance of hundreds of other slaves to freedom on the Underground Railroad.
3. A return to slavery was risked by Tubman or possibly death.
4. During the Civil War she was also a carrier of information from the South to the North.

5. After the war needy former slaves were helped by Tubman's raising of money for refugees.

23b Using sentence beginnings and endings

Readers automatically seek a writer's principal meaning in the main clause of a sentence—essentially, in the subject that names the actor and the verb that usually specifies the action (see the preceding pages). Thus you can help readers understand your intended meaning by controlling the information in your subjects and the relation of the main clause to any modifiers attached to it.

Old and new information

Generally, readers expect the beginning of a sentence to contain information that they already know or that you have already introduced. They then look to the sentence ending for new information. In the unemphatic passage below, the second and third sentences both begin with new topics, while the old topics appear at the ends of the sentences. The pattern of the passage is A→B. C→B. D→A.

Unemphatic Education [A] often means controversy [B] these days, with rising costs and constant complaints about its inadequacies. But the value [C] of schooling should not be obscured by the controversy [B]. The single best means [D] of economic advancement, despite its shortcomings, remains education [A].

emph 23b

In the more emphatic revision, old information begins each sentence and new information ends the sentence. The passage follows the pattern A→B. B→C. A→D.

Revised Education [A] often means controversy [B] these days, with rising costs and constant complaints about its inadequacies. But the controversy [B] should not obscure the value [C] of schooling. Education [A] remains, despite its shortcomings, the single best means [D] of economic advancement.

Cumulative and periodic sentences

You can call attention to information by placing it first or last in a sentence, reserving the middle for incidentals:

Unemphatic Education remains the single best means of economic advancement, despite its shortcomings. [Emphasizes shortcomings.]

Revised Despite its shortcomings, education remains the single best means of economic advancement. [Emphasizes advancement more than shortcomings.]

Revised Education remains, despite its shortcomings, the single best means of economic advancement. [De-emphasizes shortcomings.]

Many sentences begin with the main clause and then add modifiers to explain, amplify, or illustrate it. Such sentences are called **cumulative** (because they accumulate information as they proceed) or **loose** (because they are not tightly structured). They parallel the way we naturally think.

Cumulative Education has no equal in opening minds, instilling values, and creating opportunities.

Cumulative Most of the Great American Desert is made up of bare rock, rugged cliffs, mesas, canyons, mountains, separated from one another by broad flat basins covered with sun-baked mud and alkali, supporting a sparse and measured growth of sagebrush or creosote or saltbush, depending on location and elevation. —Edward Abbey

The opposite kind of sentence, called **periodic**, saves the main clause until just before the end (the period) of the sentence. Everything before the main clause points toward it.

Periodic In opening minds, instilling values, and creating opportunities, education has no equal.

Periodic With people from all over the world—Korean doctors, Jamaican cricket players, Vietnamese engineers, Haitian cabdrivers, Chinese athletes, Indian restaurant owners—the American mosaic is continually changing.

The periodic sentence creates suspense for readers by reserving important information for the end. But readers should already have an idea of the sentence's subject—because it was discussed or introduced in the preceding sentence—so that they know what the opening modifiers describe. A variation of the periodic sentence names the subject at the beginning, follows it with a modifier, and then completes the main clause:

> Dick Hayne, who works in jeans and loafers and likes to let a question cure in the air for a while before answering it, bears all the markings of what his generation used to call a laid-back kind of guy.
>
> —George Rush

Exercise 23.2 Sentence combining: Beginnings and endings

Locate the main idea in each of the following groups of sentences. Then combine each group into a single sentence that emphasizes that idea by placing it at the beginning or the end. For sentences 2–5, determine the position of the main idea by considering its relation to the previous sentences: if the main idea picks up a topic that's already been introduced, place it at the beginning; if it adds new information, place it at the end.

Example:

The storm blew roofs off buildings. It caused extensive damage. It knocked down trees. It severed power lines.

Main idea at beginning: The storm caused extensive damage, blowing roofs off buildings, knocking down trees, and severing power lines.

Main idea at end: Blowing roofs off buildings, knocking down trees, and severing power lines, the storm caused extensive damage.

1. Pat Taylor strode into the room. The room was packed. He greeted students called "Taylor's Kids." He nodded to their parents and teachers.
2. This was a wealthy Louisiana oilman. He had promised his "Kids" free college educations. He was determined to make higher education available to all qualified but disadvantaged students.
3. The students welcomed Taylor. Their voices joined in singing. They sang "You Are the Wind beneath My Wings." Their faces beamed with hope. Their eyes flashed with self-confidence.
4. The students had thought a college education was beyond their dreams. It seemed too costly. It seemed too demanding.
5. Taylor had to ease the costs and the demands of getting to college. He created a bold plan. The plan consisted of scholarships, tutoring, and counseling.

23c Arranging parallel elements effectively

Series

With parallelism, you use similar grammatical structures for ideas linked by *and, but,* and similar words: *Blustery winds and upturned leaves often signal thunderstorms.* (See Chapter 25.) In addition, you should arrange the parallel ideas in order of their importance:

Unemphatic The storm ripped the roofs off several buildings, killed ten people, and knocked down many trees in town. [Buries the most serious damage—deaths—in the middle.]

Emphatic The storm knocked down many trees in town, ripped the roofs off several buildings, and killed ten people. [Arranges items in order of increasing importance.]

You may want to use an unexpected item at the end of a series for humor or for another special effect:

Early to bed and early to rise makes a man healthy, wealthy, and dead.
—James Thurber

But be careful when creating such a series. The following series seems thoughtlessly random rather than intentionally humorous:

Unemphatic The painting has subdued tone, intense feeling, and a height of about three feet.

Emphatic The painting, about three feet high, has subdued tone and intense feeling.

Balanced sentences

A sentence is **balanced** when its clauses are parallel—that is, matched in grammatical structure (Chapter 25). When used carefully, balanced sentences can be especially effective in alerting readers to a strong comparison between two ideas. Read the following examples aloud to hear their rhythm.

> The fickleness of the women I love is equalled only by the infernal constancy of the women who love me. —George Bernard Shaw

In a pure balanced sentence two main clauses are exactly parallel: they match item for item.

> Scratch a lover, and find a foe. —Dorothy Parker

But the term *balanced* is commonly applied to sentences that are only approximately parallel or that have only some parallel parts:

> If thought corrupts language, language can also corrupt thought. —George Orwell

> As the traveler who has once been from home is wiser than he who has never left his own doorstep, so a knowledge of one other culture should sharpen our ability to scrutinize more steadily, to appreciate more lovingly, our own. —Margaret Mead

Exercise 23.3 Revising: Series and balanced elements

Revise the following sentences so that elements in a series or balanced elements are arranged to give maximum emphasis to main ideas.

Example:

The campers were stranded without matches, without food or water, and without a tent.

The campers were stranded without matches, without a tent, and without food or water.

1. Remembering her days as a "conductor" on the Underground Railroad made Harriet Tubman proud, but she got angry when she remembered her years as a slave.
2. Tubman wanted freedom regardless of personal danger, whereas for her husband, John, personal safety was more important than freedom.
3. Tubman proved her fearlessness in many ways: she led hundreds of other slaves to freedom, she was a spy for the North during the Civil War, and she disobeyed John's order not to run away.
4. To conduct slaves north to freedom, Tubman risked being returned to slavery, being hanged for a huge reward, and being caught by Southern patrollers.

5. After the war Tubman worked tirelessly for civil rights and women's suffrage; raising money for homes for needy former slaves was something else she did.

23d Repeating ideas

Repetition of words and phrases often clutters and weakens sentences, as discussed on page 522. But carefully planned repetition can be an effective means of emphasis. Such repetition often combines with parallelism. It may occur in a series of sentences (see pp. 82–83) or in a series of words, phrases, or clauses within a sentence, as in the following examples:

> There is something uneasy in the Los Angeles air this afternoon, some unnatural stillness, some tension. —Joan Didion

> We have the tools, all the tools—we are suffocating in tools—but we cannot find the actual wood to work or even the actual hand to work it. —Archibald MacLeish

23e Separating ideas

When you save important information for the end of a sentence, you can emphasize it even more by setting it off from the rest of the sentence, as in the second example below:

> Mothers and housewives are the only workers who do not have regular time off, so they are the great vacationless class.

> Mothers and housewives are the only workers who do not have regular time off. They are the great vacationless class. —Anne Morrow Lindbergh

You can vary the degree of emphasis by varying the extent to which you separate one idea from the others. A semicolon provides more separation than a comma, and a period provides still more separation. Compare the following sentences:

> Most of the reading which is praised for itself is neither literary nor intellectual**,** but narcotic.

> Most of the reading which is praised for itself is neither literary nor intellectual**;** it is narcotic.

> Most of the reading which is praised for itself is neither literary nor intellectual**.** It is narcotic. —Donald Hall

Sometimes a dash or a pair of dashes will isolate and thus emphasize a part of a statement (see also pp. 469–70):

> His schemes were always elaborate, ingenious, and exciting**—**and wholly impractical.

Athletics—that is, winning athletics—has become a profitable university operation.

Exercise 23.4 Emphasizing with repetition or separation

Emphasize the main idea in each of the following sentences or groups of sentences by following the instructions in parentheses: either combine sentences so that parallelism and repetition stress the main idea, or place the main idea in a separate sentence. Each item has more than one possible answer.

Example:

I try to listen to other people's opinions. When my mind is closed, I find that other opinions open it. And they can change my mind when it is wrong. (*Parallelism and repetition.*)

I try to listen to other people's opinions, for they can open my mind when it is closed and can change my mind when it is wrong.

1. One of the few worthwhile habits is daily reading. One can read for information. One can read for entertainment. Reading can give one a broader view of the world. (*Parallelism and repetition.*)
2. Reading introduces new words. One encounters unfamiliar styles of expression through reading. (*Parallelism and repetition.*)
3. Students who read a great deal will more likely write vividly, coherently, and grammatically, for they will have learned from other authors. (*Separation.*)
4. Reading gives knowledge. One gets knowledge about other cultures. One will know about history and current events. One gains information about human nature. (*Parallelism and repetition.*)
5. As a result of reading, writers have more resources and more flexibility, and thus reading creates better writers. (*Separation.*)

23f Being concise

Conciseness—brevity of expression—aids emphasis no matter what the sentence structure. Unnecessary words detract from necessary words. They clutter sentences and obscure ideas.

Weak In my opinion the competition in the area of grades is distracting. It distracts many students from their goal, which is to obtain an education that is good. There seems to be a belief among a few students that grades are more important than what is measured by them.

Emphatic The competition for grades distracts many students from their goal of obtaining a good education. A few students seem to believe that grades are more important than what they measure.

Techniques for tightening sentences are listed in the following box. Some of these techniques appear earlier in this chapter. All of them are covered in Chapter 39 on writing concisely.

Ways to achieve conciseness

- **Make the subject and verb of each sentence identify its actor and action** (pp. 382, 520):

  Avoid nouns made from verbs.
  Use strong verbs.
  Rewrite the passive voice as active.

- **Cut or shorten empty words or phrases** (pp. 520–21):

  Shorten filler phrases, such as *by virtue of the fact that.*
  Cut all-purpose words, such as *area, factor.*
  Cut unneeded qualifiers, such as *in my opinion, for the most part.*

- **Cut unnecessary repetition** (p. 522).
- **Reduce clauses to phrases and phrases to single words** (p. 523).
- **Avoid constructions beginning with *there is* or *it is*** (p. 524).
- **Combine sentences** (p. 524).
- **Cut or rewrite jargon** (p. 524).

emph
23f

Exercise 23.5 Revising: Conciseness

Revise the following sentences to make them more emphatic by eliminating wordiness.

Example:

The problem in this particular situation is that we owe more money than we can afford under present circumstances.

The problem is that we owe more money than we can afford.

1. As far as I am concerned, customers who are dining out in restaurants in our country must be wary of suggestive selling, so to speak.
2. In suggestive selling, diners are asked by the waiter to buy additional menu selections in addition to what was ordered by them.
3. For each item on the menu, there is another food that will naturally complement it.
4. For example, customers will be presented with the question of whether they want to order french fries along with a sandwich or whether they want to order a salad along with a steak dinner.
5. Due to the fact that customers often give in to suggestive selling, they often find that their restaurant meals are more costly than they had intended to pay.

Exercise 23.6 Revising: Emphasizing ideas

Drawing on the advice in this chapter, rewrite the following paragraph to emphasize main ideas and to de-emphasize less important information.

These days, the choice is made by people to give "alternative" gifts for birthdays and holidays. When a donation is made to a charity or an organization in honor of the recipient, that is an alternative gift. A wrapped present is not received by the giftee. Instead, a card is sent to the giftee that explains the donation given in his or her honor. As for the alternative gift itself, a common option is money. Many other types are also possible. One organization sends livestock to rural families around the world. The use of the animals is for the families to feed themselves and to generate income by selling eggs and milk. Sewing machines are provided to city dwellers by another group. The machines allow people to start small businesses and become financially independent. Alternative gifts are ways to help others without cluttering the recipient's home, so they are the perfect choice for people who already have everything they need.

Note See page 414 for an exercise involving emphasis along with parallelism and other techniques for effective sentences.

24 Using Coordination and Subordination

Chapter essentials

- Coordinate equally important ideas (next page).
- Subordinate to distinguish main ideas from less important ideas (p. 394).
- Use clear connectors to relate ideas (p. 399).

Visit MyWritingLab™ for more resources on coordination and subordination.

Two techniques can help you show relations between ideas and stress your more important ideas:

- ***Coordination*** **shows that two or more elements in a sentence are equally important in meaning.** You signal coordination with words such as *and, but,* and *or.*

  equally important

  Car insurance is costly, but health insurance seems a luxury.

- ***Subordination*** **shows that some elements in a sentence are less important than other elements for your meaning.** Usually, the main idea appears in the main clause, and supporting information appears in single words, phrases, and subordinate clauses.

  less important (subordinate clause) | more important (main clause)

  Because accidents and thefts occur frequently, car insurance is costly.

24a Coordinating to relate equal ideas

By linking equally important information, you can emphasize the relations for readers. Compare the following passages:

String of simple sentences

We should not rely so heavily on oil. Coal and natural gas are also overused. We have a substantial energy resource in the moving waters of our rivers. Smaller streams add to the total volume of water. The resource renews itself. Oil and coal are irreplaceable. Gas is also irreplaceable. The cost of water power tends to be stable over time. The costs of coal, oil, and gas fluctuate dramatically.

Ideas coordinated

We should not rely so heavily on oil, coal, and natural gas, for we have a substantial energy resource in the moving waters of our rivers and streams. Oil, coal, and gas are irreplaceable and thus subject to dramatic cost fluctuations; water, however, is self-renewing and more stable in cost.

The second passage is shorter and considerably easier to understand because it links coordinate ideas with the underlined words.

Note For punctuating coordinated constructions, see pages 347–48 and 422–24 (main clauses), 433 (items in series), and 433–34 (coordinate adjectives).

1 Using coordination effectively

coord 24a

A string of coordinated elements—especially main clauses—creates the same effect as a string of simple sentences: it obscures the relative importance of ideas and details.

Excessive coordination The weeks leading up to the resignation of President Richard Nixon were eventful, and the Supreme Court and the Congress closed in on him, and the Senate Judiciary Committee voted to begin impeachment proceedings, and finally the President resigned on August 9, 1974.

Such a passage needs editing to stress the important points (underlined below) and to de-emphasize the less important information:

Revised The weeks leading up to the resignation of President Richard Nixon were eventful, as the Supreme Court and the Congress closed in on him and the Senate Judiciary Committee voted to begin impeachment proceedings. Finally, the President resigned on August 9, 1974.

2 Coordinating logically

Coordinated sentence elements should be logically equal and related, and the relation between them should be the one expressed by the connecting word. Otherwise, the result is **faulty coordination.**

Ways to coordinate information in sentences

- **Link main clauses with a comma and a coordinating conjunction:** *and, but, or, nor, for, so, yet* (p. 422).

  Independence Hall in Philadelphia is faithfully restored, but many years ago it was in bad shape.

- **Relate main clauses with a semicolon alone or a semicolon and a conjunctive adverb:** *however, indeed, thus,* etc. (pp. 443, 445).

  The building was standing; however, it suffered from neglect.

- **Within clauses, link words and phrases with a coordinating conjunction:** *and, but, or, nor* (p. 268).

  The people and officials of the nation were indifferent to Independence Hall or took it for granted.

- **Link main clauses, words, or phrases with a correlative conjunction:** *both . . . and, not only . . . but also,* etc. (pp. 268–69).

  People not only took the building for granted but also neglected it.

Faulty John Stuart Mill was a nineteenth-century utilitarian, and he believed that actions should be judged by their usefulness or by the happiness they cause. [The two clauses are not separate and equal: the second expands on the first by explaining what a utilitarian such as Mill believed.]

Revised John Stuart Mill, a nineteenth-century utilitarian, believed that actions should be judged by their usefulness or by the happiness they cause.

Faulty Mill is recognized as a utilitarian, and he did not found the utilitarian school of philosophy. [The two clauses seem to contrast, requiring *but* or *yet* between them.]

Revised Mill is recognized as a utilitarian, but he did not found the utilitarian school of philosophy.

coord 24a

Exercise 24.1 Sentence combining: Coordination

Combine sentences in the following passages to coordinate related ideas in the ways that seem most effective to you. You will have to supply coordinating conjunctions or conjunctive adverbs and the appropriate punctuation.

1. Many chronic misspellers do not have the time to master spelling rules. They may not have the motivation. They may rely on spelling checkers and dictionaries to catch misspellings. Most dictionaries list words under their correct spellings. One kind of dictionary is designed for chronic misspellers. It lists each word under its common *mis*spellings. It then provides the correct spelling. It also provides the definition.

2. Henry Hudson was an English explorer. He captained ships for the Dutch East India Company. On a voyage in 1610 he passed by Greenland. He sailed into a great bay in today's northern Canada. He thought he and his sailors could winter there. The cold was terrible. Food ran out. The sailors mutinied. The sailors cast Hudson adrift in a small boat. Eight others were also in the boat. Hudson and his companions perished.

Exercise 24.2 Revising: Excessive or faulty coordination

Revise the following sentences to eliminate excessive or faulty coordination. Relate ideas effectively by adding or subordinating information or by forming more than one sentence. Each item has more than one possible answer.

Example:

The doctor told Sam that he was underweight, and he needed to eat more.

The doctor told Sam that he needed to eat more because he was underweight.

1. Often soldiers admired their commanding officers, and they gave them nicknames, and these names frequently contained the word "old," but not all of the commanders were old.
2. General Thomas "Stonewall" Jackson was also called "Old Jack," and he was not yet forty years old.
3. Another Southern general in the Civil War was called "Old Pete," and his full name was James Longstreet.
4. The Union general Henry W. Halleck had a reputation as a good military strategist, and he was an expert on the work of a French military authority, Henri Jomini, and Halleck was called "Old Brains."
5. General William Henry Harrison won the Battle of Tippecanoe, and he received the nickname "Old Tippecanoe," and he used the name in his presidential campaign slogan "Tippecanoe and Tyler, Too," and he won the election in 1840, but he died of pneumonia a month after taking office.

24b Subordinating to distinguish main ideas

With **subordination** you use words or word groups to indicate that some ideas in a sentence are less important than the idea in the main clause. In the following sentence, it is difficult to tell what is most important:

Excessive coordination	Computer prices have dropped, and production costs have dropped more slowly, and computer manufacturers have had to contend with shrinking profits.

The following revision places the point of the sentence (shrinking profits) in the main clause and reduces the rest of the information to a modifier (underlined):

Revised Because production costs have dropped more slowly than prices, computer manufacturers have had to contend with shrinking profits.

No rules can specify what information in a sentence you should make primary and what you should subordinate; the decision will depend on your meaning. But, in general, you should consider using subordinate structures for details of time, cause, condition, concession, purpose, and identification (size, location, and the like). Use the structures listed below to subordinate information:

Ways to subordinate information in sentences

- **Use a subordinate clause beginning with a subordinating conjunction:** *although, because, if, whereas,* etc. (p. 264).

  Although some citizens had tried to rescue Independence Hall, they had not gained substantial public support.

- **Use a subordinate clause beginning with a relative pronoun:** *who, whoever, which, that* (p. 264).

  The first strong step was taken by the federal government, which made the building a national monument.

- **Use a phrase** (p. 257).

  Like most national monuments, Independence Hall is protected by the National Park Service. [Prepositional phrase.]

  Protecting many popular tourist sites, the service is a highly visible government agency. [Verbal phrase.]

- **Use an appositive** (pp. 266–67).

  The National Park Service, a branch of the Department of Interior, also runs Yosemite and other wilderness parks.

- **Use a short modifier.**

  At the red brick Independence Hall, park rangers give guided tours and protect the irreplaceable building from vandalism.

sub 24b

In general, the shorter a subordinate structure is, the less emphasis it has. The following examples show how subordinate structures may convey various meanings with various weights. (Some appropriate subordinating words for each meaning appear in parentheses.)

Space or time (*after, before, since, until, when, while; at, in, on, until*)

The mine explosion killed six workers. The owners adopted safety measures.

After the mine explosion killed six workers, the owners adopted safety measures. [Subordinate clause.]

After six deaths in a mine explosion, the owners adopted safety measures. [Prepositional phrases.]

Cause or effect (*as, because, since, so that; because of, due to*)

Jones had been without work for six months. He was having trouble paying his bills.

Because Jones had been without work for six months, he was having trouble paying his bills. [Subordinate clause.]

Having been jobless for six months, Jones could not pay his bills. [Verbal phrase.]

Condition (*if, provided, since, unless, whenever; with, without*)

Forecasters predict a mild winter. Farmers hope for an early spring.

Whenever forecasters predict a mild winter, farmers hope for an early spring. [Subordinate clause.]

With forecasts for a mild winter, farmers hope for an early spring. [Prepositional phrase.]

Concession (*although, as if, even though, though; despite, except for, in spite of*)

The horse looked gentle. It proved hard to manage.

Although the horse looked gentle, it proved hard to manage. [Subordinate clause.]

The horse, a gentle-looking animal, proved hard to manage. [Appositive.]

The gentle-looking horse proved hard to manage. [Single word.]

Purpose (*in order that, so that, that; for, toward*)

Congress passed new immigration laws. Many Vietnamese refugees could enter the United States.

sub 24b

Congress passed new immigration laws so that many Vietnamese refugees could enter the United States. [Subordinate clause.]

Congress passed new immigration laws, permitting many Vietnamese refugees to enter the United States. [Verbal phrase.]

Identification (*that, when, where, which, who; by, from, of*)

Old barns are common in New England. They are often painted red.

Old barns, which are often painted red, are common in New England. [Subordinate clause.]

Old barns, often painted red, are common in New England. [Verbal phrase.]

Old red barns are common in New England. [Single word.]

Note For punctuating subordinate elements that introduce, interrupt, or conclude sentences, see pages 425–31 (commas), 466–68 (the colon), and 469–70 (dashes).

1 Subordinating logically

Use subordination only for the less important information in a sentence. **Faulty subordination** reverses the dependent relation the reader expects:

Faulty Ms. Angelo was in her first year of teaching, although she was a better instructor than others with many years of experience. [The sentence suggests that Angelo's inexperience is the main idea, whereas the writer meant to stress her skill *despite* her inexperience.]

Revised Although Ms. Angelo was in her first year of teaching, she was a better instructor than others with many years of experience.

2 Using subordination effectively

Subordination can do much to organize and emphasize information. But it loses that power when you try to cram too much loosely related detail into one long sentence:

Overloaded The boats that were moored at the dock when the hurricane, which was one of the worst in three decades, struck were ripped from their moorings, because the owners had not been adequately prepared, since the weather service had predicted that the storm would blow out to sea, which storms do at this time of year.

Such sentences usually have more than one idea that deserves a main clause, so they are best revised by sorting their details into more than one sentence:

Revised Struck by one of the worst hurricanes in three decades, the boats at the dock were ripped from their moorings. The owners were unprepared because the weather service had said that storms at this time of year blow out to sea.

A common form of excessive subordination occurs with a string of adjective clauses, each beginning with *which, who,* or *that*:

Stringy The company opened a new plant outside Louisville, which is in Kentucky and which is on the Ohio River, which forms the border between Kentucky and Ohio.

To revise such sentences, recast some of the subordinate clauses as other kinds of modifying structures:

Revised The company opened a new plant outside Louisville, Kentucky, a city across the Ohio River from Ohio.

Exercise 24.3 Sentence combining: Subordination

Combine each of the following pairs of sentences twice, each time using one of the subordinate structures in parentheses to make a single sentence. You will have to add, delete, change, and rearrange words.

Example:

During the late eighteenth century, workers carried beverages in brightly colored bottles. The bottles had cork stoppers. (*Clause beginning that. Phrase beginning with.*)

During the late eighteenth century, workers carried beverages in brightly colored bottles that had cork stoppers.

During the late eighteenth century, workers carried beverages in brightly colored bottles with cork stoppers.

1. The bombardier beetle sees an enemy. It shoots out a jet of chemicals to protect itself. (*Clause beginning when. Phrase beginning seeing.*)
2. The beetle's spray consists of hot and irritating chemicals. It is often fatal to other insects. (*Clause beginning because. Phrase beginning consisting.*)
3. The spray's two chemicals are stored separately in the beetle's body and mixed in the spraying gland. The chemicals resemble a nerve-gas weapon. (*Phrase beginning stored. Clause beginning which.*)
4. The tip of the beetle's abdomen sprays the chemicals. The tip revolves like a turret on a World War II bomber. (*Phrase beginning revolving. Phrase beginning spraying.*)
5. The beetle defeats most of its enemies. It is still eaten by spiders and birds. (*Clause beginning although. Phrase beginning except.*)

Exercise 24.4 Revising: Subordination

Rewrite the following paragraph in the way you think most effective to subordinate the less important ideas to the more important ones. Use subordinate clauses, phrases, and single words as you think appropriate.

Fewer students today are majoring in the liberal arts. I mean by "liberal arts" such subjects as history, English, and the social sciences. Students think a liberal arts degree will not help them get jobs. They are wrong. They may not get practical, job-related experience from the liberal arts, but they will get a broad education, and it will never again be available to them. Many employers look for more than a technical, professional education. They think such an education can make an employee's views too narrow. The employers want openminded employees. They want employees to think about problems from many angles. The liberal arts curriculum instills such flexibility. The flexibility is vital to the health of our society.

Exercise 24.5 Revising: Faulty or excessive subordination

Revise the following sentences to eliminate faulty or excessive subordination. Correct faulty subordination by reversing main and subordinate structures. Correct excessive subordination by coordinating equal ideas or by making separate sentences.

Example:

Terrified to return home, he had driven his mother's car into a cornfield.

Having driven his mother's car into a cornfield, he was terrified to return home.

1. Genaro González is a successful writer, which means that his stories and novels have been published to critical acclaim.
2. He loves to write, although he has also earned a doctorate in psychology.
3. His first story, which reflects his consciousness of his Aztec heritage and place in the world, is titled "Un Hijo del Sol."
4. González wrote the first version of "Un Hijo del Sol" while he was a sophomore at the University of Texas–Pan American, which is in the

Rio Grande valley of southern Texas, which González calls "el Valle" in the story.

5. González's latest book, which is about a teenager and is titled *A So-Called Vacation,* is a novel about how the teen and his family live for a summer as migrant fruit pickers, which was the experience his father had when he first immigrated from Mexico.

24c Choosing clear connectors

Most connecting words signal specific and unambiguous relations; for instance, *but* clearly indicates contrast, and *because* clearly indicates cause. A few connectors, however, require careful use, either because they are ambiguous in many contexts or because they are often misused.

1 Using *as* and *while* clearly

The subordinating conjunction *as* can indicate several relations, including comparison and time:

Comparison	The technicians work quickly, as the rules require them to do.
Time	One shift starts as the other stops.

Avoid using *as* to indicate cause. It is unclear.

Unclear	As the experiment was occurring, the laboratory was sealed. [Time or cause intended?]
Revised	When the experiment was occurring, the laboratory was sealed. [Time.]
Revised	Because the experiment was occurring, the laboratory was sealed. [Cause.]

The subordinating conjunction *while* can indicate either time or concession. Unless the context makes the meaning of *while* unmistakably clear, choose a more exact connector:

Unclear	While technicians work in the next room, they cannot hear the noise. [Time or concession intended?]
Revised	When technicians work in the next room, they cannot hear the noise. [Time.]
Revised	Although technicians work in the next room, they cannot hear the noise. [Concession.]

2 Using *as* and *like* correctly

The use of *as* as a substitute for *whether* or *that* is considered nonstandard (it does not conform to spoken and written standard English):

Nonstandard	They are not sure as the study was a success.
Revised	They are not sure whether [or that] the study was a success.

Although the preposition *like* is often used as a conjunction in informal speech and in advertising (*Dirt-Away works like a soap should*), writing generally requires the conjunction *as, as if, as though,* or *that*:

Speech	It seemed like it did succeed.
Writing	It seemed as if [or as though or that] it did succeed.

Exercise 24.6 Revising: Coordination and subordination

The following paragraph consists entirely of simple sentences. Use coordination and subordination to combine sentences in the ways you think most effective to emphasize main ideas.

Sir Walter Raleigh personified the Elizabethan Age. That was the period of Elizabeth I's rule of England. The period occurred in the last half of the sixteenth century. Raleigh was a courtier and poet. He was also an explorer and entrepreneur. Supposedly, he gained Queen Elizabeth's favor. He did this by throwing his cloak beneath her feet at the right moment. She was just about to step over a puddle. There is no evidence for this story. It does illustrate Raleigh's dramatic and dynamic personality. His energy drew others to him. He was one of Elizabeth's favorites. She supported him. She also dispensed favors to him. However, he lost his queen's goodwill. Without her permission he seduced one of her maids of honor. He eventually married the maid of honor. Elizabeth died. Then her successor imprisoned Raleigh in the Tower of London. Her successor was James I. The king falsely charged Raleigh with treason. Raleigh was released after thirteen years. He was arrested again two years later on the old treason charges. At the age of sixty-six he was beheaded.

Note See page 414 for an exercise involving coordination and subordination along with parallelism and other techniques for effective sentences.

25 Using Parallelism

Chapter essentials

- Use parallelism with *and, but,* and other coordinating conjunctions (opposite).
- Use parallelism with *both . . . and, not only . . . but also,* and other correlative conjunctions (p. 403).
- Use parallelism for elements being compared or contrasted (p. 403).
- Use parallelism in lists, outlines, and headings (p. 403).
- Use parallelism to increase coherence (p. 405).

Visit MyWritingLab™ for more resources on parallelism.

Parallelism gives similar grammatical form to sentence elements that have similar function and importance.

> The air is dirtied by || factories belching smoke
> and || cars spewing exhaust.

Parallel structure reinforces and highlights a close relation between compound sentence elements, whether they are words, phrases, or clauses.

The principle underlying parallelism is that form should reflect meaning: since the parts of compound constructions have the same function and importance, they should have the same grammatical form.

Note Parallel elements match each other in structure, but they do not always match word for word:

> The pioneers passed || through the town
> and || into the vast, unpopulated desert.

25a Using parallelism for equal elements

Use parallelism in all the situations described below and illustrated in the box on the next page.

1 Using parallelism for elements linked by coordinating conjunctions

The coordinating conjunctions *and, but, or, nor,* and *yet* always signal a need for parallelism:

> The industrial base was shifting and shrinking.
>
> The government seldom acknowledged the problem or proposed alternatives.
>
> Industrial workers were understandably disturbed that they were losing their jobs and that no one seemed to care.

If sentence elements linked by coordinating conjunctions are not parallel in structure, the resulting sentence will be awkward and distracting:

Nonparallel Three reasons why steel companies kept losing money were that their plants were inefficient, high labor costs, and foreign competition was increasing.

Revised Three reasons why steel companies kept losing money were inefficient plants, high labor costs, and increasing foreign competition.

All the words required by idiom or grammar must be stated in compound constructions (see also p. 268).

// 25a

Patterns of parallelism

- **Use parallel structures for elements connected by coordinating conjunctions (*and, but, or,* etc.) or correlative conjunctions (*both . . . and, neither . . . nor,* etc.):**

  In 1988 a Greek cyclist, backed up by || engineers,
  || physiologists,
  and || athletes,
  broke the world's record for human flight
  with neither || a boost
  nor || a motor.

- **Use parallel structures for elements being compared or contrasted:**

  || Pedal power
  rather than || horse power
  propelled the plane.

- **Use parallel structures for lists, outlines, or headings:**

  The four-hour flight was successful because
  || (1) the cyclist was very fit,
  || (2) he flew a straight course over water,
  and || (3) he kept the aircraft near the water's surface.

// 25a

Nonparallel Given training, workers can acquire the skills and interest in other jobs. [*Skills* and *interest* require different prepositions, so both must be stated.]

Revised Given training, workers can acquire the skills for and interest in other jobs.

Often, a word must be repeated to avoid confusion:

Confusing Thoreau stood up for his principles by not paying his taxes and spending a night in jail. [Did he spend a night in jail or not?]

Revised Thoreau stood up for his principles by not paying his taxes and by spending a night in jail.

Be sure that clauses beginning *who* or *which* are coordinated only with other *who* or *which* clauses, even when the pronoun is not repeated:

Nonparallel Thoreau is the nineteenth-century essayist who retired to the woods and he wrote about nature.

Revised Thoreau is the nineteenth-century essayist who retired to the woods and [who] wrote about nature.

2 Using parallelism for elements linked by correlative conjunctions

Correlative conjunctions are pairs of connectors. For example:

both . . . and	neither . . . nor	not only . . . but also
either . . . or	not . . . but	whether . . . or

Correlative conjunctions stress equality and balance and thus emphasize the relation between elements, even long phrases and clauses. The elements should be parallel to confirm their relation:

> It is not a tax bill but a tax relief bill, providing relief not for the needy but for the greedy. — Franklin Delano Roosevelt

> At the end of the novel, Huck Finn both rejects society's values by turning down money and a home and affirms his own values by setting out for "the territory."

Most errors in parallelism with correlative conjunctions occur when the element after the second connector does not match the element after the first connector.

Nonparallel Mark Twain refused either to ignore the moral blindness of his society or spare the reader's sensibilities. [*To* follows *either,* so it must also follow *or.*]

Revised Mark Twain refused either to ignore the moral blindness of his society or to spare the reader's sensibilities.

Nonparallel Huck Finn learns not only that human beings have an enormous capacity for folly but also enormous dignity. [The first element includes *that human beings have;* the second element does not.]

Revised Huck Finn learns that human beings have not only an enormous capacity for folly but also enormous dignity.

// 25a

3 Using parallelism for elements being compared or contrasted

Elements being compared or contrasted should ordinarily be cast in the same grammatical form.

> It is better to live rich than to die rich. — Samuel Johnson

Weak The study found that most welfare recipients wanted to work rather than handouts.

Revised The study found that most welfare recipients wanted work rather than handouts.

Revised The study found that most welfare recipients wanted to work rather than to accept handouts.

4 Using parallelism for lists, outlines, and headings

The elements of a list or outline that divides a larger subject are coordinate and should be parallel in structure. Parallelism is essential in the headings that divide a paper into sections (see p. 109) and in a formal topic outline (see pp. 38–39).

Faulty	Improved
Changes in Renaissance England	Changes in Renaissance England
1. Extension of trade routes	1. Extension of trade routes
2. Merchant class became more powerful	2. Increased power of the merchant class
3. The death of feudalism	3. Death of feudalism
4. Upsurging of the arts	4. Upsurge of the arts
5. The sciences were encouraged	5. Encouragement of the sciences
6. Religious quarrels began	6. Rise of religious quarrels

Exercise 25.1 Identifying parallel elements

Identify the parallel elements in the following sentences. How does parallelism contribute to the effectiveness of each sentence?

1. Eating an animal has not always been an automatic or an everyday affair; it has tended to be done on solemn occasions and for a special treat. — Margaret Visser
2. They [pioneer women] rolled out dough on the wagon seats, cooked with fires made out of buffalo chips, tended the sick, and marked the graves of their children, their husbands, and each other. — Ellen Goodman
3. The mornings are the pleasantest times in the apartment, exhaustion having set in, the sated mosquitoes at rest on ceiling and walls, sleeping it off, the room a swirl of tortured bedclothes and abandoned garments, the vines in their full leafiness filtering the hard light of day, the air conditioner silent at last, like the mosquitoes. — E. B. White
4. Aging paints every action gray, lies heavy on every movement, imprisons every thought. — Sharon Curtin

Exercise 25.2 Revising: Parallelism

Revise the following sentences to make coordinate, compared, or listed elements parallel in structure. Add or delete words or rephrase as necessary.

Example:

After emptying her bag, searching the apartment, and she called the library, Emma realized she had lost the book.

After emptying her bag, searching the apartment, and calling the library, Emma realized she had lost the book.

1. The ancient Greeks celebrated four athletic contests: the Olympic Games at Olympia, the Isthmian Games were held near Corinth, at Delphi the Pythian Games, and the Nemean Games were sponsored by the people of Cleonae.
2. Each day of the games consisted of either athletic events or holding ceremonies and sacrifices to the gods.

3. In the years between the games, competitors were taught wrestling, javelin throwing, and how to box.
4. Competitors participated in running sprints, spectacular chariot and horse races, and running long distances while wearing full armor.
5. The purpose of such events was to develop physical strength, demonstrating skill and endurance, and to sharpen the skills needed for war.
6. Events were held for both men and for boys.
7. At the Olympic Games the spectators cheered their favorites to victory, attended sacrifices to the gods, and they feasted on the meat not burned in offerings.
8. The athletes competed less to achieve great wealth than for gaining honor both for themselves and their cities.
9. Of course, exceptional athletes received financial support from patrons, poems and statues by admiring artists, and they even got lavish living quarters from their sponsoring cities.
10. With the medal counts and flag ceremonies, today's Olympians sometimes seem to be proving their countries' superiority more than to demonstrate individual talent.

25b Using parallelism to increase coherence

Effective parallelism will enable you to combine in a single, well-ordered sentence related ideas that you might have expressed in separate sentences. Compare the following three sentences with the original single sentence written by H. L. Mencken:

> Slang originates in the effort of ingenious individuals to make the language more pungent and picturesque. They increase the store of terse and striking words or widen the boundaries of metaphor. Thus a vocabulary for new shades and differences in meaning is provided by slang.
>
> Slang originates in the effort of ingenious individuals to make the language more pungent and picturesque—to increase the store of terse and striking words, to widen the boundaries of metaphor, and to provide a vocabulary for new shades and differences in meaning. — H. L. Mencken

Parallel structure works as well to emphasize the connections among related sentences in a paragraph:

> *Lewis Mumford stands* high in the company of [twentieth-century] sages. A scholar of cosmic cultural reach and conspicuous public conscience, a distinguished critic of life, arts, and letters, an unequaled observer of cities and civilizations, *he is* secure in the modern pantheon of great men. *He is* also an enigma and an anachronism. A legend of epic proportions in intellectual and academic circles, *he is* surprisingly little known to the public. — Ada Louise Huxtable

Here, Huxtable tightly binds her sentences with two layers of parallelism: the subject-verb patterns of all four sentences (italic and underlined) and the appositives of the second and fourth sentences (underlined). (See p. 83 for another illustration of parallelism among sentences.)

Exercise 25.3 Sentence combining: Parallelism

Combine each group of sentences below into one concise sentence in which parallel elements appear in parallel structures. You will have to add, delete, change, and rearrange words. Each item has more than one possible answer.

Example:

The new process works smoothly. It is efficient, too.
The new process works smoothly and efficiently.

1. People can develop post-traumatic stress disorder (PTSD). They develop it after experiencing a dangerous situation. They will also have felt fear for their survival.
2. The disorder can be triggered by a wide variety of events. Combat is a typical cause. Similarly, natural disasters can result in PTSD. Some people experience PTSD after a hostage situation.
3. PTSD can occur immediately after the stressful incident. Or it may not appear until many years later.
4. Sometimes people with PTSD will act irrationally. Moreover, they often become angry.
5. Other symptoms include dreaming that one is reliving the experience. They include hallucinating that one is back in the terrifying place. In another symptom one imagines that strangers are actually one's former torturers.

Exercise 25.4 Revising: Parallelism

Revise the following paragraph to create parallelism wherever it is required for grammar or for coherence.

The great white shark has an undeserved bad reputation. Many people consider the great white not only swift and powerful but also to be a cunning and cruel predator on humans. However, scientists claim that the great white attacks humans not by choice but as a result of chance. To a shark, our behavior in the water is similar to that of porpoises, seals, and sea lions—the shark's favorite foods. These sea mammals are both agile enough and can move fast enough to evade the shark. Thus the shark must attack with swiftness and noiselessly to surprise the prey and giving it little chance to escape. Humans become the shark's victims not because the shark has any preference or hatred of humans but because humans can neither outswim nor can they outmaneuver the shark. If the fish were truly a cruel human-eater, it would prolong the terror of its attacks, perhaps by circling or bumping into its intended victims before they were attacked.

Note See page 414 for an exercise involving parallelism along with other techniques for effective sentences.

26 Achieving Variety

Chapter essentials

- Vary sentence length and structure so that important ideas stand out (next page).
- Vary the beginnings of sentences (p. 409).
- Occasionally, invert the normal word order of sentences (p. 412).
- Occasionally, use a command, a question, or an exclamation (p. 412).

Visit MyWritingLab™ for more resources on achieving variety.

In a paragraph or an essay, each sentence stands in relation to those before and after it. To make sentences work together effectively and to avoid monotony for readers, writers vary sentences' length, structure, and word order to reflect the importance and complexity of ideas.

The following passage consists of eight sentences, all between twelve and sixteen words long (counting initials and dates). They are about equally detailed, and they all begin with the subject.

Unvaried sentences

Ulysses S. Grant and Robert E. Lee met on April 9, 1865. Their meeting place was the parlor of a modest house at Appomattox Court House, Virginia. They met to work out the terms for the surrender of Lee's Army of Northern Virginia. One great chapter of American life ended with their meeting, and another began. Grant and Lee were bringing the Civil War to its virtual finish. Other armies still had to surrender, and the fugitive Confederate government would struggle desperately and vainly. It would try to find some way to go on living with its chief support gone. Grant and Lee had signed the papers, however, and it was all over in effect.

Overall, the passage is monotonous and ineffective: we get a sense of names, dates, and events but no immediate sense of how they relate or what is most important.

Now compare the preceding passage with the actual passage written by Bruce Catton. Here the four sentences range from eleven to fifty-five words, and only one sentence begins with its subject:

Varied sentences

When Ulysses S. Grant and Robert E. Lee met in the parlor of a modest house at Appomattox Court House, Virginia, on April 9, 1865, to work out the terms for the surrender of Lee's Army of Northern Virginia, a great chapter in American life came to a close, and a great new chapter began.

> Suspenseful periodic sentence (p. 385) focuses attention on meeting; details of place, time, and cause are in opening subordinate clause

These men were bringing the Civil War to its virtual finish. To be sure, other armies had yet

> Short sentence sums up

to surrender, and for a few days the fugitive Confederate government would struggle desperately and vainly, trying to find some way to go on living now that its chief support was gone. But in effect it was all over when Grant and Lee signed the papers.

— Bruce Catton, "Grant and Lee"

Cumulative sentence (p. 385) reflects lingering obstacles to peace

Short final sentence indicates futility of further struggle

26a Varying sentence length and structure

The sentences of a stylistically effective essay will vary most obviously in their length and the arrangement of main clauses and modifiers. The variation in length and structure makes writing both readable and clear.

1 Varying length

Sentences generally vary from about ten to about forty words. When sentences are all at one extreme or the other, readers may have difficulty focusing on main ideas and seeing the relations among them:

- **Long sentences.** If most of your sentences contain thirty-five words or more, your main ideas may not stand out from the details that support them. Break some of the long sentences into shorter, simpler ones.
- **Short sentences.** If most of your sentences contain fewer than ten or fifteen words, all your ideas may seem equally important and the links between them may not be clear. Try combining them with coordination (p. 392) and subordination (p. 394) to show relationships and to stress main ideas.

var 26a

2 Rewriting strings of brief and simple sentences

A series of brief and simple sentences is both monotonous and hard to understand because it forces the reader to sort out relations among ideas. If you find that you depend on brief, simple sentences, work to increase variety by combining some of them into longer units that emphasize and link important ideas while de-emphasizing incidental information. (See Chapter 24.)

The following examples show how a string of simple sentences can be revised into an effective piece of writing:

Monotonous The moon is now drifting away from the earth. It moves away at the rate of about one inch a year. This movement is lengthening our days. They increase a thousandth of a second every century. Forty-seven of our present days will someday make up a month. We might eventually lose the moon altogether. Such great planetary movement rightly concerns astronomers, but it need not worry us. It will take 50 million years.

Revised The moon is now drifting away from the earth about one inch a year. At a thousandth of a second every century, this movement is lengthening our days. Forty-seven of our present days will someday make up a month, if we don't eventually lose the moon altogether. Such great planetary movement rightly concerns astronomers, but it need not worry us. It will take 50 million years.

In the revision, underlining indicates subordinate structures that were simple sentences in the original. With five sentences instead of the original eight, the revision emphasizes the moon's movement, the lengthening days, and the enormous span of time involved.

3 Rewriting strings of compound sentences

Compound sentences are usually just simple sentences linked with conjunctions. Thus a series of them will be as weak as a series of brief, simple sentences, especially if the clauses of the compound sentences are all about the same length:

Monotonous Physical illness may involve more than the body, for the mind may also be affected. Disorientation is common among sick people, but they are often unaware of it. They may reason abnormally, or they may behave immaturely.

Revised Physical illness may involve the mind as well as the body. Though often unaware of it, sick people are commonly disoriented. They may reason abnormally or behave immaturely.

The first passage creates a seesaw effect. The revision, with some main clauses shortened or changed into modifiers (underlined), is both clearer and more emphatic. (See p. 392 for more on avoiding excessive coordination.)

Exercise 26.1 Revising: Varied sentence structures

Rewrite the following paragraph to increase variety so that important ideas receive greater emphasis than supporting information does. You will have to change some main clauses into modifiers and then combine and reposition the modifiers and the remaining main clauses.

Charlotte Perkins Gilman was a leading intellectual in the women's movement during the first decades of the twentieth century. She wrote *Women and Economics.* This book challenged Victorian assumptions about differences between the sexes, and it explored the economic roots of women's oppression. Gilman wrote little about gaining the vote for women, but many feminists were then preoccupied with this issue, and historians have since focused on it. As a result, Gilman's contribution to today's women's movement has often been overlooked.

26b Varying sentence beginnings

An English sentence often begins with its subject, which generally captures old information from a preceding sentence (see pp. 384–85):

The defendant's lawyer was determined to break the prosecution's witness. She relentlessly cross-examined the stubborn witness for a week.

However, an unbroken sequence of sentences beginning with the subject quickly becomes monotonous, as shown by the unvaried passage on Grant and Lee that opened this chapter (p. 407). You can vary this subject-first pattern by adding modifiers or other elements before the subject.

Note The final arrangement of sentence elements should always depend on two concerns: the relation of a sentence to those preceding and following it and the emphasis required by your meaning.

Adverb modifiers

Adverbs modify verbs, adjectives, other adverbs, and whole clauses. They can often fall in a variety of spots in a sentence. Consider these different emphases:

For a week, the defendant's lawyer relentlessly cross-examined the stubborn witness.

Relentlessly, the defendant's lawyer cross-examined the stubborn witness for a week.

Relentlessly, for a week, the defendant's lawyer cross-examined the stubborn witness.

Notice that the last sentence, with both modifiers at the beginning, is periodic and thus highly emphatic (see p. 385).

var 26b

CULTURE LANGUAGE In standard American English, placing some negative adverb modifiers at the beginning of a sentence requires you to use the word order of a question, in which the verb or a part of it precedes the subject (see p. 270). These modifiers include *never, rarely, seldom,* and adverb phrases beginning in *no, not since,* and *not until.*

adverb subject verb phrase
Faulty Seldom a witness has held the stand for so long.

adverb helping verb subject main verb
Revised Seldom has a witness held the stand for so long.

Adjective modifiers

Adjectives and adjective phrases modify nouns and pronouns. They may sometimes fall at the beginning of a sentence to postpone the subject:

Exhausted from his testimony, the witness did not cooperate.
Scowling, he responded irritably to the lawyer's questions.

Coordinating conjunctions and transitional expressions

When the relation between two successive sentences demands, you may begin the second with a coordinating conjunction such as *and* or *but* (p. 268) or with a transitional expression such as *first, for instance, however,* or *therefore* (pp. 85–86).

> The witness had expected to be dismissed after his first long day of cross-examination. But he was not.
>
> The price of a college education has risen astronomically. For example, annual tuition at one state university climbed from $7400 to $9300 in just two years.

Occasional expletive constructions

An expletive construction—*it* or *there* plus a form of *be*—may occasionally be useful to delay and thus emphasize the subject of the sentence:

> His judgment seems questionable, not his desire.
> It is his judgment that seems questionable, not his desire.

However, expletive constructions are more likely to flatten writing by adding extra words. You should use them rarely, only when you can justify doing so. (See also p. 524.)

Exercise 26.2 Revising: Varied sentence beginnings

Follow the instructions in parentheses to revise each group of sentences below: either create a single sentence that begins with an adverb or adjective modifier, or make one sentence begin with an appropriate connector.

> *Example:*
> The *Seabird* took first place. It moved quickly in the wind. (*One sentence with adjective modifier beginning Moving.*)
> Moving quickly in the wind, the *Seabird* took first place.

1. Some people are champion procrastinators. They seldom complete their work on time. (*Two sentences with transitional expression.*)
2. Procrastinators may fear criticism. They may fear rejection. They will delay completing an assignment. (*One sentence with adverb modifier beginning If.*)
3. Procrastinators often desire to please a boss or a teacher. They fear failure so much that they cannot do the work. (*Two sentences with coordinating conjunction.*)
4. Procrastination seems a hopeless habit. It is conquerable. (*One sentence with adverb modifier beginning Although.*)
5. Teachers or employers can be helpful. They can encourage procrastinators. They can give procrastinators the confidence to do good work on time. (*One sentence with adjective modifier beginning Helpfully encouraging.*)

Exercise 26.3 Revising: Varied sentence beginnings

Revise the following paragraph to vary sentence beginnings by using each of the following at least once: an adverb modifier, an adjective modifier, a coordinating conjunction, and a transitional expression.

> Scientists in Egypt dug up 40-million-year-old fossil bones. They had evidence of primitive whales. The whale ancestors are called mesonychids. They were small, furry land mammals with four legs. These limbs were complete with kneecaps, ankles, and little toes. Gigantic modern whales have tiny hind legs inside their bodies and flippers instead of front legs. Scientists are certain that these two very different creatures share the same family tree.

26c Inverting the normal word order

The word order of subject, verb, and object or complement is strongly fixed in English (see pp. 251–54). Thus an inverted sentence can be emphatic:

> Voters once had some faith in politicians, and they were fond of incumbents. But now all politicians, especially incumbents, voters seem to detest. [The object *all politicians* precedes the verb *detests*.]

Inverting the normal order of subject, verb, and complement can be useful in two successive sentences when the second expands on the first:

> Critics have not been kind to Presidents who have tried to apply the ways of private business to public affairs. Particularly explicit was the curt verdict of one critic of President Hoover: Mr. Hoover was never President of the United States; he was four years chairman of the board.
>
> —Adapted from Emmet John Hughes

var 26d

Inverted sentences used without need are artificial. Avoid descriptive sentences such as *Up came Ben and down went Katie's spirits.*

26d Mixing types of sentences

Most written sentences make statements. Occasionally, however, you may want to use questions, commands, or exclamations to enhance variety.

Questions may set the direction of a paragraph, as in *What does a detective do?* or *How is the percentage of unemployed workers calculated?* More often, though, the questions used in exposition or argument do not require answers but simply emphasize ideas that readers can be expected to agree with. Such **rhetorical questions** are illustrated in the following passage:

> Another word that has ceased to have meaning due to overuse is *attractive. Attractive* has become verbal chaff. Who, by some stretch of language and imagination, cannot be described as attractive? And just what is it that attractive individuals are attracting? — Diane White

Commands occur frequently in an explanation of a process, particularly in directions, as this passage on freewriting illustrates:

The idea is simply to write for ten minutes (later on, perhaps fifteen or twenty). Don't stop for anything. Go quickly, without rushing. Never stop to look back, to cross something out, to wonder how to spell something, to wonder what word or thought to use, or to think about what you are doing. — Peter Elbow

Notice that the authors of these examples use questions and commands to achieve some special purpose. Variety occurs because a particular sentence type is effective for the context, not because the writer set out to achieve variety for its own sake.

Exercise 26.4 Writing varied sentences

Imagine that you are writing an essay on a transportation problem at your school. Practice varying your sentences by composing a sentence or passage to serve each purpose listed below.

1. Write a question that could open the essay.
2. Write a command that could open the essay.
3. Write an exclamation that could open the essay.
4. For the body of the essay, write an appropriately varied paragraph of at least five sentences, including at least one short and one long sentence beginning with the subject; at least one sentence beginning with an adverb modifier; at least one sentence beginning with a coordinating conjunction or transitional expression; and one rhetorical question or command.

Exercise 26.5 Analyzing variety

Examine the following paragraph for sentence variety. Try to explain why the author wrote each short or long sentence, each cumulative or periodic sentence, each sentence beginning with its subject or beginning some other way, and each question.

My earliest memory of learning to read is sitting with my grandmother on her livingroom sofa as her finger underlined the words of *Go, Dog. Go!* and I struggled to decipher them. Why did she spend so much time with me when she knew I would have every opportunity to finish high school and go to college? She listened patiently because she didn't take my education—or anyone's—for granted. The only one of her ten siblings to graduate from college, she had beaten the odds. She finished high school at the top of her class, held a full-time job while commuting to her college classes, and graduated with honors. Then she took a job at a public high school where she taught for more than thirty years. She knew that I was unaware of my opportunities, and she did not assume that I would succeed as she had. In her years of teaching, she had seen enough students struggle and drop out to know that failure often comes more easily than success. She was determined that I would be one of the successes—indeed, that I would soar. And soar I did.

Exercise 26.6 Revising: Variety

The following paragraph consists entirely of simple sentences that begin with their subjects. As appropriate, use the techniques discussed in this chapter to vary sentences. Your goal is to make the paragraph more readable and make its important ideas stand out clearly. You will have to delete, add, change, and rearrange words.

The Italian volcano Vesuvius had been dormant for many years. It then exploded on August 24 in the year AD 79. The ash, pumice, and mud from the volcano buried two busy towns. Herculaneum is one. The more famous is Pompeii. Both towns lay undiscovered for many centuries. Herculaneum and Pompeii were discovered in 1709 and 1748, respectively. The excavation of Pompeii was the more systematic. It was the occasion for initiating modern methods of conservation and restoration. Herculaneum was simply looted of its most valuable finds. It was then left to disintegrate. Pompeii appears much as it did before the eruption. A luxurious house opens onto a lush central garden. An election poster decorates a wall. A dining table is set for breakfast.

Exercise on Chapters 23–26 Revising: Effective sentences

Revise the paragraphs below to emphasize main ideas, de-emphasize supporting information, and achieve variety in sentences. As appropriate, employ the techniques discussed in Chapters 23–26, such as effective subjects and verbs, subordination and coordination, parallelism, and varied sentence beginnings. Edit the finished product for punctuation.

Modern Americans owe many debts to Native Americans. Several pleasures are among the debts. Native Americans originated two fine junk foods. They discovered popcorn. Potato chips were also one of their contributions.

The introduction of popcorn to the European settlers came from Native Americans. Massasoit provided popcorn at the first Thanksgiving feast. The Aztecs offered popcorn to the Spanish explorer Hernando Cortés. The Aztecs wore popcorn necklaces. So did the natives of the West Indies. There were three ways that the Native Americans popped the corn. First, they roasted an ear over fire. The ear was skewered on a stick. They ate only some of the popcorn. They ate the corn that fell outside the flames. Second, they scraped the corn off the cob. The kernels would be thrown into the fire. Of course, the fire had to be low. Then the popped kernels that did not fall into the fire were eaten. The third method was the most sophisticated. It involved a shallow pottery vessel. It contained sand. The vessel was heated. The sand soon got hot. Corn kernels were stirred in. They popped to the surface of the sand and were eaten.

A Native American chef was responsible for devising the crunchy potato chip. His name was George Crum. In 1853 Crum was cooking at Moon Lake Lodge. The lodge was in Saratoga Springs, New York. Complaints were sent in by a customer. The man thought Crum's french-fried potatoes were too thick. Crum tried a thinner batch. These were also unsuitable. Crum became frustrated. He deliberately made the potatoes thin and crisp. They could not be cut with a knife and fork. Crum's joke backfired. The customer raved about the potato chips. The chips were named Saratoga Chips. Soon they appeared on the lodge's menu. They also appeared throughout New England. Crum later opened his own restaurant. Of course, he offered potato chips.

Now all Americans munch popcorn in movies. They crunch potato chips at parties. They gorge on both when alone and bored. They can be grateful to Native Americans for these guilty pleasures.

PART 6

Punctuation

Commas, semicolons, colons, dashes, parentheses

(For explanations, consult the pages in parentheses.)

Sentences with two main clauses

The bus stopped, but no one got off. (p. 422)
The bus stopped; no one got off. (p. 443)
The bus stopped; however, no one got off. (p. 445)
The mechanic replaced the battery, the distributor cap, and the starter; but still the car would not start. (p. 447)
Her task was clear: she had to find the problem. (p. 466)

Introductory elements

Modifiers (p. 425)

After the argument was over, we laughed at ourselves.
Racing over the plain, the gazelle escaped the lion.
To dance in the contest, he had to tape his knee.
Suddenly, the door flew open.
With 125 passengers aboard, the plane was half full.
In 1983 he won the Nobel Prize.

Absolute phrases (p. 432)

Its wing broken, the bird hopped around on the ground.

Interrupting and concluding elements

Nonessential modifiers (p. 427)

Michael's car, which barely runs, has been impounded.
We consulted the dean, who had promised to help us.
The boy, like his sister, wants to be a pilot.
They moved across the desert, shielding their eyes from the sun.
The men do not speak to each other, although they share a car.

p

Nonessential appositives

Bergen's only daughter, Candice, became an actress. (p. 429)
The residents of three counties—Suffolk, Springfield, and Morrison—were urged to evacuate. (p. 469)
My father demanded one promise: that we not lie to him. (p. 467)

Essential modifiers (p. 440)

The car that hit mine was uninsured.
We consulted a teacher who had promised to help us.
The boy in the black hat is my cousin.
They were surprised to find the desert teeming with life.
The men do not speak to each other because they are feuding.

Essential appositives (p. 441)

Shaw's play *Saint Joan* was performed last year.

Their sons Tony, William, and Steve all chose military careers, leaving only Matthew to run the family business.

Transitional or parenthetical expressions

We suspect, however, that he will not come. (p. 429)

Jessica is respected by many people—including me. (p. 470)

George Balanchine (1904–83) was a brilliant choreographer of classical ballet. (p. 471)

Absolute phrases (p. 432)

The bird, its wing broken, hopped about on the ground.

The bird hopped about on the ground, its wing broken.

Phrases expressing contrast (p. 432)

The humidity, not just the heat, gives me headaches.

My headaches are caused by the humidity, not just the heat.

Concluding summaries and explanations

The movie opened to bad reviews: the characters were judged shallow and unrealistic. (p. 467)

We had gumbo and jambalaya for dinner—a Cajun feast. (p. 470)

Items in a series

Three or more items

Chimpanzees, gorillas, orangutans, and gibbons are all apes. (p. 433)

The cities singled out for praise were Birmingham, Alabama; Lincoln, Nebraska; Austin, Texas; and Troy, New York. (p. 447)

Two or more adjectives before a noun (p. 433)

Dirty, smelly clothes decorated their room.

Dessert consisted of one tiny scoop of ice cream.

Introductory series (p. 470)

Appropriateness, accuracy, and necessity—these criteria should govern your selection of words.

Concluding series

Every word should be appropriate, accurate, and necessary. (p. 441)

Every word should meet three criteria: appropriateness, accuracy, and necessity. (p. 467)

Pay attention to your words—to their appropriateness, their accuracy, and their necessity. (p. 470)

27 End Punctuation

Chapter essentials

- Use periods after most sentences and with some abbreviations (below).
- Use a question mark after a direct question and sometimes to indicate doubt (opposite).
- Use an exclamation point occasionally for emphasis (p. 420).

Visit MyWritingLab™ for more resources on end punctuation.

End punctuation marks—the period, the question mark, and the exclamation point—signal the ends of sentences.

27a Use periods after most sentences and with some abbreviations.

1 Use a period to end a statement, mild command, or indirect question.

Statements

These are exciting and trying times.
The airline went bankrupt.

Mild commands

Please do not smoke.
Think of the possibilities.

If you are unsure whether to use an exclamation point or a period after a command, use a period. The exclamation point should be used only rarely (see p. 420).

An **indirect question** reports what someone has asked but not in the form or the exact words of the original:

Indirect questions

Students sometimes wonder whether their teachers read the papers they write.

Abused children eventually stop asking why they are being punished.

CULTURE LANGUAGE In standard American English, the reporting verb in an indirect question (for example, *asked* or *said*) usually precedes a clause that contains a subject and verb in normal order, not question order: *The reporter asked why the negotiations failed*, not *why did the negotiations fail*.

2 Use periods with some abbreviations.

Use periods with abbreviations that consist of or end in small letters. Otherwise, omit periods from abbreviations.

Dr.	Mr., Mrs.	e.g.	Feb.	ft.
St.	Ms.	i.e.	p.	a.m., p.m.
PhD	BC, BCE	USA	IBM	AM, PM
BA	AD, CE	US	USMC	AIDS

Note When a sentence ends in an abbreviation with a period, don't add a second period: *My first class is at 8 a.m.*

See also pages 489–92 on uses of abbreviations in writing.

Exercise 27.1 Revising: Periods

Revise the following sentences so that periods are used correctly.

Example:

Several times I wrote to ask when my subscription ended?
Several times I wrote to ask when my subscription ended.

1. The instructor asked when Plato wrote *The Republic*?
2. Give the date within one century
3. The exact date is not known, but it is estimated at 370 BCE
4. Dr Arn will lecture on Plato at 7:30 p.m..
5. The area of the lecture hall is only 1600 sq ft

27b Use question marks after direct questions and sometimes to indicate doubt.

1 Use a question mark with a direct question.

What is the difference between these two people?
Will economists ever really understand the economy?

After an indirect question, use a period: *The senator asked why the bill had passed.* (See opposite.)

Questions in a series are each followed by a question mark:

The officer asked how many times the suspect had been arrested. Three times? Four times? More than that?

The use of capital letters for questions in a series is optional (see p. 481).

Note Question marks are never combined with other question marks, exclamation points, periods, or commas:

Faulty "What is the point?," readers ask.
Revised "What is the point?" readers ask.

2 Use a question mark within parentheses to indicate doubt about a number or date.

The Greek philosopher Socrates was born in 470 (?) BC and died in 399 BC from drinking poison after having been condemned to death.

Note Don't use a question mark within parentheses to express sarcasm or irony. Express these attitudes through sentence structure and word choice. (See Chapters 23 and 38.)

Faulty Stern's friendliness (?) bothered Crane.

Revised Stern's insincerity bothered Crane.

Exercise 27.2 Revising: Question marks

Revise the following sentences so that question marks (along with other punctuation marks) are used correctly.

Example:
"Why should I vote for you?," the woman asked the candidate.
"Why should I vote for you?" the woman asked the candidate.

1. In Homer's *Odyssey,* Odysseus took seven years to travel from Troy to Ithaca. Or was it eight years. Or more?
2. Odysseus must have wondered whether he would ever make it home?
3. "What man are you and whence?," asks Odysseus's wife, Penelope.
4. Why does Penelope ask, "Where is your city? Your family?"?
5. Penelope does not recognize Odysseus and asks who this stranger is?

27c Use an exclamation point after an emphatic statement, interjection, or command.

No! We must not lose this election!
Come here immediately!

Follow mild interjections and commands with commas or periods, as appropriate:

No, the response was not terrific.
To prolong your car's life, change its oil regularly.

! 27c

Use exclamation points sparingly, not to express sarcasm, irony, or amazement. Rely on sentence structure and word choice to express these attitudes. (See Chapters 23 and 38.)

Faulty After traveling 4.4 billion miles through space, *Voyager 2* was off-target by 21 miles (!).

Revised After traveling 4.4 billion miles through space, *Voyager 2* was off-target by a mere 21 miles.

Relying on the exclamation point for emphasis is like crying wolf: the mark loses its power to impress the reader. Frequent exclamation points can also make writing sound overemotional:

Overused exclamation points

Our city government is a mess! After just six months in office, the mayor has had to fire four city officials! In the same period the city councilors have done nothing but argue! And city services decline with each passing day!

Note Exclamation points are never combined with other exclamation points, question marks, periods, or commas:

Faulty "This will not be endured!," he roared.

Revised "This will not be endured!" he roared.

Exercise 27.3 Revising: Exclamation points

Revise the following sentences so that exclamation points (along with other punctuation marks) are used correctly. If a sentence is punctuated correctly as given, mark the number preceding it.

Example:

"Well, now!," he said loudly.
"Well, now!" he said loudly.

1. As the firefighters moved their equipment into place, the police shouted, "Move back!".
2. A child's cries could be heard from above: "Help me. Help."
3. When the child was rescued, the crowd called, "Hooray."
4. The rescue was the most exciting event of the day!
5. Let me tell you about it.

Exercise 27.4 Revising: End punctuation

Insert appropriate punctuation (periods, question marks, or exclamation points) where needed in the following paragraph.

When visitors first arrive in Hawaii, they often encounter an unexpected language barrier Standard English is the language of business and government, but many of the people speak Pidgin English Instead of an excited "Aloha" the visitors may be greeted with an excited Pidgin "Howzit" or asked if they know "how fo' find one good hotel" Many Hawaiians question whether Pidgin will hold children back because it prevents communication with the *haoles,* or Caucasians, who run many businesses Yet many others feel that Pidgin is a last defense of ethnic diversity on the islands To those who want to make standard English the official language of the state, these Hawaiians may respond, "Just 'cause I speak Pidgin no mean I dumb" They may ask, "Why you no listen" or, in standard English, "Why don't you listen"

Note See page 477 for a punctuation exercise combining periods with other marks of punctuation.

28 The Comma

Chapter essentials

To use the comma correctly,

- Separate main clauses linked by *and, but,* or another coordinating conjunction (below).
- Set off most introductory elements (p. 425).
- Set off nonessential elements (p. 427).
- Set off absolute phrases and phrases expressing contrast (p. 432).
- Separate items in a series and coordinate adjectives (p. 433).
- Separate parts of dates, addresses, place names, and long numbers (p. 435).
- Separate signal phrases and quotations (p. 436).
- Add a comma to prevent misreading (p. 438).
- Avoid common misuses, especially between subjects and verbs, in most compounds, after conjunctions, and around essential elements (p. 438).

Visit MyWritingLab™ for more resources on the comma.

Commas usually function within sentences to separate elements (see the box on the next page). Omitting needed commas or inserting needless ones can confuse the reader:

Comma needed	Though very tall Abraham Lincoln was not an overbearing man.
Revised	Though very tall, Abraham Lincoln was not an overbearing man.
Unneeded commas	The hectic pace of Beirut, broke suddenly into frightening chaos when the city became, the focus of civil war.
Revised	The hectic pace of Beirut broke suddenly into frightening chaos when the city became the focus of civil war.

28a Use a comma before *and, but,* or another coordinating conjunction linking main clauses.

The coordinating conjunctions are *and, but, or, nor, for, so,* and *yet.* When one of them links words or phrases, do not use a comma: *Dugain plays and sings Irish and English folk songs.* However, *do* use a comma when a coordinating conjunction joins main clauses. A **main clause** has a subject and a predicate (but no subordinating word at the beginning) and makes a complete statement (see p. 263).

Caffeine can keep coffee drinkers alert, and it may make them feel more energetic.

Principal uses of the comma

- **Separate main clauses linked by a coordinating conjunction** (previous and next pages):

  Main clause , *for and or so but nor yet* **main clause** .

  The building is finished, but it has no tenants.

- **Set off most introductory elements** (p. 425):

  Introductory element , **main clause** .

  Unfortunately, the only tenant pulled out.

- **Set off nonessential elements** (p. 427):

  Main clause , **nonessential element** .

  The empty building symbolizes a weak local economy, which affects everyone.

  Beginning of main clause , **nonessential element** , **end of main clause** .

  The primary cause, the decline of local industry, is not news.

- **Separate items in a series** (p. 433):

  . . . **item 1** , **item 2** , *and or* **item 3** . . .

  The city needs more jobs, new schools, and better housing.

- **Separate coordinate adjectives** (p. 433):

  . . . **first adjective** , **second adjective** **word modified** . . .

  A tall, sleek skyscraper is not needed.

Other uses of the comma:

Set off absolute phrases (p. 432).
Set off phrases expressing contrast (p. 432).
Separate parts of dates, addresses, place names, long numbers (p. 435).
Separate quotations and signal phrases (p. 436).
Prevent misreading (p. 438).

See also page 438 for when *not* to use the comma.

Caffeine was once thought to be safe, but now researchers warn of harmful effects.

Coffee drinkers may suffer sleeplessness, for the drug acts as a stimulant to the nervous system.

Note Do not add a comma *after* a coordinating conjunction between main clauses (see also p. 440):

Not Caffeine increases the heart rate, and, it constricts the blood vessels.
But Caffeine increases the heart rate, and it constricts the blood vessels.

Exceptions When the main clauses in a sentence are very long or grammatically complicated, or when they contain internal punctuation, a semicolon before the coordinating conjunction will clarify the division between clauses (see p. 447):

Caffeine may increase alertness, elevate mood, and provide energy; but it may also cause irritability, anxiety, stomach pains, and other ills.

When main clauses are very short and closely related in meaning, you may omit the comma between them as long as the resulting sentence is clear:

Caffeine helps but it also hurts.

If you are in doubt about whether to use a comma in such a sentence, use it. It will always be correct.

Exercise 28.1 Punctuating linked main clauses

Insert a comma before each coordinating conjunction that links main clauses in the following sentences.

Example:

I would have attended the concert and the reception but I had to baby-sit for my niece.

I would have attended the concert and the reception, but I had to baby-sit for my niece.

^ 28a

1. Parents once automatically gave their children the father's surname but some no longer do.
2. Instead, they bestow the mother's name for they believe that the mother's importance should be recognized.
3. The child's surname may be just the mother's or it may link the mother's and the father's with a hyphen.
4. Sometimes the first and third children will have the mother's surname and the second child will have the father's.
5. Occasionally the mother and father combine parts of their names and a new hybrid surname is born.

Exercise 28.2 Sentence combining: Linked main clauses

Combine each group of sentences below into one sentence that contains only two main clauses connected by the coordinating conjunction in parentheses. Separate the main clauses with a comma. You will have to add, delete, and rearrange words.

Example:

The circus had come to town. The children wanted to see it. Their parents wanted to see it. (*and*)

The circus had come to town, and the children and their parents wanted to see it.

1. Parents were once legally required to bestow the father's surname on their children. These laws have been contested in court. They have been found invalid. (*but*)
2. Parents may now give their children any surname they choose. The arguments for bestowing the mother's surname are often strong. They are often convincing. (*and*)
3. Critics sometimes question the effects of unusual surnames on children. They wonder how confusing the new surnames will be. They wonder how fleeting the surnames will be. (*or*)
4. Children with surnames different from their parents' may suffer embarrassment. They may suffer identity problems. Giving children their father's surname is still very much the norm. (*for*)
5. Hyphenated names are awkward. They are also difficult to pass on. Some observers think they will die out in the next generation. Or they may die out before. (*so*)

28b Use a comma to set off most introductory elements.

An introductory element modifies a word or words in the main clause that follows. These elements are usually set off from the rest of the sentence with a comma:

Subordinate clause (p. 263)

Even when identical twins are raised apart, they grow up very like each other.

Because they are similar, such twins interest scientists.

Verbal or verbal phrase (p. 261)

Explaining the similarity, some researchers claim that one's genes are one's destiny.

Concerned, other researchers deny the claim.

Prepositional phrase (p. 257)

In a debate that has lasted centuries, scientists use identical twins to argue for or against genetic destiny.

Transitional or parenthetical expression (pp. 85–86)

Of course, scientists can now look directly at the genes themselves.

The comma may be omitted after short introductory elements if its omission does not create confusion. (If you are in doubt, however, the comma is always correct.)

Clear	In a hundred years genetics may no longer be a mystery.
Confusing	Despite intensive research scientists still have more questions than answers.
Clear	Despite intensive research, scientists still have more questions than answers.

Commas may also be omitted after some transitional expressions when they start sentences. (See p. 430.)

Thus the debate continues.

Note Take care to distinguish *-ing* words used as modifiers from *-ing* words used as subjects, as shown in the following examples. The former almost always take a comma; the latter never do.

[modifier: Studying identical twins] [subject: geneticists] [verb: learn]
Studying identical twins, geneticists learn about inheritance.

[subject: Studying identical twins] [verb: helps]
Studying identical twins helps geneticists learn about inheritance.

Exercise 28.3 Punctuating introductory elements

Insert commas where needed after introductory elements in the following sentences. If a sentence is punctuated correctly as given, mark the number preceding it.

Example:

After the new library opened the old one became a student union.
After the new library opened, the old one became a student union.

1. Moving in a fluid mass is typical of flocks of birds and schools of fish.
2. Because it is sudden and apparently well coordinated the movement of flocks and schools has seemed to be directed by a leader.
3. However new studies have discovered that flocks and schools are leaderless.
4. When each bird or fish senses a predator it follows individual rules for fleeing.
5. Multiplied over hundreds of individuals these responses look as if they have been choreographed.

^ 28b

Exercise 28.4 Sentence combining: Introductory elements

Combine each pair of sentences below into one sentence that begins with an introductory phrase or clause as specified in parentheses. Follow the introductory element with a comma. You will have to add, delete, change, and rearrange words.

Example:

The girl was humming to herself. She walked upstairs. (*Phrase beginning* Humming.)

Humming to herself, the girl walked upstairs.

1. Biologists have made an effort to explain the mysteries of flocks and schools. They have proposed bizarre magnetic fields and telepathy. (*Phrase beginning* In.)

2. Biologists developed computer models. They have abandoned earlier explanations. (*Clause beginning Since.*)
3. The movement of a flock or school starts with each individual. It is rapidly and perhaps automatically coordinated among individuals. (*Phrase beginning Starting.*)
4. One biologist observes that human beings seek coherent patterns. He suggests that investigators saw purpose in the movement of flocks and schools where none existed. (*Phrase beginning Observing.*)
5. One may want to study the movement of flocks or schools. Then one must abandon a search for purpose or design. (*Phrase beginning To.*)

28c Use a comma or commas to set off nonessential elements.

Commas around part of a sentence often signal that the element is not necessary to the meaning of the sentence:

Nonessential element

The company, which is located in Oklahoma, has a good reputation.

This **nonessential element** may modify or rename the word it refers to (*company* in the example), but it does not limit the word to a particular individual or group. (Because it does not restrict meaning, a nonessential element is also called a **nonrestrictive element.**) Nonessential elements are *not* essential, but punctuation *is.*

In contrast, an **essential** (or **restrictive**) element *does* limit the word it refers to:

Essential element

The company rewards employees who work hard.

In this example the underlined essential element cannot be omitted without leaving the meaning of *employees* too general. Because it is essential, such an element is *not* set off with commas.

Meaning and context

The same element in the same sentence may be essential or nonessential depending on your intended meaning and the context in which the sentence appears. For example, look at the second sentence in each of the following passages:

Essential

Not all the bands were equally well received, however. The band playing old music held the audience's attention. The other groups created much less excitement. [*Playing old music* identifies a particular band.]

Nonessential

A new band called Fats made its debut on Saturday night. The band, playing old music, held the audience's attention. If this performance is typical, the group has a bright future. [*Playing old music* adds information about a band already named.]

A test for essential and nonessential elements

1. **Identify the element.**

   Hai Nguyen who emigrated from Vietnam lives in Denver.
   Those who emigrated with him live elsewhere.

2. **Remove the element. Does the fundamental meaning of the sentence change?**

   Hai Nguyen lives in Denver. ***No.***
   Those live elsewhere. ***Yes.*** [Who are *Those*?]

3. **If *no,* the element is *nonessential* and should be set off with punctuation.**

   Hai Nguyen, who emigrated from Vietnam, lives in Denver.

   If *yes,* the element is *essential* and should *not* be set off with punctuation.

   Those who emigrated with him live elsewhere.

Punctuation of interrupting nonessential elements

When a nonessential element falls in the middle of a sentence, be sure to set it off with a pair of commas, one *before* and one *after* the element. Dashes or parentheses may also set off nonessential elements (see pp. 469 and 471).

1 Use a comma or commas to set off nonessential clauses and phrases.

Clauses and phrases serving as adjectives and adverbs may be either nonessential or essential. In the following examples the underlined clauses and phrases are nonessential: they could be omitted without changing the meaning of the words they modify.

28c

Nonessential

Elizabeth Blackwell was the first woman to graduate from an American medical school, in 1849. [Adverb phrase.]

She was a medical pioneer, helping to found the first medical college for women. [Adjective phrase.]

She taught at the school, which was affiliated with the New York Infirmary. [Adjective clause.]

Blackwell, who published books and papers on medicine, practiced pediatrics and gynecology. [Adjective clause.]

She moved to England in 1869, when she was forty-eight. [Adverb clause.]

Note Most adverb clauses are essential because they describe conditions necessary to the main clause. (Adverb clauses begin with *if, because,* or another subordinating conjunction.) Set an adverb clause off with a comma or commas only when it introduces a sentence (see p. 425) or when it is truly nonessential, adding incidental information (as in the last example on the previous page) or expressing a contrast beginning *although, whereas,* and the like.

In the following sentences, the underlined elements limit the meaning of the words they modify. Removing the elements would leave the meaning too general.

Essential

The history of aspirin began with the ancient Greeks.

Physicians who sought to relieve their patients' pains recommended chewing willow bark.

Willow bark contains a chemical that is similar to aspirin.

Aspirin is widely prescribed for pain because it is generally safe.

Note Whereas both nonessential and essential clauses may begin with *which,* only essential clauses begin with *that.* Some writers prefer *that* exclusively for essential clauses and *which* exclusively for nonessential clauses. See the Glossary of Usage, page 821, for advice on the use of *that* and *which.*

2 Use a comma or commas to set off nonessential appositives.

An **appositive** is a noun or noun substitute that renames another noun just before it. (See pp. 266–67.) Many appositives are nonessential; thus they are set off, usually with commas.

Nonessential

Toni Morrison's fifth novel, *Beloved*, won the Pulitzer Prize in 1988.
Morrison, a native of Ohio, won the Nobel Prize in 1993.

Take care *not* to set off essential appositives; like other essential elements, they limit or define the word to which they refer.

Essential

Morrison's novel The Bluest Eye is about an African American girl who longs for blue eyes.

The critic Michiko Kakutani says that Morrison's work "stands radiantly on its own as an American epic."

3 Use a comma or commas to set off transitional or parenthetical expressions.

Transitional expressions

Transitional expressions form links between ideas. They include conjunctive adverbs such as *however* and *moreover* as well as other words or phrases such as *for example* and *of course.* (See pp. 85–86 for a list of transitional words and phrases.) Transitional expressions are nonessential, and most of them are set off with a comma or commas:

> US workers, for example, receive fewer holidays than European workers do.

When a transitional expression links main clauses, precede it with a semicolon and follow it with a comma. (See p. 445.)

> European workers often have long paid vacations; indeed, they may receive a full month.

Exceptions The conjunctions *and, but,* and *yet* are sometimes used as transitional expressions but are never followed by commas (see p. 440). Usage varies with some other transitional expressions, depending on the expression and the writer's judgment. Many writers omit commas with expressions that we read without pauses, such as *also, hence, next, now, then,* and *thus.* The same applies to *therefore* and *instead* when they fall inside or at the ends of clauses.

> US workers therefore put in more work days. But the days themselves may be shorter.
>
> Then the total hours worked come out roughly the same.

Parenthetical expressions

Parenthetical expressions provide comments, explanations, digressions, or other supplementary information not essential to meaning—for example, *fortunately, unfortunately, all things considered, to be frank, in other words.* Like transitional expressions, most parenthetical expressions are set off, often with commas:

> Surprisingly, the most celebrated holiday in the world is New Year's Day.

Dashes and parentheses may also set off parenthetical expressions. (See pp. 470 and 471, respectively.)

4 Use a comma or commas to set off *yes* and *no,* tag questions, words of direct address, and mild interjections.

Yes and *no*

Yes, the writer did have a point.
No, that can never be.

Tag questions

They don't stop to consider others, do they?
Jones should be allowed to vote, shouldn't he?

Direct address

Cody, please bring me the newspaper.
With all due respect, sir, I will not do that.

Mild interjections

Well, you will never know who did it.
Oh, she forgot about the test.

(You may want to use an exclamation point to set off a forceful interjection. See p. 420.)

Exercise 28.5 Punctuating essential and nonessential elements

Insert commas in the following sentences to set off nonessential elements, and delete any commas that incorrectly set off essential elements. If a sentence is correct as given, mark the number preceding it.

Example:

Our language has adopted the word, *garage*, from the French.
Our language has adopted the word *garage* from the French.

1. Many colleges have started campus garden programs, that aim to teach students about the benefits of sustainable farming methods and locally grown food.
2. These gardens which use organic farming techniques also provide fresh produce for the college cafeteria.
3. A garden, that is big enough to grow produce for a college cafeteria, requires a large piece of land.
4. Such a garden also needs a leader, who can choose crops that will thrive in local growing conditions.
5. Volunteers, willing to work in the garden every week, are essential as well.
6. Some campus gardeners distribute produce to people in the community who live far from a grocery store.
7. Some urban neighborhoods are called "food deserts," because they lack grocery stores that residents can reach easily on foot.
8. The colleges may distribute produce with special trucks or "veggie wagons" that drive through the urban neighborhoods.
9. The wagons deliver produce once a week although they may make two deliveries during peak harvest time.
10. A community garden planted during the academic year will fare better in the southern states where the growing season is longer than in northern states.

Exercise 28.6 Sentence combining: Essential and nonessential elements

Combine each of the following pairs of sentences into one sentence that uses the element described in parentheses. Insert commas as appropriate. You will have to add, delete, change, and rearrange words. Some items have more than one possible answer.

Example:

Mr. Ward's oldest sister helped keep him alive. She was a nurse. (*Nonessential clause beginning who.*)

Mr. Ward's oldest sister, who was a nurse, helped keep him alive.

1. American colonists first imported pasta from the English. The English had discovered it as tourists in Italy. (*Nonessential clause beginning who.*)
2. The English returned from their grand tours of Italy. They were called macaronis because of their fancy airs. (*Essential phrase beginning returning.*)
3. A hair style was also called *macaroni.* It had elaborate curls. (*Essential phrase beginning with.*)
4. The song "Yankee Doodle" refers to this hairdo. It reports that Yankee Doodle "stuck a feather in his cap and called it macaroni." (*Essential clause beginning when.*)
5. The song was actually intended to poke fun at unrefined American colonists. It was a creation of the English. (*Nonessential appositive beginning a creation.*)

28d Use a comma or commas to set off absolute phrases.

An **absolute phrase** modifies a whole main clause rather than any word in the clause, and it usually consists of at least a participle (such as *done* or *having torn*) and its subject (a noun or pronoun). (See p. 262.) Absolute phrases can occur at almost any point in the sentence, and they are always set off by a comma or commas:

Household recycling having succeeded, the city now wants to extend the program to businesses.

Many of the city's businesses, their profits already squeezed, have resisted recycling.

28e Use a comma or commas to set off phrases expressing contrast.

The essay needs less wit, more pith.
The substance, not the style, is important.
Substance, unlike style, cannot be faked.

Note Writers often omit commas around contrasting phrases beginning with *but*: *A full but hazy moon shone down.*

Exercise 28.7 Punctuating absolute phrases and phrases of contrast

Insert commas in the following sentences to set off absolute phrases and phrases of contrast.

Example:

The recording contract was canceled the band having broken up.
The recording contract was canceled, the band having broken up.

1. Prices having risen rapidly the government debated a price freeze.
2. A price freeze unlike a rise in interest rates seemed a sure solution.

3. The President would have to persuade businesses to accept a price freeze his methods depending on their resistance.
4. No doubt the President his advisers having urged it would first try a patriotic appeal.
5. The President not his advisers insisted on negotiations with businesses.

28f Use commas between items in a series and between coordinate adjectives.

1 Use commas between words, phrases, or clauses forming a series.

Place commas between all elements of a **series**—that is, three or more items of equal importance:

> Anna Spingle married at the age of seventeen, had three children by twenty-one, and divorced at twenty-two.
>
> She worked as a cook, a baby-sitter, and a crossing guard.

Some writers omit the comma before the coordinating conjunction in a series (*Breakfast consisted of coffee, eggs and kippers*). But the final comma is never wrong, and it always helps the reader see the last two items as separate:

Confusing	In her new job Spingle updates the Web site, organizes files and responds to customers' questions.
Clear	In her new job Spingle updates the Web site, organizes files, and responds to customers' questions.

Exception When series items are long and grammatically complicated, they may be separated by semicolons. When they contain commas, they must be separated by semicolons. (See p. 447.)

2 Use commas between two or more adjectives that equally modify the same words.

When two or more adjectives modify the same word equally, they are said to be **coordinate.** The adjectives may be separated either by *and* or by a comma, as in the following examples.

> Spingle's scratched and dented car is old, but it gets her to work.
> She dreams of buying a sleek, shiny car.

Adjectives are not coordinate—and should *not* be separated by commas—when the one nearer the noun is more closely related to the noun in meaning. In each of the next examples, the second adjective and the noun form a unit that is modified by the first adjective:

> Spingle's children work at various part-time jobs.
> They all expect to go to a nearby community college.

See the following box for a test to use in punctuating adjectives.

Punctuating two or more adjectives

1. **Identify the adjectives.**

   She was a faithful sincere friend.
   They are dedicated medical students.

2. **Can the adjectives be reversed without changing meaning?**

   She was a sincere faithful friend. ***Yes.***
   They are medical dedicated students. ***No.***

3. **Can the word *and* be sensibly inserted between the adjectives?**

   She was a faithful and sincere friend. ***Yes.***
   They are dedicated and medical students. ***No.***

4. **If *yes* to both questions, the adjectives are coordinate and *should* be separated by a comma.**

   She was a faithful, sincere friend.

   If *no* to both questions, the adjectives are *not* coordinate and should *not* be separated by a comma.

   They are dedicated medical students.

Note Numbers are not coordinate with other adjectives:

Faulty Spingle has three, teenaged children.
Revised Spingle has three teenaged children.

Do not use a comma between the final adjective and the noun:

Faulty The children hope to achieve good, well-paying, jobs.
Revised The children hope to achieve good, well-paying jobs.

Exercise 28.8 Punctuating series and coordinate adjectives

Insert commas in the following sentences to separate elements in series and coordinate adjectives. Mark the number preceding any sentence whose punctuation is already correct.

Example:

Quiet by day, the club became a noisy smoky dive at night.
Quiet by day, the club became a noisy, smoky dive at night.

1. Shoes with high heels originated to protect feet from the mud garbage and animal waste in the streets.
2. The first known high heels worn strictly for fashion appeared in the sixteenth century.
3. The heels were worn by men and made of colorful silk brocades soft suedes or smooth leathers.
4. High-heeled shoes received a boost when the short powerful King Louis XIV of France began wearing them.
5. Eventually only wealthy fashionable French women wore high heels.

28g Use commas according to convention in dates, addresses, place names, and long numbers.

Use commas to separate most parts of dates, addresses, and place names: *June 20, 1950*; *24 Fifth Avenue, Suite 601*; *Cairo, Illinois*. Within a sentence, any element preceded by a comma should be followed by a comma as well, as in the following examples.

Dates

July 4, 1776, is the date the Declaration of Independence was signed.

The bombing of Pearl Harbor on Sunday, December 7, 1941, prompted American entry into World War II.

Do not use commas between the parts of a date in inverted order: *Their anniversary on 15 December 2005 was their fiftieth.* You need not use commas in dates consisting of a month or season and a year: *For the United States the war ended in August 1945.*

Addresses and place names

Columbus, Ohio, is the state capital and the location of Ohio State University.

The population of Garden City, Long Island, New York, is 22,000.

Use the address 220 Cornell Road, Woodside, California 94062, for all correspondence.

Do not use a comma between a state and a zip code.

Long numbers

Use the comma to separate the figures in long numbers into groups of three, counting from the right. With numbers of four digits, the comma is optional.

A kilometer is 3,281 feet [*or* 3281 feet].
The new assembly plant cost $7,535,000 to design and build.

CULTURE LANGUAGE Usage in American English differs from that in some other languages and dialects, which use a period, not a comma, to separate the figures in long numbers.

Exercise 28.9 Punctuating dates, addresses, place names, numbers

Insert commas as needed in the following sentences.

Example:
The house cost $27000 forty years ago.
The house cost $27,000 forty years ago.

1. The festival will hold a benefit dinner and performance on March 10 2015 in Asheville.
2. The organizers hope to raise more than $100000 from donations and ticket sales.
3. Performers are expected from as far away as Milan Italy and Kyoto Japan.

4. All inquiries sent to Mozart Festival PO Box 725 Asheville North Carolina 28803 will receive a quick response.
5. The deadline for ordering tickets by mail is Monday December 16 2014.

28h Use commas with quotations according to standard practice.

The words *he said, she writes,* and so on identify the source of a quotation. These **signal phrases** may come before, after, or in the middle of the quotation. A signal phrase must always be separated from the quotation by punctuation, usually a comma or commas.

Note Additional issues with quotations are discussed elsewhere in this book:

- **Using quotation marks conventionally,** pages 458–65.
- **Selecting and transcribing quotations from sources,** pages 603–05.
- **Integrating source material into your text,** pages 608–12.
- **Acknowledging the sources of quotations to avoid plagiarism,** pages 618–19.
- **Formatting long prose quotations and poetry quotations** in MLA style, pages 681–82; Chicago style, page 758; and APA style, page 783.

1 Ordinarily, use a comma with a signal phrase before or after a quotation.

In her book *You Learn by Living,* Eleanor Roosevelt says**,** "You must do the thing you think you cannot do."

"Knowledge is power**,**" writes Francis Bacon.

Exceptions Do not use commas with signal phrases in some situations:

28h

- **Omit a comma when a signal phrase follows a quotation ending in an exclamation point or a question mark:**

  "Claude**!**" Mrs. Harrison called.

  "Why must I come home**?**" he asked.

- **Use a colon when a complete sentence introduces a quotation:**

  Her statement hedged**:** "I will not resign unless circumstances force me to reconsider at a later time."

- **Omit commas when a quotation is integrated into your sentence structure,** including a quotation introduced by *that*:

  James Baldwin insists that "one must never, in one's life, accept . . . injustices as commonplace."

  Baldwin thought that the violence of a riot "had been devised as a corrective" to his own violence.

2 With an interrupted quotation, precede the signal phrase with a comma and follow it with the punctuation required by the quotation.

Original quotation

"The shore has a dual nature, changing with the swing of the tides."

Signal phrase interrupts at comma, ends with comma

"The shore has a dual nature," observes Rachel Carson, "changing with the swing of the tides."

Original quotation

"However mean your life is, meet it and live it; do not shun it and call it hard names."

Signal phrase interrupts at semicolon, ends with semicolon

"However mean your life is, meet it and live it," Thoreau advises in *Walden*; "do not shun it and call it hard names."

Original quotation

"This is the faith with which I return to the South. With this new faith we will be able to hew out of the mountain of despair a stone of hope."

Signal phrase interrupts at end of sentence, ends with period

"This is the faith with which I return to the South," Martin Luther King, Jr., proclaimed. "With this new faith we will be able to hew out of the mountain of despair a stone of hope."

Note Using a comma instead of a semicolon or a period after the Thoreau and King signal phrases would result in the error called a comma splice: two main clauses separated only by a comma. (See pp. 345–49.)

3 Place commas that follow quotations within quotation marks.

"Death is not the greatest loss in life," claims Norman Cousins.

"The greatest loss," Cousins says, "is what dies inside us while we live."

Exercise 28.10 Punctuating quotations

Insert commas or semicolons in the following sentences to correct punctuation with quotations. Mark the number preceding any sentence whose punctuation is already correct.

Example:

The shoplifter declared "I didn't steal anything."
The shoplifter declared, "I didn't steal anything."

1. The writer and writing teacher Peter Elbow proposes an "open-ended writing process" that "can change you, not just your words."
2. "I think of the open-ended writing process as a voyage in two stages" Elbow says.
3. "The sea voyage is a process of divergence, branching, proliferation, and confusion" Elbow continues "the coming to land is a process of convergence, pruning, centralizing, and clarifying."

4. "Keep up one session of writing long enough to get loosened up and tired" advises Elbow "long enough in fact to make a bit of a voyage."
5. "In coming to new land" Elbow says "you develop a new conception of what you are writing about."

28i Use commas to prevent misreading.

In some sentences words may run together in unintended and confusing ways unless a comma separates them:

Confusing Soon after the business closed its doors.

Clear Soon after, the business closed its doors.

Always check whether a comma added to prevent misreading might cause some other confusion or error. In the first example below, the comma prevents *pasta* and *places* from running into each other as *pasta places*, but it separates the subject (*historian*) and the verb (*places*). The revision solves both problems.

Faulty A historian who studied pasta, places its origin in the Middle East.

Revised A historian who studied pasta says that it originated in the Middle East.

Exercise 28.11 Punctuating to prevent misreading

Insert commas in the following sentences to prevent misreading.

Example:

To Jasmine MacKenzie symbolized decadence.
To Jasmine, MacKenzie symbolized decadence.

1. Though happy people still have moments of self-doubt.
2. In research subjects have reported themselves to be generally happy people.
3. Among those who have life has included sufferings as well as joys.
4. Of fifty eight subjects reported bouts of serious depression.
5. For half the preceding year had included at least one personal crisis.

no ^, 28j

28j Use commas only where required.

Commas can make sentences choppy and even confusing if they are used more often than needed. The main misuses of commas are summarized in the box on the next page.

1 Delete any comma after a subject or a verb.

Commas interrupt the movement from subject to verb to object or complement, as in the following faulty examples.

Principal misuses of the comma

- **Don't use a comma after a subject or verb:**

Faulty Anyone with breathing problems, should not exercise during smog alerts.

Revised Anyone with breathing problems should not exercise during smog alerts.

- **Don't separate a pair of words, phrases, or subordinate clauses joined by *and, or,* or *nor*:**

Faulty Asthmatics are affected by ozone, and sulfur oxides.

Revised Asthmatics are affected by ozone and sulfur oxides.

- **Don't use a comma after *and, but, although, because,* or another conjunction:**

Faulty Smog is dangerous and, sometimes even fatal.

Revised Smog is dangerous and sometimes even fatal.

- **Don't set off essential elements:**

Faulty The pollutant, sulfur oxide, is especially dangerous.

Revised The pollutant sulfur oxide is especially dangerous.

Faulty Even people, who are healthy, should be careful.

Revised Even people who are healthy should be careful.

- **Don't set off a series:**

Faulty Cars, factories, and even bakeries, contribute to smog.

Revised Cars, factories, and even bakeries contribute to smog.

- **Don't set off an indirect quotation:**

Faulty Experts say, that smog is increasing.

Revised Experts say that smog is increasing.

no ,
28j

Faulty The returning soldiers, received a warmer welcome than they expected. [Separation of subject and verb.]

Revised The returning soldiers received a warmer welcome than they expected.

Faulty They had chosen, to fight for their country. [Separation of verb *chosen* and object *to fight.*]

Revised They had chosen to fight for their country.

Exception Use commas between subject, verb, and object or complement only when other words between these elements require punctuation:

Americans, who are preoccupied with other sports, have only recently developed an interest in professional soccer. [Commas set off a nonessential clause.]

2 Delete any comma that separates a pair of words, phrases, or subordinate clauses joined by a coordinating conjunction.

When linking elements with *and, or,* or another coordinating conjunction, do not use a comma unless the elements are main clauses (see p. 422):

Faulty Banks could, and should help older people manage their money. [Compound helping verb.]

Revised Banks could and should help older people manage their money.

Faulty Older people need special assistance because they live on fixed incomes, and because they are not familiar with new accounts, and rates. [Compound subordinate clauses *because . . . because* and compound object of preposition *with.*]

Revised Older people need special assistance because they live on fixed incomes and because they are not familiar with new accounts and rates.

Faulty Banks, and community groups can assist the elderly, and eliminate the confusion they often feel. [Compound subject and compound predicate.]

Revised Banks and community groups can assist the elderly and eliminate the confusion they often feel.

3 Delete any comma after a conjunction.

The coordinating conjunctions (*and, but,* and so on) and the subordinating conjunctions (*although, because,* and so on) are not followed by commas:

Faulty Parents of adolescents notice increased conflict at puberty, and, they complain of bickering.

Revised Parents of adolescents notice increased conflict at puberty, and they complain of bickering.

no ^ 28j

Faulty Although, other primates leave the family at adolescence, humans do not.

Revised Although other primates leave the family at adolescence, humans do not.

4 Delete any commas that set off essential elements.

Commas do not set off an essential element, which limits the meaning of the word to which it refers (see p. 427):

Faulty Hawthorne's work, *The Scarlet Letter,* was the first major American novel. [The title is essential to distinguish the novel from the rest of Hawthorne's work.]

Revised Hawthorne's work *The Scarlet Letter* was the first major American novel.

Faulty The symbols, that Hawthorne uses, have influenced other novelists. [The clause identifies which symbols have been influential.]

Revised The symbols that Hawthorne uses have influenced other novelists.

Faulty Published in 1850, *The Scarlet Letter* is still popular, because its theme of secret sin resonates with contemporary readers. [The clause is essential to explain why the novel is still popular.]

Revised Published in 1850, *The Scarlet Letter* is still popular because its theme of secret sin resonates with contemporary readers.

Quoted or italicized words are essential appositives when they limit the word they refer to (see p. 429). Do not use commas around an essential appositive:

Faulty James Joyce's short story, "The Dead," was made into a film. [The commas imply wrongly that Joyce wrote only one story.]

Revised James Joyce's short story "The Dead" was made into a film.

Faulty The word, *open,* can be either a verb or an adjective.

Revised The word *open* can be either a verb or an adjective.

The following sentence requires commas because the quoted title is a nonessential appositive:

Her only poem about death, "Henry," was printed in the *New Yorker.*

5 Delete any comma before or after a series unless a rule requires it.

Commas separate the items *within* a series (p. 433) but do not separate the series from the rest of the sentence:

Faulty The skills of, hunting, herding, and agriculture, sustained the Native Americans.

Revised The skills of hunting, herding, and agriculture sustained the Native Americans.

In the sentence below, the commas around the series are appropriate because the series is a nonessential appositive (p. 429):

The four major broadcast networks, ABC, CBS, Fox, and NBC, face fierce competition from cable, satellite, and the Internet.

However, many writers prefer to use dashes rather than commas to set off series functioning as appositives (see p. 469).

6 Delete any comma setting off an indirect quotation.

Faulty The report concluded, that dieting could be more dangerous than overeating.

Revised The report concluded that dieting could be more dangerous than overeating.

Exercise 28.12 Revising: Needless or misused commas

Revise the following sentences to eliminate needless or misused commas. Mark the number preceding any sentence that is already punctuated correctly.

Example:

The portrait of the founder, that hung in the dining hall, was stolen by pranksters.

The portrait of the founder that hung in the dining hall was stolen by pranksters.

1. Nearly 40 million US residents, speak a first language other than English.
2. After English the languages most commonly spoken in the United States are, Spanish, Chinese, and French.
3. Almost 75% of the people, who speak foreign languages, used the words, "good" or "very good," when judging their proficiency in English.
4. Recent immigrants, especially those speaking Spanish, Chinese, and Korean, tended to judge their English more harshly.
5. The states with the highest proportion of foreign language speakers, are New Mexico, and California.

Exercise 28.13 Revising: Commas

Insert commas in the following paragraphs wherever they are needed, and eliminate any misused or needless commas.

Ellis Island New York reopened for business in 1990 but now the customers are tourists not immigrants. This spot which lies in New York Harbor was the first American soil seen, or touched by many of the nation's immigrants. Though other places also served as ports of entry for foreigners none has the symbolic power of, Ellis Island. Between its opening in 1892 and its closing in 1954, over 20 million people about two-thirds of all immigrants were detained there before taking up their new lives in the United States. Ellis Island processed over 2000 newcomers a day when immigration was at its peak between 1900 and 1920.

As the end of a long voyage and the introduction to the New World Ellis Island must have left something to be desired. New arrivals were herded about kept standing in lines for hours or days yelled at and abused. Assigned numbers they submitted their bodies to the pokings and proddings of the silent nurses and doctors, who were charged with ferreting out the slightest sign of sickness, disability or insanity. That test having been passed the immigrants faced interrogation by an official through an interpreter. Those, with names deemed inconveniently long or difficult to pronounce, often found themselves permanently labeled with abbreviations, of their names, or with the names, of their hometowns. But, millions survived the examination humiliation and confusion, to take the last short boat ride to New York City. For many of them and especially for their descendants Ellis Island eventually became not a nightmare but the place where life began.

Note See page 477 for a punctuation exercise combining commas with other marks of punctuation.

29 The Semicolon

Chapter essentials

To use the semicolon correctly,

- Separate main clauses that are not joined by *and, but,* or another coordinating conjunction (below).
- Separate main clauses related by *however, for example,* or a similar expression (p. 445).
- Separate main clauses or series items that contain commas (p. 447).
- Avoid misuses of the semicolon: with phrases and subordinate clauses and before series and explanations (p. 448).

Visit MyWritingLab™ for more resources on the semicolon.

The semicolon separates equal and balanced sentence elements, usually main clauses, sometimes items in series.

29a Use a semicolon between main clauses not joined by *and, but,* or another coordinating conjunction.

Main clauses contain a subject and a predicate and do not begin with a subordinating word (see p. 263). When you join two main clauses in a sentence, you have two primary options for separating them:

- **Insert a comma and a coordinating conjunction:** *and, but, or, nor, for, so, yet.* (See p. 422.)

  The drug does little to relieve symptoms, and it can have negative side effects.

- **Insert a semicolon:**

  The side effects are not minor; some leave the patient quite ill.

Note If you do not link main clauses with a coordinating conjunction and you separate them only with a comma or with no punctuation at all, you will produce a comma splice or a fused sentence. (See Chapter 18.)

Exercise 29.1 Punctuating between main clauses

Insert semicolons to separate main clauses in the following sentences.

Example:
One man at the auction bid prudently another spent his savings.
One man at the auction bid prudently; another spent his savings.

1. More and more musicians are playing computerized instruments more and more listeners are worrying about the future of acoustic instruments.

Distinguishing the comma, the semicolon, and the colon

Comma

The *comma* chiefly separates both equal and unequal sentence elements.

- **It separates main clauses when they are linked by a coordinating conjunction** (p. 422):

  An airline once tried to boost sales by advertising the tense alertness of its crews**,** but nervous fliers did not want to hear about pilots' sweaty palms.

- **It separates subordinate information that is part of or attached to a main clause,** such as an introductory element or a nonessential modifier (pp. 425, 427):

  Although the airline campaign failed**,** many advertising agencies**,** including some clever ones**,** copied its underlying message.

Semicolon

The *semicolon* chiefly separates equal and balanced sentence elements. Often the first clause creates an expectation, and the second clause fulfills the expectation.

- **It separates complementary main clauses that are *not* linked by a coordinating conjunction** (previous page):

  The airline campaign had highlighted only half the story**;** the other half was buried in the copy.

- **It separates complementary main clauses that are related by a conjunctive adverb or other transitional expression** (opposite):

  The campaign should not have stressed the pilots' insecurity**;** instead, the campaign should have stressed the improved performance resulting from that insecurity.

; 29a

Colon

The *colon* chiefly separates unequal sentence elements.

- **It separates a main clause from a following explanation or summary,** which may or may not be a main clause (pp. 466–68):

  Many successful advertising campaigns have used this message**:** the anxious seller is harder working and smarter than the competitor.

2. The computer is not the first new technology in music the pipe organ and saxophone were also technological breakthroughs in their day.
3. Musicians have always experimented with new technology audiences have always resisted the experiments.
4. Most computer musicians are not merely following the latest fad they are discovering new sounds and new ways to manipulate sound.

5. Few musicians have abandoned acoustic instruments most value acoustic sounds as much as electronic sounds.

Exercise 29.2 Sentence combining: Related main clauses

Combine each of the following sets of three sentences into one sentence containing only two main clauses, and insert a semicolon between the clauses. You will have to add, delete, change, and rearrange words. Most items have more than one possible answer.

Example:

The painter Andrew Wyeth is widely admired. He is not universally admired. Some critics view his work as sentimental.

The painter Andrew Wyeth is widely but not universally admired; some critics view his work as sentimental.

1. Electronic instruments are prevalent in jazz. They are also prevalent in rock music. They are less common in classical music.
2. Jazz and rock change rapidly. They nourish experimentation. They nourish improvisation.
3. Traditional classical music does not change. Its notes and instrumentation were established by a composer. The composer was writing decades or centuries ago.
4. Contemporary classical music can not only draw on tradition. It can also respond to innovations. These are innovations such as jazz rhythms and electronic sounds.
5. Much contemporary electronic music is more than just one type of music. It is more than just jazz, rock, or classical. It is a fusion of all three.

29b Use a semicolon between main clauses related by *however, for example,* and so on.

Two kinds of words can relate main clauses: **conjunctive adverbs,** such as *consequently, hence, however, indeed,* and *thus* (see p. 269), and other **transitional expressions,** such as *even so, for example,* and *of course* (see pp. 85–86). When either type of word connects two main clauses, the clauses should be separated by a semicolon:

An American immigrant, Levi Strauss, invented blue jeans in the 1860s; eventually, his product clothed working men throughout the West.

The position of the semicolon between main clauses never changes, but the conjunctive adverb or transitional expression may move around within a clause. The adverb or expression is usually set off with a comma or commas (see pp. 429–30):

Blue jeans have become fashionable all over the world; however, the American originators still wear more jeans than anyone else.

Blue jeans have become fashionable all over the world; the American originators, however, still wear more jeans than anyone else.

Its mobility distinguishes a conjunctive adverb or transitional expression from other connecting words, such as coordinating and subordinating conjunctions. See page 269 on this distinction.

Note If you use a comma or no punctuation at all between main clauses connected by a conjunctive adverb or transitional expression, you will produce a comma splice or a fused sentence. (See Chapter 18.)

Exercise 29.3 Punctuating main clauses related by conjunctive adverbs or transitional expressions

Insert a semicolon in each of the following sentences to separate main clauses related by a conjunctive adverb or transitional expression. Also insert a comma or commas where needed to set off the adverb or expression.

Example:

He knew that tickets for the movie would sell out quickly therefore he bought tickets online in advance.

He knew that tickets for the movie would sell out quickly; therefore, he bought tickets online in advance.

1. Music is a form of communication like language the basic elements however are not letters but notes.
2. Computers can process any information that can be represented numerically as a result they can process musical information.
3. A computer's ability to process music depends on what software it can run it must moreover be connected to a system that converts electrical vibration into sound.
4. Computers and their sound systems can produce many different sounds indeed the number of possible sounds is infinite.
5. The powerful music computers are very expensive therefore they are used only by professional musicians.

Exercise 29.4 Sentence combining: Main clauses related by conjunctive adverbs or transitional expressions

; 29b

Combine each set of three sentences below into one sentence containing only two main clauses. Connect the clauses with the conjunctive adverb or transitional expression in parentheses, and separate them with a semicolon. Be sure the adverbs and expressions are punctuated appropriately. You will have to add, delete, change, and rearrange words. Each item has more than one possible answer.

Example:

The Albanians censored their news. We got little news from them. And what we got was unreliable. (*therefore*)

The Albanians censored their news; therefore, the little news we got from them was unreliable.

1. Most music computers are too expensive for the average consumer. Digital keyboard instruments can be inexpensive. They are widely available. (*however*)

2. Inside the keyboard is a small computer. The computer controls a sound synthesizer. The instrument can both process and produce music. (*consequently*)
3. The person playing the keyboard presses keys or manipulates other controls. The computer and synthesizer convert these signals. The signals are converted into vibrations and sounds. (*immediately*)
4. The inexpensive keyboards can perform only a few functions. To the novice computer musician, the range is exciting. The range includes drum rhythms and simulated instruments. (*still*)
5. Would-be musicians can orchestrate whole songs. They start from just the melody lines. They need never again play "Chopsticks." (*thus*)

29c Use a semicolon to separate main clauses when they are long or contain commas, even with a coordinating conjunction.

We normally use a comma with a coordinating conjunction such as *and* or *but* between main clauses (see p. 422). But a semicolon makes a sentence easier to read when the main clauses are long and complicated or contain commas:

> By a conscious effort of the mind, we can stand aloof from actions and their consequences; and all things, good and bad, go by us like a torrent.
>
> —Henry David Thoreau

> I doubt if the texture of Southern life is any more grotesque than that of the rest of the nation, but it does seem evident that the Southern writer is particularly adept at recognizing the grotesque; and to recognize the grotesque, you have to have some notion of what is not grotesque and why.
>
> —Flannery O'Connor

29d Use semicolons to separate items in a series when they are long or contain commas.

; 29d

We normally use commas to separate items in a series (see p. 433). But when the items are long or contain commas, semicolons help readers identify the items:

> The custody case involved Amy Dalton, the child; Ellen and Mark Dalton, the parents; and Ruth and Hal Blum, the grandparents.

> One may even reasonably advance the claim that the sort of communication that really counts, and is therefore embodied into permanent records, is primarily written; that "words fly away, but written messages endure," as the Latin saying put it two thousand years ago; and that there is no basic significance to at least fifty percent of the oral interchange that goes on among all sorts of persons, high and low.
>
> —Mario Pei

Exercise 29.5 Punctuating long main clauses and series items

Substitute semicolons for commas in the following sentences to separate main clauses or series items that are long or contain commas.

Example:

After graduation he debated whether to settle in San Francisco, which was temperate but far from his parents, New York City, which was exciting but expensive, or Atlanta, which was close to home but already familiar.

After graduation he debated whether to settle in San Francisco, which was temperate but far from his parents; New York City, which was exciting but expensive; or Atlanta, which was close to home but already familiar.

1. The Indian subcontinent is separated from the rest of the world by clear barriers: the Bay of Bengal and the Arabian Sea to the east and west, respectively, the Indian Ocean to the south, and 1600 miles of mountain ranges to the north.
2. In the north of India are the world's highest mountains, the Himalayas, and farther south are fertile farmlands, unpopulated deserts, and rain forests.
3. India is a nation of ethnic and linguistic diversity, with numerous religions, including Hinduism, Islam, and Christianity, with distinct castes and ethnic groups, and with sixteen languages, including the official Hindi and the "associate official" English.
4. Between the seventeenth and nineteenth centuries, the British colonized most of India, taking control of government, the bureaucracy, and industry, and they assumed a social position above all Indians.
5. During British rule the Indians' own unresolved differences and their frustrations with the British erupted in violent incidents such as the Sepoy Mutiny, which began on February 26, 1857, and lasted two years, the Amritsar Massacre on April 13, 1919, and violence between Hindus and Muslims during World War II that resulted in the separation of Pakistan from India.

29e Use the semicolon only where required.

Semicolons do not separate unequal sentence elements and should not be overused.

1 Delete or replace any semicolon that separates a subordinate clause or a phrase from a main clause.

The semicolon does not separate subordinate clauses from main clauses or phrases from main clauses:

Faulty Pygmies are in danger of extinction; because of encroaching development.

Revised Pygmies are in danger of extinction because of encroaching development.

Faulty According to African authorities; only about 35,000 Pygmies exist today.

Revised According to African authorities, only about 35,000 Pygmies exist today.

Note Many readers regard a phrase or subordinate clause set off with a semicolon as a kind of sentence fragment. (See Chapter 17.)

2 Delete or replace any semicolon that introduces a series or explanation.

Colons and dashes, not semicolons, introduce series, explanations, and so forth. (See pp. 466 and 469.)

Faulty Teachers have heard all sorts of reasons why students do poorly; psychological problems, family illness, too much work, too little time.

Revised Teachers have heard all sorts of reasons why students do poorly: psychological problems, family illness, too much work, too little time.

Revised Teachers have heard all sorts of reasons why students do poorly—psychological problems, family illness, too much work, too little time.

3 Use the semicolon sparingly.

Use the semicolon only occasionally. Many semicolons in a passage, even when they are required by rule, often indicate repetitive sentence structure. To revise a passage with too many semicolons, you'll need to restructure your sentences, not just remove the semicolons. (See Chapter 26 for tips on varying sentences.)

Semicolon overused

The Make-a-Wish Foundation helps sick children; it grants the wishes of children who are terminally ill. The foundation learns of a child's wish; the information usually comes from parents, friends, or hospital staff; the wish may be for a special toy, a trip to the circus, or a visit to Disneyland. The foundation grants some wishes with its own funds; for other wishes it appeals to those who have what the child desires.

Revised

The Make-a-Wish Foundation grants the wishes of children who are terminally ill. From parents, friends, or hospital staff, the foundation learns of a child's wish for a special toy, a trip to the circus, or a visit to Disneyland. It grants some wishes with its own funds; for other wishes it appeals to those who have what the child desires.

; 29e

Exercise 29.6 Revising: Misused or overused semicolons

Revise the following sentences to eliminate misused or overused semicolons, substituting other punctuation as appropriate.

Example:

The doctor gave everyone the same advice; get exercise.
The doctor gave everyone the same advice: get exercise.

1. The main religion in India is Hinduism; a way of life as well as a theology and philosophy.
2. Unlike Christianity and Judaism; Hinduism is a polytheistic religion; with deities numbering in the hundreds.
3. Hinduism is unlike many other religions; it allows its creeds and practices to vary widely from place to place and person to person. Other religions have churches; Hinduism does not. Other religions have principal prophets and holy books; Hinduism does not. Other religions center on specially trained priests or other leaders; Hinduism promotes the individual as his or her own priest.
4. In Hindu belief there are four types of people; reflective, emotional, active, and experimental.
5. Each type of person has a different technique for realizing the true, immortal self; which has infinite existence, infinite knowledge, and infinite joy.

Exercise 29.7 Revising: Semicolons

Insert semicolons in the following paragraph wherever they are needed. Eliminate any misused or needless semicolons, substituting other punctuation as appropriate.

The set, sounds, and actors in the movie captured the essence of horror films. The set was ideal; dark, deserted streets, trees dipping their branches over the sidewalks, mist hugging the ground and creeping up to meet the trees, looming shadows of unlighted, turreted houses. The sounds, too, were appropriate, especially terrifying was the hard, hollow sound of footsteps echoing throughout the film. But the best feature of the movie was its actors; all of them tall, pale, and thin to the point of emaciation. With one exception, they were dressed uniformly in gray and had gray hair. The exception was an actress who dressed only in black; as if to set off her pale yellow, nearly white, long hair; the only color in the film. The glinting black eyes of another actor stole almost every scene, indeed, they were the source of all the film's mischief.

Note See page 477 for a punctuation exercise combining semicolons with other marks of punctuation.

30 The Apostrophe

Chapter essentials

- Use the apostrophe to show possession in singular and plural words (below).
- Do not use the apostrophe in plural nouns or in singular verbs ending in *-s* (p. 454).
- Do not use the apostrophe in personal or relative pronouns (p. 455).
- Use the apostrophe to show omissions in contractions (p. 455).

Visit MyWritingLab™ for more resources on the apostrophe.

Unlike other punctuation marks, which separate words, the apostrophe (') appears as *part* of a word to indicate possession or the omission of one or more letters.

30a Use the apostrophe to show possession.

In English the **possessive case** shows ownership or possession of one person or thing by another. For nouns and indefinite pronouns, possession may be shown with an *of* phrase (*the hair of the dog, the interest of everyone*), or it may be shown with the addition of an apostrophe and, usually, an *-s* (*the dog***'s** *hair, everyone***'s** *interest*). Only certain pronouns do not use apostrophes for possession: *mine, yours, his, hers, its, ours, theirs,* and *whose* (p. 455).

Note Apostrophes are easy to misuse. Always check your drafts to ensure the following:

- **Every word ending in *-s* neither omits a needed apostrophe nor adds an unneeded one.**
- **The apostrophe or apostrophe-plus-*s* is an *addition*.** Before this addition, always spell the name of the owner or owners without dropping or adding letters: *girls* becomes *girls',* not *girl's.*

1 Add -'s to singular nouns and indefinite pronouns.

Bill Boughton**'s** skillful card tricks amaze children.

Some of the earth**'s** forests are regenerating.

Everyone**'s** fitness can be improved through exercise. [Indefinite pronoun.]

Add *-'s* as well to singular nouns that end in *-s*:

Henry James**'s** novels reward the patient reader.

Los Angeles**'s** weather is mostly warm.

The business**'s** customers filed suit.

Uses and misuses of the apostrophe

Uses of the apostrophe

- **Use an apostrophe to form the possessives of nouns and indefinite pronouns** (previous page and opposite).

Singular	Plural
Ms. Park's	the Parks'
lawyer's	lawyers'
everyone's	two weeks'

- **Use an apostrophe to form contractions** (p. 455).

it's a girl	shouldn't
you're	won't

- **The apostrophe is optional for plurals of abbreviations, dates, and words or characters named as words** (p. 457).

MAs or MA's	Cs or C's
1960s or 1960's	*ifs* or *if*'s

Misuses of the apostrophe

- **Do not use an apostrophe plus -*s* to form the possessives of plural nouns** (p. 454). Instead, first form the plural with -*s* and *then* add the apostrophe.

Not	But
the Kim's car	the Kims' car
boy's fathers	boys' fathers
babie's care	babies' care

- **Do not use an apostrophe to form plurals of nouns** (p. 454).

Not	But
book's are	books are
the Freed's	the Freeds

- **Do not use an apostrophe with verbs ending in -*s*** (p. 454).

Not	But
swim's	swims

- **Do not use an apostrophe to form the possessives of personal and relative pronouns** (p. 455).

Not	But
it's toes	its toes
who's car	whose car

30a

Exception We often do not pronounce the possessive -*s* of a few singular nouns ending in an *s* or *z* sound: names with more than one *s* sound (*Moses*), names that sound like plurals (*Rivers, Bridges*), and nouns followed by a word beginning in *s*. In these cases, many writers add only the apostrophe to show possession.

Moses' mother concealed him in the bulrushes.

Joan Rivers' career spanned nearly six decades.

For conscience' sake Shawn confessed his lie.

However, usage varies widely, and the final *-s* is not wrong with words like these (*Moses's*, *Rivers's*, *conscience's*).

2 Add *-'s* to plural nouns not ending in *-s*.

The bill establishes children's rights.

Publicity grabbed the media's attention.

3 Add only an apostrophe to plural nouns ending in *-s*.

Workers' incomes have not risen much over the past decade.

Many students benefit from several years' work after high school.

The Jameses' talents are extraordinary.

Note the difference in the possessives of singular and plural words ending in *-s*. The singular form usually takes the apostrophe and *-s*: *James's*. The plural takes only the apostrophe: *Jameses'*.

4 Add *-'s* only to the last word of compound words or word groups.

The council president's speech was a bore.

The brother-in-law's business failed.

Taxes are always somebody else's fault.

5 With two or more words, add *-'s* to one or both depending on meaning.

Individual possession

Zimbale's and Mason's comedy techniques are similar. [Each comedian has his own technique.]

Joint possession

The children recovered despite their mother and father's neglect. [The mother and father were jointly neglectful.]

Exercise 30.1 Forming possessives

Form the possessive case of each word or word group in brackets.

Example:

The [men] blood pressures were higher than the [women].

The men's blood pressures were higher than the women's.

1. In works for adults and teens, fiction writers often explore [people] relationship to nature and the environment.
2. For example, [Carl Hiaasen] inventive and humorous plots often revolve around endangered [species] habitats.
3. His [characters] personalities are often eccentric and extreme.

4. Most of [Hiaasen] books for adults and younger readers address [Florida] natural landscape and challenges to it.
5. For instance, in *Hoot*, [Hiaasen] first novel for younger readers, endangered [owls] habitat will be destroyed if a [business] plans to build a new restaurant proceed.
6. In *Flush* the main [character] father is in jail for sinking a casino boat that regularly emptied raw sewage into [Florida] water.
7. In *Scat* two [students] investigation into a [teacher] disappearance leads to an environmental mystery.
8. Two of [Margaret Atwood] recent novels are about several [individuals] survival following a devastating environmental crisis and a plague that has killed nearly all of the residents of a city.
9. The first of the two books, *Oryx and Crake*, involves characters with those names but is told from one [man] perspective, that of a character named Jimmy.
10. Readers learn [Jimmy] version of the events that have occurred.
11. Gradually readers learn about [Oryx and Crake] lives and why they are not struggling for survival along with Jimmy.
12. In the second Atwood book, *The Year of the Flood*, readers encounter a similar story, but through two [women] experiences.
13. In both books, most of the [city] residents have died from an outbreak of disease.
14. [Everyone] home is empty.
15. Some readers may be unsettled by these two [books] visions of the future.

30b Delete apostrophes where they are not required.

Not all words ending in *-s* take an apostrophe. Three kinds of words are especially likely to attract unneeded apostrophes.

Plural nouns

Form most plural nouns by adding *-s* or *-es* (*boys, Smiths, families, Joneses*). Never add an apostrophe to form the plural:

Faulty The unleashed dog's began traveling in a pack.
Revised The unleashed dogs began traveling in a pack.

Faulty The Jones' and Bass' were feuding.
Revised The Jones**es** and Bass**es** were feuding.

Singular verbs

Do not add an apostrophe to present-tense verbs used with *he, she, it,* and other third-person singular subjects. These verbs always end in *-s* but *never* with an apostrophe:

Faulty The subway break's down less often now.
Revised The subway breaks down less often now.

Faulty It run's more reliably.

Revised It runs more reliably.

Possessive personal and relative pronouns

His, hers, its, ours, yours, and *theirs* are possessive forms of the personal pronouns *he, she, it, we, you,* and *they. Whose* is the possessive form of the relative pronoun *who.* These possessives do not take apostrophes:

Faulty The frog is her's, not their's. It's skin is speckled.

Revised The frog is hers, not theirs. Its skin is speckled.

The possessive pronouns are often confused with contractions, such as *it's, you're,* and *who's.* See below.

Exercise 30.2 Distinguishing between plurals and possessives

Supply the appropriate form—possessive or plural—of each word given in brackets. Some answers require apostrophes, and some do not.

Example:

Hawaiian [shirt], each with [it] own loud design, hung in the window.

Hawaiian shirts, each with its own loud design, hung in the window.

1. Demeter may be the oldest of the Greek [god], older than Zeus.
2. Many prehistoric [culture] had earth [goddess] like Demeter.
3. In myth she is the earth mother, which means that the responsibility for the fertility of both [animal] and [plant] is [she].
4. The [goddess] festival came at harvest time, with [it] celebration of bounty.
5. The [people] [prayer] to Demeter thanked her for grain and other [gift].

30c Use an apostrophe to indicate the omission in a standard contraction.

Contractions are common in speech and in informal writing. They may also be used to relax style in more formal kinds of writing, as they are in this handbook. But be aware that some readers disapprove of contractions in any kind of formal writing.

Standard contractions

it is, it has	it's	let us	let's
he is	he's	does not	doesn't
she is	she's	were not	weren't
they are	they're	class of 2014	class of '14
you are	you're	of the clock	o'clock
who is, who has	who's	madam	ma'am

Contractions vs. possessive pronouns

Contractions are easily confused with possessive pronouns:

Contraction	Possessive pronoun
it's	its
they're	their
you're	your
who's	whose

Faulty Legislators know their going to have to cut the budget to eliminate it's deficit.

Revised Legislators know they're going to have to cut the budget to eliminate its deficit.

If you tend to confuse these forms, search for both spellings throughout your drafts. Then test for correctness:

- **If you intend the word to contain the verb *is, has,* or *are,* use an apostrophe.**

It's [It is] a great party.
They're [They are] my friends.
Who's [Who is] coming with us?
It's [It has] happened again.
You're [You are] right.
Who's [Who has] responded?

- **If you intend the word to show possession, don't use an apostrophe.**

Its tail was wagging.
Their car broke down.
Your eyes are brown.
Whose book is that?

Exercise 30.3 Forming contractions

Form contractions from each set of words below. Use each contraction in a complete sentence.

Example:

we are: we're
We're open to ideas.

30c

1. she would
2. could not
3. they are
4. he is
5. do not
6. she will
7. hurricane of 1962
8. is not
9. it is
10. will not

Exercise 30.4 Revising: Contractions and possessive pronouns

Revise the following sentences to correct mistakes in the use of contractions and possessive pronouns. Mark the number preceding any sentence that is already correct.

Example:

The agencies give they're employees they're birthdays off.
The agencies give their employees their birthdays off.

1. Many students seek help from the college writing center when their writing papers for their classes.

2. The writing center has expanded it's hours: it's now open until 10 PM every night.
3. The writing center also offers online tutoring to students whose schedules make face-to-face meetings difficult.
4. For online tutoring, students can submit they're papers by computer when they're ready to receive help.
5. In a survey, students who use the writing center responded that it's a good source of feedback for they're writing.

30d The apostrophe is optional to mark plural abbreviations, dates, and words or characters named as words.

You'll sometimes see apostrophes used to form the plurals of abbreviations (BA's), dates (1900's), and words or characters named as words (*but*'s). However, most current style guides do not recommend the apostrophe in these cases.

BAs PhDs
1990s 2000s

The sentence has too many *but*s.
Two *3*s end the zip code.

Note Italicize or underline a word or character named as a word (see p. 488), but not the added *-s*.

Exercise 30.5 Revising: Apostrophes

In the following paragraph correct any mistakes in the use of the apostrophe or any confusion between contractions and possessive pronouns.

People who's online experiences include blogging, Web cams, and social-networking sites are often used to seeing the details of other peoples private lives. Many are also comfortable sharing they're own opinions, photographs, and videos with family, friend's, and even stranger's. However, they need to realize that employers and even the government can see they're information, too. Employers commonly search for applicants' names on social-networking Web sites such as *Twitter* and *Facebook*. Many large companies read their employees outbound e-mail. People can take steps to protect their personal information by adjusting the privacy settings on their social-networking pages. They can avoid posting photos of themselves that they wouldnt want an employer to see. They can avoid sending personal e-mail while their at work. Its the individuals responsibility to keep certain information private.

Note See page 477 for a punctuation exercise involving apostrophes along with other marks of punctuation.

31 Quotation Marks

Chapter essentials

- Use quotation marks to enclose direct quotations (below and pp. 460–61).
- Use quotation marks to enclose titles of works that are parts of other works (p. 462).
- Use quotation marks to enclose words being used in a special sense (p. 463).
- Do not use quotation marks with the title of your own paper, a common nickname, or slang (p. 463).
- Place quotation marks inside or outside other marks according to standard practice (p. 464).

Visit MyWritingLab™ for more resources on quotation marks.

Quotation marks—either double (" ") or single (' ')—mainly enclose direct quotations from speech and from writing. The box on the next two pages summarizes this use and the combination of quotation marks with commas, semicolons, ellipsis marks, and other punctuation. Additional information on using quotations appears elsewhere in this book:

- **Using commas with signal phrases introducing quotations,** pages 436–37.
- **Using brackets and the ellipsis mark to indicate changes in quotations,** pages 472–75.
- **Quoting sources versus paraphrasing or summarizing them,** pages 599–606.
- **Integrating quotations into your text,** pages 608–12.
- **Acknowledging the sources of quotations to avoid plagiarism,** pages 618–19.
- **Formatting long prose quotations and poetry quotations** in MLA style, pages 681–82; Chicago style, page 758; and APA style, page 783.

Note Always use quotation marks in pairs, one at the beginning of a quotation and one at the end.

31a Use double quotation marks to enclose direct quotations.

Direct quotations report what someone has said or written in the exact words of the original. Enclose most direct quotations in quotation marks.

Handling quotations from speech or writing

Direct and indirect quotation

Direct quotation

According to Lewis Thomas, "We are, perhaps uniquely among the earth's creatures, the worrying animal. We worry away our lives."

Note Do not use quotation marks with a direct quotation that is set off from your text. See the note on the next page.

Quotation within quotation

Quoting a phrase by Lewis Thomas, the author adds, "We are 'the worrying animal.'"

Indirect quotation

Lewis Thomas says that human beings are unique among animals in their worrying.

Quotation marks with other punctuation marks

Commas and periods

Human beings are the "worrying animal," says Thomas.
Thomas calls human beings "the worrying animal."

Semicolons and colons

Machiavelli says that "the majority of men live content"; in contrast, Thomas calls us "the worrying animal."

Thomas believes that we are "the worrying animal": we spend our lives afraid and restless.

Question marks, exclamation points, dashes

When part of your own sentence:

Who said that human beings are "the worrying animal"?
Imagine saying that we human beings "worry away our lives"!
Thomas's phrase—"the worrying animal"—seems too narrow.

When part of the original quotation:

"Will you discuss this with me?" she asked.
"I demand that you discuss this with me!" she yelled.
"Please, won't you—" She paused.

Altering quotations

Brackets for additions

"We [human beings] worry away our lives," says Thomas.

Brackets for altered capitalization

"[T]he worrying animal" is what Thomas calls us. He says that "[w]e worry away our lives."

(continued)

" " 31a

Handling quotations from speech or writing
(continued)

Ellipsis marks for omissions

"We are . . . the worrying animal," says Thomas.

Worrying places us "uniquely among the earth's creatures. . . . We worry away our lives."

Punctuating signal phrases with quotations

Introductory signal phrase

He says, "We worry away our lives."

She quotes these words by Lewis Thomas: "We are, perhaps uniquely among the earth's creatures, the worrying animal."

Thomas says that "the worrying animal" is afraid and restless.

Concluding signal phrase

We are "the worrying animal," says Thomas.

"Who says?" she demanded.

"I do!" he shouted.

Interrupting signal phrase

"We are," says Thomas, "perhaps uniquely among the earth's creatures, the worrying animal."

"I do not like the idea," she said; "however, I agree with it."

Human beings are "the worrying animal," says Thomas. "We worry away our lives."

> "Fortunately," said the psychoanalyst Karen Horney, "analysis is not the only way to resolve inner conflicts. Life itself still remains a very effective therapist."

" "
31b

Notes Do not use quotation marks with a direct quotation that is set off from your text. For handling such quotations, see pages 681–82 (MLA style), 758 (Chicago style), and 783 (APA style).

Also do not use quotation marks with an **indirect quotation**, which reports what someone said or wrote but not in the exact words:

> The psychoanalyst Karen Horney remarked that analysis is but one solution to personal problems, for life is a good therapist.

(See also pp. 600–03 on paraphrasing quotations.)

31b Use single quotation marks to enclose a quotation within a quotation.

When you quote someone, use double quotation marks. When the material you quote contains yet another quotation, distinguish the two by enclosing the second one in single quotation marks:

"In formulating any philosophy," Woody Allen writes, "the first consideration must always be: What can we know? Descartes hinted at the problem when he wrote, 'My mind can never know my body, although it has become quite friendly with my leg.'"

Notice that two different quotation marks appear at the end of the sentence—one single (to finish the interior quotation) and one double (to finish the main quotation).

Exercise 31.1 Using double and single quotation marks

Insert double and single quotation marks as needed in the following sentences. Mark the number preceding any sentence that is already correct.

Example:

The purpose of this book, explains the preface, is to examine the meaning of the expression Dance is poetry.

"The purpose of this book," explains the preface, "is to examine the meaning of the expression 'Dance is poetry.'"

1. Why, the lecturer asked, do we say Bless you! or something else when people sneeze but not acknowledge coughs, hiccups, and other eruptions?
2. She said that sneezes have always been regarded differently.
3. Sneezes feel more uncontrollable than some other eruptions, she said.
4. Unlike coughs and hiccups, she explained, sneezes feel as if they come from inside the head.
5. She concluded, People thus wish to recognize a sneeze, if only with a Gosh.

31c Set off quotations of dialog according to standard practice.

" " 31c

When quoting conversations, begin a new paragraph for each speaker:

> "What shall I call you? Your name?" Andrews whispered rapidly, as with a high squeak the latch of the door rose.
>
> "Elizabeth," she said. "Elizabeth."
>
> —Graham Greene, *The Man Within*

When you quote a single speaker for more than one paragraph, put quotation marks at the beginning of each paragraph but at the end of only the last paragraph. The absence of quotation marks at the end of a paragraph tells readers that the speech is continuing.

Note Quotation marks are optional for unspoken thoughts or imagined dialog:

I asked myself, "How can we solve this?"
I asked myself, How can we solve this?

31d Put quotation marks around the titles of works that are parts of other works.

Use quotation marks to enclose the titles of works that are published or released within larger works: see the following box. As in the second article title in the box, use single quotation marks for a quotation within a quoted title, and enclose all punctuation in the title within the quotation marks. Use italics or underlining for all other titles, such as books, plays, periodicals, and movies. (See pp. 486–87.)

Titles to be enclosed in quotation marks

Other titles should be italicized or underlined. (See pp. 486–87.)

Songs
"Let It Be"
"America the Beautiful"

Short poems
"On Virtue"
"Sunday Morning"

Articles in periodicals
"Comedy and Tragedy Transposed"
"Does 'Scaring' Work?"

Essays
"Politics and the English Language"
"Joey: A 'Mechanical Boy'"

Unpublished speeches
"Horses and Healing"

Short stories
"The Battler"
"The Gift of the Magi"

Pages or documents on Web sites
"Readers' Page" (on site *Friends of Prufrock*)

Episodes of television and radio programs
"The Mexican Connection" (on *60 Minutes*)
"Cooking with Clams" (on *Eating In*)

Subdivisions of books
"Voyage to the Houyhnhnms" (Part 4 of *Gulliver's Travels*)
"The Mast Head" (Chapter 35 of *Moby-Dick*)

" " 31d

Note Some academic disciplines do not require quotation marks for titles within source citations. See pages 766–67 (APA style) and 797–98 (CSE style).

Exercise 31.2 Quoting titles

Insert quotation marks as needed for titles in the following sentences. If quotation marks should be used instead of italics, insert them.

Example:

She published an article titled Marriage in Grace Paley's An Interest in Life.

She published an article titled "Marriage in Grace Paley's 'An Interest in Life.'"

1. In Chapter 8, titled *How to Be Interesting,* the author explains the art of conversation.
2. The Beatles' song Let It Be reminds Martin of his uncle.
3. The article that appeared in *Mental Health* was titled *Children of Divorce Ask, "Why?"*
4. In the encyclopedia the discussion under Modern Art fills less than a column.
5. One prizewinning essay, *Cowgirls on Wall Street,* first appeared in *Entrepreneur* magazine.

31e Quotation marks may be used to enclose words used in a special sense.

On film sets, movable "wild walls" make a one-walled room seem four-walled on film.

Writers often put quotation marks around a word they are using with irony—that is, with a different or even opposite meaning than usual:

With all the "compassion" it could muster, the agency turned away two-thirds of those seeking help. —Joan Simonson

Readers quickly tire of such irony, though, so use it sparingly. Prefer language that expresses your meaning exactly. (See Chapter 38.)

Note For words you are defining, use italics or underlining. (See p. 488.)

31f Use quotation marks only where they are required.

Don't use quotation marks in the titles of your papers unless they contain or are themselves direct quotations:

Not "The Death Wish in One Poem by Robert Frost"
But The Death Wish in One Poem by Robert Frost
Or The Death Wish in "Stopping by Woods on a Snowy Evening"

Don't use quotation marks to enclose common nicknames or technical terms that are not being defined:

Not As President, "Jimmy" Carter preferred to use his nickname.
But As President, Jimmy Carter preferred to use his nickname.

Not "Mitosis" in a cell is fascinating to watch.
But Mitosis in a cell is fascinating to watch.

Don't use quotation marks in an attempt to justify or apologize for slang and trite expressions that are inappropriate to your writing. If slang is appropriate, use it without quotation marks.

Not We should support the President in his "hour of need" rather than "wimp out" on him.

But We should give the President the support he needs rather than turn away like cowards.

(See pp. 500 and 517 for more on slang and trite expressions.)

31g Place other punctuation marks inside or outside quotation marks according to standard practice.

The position of another punctuation mark inside or outside a closing quotation mark depends on what the other mark is, whether it appears in the quotation, and whether a source citation immediately follows the quotation.

1 Place commas and periods inside quotation marks.

Commas or periods fall *inside* closing quotation marks, even when (as in the third example) single and double quotation marks are combined:

Swift uses irony in his essay "A Modest Proposal."

Many first-time readers are shocked to see infants described as "delicious."

"'A Modest Proposal,'" writes one critic, "is so outrageous that it cannot be believed."

(See pp. 436–37 for the use of commas, as in the preceding example, to separate a quotation from a signal phrase such as *writes one critic.*)

Exception When a parenthetical source citation immediately follows a quotation, place any period or comma *after* the citation:

One critic calls the essay "outrageous" (Olms 26).

Partly because of "the cool calculation of its delivery" (Olms 27), Swift's satire still chills a modern reader.

See pages 641–43 for more on placing parenthetical citations.

2 Place colons and semicolons outside quotation marks.

Some years ago the slogan in elementary education was "learning by playing"; now educators are concerned with basic skills.

We all know what is meant by "inflation": more money buys less.

3 Place dashes, question marks, and exclamation points inside quotation marks only if they belong to the quotation.

When a dash, question mark, or exclamation point is part of the quotation, put it *inside* quotation marks. Don't use any other punctuation such as a period or a comma:

"But must you—" Marcia hesitated, afraid of the answer.

"Go away!" I yelled.

Did you say, "Who is she?" [When both your sentence and the quotation would end in a question mark or exclamation point, use only the mark in the quotation.]

When a dash, question mark, or exclamation point applies only to the larger sentence, not to the quotation, place it *outside* quotation marks—again, with no other punctuation:

One evocative line in English poetry—"After many a summer dies the swan"—comes from Alfred, Lord Tennyson.

Who said, "Now cracks a noble heart"?

The woman called me "stupid"!

Exercise 31.3 Revising: Quotation marks

The italic words in the following sentences are titles or direct quotations. Insert quotation marks where italics should not be used. Be sure that other marks of punctuation are correctly placed inside or outside the quotation marks.

Example:

The award-winning essay is *Science and Values.*
The award-winning essay is "Science and Values."

1. In the title essay of her book *The Death of the Moth and Other Essays,* Virginia Woolf describes the last moments of a *frail and diminutive body.*
2. An insect's death may seem insignificant, but the moth is, in Woolf's words, *life, a pure bead.*
3. The moth's struggle against death, *indifferent, impersonal,* is heroic.
4. Where else but in such a bit of life could one see a protest so *superb*?
5. At the end Woolf sees the moth lying *most decently and uncomplainingly composed*; in death it finds dignity.

Exercise 31.4 Revising: Quotation marks

Insert quotation marks as needed in the following paragraphs.

In a history class we talked about a passage from the *Gettysburg Address,* the speech delivered by President Abraham Lincoln on November 19, 1863:

> Four score and seven years ago our fathers brought forth on this continent, a new nation, conceived in Liberty, and dedicated to the proposition that all men are created equal. Now we are engaged in a great civil war, testing whether that nation, or any nation so conceived and so dedicated, can long endure.

What was Lincoln referring to in the first sentence? the teacher asked. Perhaps we should define *score* first. Explaining that a score is twenty years, she said that Lincoln was referring to the document in which the colonies had declared independence from England eighty-seven years earlier, in 1776.

One student commented, Lincoln's decision to end slavery is implied in that first sentence. The President was calling on the authority of the Founding Fathers.

Lincoln gave the speech at the dedication of the National Cemetery in Gettysburg, Pennsylvania, another student added. It was the site of a very bloody Civil War battle.

A third student noted that in the second sentence Lincoln was posing the central question of the war: whether a nation founded on equality can long endure.

Note See page 477 for a punctuation exercise involving quotation marks along with other marks of punctuation.

32 Other Punctuation Marks

Chapter essentials

- Use the colon (:) to introduce and to separate (below).
- Use the dash (—) to set off interruptions (p. 469).
- Use parentheses (( )) to enclose parenthetical expressions and labels for lists within sentences (p. 471).
- Use brackets ([ ]) mainly to indicate changes in quotations (p. 472).
- Use the ellipsis mark (. . .) mainly to indicate omissions from quotations (p. 473).
- Use the slash (/) to separate options and lines of poetry (p. 476).

Visit MyWritingLab™ for more resources on other punctuation marks.

32a Use the colon to introduce and to separate.

The colon is mainly a mark of introduction: it signals that the words following will explain or amplify. The colon also has several conventional uses, such as in expressions of time.

In its main use as an introducer, a colon is *always* preceded by a complete **main clause**—a word group that can stand alone as a sentence because it contains a subject and a predicate and does not start with a subordinating word (see p. 263 for more on main clauses). A colon may or may not be followed by a main clause. This is one way the colon differs from the semicolon (see the box opposite). The colon is interchangeable with the dash, though the dash is more informal and more abrupt (see p. 469).

Distinguishing the colon and the semicolon

Colon

The colon is a mark of introduction that separates elements of *unequal* importance, such as statements and explanations or introductions and quotations. The first element must be a complete main clause; the second element need not be.

The business school caters to working students: it offers special evening courses in business writing, finance, and management.

The school has one goal: to train students to be responsible, competent businesspeople.

Semicolon

The semicolon separates elements of *equal* importance, almost always complete main clauses. (See p. 443.)

Few enrolling students know exactly what they want from the school; most hope generally for a managerial career.

Note Don't use a colon more than once in a sentence. The sentence should end with the element introduced by the colon.

1 Use a colon to introduce a concluding explanation, a series, an appositive, and some quotations.

Depending on your preference, a complete sentence *after* the colon may begin with a capital letter or a small letter. Just be consistent throughout an essay.

Explanation

Soul food is a varied cuisine: it includes spicy gumbos, black-eyed peas, and collard greens.

Soul food has a deceptively simple definition: the ethnic cooking of African Americans.

Sometimes a concluding explanation is preceded by *the following* or *as follows* and a colon:

A more precise definition might be the following: soul food draws on ingredients, cooking methods, and dishes that originated in Africa, were brought to the New World by slaves, and were modified or supplemented in the Caribbean and the American South.

Series (p. 433)

At least three soul food dishes are familiar to most Americans: fried chicken, barbecued spareribs, and sweet potato pie.

Appositive (pp. 266–67)

Soul food has one disadvantage: fat.

Certain expressions commonly introduce appositives, such as *namely* and *that is.* These expressions should *follow* the colon: *Soul food has one disadvantage: namely, fat.*

Quotation

The comma generally separates a signal phrase from a quotation (see pp. 436–37). But when you introduce a quotation with a complete sentence, use a colon instead:

> One soul food chef has a solution: "Soul food doesn't have to be greasy to taste good. Instead of using ham hocks to flavor beans, I use smoked turkey wings. The soulful, smoky taste remains, but without all the fat of pork."

2 Use a colon to separate titles and subtitles and the subdivisions of time.

Titles and subtitles	Time
Charles Dickens: An Introduction to His Novels	1:30 AM
Eros and Civilization: An Inquiry into Freud	12:26 PM

3 Use the colon only where required.

Use the colon only at the *end* of a main clause. Do not use it directly after a verb or preposition.

Not Two critically acclaimed movies directed by Steven Spielberg are: *Schindler's List* and *Saving Private Ryan.*

But Two critically acclaimed movies directed by Steven Spielberg are *Schindler's List* and *Saving Private Ryan.*

Not Shakespeare had the qualities of a Renaissance thinker, such as: humanism and an interest in Greek and Roman literature.

But Shakespeare had the qualities of a Renaissance thinker, such as humanism and an interest in Greek and Roman literature.

Exercise 32.1 Revising: Colons

Insert colons as needed in the following sentences, or delete colons that are misused.

Example:

Mix the ingredients as follows sift the flour and salt together, add the milk, and slowly beat in the egg yolk.

Mix the ingredients as follows: sift the flour and salt together, add the milk, and slowly beat in the egg yolk.

1. In remote areas of many developing countries, simple signs mark human habitation a dirt path, a few huts, smoke from a cooking fire.
2. In the built-up sections of industrialized countries, nature is all but obliterated by signs of human life, such as: houses, factories, skyscrapers, and highways.

3. The spectacle makes many question the words of Ecclesiastes 1.4 "One generation passeth away, and another cometh; but the earth abideth forever."
4. Yet many scientists see the future differently they hold that human beings have all the technology necessary to clean up the earth and restore the cycles of nature.
5. All that is needed is: a change in the attitudes of those who use technology.

32b Use a dash to indicate shifts in tone or thought and to set off some sentence elements.

The dash is mainly a mark of interruption: it signals an insertion or break.

Note In your papers, form a dash with two hyphens (--) or use the character called an em dash on your word processor. Do not add extra space around or between the hyphens or around the em dash.

1 Use a dash or dashes to indicate shifts and hesitations.

Shift in tone

The novel—if one can call it that—appeared in 2010.

Unfinished thought

If the book had a plot—but a plot would be conventional.

Hesitation in dialog

"I was worried you might think I had stayed away because I was influenced by—" He stopped and lowered his eyes.

Astonished, Howe said, "Influenced by what?"

"Well, by—" Blackburn hesitated and for an answer pointed to the table.

—Lionel Trilling

— 32b

2 Use a dash or dashes to emphasize nonessential elements.

Dashes may be used in place of commas or parentheses to set off and emphasize nonessential elements. (See the box on the next page.) Dashes are especially useful when these elements are internally punctuated. Be sure to use a pair of dashes when the element interrupts a main clause.

Appositive (p. 429)

The qualities Monet painted—bright sunlight, rich shadows, deep colors—abounded near the rivers and gardens he used as subjects.

Modifier

Though they are close together—separated by only a few blocks—the two neighborhoods could be in different countries.

Distinguishing dashes, commas, and parentheses

Dashes, commas, and parentheses may all set off nonessential elements.

Dashes

Dashes give the information the greatest emphasis:

Many students—including some employed by the college—disapprove of the new work rules.

Commas

Commas are less emphatic (p. 427):

Many students, including some employed by the college, disapprove of the new work rules.

Parentheses

Parentheses are the least emphatic, signaling that the information is just worth a mention (next page):

Many students (including some employed by the college) disapprove of the new work rules.

Parenthetical expression (opposite)

At any given time there exists an inventory of undiscovered embezzlement in—or more precisely not in—the country's businesses and banks.
—John Kenneth Galbraith

3 Use a dash to set off introductory series and concluding series and explanations.

Introductory series

Shortness of breath, skin discoloration or the sudden appearance of moles, persistent indigestion, the presence of small lumps—all these may signify cancer.

32b

A dash sets off concluding series and explanations more informally and more abruptly than a colon does (see p. 467):

Concluding series

The patient undergoes a battery of tests—imaging, blood work, perhaps even biopsy.

Concluding explanation

Many patients are disturbed by MRI imaging—by the need to keep still for long periods in an exceedingly small space.

4 Use the dash only where needed.

Don't use the dash when commas, semicolons, and periods are more appropriate. And don't use too many dashes. They can create a jumpy or breathy quality in writing.

Not In all his life—eighty-seven years—my great-grandfather never allowed his picture to be taken—not even once. He claimed the "black box"—the camera—would steal his soul.

But In all his eighty-seven years my great-grandfather did not allow his picture to be taken even once. He claimed the "black box"—the camera—would steal his soul.

Exercise 32.2 Revising: Dashes

Insert dashes as needed in the following sentences.

Example:

What would we do if someone like Adolf Hitler that monster appeared among us?

What would we do if someone like Adolf Hitler—that monster—appeared among us?

1. The movie-theater business is undergoing dramatic changes changes that may affect what movies are made and shown.
2. The closing of independent theaters, the control of theaters by fewer and fewer owners, and the increasing ownership of theaters by movie studios and distributors these changes may reduce the availability of noncommercial films.
3. Yet at the same time the number of movie screens is increasing primarily in multiscreen complexes so that smaller films may find more outlets.
4. The number of active movie screens that is, screens showing films or booked to do so is higher now than at any time since World War II.
5. The biggest theater complexes seem to be something else as well art galleries, amusement arcades, restaurants, spectacles.

32c Use parentheses to enclose parenthetical expressions and labels for lists within sentences.

( ) 32c

Parentheses *always* come in pairs: one before and one after the punctuated material.

1 Use parentheses to enclose parenthetical expressions.

Parenthetical expressions include explanations, digressions, and examples that may be helpful or interesting but are not essential to meaning. They are emphasized least when set off with a pair of parentheses instead of commas or dashes. (See the box on the facing page.)

The population of Philadelphia (now about 1.5 million) has declined since 1950.

Ariel (published in 1965) contains Sylvia Plath's last poems.

Note Don't put a comma before a parenthetical expression enclosed in parentheses:

Not The population of Philadelphia compares with that of Phoenix, (about 1.5 million).

But The population of Philadelphia compares with that of Phoenix (about 1.5 million).

If you use a comma, semicolon, or period after a parenthetical expression, place the mark *outside* the closing parenthesis:

Philadelphia has a larger African American population (over 40%), while Phoenix has a larger Latino population (over 40%).

If you enclose a complete sentence in parentheses, capitalize the sentence and place the closing period *inside* the closing parenthesis:

In general, coaches will tell you that scouts are just guys who can't coach. (But then, so are brain surgeons.) —Roy Blount

2 Use parentheses to enclose labels for lists within sentences.

Outside the Middle East, the countries with the largest oil reserves are (1) Venezuela (297 billion barrels), (2) Canada (179 billion barrels), and (3) Russia (116 billion barrels).

When you set a list off from your text, do not enclose such labels in parentheses.

Exercise 32.3 Revising: Parentheses

Insert parentheses as needed in the following sentences.

Example:

Students can find good-quality, inexpensive furniture for example, desks, tables, chairs, sofas, even beds in thrift shops.

Students can find good-quality, inexpensive furniture (for example, desks, tables, chairs, sofas, even beds) in thrift shops.

1. Many of those involved in the movie business agree that multiscreen complexes are good for two reasons: 1 they cut the costs of exhibitors, and 2 they offer more choices to audiences.
2. Those who produce and distribute films and not just the big studios argue that the multiscreen theaters give exhibitors too much power.
3. The major studios are buying movie theaters to gain control over important parts of the distribution process what gets shown and for how much money.
4. For twelve years 1938–50 the federal government forced the studios to sell all their movie theaters.
5. But because they now have more competition DVDs and the Internet, for instance, the studios are permitted to own theaters.

[ ]
32d

32d Use brackets within quotations to indicate your own comments or changes.

Brackets have specialized uses in mathematical equations, but their main use for all kinds of writing is to indicate that you have altered a quotation. If you need to explain, clarify, or correct the words of the writer you quote, place your additions in a pair of brackets:

> "That Chevron station [just outside Dallas] is one of the busiest in the nation," said a company spokesperson.

Use brackets if you need to alter the capitalization of a quotation so that it will fit into your sentence. (See also p. 474.)

> "[O]ne of the busiest in the nation" is how a company spokesperson described the station.

You may also use a bracketed word or words to substitute for parts of a quotation that would otherwise be unclear. In the following sentence, the bracketed word substitutes for *they* in the original:

> "Despite considerable achievements in other areas, [humans] still cannot control the weather and probably will never be able to do so."

See page 609 for more examples of using brackets with quotations.

The word *sic* (Latin for "in this manner") in brackets indicates that an error in the quotation appeared in the original and was not made by you. When following MLA style, do not italicize sic in brackets. Most other styles—including Chicago, APA, and CSE—do italicize *sic*.

> According to the newspaper report, "The car slammed thru [sic] the railing and into oncoming traffic."

Don't use *sic* to make fun of a writer or to note errors in a passage that is clearly nonstandard or illiterate.

Note Always acknowledge the sources of quotations in order to avoid plagiarism. (See pp. 603–05 and 618–20.)

32e Use the ellipsis mark to indicate omissions from quotations and pauses in speech.

. . . 32e

The **ellipsis mark** consists of three periods separated by space (. . .). The ellipsis mark usually indicates an omission from a quotation, although it may also show an interruption in dialog.

Note Additional issues with quotations are discussed elsewhere in this book:

- **Choosing and editing quotations,** pages 603–05.
- **Integrating source material into your text,** pages 608–12.
- **Acknowledging the sources of quotations to avoid plagiarism,** pages 618–20. See also example 3 on the next page.

1 The ellipsis mark substitutes for omissions from quotations.

When you omit a part of a quotation, show the omission with an ellipsis mark. All the examples on the next two pages quote from the following passage about environmentalism.

Original quotation

"At the heart of the environmentalist world view is the conviction that human physical and spiritual health depends on sustaining the planet in a relatively unaltered state. Earth is our home in the full, genetic sense, where humanity and its ancestors existed for all the millions of years of their evolution. Natural ecosystems—forests, coral reefs, marine blue waters—maintain the world exactly as we would wish it to be maintained. When we debase the global environment and extinguish the variety of life, we are dismantling a support system that is too complex to understand, let alone replace, in the foreseeable future." —Edward O. Wilson, "Is Humanity Suicidal?"

1. Omission of the middle of a sentence

"Natural ecosystems . . . maintain the world exactly as we would wish it to be maintained."

2. Omission of the end of a sentence, without source citation

"Earth is our home. . . ." [The sentence period, closed up to the last word, precedes the ellipsis mark.]

3. Omission of the end of a sentence, with source citation

"Earth is our home . . ." (Wilson 27). [The sentence period follows the source citation.]

4. Omission of parts of two or more sentences

Wilson writes, "At the heart of the environmentalist world view is the conviction that human physical and spiritual health depends on sustaining the planet . . . where humanity and its ancestors existed for all the millions of years of their evolution."

5. Omission of one or more sentences

As Wilson puts it, "At the heart of the environmentalist world view is the conviction that human physical and spiritual health depends on sustaining the planet in a relatively unaltered state. . . . When we debase the global environment and extinguish the variety of life, we are dismantling a support system that is too complex to understand, let alone replace, in the foreseeable future."

6. Omission from the middle of a sentence through the end of another sentence

"Earth is our home. . . . When we debase the global environment and extinguish the variety of life, we are dismantling a support system that is too complex to understand, let alone replace, in the foreseeable future."

7. Omission of the beginning of a sentence, leaving a complete sentence

a. Bracketed capital letter

"[H]uman physical and spiritual health," Wilson writes, "depends on sustaining the planet in a relatively unaltered state." [No ellipsis mark is needed because the brackets around the *H* indicate that the letter was not capitalized originally and thus that the beginning of the sentence has been omitted.]

b. Small letter

According to Wilson, "human physical and spiritual health depends on sustaining the planet in a relatively unaltered state." [No ellipsis mark is needed because the small *h* indicates that the beginning of the sentence has been omitted.]

c. Capital letter from the original

One reviewer comments, ". . . Wilson argues eloquently for the environmentalist world view"(Hami 28). [An ellipsis mark is needed because the quoted part of the sentence begins with a capital letter and it's otherwise not clear that the beginning of the original sentence has been omitted.]

8. Use of a word or phrase

Wilson describes the earth as "our home." [No ellipsis mark needed.]

Note the following features of the examples:

- **Use an ellipsis mark when it is not otherwise clear that you have left out material from the source,** as when you omit one or more sentences (examples 5 and 6) or when the words you quote form a complete sentence that is different in the original (examples 1–4 and 7c).
- **You don't need an ellipsis mark when it is obvious that you have omitted something,** such as when a bracketed capital letter or a small letter indicates omission (examples 7a and 7b) or when a phrase clearly comes from a larger sentence (example 8).
- **Place an ellipsis mark after any sentence period *except* when a parenthetical source citation follows the quotation,** as in examples 3 and 7c. Then the sentence period falls after the citation.

If you omit one or more lines of poetry or paragraphs of prose from a quotation, use a separate line of ellipsis marks across the full width of the quotation to show the omission:

In "Song: Love Armed" from 1676, Aphra Behn contrasts two lovers' experiences of a romance:

Love in fantastic triumph sate,
Whilst bleeding hearts around him flowed,
. . . .
But my poor heart alone is harmed,
Whilst thine the victor is, and free. (lines 1-2, 15-16)

(See pp. 681–82 for the format of displayed quotations like this one. And see p. 640 on the source-citation form illustrated here.)

2 The ellipsis mark indicates pauses or unfinished statements.

When writing dialog or when writing informally (not in academic writing), you can show hesitation or interruption with an ellipsis mark instead of a dash (p. 469).

"I wish . . ." His voice trailed off.

Exercise 32.4 Using ellipsis marks

Use ellipsis marks and any other needed punctuation to follow the numbered instructions for quoting from the following paragraph.

Women in the sixteenth and seventeenth centuries were educated in the home and, in some cases, in boarding schools. Men were educated at home, in grammar schools, and at the universities. The universities were closed to female students. For women, "learning the Bible," as Elizabeth Joceline puts it, was an impetus to learning to read. To be able to read the Bible in the vernacular was a liberating experience that freed the reader from hearing only the set passages read in the church and interpreted by the church. A Protestant woman was expected to read the scriptures daily, to meditate on them, and to memorize portions of them. In addition, a woman was expected to instruct her entire household in "learning the Bible" by holding instructional and devotional times each day for all household members, including the servants.

—Charlotte F. Otten, *English Women's Voices, 1540–1700*

1. Quote the fifth sentence, but omit everything from *that freed the reader* to the end.
2. Quote the fifth sentence, but omit the words *was a liberating experience that.*
3. Quote the first and sixth sentences together.

32f Use the slash between options and between lines of poetry.

Option

I don't know why some teachers oppose pass/fail courses.

Between options, the slash is not surrounded by extra space.

Note The options *and/or* and *he/she* should be avoided. (See the Glossary of Usage, pp. 808 and 814.)

/ 32f

Poetry

Many readers have sensed a reluctant turn away from death in Frost's lines "The woods are lovely, dark and deep, / But I have promises to keep" (13–14).

When you run lines of poetry into your text, separate them with a slash surrounded by space. (See pp. 681–82 for more on quoting poetry.)

Exercise 32.5 Revising: Colons, dashes, parentheses, brackets, ellipsis marks, slashes

Insert colons, dashes, parentheses, brackets, ellipsis marks, or slashes as needed in the following paragraph. When different marks would be appropriate in the same place, be able to defend the choice you make.

"Let all the learned say what they can, 'Tis ready money makes the man." These two lines of poetry by the Englishman William Somerville

1645–1742 may apply to a current American economic problem. Non-American investors with "ready money" pour some of it as much as $1.3 trillion in recent years into the United States. The investments of foreigners are varied stocks and bonds, savings deposits, service companies, factories, artworks, even the campaigns of political candidates. Proponents of foreign investment argue that it revives industry, strengthens the economy, creates jobs more than 3 million, they say, and encourages free trade among nations. Opponents discuss the risks of heavy foreign investment it makes the American economy vulnerable to outsiders, sucks profits from the country, and gives foreigners an influence in governmental decision making. On both sides, it seems, "the learned say 'Tis ready money makes the man or country." The question is, whose money?

Exercise on Chapters 27–32 Revising: Punctuation

The following paragraphs are unpunctuated except for end-of-sentence periods. Insert periods, commas, semicolons, apostrophes, quotation marks, colons, dashes, or parentheses where they are required. When different marks would be appropriate in the same place, be able to defend the choice you make.

Brewed coffee is the most widely consumed beverage in the world. The trade in coffee beans alone amounts to well over $6000000000 a year and the total volume of beans traded exceeds 4250000 tons a year. Its believed that the beverage was introduced into Arabia in the fifteenth century CE probably by Ethiopians. By the middle or late sixteenth century the Arabs had introduced the beverage to the Europeans who at first resisted it because of its strong flavor and effect as a mild stimulant. The French Italians and other Europeans incorporated coffee into their diets by the seventeenth century the English however preferred tea which they were then importing from India. Since America was colonized primarily by the English Americans also preferred tea. Only after the Boston Tea Party 1773 did Americans begin drinking coffee in large quantities. Now though the US is one of the top coffee-consuming countries consumption having been spurred on by familiar advertising claims Good till the last drop Rich hearty aroma Always rich never bitter and by ubiquitous coffee bars.

Produced from the fruit of an evergreen tree coffee is grown primarily in Latin America southern Asia and Africa. Coffee trees require a hot climate high humidity rich soil with good drainage and partial shade consequently they thrive on the east or west slopes of tropical volcanic mountains where the soil is laced with potash and drains easily. The coffee beans actually seeds grow inside bright red berries. The berries are picked by hand and the beans are extracted by machine leaving a pulpy fruit residue that can be used for fertilizer. The beans are usually roasted in ovens a chemical process that releases the beans essential oil caffeol which gives coffee its distinctive aroma. Over a hundred different varieties of beans are produced in the world each with a different flavor attributable to three factors the species of plant *Coffea arabica* and *Coffea robusta* are the most common and the soil and climate where the variety was grown.

PART 7
Mechanics

33 Capitals

Chapter essentials

- Capitalize the first word of every sentence (below).
- Capitalize most words in titles and subtitles of works (facing page).
- Always capitalize *I* and *O* (facing page).
- Capitalize proper nouns, proper adjectives, and words used as essential parts of proper nouns (p. 482).
- Capitalize most titles of persons when they precede the persons' names (p. 484).
- Avoid misusing capital letters in common nouns, compass directions, names of seasons, and names of relationships (p. 484).
- Avoid using all capitals or all small letters in texts, e-mails, and other electronic communication (p. 485).

Visit MyWritingLab™ for more resources on capitals.

Generally, capitalize a word only when a dictionary or conventional use says you must. Consult one of the style guides listed on pages 762 and 795–96 for special uses of capitals in the social, natural, and applied sciences.

CULTURE LANGUAGE Conventions of capitalization vary from language to language. English, for instance, is the only language to capitalize the first-person singular pronoun (*I*), and its practice of capitalizing proper nouns but not most common nouns also distinguishes it from some other languages.

My **f**riend (common noun) **N**athaniel (proper noun) and **I** (pronoun) both play the **d**rums (common noun).

33a Capitalize the first word of every sentence.

Every writer should own a good dictionary.
Will inflation be curbed?
Watch out!

When quoting other writers, you must either reproduce the capital letters beginning their sentences or indicate with brackets that you have altered the source. Whenever possible, integrate the quotation into your own sentence so that its capital letters coincide with your own:

"**P**sychotherapists often overlook the benefits of self-deception," the author argues (122).

The author argues that "**t**he benefits of self-deception" are not always recognized by psychotherapists (122).

If you need to alter the capitalization in the source, indicate the change with brackets (see pp. 472–73):

> "**[T]**he benefits of self-deception" are not always recognized by psychotherapists, the author argues (122).
>
> The author argues that "**[p]**sychotherapists often overlook the benefits of self-deception" (122).

Note Capitalization of questions in a series is optional. Both examples below are correct:

> Is the population a hundred? Two hundred? More?
> Is the population a hundred? two hundred? more?

Also optional is capitalization of the first word in a complete sentence after a colon (see p. 467).

33b Capitalize most words in titles and subtitles of works.

Within your text, capitalize all the words in a title *except* the following: articles (*a, an, the*), *to* in infinitives, coordinating conjunctions (*and, but,* etc.), and prepositions (*with, between,* etc.). Capitalize even these words when they are the first or last word in a title or when they fall after a colon or semicolon.

> *The Sound and the Fury*
> "Courtship through the Ages"
> *A Diamond Is Forever*
> "Knowing Whom to Ask"
> *Learning from Las Vegas*
> "The Truth about AIDS"
> *Management: A New Theory*
> "Once More to the Lake"
> *An End to Live For*
> "Power: How to Get It"
> *File under Architecture*
> *Only When I Laugh*

Always capitalize the prefix or first word in a hyphenated word within a title. Capitalize the second word only if it is a noun or an adjective or is as important as the first word.

> "Applying Stage Make-up"
> *The Pre-Raphaelites*
> *Through the Looking-Glass*

Note The style guides of the academic disciplines have their own rules for capitals in titles. For instance, the preceding guidelines reflect MLA style for English and some other humanities. In contrast, APA style for the social sciences and CSE style for the sciences capitalize only the first word and proper names in book and article titles within source citations. See pages 766–67 (APA) and 798 (CSE).

33c Always capitalize the pronoun *I* and the interjection *O*. Capitalize *oh* only when it begins a sentence.

> I love to stay up at night, but, oh, I hate to get up in the morning.
>
> He who thinks himself wise, O heavens, is a great fool. —Voltaire

33d Capitalize proper nouns, proper adjectives, and words used as essential parts of proper nouns.

Proper nouns name specific persons, places, and things: *Shakespeare, California, World War I.* **Proper adjectives** are formed from some proper nouns: *Shakespearean, Californian.*

1 Capitalize proper nouns and proper adjectives.

Capitalize all proper nouns and proper adjectives but not the articles (*a, an, the*) that precede them.

Proper nouns and adjectives to be capitalized

Specific persons and things

Stephen King	the Leaning Tower of Pisa
Napoleon Bonaparte	Boulder Dam
Lady Gaga	the Empire State Building

Specific places and geographical regions

New York City	the Mediterranean Sea
China	Lake Victoria
Europe	the Northeast, the South
North America	the Rocky Mountains

But: northeast of the city, going south

Days of the week, months, holidays

Monday	Yom Kippur
May	Christmas
Thanksgiving	Labor Day

Historical events, documents, periods, movements

World War II	Middle Ages
Vietnam War	Age of Reason
Boston Tea Party	Renaissance
Treaty of Ghent	Great Depression
Constitution	Romantic Movement
Bill of Rights	Cultural Revolution

Government offices, departments, and institutions

House of Representatives	Polk Municipal Court
Department of Defense	Warren County Hospital
Appropriations Committee	Palo Alto City Council

Academic institutions and departments

University of Kansas	Department of Nursing
Santa Monica College	Haven High School

But: the university, college course, high school diploma

Political, social, athletic, and other organizations and associations and their members

Democratic Party, Democrats	Rotary Club, Rotarians
Sierra Club	League of Women Voters
Girl Scouts of America, Scout	Boston Celtics
B'nai B'rith	Chicago Symphony Orchestra

Races, nationalities, and their languages

Native American	Germans
African American	Swahili
Caucasian	Italian

But: blacks, whites

Religions and their followers

Christianity, Christians	Judaism, Orthodox Jews
Protestantism, Protestants	Hinduism, Hindus
Catholicism, Catholics	Islam, Muslims

Religious terms for the sacred

God	Buddha
Allah	Bible [*but:* biblical]
Christ	Koran, Qur'an

2 Capitalize common nouns used as essential parts of proper nouns.

Common nouns name general classes of persons, places, or things, and they usually are not capitalized. However, capitalize common nouns such as *street, avenue, park, river, ocean, lake, company, college, county,* and *memorial* when they are part of proper nouns naming specific places or institutions:

Main Street	Crum Creek
Park Avenue	Lake Superior
Garland Place	Ford Motor Company
Central Park	Madison College
Mississippi River	San Mateo County
Pacific Ocean	George Washington Memorial

3 Capitalize trade names.

Trade names identify individual brands of certain products. When a trade name loses its association with a brand and comes to refer to a product in general, it is not capitalized. Refer to a dictionary for current usage when you are in doubt about a name.

Scotch tape	Xerox
Chevrolet	Bunsen burner

But: nylon, thermos

33e Capitalize most titles of persons only when they precede the persons' names.

Professor Otto Osborne	Otto Osborne, a professor of English
Doctor Jane Covington	Jane Covington, a medical doctor
Governor Ella Moore	Ella Moore, the governor

Not The Senator supported the bill.

But The senator supported the bill.

Or Senator Carmine supported the bill.

Exception Many writers capitalize a title denoting very high rank even when it follows a proper name or is used alone:

Ronald Reagan, past President of the United States, died in 2004.
John Roberts is Chief Justice of the United States.

33f Avoid common misuses of capital letters.

1 Use small letters for common nouns replacing proper nouns.

Not I am determined to take an Economics course before I graduate from College.

But I am determined to take an economics course before I graduate from college.

Or I am determined to take Economics 101 before I graduate from Madison College.

2 Capitalize compass directions only when they refer to specific geographical areas.

The storm blew in from the northeast and then veered south along the coast. [Here *northeast* and *south* refer to general directions.]

Students from the South have trouble adjusting to the Northeast's bitter winters. [Here *South* and *Northeast* refer to specific regions.]

3 Use small letters for the names of seasons and the names of academic years and terms.

spring	autumn	senior year
summer	fall quarter	winter term

4 Capitalize the names of relationships only when they form part of or substitute for proper names.

my mother	the father of my friend
my uncle Brad	Brad's brother

I remember how Dad scolded us.
Aunt Annie and Uncle Jake died within two months of each other.

5 Avoid using all capitals or all small letters in electronic communication.

Online messages written in all-capital letters or with no capital letters are difficult to read. Further, messages in all-capital letters may be considered rude.

Exercise 33.1 Revising: Capitals

Capitalize words as necessary in the following sentences, or substitute small letters for unnecessary capitals. Consult a dictionary if you are in doubt. If the capitalization in a sentence is already correct, mark the number preceding the sentence.

Example:

The first book on the reading list is mark twain's *a connecticut yankee in king arthur's court.*

The first book on the reading list is Mark Twain's *A Connecticut Yankee in King Arthur's Court.*

1. San Antonio, texas, is a thriving city in the southwest.
2. The city has always offered much to tourists interested in the roots of spanish settlement of the new world.
3. The alamo is one of five Catholic Missions built by Priests to convert native americans and to maintain spain's claims in the area.
4. But the alamo is more famous for being the site of an 1836 battle that helped to create the republic of Texas.
5. Many of the nearby Streets, such as Crockett street, are named for men who gave their lives in that Battle.
6. The Hemisfair plaza and the San Antonio river link tourist and convention facilities developed during mayor Cisneros's terms.
7. Restaurants, Hotels, and shops line the River. the haunting melodies of "Una paloma blanca" and "malagueña" lure passing tourists into Casa rio and other excellent mexican restaurants.
8. The university of Texas at San Antonio has expanded, and a Medical Center has been developed in the Northwest part of the city.
9. A marine attraction on the west side of San Antonio entertains grandparents, fathers and mothers, and children with the antics of dolphins and seals.
10. The City has attracted high-tech industry, creating a corridor of economic growth between san antonio and austin and contributing to the texas economy.

Note See pages 495–96 for an exercise involving capitals along with italics or underlining and other mechanics.

34 Italics or Underlining

Chapter essentials

Italicize or underline the following:

- Titles of works that appear independently (below).
- Names of ships, aircraft, spacecraft, and trains (facing page).
- Foreign words that are not part of the English language (facing page).
- Words or characters named as words (p. 488).
- Occasionally, words that you are emphasizing (p. 488).

Visit MyWritingLab™ for more resources on italics or underlining.

Italic type and underlining indicate the same thing: the word or words are being distinguished or emphasized. Always use one or the other consistently throughout a document in both text and source citations:

Text

Growing older is one of several themes Joan Didion explores in *Blue Nights*.

Source citation (MLA style)

Didion, Joan. *Blue Nights*. Vintage, 2011.

34a Italicize or underline the titles of works that appear independently.

Within your text, italicize or underline the titles of works that are published, released, or produced separately from other works (see the following box). Use quotation marks for all other titles (see p. 462).

Titles to be italicized or underlined

Other titles should be placed in quotation marks. (See p. 462.)

Books

War and Peace
Psychology: An Introduction

Plays

Hamlet
The Phantom of the Opera

Computer software

Microsoft Word
Google Chrome

Web sites

YouTube
Friends of Prufrock

Pamphlets

The Truth about Alcoholism
Plants of the Desert

Long musical works

Tchaikovsky's *Swan Lake*
The Beatles' *Revolver*
But: Symphony in C

Television and radio programs
All Things Considered
NBC Sports Hour

Long poems
Beowulf
Paradise Lost

Periodicals
Time
Boston Globe
Yale Law Review

Published speeches
Lincoln's *Gettysburg Address*
Pericles's *Funeral Oration*

Movies, DVDs, and videos
Schindler's List
How to Relax

Works of visual art
Michelangelo's *David*
Picasso's *Guernica*

Note In newspaper titles, highlight the name of the city only when it is part of the title. And for all periodical titles, do not capitalize or highlight the article *the* when it begins the title.

> Who is the publisher of the Manchester *Guardian*?
>
> The national edition of the *New York Times* often differs substantially from the late edition.

Exceptions Legal documents, the Bible, the Koran, and their parts are generally not italicized or underlined.

> **Not** They registered their *deed*.
> **But** They registered their deed.
>
> **Not** We studied the *Book of Revelation* in the *Bible*.
> **But** We studied the Book of Revelation in the Bible.

Many sciences do not use italics or underlining for some or all titles within source citations. (See pp. 795–96 on CSE style.)

34b Italicize or underline the names of ships, aircraft, spacecraft, and trains.

Queen Mary 2	*Orient Express*	*Apollo XI*
Challenger	*Spirit of St. Louis*	*Montrealer*

34c Italicize or underline foreign words and phrases that have not been absorbed into English.

English has adopted many foreign words and phrases—such as the French "bon voyage"—and they need not be italicized or underlined. Do italicize or underline words considered foreign, consulting a dictionary if needed.

> The scientific name for the brown trout is *Salmo trutta*. [The Latin scientific names for plants and animals are always italicized or underlined.]

The Latin *De gustibus non est disputandum* translates roughly as "There's no accounting for taste."

34d Italicize or underline words or characters named as words.

Use italics or underlining to indicate that you are citing a character or word as a word rather than using it for its meaning. Words you are defining fall under this convention:

The word *syzygy* refers to a straight line formed by three celestial bodies, as in the alignment of the earth, sun, and moon.

Some people say *th,* as in *thought,* with a faint *s* or *f* sound.

Carved into the column, twenty feet up, was a mysterious *7.*

34e Occasionally, italics or underlining may be used for emphasis.

Italics or underlining can stress an important word or phrase, especially in reporting how someone said something:

"Why on earth would *you* do that?" she cried.

But use such emphasis very rarely. Excessive underlining or italics will make your writing sound immature or hysterical:

The settlers had *no* firewood and *no* food. Many of them *starved* or *froze to death* that first winter.

34f In electronic communication, use alternatives for italics or underlining.

Some forms of online communication do not allow italics or underlining for the purposes described in this chapter. On Web sites, for instance, underlining often indicates a link to another site.

If you can't use italics or underlining for highlighting, type an underscore before and after the element: *Measurements coincide with those in _Joule's Handbook_.* You can also emphasize words with asterisks: *I *will not* be able to attend.*

Avoid using all-capital letters for emphasis. (See also p. 485.)

Exercise 34.1 Revising: Italics or underlining

In the following sentences, underline the words and phrases that need highlighting with italics or underlining and place a check mark next to words and phrases that are highlighted unnecessarily. Note that some highlighting is correct as given.

Example:

Of Hitchcock's movies, Psycho is the scariest.

Of Hitchcock's movies, <u>Psycho</u> is the scariest.

1. Of the many Vietnam veterans who are writers, Oliver Stone is perhaps the most famous for writing and directing the films Platoon and Born on the Fourth of July.
2. Tim O'Brien has written short stories for Esquire, GQ, and Massachusetts Review.
3. Going after Cacciato is O'Brien's dreamlike novel about the horrors of combat.
4. The word Vietnam is technically two words (*Viet* and *Nam*), but most American writers spell it as *one* word.
5. American writers use words or phrases borrowed from Vietnamese, such as di di mau ("go quickly") or dinky dau ("crazy").
6. Philip Caputo's *gripping* account of his service in Vietnam appears in the book A Rumor of War.
7. Caputo's book was made into a television movie, also titled *A Rumor of War.*
8. David Rabe's plays—including The Basic Training of Pavlo Hummel, Streamers, and Sticks and Bones—depict the effects of the war *not only* on the soldiers *but also* on their families.
9. Called "the poet laureate of the Vietnam war," Steve Mason has published two volumes of poems: Johnny's Song and Warrior for Peace.
10. The Washington Post published *rave* reviews of Veteran's Day, an autobiography by Rod Kane.

Note See pages 495–96 for an exercise involving italics or underlining along with capitals and other mechanics.

35 Abbreviations

Chapter essentials

- Abbreviate titles that fall just before and after proper names (next page).
- Use only abbreviations that are familiar to your readers (next page).
- Use *BC, BCE, AD, CE, AM, PM, no.*, and *$* only with specific dates and numbers (p. 491).
- Reserve most Latin abbreviations for source citations and parenthetical expressions (p. 491).
- Use *Inc., Bros., Co.*, or *&* (for *and*) only in names of business firms (p. 491).
- Generally spell out units of measurement and names of places, calendar designations, people, and courses (p. 491).

Visit MyWritingLab™ for more resources on abbreviations.

The following guidelines on abbreviations pertain to the text of a nontechnical document. All academic disciplines use abbreviations in source citations, and much technical writing, such as in the sciences and engineering, uses many abbreviations in the document text. For the requirements of the discipline you are writing in, consult one of the style guides listed on pages 744 (humanities), 762 (social sciences), and 795–96 (natural and applied sciences).

Usage varies, but writers increasingly omit periods from abbreviations that consist of or end in capital letters: *US, BA, USMC, PhD.* See pages 418–19 on punctuating abbreviations.

35a Use standard abbreviations for titles immediately before and after proper names.

Before the name	After the name
Dr. James Hsu	James Hsu, MD
Mr., Mrs., Ms., Hon., St., Rev., Msgr., Gen.	DDS, DVM, PhD, EdD, OSB, SJ, Sr., Jr.

Use abbreviations such as *Rev., Hon., Prof., Rep., Sen., Dr.,* and *St.* (for *Saint*) only if they appear before a proper name. Spell them out in the absence of a proper name:

Not We learned to trust the Dr.

But We learned to trust the doctor.

Or We learned to trust Dr. Kaplan.

The abbreviations for academic degrees—*PhD, MA, BA, DDS,* and the like—may be used without a proper name: *My brother took seven years to get his PhD. It seems that I will take as long to earn my BA.*

35b Familiar abbreviations and acronyms are acceptable in most writing.

An **acronym** is an abbreviation that spells a pronounceable word, such as NATO, AIDS, and NASA. These and other abbreviations that use initials are acceptable in most writing as long as they are familiar to readers.

ab 35b

Institutions	LSU, UCLA, TCU
Organizations	CIA, FBI, YMCA, AFL-CIO
Corporations	IBM, CBS, ITT
People	JFK, LBJ, FDR
Countries	US, USA

Note If a name or term (such as *operating room*) appears often in a piece of writing, you can use its abbreviation (*OR*) can cut down on extra words. Spell out the full term at its first appearance, give its abbreviation in parentheses, and use the abbreviation from then on.

35c Use *BC, BCE, AD, CE, AM, PM, no.,* and *$* only with specific dates and numbers.

44 BC	AD 1492	8:05 PM (*or* p.m.)	no. 36 (*or* No. 36)
44 BCE	1492 CE	11:26 AM (*or* a.m.)	$7.41

Not Hospital routine is easier to follow in the AM than in the PM.

But Hospital routine is easier to follow in the morning than in the afternoon or evening.

Note The abbreviation BC ("before Christ") always follows a date, whereas AD (*anno Domini,* Latin for "in the year of the Lord") precedes a date. Increasingly, these abbreviations are being replaced by BCE ("before the common era") and CE ("common era"), respectively. Both follow the date.

35d Generally, reserve Latin abbreviations for source citations and comments in parentheses.

The following common Latin abbreviations are generally not italicized or underlined.

i.e. *id est:* that is
cf. *confer:* compare
e.g. *exempli gratia:* for example
et al. *et alii:* and others
etc. *et cetera:* and so forth
NB *nota bene:* note well

He said he would be gone a fortnight (i.e., two weeks).
Trees, too, are susceptible to disease (e.g., Dutch elm disease).
Bloom et al., editors, *Anthology of Light Verse*

Some writers avoid these Latin abbreviations in formal writing, even within parentheses.

35e Use *Inc., Bros., Co.,* or *&* (for *and*) only in official names of business firms.

Not The Santini bros. operate a large moving firm in New York City.

But The Santini brothers operate a large moving firm in New York City.

Or Santini Bros. is a large moving firm in New York City.

Not We read about the Hardy Boys & Nancy Drew.

But We read about the Hardy Boys and Nancy Drew.

35f Spell out most units of measurement and names of places, calendar designations, people, and courses.

In most academic, general, and business writing, certain words should always be spelled out. (In source citations and technical writing, however, these words are more often abbreviated.)

Units of measurement

The dog is thirty inches [not in.] high.
The building is 150 feet [not ft.] tall.

Exception Long phrases such as *miles per hour* (*m.p.h.*) or *cycles per second* (*c.p.s.*) are usually abbreviated, with or without periods: *The speed limit on that road has been 30 m.p.h.* [or *mph*] *since I've lived there*.

Geographical names

The publisher is in Massachusetts [not Mass. or MA].
He came from Auckland, New Zealand [not NZ].
She lived on Morrissey Boulevard [not Blvd.].

Exceptions The United States is often referred to as the USA or the US. In writing of the US capital, use the abbreviation DC for District of Columbia when it follows the city's name: Washington, DC.

Names of days, months, and holidays

The truce was signed on Tuesday [not Tues.], April [not Apr.] 16.
The Christmas [not Xmas] holidays were uneventful.

Names of people

Virginia [not Va.] Woolf was British.
Robert [not Robt.] Frost wrote accessible poems.

Courses of instruction

I'm majoring in political science [not poli. sci.].
Economics [not Econ.] is a difficult course.

Exercise 35.1 Revising: Abbreviations

Revise the following sentences as needed to correct inappropriate use of abbreviations for nontechnical writing. Mark the number preceding any sentence in which abbreviations are appropriate as written.

Example:

One prof. lectured for five hrs.
One professor lectured for five hours.

1. In the Sept. 17, 2003, issue of *Science* magazine, Virgil L. Sharpton discusses a theory that could help explain the extinction of dinosaurs.
2. About 65 mill. yrs. ago, a comet or asteroid crashed into the earth.
3. The result was a huge crater about 10 km. (6.2 mi.) deep in the Gulf of Mex.
4. Sharpton's new measurements suggest that the crater is 50 pct. larger than scientists previously believed.
5. Indeed, 20-yr.-old drilling cores reveal that the crater is about 186 mi. wide, roughly the size of Conn.
6. The space object was traveling more than 100,000 m.p.h. and hit earth with the impact of 100 to 300 million megatons of TNT.
7. On impact, 200,000 cubic km. of rock and soil were vaporized or thrown into the air.

8. That's the equivalent of 2.34 bill. cubic ft. of matter.
9. The impact would have created 400-ft. tidal waves across the Atl. Ocean, temps. higher than 20,000 degs., and powerful earthquakes.
10. Sharpton theorizes that the dust, vapor, and smoke from this impact blocked the sun's rays for mos., cooled the earth, and thus resulted in the death of the dinosaurs.

Note See pages 495–96 for an exercise involving abbreviations along with capitals and other mechanics.

36 Numbers

Chapter essentials

- Use numerals according to standard practice in your field (below).
- Use numerals according to convention for dates, addresses, and other information (next page).
- Spell out numbers that begin sentences (p. 495).

Visit MyWritingLab™ for more resources on numbers.

Expressing numbers in numerals (*28*) or in words (*twenty-eight*) is often a matter of style in a discipline: the technical disciplines more often prefer numerals, and the nontechnical disciplines more often prefer words. All disciplines use many more numerals in source citations than in the document texts.

36a Use numerals according to standard practice in the field you are writing in.

Always use numerals for numbers that require more than two words to spell out:

> The leap year has 366 days.
> The population of Minot, North Dakota, is about 36,500.

In nontechnical academic writing, spell out numbers of one or two words. A hyphenated number may be considered one word.

> Twelve nations signed the treaty.
> The ball game drew forty-two thousand people.
> Jenson lived to be ninety-nine or one hundred.

In much business writing, use numerals for all numbers over ten (*five reasons, 11 participants*). In technical academic and business writing, such as in science and engineering, use numerals for all numbers over ten, and use numerals for zero through nine when they refer to exact measurements (*2 milliliters, 1 kilosecond*). (Consult one of the style guides listed on pp. 762 and 795–96 for more details.)

Notes Use a combination of numerals and words for round numbers over a million: *26 million, 2.45 billion*. And use either all numerals or all words when several numbers appear together in a passage, even if convention would require a mixture:

Inconsistent	The satellite Galatea is about twenty-six thousand miles from Neptune. It is 110 miles in diameter and orbits Neptune in just over ten hours.
Revised	The satellite Galatea is about 26,000 miles from Neptune. It is 110 miles in diameter and orbits Neptune in just over 10 hours.

Avoid using two numbers in a row, which can be confusing. Rewrite to separate the numbers:

Confusing	Out of 530 101 children caught the virus.
Clear	Out of 530 children 101 caught the virus.

CULTURE LANGUAGE In American English a comma separates the numerals in long numbers (*26,000*), and a period functions as a decimal point (*2.06*).

36b Use numerals according to convention for dates, addresses, and other information.

Even when a number requires one or two words to spell out, we conventionally use numerals in the following situations:

Days and years

June 18, 2000 AD 12 456 BCE 1999

Exception The day of a month may be expressed in words when it is not followed by a year (*June fifth; October first*).

Pages, chapters, volumes, acts, scenes, lines

Chapter 9, page 123
Hamlet, act 5, scene 3, lines 35–40

Decimals, percentages, and fractions

22.5
48% (*or* 48 percent)
3½

Addresses

RD 2
419 Stonewall Street
Washington, DC 20036

Scores and statistics

21 to 7
a mean of 26
a ratio of 8 to 1

Exact amounts of money

$4.50
$3.5 million (*or* $3,500,000)

The time of day

9:00 AM
2:30 PM

Exceptions Round dollar or cent amounts of only a few words may be expressed in words: *seventeen dollars; fifteen hundred dollars; sixty cents.* When the word *o'clock* is used for the time of day, also express the number in words: *two o'clock* (not *2 o'clock*).

36c Always spell out numbers that begin sentences.

For clarity, spell out any number that begins a sentence. If the number requires more than two words, reword the sentence so that the number falls later and can be expressed as a numeral:

Not 3.9 billion people live in Asia.

But The population of Asia is 3.9 billion.

Exercise 36.1 Revising: Numbers

Revise the following sentences so that numbers are used appropriately for nontechnical writing. Mark the number preceding any sentence in which numbers are already used appropriately.

Example:
Charlie paid two hundred five dollars for used scuba gear.
Charlie paid $205 for used scuba gear.

1. The planet Saturn is nine hundred million miles, or nearly one billion five hundred million kilometers, from the sun.
2. A year on Saturn equals almost thirty of our years.
3. Thus, Saturn orbits the sun only two and four-tenths times during the average human life span.
4. It travels in its orbit at about twenty-one thousand six hundred miles per hour.
5. 15 to 20 times denser than Earth's core, Saturn's core measures 17,000 miles across.
6. The temperature at Saturn's cloud tops is minus one hundred seventy degrees Fahrenheit.
7. In nineteen hundred thirty-three, astronomers found on Saturn's surface a huge white spot 2 times the size of Earth and 7 times the size of Mercury.
8. Saturn's famous rings reflect almost seventy percent of the sunlight that approaches the planet.
9. The ring system is almost forty thousand miles wide, beginning 8800 miles from the planet's visible surface and ending forty-seven thousand miles from that surface.
10. Saturn also has at least sixty-two moons, ranging in size from less than one mile across to more than one-half the size of Earth's moon.

Exercise on Chapters 33–36 Revising: Mechanics

Revise the following paragraphs to correct any errors in the use of capital letters, italics or underlining, abbreviations, and numbers. (For abbreviations and numbers, follow standard practice for nontechnical writing.) Consult a dictionary as needed.

According to many sources—e.g., the Cambridge Ancient History and Gardiner's Egypt of the Pharaohs—the ancient egyptians devoted much attention to making Life more convenient and pleasurable for themselves.

Our word pharaoh for the ancient egyptian rulers comes from the egyptian word pr'o, meaning "great house." Indeed, the egyptians placed great emphasis on family residences, adding small bedrms. as early as 3500 yrs. bce. By 3000 bce, the egyptians made ice through evaporation of water at night and then used it to cool their homes. About the same time they used fans made of palm fronds or papyrus to cool themselves in the day. To light their homes, the egyptians abandoned the animal-fat lamps Humans had used for 50 thousand yrs. Instead, around 1300 bce the people of Egt. devised the 1st oil lamps.

egyptians found great pleasure in playing games. Four thousand three hundred yrs. ago or so they created one of the oldest board games known. the game involved racing ivory or stone pieces across a papyrus playing board. By three thousand bce, egyptian children played marbles with semi-precious stones, some of which have been found in gravesites at nagada, EG. Around one thousand three hundred sixty bce, small children played with clay rattles covered in silk and shaped like animals.

To play the game of love, egyptian men and women experimented with cosmetics applied to skin and eyelids. kohl, history's first eyeliner, was used by both sexes to ward off evil. 5000 yrs. ago egyptians wore wigs made of vegetable fibers or human hair. In 9 hundred bce, queen Isimkheb wore a wig so heavy that she needed assistance in walking. To adjust their make-up and wigs, egyptians adapted the simple metal mirrors devised by the sumerians in the bronze age, ornamenting them with carved handles of ivory, gold, or wood. Feeling that only those who smelled sweet could be attractive, the egyptians made deodorants from perfumed oils, e.g., cinnamon and citrus.

PART 8

Effective Words

37 Using Appropriate Language

Chapter essentials

- Choose standard American English for most academic writing (below).
- Revise spellings and shortcuts common in texting and other electronic communication (p. 500).
- Use slang, colloquial language, and regionalisms only when appropriate (pp. 500, 501).
- Use technical words with care (p. 502).
- Revise indirect or pretentious writing (p. 502).
- Revise sexist and other biased language (p. 503).

Visit MyWritingLab™ for more resources on using appropriate language.

Appropriate language suits your writing situation—your subject, purpose, and audience. Like everyone, you vary your words depending on the context in which you are speaking and writing. Look, for example, at the underlined words in these two sentences:

> Kids who dis their teachers usually get in hot water.
>
> Children who disrespect their teachers usually face discipline.

The first sentence might be addressed to friends in casual conversation. The second is more suitable for an academic audience.

The more formal language of the second example is typical of **standard American English.** This is the dialect of English normally expected and used in school, business, government, the professions, and the communications media. (For more on its role in academic writing, see pp. 141–43.)

The vocabulary of written standard English is huge, allowing you to express an infinite range of ideas and feelings. However, it does exclude words that only some groups of people use, understand, or find inoffensive. It also excludes words and expressions that are commonly spoken but are too imprecise for writing. Whenever you doubt a word's status, consult a dictionary (see p. 507). A label such as *nonstandard, slang,* or *colloquial* tells you that the word is not generally appropriate in academic or business writing.

37a Choosing standard English for most academic writing

Like many countries, the United States consists of scores of regional, social, and ethnic groups with their own distinct dialects, or versions of English. Standard American English is one of these dialects, and so are African American Vernacular English, Appalachian English, Creole, and the English of coastal Maine. All the dialects of

Appropriate language in academic writing

- **Use standard American English,** the dialect recommended by this handbook. Other dialects, slang, and colloquial language are sometimes appropriate in academic writing. Pretentious writing and the shortcuts common in electronic communication are rarely or never appropriate. (See pp. 498–503.)

Inappropriate	In many young-adult novels, characters who are supposed to be best buds often turn out to be frenemies.
Revised	In many young-adult novels, characters who are supposed to be good friends often turn out to be enemies posing as friends.

- **Avoid stereotypes.** (See pp. 503–04.)

Stereotype	Football players need tutors and counselors.
Revised	Football players with poor grades need tutors and counselors.

- **Avoid sexist language.** (See pp. 504–05.)

Sexist	Teenage girls are ideal babysitters.
Revised	Teenagers who enjoy young children are ideal babysitters.

- **Be sensitive when labeling groups.** (See pp. 505–06.)

Inappropriate	The hurricane victims needed immediate help.
Revised	The people affected by the hurricane needed immediate help.

English share many features, but each also has its own vocabulary, pronunciation, and grammar.

If you speak a dialect other than standard English, you are probably already adept at code switching—that is, moving between your dialect and standard English in speech and writing. Dialects are not wrong in themselves, but forms imported from one dialect into another may still be perceived as unclear or incorrect. When standard English is expected, such as in academic or public writing, edit your work to revise expressions that you know (or have been told) differ from standard English. These expressions may include *theirselves, hisn, them books,* and others labeled *nonstandard* by a dictionary. They may also include certain verb forms, as discussed on pages 285–92. For help identifying and editing nonstandard language, see "CULTURE LANGUAGE Guide" inside the back cover of this book.

Your participation in the community of standard English does not require you to abandon your own dialect. You may want to use it in writing you do for yourself, such as journals, notes, and drafts, which should be composed as freely as possible. You may want to quote it in an academic paper, as when analyzing or reporting conversation in dialect. And, of course, you will want to use it with others who speak it.

37b Revising the shortcuts of texting and other electronic communication

Rapid communication by e-mail and text or instant messaging encourages some informalities that are inappropriate for academic writing. If you use these media frequently, you may need to proofread your academic papers especially to identify and revise errors such as the following:

- **Sentence fragments.** Make sure every sentence has a subject and a predicate. (See pp. 338–44.)

  Not Observed the results.

  But Researchers observed the results.

- **Missing punctuation.** Between and within sentences, use standard punctuation marks. Check especially for missing commas within sentences and missing apostrophes in possessives and contractions. (See pp. 422–38 and 451–57.)

  Not The dogs bony ribs visible through its fur were evidence of neglect.

  But The dog's bony ribs, visible through its fur, were evidence of neglect.

- **Missing capital letters.** Use capital letters at the beginnings of sentences, for proper nouns and adjectives, and in titles. (See pp. 480–85.)

  Not scholars have written about abraham lincoln more than any other american.

  But Scholars have written about Abraham Lincoln more than any other American.

- **Nonstandard abbreviations and spellings.** Write out most words, avoiding forms such as *2* for *to* or *too, b4* for *before, bc* for *because, ur* for *you are* or *you're,* and + or & for *and.* (See pp. 490–92.)

  Not Students + tutors need to meet b4 the third week of the semester.

  But Students and tutors need to meet before the third week of the semester.

37c Using slang only when appropriate

All groups of people—from musicians and computer scientists to vegetarians and golfers—create novel and colorful expressions called **slang.** The following quotation, for instance, is from an essay on the slang of "skaters" (skateboarders):

> Curtis slashed ultra-punk crunchers on his longboard, while the Rubeman flailed his usual Gumbyness on tweaked frontsides and lofty fakie ollies.
>
> —Miles Orkin, "Mucho Slingage by the Pool"

Among those who understand it, slang may be vivid and forceful. It often occurs in dialog, and an occasional slang expression can enliven an informal essay. But most slang is too flippant and imprecise for effective communication, and it is generally inappropriate for college or business writing:

Slang	Many students start out pretty together but then get weird.
Revised	Many students start out with clear goals but then lose their direction.

37d Using colloquial language only when appropriate

Colloquial language designates the words and expressions appropriate to everyday spoken language, such as *chill out, go nuts,* or *get off on.*

When you write informally, colloquial language may be appropriate to achieve the casual, relaxed effect of conversation. But colloquial language generally is not exact enough for more formal college, public, and professional writing. In such writing, avoid any words and expressions labeled *informal* or *colloquial* in your dictionary.

Take special care to avoid **mixed diction,** a combination of standard and colloquial words:

Mixed diction	According to a Native American myth, the Great Creator had a dog hanging around with him when he created the earth.
Revised	According to a Native American myth, the Great Creator was accompanied by a dog when he created the earth.

Note See also pages 141–43 for a discussion of formal and informal language in academic writing.

37e Using regionalisms only when appropriate

Regionalisms are expressions or pronunciations peculiar to a particular area. Southerners may say they *reckon,* meaning "think" or "suppose." People in Maine invite their Boston friends to come *down* rather than *up* (north) to visit. New Yorkers stand *on* rather than *in* line for a movie.

Regional expressions are appropriate in writing addressed to local readers and may lend realism to regional description, but they should be avoided in writing intended for a general audience.

37f Using technical words with care

All disciplines and professions rely on specialized language, often called **jargon**, that allows members to communicate precisely and efficiently with each other. Chemists speak of *esters* and *phosphatides,* geographers and mapmakers refer to *isobars* and *isotherms,* and literary critics write about *motifs* and *subtexts.*

Technical language can be economical among those who share the vocabulary. But without explanation it is generally meaningless to nonspecialists. When you are writing for nonspecialists, avoid unnecessary technical terms and carefully define terms you must use.

For revising the overly complicated language that is also sometimes called jargon, see page 524.

37g Revising indirect or pretentious writing

In most writing, small, plain, and direct words are preferable to evasive or showy words.

- **Euphemisms** are presumably inoffensive words that substitute for words deemed potentially offensive or too blunt, such as *passed away* for "died." Euphemisms can soften the truth, but they are appropriate only when blunt, truthful words would needlessly hurt or offend your audience.
- **Double talk** (also called *doublespeak* or *weasel words*) is language intended to confuse or be misunderstood. It is unfortunately common in politics and advertising—the *revenue enhancement* that is really a tax, for example. Double talk has no place in honest writing.
- **Pretentious writing** is excessively showy. Such writing is more fancy than its subject requires. Choose your words for their exactness and economy. The big, ornate word may be tempting, but pass it up. Your readers will be grateful.

Pretentious Hardly a day goes by without a new revelation about the devastation of the natural world, and to a significant extent our dependence on the internal combustion engine is the culprit. Respected scientific minds coalesce around the argument that carbon dioxide emissions, such as those from automobiles imbibing gasoline, are responsible for a gradual escalation in temperatures on the earth.

Revised Much of the frequent bad news about the environment can be blamed on the internal combustion engine. Respected scientists argue that carbon dioxide emissions, such as those from gas-powered cars, are warming the earth.

37h Revising sexist and other biased language

Even when we do not mean it to, our language can reflect and perpetuate hurtful prejudices toward groups of people, especially racial, ethnic, religious, age, and sexual groups. Such biased language can be obvious—words such as *nigger, whitey, mick, kike, fag, dyke,* and *broad.* But it can also be subtle, generalizing about groups in ways that may be familiar but that are also inaccurate or unfair. For instance, people with physical disabilities are as varied a group as any other: the only thing they have in common is some form of impairment. To assume that people with disabilities share certain attitudes (shyness, helplessness, victimization, whatever) is to disregard the uniqueness of each person.

Biased language reflects poorly on the user, not on the person or persons whom it mischaracterizes or insults. Unbiased language does not submit to false generalizations. It treats people as individuals and labels groups as they wish to be labeled.

1 Avoiding stereotypes of race, ethnicity, religion, age, and other characteristics

A **stereotype** is a generalization based on poor evidence, a kind of formula for understanding and judging people simply because of their membership in a group:

Men are uncommunicative.
Women are emotional.
Liberals want to raise taxes.
Conservatives are affluent.

At best, stereotypes betray an uncritical writer, one who is not thinking beyond notions received from others. Worse, they betray a writer who does not mind hurting others or even *wants* to hurt others.

In your writing, be alert for any general statements about people based on only one or a few characteristics. Be especially cautious about substituting such statements for the evidence you should be providing instead.

Stereotype Elderly drivers should have their licenses limited to daytime driving. [Implies that all elderly people are poor night drivers.]

Revised Drivers with impaired night vision should have their licenses limited to daytime driving.

Some stereotypes have become part of the language, but they are still potentially offensive.

Stereotype The administrators are too blind to see the need for a new gymnasium. [Equates vision loss and lack of understanding.]

Revised The administrators do not understand the need for a new gymnasium.

2 Avoiding sexist language

Among the most subtle and persistent biased language is that expressing narrow ideas about men's and women's roles, position, and value in society. This **sexist language** distinguishes needlessly between men and women in such matters as occupation, ability, behavior, temperament, and maturity. Like other stereotypes, it can wound or irritate readers, and it indicates the writer's thoughtlessness or unfairness. The following box suggests ways of eliminating sexist language.

Eliminating sexist language

- **Avoid demeaning and patronizing language**—for instance, identifying women and men differently or trivializing either gender:

  Sexist Dr. Keith Kim and Lydia Hawkins wrote the article.
  Revised Dr. Keith Kim and Dr. Lydia Hawkins wrote the article.
  Revised Keith Kim and Lydia Hawkins wrote the article.

  Sexist Ladies are entering formerly male occupations.
  Revised Women are entering formerly male occupations.

- **Avoid occupational or social stereotypes**, assuming that a role or profession is exclusively male or female:

  Sexist The considerate doctor commends a nurse when she provides his patients with good care.
  Revised The considerate doctor commends a nurse who provides good care for patients.

- **Avoid referring needlessly to gender:**

  Sexist Marie Curie, a woman chemist, discovered radium.
  Revised Marie Curie, a chemist, discovered radium.

  Sexist The patients were tended by a male nurse.
  Revised The patients were tended by a nurse.

  However, don't overcorrect by avoiding appropriate references to gender: *Pregnant women* [not *people*] *should avoid drinking alcohol.*

- **Avoid using *man* or words containing *man* to refer to all human beings.** Here are a few alternatives:

businessman	businessperson
chairman	chair, chairperson
congressman	congressperson, legislator
craftsman	craftsperson, artisan
layman	layperson
mankind	humankind, humanity, human beings, people
policeman	police officer
salesman	salesperson

Sexist — Man has not reached the limits of social justice.

Revised — Humankind [or Humanity] has not reached the limits of social justice.

Sexist — The furniture consists of manmade materials.

Revised — The furniture consists of synthetic materials.

- **Avoid the generic *he*,** the male pronoun used to refer to both genders. (See also pp. 321–22.)

Sexist — The newborn child explores his world.

Revised — Newborn children explore their world. [Use the plural for the pronoun and the word it refers to.]

Revised — The newborn child explores the world. [Avoid the pronoun altogether.]

Revised — The newborn child explores his or her world. [Substitute male and female pronouns.]

Use the last option sparingly—only once in a group of sentences and only to stress the singular individual.

CULTURE LANGUAGE Forms of address vary widely from culture to culture. In some cultures, for instance, one shows respect by referring to all older women as if they were married, using the equivalent of the title *Mrs.* Usage in the United States is changing toward making no assumptions about marital status, rank, or other characteristics—for instance, using the title *Ms.* for a woman unless she is known to prefer *Mrs.* or *Miss.*

3 Using appropriate labels

We often need to label groups: *swimmers, politicians, mothers, Christians, westerners, students.* But labels can be shorthand stereotypes that slight the person labeled and ignore the preferences of the group members themselves. Showing sensitivity when applying labels reveals you to be alert to readers' needs and concerns. Although sometimes dismissed as "political correctness," such sensitivity hurts no one and helps gain your readers' trust and respect.

- **Avoid labels that (intentionally or not) insult the person or group you refer to.** A person with emotional problems is not a *mental patient.* A person with cancer is not a *cancer victim.* A person using a wheelchair is not *wheelchair-bound.*
- **Use names for racial, ethnic, and other groups that reflect the preferences of each group's members,** or at least many of them. Examples of current preferences include *African American* or *black* and *people with disabilities* (rather than *the disabled* or *the handicapped*). But labels change often. To learn how a group's members wish to be labeled, ask them directly, attend to usage in reputable periodicals, or check a recent dictionary.
- **Identify a person's group only when it is relevant to the point you're making.** Consider the context of the label: Is it a necessary piece of information? If not, don't use it.

Exercise 37.1 Revising: Appropriate words

Rewrite the following sentences as needed for standard American English. Consult a dictionary to determine whether particular words are appropriate and to find suitable substitutes.

Example:

If negotiators blow up during contract discussions, they may mess up chances for a settlement.

If negotiators become angry during contract discussions, they may harm chances for a settlement.

1. Acquired immune deficiency syndrome (AIDS) is a major deal all over the world.
2. The disease gets around primarily by sexual intercourse, exchange of bodily fluids, shared needles, and blood transfusions.
3. Those who think the disease is limited to homos, mainliners, and foreigners are quite mistaken.
4. Stats suggest that in the United States one in every five hundred college kids carries the virus.
5. A person with AIDS does not deserve to be subjected to exclusionary behavior or callousness on the part of his fellow citizens. Instead, he has the necessity for all the compassion, medical care, and financial assistance due those who are in the extremity of illness.
6. An AIDS victim often sees a team of doctors or a single doctor with a specialized practice.
7. The doctor may help his patients by obtaining social services for them as well as by providing medical care.
8. The AIDS sufferer who loses his job may need public assistance.
9. For someone who is very ill, a full-time nurse may be necessary. She can administer medications and make the sick person as comfortable as possible.
10. Some people with AIDS have insurance, but others lack the bucks for premiums.

38 Using Exact Language

Chapter essentials

- Rely on a dictionary and a thesaurus for word meanings and synonyms (below).
- Use the right word for your meaning (p. 510).
- Balance abstract and general words with concrete and specific words (p. 511).
- Use correct idioms, especially with prepositions (p. 513).
- Use figurative language with care (p. 515).
- Avoid trite expressions (clichés) (p. 517).

Visit MyWritingLab™ for more resources on using exact language.

To write clearly and effectively, you will want to find the words that fit your meaning exactly and convey your attitude precisely. However, don't worry too much about choosing the right words while you are drafting an essay. If the right word doesn't come to you, leave a blank. During revision or editing, you can consider tone, specificity, and precision as described in this chapter.

Avoiding common mistakes in word choice

- **Make sure words have the meanings you intend.** Check a dictionary if you aren't sure of a word's meanings.

  Incorrect Increased global temperatures will effect everyone.

  Revised Increased global temperatures will affect everyone.

- **Before you select a word suggested by a spelling checker, make sure it's the one you mean.** (See p. 65 for more on spelling checkers.)

  Incorrect The results were defiant: the experiment was a failure.

  Revised The results were definite: the experiment was a failure.

- **Use idioms correctly.** (See pp. 513–15 for more on idioms.)

  Incorrect The planners agreed over the details of the evacuation plan.

  Revised The planners agreed **on** the details of the evacuation plan.

38a Using a dictionary and a thesaurus

A dictionary and a thesaurus can help you choose exact words and avoid errors in word use.

1 Using a dictionary

A dictionary defines words and provides pronunciation, grammatical functions, etymology (word history), and other information. The following sample is from *Merriam-Webster's Collegiate Dictionary*:

Print dictionary entry

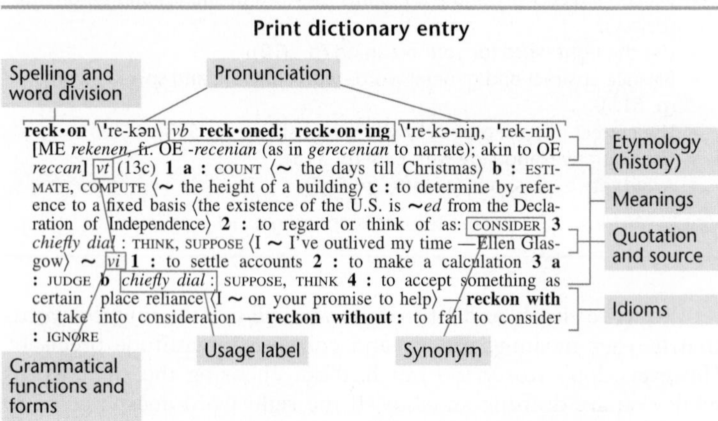

This sample is from a print dictionary, but Merriam-Webster and others provide online dictionaries that give the same information in less abbreviated form and also allow you to hear how a word is pronounced. Here is part of the entry for *reckon* from *Merriam-Webster Online*:

Partial online dictionary entry

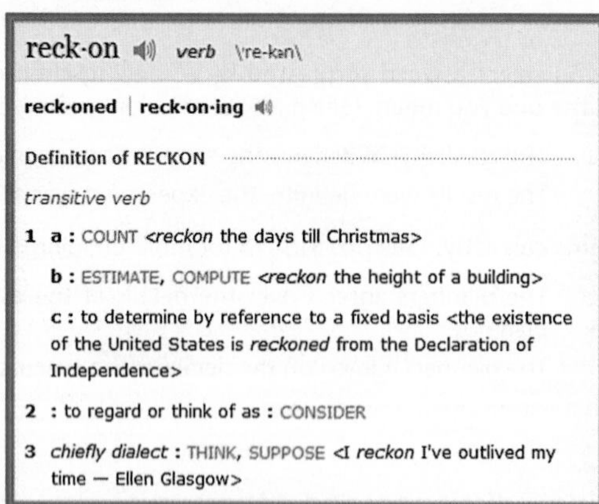

reck·on *verb* \'re-kən\

reck·oned | **reck·on·ing**

Definition of RECKON

transitive verb

1 a : COUNT <*reckon* the days till Christmas>

b : ESTIMATE, COMPUTE <*reckon* the height of a building>

c : to determine by reference to a fixed basis <the existence of the United States is *reckoned* from the Declaration of Independence>

2 : to regard or think of as **:** CONSIDER

3 *chiefly dialect* **:** THINK, SUPPOSE <I *reckon* I've outlived my time — Ellen Glasgow>

Other useful online resources are *Dictionary.com* and *The Free Dictionary,* which provide entries from several dictionaries at once. *Dictionary.com* also offers a translator that converts text between languages, such as English to Spanish. *The Free Dictionary* offers dictionaries in more than a dozen languages besides English.

If you prefer a print dictionary, good ones, in addition to *Merriam-Webster's Collegiate*, include *American Heritage College Dictionary, Random House Webster's College Dictionary*, and *Webster's New World College Dictionary*.

CULTURE LANGUAGE If English is not your native language, you probably should have a dictionary prepared especially for students using English as a second language (ESL). Such a dictionary contains special information on prepositions, count versus noncount nouns, and many other matters. The following are reliable print ESL dictionaries, each with an online version: *Longman Dictionary of Contemporary English, Oxford Advanced Learner's Dictionary*, and *Merriam-Webster Advanced Learner's English Dictionary*.

2 Using a thesaurus

To find a word with the exact shade of meaning you intend, you may want to consult a thesaurus, or collection of **synonyms**—words with approximately the same meaning. For instance, here is the listing of synonyms for just one meaning of *reckon* on the site *Thesaurus.com*:

Partial online thesaurus entry

Main Entry:	**reckon**
Part of Speech:	*verb*
Definition:	add up; evaluate
Synonyms:	account, appraise, approximate, calculate, call, cast, cipher, compute, conjecture, consider, count, count heads, count noses, deem, enumerate, esteem, estimate, figure, figure out, foot, gauge, guess, hold, judge, keep tabs, look upon, number, place, put, rate, regard, run down, square, sum, surmise, take account of, tally, think of, tick off, tot, tot up, total, tote, tote up, view

Because a thesaurus aims to open up possibilities, its lists of synonyms include approximate as well as precise matches. The thesaurus does not define synonyms or distinguish among them, however, so you need a dictionary to discover exact meanings. In general, don't use a word from a thesaurus—even one you like the sound of—until you are sure of its appropriateness for your meaning.

Exercise 38.1 Using a dictionary

Consult your dictionary on five of the following words. For each word, write down (*a*) the division into syllables, (*b*) the pronunciation, (*c*) the grammatical functions and forms, (*d*) the etymology, (*e*) each meaning, and (*f*) any special uses indicated by labels. Finally, use the word in at least two sentences of your own.

1. depreciation	4. manifest	7. potlatch	10. toxic
2. secretary	5. assassin	8. plain (*adj.*)	11. steal
3. grammar	6. astrology	9. ceremony	12. obelisk

38b Using the right word for your meaning

Precisely expressing your meaning requires understanding both the denotations and the connotations of words. A word's **denotation** is the thing or idea it refers to, the meaning listed in the dictionary without reference to the emotional associations it may arouse in a reader. Using words according to their established denotations is essential if readers are to grasp your meaning. Here are a few guidelines:

- **Consult a dictionary whenever you are unsure of a word's meaning.**
- **Distinguish between similar-sounding words that have widely different denotations:**

  Inexact Older people often suffer infirmaries [places for the sick].

  Exact Older people often suffer infirmities [disabilities].

  Some words, called **homonyms** (from the Greek meaning "same name"), sound exactly alike but differ in meaning: for example, *principal/principle* and *rain/reign/rein*. (See pp. 527–28 for a list of commonly confused homonyms.)
- **Distinguish between words with related but distinct denotations:**

  Inexact Television commercials continuously [unceasingly] interrupt programming.

  Exact Television commercials continually [regularly] interrupt programming.

In addition to their emotion-free denotations, many words carry related meanings that evoke specific feelings. These **connotations** can shape readers' responses and are thus a powerful tool for writers. (At the same time they are a potential snare for readers. See p. 190.) Some connotations are personal: the word *dog,* for instance, may have negative connotations for the letter carrier who has been bitten three times. Usually, though, people agree about connotations. The following word pairs are just a few of many that have related denotations but very different connotations:

pride: sense of self-worth
vanity: excessive regard for oneself

firm: steady, unchanging, unyielding
stubborn: unreasonable, bullheaded

enthusiasm: excitement
mania: excessive interest or desire

exact 38b

Understanding connotation is especially important in choosing among **synonyms,** or words with approximately the same meanings.

For instance, *cry* and *weep* both denote the shedding of tears, but *cry* more than *weep* connotes a sobbing sound accompanying the tears. *Sob* itself connotes broken, gasping crying, with tears, whereas *wail* connotes sustained sound, perhaps without tears.

Exercise 38.2 Revising: Denotation

Revise any underlined word below that is not used according to its established denotation. Circle any word used correctly. Consult a dictionary if you are uncertain of a word's precise meaning.

Example:

Sam and Dave are going to Bermuda and Hauppauge, respectfully, for spring vacation.

Sam and Dave are going to Bermuda and Hauppauge, respectively, for spring vacation.

1. Maxine Hong Kingston was rewarded many prizes for her first two books, *The Woman Warrior* and *China Men*.
2. Kingston sites her mother's tales about ancestors and ancient Chinese customs as the sources of these memoirs.
3. In her childhood Kingston was greatly effected by her mother's tale about a pregnant aunt who was ostracized by villagers.
4. The aunt gained avengeance by drowning herself in the village's water supply.
5. Kingston decided to make her nameless relative infamous by giving her immortality in *The Woman Warrior*.

Exercise 38.3 Considering the connotations of words

Fill the blank in each sentence below with the most appropriate word from the list in parentheses. Consult a dictionary to be sure of your selections.

Example:

Channel 5 _____ Oshu the winner before the polls closed. (*advertised, declared, broadcast, promulgated*)

Channel 5 declared Oshu the winner before the polls closed.

1. AIDS is a serious health _____. (*problem, worry, difficulty, plight*)
2. Once the virus has entered the blood system, it _____ T-cells. (*murders, destroys, slaughters, executes*)
3. The _____ of T-cells is to combat infections. (*ambition, function, aim, goal*)
4. Without enough T-cells, the body is nearly _____ against infections. (*defenseless, hopeless, desperate*)
5. To prevent exposure to the disease, one should be especially _____ in sexual relationships. (*chary, circumspect, cautious, calculating*)

38c Balancing the abstract and concrete, the general and specific

To understand a subject as you understand it, your readers need ample guidance from your words. When you describe a building as *beautiful* and nothing more, you force readers to provide their own ideas of what makes a building beautiful. If readers bother (and they may not), they surely will not conjure up the image you had in mind. Use words to tell readers what you want them to know, that the beautiful building is *a sleek, silver skyscraper with blue-tinted windows,* for instance, or *a Victorian brick courthouse with tall, arched windows.*

Clear, exact writing balances abstract and general words, which outline ideas and objects, with concrete and specific words, which sharpen and solidify.

- **Abstract words** name ideas: *beauty, inflation, management, culture, liberal.* **Concrete words** name qualities and things we can know by our five senses of sight, hearing, touch, taste, and smell: *sleek, humming, rough, salty, musty.*
- **General words** name classes or groups of things, such as *buildings, weather, plants,* and *birds,* and include all the varieties of the class. **Specific words** limit a general class, such as *buildings,* by naming a variety, such as *skyscraper, courthouse,* or *hut.*

Note that *general* and *specific* are relative terms: the same word may be more general than some words but more specific than others.

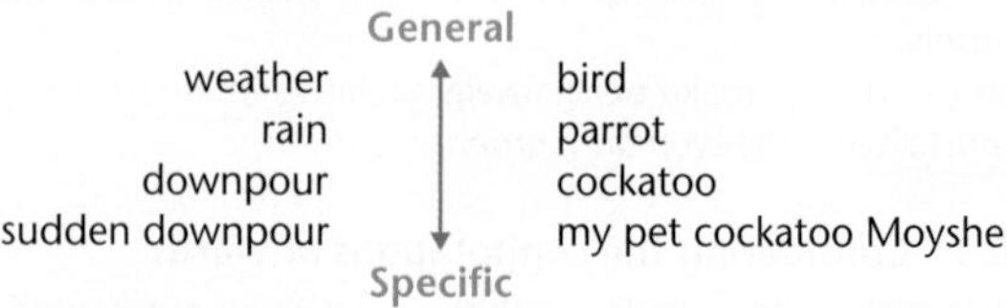

Abstract and general words are useful in the broad statements that set the course for your writing:

> The wild horse in America has a romantic history.
>
> We must be free from government interference in our affairs.
>
> Relations between the sexes today are only a little more relaxed than they were in the past.

But the sentences following these would have to develop the ideas with concrete and specific details. When your meaning calls for an abstract or general word, make sure you define it, explain it, and narrow it. Look at how concrete and specific information turns vague sentences into exact ones in the following examples:

Vague The size of his hands made his smallness real. [How big were his hands? How small was he?]

Exact Not until I saw his delicate, doll-like hands did I realize that he stood a full head shorter than most other men.

Vague The long flood caused a lot of awful destruction in the town. [How long did the flood last? What destruction did it cause? Why was the destruction awful?]

Exact The flood waters, which rose swiftly and then stayed stubbornly high for days, killed at least six townspeople and made life a misery for the hundreds who had to evacuate their ruined homes and stores.

Note You can use your computer's Find function to help you find and revise abstract and general words that you tend to overuse. Examples of such words might include *nice, interesting, things, very, good, a lot, a little,* and *some.*

Exercise 38.4 Revising: Concrete and specific words

Make the following paragraph vivid by expanding the sentences with appropriate details of your own choosing. Substitute concrete and specific words for the abstract and general ones that are underlined.

I remember clearly how awful I felt the first time I attended Mrs. Murphy's second-grade class. I had recently moved from a small town in Missouri to a crowded suburb of Chicago. My new school looked big from the outside and seemed dark inside as I walked down the long corridor toward the classroom. The class was noisy as I neared the door; but when I entered, everyone became quiet and looked at me. I felt uncomfortable and wanted a place to hide. However, in a loud voice Mrs. Murphy directed me to the front of the room to introduce myself.

Exercise 38.5 Using concrete and specific words

For each abstract or general word below, give at least two other words or phrases that illustrate increasing specificity or concreteness. Consult a dictionary as needed. Use the most specific or concrete word from each group in a sentence of your own.

Example:

awake, watchful, vigilant

Vigilant guards patrol the buildings.

1. fabric
2. delicious
3. car
4. narrow-minded
5. reach (*verb*)
6. green
7. walk (*verb*)
8. flower
9. serious
10. pretty
11. teacher
12. nice
13. virtue
14. angry
15. crime

38d Using idioms

Idioms are expressions in any language whose meanings cannot be determined simply from the words in them or whose component words cannot be predicted by any rule of grammar; often, they violate conventional grammar. Examples of English idioms include *put up with, plug away at,* and *make off with.*

Idioms involving prepositions can be especially confusing for both native and nonnative speakers of English. Some idioms with prepositions are listed in the following box.

Idioms with prepositions

abide by a rule
  in a place or state
accords with
according to
accuse of a crime
adapt from a source
  to a situation
afraid of
agree on a plan as a group
  to someone else's plan
  with a person
angry with
aware of
based on
capable of
certain of
charge for a purchase
  with a crime
concur in an opinion
  with a person
contend for a principle or prize
  with an obstacle
dependent on
differ about or over a question
  from in some quality
  with a person
disappointed by or in a person
  in or with a thing

familiar with
identical with or to
impatient for a raise
  with a person
independent of
infer from
inferior to
involved in a task
  with a person
oblivious of or to one's surroundings
  of something forgotten
occupied by a person
  in study
  with a thing
opposed to
part from a person
  with a possession
prior to
proud of
related to
rewarded by the judge
  for something done
  with a gift
similar to
superior to
wait at, by, under a place or thing
  for a train, a person
  on a customer

CULTURE LANGUAGE If you are learning standard American English, you may find its prepositions difficult: their meanings can shift depending on context, and they have many idiomatic uses. In mastering the prepositions of standard English, you probably can't avoid memorization. But you can help yourself by memorizing related groups, such as those below for the very common *at, in, on, for,* and *since*.

At, in, or *on* in expressions of time

- **Use *at* before actual clock time:** *at 8:30.*
- **Use *in* before a month, year, century, or period:** *in April, in 2016, in the twenty-first century, in the next month.*
- **Use *on* before a day or date:** *on Tuesday, on August 3, on Labor Day.*

At, in, or *on* in expressions of place

- **Use *at* before a specific place or address:** *at the school, at 511 Iris Street.*
- **Use *in* before a place with limits or before a city, state, country, or continent:** *in the house, in a box, in Tulsa, in China, in Asia.*
- **Use *on* to mean "supported by" or "touching the surface of":** *on the table, on Iris Street, on page 150.*

For or *since* in expressions of time

- **Use *for* before a period of time:** *for an hour, for two years.*
- **Use *since* before a specific point in time:** *since 1999, since Friday.*

A dictionary of English as a second language is the best source for the meanings of prepositions; see the recommendations on page 509. In addition, some reference works focus on prepositions. See *Essential Idioms in English* or volume 1 (*Verbs with Prepositions and Particles*) of the *Oxford Dictionary of Current Idiomatic English.*

Exercise 38.6 Using prepositions in idioms

Insert the preposition that correctly completes each idiom in the following sentences. Consult the box opposite or a dictionary as needed.

Example:

I disagree _____ many feminists who say women should not be homemakers.

I disagree with many feminists who say women should not be homemakers.

1. Children are waiting longer to become independent _____ their parents.
2. According _____ US Census data for young adults ages eighteen to twenty-four, 57% of men and 47% of women live full-time with their parents.
3. Some of these adult children are dependent _____ their parents financially.
4. In other cases, the parents charge their children _____ housing, food, and other living expenses.
5. Many adult children are financially capable _____ living independently but prefer to save money rather than contend _____ high housing costs.

38e Using figurative language

Figurative language (or a **figure of speech**) departs from the literal meanings (the denotations) of words, usually by comparing very different ideas or objects:

Literal	As I try to write, I can think of nothing to say.
Figurative	As I try to write, my mind is a slab of black slate.

When you use figurative language imaginatively and carefully, it can capture your meaning more precisely and emotionally than literal language.

Figurative language is common in speech. Having *slept like a log,* you may get up to find it *raining cats and dogs*. But the rapid exchange of speech leaves little time for inventiveness, and most figures of daily conversation, like those above, are worn and hackneyed. Writing gives you time to reject the tired figure and to search out fresh, concrete words and phrases.

Following are the most common figures of speech:

- **Simile and metaphor** both compare two things of different classes, often one abstract and the other concrete. A **simile** makes the comparison explicit and usually begins with *like* or *as*:

  Whenever we grow, we tend to feel it, as a young seed must feel the weight and inertia of the earth when it seeks to break out of its shell on its way to becoming a plant. —Alice Walker

  To hold America in one's thoughts is like holding a love letter in one's hand—it has so special a meaning. —E. B. White

  Instead of stating a comparison, a **metaphor** implies it, omitting such words as *like* or *as*:

  I cannot and will not cut my conscience to fit this year's fashions. —Lillian Hellman

  A school is a hopper into which children are heaved while they are young and tender; therein they are pressed into certain standard shapes and covered from head to heels with official rubber stamps. —H. L. Mencken

- **Personification** treats ideas and objects as if they were human:

  The economy consumes my money and gives me little in return.

  I could hear the whisper of snowflakes, nudging each other as they fell.

- **Hyperbole** deliberately exaggerates:

  She appeared in a mile of billowing chiffon, flashing a rhinestone as big as an ostrich egg.

  He yelled so loud that his voice carried to the next county.

To be successful, figurative language must be not only fresh but unstrained, calling attention not to itself but to the writer's meaning. One kind of figurative language gone wrong is the **mixed metaphor**, in which the writer combines two or more incompatible figures. Since metaphors often generate visual images in the reader's mind, a mixed metaphor can be laughable:

Mixed Various thorny problems that we try to sweep under the rug continue to bob up all the same.

To revise a mixed metaphor, follow through consistently with just one image:

Improved Various thorny problems that we try to weed out continue to thrive all the same.

Exercise 38.7 Analyzing figurative language

Identify each figure of speech in the following sentences as a simile or a metaphor, and analyze how it adds to the writer's meaning.

1. A distant airplane, a delta wing out of nightmare, made a gliding shadow on the creek's bottom that looked like a stingray crossing upstream. —Annie Dillard
2. Her roots ran deep into the earth, and from those roots she drew strength enough to hold still against all the forces of chance and disorder. —N. Scott Momaday
3. As a member of the winning team (the graduating class of 1940) I had outdistanced unpleasant sensations by miles. I was headed for the freedom of open fields. —Maya Angelou
4. All artists quiver under the lash of adverse criticism. —Catherine Drinker Bowen
5. Every writer, in a roomful of writers, wants to be the best, and the judge, or umpire, or referee is soon overwhelmed and shouted down like a chickadee trying to take charge of a caucus of crows. —James Thurber

Exercise 38.8 Using figurative language

Invent appropriate figurative language of your own (simile, metaphor, hyperbole, or personification) to describe each of the following scenes or qualities, and use each figure in a sentence.

Example:

The attraction of a lake on a hot day

The small waves like fingers beckoned us irresistibly.

1. The sound of a kindergarten classroom
2. People waiting for something, such as a bus or plane
3. The politeness of strangers meeting for the first time
4. A streetlight seen through dense fog
5. The effect of watching television for ten hours straight

38f Using fresh, not trite, expressions

Trite expressions, or **clichés,** are phrases so old and so often repeated that they have become stale. They include the following:

acid test
add insult to injury
better late than never
beyond the shadow of a doubt
brought back to reality
cold, hard facts
cool as a cucumber
crushing blow
easier said than done
face the music

flat as a pancake
green with envy
hard as a rock
heavy as lead
hit the nail on the head
hour of need
ladder of success
moving experience
needle in a haystack
point with pride
ripe old age
shoulder the burden
smart as a whip
sneaking suspicion
sober as a judge
stand in awe
strong as an ox
thin as a rail
tired but happy
tried and true
untimely death
wise as an owl

Besides these old phrases, stale writing may also depend on fashionable words that are losing their effect: for instance, *lifestyle, enhance, awesome, fantastic,* and *caring.*

Many trite expressions were once fresh and forceful, but constant use has dulled them. They, in turn, will dull your writing by suggesting that you have not thought about what you are saying and have resorted to the easiest phrase.

Clichés may slide into your drafts while you are trying to express your meaning. In editing, then, be wary of any expression you have heard or used before. Substitute fresh words of your own or restate the idea in plain language.

Trite A healthful lifestyle enhances your ability to go for the gold and allows you to enjoy life to the fullest.

Revised Living healthfully helps you perform well and enjoy life thoroughly.

Exercise 38.9 Revising: Trite expressions

Revise the following sentences to eliminate trite expressions.

Example:

The basketball team had almost seized victory, but it faced the test of truth in the last quarter of the game.

The basketball team seemed about to win, but the real test came in the last quarter of the game.

1. The disastrous consequences of the war have shaken the small nation to its roots.
2. Prices for food have shot sky high, and citizens have sneaking suspicions that others are making a killing on the black market.
3. Medical supplies are so few and far between that even civilians who are as sick as dogs cannot get treatment.
4. With most men fighting or injured or killed, women have had to bite the bullet and bear the men's burden in farming and manufacturing.
5. Last but not least, the war's heavy drain on the nation's pocketbook has left the economy in a shambles.

39 Writing Concisely

Chapter essentials

- Focus on the subject and verb (next page).
- Cut empty words and unneeded repetition (pp. 520, 522).
- Tighten modifiers (p. 523).
- Revise *there is* or *it is* constructions (p. 524).
- Combine sentences (p. 524).
- Rewrite jargon (p. 524).

Visit MyWritingLab™ for more resources on writing concisely.

Concise writing makes every word count. Conciseness is not the same as mere brevity: detail and originality should not be cut along with needless words. Rather, the length of an expression should be appropriate to the thought.

You may find yourself writing wordily when you are unsure of your subject or when your thoughts are tangled. It's fine, even necessary, to stumble and grope while drafting. But you should

Ways to achieve conciseness

Wordy (87 words)

The highly pressured nature of critical-care nursing is due to the fact that the patients have life-threatening illnesses. Critical-care nurses must have possession of steady nerves to care for patients who are critically ill and very sick. The nurses must also have possession of interpersonal skills. They must also have medical skills. It is considered by most health-care professionals that these nurses are essential if there is to be improvement of patients who are now in critical care from that status to the status of intermediate care.

- Focus on subject and verb, and cut or shorten empty words and phrases.
- Avoid nouns made from verbs.
- Cut unneeded repetition.
- Combine sentences.
- Change passive voice to active voice.
- Revise *there is* constructions.
- Cut unneeded repetition, and tighten modifiers.

Concise (37 words)

Critical-care nursing is highly pressured because the patients have life-threatening illnesses. Critical-care nurses must possess steady nerves and interpersonal and medical skills. Most health-care professionals consider these nurses essential if patients are to improve to intermediate care.

straighten out your ideas and eliminate wordiness during revision and editing.

CULTURE LANGUAGE As you'll see in this chapter's examples, wordiness is not a problem of incorrect grammar. A sentence may be perfectly grammatical but still contain unneeded words that make it unclear or awkward.

39a Focusing on the subject and verb

Using the subjects and verbs of your sentences for the key actors and actions will reduce words and emphasize important ideas. (See pp. 382–83 for more on this topic.)

Wordy The reason why most of the country shifts to daylight time is that summer days are much longer than winter days.

Concise Most of the country shifts to daylight time because summer days are much longer than winter days.

Focusing on subjects and verbs will also help you avoid several other causes of wordiness discussed further on pages 382–83:

Nouns made from verbs

Wordy The occurrence of the winter solstice, the shortest day of the year, is an event occurring about December 22.

Concise The winter solstice, the shortest day of the year, occurs about December 22.

Weak verbs

Wordy The earth's axis has a tilt as the planet is in orbit around the sun so that the northern and southern hemispheres are alternately in alignment toward the sun.

Concise The earth's axis tilts as the planet orbits the sun so that the northern and southern hemispheres alternately align toward the sun.

Passive voice

Wordy During its winter the northern hemisphere is tilted farthest away from the sun, so the nights are made longer and the days are made shorter.

Concise During its winter the northern hemisphere tilts away from the sun, which makes the nights longer and the days shorter.

See also pages 307–08 on changing the passive voice to the active voice, as in the example above.

39b Cutting or shortening empty words and phrases

Empty words and phrases walk in place, gaining little or nothing in meaning. When you cut or shorten them, your writing will move faster and work harder.

Many empty phrases can be cut entirely:

all things considered	in a manner of speaking
as far as I'm concerned	in my opinion
for all intents and purposes	last but not least
for the most part	more or less

Wordy In my opinion, the council's proposal to improve the city center is inadequate, all things considered.

Concise The council's proposal to improve the city center is inadequate.

Other empty words can be cut along with some words around them:

angle	character	kind	situation
area	element	manner	thing
aspect	factor	nature	type
case	field		

Wordy The type of large expenditures on advertising that manufacturers must make is a very important aspect of the cost of detergents.

Concise Manufacturers' large advertising expenditures increase the cost of detergents.

Still other empty phrases can be reduced from several words to a single word:

For	Substitute
at all times	always
at the present time	now
at this point in time	now
in today's society	now
in the nature of	like
for the purpose of	for
in order to	to
until such time as	until
for the reason that	because
due to the fact that	because
because of the fact that	because
by virtue of the fact that	because
despite the fact that	although
in the event that	if
by means of	by
in the final analysis	finally

Wordy At this point in time, the software is expensive due to the fact that it has no competition.

Concise The software is expensive now because it has no competition.

Exercise 39.1 Revising: Subjects and verbs; empty words and phrases

Revise the following sentences to achieve conciseness by focusing on subjects and verbs and by cutting or reducing empty words and phrases.

w 39b

See also page 383 for an additional exercise in focusing on subjects and verbs.

Example:

I made college my destination because of many factors, but most of all because of the fact that I want a career in medicine.

I came to college mainly because I want a career in medicine.

1. *Gerrymandering* refers to a situation in which the lines of a voting district are redrawn so that a particular party or ethnic group has benefits.
2. The name is a reference to the fact that Elbridge Gerry, the governor of Massachusetts in 1812, redrew voting districts in Essex County.
3. On the map one new district was seen to resemble something in the nature of a salamander.
4. Upon seeing the map, a man who was for all intents and purposes a critic of Governor Gerry's administration cried out, "Gerrymander!"
5. At the present time, changes may be made in the character of a district's voting pattern by a political group by gerrymandering to achieve the exclusion of rival groups' supporters.

39c Cutting unnecessary repetition

Planned repetition and restatement can make writing more coherent (p. 82) or emphatic (p. 388). But unnecessary repetition weakens sentences:

Wordy Many unskilled workers without training in a particular job are unemployed and do not have any work.

Concise Many unskilled workers are unemployed.

The use of one word two different ways within a sentence is confusing:

Confusing Preschool instructors play a role in the child's understanding of male and female roles.

Clear Preschool instructors contribute to the child's understanding of male and female roles.

The simplest kind of useless repetition is the phrase that says the same thing twice. In the following examples, the unneeded words are underlined:

biography of his life
circle around
consensus of opinion
continue on
cooperate together
few in number
final completion
frank and honest exchange
the future to come
habitual custom
important [basic] essentials
large in size
puzzling in nature
repeat again
return again
revert back
square [round] in shape
surrounding circumstances

w 39c

CULTURE LANGUAGE Phrases like those above are redundant because the main word already implies the underlined word or words. The repetition is not emphatic but tedious. A dictionary will tell you what meanings a word implies. *Assassinate,* for instance, means "murder someone well known," so the following sentence is redundant: *Abraham Lincoln was assassinated and killed at a theater.*

Exercise 39.2 Revising: Unnecessary repetition

Revise the following sentences to achieve conciseness. Concentrate on eliminating repetition and redundancy.

Example:

Because the circumstances surrounding the cancellation of classes were murky and unclear, the editor of the student newspaper assigned a staff reporter to investigate and file a report on the circumstances.

Because the circumstances leading to the cancellation of classes were unclear, the editor of the student newspaper assigned a staffer to investigate and report the story.

1. Some Vietnam veterans coming back to the United States after their tours of duty in Vietnam had problems readjusting again to life in America.
2. Afflicted with post-traumatic stress disorder, a psychological disorder that sometimes arises after a trauma, some veterans had psychological problems that caused them to have trouble holding jobs and maintaining relationships.
3. Some who used to use drugs in Vietnam could not break their drug habits after they returned back to the United States.
4. The few veterans who committed crimes and violent acts gained so much notoriety and fame that many Americans thought all veterans were crazy, insane maniacs.
5. As a result of such stereotyping of Vietnam-era veterans, veterans are included in the same antidiscrimination laws that protect other victims of discrimination.

39d Tightening modifiers

Modifiers—subordinate clauses, phrases, and single words—can be expanded or contracted depending on the emphasis you want to achieve. (See pp. 257–67 on phrases and clauses and 394–96 on working with modifiers.) When editing your sentences, consider whether any modifiers can be tightened without loss of emphasis or clarity:

Wordy The weight-loss industry faces new competition from lipolysis, which is a cosmetic procedure that is relatively noninvasive.

Concise The weight-loss industry faces new competition from lipolysis, a relatively noninvasive cosmetic procedure.

39e Revising *there is* and *it is* constructions

You can postpone the sentence subject with the words *there* and *it*: *There are three points made in the text. It was not fair that only seniors could vote.* (See pp. 270–71.) These constructions can be useful to emphasize the subject (as when introducing it for the first time) or to indicate a change in direction. But often they just add words and weaken sentences:

Wordy There is a completely noninvasive laser treatment that makes people thinner by rupturing fat cells and releasing the fat into the spaces between cells. It is the expectation of some doctors that the procedure will replace liposuction.

Concise A completely noninvasive laser treatment makes people thinner by rupturing fat cells and releasing the fat into the spaces between cells. Some doctors expect that the procedure will replace liposuction.

39f Combining sentences

Often the information in two or more sentences can be combined into one tight sentence:

Wordy People who receive fat-releasing laser treatments can lose inches from their waists. They can also lose inches from their hips and thighs. They do not lose weight. The released fat remains in their bodies.

Concise People who receive fat-releasing laser treatments can lose inches from their waists, hips, and thighs; but they do not lose weight because the released fat remains in their bodies.

A number of exercises in this handbook give you practice in sentence combining. For a list, see "Sentence combining" in the book's index.

39g Rewriting jargon

Jargon can refer to the special vocabulary of any discipline or profession (see p. 502). But the term has also come to describe vague, inflated language that is overcomplicated, even incomprehensible. When it comes from government or business, we call it *bureaucratese.*

Jargon The weekly social gatherings stimulate networking by members of management from various divisions, with the aim of developing contacts and maximizing the flow of creative information.

Translation The weekly parties give managers from different divisions a chance to meet and to share ideas.

Exercise 39.3 Revising: Conciseness

Rewrite each of the following passages into a single concise sentence, using the techniques described in this chapter.

Example:

He was taking some exercise in the park. Then several thugs were suddenly ahead of him in his path.

He was exercising [or jogging or strolling] in the park when several thugs suddenly loomed in his path.

1. Chewing gum was originally introduced to the United States by Antonio López de Santa Anna. He was the Mexican general.
2. After he had been defeated by the Texans in 1845, the general, who was exiled, made the choice to settle in New York.
3. A piece of chicle had been stashed by the general in his baggage. Chicle is the dried milky sap of the Mexican sapodilla tree.
4. There was more of this resin brought into the country by Santa Anna's friend Thomas Adams. Adams had a plan to make rubber.
5. The plan failed. Then the occasion arose for Adams to get a much more successful idea on the basis of the use to which the resin was put by General Santa Anna. That is, Adams decided to make a gum that could be chewed.

Exercise 39.4 Revising: Conciseness

Make the following passage as concise as possible. Be merciless.

At the end of a lengthy line of reasoning, he came to the conclusion that the situation with carcinogens [cancer-causing substances] should be regarded as similar to the situation with the automobile. Instead of giving in to an irrational fear of cancer, we should consider all aspects of the problem in a balanced and dispassionate frame of mind, making a total of the benefits received from potential carcinogens (plastics, pesticides, and other similar products) and measuring said total against the damage done by such products. This is the nature of most discussions about the automobile. Instead of responding irrationally to the visual, aural, and air pollution caused by automobiles, we have decided to live with them (while simultaneously working to improve on them) for the benefits brought to society as a whole.

40 Spelling and the Hyphen

Chapter essentials

- Recognize typical causes of misspelling, such as misleading pronunciation (below).
- Follow spelling rules for *ie* vs. *ei,* attaching endings or prefixes to words, and forming plurals (p. 529).
- Develop skills such as careful proofreading, using a dictionary, and memorizing tricky spellings (p. 533).
- Use the hyphen correctly to form or divide words (p. 537).

Visit MyWritingLab™ for more resources on spelling and the hyphen.

English spelling is difficult, even for very experienced and capable writers. You can train yourself to spell better, and the advice in this chapter will help you. But you can also improve instantly by adopting these habits:

Ways to improve your spelling

- **Carefully proofread all your writing.** Use the proofreading tips on pages 66–67 to help you find spelling errors.
- **Check a dictionary *every time* you doubt a spelling.** Being suspicious of your spellings and relying on a dictionary will take care of many potential spelling errors.
- **Create a list of your spelling errors.** Keep a record of words you misspell, and check the list every time you write a paper. With experience, you'll learn to recognize and correct the words you typically misspell.
- **Use a spelling checker critically.** A spelling checker can help you find spelling errors in your papers. However, its usefulness is limited because it can't spot the common error of confusing words with similar spellings, such as *now/not, to/too, their/they're/there,* and *principal/principle.* See page 65 for more on spelling checkers.

40a Recognizing typical spelling problems

Spelling well involves recognizing situations that commonly lead to misspelling: pronunciation can mislead you in several ways; different forms of the same word may have different spellings; and some words have more than one acceptable spelling.

1 Being wary of pronunciation

In English, unlike some other languages, the pronunciation of words is an unreliable guide to their spelling. The same letters may have different sounds in different words. (Say aloud these different ways of pronouncing the letters *ough*: *tough, dough, cough, through, bough.*) In addition, some words contain letters that are not pronounced clearly or at all, such as the *ed* in *asked,* the silent *e* in *swipe,* or the unpronounced *gh* in *tight.*

Pronunciation is a particularly unreliable guide in spelling **homonyms,** words that are pronounced the same although they have different spellings and meanings: *great/grate, to/too/two.* Some commonly confused homonyms and near-homonyms, such as *accept/except,* are listed below. (See pp. 535–37 for tips on using spelling lists.)

Words commonly confused

accept (to receive)
except (other than)

advice (a recommendation)
advise (to recommend)

affect (to have an influence on)
effect (a result)

all ready (prepared)
already (by this time)

allude (to refer to indirectly)
elude (to avoid)

allusion (an indirect reference)
illusion (an erroneous belief or perception)

ascent (a movement up)
assent (to agree, or an agreement)

bare (unclothed)
bear (to carry, or an animal)

board (a plane of wood)
bored (uninterested)

born (brought into life)
borne (carried)

brake (to stop)
break (to smash)

buy (to purchase)
by (next to)

capital (the seat of a government)
capitol (the building where a legislature meets)

cite (to quote an authority)
sight (the ability to see)
site (a place)

desert (to abandon)
dessert (after-dinner course)

discreet (reserved, respectful)
discrete (individual or distinct)

elicit (to bring out)
illicit (illegal)

eminent (well known)
imminent (soon to happen)

fair (average, or lovely)
fare (a fee for transportation)

forth (forward)
fourth (after *third*)

gorilla (a large primate)
guerrilla (a kind of soldier)

hear (to perceive by ear)
here (in this place)

heard (past tense of *hear*)
herd (a group of animals)

hole (an opening)
whole (complete)

its (possessive of *it*)
it's (contraction of *it is* or *it has*)

lead (heavy metal)
led (past tense of *lead*)

lessen (to make less)
lesson (something learned)

meat (flesh)
meet (to encounter, or a competition)

no (the opposite of *yes*)
know (to be certain)

(continued)

Words commonly confused

(continued)

passed (past tense of *pass*)
past (after, or a time gone by)

patience (forbearance)
patients (persons under medical care)

peace (the absence of war)
piece (a portion of something)

persecute (to oppress, to harass)
prosecute (to pursue, to take legal action against)

plain (clear)
plane (a carpenter's tool, or an airborne vehicle)

presence (the state of being at hand)
presents (gifts)

principal (most important, or the head of a school)
principle (a basic truth or law)

rain (precipitation)
reign (to rule)
rein (a strap for controlling an animal)

raise (to build up)
raze (to tear down)

right (correct)
rite (a religious ceremony)
write (to make letters)

road (a surface for driving)
rode (past tense of *ride*)

scene (where an action occurs)
seen (past participle of *see*)

seam (a junction)
seem (to appear)

stationary (unmoving)
stationery (writing paper)

straight (unbending)
strait (a water passageway)

their (possessive of *they*)
there (opposite of *here*)
they're (contraction of *they are*)

to (toward)
too (also)
two (following *one*)

waist (the middle of the body)
waste (discarded material)

weak (not strong)
week (Sunday through Saturday)

weather (climate)
whether (*if*, or introducing a choice)

which (one of a group)
witch (a sorcerer)

who's (contraction of *who is* or *who has*)
whose (possessive of *who*)

your (possessive of *you*)
you're (contraction of *you are*)

2 Distinguishing between different forms of the same word

Spelling problems may occur when forms of the same word have different spellings, as in the following examples.

Verbs and nouns

Verb	Noun	Verb	Noun
advise	advice	enter	entrance
describe	description	marry	marriage
speak	speech	omit	omission

sp 40a

Nouns and adjectives

Noun	Adjective	Noun	Adjective
comedy	comic	height	high
courtesy	courteous	Britain	British
generosity	generous		

Irregular verbs

begin, began, begun	know, knew, known
break, broke, broken	ring, rang, rung

Irregular nouns

child, children	shelf, shelves
goose, geese	tooth, teeth
mouse, mice	woman, women

Other differences

four, forty	thief, theft

3 Using preferred spellings

When writing for an American audience, use American spellings instead of their British equivalents. An American dictionary will show a British spelling as a variant or give it a label such as *chiefly British*.

American	British
color, humor	colour, humour
theater, center	theatre, centre
canceled, traveled	cancelled, travelled
judgment	judgement
realize	realise

40b Following spelling rules

Misspelling is often a matter of misspelling a syllable rather than the whole word. The following general rules focus on troublesome syllables, with notes for the occasional exceptions.

1 Distinguishing between *ie* and *ei*

Words like *believe* and *receive* sound alike in the second syllable, but the syllable is spelled differently. Use the familiar jingle to distinguish between *ie* and *ei*:

> *I* before *e,* except after *c,* or when pronounced "ay" as in *neighbor* and *weigh.*

i* before *e	believe	bier	hygiene
	grief	thief	friend

ei after c	ceiling receive	conceive deceit	perceive conceit
ei sounded as "ay"	neighbor sleigh	weight freight	eight vein

Exceptions In some words an *ei* combination neither follows *c* nor is pronounced "ay." These words include *either, neither, foreign, forfeit, height, leisure, weird, seize,* and *seizure*. This sentence might help you remember some of them: *The weird foreigner neither seizes leisure nor forfeits height.*

Exercise 40.1 Distinguishing between *ie* and *ei*

Insert *ie* or *ei* in the words below. Check doubtful spellings in a dictionary.

1. br__f	5. for__gn	9. l__surely	13. h__ght
2. dec__ve	6. pr__st	10. ach__ve	14. fr__ght
3. rec__pt	7. gr__vance	11. pat__nce	15. f__nt
4. s__ze	8. f__nd	12. p__rce	16. s__ve

2 Keeping or dropping a final *e*

Many words end with an unpronounced or silent *e*: *move, brave, late, rinse.* Drop the final *e* when adding an ending that begins with a vowel:

advise + able = advisable
force + ible = forcible
surprise + ing = surprising
guide + ance = guidance

Keep the final, silent *e* when adding an ending that begins with a consonant:

battle + ment = battlement
accurate + ly = accurately
care + ful = careful
like + ness = likeness

Exceptions The silent *e* is sometimes retained before an ending beginning with a vowel. It is kept when *dye* becomes *dyeing,* to avoid confusion with *dying.* It is kept to prevent mispronunciation of words like *shoeing* (not *shoing*) and *mileage* (not *milage*). And the final *e* is often retained after a soft *c* or *g,* to keep the sound of the consonant soft rather than hard:

courageous	changeable	noticeable
outrageous	manageable	embraceable

The silent *e* is also sometimes *dropped* before an ending beginning with a consonant, when the *e* is preceded by another vowel:

argue + ment = argument
true + ly = truly

Exercise 40.2 Keeping or dropping a final *e*

Combine the following words and endings, keeping or dropping a final *e* as necessary to make correctly spelled words. Check doubtful spellings in a dictionary.

1. malice + ious	4. retire + ment	7. note + able
2. love + able	5. sue + ing	8. battle + ing
3. service + able	6. virtue + ous	9. suspense + ion

3 Keeping or dropping a final *y*

Words ending in *y* often change their spelling when an ending is added. Change the final *y* to an *i* when it follows a consonant:

beauty, beauties	worry, worried	supply, supplies
folly, follies	merry, merrier	deputy, deputize

But keep the *y* when it follows a vowel, when the added ending is *ing,* or when the *y* ends a proper name:

day, days	cry, crying	May, Mays
obey, obeyed	study, studying	Minsky, Minskys

Exercise 40.3 Keeping or dropping a final *y*

Combine the following words and endings, changing or keeping a final *y* as necessary to make correctly spelled words. Check doubtful spellings in a dictionary.

1. imply + s	4. delay + ing	7. solidify + s
2. messy + er	5. defy + ance	8. Murphy + s
3. apply + ing	6. say + s	9. supply + ed

4 Doubling consonants

Whether to double a word's final consonant depends first on the number of syllables in the word. In one-syllable words, double the final consonant when a single vowel precedes the final consonant. Otherwise, don't double the consonant.

slap, slapping	pair, paired
tip, tipping	park, parking

In words of more than one syllable, double the final consonant when a single vowel precedes the final consonant *and* the consonant ends a stressed syllable once the ending is added. Otherwise, don't double the consonant.

refer, referring	refer, reference
begin, beginning	relent, relented
occur, occurrence	despair, despairing

Exercise 40.4 Doubling consonants

Combine the following words and endings, doubling final consonants as necessary to make correctly spelled words. Check doubtful spellings in a dictionary.

1. repair + ing	4. shop + ed	7. drip + ing
2. admit + ance	5. conceal + ed	8. declaim + ed
3. benefit + ed	6. allot + ed	9. parallel + ing

5 Attaching prefixes

Adding a prefix such as *dis, mis,* and *un* does not change the spelling of a word. When adding a prefix, do not drop a letter from or add a letter to the original word:

uneasy	anti-intellectual	defuse	misstate
unnecessary	disappoint	de-emphasize	misspell
antifreeze	dissatisfied	misinform	

(See also p. 539 for when to use hyphens with prefixes: *prehistory* versus *ex-student.*)

6 Forming plurals

Nouns

Most nouns form plurals by adding *s* to the singular form:

table, tables	boy, boys
carnival, carnivals	Murphy, Murphys

Boys and *Murphys* above add *s* to a *y* ending because the *y* follows a vowel (*boy*) or ends a proper noun (*Murphy*). When a final *y* follows a consonant in a common noun, change the *y* to *ie* before adding *s*:

baby, babies	lady, ladies

Some nouns ending in *f* or *fe* form the plural by changing the ending to *ve* before adding *s*:

leaf, leaves	wife, wives
life, lives	yourself, yourselves

Singular nouns ending in *s, sh, ch,* or *x* form the plural by adding *es*:

kiss, kisses	church, churches
wish, wishes	Jones, Joneses

(Notice that verbs ending in *s, sh, ch,* or *x* form the third-person singular in the same way. *Taxes* and *lurches* are examples.)

Nouns ending in *o* preceded by a vowel usually form the plural by adding *s*:

ratio, ratios	zoo, zoos

Nouns ending in *o* preceded by a consonant usually form the plural by adding *es*:

hero, heroes	tomato, tomatoes

Exceptions Some very common nouns form irregular plurals:

child, children	man, men
mouse, mice	woman, women

Some English nouns that were originally Italian, Greek, Latin, or French form the plural according to their original language:

analysis, analyses	datum, data
basis, bases	medium, media
beau, beaux	phenomenon, phenomena
crisis, crises	piano, pianos
criterion, criteria	thesis, theses

A few such nouns may form irregular or regular plurals: for instance, *index, indices, indexes; curriculum, curricula, curriculums*. The regular plural is more contemporary.

CULTURE LANGUAGE Noncount nouns do not form plurals, either regularly (with an added *s*) or irregularly. Examples of noncount nouns include *equipment, courage,* and *wealth.* (See p. 332.)

Compound nouns

Form plurals of compound nouns in one of two ways. Add *s* to the last word when the component words are roughly equal in importance, whether or not they are hyphenated:

city-states	breakthroughs
painter-sculptors	bucket seats

Add *s* to a noun combined with other parts of speech:

fathers-in-law	passersby

Note, however, that most modern dictionaries give the plural of *spoonful* as *spoonfuls.*

Exercise 40.5 Forming plurals

Make the correct plural of each of the following singular words. Check doubtful spellings in a dictionary.

1. pile	5. mile per hour	9. Bales	13. thief
2. donkey	6. box	10. cupful	14. goose
3. beach	7. switch	11. libretto	15. hiss
4. summary	8. sister-in-law	12. video	16. appendix

40c Developing spelling skills

The following techniques can help you improve your spelling. In addition, do not overrely on your computer's spelling checker (see p. 65).

1 Editing and proofreading carefully

If spelling is a problem for you, give it high priority while editing your writing (p. 61) and again while proofreading, your last chance to catch misspelled words (p. 66). Reading a draft backward, word by word, can help you spot mistakes such as switched or omitted letters in words you know. Because the procedure forces you to consider each word in isolation, it can also highlight spellings you may be less sure of. A sense of uncertainty is crucial in spotting and correcting spelling errors, even for good spellers who make relatively few errors. Listen to your own uncertainty, and let it lead you to the dictionary.

2 Using a dictionary

How can you look up a word you can't spell? Start by guessing at the spelling and looking up your guess. If that doesn't work, pronounce the word aloud to come up with other possible spellings, and look them up. Unless the word is too specialized to be included in your dictionary, trial and error will eventually pay off.

If you're using a spelling checker, it may do the guessing for you by providing alternatives for a misspelled word and highlighting a likely option. But you may still need to check a dictionary to verify your choice.

3 Pronouncing carefully

Careful pronunciation is not always a reliable guide to spelling (see p. 527), but it can keep you from misspelling words that are often mispronounced. For example:

athletics (*not* atheletics)
disastrous (*not* disasterous)
environment (*not* envirnment)
frustrate (*not* fustrate)
government (*not* goverment)
height (*not* heighth)
history (*not* histry)
irrelevant (*not* irrevelant)
laboratory (*not* labratory)
library (*not* libary)
lightning (*not* lightening)
mischievous (*not* mischievious)
nuclear (*not* nucular)
recognize (*not* reconize)
representative (*not* representive)
strictly (*not* stricly)

4 Tracking and analyzing your errors

Keep a list of the words marked "misspelled" or "spelling" or "sp" in your papers. This list will contain hints about your particular spelling problems, such as confusing *affect* and *effect* or forming plurals incorrectly. (If you need help analyzing the list, consult your writing instructor.) The list will also provide a personalized study guide, a focus for your efforts to spell better.

5 Using mnemonics

Mnemonics (pronounced with an initial *n* sound) are techniques for assisting your memory. The *er* in *letter* and *paper* can remind you that *stationery* (meaning "writing paper") has an *er* near the end;

stationary with an *a* means "standing in place." Or the word *dome* with its long *o* sound can remind you that the building in which the legislature meets is spelled *capitol,* with an *o.* The *capital* city is spelled with *al* like *Albany,* the capital of New York. If you identify the words you have trouble spelling, you can create your own mnemonics, which may work better for you than someone else's.

6 Studying spelling lists

Learning to spell commonly misspelled words will reduce your spelling errors. For general improvement, work with the following list of commonly misspelled words. Study only six or seven words at a time. If you are unsure of the meaning of a word, look it up in a dictionary and try using it in a sentence. Pronounce the word out loud, syllable by syllable, and write the word out. (The list of similar-sounding words on pp. 527–28 should be considered an extension of the following list.)

absence
abundance
acceptable
accessible
accidentally
accommodate
accomplish
accumulate
accuracy
accustomed
achieve
acknowledge
acquire
across
actually
address
admission
adolescent
advice
advising
against
aggravate
aggressive
all right
all together
allegiance
almost
a lot
already
although
altogether
amateur
among

amount
analysis
analyze
angel
annual
answer
apology
apparent
appearance
appetite
appreciate
appropriate
approximately
argument
arrest
ascend
assassinate
assimilation
assistance
associate
atheist
athlete
attendance
audience
average

bargain
basically
because
beginning
belief
believe
beneficial
benefited
boundary
breath
Britain
bureaucracy
business

calculator
calendar
caricature
carrying
cede
ceiling
cello
cemetery
certain
changeable
changing
characteristic
chief
chocolate
choose
chose
climbed
coarse
column
coming
commercial
commitment
committed
committee
competent
competition

complement
compliment
conceive
concentrate
concert
condemn
conquer
conscience
conscious
consistency
consistent
continuous
controlled
controversial
convenience
convenient
coolly
course
courteous
criticism
criticize
crowd
cruelty
curiosity
curious
curriculum

deceive
deception
decide
decision
deductible
definitely

degree
dependent
descend
descendant
describe
description
desirable
despair
desperate
destroy
determine
develop
device
devise
dictionary
difference
dining
disagree
disappear
disappoint
disapprove
disastrous
discipline
discriminate
discussion
disease
disgusted
dissatisfied
distinction
divide
divine
division
doctor
drawer

easily
ecstasy
efficiency
efficient
eighth
either
eligible
embarrass
emphasize
empty
enemy
entirely
entrepreneur
environment
equipped
especially
essential
every
exaggerate
exceed
excellent
exercise
exhaust
exhilarate
existence
expense
experience
experiment
explanation
extremely

familiar
fascinate
favorite
February
fiery
finally
forcibly
foreign
foresee
forty
forward
friend
frightening
fulfill

gauge
generally
ghost
government
grammar
grief
guarantee
guard
guidance

happily
harass
height
heroes
hideous
humorous
hungry
hurriedly
hurrying
hypocrisy
hypocrite

ideally
illogical
imaginary
imagine
imitation
immediately
immigrant
incidentally
incredible
independence
independent
individually
inevitably
influential
initiate
innocuous
inoculate
insistent
integrate
intelligence
interest
interference
interpret
irrelevant
irresistible
irritable
island

jealousy
judgment

kindergarten
knowledge

laboratory
leisure
length
library
license
lieutenant
lightning
likelihood
literally
livelihood
loneliness
loose
lose
luxury
lying

magazine
maintenance
manageable
marriage
mathematics
meant
medicine
miniature
minor
minutes
mirror
mischievous
missile
misspelled
morale
morals
mortgage
mournful
muscle
mysterious

naturally
necessary
neighbor
neither
nickel
niece
ninety
ninth
noticeable
nuclear
nuisance
numerous

obstacle
occasion
occasionally
occur
occurrence
official
omission
omit
omitted
opinion
opponent
opportunity
opposite
ordinary
originally

paid
panicky

paralleled
parliament
particularly
peaceable
peculiar
pedal
perceive
perception
performance
permanent
permissible
persistence
personnel
perspiration
persuade
persuasion
physical
physiology
physique
pitiful
planning
playwright
pleasant
poison
politician
pollute
possession
possibly
practically
practice
prairie
precede
preference
preferred
prejudice
preparation
prevalent
primitive
privilege
probably
procedure
proceed
process
professor

prominent
pronunciation
psychology
purpose
pursue
pursuit

quandary
quantity
quarter
questionnaire
quiet
quizzes

realistically
realize
really
rebel
rebelled
recede
receipt
receive
recognize
recommend
reference
referred
relief
relieve
religious
remembrance
reminisce
renown
repetition
representative
resemblance
resistance
restaurant
rhyme
rhythm
ridiculous
roommate

sacrifice
sacrilegious

safety
satellite
scarcity
schedule
science
secretary
seize
separate
sergeant
several
sheriff
shining
shoulder
siege
significance
similar
sincerely
sophomore
source
speak
specimen
speech
sponsor
strategy
strength
strenuous
stretch
strict
strictly
studying
succeed
successful
sufficient
summary
superintendent
supersede
suppress
surely
surprise
suspicious

teammate
technical
technique

temperature
tendency
than
then
thorough
though
throughout
together
tomatoes
tomorrow
tragedy
transferred
truly
twelfth
tyranny

unanimous
unconscious
undoubtedly
unnecessary
until
usable
usually

vacuum
vegetable
vengeance
vicious
villain
visible

weather
Wednesday
weird
wherever
whether
wholly
woman
women
writing

yacht

40d Using the hyphen to form or divide words

The hyphen (-) is a mark of punctuation used either to form words or to divide them at the ends of lines.

1 Forming compound adjectives

When two or more words serve together as a single modifier before a noun, a hyphen or hyphens form the modifying words clearly into a unit:

She is a well-known actor.
The conclusions are based on out-of-date statistics.
Some Spanish-speaking students work as translators.

When the same compound adjectives follow the noun, hyphens are unnecessary and are usually left out.

The actor is well known.
The statistics were out of date.
Many students are Spanish speaking.

Hyphens are also unnecessary in compound modifiers containing an *-ly* adverb, even when the modifiers fall before the noun: *clearly defined terms; swiftly moving train.*

When part of a compound adjective appears only once in two or more parallel compound adjectives, hyphens indicate which words the reader should mentally join with the missing part:

School-aged children should have eight- or nine-o'clock bedtimes.

2 Writing fractions and compound numbers

Hyphens join the numerator and denominator of fractions and the parts of the whole numbers twenty-one to ninety-nine:

three-fourths	twenty-four
one-half	eighty-seven

3 Forming coined compounds

Writers sometimes create (coin) temporary compounds and join the words with hyphens:

Muhammad Ali gave his opponent a come-and-get-me look.

4 Attaching some prefixes and suffixes

Do not use hyphens with prefixes except as follows:

- **With the prefixes *self-*, *all-*, and *ex-*:** *self-control, all-inclusive, ex-student.*
- **With a prefix before a capitalized word:** *un-American.*
- **With a capital letter before a word:** *T-shirt.*
- **To prevent misreading:** *de-emphasize, anti-intellectual.*

The only suffix that regularly requires a hyphen is *-elect,* as in *president-elect.*

5 Eliminating confusion

Hyphens can prevent possible confusion:

Confusing Doonesbury is a comic strip character. [Is Doonesbury a comic (funny) character who strips or a character in a comic strip?]

Clear Doonesbury is a comic-strip character.

Hyphens can also clarify words with added prefixes. For example, *recreation* (*creation* with the prefix *re-*) could mean either "a new creation" or "diverting, pleasurable activity." The use of a hyphen, *re-creation,* limits the word to the first meaning. Without a hyphen the word suggests the second meaning.

6 Dividing words at the ends of lines

You can avoid occasional short lines in your documents by dividing some words between the end of one line and the beginning of the next. On a word processor, you can set the program to divide words automatically at appropriate breaks (in the Tools menu, select Language and then Hyphenation). To divide words manually, follow these guidelines:

- **Divide words only between syllables**—for instance, *win-dows*, not *wi-ndows*. Check a dictionary for correct syllable breaks.
- **Never divide a one-syllable word.**
- **Leave at least two letters on the first line and three on the second line.** If a word cannot be divided to follow this rule (for instance, *a-bus-er*), don't divide it.
- **Do not use a hyphen in breaking an electronic address** because readers may perceive any added hyphens as part of the address. The documentation styles differ in where they allow breaks in URLs. For example, MLA style allows a break only after a slash, while APA style allows a break before most punctuation marks.

Exercise 40.6 Using hyphens in compound words

Insert hyphens as needed in the following compounds. Mark all compounds that are correct as given. Consult a dictionary as needed.

1. reimburse
2. deescalate
3. forty odd soldiers
4. little known bar
5. seven eighths
6. seventy eight
7. happy go lucky
8. preexisting
9. senator elect
10. postwar
11. two and six person cars
12. ex songwriter
13. V shaped
14. reeducate

PART 9

Research Writing

41 Planning a Research Project

Chapter essentials

- Get started on your project (below).
- Find a researchable subject and question (p. 544).
- Develop a research strategy (p. 548).
- Make a working bibliography by tracking and recording source information (p. 551).
- Summarize and assess sources using annotations (p. 554).

Visit MyWritingLab™ for more resources on planning a research project.

Like most of the writing you do in college, research writing is a process that involves stages. Generally, you will pass through and return to the following stages while you work on a research project:

- **Choosing a subject and posing a question about it**
- **Finding information about the subject to answer the question**
- **Evaluating source information and synthesizing the ideas of others with your own**
- **Integrating source information into your writing**
- **Documenting the ideas of others in source citations**
- **Drafting, revising, and editing the project**

These topics and others are covered throughout Chapters 41–46. We will follow the development of research papers by two students, Justin Malik and Vanessa Haley. Malik's work, emphasizing interpretation, receives somewhat more attention; Haley's work, emphasizing analysis, enters the discussion whenever her process differed significantly from Malik's. Both students' final papers appear in Chapter 48.

41a Starting out

With its diverse and overlapping activities, research writing demands more planning than other kinds of writing. You'll need to understand your instructor's assignment, schedule and manage your time, and keep a record of your evolving ideas.

1 Understanding your assignment

Read your assignment carefully to be sure you understand what it requires and what leeway you have. The kind of paper or project you pursue will be influenced by whether you are expected to report, to interpret, or to analyze sources:

- **Report:** Survey, organize, and objectively present the available evidence about a topic.
- **Interpret:** Examine a range of views on a topic and argue your own conclusion about it.
- **Analyze:** Argue for the solution to a problem or the answer to a question based on critical thinking about texts such as scholarly or literary works. (In this context, *analysis* stands for the entire process of critical reading and writing. See pp. 146–74.)

No matter what kind of paper you write, always focus on developing your own ideas, using sources as support. Avoid the temptation to seek a "silver bullet"—that is, to locate two or three perfect sources that already say everything you want to say about your subject. Instead of merely repeating others' ideas, read and synthesize many sources so that you enter into a dialog with them and develop your own ideas.

2 Preparing a schedule

As soon as you receive an assignment for a research project, you can begin developing a strategy for completing it. The first step should be making a schedule that apportions the available time to the necessary work. A possible schedule appears on the next page. In it the research-writing process corresponds to the general writing process discussed in Chapters 1–3: planning or developing (steps 1–9), drafting (step 10), and revising and editing (step 12), plus the additional important stage of documenting the sources you use (steps 11 and 13).

3 Keeping a research journal

To keep track of your activities and ideas during research, maintain a research journal throughout the process. (See pp. 20–21 and 148–49 on journal keeping.) Make your journal portable so that you can carry it with you conveniently. Many researchers use paper notebooks, notebook computers, or mobile devices. Some schools offer students blog space for recording research and other learning activities.

In the research journal's dated entries, you can write about the sources you consult, the leads you want to pursue, and any difficulties you encounter. Most important, you can record your thoughts about sources, leads, dead ends, new directions, relationships, and anything else that strikes you. The very act of writing in your journal can expand and clarify your thinking.

Note The research journal is the place to track and develop your own ideas. To avoid mixing up your thoughts and those of others, keep separate notes on what your sources actually say, using one of the methods discussed on pages 597–98.

41b

Scheduling steps in research writing

(See the pages in parentheses for discussion of the steps.)

Complete by:

_____ 1. Setting a schedule and beginning a research journal (previous page)
_____ 2. Finding a researchable subject and question (below)
_____ 3. Developing a research strategy (p. 548)
_____ 4. Finding sources, both print and electronic (p. 555), and making a working bibliography (p. 551)

_____ 5. Evaluating and synthesizing sources (pp. 580, 593)
_____ 6. Mining and interacting with sources (p. 596), often using summary, paraphrase, and direct quotation (p. 599)
_____ 7. Taking steps to avoid plagiarism (p. 614)
_____ 8. Developing a thesis statement (p. 625)

_____ 9. Creating a structure (p. 629)
_____ 10. Drafting the paper (p. 629), integrating summaries, paraphrases, and direct quotations into your ideas (p. 608)
_____ 11. Citing sources in your text (p. 623)

_____ 12. Revising and editing the paper (p. 631)
_____ 13. Finalizing text citations and preparing the list of works cited (p. 623)
_____ 14. Preparing and proofreading the final manuscript (p. 633)
_____ Final paper due

Each segment marked off by a horizontal line will occupy *roughly* one-fourth of the total time. The most unpredictable segments are the first two, so get started early enough to accommodate the unexpected.

41b Finding a researchable subject and question

Before reading this section, review the suggestions on pages 6–9 for finding and limiting an essay subject. Generally, the same procedure applies to writing any kind of research paper: begin with an assigned subject or one that you want to explore and learn more about (perhaps one you've already written about without benefit of research); then narrow the subject to manageable size by asking questions about it, such as those on page 8. However, selecting and limiting a subject for a research paper can present special opportunities and problems.

1 Choosing an appropriate subject

A subject for a research paper has four primary requirements, each with corresponding pitfalls:

1. **Ample sources of information are available on the subject.** Other researchers should have had a chance to produce evidence on the subject, weigh the evidence, and publish their conclusions. And the sources should be accessible.

   Avoid a very recent subject, such as a new medical discovery or a breaking story in today's newspaper, unless you are placing the subject in a larger context. For example, you might discuss yesterday's theft of online credit-card information if you are placing it in the context of the overall security of consumers' data.

2. **The subject encourages research in the kinds and number of sources required by the assignment.**

   Avoid (*a*) a subject that depends entirely on personal opinion and experience, such as the virtues of your hobby; and (*b*) a subject that requires research in only one source, such as a straight factual biography or a how-to like "Making Lenses for Eyeglasses." (An exception to *b* is a paper in which you analyze a single work such as a novel or painting.)

3. **The subject will lead you to an objective assessment of sources and to defensible conclusions.** Even when you write a persuasive research paper, arguing your own point of view, the success of the argument will depend on your presenting multiple views responsibly and fairly.

   Avoid a controversial subject that rests entirely on belief or prejudice, even a subject you are passionate about, such as when human life begins or why women (or men) are superior. Such a subject may certainly be disputed; however, your own views could slant your research or conclusions, and your readers are unlikely to be swayed from their own beliefs.

4. **The subject suits the length of paper assigned and the time given for research and writing.**

   Avoid a broad subject that has too many sources to survey adequately, such as a major event in history or the collected works of a poet.

Checklist for a good research subject

1. **Published sources are ample:** the subject is not so recent that other researchers will still be discovering it.
2. **Sources are diverse:** the subject is neither wholly personal nor wholly factual.
3. **Sources can be assessed objectively:** the subject is not solely a matter of belief or prejudice.
4. **Sources can be examined thoroughly** in the assigned time and length: the subject is not too broad.

2 Posing a research question

Asking a question or questions about your subject opens avenues of inquiry. In asking questions, you can consider what you already know about the subject, explore what you don't know, and begin to develop your own perspective.

The students Justin Malik and Vanessa Haley both wrote on environmental topics, but they arrived at their research questions by slightly different paths. For a composition course, Malik's instructor assigned an interpretation with a persuasive purpose but left the selection of the subject to the student. Malik had recently read newspaper articles on a subject that intrigued him: how big businesses are trying to improve their environmental records. Taking the broad subject of business and the environment as his starting point, he used clustering (see pp. 24–25) to pursue some ideas. While generating the clusters below, Malik found himself giving the most thought to green products—consumer goods that are promoted as friendly to the environment. Malik posed questions until he hit on a question that seemed interesting and significant: *Can buying green products make a real difference for the environment?*

Clustering for a research question

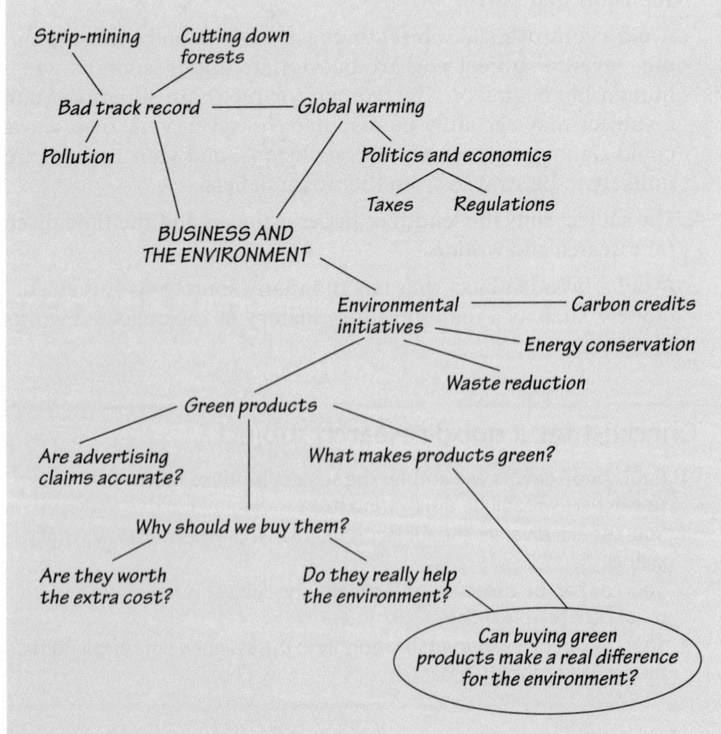

In developing a topic and question for an analysis paper assigned in a composition course, Vanessa Haley followed a somewhat different procedure. Instead of starting with a general subject, as Malik did, Haley began by looking for an unresolved question, an interesting problem, or a disagreement among the experts in some field of study. She had recently been reading an anthology of writings on the environment, and she had been disturbed by how many naturalists and environmentalists view human beings not as part of "nature" but as something separate from it, usually as its destroyer. In her journal, Haley wrote this entry:

> Many writers see nature as a place for humans to retreat to, or a wonderful thing that humans are ruining. Humans aren't considered natural themselves—human civilization isn't considered natural. Human civ. is "anti-natural." Isn't such a separation unrealistic and damaging? We *are* natural. We're here to stay, and we're not going back to the Stone Age, so we'd better focus on the connections between "us" and "it" (nature) rather than just the differences. Dillard seems to do this—seems to connect human and natural worlds. People are neither better nor worse than nature but just bound up in it. "Nature is as careless as it is bountiful, and . . . with that extravagance goes a crushing waste that will one day include our own cheap lives" (*Pilgrim* 160).

At the end of her journal entry, Haley refers to and quotes the writer Annie Dillard, one of the authors represented in the anthology. Haley decided to explore Dillard's views further by reading and analyzing more of her work. Haley's opening question for investigation, then, was *How does Annie Dillard see the place of humanity in nature?*

Exercise 41.1 Finding a topic and question

Choose three of the following subjects (or three subjects of your own), and narrow each one to at least one subject and question suitable for beginning work on a research paper. (This exercise can be the first step in a research-writing project that continues through Chapters 41–46.)

1. National security and civil rights
2. Distribution of books by conventional versus electronic means
3. Bilingual education
4. Dance in America
5. The history of women's suffrage
6. Genetically modified foods
7. Immigrants in the United States
8. Space exploration
9. Business espionage
10. The effect of television on college sports
11. Child abuse
12. African Americans and civil rights
13. Successes in cancer research
14. Computer piracy
15. The European exploration of North America before Columbus
16. Hazardous substances in the workplace
17. Television evangelism
18. Treatment or prevention of AIDS in the United States or Africa
19. Water pollution
20. Science fiction
21. Women writers
22. Campaign financing
23. Comic film actors

24. An unsolved crime
25. Alternative fuels
26. Male and female heroes in modern fiction
27. Computers and the privacy of the individual
28. Gothic or romance novels in the nineteenth and twenty-first centuries
29. The social responsibility of business
30. Stem-cell research

41c Developing a research strategy

Before you start looking for sources, consider what you already know about your subject and where you are likely to find information on it.

1 Tapping into your own knowledge

Discovering what you already know about your subject will guide you in discovering what you don't know. Take some time at the start to write down everything you know about the subject: facts you have learned, opinions you have heard or read elsewhere, and of course your own opinions. Use one of the discovery techniques discussed in Chapter 2 to explore and develop your ideas: keeping a journal, observing your surroundings, freewriting, list making, drawing, asking the journalist's questions, using the patterns of development, or thinking critically.

When you've explored your thoughts, make a list of questions for which you don't have answers, whether factual (*How much do Americans spend on green products?*) or more open-ended (*Are they worth the higher prices?*). These questions will give you clues about the sources you need to look for first.

2 Setting goals for sources

For many research projects, you'll want to consult a mix of sources, as described on the following pages. You may start by seeking the outlines of your topic—the range and depth of opinions about it—in reference works and articles in popular periodicals or through a Web search. Then, as you refine your views and your research question, you'll move on to more specialized sources, such as scholarly books and periodicals and your own interviews or surveys. (See pp. 561–78 for more on each kind of source.)

The mix of sources you choose depends heavily on your subject. For example, Justin Malik's paper on green consumerism required the use of recent sources because environmentally friendly products are fairly new to the marketplace. Your mix of sources may also be specified by your instructor or limited by the requirements of your assignment.

Sources through the library or the open Web

The print and electronic sources available at your library or through its Web site—mainly reference works, books, and articles in periodicals—have two big advantages over most of what you'll find on the open Web: library sources are cataloged and indexed for easy retrieval; and they are generally reliable, having been screened first by their publishers and then by the library's staff. In contrast, the retrieval systems of the open Web are more difficult to use effectively, and the sources themselves tend to be less reliable because most do not pass through any screening before being posted. (There are many exceptions, such as online scholarly journals and reference works. But these sources are generally available through your library's Web site as well.)

Most instructors expect research writers to consult sources found in and through the library, including print sources. But most will accept sources from the open Web, too, if you have used them judiciously. Even with its disadvantages, the Internet can be a valuable resource for primary sources, current information, and a diversity of views. For guidelines on evaluating both library and open-Web sources, see pages 580–93.

Primary and secondary sources

Use **primary sources** when they are required by the assignment or are appropriate for your subject. Primary sources are documents and objects that were created during the period you are studying. They consist of firsthand or original accounts, such as historical documents (letters, speeches, and so on), eyewitness reports (including articles by journalists who are on location), works of literature, reports on experiments or surveys conducted by the writer, and sources you originate (interviews, experiments, observations, or correspondence).

Many assignments will allow you to use **secondary sources**, which report and analyze information drawn from other sources, often primary ones. Examples include a reporter's summary of a controversial issue, a historian's account of a battle, a critic's reading of a poem, and a psychologist's evaluation of several studies. (Sometimes a secondary source may actually be your primary source, as when you analyze a historian's account or respond to a critic's interpretation.) In themselves, secondary sources may contain helpful summaries and interpretations that direct, support, and extend your own thinking. However, most research-writing assignments expect your own ideas to go beyond those in such sources.

Scholarly and popular sources

The scholarship of acknowledged experts is essential for depth, authority, and specificity. Most instructors expect students to emphasize scholarly sources in their research. But the general-interest views and information of popular sources can provide everyday examples, anecdotes, and stories that can help you apply scholarly approaches to your subject, and they can provide context for very recent topics.

Use the following guidelines to determine whether a source is scholarly or popular. (For more on the distinction between scholarly and popular periodicals, see pp. 563–64.)

- **Check the title.** Is it technical, or does it use a general vocabulary?
- **Check the publisher.** Is it a scholarly journal (such as *Cultural Geographies*) or a publisher of scholarly books (such as Harvard University Press), or is it a popular magazine (such as *Consumer Reports* or *National Geographic*) or a publisher of popular books (such as Little, Brown)?
- **Check the length of periodical articles.** Scholarly articles are generally much longer than magazine and newspaper articles.
- **Check the author.** Search the Web for the author. Is he or she an expert on the topic?
- **Check for sources.** Scholarly authors cite their sources formally in notes or a bibliography.
- **Check the URL.** A Web site's URL, or electronic address, includes an abbreviation that can tell you something about the origin of the source: scholarly sources usually end in *edu*, *org*, or *gov*, while popular sources usually end in *com*. See pages 588–89 for more on types of Web sources.

Older and newer sources

- **Check the publication date.** For most subjects a combination of older, established sources (such as books) and current sources (such as newspaper articles and Web sites) will provide both background and up-to-date information. Only historical subjects or very current subjects (such as social-networking Web sites) require an emphasis on one extreme or another.

Impartial and biased sources

Seek a range of viewpoints. Sources that attempt to be impartial can offer trustworthy facts and an overview of your subject. Sources with clear biases can give you a range of views about a subject and enrich your understanding of it. Of course, to discover bias, you may have to read the source carefully (see p. 582); but you can infer quite a bit just from a bibliographical listing.

- **Check the title.** It may reveal something about point of view. (Consider these contrasting titles uncovered by Justin Malik: "Go for the Green" versus "Where the Green Is: Examining the Paradox of Environmentally Conscious Consumption.")

- **Check the author.** Do a Web search to find out more about the author. Is he or she a respected researcher (thus more likely to be objective) or a leading proponent of a certain view (less likely to be objective)?

Sources with helpful features

Depending on your topic and how far along your research is, you may want to look for sources with features such as illustrations (which can clarify important concepts), bibliographies (which can direct you to other sources), and indexes (which can help you develop keywords for electronic searches; see pp. 557–60).

Exercise 41.2 Developing a research strategy

Following the suggestions on page 548, write what you already know about the topic you selected in Exercise 41.1 (pp. 547–48), and then frame some questions for which you'll need to find answers. Also in writing, consider the kinds of sources you'll probably need to consult, using the categories given on the preceding pages.

41d Making a working, annotated bibliography

When you begin searching for sources, it may be tempting to pursue each possibility as you come across it. But that approach would prove inefficient and probably ineffective. Instead, you'll want to find out the *full range* of sources available—from scholarly and popular articles to books and Web sites—and then decide on a good number to consult. For a paper of 1800 to 2500 words, try for ten to thirty promising titles as a start.

To keep track of where sources are, compile a **working bibliography** as you uncover possibilities. Record the information for a source as soon as you think you may want to use it, following the guidelines in this section. Then you'll be able to find the source when you're ready to consult it, and you'll have the information needed to cite the source in your paper.

As you look for and assess sources, your instructor may ask you to prepare an **annotated bibliography** as part of the research process or as a separate assignment. In an annotated bibliography, you summarize sources and evaluate their usefulness for your research.

1 Tracking source information

You can create a working bibliography by hand, on a computer or tablet, or even on your smartphone. If you use your computer, tablet, or phone, you can type the information, copy and paste it from your search results, or take a photograph of it. If you create the bibliography by hand, you can record source information as long as you have paper and a pen or pencil. Whatever method you use, be sure to record all the information you will need.

The two records below come from Justin Malik's working bibliography. The first, for a book, Malik handwrote in his research notebook. The second, for a magazine article, Malik downloaded from an online database, printed out, and then annotated with information he knew he would need.

Basic entries for a working bibliography

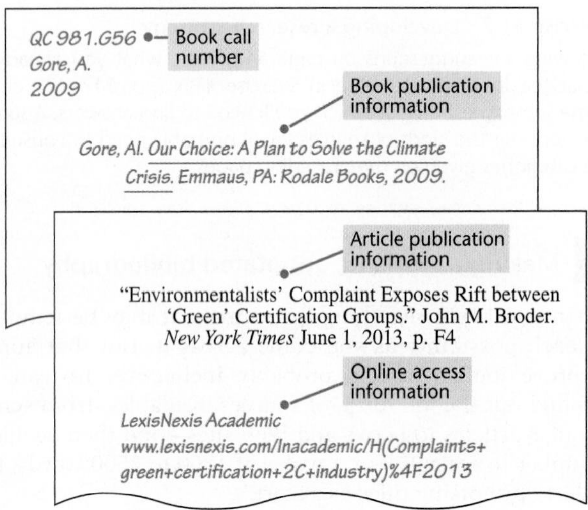

QC 981.G56
Book call number
Gore, A.
2009
Book publication information
Gore, Al. Our Choice: A Plan to Solve the Climate Crisis. Emmaus, PA: Rodale Books, 2009.
Article publication information
"Environmentalists' Complaint Exposes Rift between 'Green' Certification Groups." John M. Broder. New York Times June 1, 2013, p. F4
Online access information
LexisNexis Academic
www.lexisnexis.com/lnacademic/H(Complaints+green+certification+2C+industry)%4F2013

2 Recording source information

When you turn in your paper, you will be expected to attach a list of the sources you have used. Your list must include all the information needed to find the sources, in a format readers can understand. The box opposite shows the information you should record for each type of source so that you will not have to retrace your steps later. See later pages for illustrations of how to locate this information for journal articles (654, 772), newspaper articles (657), books (662), and Web sites (669).

Note Recording source information meticulously will help you avoid careless plagiarism because you will be less likely to omit the information in your paper. Whenever possible, record source information in the correct format for the documentation style you will be using. That will help you avoid omitting or mixing up

Information for a working bibliography

For a print or electronic book

Library call number
Name(s) of author(s), editor(s), translator(s), and other contributors
Title and subtitle
Publication data: (1) place of publication; (2) publisher's name; (3) date of publication; (4) title of any database or Web site used to reach the book; (5) publisher and date of any Web site used to find the book
Other important data, such as edition or volume number
Format (print, Web, Kindle file, etc.)
DOI or complete URL (see the note below)

For periodical articles in print, in online databases, or in Web journals

Name(s) of author(s)
Title and subtitle of article
Title of periodical
Publication data: (1) volume number and issue number (if any) in which the article appears; (2) date of issue; (3) page numbers on which article appears
Title of any database used to reach the source
DOI or complete URL (see the note below)

For Web material and other electronic sources

Name(s) of author(s) and other contributors
Title and subtitle of source
Title of Web site
Publication data: publisher and date of publication
Any publication data for the source in another medium (print, film, etc.)
Format of online source (Web site or page, podcast, e-mail, etc.)
Date you consulted the source
Title of any database used to reach the source
Complete URL or DOI (see the note below)

For other sources

Name(s) of author(s) or creator(s) and other contributors
Title of the source
Title of any larger work of which the source is a part (television series, album, etc.)
Publication or production data: (1) publisher's or producer's name; (2) date of publication, release, or production; (3) identifying numbers (if any)
Format or medium (live performance, lecture, DVD, map, TV episode, etc.)

Note Documentation styles generally require DOIs (Digital Object Identifiers) or URLs for citations of electronic sources. Always record the DOI (if one is available) and the complete URL so that you'll have whatever is needed for your final citation of a source. For more on DOIs and URLs, see pages 648 (MLA style), 749 (Chicago style), 767 (APA style), and 800 (CSE style).

dates, numbers, and other data when it's time to write your citations. This book describes four documentation styles: MLA (p. 634),

Chicago (p. 744), APA (p. 761), and CSE (p. 795). See also page 624 for tips on using bibliography software to format source information.

3 Annotating your bibliography

Your instructor may ask you to prepare an **annotated bibliography** as part of the research process or as a separate assignment. Creating annotations converts your bibliography into a tool for assessing sources, helping you discover gaps that may remain in your sources and helping you decide which sources to pursue in depth. As you find and evaluate each source, record not only its publication information but also the following:

- **What you know about the source's content.** Periodical databases and book catalogs generally include abstracts, or summaries, of sources that can help you with this part of the annotation.
- **How you think the source may be helpful in your research.** Does it offer expert opinion, statistics, an important example, or a range of views? Does it place your subject in a historical, social, or economic context?
- **Your assessment of the source.** Consider how reliable the source is and how it might fit into your research. (See pp. 593–95 for more on evaluating and synthesizing sources.)

The following example shows a summary, a list of potentially useful features, and an assessment:

Annotated bibliography entry with assessment

Publication information for source	Gore, Al. *Our Choice: A Plan to Solve the Climate Crisis.* Emmaus, PA: Rodale Books, 2009.
Summary of source (from working bibliography)	A sequel to Gore's *An Inconvenient Truth* that emphasizes solutions to global warming. Expands on the argument that global warming is a serious threat, with recent examples of natural disasters. Proposes ways that governments, businesses, and individuals can reduce or reverse the risks of global warming.
Ideas on use of source	Includes helpful summaries of scientific studies, short essays on various subjects, and dozens of images, tables, charts, and graphs.
Assessment of source	Compelling overview of possible solutions, with lots of data that seem thorough and convincing. But the book is aimed at a general audience and doesn't have formal source citations. Can use it for broad concepts, but for data I'll have to track down Gore's scholarly sources.

Exercise 41.3 Compiling an annotated working bibliography

Prepare an annotated working bibliography of at least ten sources for a research paper on one of the following people or on someone of your own choosing. Begin by limiting the subject to a manageable size, posing a question about a particular characteristic or achievement of the person. Then consult reference works, periodical databases, the library's book catalog, and the Web. (See pp. 560–76 for more on these resources.) For each source, record complete publication information as well as a summary and a note on the source's potential use.

1. Steven Jobs (a founder of Apple Computer), or another business entrepreneur
2. Sonia Sotomayor, or another Supreme Court justice
3. Emily Dickinson, or another writer
4. Serena Williams, or another sports figure
5. Isamu Noguchi, or another artist

42 Finding Sources

Chapter essentials

- Start with your library's Web site (next page).
- Plan electronic searches (next page).
- Consult reference works (p. 560).
- Consult books (p. 561).
- Find articles in periodicals (p. 563).
- Explore the Web and social media (p. 569).
- Consult government publications (p. 573).
- Locate visuals, audio, and video (p. 574).
- Generate your own sources through interviews, surveys, and observation (p. 576).

Visit MyWritingLab™ for more resources on finding sources.

Once you have discovered a research subject and question, have developed a research strategy, and know how to make an annotated working bibliography, you're ready to find sources. This chapter discusses electronic searches and the kinds of sources, both print and electronic, that are available to you.

Note If you want print or digital sources that are not available from your library, you can often get them through interlibrary loan. Check your library's Web site, and ask a librarian for help if necessary.

42a Starting with your library's Web site

As you conduct academic research, your library's Web site will be your gateway to ideas and information. Always start with your library's site, not with a public search engine such as *Google*. (See the next page for information about *Google Scholar*, a tool that searches for scholarly articles.)

Advantages of a library search

The library's site will lead you to vast resources, including books, periodical articles, and reference works that aren't available on the open Web. More important, every source you find on the library's site will have passed through filters to ensure its value. A scholarly journal article, for instance, undergoes at least three successive reviews: first, subject-matter experts deem it worth publishing in the journal; next, a database vendor deems the journal worth including in the database; and finally, your school's librarians deem the database worth subscribing to.

Note Start with your library's Web site, but don't stop there. Many books, periodicals, and other excellent sources are available only on library shelves, not online, and most instructors expect research papers to be built to some extent on these resources. When you spot promising print sources while browsing a library's online databases, make records of them and then look them up at the library. You can also browse the bookshelves to discover sources.

Disadvantages of an open-Web search

Google and other public search engines do have some benefits: they may seem more user-friendly than the library's Web site, they can help you get a sense of how your subject is talked about, and they may locate some reliable and relevant sources for your research.

However, for academic research these search engines have more drawbacks than benefits. They are not geared to academic research, so most of the sources they find will be unusable for your project. And the sources will not be filtered as library materials are: no one ensures their basic reliability.

In the end, a library Web search will be more efficient and more effective than an open-Web search. (For help with evaluating sources from any resource, see pp. 580–93.)

42b Searching electronically

An electronic search requires planning. A search that is too broad can miss helpful sources while returning hundreds, even thousands, of irrelevant sources. A search that is too narrow can exclude important sources.

A tip for researchers

Take advantage of these valuable resources offered by your library:

- **An orientation,** which will introduce you to the resources available through your library and help you navigate the library's Web site.
- **Reference librarians,** whose job it is to help you and others navigate the library's resources. All libraries offer face-to-face consultations, and many offer e-mail and chat services. Even very experienced researchers often consult reference librarians.

1 Finding print and electronic resources through your library

Your library's Web site will lead you to many kinds of print and electronic resources suitable for academic research.

- **The library catalog.** Searchable from the library's Web site, the catalog is a database that lists all the resources the library owns or subscribes to. At many libraries, the catalog finds books, e-books, and the titles of periodicals but not individual articles within online databases. At other libraries, the catalog functions as a centralized search engine that covers all the library's holdings and subscriptions and locates articles in online databases. Either type of catalog may also include the holdings at other libraries in your college's system or in your state.
- **Online databases.** Also searchable from the library's Web site, databases include a wide range of source types, from journal collections and full-text resources to reference works and primary sources. Your library's Web site will likely list databases alphabetically and by discipline. (You may discover some of the same databases on the open Web, but unless you retrieve articles through your library's Web site, you will probably have to pay for what you find.) As you use a database, be aware of what it does and does not offer, and keep track of whether you are looking at an article, a book, an archival document, or something else. Ask a librarian if you're not sure. For help with selecting databases, see pages 564–65.
- **Research guides.** Some libraries provide guides that direct users to resources on particular subjects, such as twentieth-century English literature or social psychology.
- ***Google Scholar.*** Available on the open Web, *Google Scholar* is a search engine that seeks out scholarly books and articles. It is particularly useful for subjects that range across disciplines, for which discipline-specific databases can be too limited. *Google Scholar* can connect to your library's holdings if you set it to

do so under Scholar Preferences. Keep in mind, however, that *Google Scholar*'s searches may list books that are unavailable to you and articles that you cannot obtain in full text. Your library is still the best resource for material that is easily available to you, so begin there.

2 Developing search terms

Take time early in your research to develop search terms that describe your subject effectively. For this step, it helps to understand the difference between keywords and subject headings:

- **Keywords** are the terms you type when you begin a search. In a library catalog or an online database, a keyword search looks for that word (or words) in titles, authors, and subject headings (described below) and sometimes within lists of keywords supplied by the author or in user tags added by readers. On the open Web, a keyword search looks for your terms anywhere in the record. In any case, the process is entirely automatic, so your challenge as a researcher is to find keywords that others have used to describe the same subject.
- **Subject headings** (also called *subject terms*) tell you what a source is about. They are assigned to books and articles by people who have read the sources and categorized them, so they can be more efficient than keywords at finding relevant sources. To find subject headings, use and refine your keywords until you discover a promising source. On the source's full record, check the list of subject headings to see how the source is categorized. (See p. 567 for an illustration.) Building the subject headings that most closely match your subject into your search terms can improve your searches.

3 Refining search terms

Databases, catalogs, and search engines provide systems that you can use to refine your search terms for your purposes. The basic operations appear in the following box, but resources do differ. For instance, some assume that *AND* should link two or more keywords, while others provide options specifying "Must contain all the words" and other equivalents for the operations in the box. To learn a search engine's system, consult its Advanced Search page.

Ways to refine keywords

Most databases and many search engines work with **Boolean operators,** terms or symbols that allow you to expand or limit your keywords and thus your search.

- **Use *AND* or + to narrow the search by including only sources that use all the given words.** The keywords *green AND products* request only the sources in the shaded area:

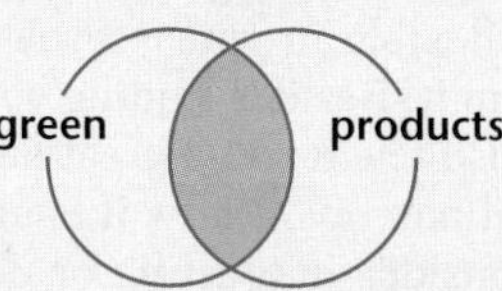

- **Use *NOT* or – ("minus") to narrow the search by excluding irrelevant words.** *Green AND products NOT guide* excludes sources that use the word *guide*:

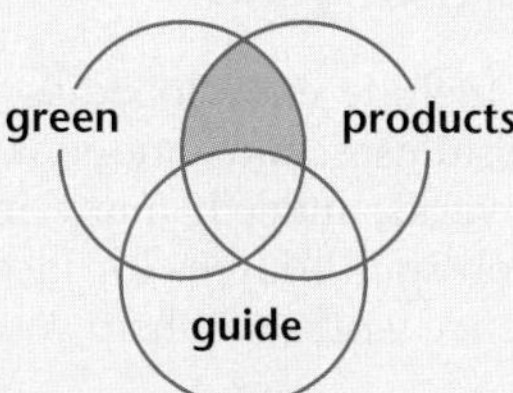

- **Use *OR* to broaden the search by giving alternative keywords.** *Green AND products OR goods* allows for sources that use a synonym for *products*:

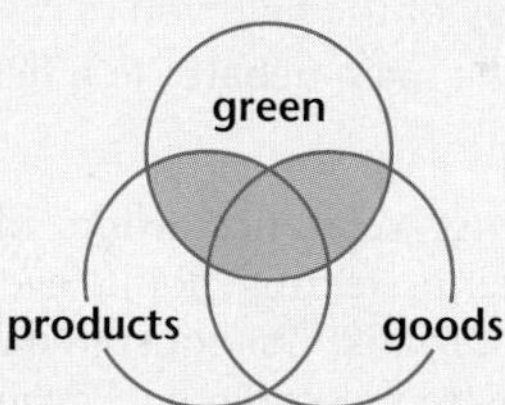

- **Use quotation marks or parentheses to form search phrases.** For instance, *"green products"* requests the exact phrase, not the separate words. Only sources using *green products* would turn up.
- **Use wild cards to permit different versions of the same word.** In *consum**, for instance, the wild card * indicates that sources may include *consume, consumer, consumerism,* and *consumption* as well as *consumptive, consumedly,* and *consummate.* The example suggests that you have to consider all the variations allowed by a wild card and whether it opens up your search too much. If you seek only two or three from many variations, you may be better off using *OR*: *consumption OR consumerism.* (Note that some systems use ?, :, or + for a wild card instead of *.)
- **Be sure to spell your keywords correctly.** Some search tools will look for close matches or approximations, but correct spelling gives you the best chance of finding relevant sources.

Note You will probably have to use trial and error in developing search terms because library catalogs, databases, and search engines may all use slightly different words to describe your subject. If you are having trouble finding appropriate sources, try using subject headings, and be flexible in your search terms. The process is not busywork—far from it. Besides leading you eventually to worthwhile sources, it can also teach you a great deal about your subject: how you can or should narrow it, how it is and is not described by others, what others consider interesting or debatable about it, and what the major arguments are.

42c Finding reference works

Reference works include encyclopedias, dictionaries, digests, bibliographies, indexes, atlases, and handbooks. Your research *must* go beyond reference works; indeed, many instructors discourage students from relying on such sources for ideas and information in final papers. But reference works can help you get started:

- **They can help you decide whether your subject interests you and meets the requirements for a research paper** (pp. 544–45).
- **They can direct you to more detailed sources on your subject.**
- **They can help you refine keywords for electronic searches,** giving you the terminology of the field you're researching.
- **They can identify the main debates in a field and the proponents of each side.**

Justin Malik's use of reference works illustrates how helpful such sources can be as a starting point, even for a current topic such as green products. Malik first consulted *Dictionary of Environment and Development* (to get some background on environmental issues) and *Encyclopedia of Advertising* (to explore the recent history of promotional campaigns for green products).

The following list describes the types of reference works. Ask a reference librarian if you're unsure of where to start. The librarian can also advise you which sources are available through the library's Web site, in print at the library, or directly via the open Web.

- **General encyclopedias**, such as *Encyclopaedia Brittanica*, give brief overviews and bibliographies. Covering all fields, they are convenient but limited. The Web-based encyclopedia *Wikipedia* has an added limitation in that it is a **wiki**, a kind of Web site that can by contributed to or edited by anyone, not just reliable experts. Ask your instructor whether *Wikipedia* is an acceptable source before you use it. If you do use it, you must carefully evaluate any information you find, using the guidelines on pages 583–90.

- **Specialized encyclopedias, dictionaries, and bibliographies** generally cover a single field or subject. These works give more detailed and more technical information than a general reference, and many of them (especially bibliographies) direct you to particular books and articles on your subject.
- **Unabridged dictionaries**, such as the *Oxford English Dictionary,* give detailed entries for words and are far more comprehensive than college or abridged dictionaries.
- **Special dictionaries on language**, such as the *Dictionary of American Regional English,* give authoritative information on usage, dialects, and other aspects of language.
- **Biographical reference works**, such as *American Men and Women of Science,* give information about the lives and achievements of individuals.
- **Atlases and gazetteers** provide information about geography. Atlases, such as the *National Geographic Atlas of the World,* are collections of maps. Gazetteers, such as *Webster's New Geographical Dictionary,* give maps as well as social data about locations, such as population, literacy rates, and household incomes.
- **Almanacs and yearbooks**, such as the *World Almanac and Book of Facts* and the *Statistical Abstract of the United States,* are annual compilations of facts and statistics.

42d Finding books

Books can provide background information, subject surveys, popular views of culture, statements of scholarly theory, research results—in short, a broad range of secondary and primary sources (see p. 549).

1 Using the library catalog

Your library's catalog is searchable via the library's Web site. It lists the books available in your library and may also list books in other libraries in your area. Ask a librarian if you want to obtain a book from another library, and allow time for the book to be sent after your request.

All book catalogs contain similar information, though they may be organized differently from one library to the next. By far the most widely used format derives from the Library of Congress cataloging system and includes author, title, publisher, date of publication, description (number of pages, size, and other data), subject headings the book is listed under, and the library's call number (which directs you to the book's location in the stacks). See the next page for a complete book record showing all this information.

2 Using a search strategy

Unless you seek a specific author or title, you'll want to search for books by using keywords or subject headings with the library's catalog. In a keyword search, you start with your own search terms. In a subject-heading search, you use the headings on the records of promising sources to locate similar sources.

Both approaches are illustrated here by part of Justin Malik's catalog search. His initial keyword search (screen 1) produced a

1. Initial keyword search of the library catalog

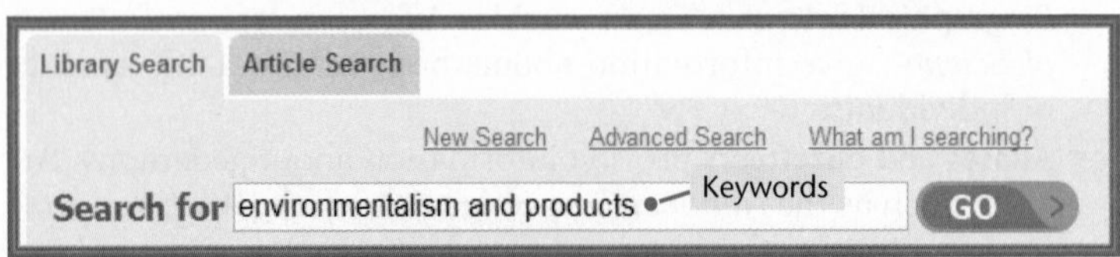

2. Catalog search results

1
Green gone wrong : how our economy is undermining the environmental revolution (View details)
Heather Rogers 1970- New York : Scribner 2010
Book
Add to e-Shelf
Checked out (HC79.E5 R6312 2010) (Get It)
Locations

2
Building the green economy : success stories from the grassroots (View details)
Kevin Danaher 1950- Shannon Biggs; Jason Mark Sausalito, CA : PoliPointPress : Distributed by Ingram Publisher Services c2007
Book
Add to e-Shelf
Available (HC79.E5 D3252 2007) (Get It)
Locations

3
Simple steps to a greener home (View details)
Danny Seo; Gaiam Media. Louisville, CO : Gaiam Americas c2007
Audio/Visual
Add to e-Shelf
Available (TH4860 .S56 2007) (Get It)
Locations

3. Full catalog record

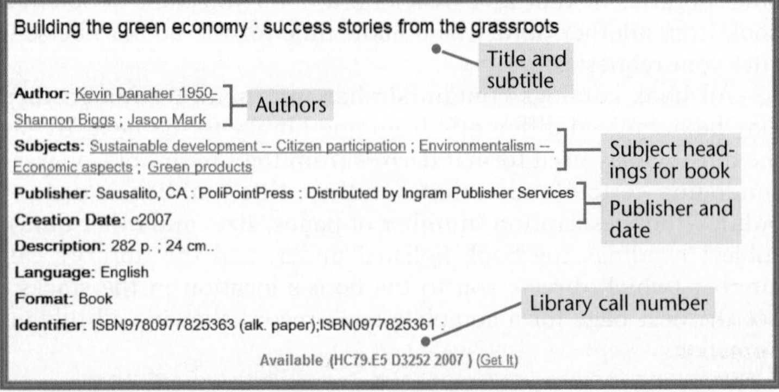

number of promising books (screen 2). The complete record for one of those books (screen 3) gave three subject headings—for instance, *Green products*—that Malik then used to search the catalog further.

Note In addition to searching the book catalog, you can also browse the library shelves. The first part of the call number for a promising title (*HC79.E5* in the full record opposite) will lead you to other books on the same subject that a catalog search might miss. However, be aware that some books in your library's collection may be on loan or stored elsewhere. The shelves may not represent the library's complete book collection.

3 Using references to books

The following can help you identify books that have information about your topic:

- ***WorldCat*** allows you to conduct subject, author, title, and keyword searches of library catalogs around the world. You might, for example, use *WorldCat* to find out if the author of an encyclopedia article has published any relevant books since the date of the encyclopedia.
- **Review indexes** list published reviews of books and can help you evaluate whether a book is relevant to your subject.

42e Finding periodicals

Periodicals include newspapers, academic journals, and magazines, either print or online. Newspapers are useful for detailed accounts of past and current events. Journals and magazines can be harder to distinguish, but their differences are important. Most college instructors expect students' research to rely more on journals than on magazines.

	Journals	Magazines
Examples	*American Anthropologist, Journal of Black Studies, Journal of Chemical Education*	*The New Yorker, Time, Rolling Stone, People*
Availability	Mainly college and university libraries, either on library shelves or in online databases	Public libraries, newsstands, bookstores, the open Web, and online databases
Purpose	Advance knowledge in a particular field	Express opinion, inform, or entertain
Authors	Specialists in the field	May or may not be specialists in their subjects

	Journals	Magazines
Readers	Often specialists in the field	Members of the general public or a subgroup with a particular interest
Source citations	Source citations always included	Source citations rarely included
Length of articles	Usually long, ten pages or more	Usually short, fewer than ten pages
Frequency of publication	Quarterly or less often	Weekly, biweekly, or monthly
Pagination of issues	May be paged separately (like a magazine) or may be paged sequentially throughout an annual volume, so that issue number 3 (the third issue of the year) could open on page 327.	Paged separately, each beginning on page 1

1 Using periodical databases

Periodical databases index the articles in journals, magazines, and newspapers. Often these databases include abstracts, or summaries, of the articles, and they may offer the full texts of the articles as well. Your library subscribes to many periodical databases and to services that offer multiple databases. (See p. 568 for a list.) Most databases and services will be searchable through the library's Web site.

Selection of databases

To decide which databases to consult, you'll need to consider what you're looking for:

- **Does your research subject span more than one discipline?** Then start with a broad database such as *Academic Search Complete, ProQuest Research Library,* or *JSTOR*. A broad database covers many subjects and disciplines but does not index the full range of periodicals in each subject. If your library offers a centralized search engine that searches across multiple databases, you can start there.
- **Does your research subject focus on a single discipline?** Then start with a discipline-specific database such as *Historical Abstracts, MLA International Bibliography, Biological Abstracts*, or *Education Search Complete*. A specific database covers few subjects but includes most of the available periodicals in each subject. If you don't know the name of an appropriate database, the library's Web site probably lists possibilities by discipline.

- **Do you need primary sources?** Some specialized databases collect primary sources—for instance, historical newspapers, literary works not available in print, diaries, letters, music recordings, album liner notes. To determine whether you have access to such materials through your library, consult the list of databases on your library's Web site and read the descriptions to find out what each offers.
- **Which databases most likely include the kinds of resources you need?** The Web sites of most libraries provide lists of databases organized alphabetically and by discipline. Some libraries also provide research guides, which list potentially helpful databases for your search terms. To determine each database's focus, check the description of the database or the list of indexed resources. The description will also tell you the time period the database covers, so you'll know whether you also need to consult older print indexes at the library.

Database searches

When you first search a database, use your own keywords to locate sources. The general procedure is discussed on pages 557–59. Your goal is to find at least one source that seems just right for your subject, so that you can then see what subject headings the database itself uses for such sources. Picking up one or more of those headings for your search terms will focus and speed your search.

Justin Malik first searched *EBSCOhost Academic Search Complete,* a broad database covering more than 4500 periodicals. His keywords *green* and *products* returned more than 7000 articles, and none on the first page dealt with his subject. He stopped to brainstorm other terms that might work better, some of them synonyms and some narrower:

green	products	environment
responsible	shopping	environmentalism
conscious	consumption	pollution
eco-friendly	advertising	waste
sustainable	economics	
	business	

The screen shots on the next two pages show Malik's use of one combination of these terms—*green products* and *shopping*—along with some results and the full record for one article. Malik searched further by using some of the database subject headings shown on the full records of likely sources.

Many databases allow you to limit your search to peer-reviewed or refereed journals—that is, scholarly journals whose articles have been reviewed before publication by experts in the field and then revised by the author. (Malik's initial search on *Academic Search*

Complete included this limitation, as shown in screen 1.) Limiting your search to peer-reviewed journals can help you navigate huge databases that might otherwise return scores of unusable articles from other kinds of periodicals.

Note As you follow leads in online research, it's easy to lose track of what database you're using. You'll need this information to cite any article you obtain online, so make sure you have it. When

1. Initial keyword search of a periodical database

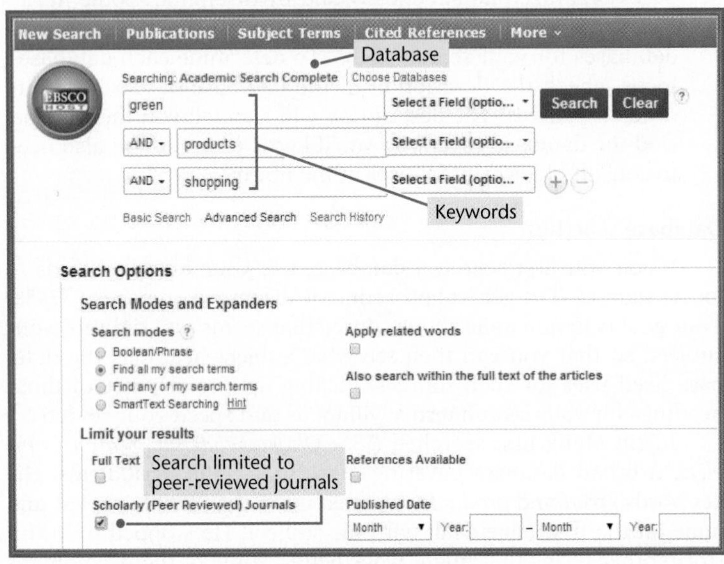

2. Partial keyword search results

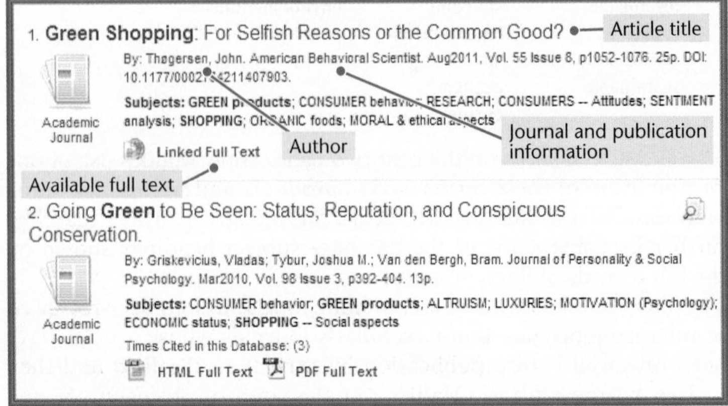

3. Full article record with abstract

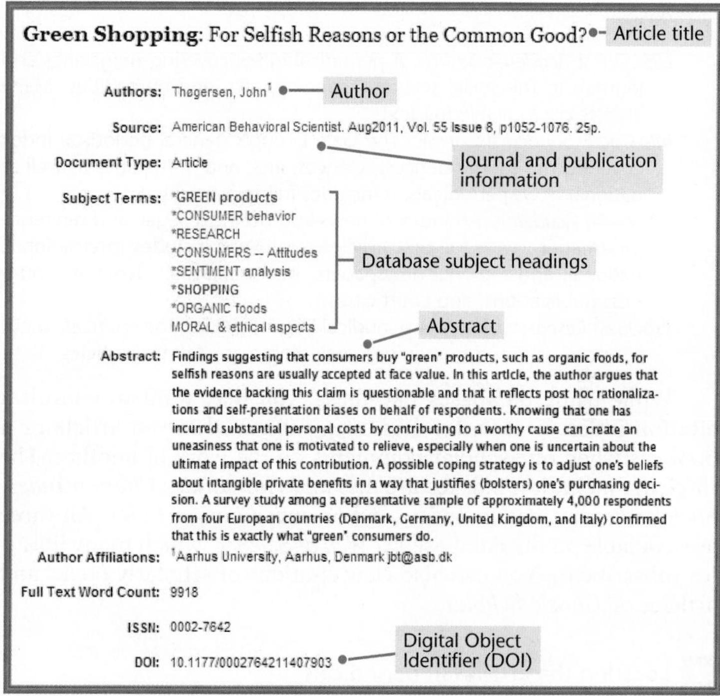
Green Shopping: For Selfish Reasons or the Common Good?
Article title

Authors: Thøgersen, John[1]
Author

Source: American Behavioral Scientist. Aug2011, Vol. 55 Issue 8, p1052-1076. 25p.
Journal and publication information

Document Type: Article

Subject Terms: *GREEN products
*CONSUMER behavior
*RESEARCH
*CONSUMERS -- Attitudes
*SENTIMENT analysis
*SHOPPING
*ORGANIC foods
MORAL & ethical aspects
Database subject headings

Abstract
Abstract: Findings suggesting that consumers buy "green" products, such as organic foods, for selfish reasons are usually accepted at face value. In this article, the author argues that the evidence backing this claim is questionable and that it reflects post hoc rationalizations and self-presentation biases on behalf of respondents. Knowing that one has incurred substantial personal costs by contributing to a worthy cause can create an uneasiness that one is motivated to relieve, especially when one is uncertain about the ultimate impact of this contribution. A possible coping strategy is to adjust one's beliefs about intangible private benefits in a way that justifies (bolsters) one's purchasing decision. A survey study among a representative sample of approximately 4,000 respondents from four European countries (Denmark, Germany, United Kingdom, and Italy) confirmed that this is exactly what "green" consumers do.

Author Affiliations: [1]Aarhus University, Aarhus, Denmark jbt@asb.dk

Full Text Word Count: 9918

ISSN: 0002-7642

DOI: 10.1177/0002764211407903
Digital Object Identifier (DOI)

you print search records or save them as a file, the database name may appear on the record. If not, you will have to add the database name to the printout or file. (For help with citing articles you find in online databases, see pp. 652–58.)

The use of abstracts

The full article record above shows a key feature of many databases' periodical listings: an abstract that summarizes the article. Describing research methods, conclusions, and other information, an abstract can tell you whether you want to pursue an article and thus save you time. However, the abstract cannot replace the actual article. If you want to use the work as a source, you must consult the full text.

Helpful databases

The following list includes databases to which academic libraries commonly subscribe. Some of these databases—for instance, *ProQuest Research Library* and *EBSCOhost Academic Search*—cover much the same material, so your library may not subscribe to all of them. See also pages 564–65 for tips on finding and selecting databases.

EBSCOhost Academic Search. A periodical index covering magazines and journals in the social sciences, sciences, arts, and humanities. Many articles are available full-text.

InfoTrac Expanded Academic. The Gale Group's general periodical index covering the social sciences, sciences, arts, and humanities as well as national news periodicals. It includes full-text articles.

LexisNexis Academic. An index of news and business, legal, and reference information, with full-text articles. *LexisNexis* includes international, national, and regional newspapers, newsmagazines, legal and business publications, and court cases.

ProQuest Research Library. A periodical index covering the sciences, social sciences, arts, and humanities, including many full-text articles.

While using databases like these, you may want to consult a **citation index** to see what has been written *about* an article or a book, as when one scholar comments on the work of another. The three main citation indexes are *Arts and Humanities Citation Index, Social Science Citation Index,* and *Science Citation Index.* All three are available on the database *ISI Web of Science,* which many libraries subscribe to. You can also view citations of scholarly books and articles on *Google Scholar.*

2 Locating the articles in periodicals

Many article listings you find will include or link directly to the full text of the article, which you'll be able to read online and print or e-mail to yourself. If the full text is not available online, usually you can click on a link within the article record to see whether your library has the article in print or another format.

Your library probably holds recent issues of print periodicals in the periodicals room. Back issues are usually stored elsewhere, in one of three forms:

- **In bound volumes**
- **On *microfilm,*** a filmstrip showing pages side by side
- **On *microfiche,*** a sheet of film with pages arranged in rows and columns.

Consulting periodicals stored on microfilm or microfiche requires using a special machine, or "reader," with which you locate the page and project it on a screen. (Some readers are also attached to scanners or photocopiers.) Any member of the library's staff will show you how to operate the reader.

If the periodical you seek is not available in your library, you may be able to obtain the article by interlibrary loan. The article will probably arrive online. Even electronic loans can sometimes take a week or more, so place your order early.

Note Many periodicals are available both online and in print, and most documentation styles require you to specify which version you consulted. For scholarly journals, the two versions are likely to be identical in content though not in format: for instance, the online version may not include the print version's page breaks and numbers. (However, a full-text version in PDF format reproduces the actual pages of the print journal.) For newspapers and magazines, the two versions often differ more: for instance, the online version may be more or less detailed than the print version, may contain fewer illustrations, or may include links to other resources.

42f Finding sources on the Web

As an academic researcher, you enter the Web in two ways: through your library's Web site and through public search engines such as *Firefox* and *Google.* The library entrance, covered in the preceding sections, is your main path to the books and periodicals that, for most subjects, should make up most of your sources. The open Web, discussed here, can lead to a wealth of information and ideas, but it also has disadvantages that limit its usefulness for academic research:

- **The Web is a wide-open network.** Anyone with the right tools can place information on the Internet, and even a carefully conceived search can turn up sources with widely varying reliability: journal articles, government documents, scholarly data, term papers written by high school students, sales pitches masked as objective reports, wild theories. You must be especially diligent about evaluating Internet sources (see pp. 583–93).
- **The Web changes constantly.** No search engine can keep up with the Web's daily additions and deletions, and a source you find today may be updated or gone tomorrow. You should not put off consulting an online source that you think you may want to use. If it seems appropriate for your needs, take notes from it or (if the source allows) download it to your own computer. Be sure to record complete source information at the same time, and note the date you found the source. (See p. 553 for a complete list of what to record.)
- **The Web is not all-inclusive.** Most books and many periodicals are available only via the library, not directly via the Web.

Clearly, the Web warrants cautious use. It should not be the only resource you work with.

1 Using a public search engine

To find sources on the Web, you use a **search engine** that catalogs Web sites in a series of directories and conducts keyword searches. For a good range of sources, try out more than a single search engine, perhaps as many as four or five, because no engine can catalog the entire Web. In addition, most search engines accept paid placements, giving higher billing to sites that pay a fee. These so-called sponsored links are usually marked as such, but they can compromise a search engine's method for arranging sites in response to your keywords.

Customized searches

The home page of a search engine includes a field for you to type your keywords into. Generally, it will also include an Advanced Search link that you can use to customize your search. For instance, you may be able to select a range of dates, a language, or a number of results to see. Advanced Search will also explain how to use operators such as *AND* and *NOT* to limit or expand your search.

Search records

No matter which search engines you use, your Web browser includes functions that allow you to keep track of Web sources and your search:

- **Use *Favorites* or *Bookmarks* to save site addresses as links.** Click one of these terms near the top of the browser screen to add a site you want to return to. A favorite or bookmark remains on file until you delete it.
- **Use *History* to locate sites you have visited before.** The browser records sites for a certain period, such as a day, a week, or a month. (You can set the period in the browser's Tools menu.) If you forgot to bookmark a site, click History or Go to recover the site from the search history.

Note If you do Web research on a public computer, such as in a lab at school, your favorites and history probably will not be saved from one day to the next. To track sources that you may want to return to, copy the site URLs and e-mail them to yourself or save them in a file.

2 Following a sample Web search

For his initial search of the Web, Justin Malik started on *Google* with the keywords *green products*. But the search returned more than *1.5 billion* items, with the first page consisting entirely of sites selling products, including sponsored sites and other advertisers (see screen 1). Malik realized he had to alter his strategy to get more

1. First *Google* search results

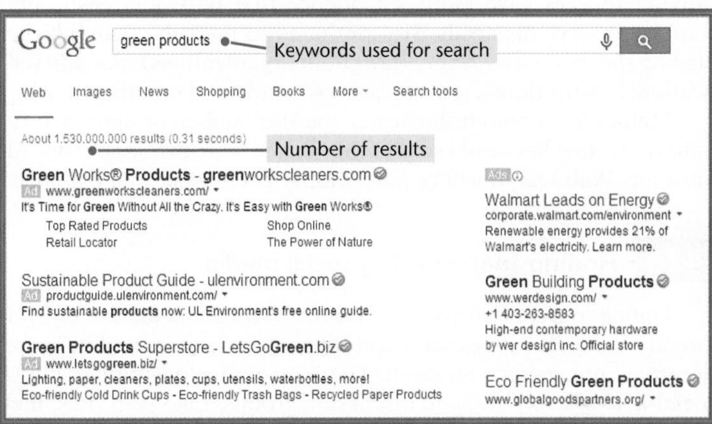

useful results. Following the same procedure he had used with a periodical database, he experimented with combinations of synonyms and narrower terms. The keywords *"green consumerism" products* did refine the search but still produced 130,000 results.

From *Google*'s Advanced Search help, Malik learned that he could specify what he wanted to see in the URLs of sources. Adding *site:.gov* limited the results to government sites, whose URLs end in *.gov*. With *"green consumerism" products site:.gov,* Malik received 8,780 results (see screen 2 below). Although the number was still

2. *Google* results with refined keywords

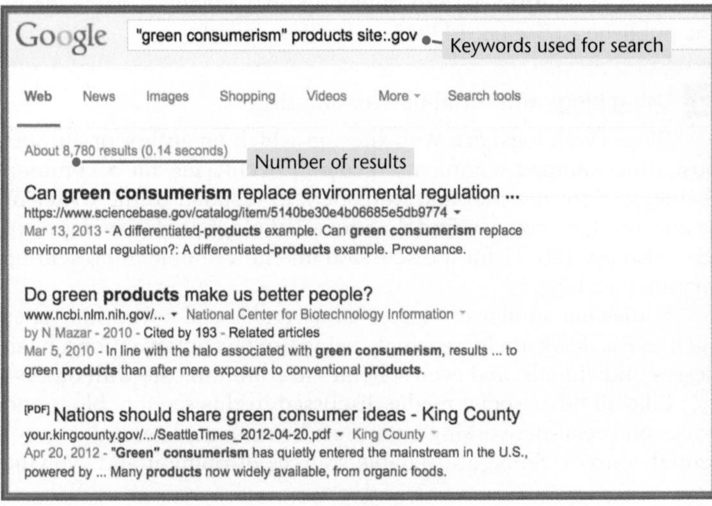

large, the government origin combined with *Google*'s criteria for ranking sources gave Malik confidence that he would easily find sources to serve his needs. He continued to limit the search by replacing *site:.gov* with *site:.org* (nonprofit organizations), *site:.edu* (educational institutions), and *site:.com* (commercial organizations).

Malik's Web search illustrates the trial-and-error approach required to refine keywords so that they locate worthwhile sources. Almost any Web search will require similar persistence and patience.

42g Finding sources using social media

Online sources that you reach through social media can put you directly in touch with experts and others whose ideas and information may inform your research. These media include e-mail, blogs, social-networking sites, and discussion groups. Like Web sites, they are unfiltered, so you must always evaluate them carefully. (See pp. 590–93.)

Note If your paper includes social-media correspondence that is not already public—for instance, an e-mail or a discussion-group posting—ask the author for permission to use it. Doing so advises the author that his or her ideas are about to be distributed more widely and lets the author verify that you have not misrepresented the ideas. (See also pp. 576–77 on interviews.)

1 Using e-mail

As a research tool, e-mail allows you to communicate with others who are interested in your topic. You might, for instance, carry on an e-mail conversation with a teacher at your school or interview an expert in another state to follow up on a scholarly article he or she published. (See pp. 144–45 on writing e-mail.)

2 Using blogs and social-networking sites

Blogs (Web logs) are Web sites on which an author or authors post time-stamped comments, generally centering on a common theme, in a format that allows readers to respond to the writer or to one another. You can find directories of blogs at *blogcatalog.com*. (See also pp. 120–21 for a discussion and an example of presenting writing on a blog.)

Somewhat similar to blogs, *Twitter* and social-networking sites such as *Facebook* are increasingly being used by organizations, businesses, individuals, and even scholars to communicate with others.

Like all other social media discussed in this section, blogs and pages on social-networking sites must be evaluated carefully as potential sources. Some are reliable sources of opinion and evolving scholarship, and many refer to worthy books, articles, Web sites, and other resources. But just as many are little more than outlets for their authors' gripes or self-marketing. See pages 590–93 for tips on telling the good from the bad.

3 Using discussion lists

A **discussion list** (sometimes called a **listserv** or just a **list**) uses e-mail to connect individuals who are interested in a common subject, often with a scholarly or technical focus. By sending a question to an appropriate list, you may be able to reach scores of people who know something about your topic. For an index of discussion lists, see *tile.net.*

Begin research on a discussion list by consulting the list's archive to ensure that the discussion is relevant to your topic and to see whether your question has already been answered. When you write to the list, follow the guidelines for writing e-mail on pages 144–45. And always evaluate messages you receive, following the guidelines on pages 590–93. Although many contributors are reliable experts, almost anyone with an Internet connection can post a message.

4 Using Web forums and newsgroups

Web forums and newsgroups are more open and less scholarly than discussion lists, so their messages require even more diligent evaluation. **Web forums** allow participants to join a conversation simply by selecting a link on a Web page. For a directory of forums, see *delphiforums.com.* **Newsgroups** are organized under subject headings such as *soc* for social issues and *biz* for business. For a directory of newsgroups, see *giganews.com.*

42h Finding government publications

Government publications provide a vast array of data compilations, reports, policy statements, public records, and other historical and contemporary information. For US government publications, by far the most numerous, consult the Government Printing Office's *GPO Access* at *www.gpoaccess.gov*. Also helpful is *www.usa .gov*, a portal to a range of documents and information.

Many federal, state, and local government agencies post important publications—legislation, reports, press releases—on their own Web sites. You can find lists of sites for various federal agencies by using the keywords *United States federal government* with any search engine. Use the name of a state, city, or town with *government* for state and local information. With the keywords *US Environmental Protection Agency*, Justin Malik found the following graph of the volume of municipal solid waste (MSW) produced in the United States:

Government Web sites can be sources for data, policy, consumer advice, and other information.

Graph from a government publication

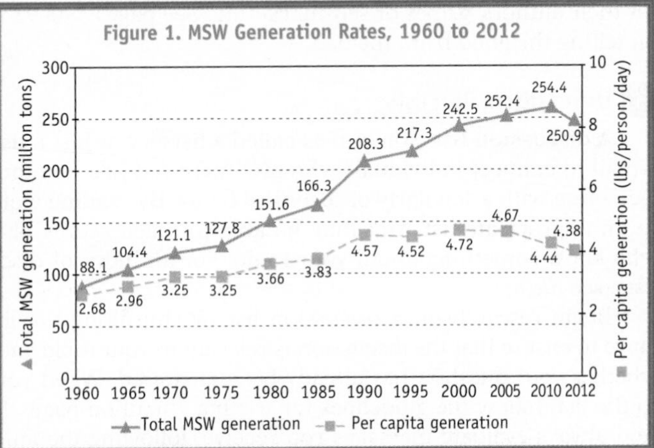

Besides what's available online, your library will have a large collection of printed government publications only if it is a depository library (that is, designated to receive such documents). If yours is a depository library, ask a librarian to help you locate the documents you seek.

42i Finding visuals, audio, and video

Visuals, audio, and video can be used as both primary and secondary sources in a research project. A painting, an advertisement, or a video of a speech might be the subject of your writing and thus a primary source. A college lecture or a podcast of a radio interview with an expert on your subject might serve as a secondary source. Because many of these sources are unfiltered—they can be posted by anyone—you must always evaluate them as carefully as you would any source you find on the open Web. (See pp. 583–93.)

Caution You must also cite every visual, audio, and video source fully in your paper, just as you cite text sources, with author, title, and publication information. In addition, some sources will require that you seek permission from the copyright holder, such as a publisher or a photographer. (See pp. 621–22.) To avoid having to seek permission, you can search Web sites such as *Google, Flickr Creative Commons,* and *Wikimedia Commons* for media that are not protected by copyright. On *Google,* for instance, go to "Search tools" and select "Labeled for reuse." Consult a librarian at your school if you have questions.

1 Finding visuals

Pages 114–16 discuss the use of visuals as evidence in your writing. To find visuals, you have a number of options:

- **Scout for visuals while reading print or online sources.** Your sources may include charts, photographs, and other visuals that can support your ideas. When you find a visual you may want to use, photocopy or download it so you'll have it available later.
- **Create your own visuals,** such as photographs or charts. See pages 110–13 for suggestions on creating visuals.
- **Use an image search engine.** Web search engines can be set to find visuals, and they allow you to restrict your search to visuals that don't require reuse permission. Although search engines can find scores of visuals, the results may be inaccurate or incomplete because the sources surveyed often do not include descriptions of the visuals. (The engines search file names and any text accompanying the visuals.)
- **Use a public image database.** The following sites generally conduct accurate searches because their images are filed with information such as a description of the visual, the artist's name, and the visual's date:

  Digital Public Library of America. Maps, documents, photographs, advertisements, and more from libraries throughout the United States.

  Duke University, *Ad*Access.* Print advertisements spanning 1911–55.

  Library of Congress, *American Memory.* Maps, photographs, prints, cartoons, and advertisements documenting the American experience.

  Library of Congress, *Prints and Photographs Online Catalog.* Visuals from the library's collection, including those available through *American Memory.*

  New York Public Library Digital Gallery. Maps, drawings, photographs, and paintings from the library's collection.

- **Use a public image directory.** The following sites collect links to image sources:

  Art Project—Google Cultural Institute. Selections of fine art from major museums in the United States and Europe.

  MuseumLink's Museum of Museums. Links to museums all over the world.

  Cultural Politics: Resources for Critical Analysis. Sources on advertising, fashion, magazines, toys, and other artifacts of popular culture.

  Yale University Robert B. Haas Family Arts Library, *Image Resources.* Sources on the visual and performing arts.

- **Use a library database.** Your library may subscribe to the following resources:

  ARTstor. Museum collections and a database of images typically used in art history courses.

Associated Press, *AccuNet/AP Multimedia Archives*. Historical and contemporary news images.
Grove Art Online. Art images and links to museum sites.

Many visuals you find will be available at no charge for copying or downloading, but some sources do charge a fee for use. Before paying for a visual, check with a librarian to see if it is available elsewhere for free.

2 Finding audio and video

Audio and video, widely available on the Web and on disc, can provide you and your readers with the experience of "being there." For example, if you write about the media response to the *I Have a Dream* speech of Martin Luther King, Jr., and you submit your paper electronically, you might insert links to the speech and to TV and radio coverage of it.

- **Audio files** such as podcasts, Webcasts, and CDs record radio programs, interviews, speeches, lectures, and music. They are available on the Web and through your library. Online sources of audio include the Library of Congress's *American Memory*, the *Internet Archive*, and *Podcastdirectory.com*.
- **Video files** capture performances, speeches and public presentations, news events, and other activities. They are available on the Web and on DVD or Blu-ray disc from your library. Online sources of video include the Library of Congress's *American Memory*; *YouTube* and the *Internet Archive*, which include commercials, historical footage, current events, and much more; and search engines such as *Google*.

42j Generating your own sources

For some papers you will need to conduct primary research to support, extend, or refute the ideas of others. For example, if you were writing about cyberbullying among college students, you might want to survey students on your campus as well as consult published research on the subject. Three common forms of primary research are personal interviews, surveys, and observation.

1 Conducting personal interviews

A personal interview with an expert on the topic you are researching can provide the kind of information you won't find in books, articles, or Web documents. Because of the give-and-take of an interview, you can ask questions precisely geared to your topic and follow up on points of confusion and unexpected leads. In addition, quotations and paraphrases from an interview can give your paper immediacy and authority.

You can conduct an interview in person, over the telephone, or online. A personal interview is preferable if you can arrange it because you can see the person's expressions and gestures as well as hear his or her tone. But telephone and online interviews allow you to consult someone who resists a personal interview or who lives far away from you, while still retaining most advantages of interaction.

A few precautions will help you get the maximum information from an interview with the minimum disruption to the person you are interviewing:

- **Choose your interviewee carefully.** If you do not already know whom to consult for an interview, ask a teacher in the field or do some telephone or library research. Likely sources, depending on your topic, are those who have written about your topic or something closely related, officials in government, businesspeople, even a relative, if he or she is an expert on your topic because of experience, scholarship, or both.
- **Call or write for an appointment.** Tell the person exactly why you are calling, what you want to discuss, and how long you expect the interview to take. Be true to your word on all points.
- **Prepare a list of open-ended questions to ask**—perhaps ten or twelve for a one-hour interview. Do some research on these questions ahead of the interview to discover background on the issues and your subject's published views on the issues.
- **Pay attention to your subject's answers** so that you can ask appropriate follow-up questions. Take care in interpreting answers, especially if you are online and thus can't depend on facial expressions, gestures, and tone of voice to convey the subject's attitudes. Ask for clarification when you need it.
- **Keep thorough notes.** Take notes during an in-person or telephone interview, or record the interview if you have the equipment and your subject agrees. For online interviews, save the discussion in a file of its own.
- **Verify quotations.** Before you quote your subject in your paper, check with him or her to ensure that the quotations are accurate.
- **Send a thank-you note immediately after the interview.** Promise your subject a copy of your finished paper, and send the paper promptly.

See page 698 for an example of an interview used as a research source.

2 Conducting surveys

Asking questions of a defined group of people can provide information about respondents' attitudes, behavior, backgrounds, and expectations. Use the following tips to plan and conduct a survey:

- **Decide what you want to find out.** The questions you ask should be dictated by your purpose. Formulating a **hypothesis** about your subject—a generalization that can be tested—will help you refine your purpose.
- **Define your population.** Think about the kinds of people your hypothesis is about—for instance, college men or preschool children. Plan to sample this population so that your findings will be representative.
- **Write your questions.** Surveys may contain closed questions that direct the respondent's answers (checklists and multiple-choice, true/false, or yes/no questions) or open-ended questions that allow brief, descriptive answers. Avoid loaded questions that reveal your own biases or make assumptions about subjects' answers, such as "Do you want the United States to support democracy in China?" or "How much more money does your father make than your mother?"
- **Test your questions.** Use a few respondents with whom you can discuss the answers. Eliminate or recast questions that respondents find unclear, discomforting, or unanswerable.
- **Tally the results.** Count the actual numbers of answers, including any nonanswers.
- **Seek patterns in the raw data.** Such patterns may confirm or contradict your hypothesis. Revise the hypothesis or conduct additional research if necessary.

See pages 786–87 for an example of a survey used as a research source.

3 Observing

Observation can be an effective way to gather fresh information on your subject. You may observe in a controlled setting—for instance, watching children at play in a child-development lab. Or you may observe in a more open setting—for instance, watching the interactions among students at a cafeteria on your campus. Use these guidelines for planning and gathering information through observation:

- **Be sure that what you want to learn *can* be observed.** You can observe people's choices and interactions, but you would need an interview or a survey to discover people's attitudes or opinions.
- **Allow ample time.** Observation requires several sessions of several hours in order to be reliable.
- **Record your impressions.** Throughout the observation sessions, take careful notes on paper, a computer, or a mobile device. Always record the date, time, and location for each session.
- **Be aware of your own bias.** Such awareness will help you avoid the common pitfall of seeing only what you expect or want to see.

Exercise 42.1 Using the library

To become familiar with the research sources available through your library, visit both the library and its Web site for answers to the following questions. Ask a librarian for help whenever necessary.

1. Which resources does the library include on its Web site? Which resources require a visit to the library?
2. Where are reference books stored in the library? How are they cataloged and arranged? Which ones are available through the Web site? Where and in what format(s) are (*a*) *Contemporary Authors,* (*b*) *Encyclopaedia Britannica,* and (*c*) *MLA International Bibliography of Books and Articles on the Modern Languages and Literatures*?
3. Where is the catalog of the library's periodicals? Where and in what format(s) does the library have current and back issues of the following periodicals: (*a*) the *New York Times,* (*b*) *Harper's* magazine, and (*c*) *Journal of Social Psychology*?
4. What tools does the library's Web site offer for finding periodical databases that are appropriate for a particular research subject?
5. Research the focus and indexed publications of two periodical databases, such as *Academic Search Complete, JSTOR, LexisNexis, PAIS,* or *ProQuest Research Library*. What disciplines does each database seem most suited for?
6. Does the catalog cover all of the library's book holdings? If not, which books are not included, and where are they cataloged?
7. What are the library call numbers of the following books: (*a*) *The Power Broker,* by Robert Caro; (*b*) *Heart of Darkness,* by Joseph Conrad; and (*c*) *The Hero with a Thousand Faces,* by Joseph Campbell?

Exercise 42.2 Finding library sources

Locate at least six promising articles and books for the subject you began working on in the previous chapter (Exercise 41.1, p. 547, and Exercise 41.2, p. 551). Consider the sources "promising" if they seem directly to address your central research question. Following the guidelines on pages 551–54, make an annotated working bibliography of the sources. Be sure to include all the information you will need to acknowledge the sources in your final paper.

Exercise 42.3 Finding Web sources

Use at least two Web search engines to locate six or seven promising sources for your research project. Begin by developing a list of keywords that can be used to query one of the search engines (see pp. 558–59). Then try your keywords on the other search engine as well. How do the results differ? What keyword strategies worked best for finding relevant information? Add promising sources to your annotated working bibliography.

43 Working with Sources

Chapter essentials

- Use the criteria for reading sources critically (below).
- Evaluate library sources (p. 582).
- Evaluate Web sources and social media (pp. 583, 590).
- Synthesize information from sources (p. 593).
- Interact with sources while reading and making notes (p. 596).
- Carefully summarize, paraphrase, and quote sources (p. 599).
- Integrate source information into your writing (p. 608).

Visit MyWritingLab™ for more resources on working with sources.

The previous chapters helped you lay the groundwork for a research project. This chapter takes you into the most personal, most intensive, and most rewarding part of research writing: using the sources you've found to extend and support your own ideas, to make your subject your own. As before, the work of Justin Malik (on green consumerism) and Vanessa Haley (on the work of Annie Dillard) will illustrate the activity and thought that go into research writing.

CULTURE LANGUAGE Making a subject your own requires thinking critically about sources and developing independent ideas. These goals may at first be uncomfortable if your native culture emphasizes understanding and respecting established authority more than questioning and enlarging it. This chapter offers guidance in working with sources so that you can become an expert in your own right and convincingly convey your expertise to others.

43a Evaluating sources

When you evaluate sources, you look at them critically and judge them with a variety of criteria. Evaluation is one of the most challenging aspects of research because it requires you to determine whether a source is worthwhile in itself and for your research project.

1 Gaining an overview

Once you have a satisfactory working bibliography, you want to get a sense of your sources' usefulness and value.

- **Look first at sources that seem most likely to define your subject.** Justin Malik started with a scholarly review of the literature on green consumption. Vanessa Haley turned first to a book by Annie Dillard, Haley's subject. (For a paper like Haley's that analyzes a writer's work, always begin with that work.)
- **Scan sources to gauge the kind and extent of their ideas and information.** Don't get bogged down collecting information at this

point. Instead, ensure that your sources are appropriately detailed and cover the full range of your subject—that together they promise to help you answer your research question.

2 Judging relevance and reliability

Not all the sources you find will prove worthwhile: some may be irrelevant to your project, and others may be unreliable. Gauging the relevance and reliability of sources is the essential task of evaluating them. If you haven't already done so, read this book's Chapters 7 and 8 on critical reading. They provide a foundation for answering the questions in the following box.

Questions for evaluating sources

For online sources, supplement these questions with those on pages 583 and 590–91.

Relevance

- **Does the source devote some attention to your subject?** Does it focus on your subject or cover it marginally? How does it compare to other sources you've found?
- **Is the source appropriately specialized for your needs?** Check the source's treatment of a topic you know something about, to ensure that it is neither too superficial nor too technical.
- **Is the source up to date enough for your subject?** When was it published? If your subject is current, your sources should be, too.

Reliability

- **Where does the source come from?** Did you find it through your library or directly through the Internet? (If the latter, see the note below.) Is it popular or scholarly?
- **Is the author an expert in the field?** Check the author's credentials in a biography (if the source includes one), in a biographical reference, or by a keyword search of the Web.
- **What is the bias of the source?** How do the author's ideas relate to those in other sources? What areas does the author emphasize, ignore, or dismiss?
- **Is the source fair, reasonable, and well written?** Does it provide sound reasoning and a fair picture of opposing views? Is the tone calm and objective? Is the source logically organized and error-free?
- **Are the claims well supported, even if you don't agree with the author?** Does the author provide accurate, relevant, representative, and adequate evidence to back up his or her claims? Does the author cite sources, and if so are they reliable?

Note In evaluating sources, you need to consider how they came to you. The sources you find through the library, both in print and on the Web, have been previewed for you by their publishers and by the library's staff. They still require your critical reading, but you can have some confidence in the information they contain. With online sources you reach directly, however, you cannot assume similar previewing, so your critical reading must be especially rigorous. Special tips for evaluating Web sites and other online sources begin on the next page.

3 Evaluating library sources

To evaluate sources you find through your library—either in print or on the library's Web site—look at dates, titles, summaries, introductions, headings, author biographies, and any source citations. The following criteria expand on the most important tips in the box on the previous page. On pages 584–85 you can see how Justin Malik applied these criteria to two print sources, a magazine article and a journal article, that he consulted during his research into green consumerism.

Identify the origin of the source.

Check whether a library source is popular or scholarly. Scholarly sources, such as refereed journals and university press books, are generally deeper and more reliable. But some popular sources, such as first-hand newspaper accounts and books for a general audience, are often appropriate for research projects.

Check the author's expertise.

The authors of scholarly publications tend to be experts whose authority can be verified. Check the source to see whether it contains a biographical note about the author, check a biographical reference, or check the author's name in a keyword search of the Web. Look for other publications by the author and for his or her job and any affiliation, such as teacher at a university, researcher with a nonprofit organization, author of general-interest books, or writer for popular magazines.

Identify the author's bias.

Every author has a point of view that influences the selection and interpretation of evidence. You may be able to learn about an author's bias from biographies, review indexes (p. 563), and citation indexes (p. 568). But also look at the source itself. How do the author's ideas relate to those in other sources? What areas does the author emphasize, ignore, or dismiss? When you're aware of sources' biases, you can acknowledge them in your writing and try to balance them.

Determine whether the source is fair, reasonable, and well written.

Even a strongly biased work should present solid reasoning and give balanced coverage to opposing views—all in an objective tone. View with suspicion any source that is not organized logically and written in clear, error-free sentences.

Analyze support for the author's claims.

Whether or not you agree with the author you should be able to find the evidence accurate, relevant to the argument, representative of its context, and adequate for the point being made. (See pp. 187–88). The author's sources should themselves be reliable.

4 Evaluating Web sites

To a great extent, the same critical reading that helps you evaluate library sources will help you evaluate Web sites that you reach directly. You would not use a popular magazine such as *People* in academic research—unless, say, you were considering it as a primary source in a paper analyzing popular culture. Similarly, you would not use a celebrity's Web site, a fan site, or a gossip site as a source unless you were placing it in a larger academic context.

Even Web sites that seem worthy pose challenges for evaluation because they have not undergone prior screening by editors and librarians. On your own, you must distinguish scholarship from corporate promotion, valid data from invented statistics, and well-founded opinion from clever propaganda.

To make such distinctions, use the strategy that is summarized in the following box and explained on pages 588–90. On pages 586–87 you can see how Justin Malik applied the strategy to two Web sites he found during his research into green consumerism.

Questions for evaluating Web sites

Supplement these questions with those on page 581.

- **What type of site are you viewing**—for example, is it scholarly, informational, or commercial? What does the type lead you to expect about the site's purpose and content?
- **Who is the author or publisher?** How credible is the person or group responsible for the site?
- **What is the purpose of the site?** What does the site's author or publisher intend to achieve? Are there ads on the site, signaling that the site is trying to make money from its content?
- **What is the bias of the site?** Does the site advocate for one side or another of a particular issue?
- **What does context tell you?** What do you already know about the site's subject that can inform your evaluation? What kinds of support or other information do the site's links provide?
- **What does presentation tell you?** Is the site's design well thought out and effective? Is the writing clear and error-free?
- **How worthwhile is the content?** Are the site's claims well supported by evidence? Is the evidence from reliable sources? When was the site last updated?

(text continues on p. 588)

43a

Evaluating library sources

Opposite are sample pages from two library sources that Justin Malik considered for his paper on green consumerism. Malik evaluated the sources using the questions in the box on page 581 and the guidelines on pages 582–83.

	Makower	Jackson
Origin	Interview with Joel Makower published in *Vegetarian Times*, a popular magazine.	Article by Tim Jackson published in *Journal of Industrial Ecology*, a scholarly journal sponsored by two reputable universities: MIT and Yale.
Author	Gives Makower's credentials at the beginning of the interview: the author of a book on green products and of a monthly newsletter on green businesses. Quotes another source that calls Makower the "guru of green business practice."	Includes a biography at the end of the article that describes Jackson as a professor at the University of Surrey (UK) and lists his professional activities related to the environment.
Bias	Describes and promotes green products. Concludes with an endorsement of a for-profit Web site that tracks and sells green products.	Presents multiple views of green consumerism. Argues that a solution to environmental problems will involve green products and less consumption but in different ways than currently proposed.
Reasonableness and writing	Presents Makower's data and perspective on distinguishing good from bad green products, using conversational writing in an informal presentation.	Presents and cites opposing views objectively, using formal academic writing.
Source citations	Lacks source citations for claims and data.	Includes more than three pages of source citations, many of scholarly and government sources and all cited within the article.
Assessment	**Unreliable for academic research:** Despite Makower's reputation, the article comes from a nonscholarly source, takes a one-sided approach to consumption, and depends on statistics credited only to Makower.	**Reliable for academic research:** The article comes from a scholarly journal, the author is an expert in the field, he discusses many views and concedes some, and his source citations confirm evidence from reliable sources.

Unreliable source for academic research:
An interview with Joel Makower, published in *Vegetarian Times*

a greater capacity than they did 10 years ago because landfill operators are more sophisticated about compacting.

The problem with landfills is the energy and resources used to make the stuff that goes into them. Over 95 percent of the things we buy—disposable razors, single-use water bottles—have a useful life of less than six weeks, and sometimes less than a day. Almost every environmental problem we face is a result of our own wastefulness. We pay a high price for being a consumer society, and not just at the checkout counter. The promise of green consumerism is that we won't have to do without things we want or need. But that means demanding that manufacturers find better ways to make these things and rewarding the companies that do by buying their products.

q:
Who are they?

q:
Can we really do much in our own homes?

a:
Sure. I live in the house where I grew up. We've made a series of eco-friendly renovations, using wood that is harvested in a sustainable way, paints that don't emit harmful chemicals, energy-efficient appliances and windows. We also asked that the contractors recycle all of the waste from the work they did. Because we live in California, which is a pretty eco-conscious state, contractors get asked to do that quite a lot. But you have to ask. That's what creates a demand for the service.

Being a green consumer isn't just passively selecting the right items at your supermarket. It involves complaining when complaining is warranted, demanding new products and services when they don't exist and buying them when they appear. It means taking action. ■

go for the green

interview by alan pell crawford

buying beer? sneakers? a car? the most eco-conscious companies aren't always the most obvious

It isn't easy being green. No fewer than 137 eco-labels appear on consumer products these days, reports Consumers Union, and that's not counting stickers such as "sweatshop-free." This explosion of claims comes from companies eager to meet the demand for healthful, environmentally friendly products—or at least to cash in on it. Figuring out which products really are green and which are mere hype can be overwhelming.

Fortunately, there's help. To find out more about the current state of green consumerism, *VT* interviewed Joel Makower, who has spent the past 20 years helping consumers become savvier shoppers and getting corporations to become more responsible corporate citizens. The author of The Green Consumer and editor of The Green Business Letter—a monthly publication that offers information to companies working to integrate environmental thinking into their operations—Makower is the "guru of green business practices," according to the Associated Press.

If anybody knows how corporations have responded to this demand for environmentally responsible products, it's Makower. General Electric, General Motors, Hewlett-Packard, Levi Strauss & Co., Nike and Procter & Gamble have all had the benefit of his counsel. Now it's your turn.

green-rated products

Alonovo.com—from the Latin alo novo for "nurturing change"—is an online eco-shopping service that's associated with Amazon.com. Find a product on Alonovo, and in addition to the description, reviews and price, you'll also see a five-dot rating for the company that produced it. Better still, Alonovo allows you to influence the ratings that products and companies receive by weighting the values most important to you—Healthy Environment, Business Ethics and so forth. Best of all, you can buy products through Alonovo at Amazon prices but 20 percent of revenues are sent to a nonprofit that you specify. Amazon processes the transaction and ships the goods.

Launched in August 2005, Alonovo (a for-profit company) is one of a number of new services designed to help consumers make smart choices. Similar in concept is Idealswork (idealswork.com), which allows you to put more emphasis on a company's animal-welfare policies, for example, than on its concern for workplace equity—or vice versa.

How good will Alonovo be? "If it catches on," says Joel Makower, "it could be one of the most powerful social change tools ever put into consumers' hands."

www.vegetariantimes.com 87

STATE OF THE DEBATE

Live Better by Consuming Less?

Is There a "Double Dividend" in Sustainable Consumption?

Tim Jackson

Keywords

consumer behavior
consumer choice
consumer culture
evolutionary psychology
industrial ecology
symbolic interactionism

Summa

Industria
the effic
tion is al
ment. Th
this. But
really be
debates
self. This article explores some of these wider debates. In particular, it draws attention to a fundamental disagreement that runs through the literature on consumption and haunts the debate on sustainable consumption: the question of whether, or to what extent, consumption can be taken as "good for us." Some approaches assume that increasing consumption is more or less synonymous with improved well-being: the more we consume the better off we are. Others argue, just as vehemently, that the scale of consumption in modern society is both environmentally and psychologically damaging, and that we could reduce consumption significantly without threatening the quality of our lives. This second viewpoint suggests that a kind of "double dividend" is inherent in sustainable consumption: the ability to live better by consuming less and reduce our impact on the environment in the process. In the final analysis, this article argues, such "win-win" solutions may exist but will require a concerted societal effort to realize.

http://mitpress.mit.edu/jie   *Journal of Industrial Ecology* 19

penter Publishing.

UNDP (United Nations Development Programme) 1998. *Human development report 1998*. Oxford, UK: Oxford University Press.

UNEP (United Nations Environment Programme) 2001. Consumption opportunities: Strategies for change. Paris: UNEP.

Van den Bergh, J. C. J. M., A. Ferrer-i-Carbonell, and G. Munda. 2000. Alternative models of individual behaviour and implications for environmental policy. *Ecological Economics* 32(1): 43–61.

About the Author

Tim Jackson is Professor of Sustainable Development at the Centre for Environmental Strategy (CES) in the University of Surrey, Guildford, United Kingdom. He currently holds a research fellowship in sustainable consumption funded by the Economic and Social Research Council and leads the Ecological Economics Research Group at CES. He is also chair of the Economics Steering Group of the U.K. Sustainable Development Commission and sits on the U.K. Round Table on Sustainable Consumption.

Reliable source for academic research:
An article by Tim Jackson, published in the *Journal of Industrial Ecology*

Evaluating Web sites

Opposite are screen shots from two Web sites that Justin Malik consulted for his paper on green consumerism. Malik evaluated the sources using the questions in the boxes on pages 581 and 583.

	Wikipedia	*Center for Climate and Energy Solutions*
Author and publisher	Author of the page is not given. Web site is *Wikipedia*, the online encyclopedia to which anyone can contribute anonymously.	Author is an expert on energy and public policy. (His biography can be found online.) Publisher is the Center for Climate and Energy Solutions, a nonprofit group specializing in energy and climate change.
Purpose and bias	Informational page with no stated or obvious bias.	Informational site with the stated purpose of "working to promote sound policy on the challenges of energy and climate change." Report expresses bias toward sustainable electricity production.
Context	An encyclopedia site publishing general information on a wide variety of topics.	Nonprofit organization's site dedicated to publishing current research on energy and climate issues.
Presentation	Clean, professional-looking page with mostly error-free writing.	Clean, professionally designed site with error-free writing.
Content	Article gives basic information about energy use and provides links to other pages that expand on its claims. Probably because of the intended general audience, the page does not link to extensive citations of scholarly research.	Report is current (date below the author's name), it describes scenarios for meeting future electricity needs, and it cites scholarly sources.
Assessment	**Unreliable for academic research:** The page has no listed author and few scholarly citations. A *Wikipedia* page is suitable for background information but not as evidence in an academic paper.	**Reliable for academic research:** The report has a bias toward sustainable electricity production, but the publisher is reputable and the author is an expert and cites scholarly sources.

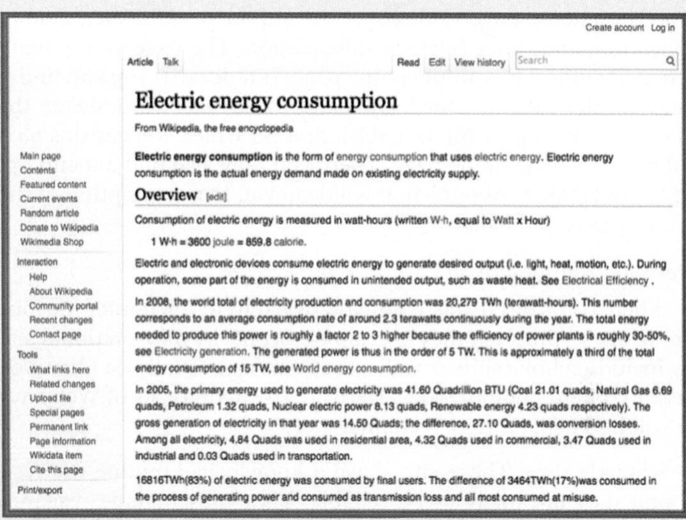

Create account Log in

Article Talk Read Edit View history Search

Electric energy consumption

From Wikipedia, the free encyclopedia

Main page
Contents
Featured content
Current events
Random article
Donate to Wikipedia
Wikimedia Shop

Interaction
Help
About Wikipedia
Community portal
Recent changes
Contact page

Tools
What links here
Related changes
Upload file
Special pages
Permanent link
Page information
Wikidata item
Cite this page

Print/export

Electric energy consumption is the form of energy consumption that uses electric energy. Electric energy consumption is the actual energy demand made on existing electricity supply.

Overview [edit]

Consumption of electric energy is measured in watt-hours (written W·h, equal to Watt x Hour)

1 W·h = 3600 joule = 859.8 calorie.

Electric and electronic devices consume electric energy to generate desired output (i.e. light, heat, motion, etc.). During operation, some part of the energy is consumed in unintended output, such as waste heat. See Electrical Efficiency .

In 2008, the world total of electricity production and consumption was 20,279 TWh (terawatt-hours). This number corresponds to an average consumption rate of around 2.3 terawatts continuously during the year. The total energy needed to produce this power is roughly a factor 2 to 3 higher because the efficiency of power plants is roughly 30-50%, see Electricity generation. The generated power is thus in the order of 5 TW. This is approximately a third of the total energy consumption of 15 TW, see World energy consumption.

In 2005, the primary energy used to generate electricity was 41.60 Quadrillion BTU (Coal 21.01 quads, Natural Gas 6.69 quads, Petroleum 1.32 quads, Nuclear electric power 8.13 quads, Renewable energy 4.23 quads respectively). The gross generation of electricity in that year was 14.50 Quads; the difference, 27.10 Quads, was conversion losses. Among all electricity, 4.84 Quads was used in residential area, 4.32 Quads used in commercial, 3.47 Quads used in industrial and 0.03 Quads used in transportation.

16816TWh(83%) of electric energy was consumed by final users. The difference of 3464TWh(17%)was consumed in the process of generating power and consumed as transmission loss and all most consumed at misuse.

Unreliable source for academic research: A page on the Web site *Wikipedia*

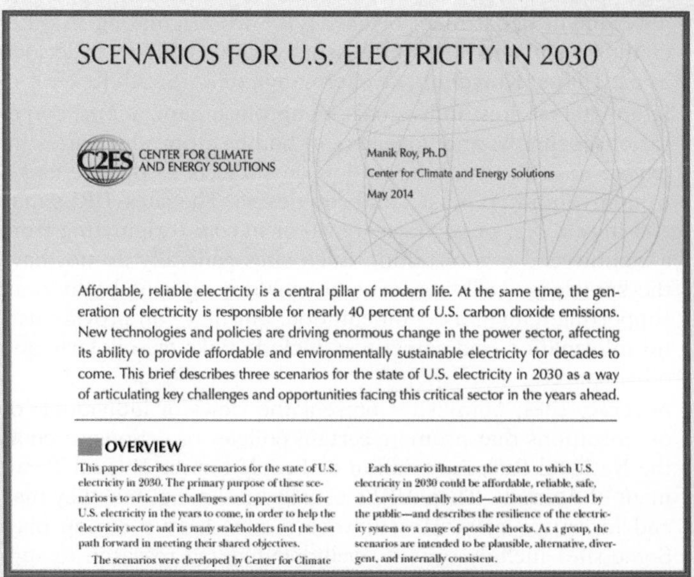

SCENARIOS FOR U.S. ELECTRICITY IN 2030

C2ES CENTER FOR CLIMATE AND ENERGY SOLUTIONS

Manik Roy, Ph.D
Center for Climate and Energy Solutions
May 2014

Affordable, reliable electricity is a central pillar of modern life. At the same time, the generation of electricity is responsible for nearly 40 percent of U.S. carbon dioxide emissions. New technologies and policies are driving enormous change in the power sector, affecting its ability to provide affordable and environmentally sustainable electricity for decades to come. This brief describes three scenarios for the state of U.S. electricity in 2030 as a way of articulating key challenges and opportunities facing this critical sector in the years ahead.

OVERVIEW

This paper describes three scenarios for the state of U.S. electricity in 2030. The primary purpose of these scenarios is to articulate challenges and opportunities for U.S. electricity in the years to come, in order to help the electricity sector and its many stakeholders find the best path forward in meeting their shared objectives.

The scenarios were developed by Center for Climate

Each scenario illustrates the extent to which U.S. electricity in 2030 could be affordable, reliable, safe, and environmentally sound—attributes demanded by the public—and describes the resilience of the electricity system to a range of possible shocks. As a group, the scenarios are intended to be plausible, alternative, divergent, and internally consistent.

Reliable source for academic research: A report published on the Web site *Center for Climate and Energy Solutions*

(continued from p. 583)

Note To evaluate a Web document, you'll often need to travel to the site's home page to discover the author or publisher, date of publication, and other relevant information. The page you're reading may include a link to the home page. If it doesn't, you can find it by editing the URL in your browser. Working backward, delete the end of the URL up to the last slash and hit Enter. Repeat this step until you reach the home page. There you may also find a menu option, often labeled "About," that will lead you to a description of the site's author or publisher.

Determine the type of site.

When you search the Web, you're likely to encounter various types of sites. Although they overlap—a primarily informational site may include scholarship as well—the types can usually be identified by their content and purposes. Here are the main types of Web sites you will find using a search engine:

- **Scholarly sites:** These sites have a knowledge-building interest, and they are likely to be reliable. They may include research reports with supporting data and extensive documentation of scholarly sources. For such sites originating in the United States, the URLs generally end in *edu* (originating from a college or university), *org* (a nonprofit organization), or *gov* (a government department or agency). Sites originating in other countries will end differently, usually with a country code such as *uk* (United Kingdom), *de* (Germany), or *kr* (South Korea).
- **Informational sites:** Individuals, nonprofit organizations, corporations, schools, and government bodies all produce sites intended to centralize information on subjects as diverse as astronomy, hip-hop music, and zoo design. The sites' URLs may end in *edu, org,* or *gov* (see above) or in *com* (originating from a commercial organization). Such sites generally do not have the knowledge-building focus of scholarly sites and may omit supporting data and documentation, but they can provide useful information and sometimes include links to scholarly and other sources.
- **Advocacy sites:** Many sites present the views of individuals or organizations that promote certain policies or actions, such as the National Rifle Association or People for the Ethical Treatment of Animals. Their URLs usually end in *org*, but they may end in *edu* or *com*. Most advocacy sites have a strong bias. Some sites include serious, well-documented research to support their positions, but others select or distort evidence.
- **Commercial sites:** Corporations and other businesses—such as automakers, electronics manufacturers, and booksellers—maintain Web sites to explain themselves, promote themselves, or sell

goods and services. URLs of commercial sites usually end in *com*; however, some end in *biz*, and those of businesses based outside the United States often end in the country code. Although business sites intend to further the publishers' profit-making purposes, they can include reliable data.

- **Personal sites:** The sites maintained by individuals range from diaries of a family's travels to opinions on political issues to reports on evolving scholarship. The sites' URLs usually end in *com* or *edu*. Personal sites are only as reliable as their authors, but some do provide eyewitness accounts, links to worthy sources, and other usable information. Personal sites are often blogs or pages on social-networking sites, discussed on pages 590–93.

Identify the author and publisher.

A reputable site lists its authors, names the group responsible for the site, and provides information or a link for contacting the author and the publisher. If none of this information is provided, you should not use the source. If you have only the author's or the publisher's name, you may be able to discover more in a biographical dictionary, through a keyword search, or in your other sources. Make sure the author and the publisher have expertise on the subject they're presenting: if an author is a doctor, for instance, what is he or she a doctor of?

Gauge purpose and bias.

A Web site's purpose determines what ideas and information it offers. Inferring that purpose tells you how to interpret what you see on the site. If a site is intended to sell a product or advocate a particular position, it may emphasize favorable ideas and information while ignoring or even distorting unfavorable information or opposing views. In contrast, if a site is intended to build knowledge—for instance, a scholarly project or journal—it will likely acknowledge diverse views and evidence.

Determining the purpose and bias of a site often requires looking beyond the first page and beneath the surface of words and images. To start, read critically what the site says about itself, usually on a page labeled "About." Be suspicious of any site that doesn't provide information about itself and its goals.

Consider context.

Your evaluation of a Web site should be informed by considerations outside the site itself. Chief among these considerations is your own knowledge. What do you already know about the site's subject and the prevailing views of it? Where does this site seem to fit into that picture? What can you learn from this site that you don't already know?

In addition, you can follow some of the site's links to see how they support, or don't support, the site's credibility. For instance, links to scholarly sources lend authority to a site—but *only* if the scholarly sources actually relate to and back up the site's claims.

Look at presentation.

Considering both the look of a site and the way it's written can illuminate its intentions and reliability. Do the site's elements all support its purpose, or is the site cluttered with irrelevant material and graphics? Is the text clearly written and focused on the purpose? Is it relatively error-free, or does it contain typos and grammatical errors? Does the site seem carefully constructed and well maintained, or is it sloppy? How intrusive are any pop-up advertisements?

Analyze content.

With information about a site's author, purpose, and context, you're in a position to evaluate its content. Are the ideas and information current, or are they dated? (Check the publication date.) Are they slanted and, if so, in what direction? Are the views and data authoritative, or do you need to balance them—or even reject them? Are claims made on the site supported by evidence drawn from reliable sources? These questions require close reading of both the text and its sources.

5 Evaluating other online sources

Social media and multimedia require the same critical scrutiny as Web sites do. Social media—including e-mail, blogs, *Twitter,* discussion groups, *Facebook* pages, and wikis—can be sources of reliable data and opinions, but they can also contain wrong or misleading data and skewed opinions. Multimedia—visuals, audio, and video—can provide valuable support for your ideas, but they can also mislead or distort. For example, a *YouTube* search using "I have a dream" brings up videos of Martin Luther King, Jr., delivering his famous speech as well as videos of people speaking hatefully about King and the speech.

Use the following strategy for evaluating such online sources. See page 592 for Justin Malik's use of this strategy with a blog he found while researching green consumerism.

Questions for evaluating social media and multimedia

Supplement these questions with those on page 581.

- **Who is the author or creator?** How credible is he or she?
- **What is the author's or creator's purpose?** What can you tell about why the author or creator is publishing the work?

- **What does the context reveal?** What do reasonable responses to the work, such as comments on a blog or a news site, indicate about the source's balance and reliability?
- **How worthwhile is the content?** Are the claims made by the author or creator supported by evidence? Is the evidence from reliable sources?
- **How does the source compare with other sources?** Do the claims made by the author or creator seem accurate and fair, given what you've seen in sources you know to be reliable?

Identify the author or creator.

Checking out the author or creator of a potential source can help you judge its reliability. The author may be identified on the source—for instance, the blog posting shown on the next page ends with a biographical note saying that the author is a professor writing on behalf of the American Anthropological Association's Task Force on Global Climate Change. You may also be able to learn about the author with a keyword search of the Web. If you can't identify the author or creator at all, you can't use the source.

You can also get a sense of the interests and biases of an author or creator by tracking down his or her other work. For instance, you might check whether a blog author cites or links to other publications, look for other postings by the same author in a discussion-group archive, or use a Web search to gain an overview of a photographer's work.

Analyze the author's or creator's purpose.

What can you tell about *why* the author or creator is publishing the work? The blog posting on the next page provides a quick answer in the title, which indicates the author's negative view of green products. You can also dig to discover purpose, looking for claims, the use (or not) of evidence, and the treatment of opposing views. All these factors convey the person's stand on the subject and general fairness, and they will help you position the source among your other sources.

Consider the context.

Social media and multimedia are often difficult to evaluate in isolation. Looking beyond a particular contribution to the responses of others can give you a sense of context by indicating how the author or creator is regarded. On a *Facebook* page or a blog, such as the posting from the *Huffington Post* on the next page, look at the comments others have posted. If you discover negative or angry responses, try to understand why: sometimes online anonymity encourages hateful responses to even quite reasonable postings.

Evaluating a blog

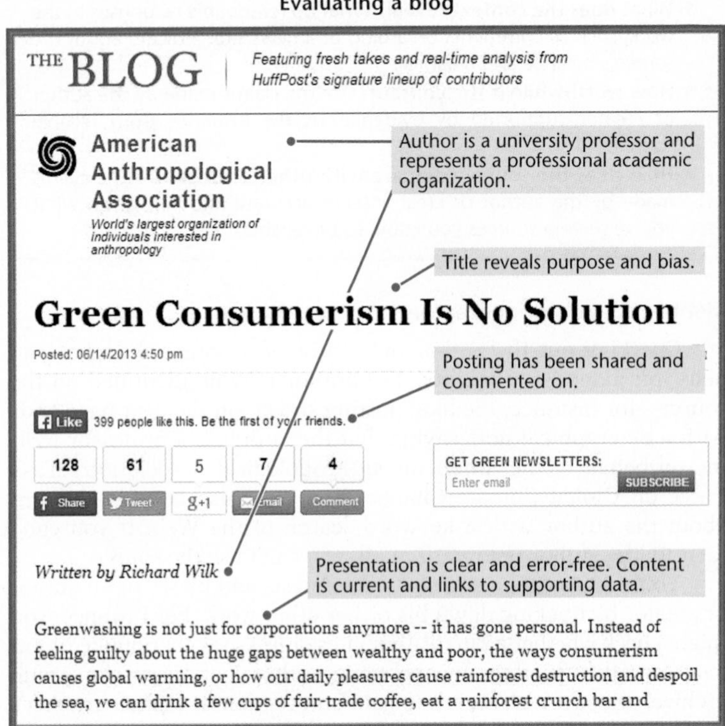

THE BLOG
Featuring fresh takes and real-time analysis from HuffPost's signature lineup of contributors
American Anthropological Association
World's largest organization of individuals interested in anthropology
Author is a university professor and represents a professional academic organization.
Title reveals purpose and bias.
Green Consumerism Is No Solution
Posted: 06/14/2013 4:50 pm
Posting has been shared and commented on.
Like 399 people like this. Be the first of your friends.
128 61 5 7 4
Share Tweet 8+1 Email Comment
GET GREEN NEWSLETTERS:
Enter email
SUBSCRIBE
Written by Richard Wilk
Presentation is clear and error-free. Content is current and links to supporting data.
Greenwashing is not just for corporations anymore -- it has gone personal. Instead of feeling guilty about the huge gaps between wealthy and poor, the ways consumerism causes global warming, or how our daily pleasures cause rainforest destruction and despoil the sea, we can drink a few cups of fair-trade coffee, eat a rainforest crunch bar and

Analyze content.

A reliable source will offer evidence for claims and will list the sources of its evidence. The blog posting above, for example, links to scholarly information about carbon dioxide emissions. If you don't see such support, then you probably shouldn't use the source. However, when the source is important to you and biographical information or context indicates that the author or creator is serious and reliable, you might ask him or her to direct you to supporting information.

The tone of writing can also be a clue to its purpose and reliability. In most social media, the writing tends to be more informal and may be more heated than in other kinds of sources; but look askance at writing that's contemptuous, dismissive, or shrill.

Compare with other sources.

Always consider social-media and multimedia sources in comparison to other sources so that you can distinguish singular, untested views from more mainstream views that have been subject to verification. Don't assume that a blog author's information and opinions are reliable just because you see them on other blogs. The technology allows content to be picked up instantly by other blogs, so widespread distribution indicates only popular interest, not reliability.

Be wary of blogs that reproduce periodical articles, reports, or other publications. Try to locate the original version of the publication to be sure it has been reproduced fully and accurately, not quoted selectively or distorted. If you can't locate the original version, don't use the publication as a source.

Exercise 43.1 Evaluating a source

Imagine that you are researching a paper on the advertising techniques that are designed to persuade consumers to buy products. You have listed the following book in your working bibliography:

Vance Packard, *The Hidden Persuaders,* revised edition, 1981.

On your own or with your classmates (as your instructor wishes), obtain this book from a library and evaluate it as a source for your paper. Use the guidelines on page 581.

Exercise 43.2 Evaluating Web sites

Find and evaluate two Web sites: a commercial site, such as Microsoft's or Apple's, and a site for a nonprofit organization, such as the American Medical Association or Greenpeace. What do you know or can you infer about each site's publisher or author? What seems to be the site's purpose or purposes? What do the site's links contribute? How effective is the site's design? How reliable do you judge the site's information to be? How do the two sites differ in these respects?

Exercise 43.3 Evaluating a blog

Visit *wordpress.com* or *blogcatalog.com* to find a blog on a controversial subject such as stem-cell research or animal research. Who is responsible for the blog? What can you tell about its purpose? How reliable do you judge its ideas and information to be?

Exercise 43.4 Evaluating an online discussion

On a social-media site, locate a discussion that interests you. (If you already participate in an online discussion group, you can use it instead.) Pick one series of at least ten related messages on a single topic. Write a brief summary of each message (see pp. 155–57 on summarizing). Then analyze and synthesize the messages to develop a one- or two-paragraph evaluation of the discussion. Which messages seem reliable? Which don't? Why?

43b Synthesizing sources

When you begin to see the differences and similarities among sources, you move into the most significant part of research writing:

forging relationships for your own purpose. This **synthesis,** an essential step in critical reading (pp. 161–62), continues through the drafting and revision of a research paper. As you read, take notes, and infer connections—say, between one writer's ideas and another's or between two works by the same author—you shape your own perspective on your subject and create new knowledge.

All kinds of connections may occur to you as you work with sources. Justin Malik, researching the environmental impacts of green consumption, uncovered a central disagreement among sources over whether changing individual consumer behavior would make a significant difference on a global scale. Vanessa Haley, writing about Annie Dillard, discovered that her view of Dillard was partly supported by some of the critics she consulted but not supported by others. She knew she would have to take account of these divergent views in her paper.

Your synthesis of sources will grow more detailed and sophisticated as you proceed through the process of working with sources described in the balance of this chapter: interacting with sources (pp. 596–97), deciding whether to summarize, paraphrase, or quote directly from sources (pp. 599–606), and integrating source material into your sentences (pp. 608–13). Unless, like Vanessa Haley, you are analyzing primary sources such as the works of a writer, read your sources quickly and selectively at first to obtain an overview of your subject and a sense of how the sources approach it. Instead of taking detailed notes about what sources say, record your own ideas about the sources in your research journal (p. 543) or your annotated bibliography (p. 554).

Respond to sources.

One way to find your own perspective on a topic is to write down what your sources make you think. Do you agree or disagree with the author? Do you find his or her views narrow, or do they open up new approaches for you? Is there anything in the source that you need to research further before you can understand it? Does the source prompt questions that you should keep in mind while reading other sources?

Connect sources.

When you notice a link between sources, write about it. Do two sources differ in their theories or their interpretations of facts? Does one source illuminate another—perhaps commenting or clarifying or supplying additional data? Do two or more sources report studies that support a theory you've read about or an idea of your own?

Heed your insights.

Apart from ideas prompted by your sources, you are sure to come up with independent thoughts: a conviction, a point of confusion that suddenly becomes clear, a question you haven't seen anyone else ask. These insights may occur at unexpected times, so it's good practice to keep a notebook or computer handy to record them.

Draw your own conclusions.

As your research proceeds, the responses, connections, and insights you form through synthesis will lead you to answer your starting research question with a statement of your thesis (see p. 625). They will also lead you to the main ideas supporting your thesis—conclusions you have drawn from your synthesis of sources, forming the main divisions of your paper. Be sure to write them down as they occur to you.

Use sources to support your conclusions.

Effective synthesis requires careful handling of evidence from sources so that it meshes smoothly into your sentences and yet is clearly distinct from your own ideas. When drafting your paper, make sure that each paragraph focuses on an idea of your own, with the support for the idea coming from your sources. Generally, open each paragraph with your own idea, provide evidence from a source or sources with appropriate citations, and close with an interpretation of the evidence. (Avoid ending a paragraph with a source citation; instead, end with your own idea.) In this way, your paper will synthesize others' work into something wholly your own. For more on structuring paragraphs in academic writing, see pages 172–74.

Exercise 43.5 Synthesizing sources

The following three passages address the same issue, the legalization of drugs. What similarities do you see in the authors' ideas? What differences? Write a paragraph of your own in which you use these authors' views as a point of departure for your own view about drug legalization.

Perhaps the most unfortunate victims of drug prohibition laws have been the residents of America's ghettos. These laws have proved largely futile in deterring ghetto-dwellers from becoming drug abusers, but they do account for much of what ghetto residents identify as the drug problem. Aggressive, gun-toting drug dealers often upset law-abiding residents far more than do addicts nodding out in doorways. Meanwhile other residents perceive the drug dealers as heroes and successful role models. They're symbols of success to children who see no other options. At the same time the increasingly harsh criminal penalties imposed on adult drug dealers have led drug traffickers to recruit juveniles. Where once children started dealing drugs only after they had been using them for a few years, today the sequence is often reversed. Many children start using drugs only after working for older drug dealers for a while. Legalization of drugs, like legalization of alcohol in the early 1930s, would drive the drug-dealing business off the streets and out of apartment buildings and into government-regulated, tax-paying stores.

It also would force many of the gun-toting dealers out of the business and convert others into legitimate businessmen.

—Ethan A. Nadelmann, "Shooting Up"

Statistics argue against legalization. The University of Michigan conducts an annual survey of twelfth graders, asking the students about their drug consumption. In 1980, 56.4% of those polled said they had used marijuana in the past twelve months, whereas in 2012 only 45.5% had done so. Cocaine use was even more reduced in the same period (22.6% to 5.2%). At the same time, twelve-month use of legally available drugs—alcohol and nicotine-containing cigarettes—remained fairly steady around 70% and 50%, respectively. The numbers of illegal drug users haven't declined nearly enough: those teenaged marijuana and cocaine users are still vulnerable to addiction and even death, and they threaten to infect their impressionable peers. But clearly the prohibition of illegal drugs has helped, while the legal status of alcohol and cigarettes has not made them less popular.

—Sylvia Smith, "The Case against Legalization"

I have to laugh at the debate over what to do about the drug problem. Everyone is running around offering solutions—from making drug use a more serious criminal offense to legalizing it. But there isn't a real solution. I know that. I used and abused drugs, and people, and society, for two decades. Nothing worked to get me to stop all that behavior except just plain being sick and tired. Nothing. Not threats, not ten-plus years in prison, not anything that was said to me. I used until I got through. Period. And that's when you'll win the war. When all the dope fiends are done. Not a minute before.

—Michael W. Posey, "I Did Drugs Till I Was Worn Out.
Why War On Drugs Won't Work."

Exercise 43.6 Evaluating and synthesizing sources

Look up the sources in the working bibliography you made in Exercises 42.2 and 42.3 (p. 593). Evaluate the sources for their relevance and reliability. If the sources seem unreliable or don't seem to give you what you need, expand your working bibliography and evaluate the new sources. In your research journal or annotated bibliography, write down your responses to sources, the connections you perceive among sources, and other original ideas that occur to you.

43c Interacting with sources

When you have decided which sources to pursue, you may be ready to gather and synthesize information, or you may want to step back and get your bearings. Your choice will depend mainly on how familiar you are with the main issues of your subject and whether you have formed a central idea about it.

- **When you know what you're looking for, proceed with information gathering.** If you've formed a good idea of your thesis and a sense of the topics you will cover, you'll have a framework for finding and synthesizing the information in your sources.

- **When you're uncertain of your direction, stop to draft a thesis statement and create an outline.** These steps (discussed on pp. 625–29) can help when you're attracted to several different theses or when you don't see how the various areas of your subject relate.

The following sections discuss reading sources and then gathering and organizing information from sources.

1 Skimming and then reading

The most efficient method of reading secondary sources during research is **skimming,** reading quickly to look for pertinent information. (Primary sources usually need to be read more carefully, especially when they are the focus of your paper.) Follow these guidelines for skimming:

- **Read with a specific question in mind,** not randomly in hopes of hitting something worthwhile.
- **Consult reference aids**—tables of contents, menus, indexes, or headings—to find what you want.
- **Concentrate on headings and main ideas,** skipping material unrelated to the specific question you are researching.

When you find something relevant, read slowly and carefully to achieve a clear understanding of what the author is saying and to interpret and evaluate the material in the context of your own and others' opinions.

2 Gathering information

You can collect and store source information in a number of ways: handwrite notes, type notes into a file, copy and paste chunks of text from online articles into a file, annotate print or electronic documents such as PDF files, or scan or photocopy pages from books and other print sources.

Whatever method you use to gather information, you have four main goals:

- **Keep accurate records of what sources say.** Accuracy helps prevent misrepresentation and plagiarism. If you write notes by hand or type them into a file, do so carefully to avoid introducing errors.
- **Keep track of others' words and ideas.** Put quotation marks around any words you take from a source, and always include a source citation that ties the quotation to the publication information you have recorded. For any idea you summarize or

paraphrase, always include a source citation that ties the idea to the publication information. For more on summarizing, paraphrasing, and quoting sources, see the next section.

- **Keep accurate records of how to find sources.** Whether you handwrite notes or work with an electronic file, always link the source material to its complete publication information. These records are essential for retracing steps and for citing sources in your drafts and in the final paper. If you have the complete information in your working bibliography (see pp. 551–54), you can use a shorthand reference to it on the source material, such as the author's name and any page or other reference number.
- **Synthesize sources.** Information gathering is a critical process in which you learn from sources, understand the relationships among them, and develop your own ideas about your subject and your sources. Analyze and interact with your sources by highlighting key information and commenting on what they say. See the sample below.

Source printout with annotations

Environmental consequences of consumption

EPA, Municipal Solid Waste... www.epa.gov/epaoswer/non-hw/muncpl/pubs/msw10.pdf

The breakdown, by weight, of waste generated in 2012 by product category is shown in Figure 8. Containers and packaging made up the largest portion of waste generated, 30% or 75 million tons. The second largest portion came from nondurable goods, which amounted to 21% or 53 million tons. Durable goods make up the third largest segment, accounting for 20% or 50 million tons.

Packaging causes almost 1/3 of all waste...

The generation and recovery of materials in the product categories, by weight and recovery as a percent of generation, are shown in Table 2. The table shows that the recovery of containers and packaging was the highest of the four product categories, with about 52% of the generated materials recycled. Steel, paper products, and aluminum were the most recycled materials by percentage in this category.

...and barely half of it is recycled.

3 Organizing information

As you're collecting ideas and information from sources, you want to manage them so that they are retrievable when you need them. One method is to divide your subject into subtopics and then label each item of source material with the relevant subtopic. (If you have previously outlined your preliminary ideas, use outline headings for these labels.)

Justin Malik divided his general subject of green consumption into these categories:

Environmental crisis
Business opportunities
Advertising messages
Benefits of green products
Environmental consequences of consumption
Activist perspectives (economic, social, and political issues)
Alternative solutions

You can see Malik's use of one of these headings in his annotated printout opposite.

43d Using summary, paraphrase, and quotation

Deciding whether to summarize, paraphrase, or quote directly from sources is an important step in synthesizing the sources' ideas and your own. You engage in synthesis when you use your own words to summarize an author's argument or paraphrase a significant example or when you select a significant passage to quote. Choosing summary, paraphrase, or quotation should depend on why you are using a source.

Caution **Summaries, paraphrases, and quotations all require source citations. A summary or paraphrase without a source citation or a quotation without quotation marks and a source citation is plagiarism.** (See pp. 614–20 for more on plagiarism.)

1 Summarizing

When you **summarize,** you condense an extended idea or argument into a sentence or more in your own words. A full discussion of summary appears on pages 155–57, and you should read that section if you have not already done so.

Summary is most useful when you want to record the gist of an author's idea without the background or supporting evidence. Justin Malik summarized the following quotation from one of his sources—the introduction by Thomas Princen, Michael Maniates, and Ken Conca to their anthology *Confronting Consumption,* page 4:

> Such intuition is even making its way, albeit slowly, into scholarly circles, where recognition is mounting that ever-increasing pressures on ecosystems, life-supporting environmental services, and critical natural cycles are driven not only by the sheer number of resource users and the inefficiencies of their resource use, but also by the patterns of resource use themselves. In global environmental policymaking arenas, it is becoming more and more difficult to ignore the fact that overdeveloped countries must restrain their consumption if they expect underdeveloped countries to embrace a more sustainable trajectory. And while global population growth still remains a huge issue in many regions around the world—both rich and poor—per-capita growth in consumption is, for many resources, expanding eight to twelve times faster than population growth.

In the following one-sentence summary, Malik picks out the kernel of the authors' passage and expresses it in his own words:

Summary of source

Environmental consequences of consumption

Princen et al. 4

Overconsumption may be a more significant cause of environmental problems than increasing population is.

Notice how Malik's note records source information for the summary: the first author's last name, *et al.* (for "and others," per MLA style for more than two authors), and the page number. This information would help Malik avoid accidentally plagiarizing the authors' idea in his paper.

The examples below show the preceding summary in the context of a draft. The first lacks proper citation and thus is plagiarism. The second has proper citation (in MLA style).

Summary with no citation (plagiarized)

Always seeking newer and better things, we consume without regard for the resources we use or the waste we leave behind. In fact, overconsumption may be a more significant cause of environmental problems than increasing population is.

Summary with proper citation (not plagiarized)

Always seeking newer and better things, we consume without regard for the resources we use or the waste we leave behind. In fact, according to Princen and his coauthors, overconsumption may be a more significant cause of environmental problems than increasing population is (4).

See pages 614–20 for more on plagiarism.

2 Paraphrasing

When you **paraphrase**, you follow much more closely the author's original presentation, but you restate it using your own words and sentence structures. Paraphrase when you want to present or examine an author's line of reasoning but you don't feel the original words merit direct quotation. Generally, a paraphrase is briefer than the original quotation and omits examples and other details.

The following note shows how Malik might have paraphrased the passage by Princen, Maniates, and Conca given on the previous page. Notice the record of the authors and the page number, which would help Malik avoid confusing the paraphrase with his own ideas and then inadvertently plagiarizing.

Complete paraphrase of source

Environmental consequences of consumption

Princen et al. 4

Scholars are coming to believe that consumption is partly to blame for changes in ecosystems, reduction of essential natural resources, and changes in natural cycles. Policy makers increasingly see that developing nations will not adopt practices that reduce pollution and waste unless weathly nations consume less. Rising population around the world does cause significant stress on the environment, but consumption is increasing even more rapidly than population.

This paraphrase uses simpler sentences and more common terms than the original passage, in effect translating it as shown below and on the next page. Only words that lack satisfactory synonyms—such as *ecosystems, natural, cycles,* and *population*—remain the same.

Source authors' words	Malik's paraphrase
Such intuition is even making its way, albeit slowly, into scholarly circles, where recognition is mounting that	Scholars are coming to believe that
ever-increasing pressures on ecosystems, life-supporting environmental services, and critical natural cycles are driven not only by the sheer number of resource users and the inefficiencies of their resource use, but also by the patterns of resource use themselves.	consumption is partly to blame for changes in ecosystems, reduction of essential natural resources, and changes in natural cycles.
In global environmental policy-making arenas, it is becoming more and more difficult to ignore the fact that	Policy makers increasingly see that
overdeveloped countries must restrain their consumption if they expect underdeveloped countries to embrace a more sustainable trajectory.	developing nations will not adopt practices that reduce pollution and waste unless wealthy nations consume less.
And while global population growth still remains a huge issue in many regions around the world—both rich and poor—	Rising population around the world does cause significant stress on the environment,

Source authors' words	Malik's paraphrase
per-capita growth in consumption is, for many resources, expanding eight to twelve times faster than population growth.	but consumption is increasing even more rapidly than population.

Follow these guidelines when paraphrasing:

- **Read the material several times to be sure you understand it.**
- **Restate the main ideas in your own words and sentence structures.** You do not have to follow the organization of the original or restate all of it. Select and restate only what you need. If complete sentences seem too detailed or cumbersome, use phrases. Justin Malik might have written the following briefer paraphrase of the quotation by Princen, Maniates, and Conca.

Abbreviated paraphrase of source

> Environmental consequences of consumption
>
> Princen et al. 4
>
> Consumption is increasing more rapidly than population + contributing to major ecological crises. Wealthy nations have to start consuming less.

- **Be careful not to distort meaning.** Don't change the source's emphasis or omit connecting words, qualifiers, and other material whose absence will confuse you later or cause you to misrepresent the source. (See also pp. 606–07.)
- **Be careful not to plagiarize the source.** Use your own words and sentence structures, and always record a citation in your notes. Especially if your source is difficult or complex, you may be tempted to change just a few words or to modify the sentence structure just a bit. But either approach is plagiarism, not paraphrase.

The following examples show the preceding abbreviated paraphrase in the context of a draft. The first example lacks proper citation and is plagiarism. The second example has proper citation (in MLA style).

Paraphrase with no citation (plagiarized)

Always seeking newer and better things, we consume without regard for the resources we use or the waste we leave behind. In fact, overconsumption is increasing more rapidly than population and contributing to major ecological crises. Wealthy nations have to start consuming less.

Paraphrase with proper citation (not plagiarized)

Always seeking newer and better things, we consume without regard for the resources we use or the waste we leave behind. In fact, according to Princen and his coauthors, overconsumption is increasing more rapidly than population and contributing to major ecological crises. Wealthy nations have to start consuming less (4).

See pages 614–20 for more on plagiarism.

CULTURE LANGUAGE If English is not your native language and you have difficulty paraphrasing the ideas in sources, try this: Before attempting a paraphrase, read the original passage several times. Then, instead of "translating" line by line, try to state the gist of the passage without looking at it. Check your effort against the original to be sure you have captured the source author's meaning and emphasis without using his or her words and sentence structures. If you need a synonym for a word, look it up in a dictionary.

3 Quoting

When you **quote** a source, you reproduce the author's exact words. Choose quotations carefully, making sure that they work for, not replace, your ideas.

Deciding when to quote

Your notes from sources may include many quotations, especially if you rely on photocopies, printouts, or downloads. Whether to use a quotation in your draft, instead of a summary or paraphrase, depends on whether the source is primary or secondary and on how important the exact words are.

- **Quote extensively only when you are analyzing primary sources,** such as literary works and historical documents. The quotations will often be both the target of your analysis and the chief support for your ideas. You may need to quote many brief passages, integrated into your sentences, and then comment on the quotations to clarify your analysis and win readers' agreement with it. For examples, see Vanessa Haley's analysis of Annie Dillard's writing (pp. 710–14) and the three literary analyses in Chapter 49 (pp. 732–33, 736–37, and 738–40).
- **Quote selectively when you are drawing on secondary sources**—reports or analyses of other sources, such as a critic's view of a poem or a historian's synthesis of several eyewitness reports. Favor summaries and paraphrases over quotations, and put every quotation to each test in the following box. Most papers of ten or so pages should not need more than two or three quotations that are longer than a few lines each.

Tests for direct quotations from secondary sources

The author's original satisfies one of these requirements:

- The language is unusually vivid, bold, or inventive.
- The quotation cannot be paraphrased without distortion or loss of meaning.
- The words themselves are at issue in your interpretation.
- The quotation represents and emphasizes a body of opinion or the view of an important expert.
- The quotation emphatically reinforces your own idea.
- The quotation is an illustration, such as a graph, diagram, or table.

The quotation is as short as possible:

- It includes only material relevant to your point.
- It is edited to eliminate examples and other unneeded material. (For editing quotations, see the bulleted list below.)

Transcribing and using quotations

When you quote a source, either in your notes or in your draft, take precautions to avoid plagiarism or misrepresentation:

- **Copy the material carefully.** Take down the author's exact wording, spelling, capitalization, and punctuation.
- **Proofread every direct quotation at least twice.**
- **Use quotation marks around the quotation** so that later you won't confuse it with a paraphrase or summary. Be sure to transfer the quotation marks into your draft as well, unless the quotation is long. See later pages for handling long quotations in MLA style (681–82), Chicago style (758), and APA style (783).
- **Use brackets** to add words for clarity or to change the capitalization of letters (see pp. 472–73, 481).
- **Use ellipsis marks** to omit irrelevant words or sentences (see pp. 473–75).
- **Cite the source of the quotation in your draft.** See pages 623–24 on documenting sources.

For a summary of conventions regarding quotations, see the chart on pages 459–60.

The note on the facing page shows how Justin Malik might have quoted part of the passage on page 599 by Princen, Maniates, and Conca, using brackets and an ellipsis mark to make the quotation more concise. Notice the record of the authors and the page number as well as the quotation marks around the authors' exact words—all of which would help Malik avoid plagiarizing the source in his paper.

Quotation of source

Environmental consequences of consumption

Princen et al. 4

"[E]ver-increasing pressures on ecosystems, life-supporting environmental services, and critical natural cycles are driven not only by the sheer number of resource users . . . but also by the patterns of resource use themselves."

The following examples show the quotation as part of a draft. The first, lacking appropriate punctuation and proper citation, is plagiarism. The second is corrected (in MLA style).

Quotation lacking quotation marks, brackets, an ellipsis mark, and a citation (plagiarized)

Increasing consumption may be as much of a threat to the environment as increasing population. Ever-increasing pressures on ecosystems, life-supporting environmental services, and critical natural cycles are driven not only by the sheer number of resource users but also by the patterns of resource use themselves.

Quotation with quotation marks, brackets, an ellipsis mark, and proper citation (not plagiarized)

Increasing consumption may be as much of a threat to the environment as increasing population. According to Princen and his coauthors, "[E]ver-increasing pressures on ecosystems, life-supporting environmental services, and critical natural cycles are driven not only by the sheer number of resource users . . . but also by the patterns of resource use themselves" (4).

See pages 614–20 for more on plagiarism.

4 Combining quotation, summary, and paraphrase

Using quotation in combination with summary or paraphrase can help you shape the material to suit your purposes (although you must be careful not to distort the author's meaning). The note on the next page shows how Justin Malik might have used a combination of quotation and paraphrase to record the statement by Princen and his coauthors. Notice the record of the authors and the page number as well as the quotation marks around the authors' exact words—all of which would help Malik avoid plagiarizing the source in his paper.

The examples after the note show the combined paraphrase and quotation in the context of a draft. The first example cites the source but passes off the quoted language as part of the paraphrase. The second example includes the needed quotation marks.

Combined paraphrase and quotation of source

Environmental consequences of consumption

Princen et al. 4

Scholars are coming to believe that consumption as much as rising population is to blame for "ever-increasing pressures on ecosystems, life-supporting environmental services, and critical natural cycles."

Combined paraphrase and quotation without quotation marks (plagiarized)

Always seeking newer and better things, we consume without regard for the resources we use or the waste we leave behind. According to Princen and his coauthors, scholars are coming to believe that overconsumption as much as rising population is to blame for ever-increasing pressures on ecosystems, life-supporting environmental services, and critical natural cycles (4).

Combined paraphrase and quotation with quotation marks (not plagiarized)

Always seeking newer and better things, we consume without regard for the resources we use or the waste we leave behind. According to Princen and his coauthors, scholars are coming to believe that overconsumption as much as rising population is to blame for "ever-increasing pressures on ecosystems, life-supporting environmental services, and critical natural cycles" (4).

See pages 614–20 for more on plagiarism.

5 Using sources accurately and fairly

When borrowing from sources, you must represent the author's meaning exactly, without distorting it. In the inaccurate summary below, the writer has stated a meaning exactly opposite that of the original. The original quotation, from the artist Henri Matisse, appears in Jack D. Flam, *Matisse on Art,* page 148.

Original For the artist creation begins with vision. To see is itself a creative operation, requiring an effort. Everything that we see in our daily life is more or less distorted by acquired habits, and this is perhaps more evident in an age like ours when cinema posters and magazines present us every day with a flood of ready-made images which are to the eye what prejudices are to the mind.

Inaccurate summary Matisse said that the artist can learn how to see creatively by looking at posters and magazines (qtd. in Flam 148).

The following revision combines summary and quotation to represent the author's meaning exactly:

Accurate summary Matisse said that the artist must overcome visual "habits" and "prejudices," particularly those developed in response to images of popular culture (qtd. in Flam 148).

Exercise 43.7 Summarizing and paraphrasing

Prepare two source notes, one summarizing the entire following paragraph and the other paraphrasing the first four sentences (ending with the word *autonomy*). Use the note format illustrated in the preceding section, omitting only the subject heading.

Federal organization [of the United States] has made it possible for the different states to deal with the same problems in many different ways. One consequence of federalism, then, has been that people are treated differently, by law, from state to state. The great strength of this system is that differences from state to state in cultural preferences, moral standards, and levels of wealth can be accommodated. In contrast to a unitary system in which the central government makes all important decisions (as in France), federalism is a powerful arrangement for maximizing regional freedom and autonomy. The great weakness of our federal system, however, is that people in some states receive less than the best or the most advanced or the least expensive services and policies that government can offer. The federal dilemma does not invite easy solutions, for the costs and benefits of the arrangement have tended to balance out.

—Peter K. Eisinger et al., *American Politics,* page 44

Exercise 43.8 Combining summary, paraphrase, and direct quotation

Prepare a source note that combines paraphrase or summary and direct quotation to state the main idea of the following passage. Use the note format illustrated in the preceding section, omitting only the subject heading.

Most speakers unconsciously duel even during seemingly casual conversations, as can often be observed at social gatherings where they show less concern for exchanging information with other guests than for asserting their own dominance. Their verbal dueling often employs very subtle weapons like mumbling, a hostile act which defeats the listener's desire to understand what the speaker claims he is trying to say (but is really not saying because he is mumbling!). Or the verbal dueler may keep talking after someone has passed out of hearing range—which is often an aggressive challenge to the listener to return and acknowledge the dominance of the speaker.

—Peter K. Farb, *Word Play,* page 107

Exercise 43.9 Gathering information from sources

Continuing from Exercise 43.6 (p. 596), as the next step in preparing a research paper, gather and organize the information from your sources. Mark every note, photocopy, printout, and download with the source's publication information and a heading related to the topics of your paper. Annotate relevant passages of photocopies, printouts, and downloads with your own ideas. For handwritten or computer notes, use direct quotation, summary, or paraphrase as seems appropriate, being careful to avoid inaccuracy and plagiarism. (If you need help recognizing plagiarism, see Chapter 44.)

43e Integrating sources into your text

Integrating source material into your sentences is key to synthesizing others' ideas with your own. Evidence drawn from sources should *back up* your conclusions, not *be* your conclusions: you don't want to let your evidence overwhelm your own voice and point of view. To emphasize your ideas, you do more than just present borrowed material; you introduce and interpret it as well.

Note Integrating borrowed material into your sentences involves several conventions discussed elsewhere in this book:

- **Using commas to punctuate signal phrases,** pages 436–37.
- **Placing other punctuation marks with quotation marks,** pages 464–65.
- **Using brackets for changes in quotations,** pages 472–73 and opposite.
- **Using ellipsis marks for omissions from quotations,** pages 473–75.
- **Punctuating and placing parenthetical citations,** pages 641–43.
- **Setting off long quotations from your text without quotation marks,** pages 681–82 (MLA style), 758 (Chicago style), and 783 (APA style).

Note The examples in this and the next section use the MLA style of source documentation and also the present-tense verbs (such as *disagrees*) that are typical of much writing in the humanities. For specific variations in documentation and verb tense within the academic disciplines, see pages 612–13.

1 Introducing borrowed material

Always introduce a summary, a paraphrase, or a quotation by identifying it and by providing a smooth transition between your words and ideas and those of your source.

Links between borrowed material and your own sentences

Readers will be distracted from your point if borrowed material does not fit into your sentence. In the passage below, the writer has identified the quotation source (*one editor . . . Lyman*) but has not meshed the structures of her own and her source's sentences:

Awkward One editor disagrees with this view and "a good reporter does not fail to separate opinions from facts" (Lyman 52).

In the following revision the writer adds words to integrate the quotation into her sentence:

Revised One editor disagrees with this view, maintaining that "a good reporter does not fail to separate opinions from facts" (Lyman 52).

Alterations of quotations

To mesh your own and your source's words, you may sometimes need to make a substitution or addition to the quotation, signaling your change with brackets:

Words added

"The tabloids [of England] are a journalistic case study in bad reporting," claims Lyman (52).

Verb form changed

A bad reporter, Lyman implies, is one who "[fails] to separate opinions from facts" (52). [The bracketed verb replaces *fail* in the original.]

Capitalization changed

"[T]o separate opinions from facts" is a goal of good reporting (Lyman 52). [In the original, *to* is not capitalized.]

Noun supplied for pronoun

The reliability of a news organization "depends on [reporters'] trustworthiness," says Lyman (52). [The bracketed noun replaces *their* in the original.]

2 Interpreting borrowed material

You need to work borrowed material into your sentences so that readers see without effort how any quotation, paraphrase, or summary contributes to the ideas you are developing. If you merely dump source material into your paper without explaining how you intend it to be understood, readers will have to struggle to understand your sentences and the relationships you are trying to establish. For example, the following passage forces us to figure out for ourselves that the writer's sentence and the quotation state opposite points of view.

Dumped Many news editors and reporters maintain that it is impossible to keep personal opinions from influencing the selection and presentation of facts. "True, news reporters, like everyone else, form impressions of what they see and hear. However, a good reporter does not fail to separate opinions from facts" (Lyman 52).

In the revision the underlined additions tell us how to interpret the quotation:

Revised Many news editors and reporters maintain that it is impossible to keep personal opinions from influencing the selection and presentation of facts. Yet not all authorities agree with

> this view. One editor grants that "news reporters, like everyone else, form impressions of what they see and hear." But, he insists, "a good reporter does not fail to separate opinions from facts" (Lyman 52).

Signal phrases

In the preceding revised passage, the words *One editor grants* and *he insists* are **signal phrases**: they tell readers who the source is and what to expect in the quotations that follow. Signal phrases usually contain (1) the source author's name (or a substitute for it, such as *One editor* and *he*) and (2) a verb that indicates the source author's attitude or approach to what he or she says. In the preceding example, *grants* implies concession and *insists* implies argument. The following box gives a list of verbs that are often used in signal phrases.

Verbs for signal phrases

Use verbs that convey information about source authors' attitudes or approaches. In the sentence *Smith* ________ *that the flood might have been disastrous,* filling the blank with *observes, finds,* or *insists* would create different meanings.

Note Disciplines vary in the tenses of verbs used within signal phrases. The verbs listed below are in the present tense, which is typical of writing about literature and in other humanities. In the social and natural sciences, the past tense (*asked*) or present perfect tense (*has asked*) is more common. See page 612.

Author is neutral	Author infers or suggests	Author argues	Author is uneasy or disparaging
comments	analyzes	claims	belittles
describes	asks	contends	bemoans
explains	assesses	defends	complains
illustrates	concludes	disagrees	condemns
notes	finds	holds	deplores
observes	predicts	insists	deprecates
points out	proposes	maintains	derides
records	reveals	**Author agrees**	laments
relates	shows	admits	warns
reports	speculates	agrees	
says	suggests	concedes	
sees	supposes	concurs	
thinks		grants	
writes			

Vary your signal phrases to suit your interpretation of borrowed material and also to keep readers' interest. A signal phrase may precede, interrupt, or follow the borrowed material:

Signal phrase precedes

Lyman insists that "a good reporter does not fail to separate opinions from facts" (52).

Signal phrase interrupts

"However," Lyman insists, "a good reporter does not fail to separate opinions from facts" (52).

Signal phrase follows

"[A] good reporter does not fail to separate opinions from facts," Lyman insists (52).

Background information

You can add information to a signal phrase to inform readers why you are using a source. In most cases, provide the author's name in the text, especially if the author is an expert or if readers will recognize the name:

Author named

Harold Lyman grants that "news reporters, like everyone else, form impressions of what they see and hear." But, Lyman insists, "a good reporter does not fail to separate opinions from facts" (52).

If the source title contributes information about the author or the context of the quotation, you can provide it in the text:

Title given

Harold Lyman, in his book *The Conscience of the Journalist*, grants that "news reporters, like everyone else, form impressions of what they see and hear." But, Lyman insists, "a good reporter does not fail to separate opinions from facts" (52).

Finally, if the quoted author's background and experience reinforce or clarify the quotation, you can provide those credentials in the text:

Credentials given

Harold Lyman, a newspaper editor for more than forty years, grants that "news reporters, like everyone else, form impressions of what they see and hear." But, Lyman insists, "a good reporter does not fail to separate opinions from facts" (52).

You need not always name the author, source, or credentials in your text. In fact, such introductions may get in the way when you are simply establishing facts or weaving together facts and opinions from varied sources. In the following passage, the information is more important than the source, so the name of the source is confined to a parenthetical acknowledgment:

To end the abuses of the British, many colonists were urging three actions: forming a united front, seceding from Britain, and taking control of their own international relations (Wills 325–36).

3 Following discipline styles for integrating sources

The preceding guidelines for introducing and interpreting borrowed material apply generally across academic disciplines, but there are differences in verb tense and documentation style.

English and some other humanities

Writers in English, foreign languages, and related disciplines use MLA style for documenting sources (see Chapter 47) and generally use the present tense of verbs in signal phrases. In discussing sources other than works of literature, the present perfect tense is also sometimes appropriate:

> Lyman insists . . . [present].
> Lyman has insisted . . . [present perfect].

In discussing works of literature, use only the present tense to describe both the work of the author and the action in the work:

> Kate Chopin builds irony into every turn of "The Story of an Hour." For example, Mrs. Mallard, the central character, finds joy in the death of her husband, whom she loves, because she anticipates "the long procession of years that would belong to her absolutely" (23).

Avoid shifting tenses in writing about literature. You can, for instance, shorten quotations to avoid their past-tense verbs:

Shift Her freedom elevates her, so that "she carried herself unwittingly like a goddess of victory" (24).

No shift Her freedom elevates her, so that she walks "unwittingly like a goddess of victory" (24).

History and other humanities

Writers in history, art history, philosophy, and related disciplines generally use the present tense or present perfect tense of verbs in signal phrases:

> Lincoln persisted, as Haworth has noted, in "feeling that events controlled him."[3]

> What Miller calls Lincoln's "severe self-doubt"[6] undermined the President's effectiveness on at least two occasions.

The raised numbers after the quotations are part of the Chicago documentation style, used in history and other disciplines and discussed on pages 744–57.

Social and natural sciences

Writers in the sciences generally use a verb's present tense just for reporting the results of a study (*The data suggest* . . .). Otherwise, they use a verb's past tense or present perfect tense in a signal phrase, as when introducing an explanation, interpretation, or other commentary. (Thus when you are writing for the sciences, generally convert the list of signal-phrase verbs on p. 610 from the present to the past or present perfect tense.)

> Lin (1999) has suggested that preschooling may significantly affect children's academic performance through high school (pp. 22–23).
>
> In an exhaustive survey of the literature published between 1990 and 2000, Walker (2001) found "no proof, merely a weak correlation, linking place of residence and rate of illness" (p. 121).

These passages conform to APA documentation style, discussed on pages 761–82. APA style, or one quite similar to it, is also used in sociology, education, nursing, biology, and many other sciences.

Exercise 43.10 Introducing and interpreting borrowed material

Drawing on the ideas in the following paragraph and using examples from your own observations and experiences, write a paragraph about anxiety. Integrate at least one direct quotation and one paraphrase from the following paragraph into your own sentences. In your paragraph identify the author by name and give his credentials: he is a professor of psychiatry and a practicing psychoanalyst.

> There are so many ways in which man is different from all the lower forms of animals, and almost all of them make us uniquely susceptible to feelings of anxiousness. Our imagination and reasoning powers facilitate anxiety; the anxious feeling is precipitated not by an absolute impending threat—such as the worry about an examination, a speech, travel—but rather by the symbolic and often unconscious representations. We do not have to be experiencing a potential danger. We can experience something related to it. We can recall, through our incredible memories, the original symbolic sense of vulnerability in childhood and suffer the feeling attached to that. We can even forget the original memory and still be stuck with the emotion—which is then compounded by its seemingly irrational quality at this time. It is not just the fear of death which pains us, but the anticipation of it; or the anniversary of a specific death; or a street, a hospital, a time of day, a color, a flower, a symbol associated with death.
>
> —Willard Gaylin, "Feeling Anxious," page 23

44 Avoiding Plagiarism

Chapter essentials

- Know what plagiarism is, and do not plagiarize sources deliberately or carelessly (below and opposite).
- Know which sources you do not need to cite (p. 617).
- Know which sources you *must* cite (p. 618).
- Obtain permission from copyright holders if you intend to publish your work (p. 621).

Visit MyWritingLab™ for more resources on avoiding plagiarism.

The knowledge building that is the focus of academic writing rests on the integrity of everyone who participates, including students, in using and crediting sources. The work of a writer or creator is his or her intellectual property. You and others may borrow the work's ideas and even its words or an image, but you *must* acknowledge that what you borrowed came from someone else.

When you acknowledge sources in your writing, you are doing more than giving credit to the writer or creator of the work you consulted. You are also showing what your own writing is based on, which in turn adds to your integrity as a researcher and writer. Acknowledging sources creates the trust among scholars, students, writers, and readers that knowledge building requires.

Plagiarism (from a Latin word for "kidnapper") is the presentation of someone else's work as your own. Whether deliberate or careless, plagiarism is a serious offense. It breaks trust, and it undermines or even destroys your credibility as a researcher and writer. In most colleges, a code of academic honesty calls for severe consequences for plagiarism: a reduced or failing grade, suspension from school, or expulsion. The way to avoid plagiarism is to acknowledge your sources: keep track of the ones you consult for each paper you write, and document them within the paper and in a list of works cited.

CULTURE LANGUAGE The concepts of originality, intellectual property, and plagiarism are not universal. In some other cultures, for instance, students may be encouraged to copy the words of scholars without acknowledgment, in order to demonstrate their mastery of or respect for the scholars' work. In the United States, however, using an author's work without a source citation is a serious offense, whether it is careless or intentional. When in doubt about the guidelines in this chapter, ask your instructor for advice.

Checklist for avoiding plagiarism

Know your source.

Are you using

- your own experience,
- common knowledge, or
- someone else's material?

You must acknowledge someone else's material.

Quote carefully.

- Check that every quotation exactly matches its source.
- Insert quotation marks around every quotation that you run into your text. (A quotation set off from the text does not need quotation marks. See pp. 681–82.)
- Indicate any omission from a quotation with an ellipsis mark and any addition with brackets.
- Acknowledge the source of every quotation.

Paraphrase and summarize carefully.

- Use your own words and sentence structures for every paraphrase and summary. If you have used the author's words, add quotation marks around them.
- Acknowledge the source of the idea(s) in every paraphrase or summary.

Cite sources responsibly.

- Acknowledge every use of someone else's material in each place you use it.
- Include all your sources in your list of works cited. See Chapters 47 and 50–52 for citing sources in MLA, Chicago, APA, and CSE documentation styles.

44a Avoiding both deliberate and careless plagiarism

Instructors usually distinguish between deliberate plagiarism, which is cheating, and careless plagiarism, which often stems from a writer's inexperience with managing sources.

1 Deliberate plagiarism

Deliberate plagiarism is intentional: the writer chooses to cheat by turning in someone else's work as his or her own. Students who deliberately plagiarize deprive themselves of an education in honest research. When their cheating is detected, the students often face stiff penalties, including expulsion.

Following are examples of deliberate plagiarism:

- Copying a phrase, a sentence, or a longer passage from a source and passing it off as your own by omitting quotation marks and a source citation.
- Summarizing or paraphrasing someone else's ideas without acknowledging the source in a citation.
- Handing in as your own work a paper you have copied off the Web, had a friend write, or accepted from another student.
- Handing in as your own work a paper you have purchased from a paper-writing service. **Paying for research or a paper does not make it your work.**

2 Careless plagiarism

Careless plagiarism is unintentional: grappling with complicated information and ideas in sources, the writer neglects to put quotation marks around a source's exact words or neglects to include a source citation for a quotation, paraphrase, or summary. Most instructors and schools do not permit careless plagiarism, but they treat it less harshly than deliberate plagiarism—at least the first time it occurs.

Here are examples of careless plagiarism:

- Reading sources without taking notes on them, and then not remembering the difference between what you recently learned and what you already knew.
- Copying and pasting material from a source into your document without placing quotation marks around the other writer's work.
- Forgetting to add a source citation for a paraphrase. Even though a paraphrase casts another person's idea in your own words, you still need to cite the source of the idea.
- Omitting a source citation for another's idea because you are unaware of the need to acknowledge the idea.

Plagiarism and the Internet

The Internet has made it easier to plagiarize than ever before: with just a few clicks, you can copy and paste passages or whole documents into your own files. If you do so without quoting and acknowledging your source, you plagiarize.

The Internet has also made plagiarism easier to detect. Instructors can use search engines to find specific phrases or sentences anywhere on the Web, including among scholarly publications, all kinds of Web sites, and term-paper collections. They can search term-paper sites as easily as students can, looking for similarities with papers they've received. They can also use detection software—such as *Turnitin*, *PlagiServe*, and *Glatt Plagiarism Services*—which compares students' work with other work anywhere on the Internet, seeking matches as short as a few words.

Some instructors suggest that their students use plagiarism-detection programs to verify that their own work does not include careless plagiarism, at least not from the Internet.

44b Knowing what you need not acknowledge

Two kinds of information do not have to be acknowledged in source citations: your own independent material and common knowledge.

1 Using your independent material

Your own independent material includes your thoughts, observations from experience, compilations of facts, or experimental results, expressed in your words or format. For example, you might offer a conclusion about crowd behavior based on watching crowds at concerts or draw a diagram from information you gathered yourself. Though you generally should describe the basis for your conclusions so that readers can evaluate your thinking, you need not cite sources for them.

Note that someone else's ideas and facts are not yours, even when you express them entirely in your own words and sentence structures. The ideas and facts require acknowledgment.

2 Using common knowledge

Common knowledge consists of the standard information of a field of study as well as folk literature and commonsense observations.

- **Standard information** includes the major facts of history, such as the dates during which Charlemagne ruled as emperor of Rome (800–14). It does *not* include interpretations of facts, such as a historian's opinion that Charlemagne was sometimes needlessly cruel in extending his power.
- **Folk literature,** such as the fairy tale "Snow White," is popularly known and cannot be traced to a particular writer. Literature traceable to a writer is *not* folk literature, even if it is very familiar.
- **Commonsense observations** are things most people know, such as that inflation is most troublesome for people with low and fixed incomes. A particular economist's idea about the effects of inflation on Chinese immigrants is *not* a commonsense observation.

As long as you express it in your own words and sentence structures, you may use common knowledge as your own.

The first time you come across an idea or a piece of information that you may want to use, record the publication information for the source. If in wider reading you repeatedly encounter the same idea or information without cited sources, then you may assume it's common knowledge. Don't take unnecessary risks, however: a source citation for common knowledge is not wrong.

44c Knowing what you *must* acknowledge

You must always acknowledge other people's independent material—that is, any facts, ideas, or opinions that are not common knowledge or your own. The source may be a formal publication or release, such as a book, an article, a movie, an interview, an artwork, a comic strip, a map, a Web page, or a blog. The source may also be informal, such as a tweet, a posting on *Facebook*, an opinion you heard on the radio, or a comment by your instructor or a classmate that substantially shaped your argument. You must acknowledge summaries or paraphrases of ideas or facts as well as quotations of the language and format in which ideas or facts appear: wording, sentence structures, arrangement, and special graphics (such as a diagram).

You need to acknowledge another's material no matter how you use it, how much of it you use, or how often you use it. Whether you are quoting a single important word, paraphrasing a single sentence, or summarizing three paragraphs, and whether you are using the source only once or a dozen times, you must acknowledge the original author every time. See pages 623–24 for how to acknowledge sources and pages 641–42 for where to place source citations in relation to cited material.

1 Using copied language: Quotation marks and a source citation

Copied words and sentence structure

The following example baldly plagiarizes the original quotation from Jessica Mitford's *Kind and Usual Punishment,* page 9. Without quotation marks or a source citation, the example matches Mitford's wording (underlined) and closely parallels her sentence structure:

Original (quotation) "The character and mentality of the keepers may be of more importance in understanding prisons than the character and mentality of the kept."

Plagiarism But the character of prison officials (the keepers) is of more importance in understanding prisons than the character of prisoners (the kept).

To avoid plagiarism, the writer can paraphrase and cite the source (see opposite) or use Mitford's actual words *in quotation marks and with a source citation* (here, in MLA style):

Revision (quotation) According to Mitford, a critic of the penal system, "The character and mentality of the keepers may be of more importance in understanding prisons than the character and mentality of the kept" (9).

Changed sentence structure but copied words

Even with a source citation and with a different sentence structure, the next example is still plagiarism because it uses some of Mitford's words (underlined) without quotation marks:

Plagiarism According to Mitford, a critic of the penal system, the psychology of the kept may say less about prisons than the psychology of the keepers (9).

Revision (quotation) According to Mitford, a critic of the penal system, the psychology of "the kept" may say less about prisons than the psychology of "the keepers" (9).

2 Using a paraphrase or summary: Your own words and sentence structure and a source citation

Changed sentence structure but copied words

The following example changes the sentence structure of the original Mitford quotation opposite, but it still uses Mitford's words (underlined) without quotation marks or a source citation:

Plagiarism In understanding prisons, we might focus less on the character and mentality of the kept than on those of the keepers.

To avoid plagiarism, the writer can use quotation marks and cite the source or *use his or her own words* and still *cite the source* (because the idea is Mitford's, not the writer's):

Revision (paraphrase) Mitford holds that we may learn less about prisons from the psychology of prisoners than from the psychology of prison officials (9).

Revision (paraphrase) We may understand prisons better if we focus on the personalities and attitudes of the prison workers rather than those of the inmates (Mitford 9).

Changed words but copied sentence structure

In the next example, the writer cites Mitford and does not use her words but still plagiarizes her sentence structure. The revision changes the sentence structure as well as the words.

Plagiarism Mitford, a critic of the penal system, maintains that the psychology of prison officials may be more informative about prisons than the psychology of prisoners (9).

Revision (paraphrase) Mitford, a critic of the penal system, maintains that we may learn less from the psychology of prisoners than from the psychology of prison officials (9).

3 Using online sources

Online sources are so accessible and so easy to copy into your own documents that it may seem they are freely available, exempting you from the obligation to acknowledge them. They are not. Acknowledging online sources is somewhat trickier than acknowledging print sources, but it is no less essential: when you use someone else's independent material from an online source, you must acknowledge the source.

Citing online sources is easier when you keep track of them as you work:

- **Record complete publication information each time you consult an online source.** Online sources may change from one day to the next or even disappear entirely. See page 553 for the information to record, such as the publication date. Without the proper information, you may not use the source.
- **Immediately put quotation marks around any text that you copy and paste into your document.** If you don't add quotation marks right away, you risk forgetting which words belong to the source and which are yours. If you don't know whose words you are using, recheck the source or do not use them.
- **Acknowledge linked sites.** If you use not only a Web site but also one or more of its linked sites, you must acknowledge the linked sites as well. The fact that one person has used a second person's work does not release you from the responsibility to cite the second work.

Exercise 44.1 Recognizing plagiarism

The following numbered items show various attempts to quote or paraphrase a passage by George E. Vaillant. Carefully compare each attempt with the original passage. Which attempts are plagiarized, inaccurate, or both, and which are acceptable? Why?

I would agree with the sociologists that psychiatric labeling is dangerous. Society can inflict terrible wounds by discrimination, and by confusing health with disease and disease with badness.

—George E. Vaillant, *Adaptation to Life*, p. 361

1. According to George Vaillant, society often inflicts wounds by using psychiatric labeling, confusing health, disease, and badness (361).
2. According to George Vaillant, "psychiatric labeling [such as 'homosexual' or 'schizophrenic'] is dangerous. Society can inflict terrible wounds by . . . confusing health with disease and disease with badness" (361).
3. According to George Vaillant, when psychiatric labeling discriminates between health and disease or between disease and badness, it can inflict wounds on those labeled (361).
4. Psychiatric labels can badly hurt those labeled, says George Vaillant, because they fail to distinguish among health, illness, and immorality (361).
5. Labels such as "homosexual" and "schizophrenic" can be hurtful when they fail to distinguish among health, illness, and immorality.

6. "I would agree with the sociologists that society can inflict terrible wounds by discrimination, and by confusing health with disease and disease with badness" (Vaillant 361).

Exercise 44.2 Revising plagiarized sentences

The following numbered items plagiarize sentences in a paragraph by Stephen Pinker. Analyze the problem in each item, and then rewrite it to quote or paraphrase correctly and add the proper source citation. (Consult pp. 634–36 if you need help with the citations.) Each item has more than one correct answer.

Friendship, like other kinds of altruism, is vulnerable to cheaters, and we have a special name for them: fair-weather friends. These sham friends reap the benefits of associating with a valuable person and mimic signs of warmth in an effort to become valued themselves. But when a little rain falls, they are nowhere in sight. People have an emotional response that seems designed to weed out fair-weather friends. When we are neediest, an extended hand is deeply affecting. We are moved, never forget the generosity, and feel compelled to tell the friend we will never forget it. —Steven Pinker, *How the Mind Works*, p. 509

1. Like other kinds of altruism, friendship is vulnerable to cheaters, people whom we call fair-weather friends.
2. According to Steven Pinker, sham friends draw advantages from being with someone they value, and they "mimic signs of warmth in an effort to become valued themselves."
3. Steven Pinker writes that people seem to have an emotional response designed to weed out fair-weather friends.
4. Pinker points out that when people are at their lowest, a sign of friendship is truly touching.
5. Pinker describes people who have received acts of friendship as moved. They do not forget the generosity, and they are compelled to say that they will never forget it.

44d Obtaining permission when publishing your work

When you use material from print or online sources in a project that will be published, you must not only acknowledge your sources but also take the additional precaution of observing copyright restrictions.

Publication means that your work will circulate outside the limited circle of a class or other group. It may appear in print media, such as magazines and newspapers, or it may appear on the Web, which is a publication medium as well. (The exception is a password-protected Web site, such as a course site, which many copyright holders regard as private.)

When you publish your work, borrowing certain kinds or amounts of material requires you to obtain the permission of the copyright holders. You can find information about copyright holders and permissions on the copyright page of a print publication (following the title page) and on a page labeled something like "Terms of Use" on a Web site. If you don't see an explicit release for student use or publication on private Web sites, assume that you must seek permission.

The legal convention of **fair use** allows an author to use a small portion of copyrighted material without obtaining the copyright holder's permission, as long as the author acknowledges the source. The standards of fair use are not fixed, so the following guidelines are conservative:

- **Text from print sources:** Quote without permission fewer than fifty words from an article or fewer than three hundred words from a book. You'll need permission to use any longer quotation from an article or book or any quotation at all from a play, poem, or song.
- **Text from online sources:** Quote without permission text that represents just a small portion of the whole—say, up to forty words out of three hundred. As with print texts, seek permission for any use of a play, poem, or song that you find online.
- **Visuals, audio, and video:** Seek permission to use any copyrighted media from either print or online sources: photographs, charts, maps, cartoons, diagrams, paintings, audio files, video files, and so on.

Note Much valuable material is not copyrighted and can be used without permission, although *you must still cite the source*. Uncopyrighted sources fall into two groups:

- **The creator does not claim copyright.** This category includes most government documents and material labeled for reuse, such as some of the media on *Google, Flikr Creative Commons,* and *Wikimedia Commons.*
- **The copyright has lapsed.** Material in the public domain includes most works by authors who have been dead at least fifty years.

45 Documenting Sources

Chapter essentials

- Use the documentation style appropriate for your discipline (below).
- Use bibliography software with care (next page).

Visit MyWritingLab™ for more resources on documenting sources.

Every time you borrow the words, facts, or ideas of others, you must **document** the source—that is, supply a reference (or document) telling readers that you borrowed the material and where you borrowed it from.

Editors and instructors in most academic disciplines require special documentation formats (or styles) in their scholarly journals and in students' papers. All the styles share two features described in the following box.

Key features of source documentation

- **Citations in the text signal that material is borrowed and refer readers to detailed information about the sources.** The following text citation, in MLA documentation style, gives the source author's last name and the page number in the source. Other styles add a publication date or use raised numerals instead of parenthetical citations.

  Veterans are more likely to complete college degrees if they have not only professional support but also a community of peers (Dao A16).

- **Detailed source information, either in footnotes or at the end of the paper, tells how to locate the sources.** The following source listing, also in MLA style, provides detailed publication information for the source summarized above. Most styles provide the same information, but they may organize and punctuate it differently.

  Dao, James. "Getting Them Through: Helping Veterans Graduate." *The New York Times*, 5 Feb. 2013, pp. A16+.

45a Using discipline styles for documentation

Aside from the similarities of citations in the text and detailed source information, the disciplines' documentation styles vary markedly in citation form, arrangement of source information, and other particulars. Each discipline's style reflects the needs of its practitioners for certain kinds of information presented in certain ways. For instance, the currency of a source is important in the social and natural sciences, where studies build on and correct each other; thus in-text citations in these disciplines usually include a source's year of publication. In the humanities, however, currency is less important, so in-text citations do not include the date of publication.

The disciplines' documentation formats are described in style guides listed elsewhere in this book for the humanities (p. 744), the social sciences (p. 760), and the natural and applied sciences (pp. 795–96). This book also discusses and illustrates four common documentation styles:

- **MLA style,** used in English, foreign languages, and some other humanities (pp. 634–79).
- **Chicago style,** used in history, art history, philosophy, religion, and some other humanities (pp. 744–58).
- **APA style,** used in psychology and some other social sciences (pp. 760–83).
- **CSE style,** used in the biological and some other sciences (pp. 796–802).

Ask your instructor which style you should use. If no style is specified, use the guide that's most appropriate for the discipline in which you're writing. Do follow one system for citing sources—and one system only—so that you provide all the necessary information in a consistent format.

45b Using bibliography software

Bibliography software can help you format your source citations in the style of your choice, and some programs can help you keep track of sources as you research. Your library may offer one or more bibliography programs, such as *RefWorks* or *Endnote*, or you can find free options on the Web, such as *Zotero, Bibme,* and *EasyBib*.

The programs vary in what they can do. Some simply prompt you for needed information (author's name, book title, and so on) and then format the information into a bibliography following the format of your documentation style. Others go beyond formatting to help you organize your sources, export citations from databases, and insert in-text citations as you write.

As helpful as bibliography programs can be, they don't always work the way they're advertised, and they can't substitute for your own care and attention in giving your sources accurate and complete acknowledgment. Always ask your instructors if you may use such software for your papers, and always review the citations compiled by any software to ensure that they meet your instructors' requirements.

46 Writing the Paper

Chapter essentials

- Develop a thesis statement (below).
- Create a structure for your project (next page).
- Write a first draft, including source citations (p. 629).
- Revise and edit the draft (p. 631).
- Use an appropriate document format (p. 632).
- Proofread the final draft (p. 632).

Visit MyWritingLab™ for more resources on writing the paper.

Like other kinds of writing, research writing involves focusing on a main idea, organizing ideas, expressing ideas in a draft, revising and editing drafts, and formatting the final paper. Because research writing draws on others' work, however, its stages also require attention to interpreting, integrating, and citing sources.

This chapter complements and extends the detailed discussion of the writing situation and the writing process in Chapters 1–3. If you haven't already done so, read those chapters before this one.

46a Developing a thesis statement

You began research with a question about your subject (pp. 546–47). Your question may have evolved during research, but you should be able to answer the latest version once you've consulted most of your sources. Try to state that answer in a **thesis statement**, a claim that narrows your subject to a single assertion. (See pp. 28–33 if you need guidance on developing a thesis statement.)

Justin Malik used his initial research question to draft a tentative thesis statement:

Research question

How can green consumerism help the environment?

Tentative thesis statement

Consumers need to think very carefully before buying products that claim to be green because many of them actually do more harm than good.

This statement captured Malik's preliminary idea that green products may not be as beneficial to the environment as advertised. But after further reading, Malik rethought this idea. Many of his sources quoted the environmentalists' slogan "Reduce, reuse, recycle," and he began to ask whether green products meet these basic goals. He reworked his research question: *How does consumption in general affect the environment, and can green products significantly reduce this effect?* With more research, Malik revised his thesis statement:

Revised thesis statement

Although green consumerism can help the environment, consumerism itself is the root of some of the most pressing ecological problems. To make a real difference, humans must consume less.

(Malik's thesis statement consists of two sentences, the first setting up the second. Many instructors allow statements of two or more sentences as long as they build a single idea and the final sentence presents the key assertion of the paper. However, other instructors require thesis statements of a single sentence. Ask your instructor for his or her preference.)

For Vanessa Haley, framing a thesis statement for her paper on Annie Dillard required drawing together (synthesizing) Dillard's ideas about humanity and nature into a single statement of Haley's own. The first draft of the statement merely conveyed Haley's interest in Dillard:

Tentative thesis statement

Unlike many other nature writers, Dillard does not reinforce the separation between humanity and nature.

The revision stated Haley's synthesis of Dillard's ideas:

Revised thesis statement

In her encounters with nature, Dillard probes a spiritual as well as a physical identity between human beings and nature that could help to heal the rift between them.

Exercise 46.1 Developing a thesis statement

Draft and revise a thesis statement for your developing research paper. Make sure that the revised version of the statement specifically asserts your main idea.

46b Creating a structure

Before starting to draft your research paper, organize your ideas and information so that you know the main divisions of your paper, the order you'll cover them in, and the important supporting ideas for each division. The goal is to create a structure that presents your ideas in a sensible and persuasive sequence and that supports ideas at each level with enough explanation and evidence. Consult the discussion of organization on pages 34–43 if you need help distinguishing general and specific information, arranging groups of information, or using a computer effectively for developing a structure.

1 Arranging ideas and support

Creating a structure for a research paper involves almost constant synthesis, the forging of relationships among ideas (see pp. 593–95). As you arrange and rearrange source information and your own thoughts, you find connections among ideas and determine which are most important, which are merely supportive, and which are not relevant at all.

To build a structure, follow these guidelines:

- **Arrange source information in categories.** Each category should correspond to a main section of your paper: a key idea of your own that supports the thesis. Within each category, you may have source views that differ from your own and that you intend to discuss or refute.
- **Review your research journal and annotated bibliography.** Hunt for connections between sources, opinions of sources, and other thoughts that can help you organize your paper.
- **Look objectively at your categories.** If some are skimpy, with little information, consider whether you should drop the categories or conduct more research to fill them out. If most of your information falls into one or two categories, consider whether the categories are too broad and should be divided. (Does any of this rethinking affect your thesis statement? If so, revise it accordingly.)
- **Within each category, distinguish between the main idea and the supporting ideas and evidence.** Only the support should come from your sources. The main idea should be your own.

2 Using an outline

An outline can help you shape your research and also discover potential problems, such as inadequate support and overlapping or irrelevant ideas.

Informal outline

For some research projects, you may find an **informal outline** sufficient: you list main points and supporting information in the order you expect to discuss them. Because of its informality, such an outline can help you try out different arrangements of material, even fairly early in the research process.

While examining his sources, Justin Malik used an informal outline to see how his developing ideas might fit together:

```
Environmental crisis
    Global warming
    Resource use
    Biodiversity
    Pollution
    Waste
```

Consumerism
- Rising standards of living causing more waste
- Ecological effects—American vs. global
- Inequality
- Personal issues: expenses, working hours, stress, unhappiness
- Voluntary simplicity movement

Green products
- Appeal to consumers
- Advantages for businesses
- Environmental benefits
- Problems caused by manufacturing, shipping, and discarding products, even green products

This informal outline helped Malik decide not to continue researching consumerism (the second section) because he had more than enough to work with and the topic seemed likely to overwhelm his central question of whether buying green products can solve the environmental crisis (the last and first sections).

Formal outline

Unlike an informal outline, a **formal outline** arranges ideas tightly and in considerable detail, with close attention to hierarchy and phrasing. The example below shows the formal outline's format and schematic content:

I. First main idea
  A. First subordinate idea
    1. First evidence for subordinate idea
      a. First detail of evidence
      b. Second detail of evidence
    2. Second evidence for subordinate idea
  B. Second subordinate idea
II. Second main idea

In this model, levels of headings correspond to levels of importance or detail in the paper:

- **Main ideas (Roman numerals) are the major divisions of the paper.** Each division covers a part of your thesis statement and will probably take a number of paragraphs to develop.
- **Subordinate ideas (capital letters) are the building blocks.** These ideas are your own and will probably take a paragraph or two to develop. They may serve as the topic sentences of paragraphs.
- **Evidence (Arabic numerals) and its details (small letters) support each idea.** The evidence from one or more sources will occupy much of each body paragraph. (A fourth sublevel, if needed, is labeled with Arabic numerals enclosed in parentheses.)

Each level of the outline is indented farther than the level it supports. (Your word processor may be able to format an outline automatically.)

A formal outline can help you decide not only what your main ideas are and how you will arrange them but also how you will support them. Some of this information may not emerge until you are drafting, however, so remain open to revising the outline as you proceed. And consider using a formal outline as a revision tool as well, creating a map of your completed first draft to check and improve the structure (see p. 53).

To be an effective organizer for your thoughts or an effective revision tool, a formal outline should be detailed and should adhere to several principles of logical arrangement, clarity, balance, and completeness. (See pp. 37–40 for examples and more details.)

- **The outline should indicate which ideas are primary and which are subordinate.** A long, undivided list of parallel items probably needs to be subdivided.
- **Parallel headings should represent ideas of equal importance and generality.** They should not overlap one another.
- **Single sublevels should be avoided.** They illogically divide something into only one part.

A formal outline is usually written either in phrases (a **topic outline**) or in sentences (a **sentence outline**). A complete topic outline is illustrated on page 38. A complete sentence outline accompanies Justin Malik's research paper on pages 684–85. Either is suitable for a research paper, though a sentence outline, because it requires complete statements, conveys more information.

Exercise 46.2 Creating a structure

Continuing from Exercise 46.1 (p. 626), arrange your notes into a structure. As specified by your instructor, make an informal outline or a formal sentence or topic outline to guide the drafting of your paper.

46c Drafting the paper

Beginning a draft of what will be a relatively long and complicated paper can be difficult, so it may help to remember that you do not have to proceed methodically from beginning to end.

Tips for drafting a research paper

- **Reread the assignment to review your instructor's criteria.** Make sure you have all the materials you'll need to meet the criteria.
- **Write a quick two- or three-paragraph summary of what the paper will be about.** This writing will get your juices flowing and give you a sense of direction. (Pretend you're writing to a friend if that will help loosen you up.) A version of the material you generate in this way may later prove useful for your paper's introduction or conclusion.

(continued)

Tips for drafting a research paper

(continued)

- **Start with the section of the paper you feel most confident about.** At first, skip any parts that scare you or give you undue trouble, even the introduction.
- **Work in chunks, one unit or principal idea at a time.** Fit the sections together only after you begin to see the draft take shape. (See below.)
- **Center each section on an idea of your own.** Use source material to back up the idea.
- **Take great care in working with source material.** Integrate sources into your own ideas (p. 608), and do not plagiarize (p. 614).
- **Insert source citations as you quote, paraphrase, or summarize.** Use authors' names and page numbers. (See the facing page.)

1 Working section by section

In writing a first draft, remember that a primary reason for doing a research paper is to learn how to interpret and evaluate the evidence in sources, draw your own conclusions from the evidence, and weave the two together in a way that establishes your expertise in your subject and shows your perspective on it. (See pp. 173–74 for more discussion and an example of a paragraph that accomplishes these goals.)

Integrating evidence with your own ideas will be easier if you view each principal idea of your paper (each Roman numeral of your outline) as a unit. Usually each principal idea requires a block of paragraphs to develop. Compose each unit as if it will stand alone (though of course you will pull the units together before your draft is complete).

- **Begin each unit by stating the idea,** which should be a conclusion you have drawn from reading and responding to your sources.
- **Follow the statement with specific support from your sources:** facts and examples; summaries, paraphrases, or quotations of secondary sources with your analysis; quotations of passages from primary sources with your analysis.
- **Present fairly any disagreements among experts.** Give the evidence that leads you to side with one expert or another.
- **Try to remain open to new interpretations or new arrangements of ideas that occur to you.**

Note Proceeding in this way will help you avoid a common trap of research writing: allowing your sources to control you, rather than vice versa. Make sure each unit of your paper centers on an idea of your own, not someone else's, and that your paragraphs are pointed toward demonstrating that idea, not merely presenting sources.

2 Tracking source citations

As you draft your paper, insert the source of each summary, paraphrase, and quotation in parentheses in the text—for instance, "(Matthews 43)," referring to page 43 in a work by Matthews. If you are conscientious about inserting these notes and carrying them through successive drafts, you will be less likely to plagiarize carelessly and you will have little difficulty documenting your sources in the final paper.

Exercise 46.3 Drafting your paper

Draft the research paper you have been developing in Chapters 41–45. Before beginning the draft, study your research journal and your source information. While drafting, follow your thesis statement and outline as closely as you need to, but stay open to new ideas, associations, and arrangements.

46d Revising and editing the paper

When you have written a first draft, take a break for at least a day so that you can gain some objectivity about your work and can read the draft critically when you begin to revise.

1 Revising

Always revise your draft first, satisfying yourself with the content and shape of the whole before trying to edit sentences and words. Begin with the advice and checklist on pages 51–56, and supplement them with the following checklist.

Checklist for revising a research paper

Assignment

How does the draft satisfy all of the criteria stated in your instructor's assignment?

Thesis statement

How well does your thesis statement describe your subject and your perspective as they emerged during drafting?

Structure

(Outlining your draft as suggested on p. 629 can help you see structure at a glance.)

How consistently does borrowed material illuminate and support—not lead and dominate—your own ideas? How well is the importance of ideas reflected in the emphasis they receive? Will the arrangement of ideas be clear to readers?

(continued)

Checklist for revising a research paper

(continued)

Evidence

Where might readers need more evidence in order to accept your ideas? Where might the evidence seem weak or irrelevant?

Reasonableness and clarity

How reasonable will readers find your arguments? (See pp. 208–12.) Where do you need to define terms or concepts that readers may not know or may dispute?

2 Editing

When you complete your revision—and only then—you are ready to edit. If you do not compose on a computer, copy or retype the new draft if possible so that you have a clean copy to work on. If you do compose on a computer, you can edit directly on screen or print a clean copy. (Some writers find it easier to spot errors on paper than on screen.)

For editing, consult the advice and checklist on pages 61–63. Try to read the paper from the point of view of someone who has not spent hours planning and researching but instead has come fresh to the paper. Look for lapses in sense, awkward passages, wordiness, poor transitions between ideas and evidence, unnecessary repetition, wrong or misspelled words, errors in grammar, punctuation, or mechanics—in short, anything that is likely to interfere with a reader's understanding of your meaning.

3 Completing source citations

Before you prepare your final draft (next section), you must insert final source citations into your text and prepare the list of sources for the end of the paper. See pages 625–26 on documenting sources in various disciplines' styles.

Exercise 46.4 Revising and editing your paper

Using the revision and editing checklists on pages 53–54 and 62–63 and the checklist and pointers here, revise and edit your research paper. Work to improve not only the presentation of ideas but also, if necessary, the ideas themselves. Make sure you have provided an in-text citation for every summary, paraphrase, and direct quotation of a source and that your list of sources is complete.

46e Preparing and proofreading the final draft

Prepare the final draft of your paper when you have edited the text, added the source citations, and written the list of works cited.

Most instructors expect research papers to be neatly typed with clear titling, double spacing, standard margins, and minimal handwritten corrections. Your instructor may have additional requirements, suggested by the discipline in which you are writing. This book explains four such document formats:

- **MLA format,** used in English, foreign languages, and some other humanities, pages 644 and 680–82. See also Chapter 48 for the sample research papers of Justin Malik and Vanessa Haley.
- **Chicago format**, used in history, art history, religion, philosophy, and some other humanities, pages 744–46 and 757–58.
- **APA format**, used in psychology and other social sciences, pages 766–67 and 782–83.
- **CSE format,** used in the natural and applied sciences, pages 796–97 and 802.

In any discipline, you can present your ideas effectively and attractively with readable type fonts, headings, illustrations, and other elements. See Chapter 5 for ideas.

Before you submit your paper, proofread it carefully for typographical errors, misspellings, and other errors. (See pp. 66–67 for proofreading tips.) Unless the errors are very numerous (more than several on a page), you can correct them by whiting out or crossing out (neatly) and inserting the correction (neatly) in ink. Don't let the pressure of a deadline prevent you from proofreading, for even minor errors can impair clarity or annoy readers and thus negate some of the hard work you have put into your project.

Exercise 46.5 Preparing and proofreading your final draft

Prepare the final draft of your research paper, following your instructor's requirements for document format. If your instructor does not specify a format, follow the MLA guidelines on pages 680–82. Proofread and correct the paper before submitting it.

47 Using MLA Documentation and Format

Chapter essentials

- In your text, document your sources with citations (below).
- Place text citations so that they are clear and unobtrusive (p. 641).
- Use supplemental notes as needed (p. 643).
- Prepare an MLA list of works cited (p. 644). (See the index to models on pp. 649–50.)
- Format your paper, attending to margins, spacing, long quotations, and other elements (p. 680).

Visit MyWritingLab™ for more resources on MLA documentation and format.

English, foreign languages, and some other humanities use the documentation style of the Modern Language Association, described in the *MLA Handbook* (8th ed., 2016).

In MLA style, you twice acknowledge the sources of borrowed material:

- **In your text, a brief citation adjacent to the borrowed material directs readers to a complete list of all the works you cite.** The citation consists of the author's last name and usually the page number in the source where the borrowed material appears. If the author's name is not mentioned in your sentence, it appears in parentheses with the page number:

  In-text citation

  Among African cities, says one observer, in Johannesburg "a spirit of optimism glows" (Gaddis 155).

- **At the end of your paper, the list of works cited includes complete bibliographical information for every source.**

  Works-cited entry

  Gaddis, Anicee. "Johannesburg." *Transculturalism: How the World Is Coming Together*, edited by Claude Grunitzky, True Agency, 2008, pp. 154-57.

47a Using MLA in-text citations

1 Writing in-text citations

In-text citations of sources must include just enough information for the reader to locate both of the following:

- **The *source* in your list of works cited.**
- **The *place* in the source where the borrowed material appears.**

For any kind of source, you can usually meet both these requirements by providing the author's last name and (if the source uses them) the page numbers where the material appears. The reader can find the source in your list of works cited and find the borrowed material in the source itself.

The following box is a guide to all the models of in-text citations.

MLA in-text citations

Note Models 1 and 2 show the direct relationship between what you include in your text and what you include in a parenthetical citation. If you do *not* name the author in your text, you include the name in parentheses before the page reference (model 1). If you *do* name the author in your text, you do not include the name in parentheses (model 2).

1. Author not named in your text

When you have not already named the author in your sentence, provide the author's last name and the page number(s), with no punctuation between them, in parentheses.

> One researcher concludes that "women impose a distinctive construction on moral problems, seeing moral dilemmas in terms of conflicting responsibilities" (Gilligan 105-06).

See models 6 and 8–10 for the forms to use when the source does not list an author or provide page numbers.

2. Author named in your text

When you have already given the author's name with the material you're citing, do not repeat it in the parenthetical citation. Give just the page number(s).

> Carol Gilligan concludes that "women impose a distinctive construction on moral problems, seeing moral dilemmas in terms of conflicting responsibilities" (105-06).

See models 6 and 8–10 for the forms to use when the source does not list an author or provide page numbers.

3. Work with two authors

If the source has two authors, give both of their last names in the text or in the citation. Separate the names with and:

> As Frieden and Sagalyn observe, "The poor and the minorities were the leading victims of highway and renewal programs" (29).

> According to one study, "The poor and the minorities were the leading victims of highway and renewal programs" (Frieden and Sagalyn 29).

4. Work with more than two authors

If the source has more than two authors, give only the first author's name followed by et al. (the abbreviation for the Latin *et alii*, "and others").

> Increased competition means that employees of public relations firms may find their loyalty stretched in more than one direction (Wilcox et al. 417).

5. Work by an author of two or more cited works

If your list of works cited includes two or more works by the same author, then your citation must tell the reader which of the author's works you are referring to. Give the title either in the text or in a parenthetical citation. In a parenthetical citation, omit any *A*, *An*, or *The* and shorten the title if it is longer than a noun preceded by its modifiers, if any. For instance, *Time's Arrow, Time's Cycle* shortens to *Time's Arrow*. In the following example, *Arts* is short for Gardner's full title, *The Arts and Human Development*.

> At about age seven, children begin to use appropriate gestures with their stories (Gardner, *Arts* 144-45).

If the title does not start with a noun or a noun preceded by modifiers, shorten the title to the first word (again excluding *A*, *An*, or *The*): for instance, shorten *As the Eye Moves* to *As*.

6. Anonymous work

For a work with no named author or editor (whether an individual or an organization), use a full or shortened version of the title, as explained with the previous model. In your list of works cited, you alphabetize an anonymous work by the first word of the title excluding *A*, *An*, or *The* (see p. 652), and the first word of a shortened title will be the same. The following citations refer to an unsigned source titled "The Right to Die." The title appears in quotation marks because the source is a periodical article.

> One article notes that a death-row inmate may demand his own execution to achieve a fleeting notoriety ("Right" 16).

> "The Right to Die" notes that a death-row inmate may demand execution to achieve a fleeting notoriety (16).

If two or more anonymous works have the same title, distinguish them with additional information in the text citation, such as the publication date.

7. Work with a corporate author

Some works list as author a government body, association, committee, company, or other group. Cite such a work by the organization's name except when it and the publisher are the same. When the organization and publisher have the same name, omit the author and cite the work by the title (see model 6 above).

If the organization's name is long, work it into the text to avoid an intrusive parenthetical citation:

> A 2014 report by the Nevada Department of Education provides evidence of an increase in graduation rates (12).

8. Electronic or other nonprint source

Electronic or other nonprint sources vary widely, including articles in databases, e-books, Web pages, *Facebook* posts, films or videos, and tweets. If possible, cite such a source as you would any other source, giving author and page number; but often these elements and others are lacking. The following models give a range of possibilities.

a. Work with a named author and stable page numbers

> Brannon observes that students respond readily to some poets (53).

If the work you cite has stable page numbers, like those in a PDF file, give them in your citation.

b. Work with a named author and no page numbers

> Smith reports that almost 20% of commercial banks have been audited in recent years.

When you cite a passage from a work with no page or other reference numbers, such as a Web source or an article in HTML format, try to give the author's name in your text. You will not need a parenthetical citation then, but you must list the source in your works cited.

If the author's name does not appear in your text, give it in a parenthetical citation:

Clean cars are defined as vehicles with low pollution emissions and high fuel economy (Hagedorn).

c. Work with a named author on an e-reader or other device

Writing about post-Saddam Iraq, the journalist George Packer describes the tense relationship that existed between Kurdistan and the rest of the country (ch. 1).

Page numbers are not always the same on Kindles, iPads, and other e-readers and tablets. For a book you read on such a device, give the chapter number, not the device's page numbers.

d. Work with a named author and numbered paragraphs or sections

Twins reared apart report similar feelings (Palfrey, pars. 6-7).

If the work gives numbered paragraphs or sections, use the abbreviation par., pars., sec., or secs. to tell readers that you are citing one or more paragraphs or sections rather than page numbers.

e. Work with no named author

Many decades after its release, *Citizen Kane* is still remarkable for its rich black-and-white photography.

When your works-cited entry lists the work under its title, cite the work by title in your text, as explained in model 6. This example, a film, gives the title in the text, so it omits a parenthetical citation (see model 9).

f. Audio or video

In an episode of *Master of None*, the characters recognize how little they know about the lives of their fathers in their native countries of India and China ("Parents" 14:02-27).

You may view or listen to a video or audio source on a device that displays the time span of the recording you are citing. Give the start and stop times of your source in hours (if any), minutes, and seconds, separated by colons. The numbers above cite 14 minutes, 2 to 27 seconds.

9. One-page work or entire work

When you cite a work that's a single page long or cite an entire work—for instance, a one-page article, a tweet, a Web site, a book, or a film—you may omit any page or other reference number. If the work you cite has an author, try to give the name in the text. If the work does not have an author, give the title.

> Boyd deals with the need to acknowledge and come to terms with our fear of nuclear technology.

10. Work with no page or other reference numbers

When the work you cite, print or nonprint, has no page or other reference numbers, give the author's name, if available, in your text or in a parenthetical citation. (If no author is listed, give the title.)

> In the children's classic picture book *The Very Busy Spider,* hard work and patience are rewarded when the spider catches a fly in her web (Carle).

11. Multivolume work

If you consulted only one volume of a multivolume work, your list of works cited will say so (see model 20 on p. 663), and you can treat the volume as you would any book.

If you consulted more than one volume of a multivolume work, give the appropriate volume before the page number (here volume 5):

> After issuing the Emancipation Proclamation, Lincoln said, "What I did, I did after very full deliberations, and under a very heavy and solemn sense of responsibility" (5: 438).

The number 5 indicates the volume from which the quotation was taken; the number 438 indicates the page number in that volume. When the author's name appears in such a citation, place it before the volume number with no punctuation: (Lincoln 5: 438).

If you are referring generally to an entire volume of a multivolume work and are not citing specific page numbers, add the abbreviation vol. before the volume number, as in (vol. 5) or (Lincoln, vol. 5) (note the comma after the author's name). Then readers will not misinterpret the volume number as a page number.

12. Source referred to by another source (indirect source)

When you want to use a quotation that is already in quotation marks—indicating that the author you are reading is quoting someone else—try to find the original source and quote directly from it. If you can't find the original source, then your citation must indicate that your quotation of it is indirect. In the following citation, qtd. in ("quoted in") says that Davino was quoted by Boyd.

George Davino maintains that "even small children have vivid ideas about nuclear energy" (qtd. in Boyd 22).

The list of works cited then includes only Boyd (the work consulted), not Davino.

13. Literary work

Novels, plays, and poems are often available in many editions, so your instructor may ask you to provide information that will help readers find the passage you cite no matter what edition they consult.

a. Novel

Toward the end of James's novel, Maggie suddenly feels "the thick breath of the definite—which was the intimate, the immediate, the familiar, as she hadn't had them for so long" (535; pt. 6, ch. 41).

Give the page number first, followed by a semicolon and then information on the appropriate part or chapter of the work.

b. Poem not divided into parts

In Shakespeare's Sonnet 73 the speaker identifies with the trees of late autumn, "Bare ruined choirs, where late the sweet birds sang" (line 4). "In me," Shakespeare writes, "thou seest the glowing of such fire / That on the ashes of his youth doth lie . . ." (9-10).

You may omit the page number and supply the line number(s) for the quotation. To prevent confusion with page numbers, precede the numbers with line or lines in the first citation; then use just the numbers. (See pp. 736–37 for a sample paper on a poem.)

c. Verse play or poem divided into parts

Later in Shakespeare's *King Lear* the disguised Edgar says, "The prince of darkness is a gentleman" (3.4.147).

Omit a page number and cite the appropriate part—act (and scene, if any), canto, book, and so on—plus the line number(s). Use Arabic numerals for parts, including acts and scenes (3.4), unless your instructor specifies Roman numerals (III.iv). (See pp. 739–41 for a sample paper on a verse play.)

d. Prose play

In Miller's *Death of a Salesman,* Willie Loman's wife, Linda, acknowledges her husband's failings but also the need for him to be treated with dignity: "He's not the finest character that ever lived. But he's a human being, and a terrible thing is happening to him" (56; act 1).

Provide the page number followed by the act and scene, if any.

14. The Bible

When you cite passages of the Bible in parentheses, abbreviate the title of any book longer than four letters—for instance, Gen. (Genesis), 1 Sam. (1 Samuel), Ps. (Psalms), Prov. (Proverbs), Matt. (Matthew), Rom. (Romans), 2 Cor. (2 Corinthians). Then give the chapter and verse(s) in Arabic numerals.

> According to the Bible, at Babel God "did . . . confound the language of all the earth" (Gen. 11.9).

15. Two or more works in the same citation

When you refer to more than one work in a single parenthetical citation, separate the references with a semicolon.

> Two recent articles point out that a computer badly used can be less efficient than no computer at all (Gough and Hall 201; Richards 162).

Since long citations in the text can distract the reader, you may choose to cite several or more works in an endnote or footnote rather than in the text. See page 643.

2 Positioning and punctuating parenthetical citations

The following guidelines will help you place and punctuate text citations to distinguish between your own and your sources' ideas and to make your own text readable. See also pages 608–12 on editing quotations and using signal phrases to integrate source material into your sentences.

Where to place citations

Position text citations to accomplish two goals:

- **Make it clear exactly where your borrowing begins and ends.**
- **Keep the citation as unobtrusive as possible.**

You can accomplish both goals by placing the parenthetical citation at the end of the sentence element containing the borrowed material. This sentence element may be a phrase or a clause, and it may begin, interrupt, or conclude the sentence. Usually, as in the following examples, the element ends with a punctuation mark.

> The inflation rate might climb as high as 30 percent (Kim 164), an increase that could threaten the small nation's stability.

> The inflation rate, which might climb as high as 30 percent (Kim 164), could threaten the small nation's stability.

> The small nation's stability could be threatened by its inflation rate, which, one source predicts, might climb as high as 30 percent (Kim 164).

In the last example the addition of one source predicts clarifies that Kim is responsible only for the inflation-rate prediction, not for the statement about stability.

When your paraphrase or summary of a source runs longer than a sentence, clarify the boundaries by using the author's name in the first sentence and placing the parenthetical citation at the end of the last sentence.

> Juliette Kim studied the effects of acutely high inflation in several South American and African countries since World War II. She discovered that a major change in government accompanied or followed the inflationary period in 56% of cases (22-23).

When you cite two or more sources in the same paragraph, position authors' names and parenthetical citations so that readers can see who said what. In the following example, the beginnings and ends of sentences clearly mark the different sources.

> Schools use computers extensively for drill-and-practice exercises, in which students repeat specific skills such as spelling words, using the multiplication facts, or, at a higher level, doing chemistry problems. But many education experts criticize such exercises for boring students and failing to engage their critical thinking and creativity. Jane M. Healy, a noted educational psychologist and teacher, takes issue with "interactive" software for children as well as drill-and-practice software, arguing that "some of the most popular 'educational' software . . . may be damaging to independent thinking, attention, and motivation" (20). Another education expert, Harold Wenglinsky of the Educational Testing Service, found in a well-regarded study that fourth and eighth graders who used computers frequently, including for drill and practice, actually did worse on tests than their peers who used computers less often (*Does* 21). In a later article, Wenglinsky concludes that "the quantity of use matters far less than the quality of use." In schools, he says, high-quality computer work, involving critical thinking, is still rare ("In" 17).

How to punctuate citations

Generally place a parenthetical citation *before* any punctuation required by your sentence. If the borrowed material is a quotation, place the citation *between* the closing quotation mark and the punctuation:

> Spelling argues that during the 1970s American automobile manufacturers met consumer needs "as well as could be expected" (26), but not everyone agrees with him.

The exception is a quotation ending in a question mark or exclamation point. Then use the appropriate punctuation inside the closing quotation mark, and follow the quotation with the text citation and a period.

> "Of what use is genius," Emerson asks, "if the organ . . . cannot find a focal distance within the actual horizon of human life?" ("Experience" 60). Mad genius is no genius.

When a citation appears at the end of a quotation set off from the text, place it one space *after* the punctuation ending the quotation. Do not use additional punctuation with the citation or quotation marks around the quotation.

> In Charles Dickens's *A Christmas Carol,* Scrooge and the Ghost of Christmas Past visit Scrooge's childhood boarding school. They watch as the schoolmaster offers young Ebenezer and his sister some unappealing food and drink:
>
> > Here he produced a decanter of curiously light wine, and a block of curiously heavy cake, and administered installments of those dainties to the young people: at the same time, sending out a meager servant to offer a glass of the "something" to the postboy, who answered that he thanked the gentleman, but if it was the same tap as he had tasted before, he had rather not. (34)

See the two sample research papers starting on pages 683 and 710 for further examples of placing parenthetical references in relation to summaries, paraphrases, and quotations.

3 Using footnotes or endnotes in special circumstances

Occasionally you may want to use footnotes or endnotes in place of parenthetical citations. If you need to refer to several sources at once, listing them in a long parenthetical citation could be intrusive. In that case, you use a note for the information, following the style described here.

Signal the citation with a numeral raised above the appropriate line of text and write a note beginning with the same numeral to cite the sources:

Text At least five studies have confirmed these results.[1]

Note 1. Abbott and Winger 266-68; Casner 27; Hoyenga 78-79; Marino 36; Tripp et al. 179-83.

You may also use a footnote or endnote to comment on a source or to provide information that does not fit easily in the text:

Text So far, no one has confirmed these results.[2]

Note 2. Manter tried repeatedly to replicate the experiment, but he was never able to produce the high temperatures (616).

For a footnote or an endnote, type the numeral on the text line, followed by a period, a space, and the text of the note. If the note appears as a footnote, use the footnote feature of your word processor to set it at the bottom of the page on which the citation appears. Double-space the note. If the note appears as an endnote, place it in numerical order with the other endnotes on a page between the text and the list of works cited. Double-space all the endnotes. (See pp. 704–05 for a page of endotes.)

47b Writing the MLA list of works cited

In MLA documentation style, your in-text parenthetical citations (discussed in 47a) refer the reader to complete information on your sources in a list you title Works Cited and place at the end of your paper. The list should include all the sources you quoted, paraphrased, or summarized in your paper. (If your instructor asks you to include sources you examined but did not cite, title the list Works Consulted.)

Format of the list of works cited

To format the list of works cited, use the following illustration and guidelines. For complete lists of works cited, see the papers by Justin Malik (pp. 706 and 708) and Vanessa Haley (p. 715).

MLA works-cited page

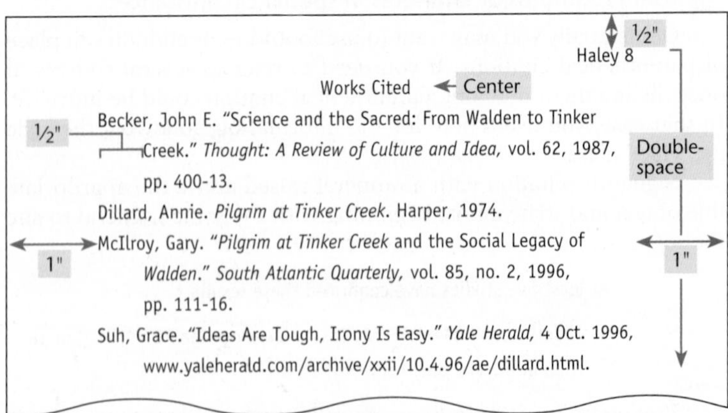

Arrangement Arrange sources alphabetically by the author's last name. If there is no author, alphabetize by the first main word of the title (excluding *A*, *An*, or *The*).

Spacing Double-space everything in the list, as shown in the sample.

Indention As shown in the sample, begin each entry at the left margin, and indent the second and subsequent lines one-half inch. Your word processor can create this so-called hanging indent automatically.

Elements of works-cited entries

The eighth edition of the *MLA Handbook* simplifies writing works-cited entries by building them on the core, visible elements in sources. In the following description and the box on the next page, these core elements are listed in order of their appearance in a works-cited entry. Few sources include all of the listed elements: as you build works-cited entries, give the elements that you find in your sources. For more information from MLA, go to *style.mla.org*.

Author Begin each entry with the author's last name, a comma, and the author's first name and middle name or initial, if any—for instance, Hohulin, John D. End the author's name with a period. See models 1–6 (pp. 650–52) for how to cite various numbers and kinds of authors.

Title of source After the author, give the full title and any subtitle of the source, separating them with a colon. End the title with a period.

- **Quotation marks for shorter works:** Use quotation marks around titles of works that are part of larger works, such as articles, pages on Web sites, and selections from anthologies: "A Rose for Emily." (See p. 462 for titles to enclose in quotation marks.)
- **Italics for longer works:** Use italics for the titles of longer, independent works such as books and films: *Do the Right Thing*. Containers (next item) also have italic titles. (See pp. 486–87 for titles to italicize.)
- **Descriptions for untitled works:** For works that do not have titles, such as interviews, give a description of the work after the name of the author. (See models 32, 34, and 50 for examples of descriptions of untitled works.)

Title of container Many sources used in research are shorter works, such as articles and Web pages, that are published in larger works, such as journals and Web sites. In MLA style, the larger publication is called the **container**. In your works-cited entry, give the title of the container in italics, followed by a comma.

- **Container 1:** Some works fall in one container. For example, if you are citing an article on a Web site, the container is the Web site (see model 34). If you are citing a short story or a chapter

Building MLA works-cited entries

Following are the core elements and their order in works-cited entries. Most sources will not contain every element. The colors correspond to the highlight colors in the models on pages 648-79.

Author's last name, First name.

"Title of Shorter Work." *or* ***Title of Longer Work.***

Container 1

Give these elements in this order if they are available. Skip "Title of Container" for self-contained works.

Title of Container 1,

Other contributors,

Version,

Number,

Publisher,

Publication date,

Location.

Container 2

Give these elements in this order if they are available.

Title of Container 2,

Other contributors,

Version,

Number,

Publisher,

Publication date,

Location.

from a print anthology, the container is the anthology (see models 27 and 28).

- **Container 2:** Many sources have more than one container—in essence, the source is inside container 1, which is inside container 2. For example, if you are citing an article from a journal that you found in a database, container 1 is the journal and container 2 is the database (see pp. 654–55). If your source is an episode of a television series that you watched on *Netflix*, container 1 is the television series and container 2 is *Netflix* (see model 48b).
- **Self-contained works:** Note that some sources are self-contained. These include books such as novels, manuals, works of nonfiction, and the like.

The models on the following pages give examples of many short works in containers such as books, journals, databases, and

Web sites, as well as longer, self-contained works such as books, films, Web sites, music albums, and so on.

Other contributors Some sources and some containers, such as anthologies and edited collections, may include the work of people besides the author. If a person's contribution to a work is important to your research, add the contributor's name to your works-cited entry preceded by a description such as adapted by, directed by, edited by, illustrated by, introduction by, narrated by, performance by, or translated by. Follow the name of a contributor with a comma. For examples of works-cited entries showing contributors, see models 16, 17, 19 (books), 48 (television episodes and series), 49 (radio programs), 51 (films and videos), 52 (sound recordings), and 54 (live performances).

Version Books, films, and computer software such as games and apps often appear in updated or revised editions and versions. If your source or its container gives a version or edition, add it to your works-cited entry, followed by a comma—for instance, version 8.1, or 3rd ed., (ed. stands for "edition"). For examples of works-cited entries showing editions and versions, see models 14 (book) and 56 (app).

Number in a sequence Some sources and containers are published in a numbered sequence. Examples include academic journals, which often have volume and issue numbers (models 7 and 8). Some books are published in sets consisting of multiple volumes (model 20). Television series and episodes are typically numbered by season and by episode (model 48). In your works-cited entry, follow a sequence number with a comma—for example, season 1, episode 6, or vol. 32, no. 6, (vol. and no. stand for "volume" and "number," respectively).

Publisher Give the publisher followed by a comma. For instance, the publisher of a book is the company that issued the book (see pp. 660–61), the publisher of a Web site is the organization that sponsors the site (see p. 669), and the publisher of a TV series is generally the main studio that produced the series (see model 48). If the source has more than one publisher, separate the names with a forward slash: Vertigo / DC Comics.

You do not need to list a publisher for some kinds of sources or containers, including periodicals (journals, newspapers, and magazines), databases, self-published works, and Web sites whose titles and publishers are the same.

Publication date Give the date of publication followed by a comma. Publication dates vary considerably depending on the type of source you are citing. To identify and cite the publication date, see the box on pages 649–50 to locate a model that most closely matches your source. See also model 37 to cite an undated source you find on the Web.

Location Give a location telling where you found the source or its container so that other researchers can find the source, too. Follow the location with a period.

- **Page numbers:** For a source within a container with page numbers, such as a chapter of a book or an article in a periodical, provide the page numbers. Use the abbreviation p. or pp. before the page numbers: p. 72 or pp. 210-13. See pages 654–55 and 657 for examples of page numbers.
- **Digital Object Identifer (DOI):** Many journal articles, books, and other documents have a DOI attached to them, a permanent URL that links to the text and functions as a unique identifier. When a DOI is available, include it at the end of your works-cited entry and follow it with a period: doi:10.1682/JRRD.2010.03.0024. Usually a DOI will follow the title of a container such as a database or a Web site. See pages 654–55 for an example of a DOI.
- **URL:** If a DOI is not available for a source you found in a database or on the Web, copy and paste the URL from your browser into your works-cited entry, deleting "http://"—for instance, harpers.org/archive/2012/10/contest-of-words/. If your source gives a stable URL, such as a *permalink*, give it instead.
- **Name and city:** If you viewed an object in a museum or an archive or attended a performance or lecture, give the name of the institution or venue and the city in which it is located—for instance, DeYoung Museum, San Francisco. For examples, see models 44, 54, and 58.

Models of MLA works-cited entries

Unlike earlier editions of the *MLA Handbook*, which gave numerous examples of works-cited entries organized by the type of source, the eighth edition emphasizes building entries based on the elements described in the preceding section. This chapter blends the two approaches, applying the new guidelines to a wide variety of sources you may encounter during your research. The models here are extensive but not exhaustive, and you will surely come across sources that do not match exactly. For such sources, refer to the list of core elements on page 646 and give whatever information you can find in the source.

The box on the next two pages will help you find appropriate MLA works-cited models for your sources.

1 Authors

The models begining on page 650 show how to handle authors' names in citing any kind of source.

Index to models of MLA works-cited entries

(continued)

MLA 47b

Index to models of MLA works-cited entries

(continued)

1. One author

Ehrenreich, Barbara. *Dancing in the Streets: A History of Collective Joy*. Henry Holt, 2006.

Give the author's full name—last name first, a comma, first name, and any middle name or initial. Omit any title, such as *Dr.* or *PhD.* End the name with a period. If your source lists an editor as author, see model 15, page 662.

2. Two authors

Lifton, Robert Jay, and Greg Mitchell. *Who Owns Death: Capital Punishment, the American Conscience, and the End of Executions*. William Morrow, 2000.

Give the authors' names in the order provided on the title page. Reverse the first and last names of the first author *only,* not of the other author. Separate the authors' names with a comma and and. If your source lists two editors as authors, see model 15, page 662.

3. More than two authors

Wilcox, Dennis L., et al. *Think Public Relations*. 2nd ed., Allyn & Bacon, 2013.

Give the name of the first author only, and follow the name with a comma and the abbreviation et al. (for the Latin *et alii,* meaning "and others"). If your source lists more than two editors as authors, see model 15, page 662.

4. The same author(s) for two or more works

Gardner, Howard. *The Arts and Human Development*. John Wiley & Sons, 1973.

---. *Five Minds for the Future*. Harvard Business School P, 2007.

Give the author's name only in the first entry. For the second and any subsequent works by the same author, substitute three hyphens for the author's name, followed by a period. Note that the three hyphens may substitute only for *exactly* the same name or names. If the second Gardner source were by Gardner and somebody else, both names would have to be given in full.

Place an entry or entries using three hyphens immediately after the entry that names the author. Within the set of entries by the same author, arrange the sources alphabetically by the first main word of the title, as in the Gardner examples (*Arts*, then *Five*).

If you cite two or more sources that list as author(s) exactly the same editor(s), follow the hyphens with a comma and editor or editors as appropriate. (See model 15, p. 662.)

5. A corporate author

Corporate authors include associations, committees, institutions, government bodies, companies, and other groups. When a source gives only the name of the organization as author and not an individual's name, the source has a corporate author.

a. Source cited by author

Vault Technologies. *Turnkey Parking Solutions*. Mills, 2014.

When the corporate author and the publisher are different, start with the name of the author.

b. Source cited by title

"Thailand's Campaign for Tobacco Control." *Center for Global Development*, 2015, millionssaved.cgdev.org/case-studies/thailands-campaign-for-tobacco-control.

When the corporate author and the publisher are the same, omit the author and start with the title. Omit the publisher as well when its name is the Web site title, as in the preceding example. (For examples of government documents cited in this way, see model 33b.)

6. Author not named (anonymous)

The Dorling Kindersley World Atlas. DK Publishing, 2013.

List a work that names no author—neither an individual nor a group—by its full title. If the work is a book, italicize the title. If the work is a periodical article or other short work, enclose the title in quotation marks:

"Drilling in the Wilderness." *The Economist*, 24 Apr. 2014, p. 32.

Alphabetize the work by the title's first main word, excluding *A*, *An*, or *The* (*Dorling* in the first example and Drilling in the second).

2 Articles in journals, newspapers, and magazines

Articles in scholarly journals, in newspapers, and in magazines appear in print periodicals, in online databases available through your library, and on the Web.

Articles in scholarly journals

To cite an article in a scholarly journal, give the author and the title of the article. Enclose the title in quotation marks. Then give information about the container(s), depending on what is available. In container 1, give the title of the journal, any volume and issue numbers, the publication date (abbreviate all months except May, June, and July), and the location of the source, such as page numbers of the article or possibly a URL. Add a container 2 if you reached the source electronically—for instance, through a library database—and give the source's location, such as a Digital Object Identifier (DOI) or a URL.

You do not need to give a publisher for articles in academic journals in print, in online databases such as *Academic Search Complete* or *ProQuest,* or on Web sites.

7. Article in a scholarly journal with volume and issue numbers

a. Print journal article

Mattingly, Carol. "Telling Evidence: Rethinking What Counts in Rhetoric." *Rhetoric Society Quarterly*, vol. 32, no. 1, Winter 2002, pp. 99-108.

See the next two pages for an explanation of this format and where to find the required information in a print journal.

b. Database journal article

Neves, Joshua. "Cinematic Encounters in Beijing." *Film Quarterly*, vol. 67, no. 1, Fall 2013, pp. 27-40. *Academic Search Complete,* doi:10.1525/FQ.2.13.67.1.27.

See the next two pages for an explanation of this format and where to find the required information in a database. Basically, start with the information for a print article (previous model), and add the information for container 2—the title of the database and the DOI or URL.

c. Web journal article

Aulisio, George J. "Green Libraries Are More Than Just Buildings." *Electronic Green Journal,* vol. 35, no. 1, 2013, escholarship.org/uc/item/3x11862z#page-1.

For a scholarly article you find in a Web journal, begin with the author and title. Then give available information about the container: the title of the journal, the volume and issue numbers, the publication date, and a URL, as here, or a DOI. If the journal article does not have page numbers, omit them from the works-cited entry.

8. Article in a journal with only issue numbers

Dobozy, Tomas. "The Writing of Trespass." *Canadian Literature,* no. 218, Autumn 2013, pp. 11-28. *Academic Search Premier,* web.a.ebscohost.com/ehost/detail/AN=94425037&db=aph.

If a scholarly journal numbers only issues, not volumes, give the issue alone after the journal title.

Articles in newspapers

To cite an article in a newspaper, give the author and the title of the article. Enclose the title in quotation marks. Then give information about the container(s), depending on what is available. In container 1, give the title of the newspaper, the publication date (abbreviate all months except May, June, and July), and the location of the article (generally page numbers or a URL). Add information for a container 2 if you used another source, such as a library database, to reach the article.

(text continues on p. 656)

MLA 47b

Citing journal articles: Print and database

Print journal article

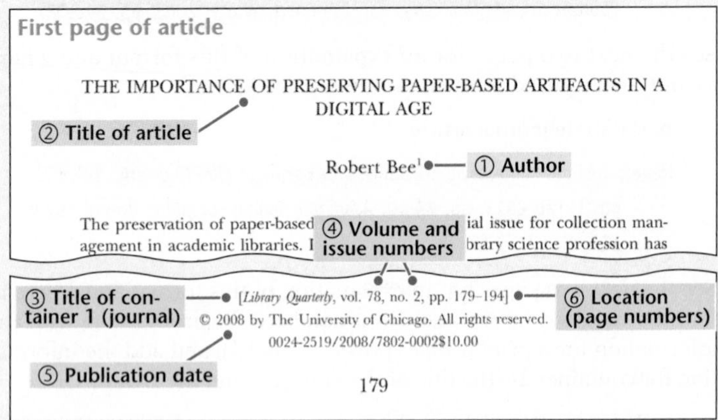

Database journal article

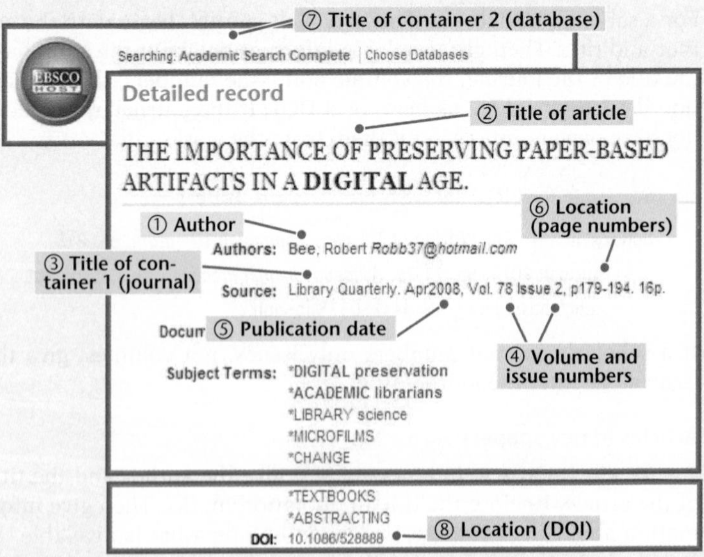

Works-cited entry: Print journal article

① Bee, Robert. ② "The Importance of Preserving Paper-Based Artifacts in a Digital Age." ③ *Library Quarterly,* ④ vol. 78, no. 2, ⑤ Apr. 2008, ⑥ pp. 179-94.

Works-cited entry: Database journal article

① Bee, Robert. ② "The Importance of Preserving Paper-Based Artifacts in a Digital Age." ③ *Library Quarterly,* ④ vol. 78, no. 2, ⑤ Apr. 2008, ⑥ pp. 179-94. ⑦ *Academic Search Complete,* ⑧ doi:10.1086/528888.

① **Author.** Give the full name—last name first, a comma, first name, and any middle name or initial. Omit *Dr., PhD,* or any other title. End the name with a period.

② **Title of article,** in quotation marks. Give the full title and any subtitle, separating them with a colon. End the title with a period inside the final quotation mark.

③ **Title of container 1 (journal),** in italics. End with a comma.

④ **Volume and issue numbers,** in Arabic numerals, preceded by vol. and no. and followed by commas.

⑤ **Publication date,** preceded by the month or season, if available. Abbreviate all months except May, June, and July. End with a comma.

⑥ **Location (page numbers of the article),** preceded by pp. and ending with a period. Provide only as many digits in the last number as needed for clarity, usually two.

⑦ **Title of container 2 (database),** in italics. End with a comma.

⑧ **Location.** If available, give a Digital Object Identifier (DOI), preceded by doi:. End with a period. If no DOI is available, give the URL without "http://." (For more on DOIs and URLs, see p. 648.)

See p. 653 for how to cite a journal article you find on the open Web.

(continued from p. 653)

You do not need to give a publisher for newspaper articles that appear in print, in online databases such *LexisNexis,* or on Web sites.

9. Article in a national newspaper

a. Print newspaper article

Lowery, Annie. "Cities Advancing Inequality Fight." *The New York Times,* 7 Apr. 2014, pp. A1+.

If the newspaper is divided into lettered sections, provide the section designation before the page number when the newspaper does the same: A1+ above. The plus sign indicates that the article continues on a later page.

b. Database newspaper article

Stein, Rob. "Obesity May Stall Trend of Increasing Longevity." *The Washington Post,* 15 Mar. 2015, p. A2. *LexisNexis Academic,* www.lexisnexis.com/lnacademic/HEADLINE(Obesity+may+stall%2C+trend+of+increasing%2C+longevity)%2BDATE%2B2015.

See the next page for an explanation of this format and where to find the required information in a database. Basically, start with the information for a print article (previous model), and add the information for container 2—the title of the database and the URL or DOI.

c. Web news article

Jarvie, Jenny. "What Life Is Like on $7.25 Per Hour." *Los Angeles Times,* 6 Apr. 2016, www.latimes.com/nation/la-na-minimum-wage-life-20160405-story.html.

To cite a newspaper article that you find on the open Web, follow the author and title with the information for the container: the title of the newspaper, the publication date (day, month, year), and the URL. To cite a reader's comment on an article, see model 40, page 671.

10. Article in a local newspaper

Beckett, Lois. "The Ignored PTSD Crisis: Americans Wounded in Their Own Neighborhoods." *The Louisiana Weekly* [New Orleans], 17 Feb. 2014, pp. 12-13.

If the city of publication does not appear in the title of a local newspaper, follow the title with the city name in brackets, not italicized.

Citing a newspaper article: Database

www.lexisnexis.com/lnacademic/?HEADLINE(A+combat+role+and+anguish+too.)%2BDATE%2B2009

⑦ Location

LexisNexis® Academic

⑥ Title of container 2 (database)

Results | Web News

④ Publication date

The New York Times

③ Title of container 1 (newspaper)

November 1, 2009 Sunday
Late Edition - Final

② Title of article

A Combat Role, and Anguish, Too

① Author

BYLINE: By DAMIEN CAVE; Diana Oliva Cave contributed reporting.

SECTION: Section A; Column 0; National Desk; **WOMEN AT ARMS**; Pg. 1

LENGTH: 3198 words

⑤ Location (page number)

For Vivienne Pacquette, being a combat **veteran** with post-traumatic stress disorder means avoiding phone calls to her sons, dinner out with her husband and therapy sessions that make her talk about seeing the reds and whites of her friends' insides after a mortar attack in 2004.

① Cave, Damien. ② "A Combat Role, and Anguish, Too." ③ *The New York Times,* ④ 1 Nov. 2009, ⑤ p. A1. ⑥ *LexisNexis Academic,* ⑦ www.lexisnexis.com/lnacademic/?HEADLINE(A+combat+role+and+anguish+too.)%2BDATE%2B2009.

① **Author.** Give the full name—last name first, a comma, first name, and any middle name or initial. End the name with a period.

② **Title of article**, in quotation marks. Give the full title and any subtitle, separating them with a colon. End the title with a period inside the final quotation mark.

③ **Title of container 1 (newspaper),** in italics. End with a comma.

④ **Publication date,** giving month, day and year. Abbreviate all months except May, June, and July. End with a comma.

⑤ **Location (page number),** preceded by p. and ending with a period. (Use pp. if the article runs on more than one page.) Include a section designation before the page number, as in A1 here, if the newspaper does.

⑥ **Title of container 2 (database),** in italics. End with a comma.

⑦ **Location.** Give the URL without "http://." End with a period.

Articles in magazines

To cite an article in a magazine, give the author and the title of the article. Enclose the title in quotation marks. Then give information about the container(s), depending on what is available. For container 1, give the title of the magazine, the publication date (abbreviate all months except May, June, and July), and the location of the article (page numbers, a URL, or a DOI). Add information for a container 2 if you used another source, such as a library database, to reach the article.

You do not need to give a publisher for magazine articles that appear in print, in online databases such *Academic Search Complete,* or on Web sites.

11. Article in a weekly or biweekly magazine

a. Print magazine article

Toobin, Jeffrey. "This Is My Jail." *The New Yorker,* 14 Apr. 2014, pp. 26-32.

Following the author and title, give information for the container: the title of the magazine, the publication date (day, month, year), and the page numbers.

b. Database magazine article

Barras, Colin. "Right on Target." *New Scientist,* 25 Jan. 2014, pp. 40-43. *Academic Search Complete,* web.a.ebscohost.com/ehost/detail/AN=93983067&db=aph.

To cite a magazine article you found in an online database, start with the information for a print article (previous model). Then add the information for the second container—the title of the database and the DOI or URL.

c. Web magazine article

Stampler, Laura. "These Cities Have the Most Open-Minded Daters." *Time,* 14 Apr. 2014, time.com/61947/these-cities-have-the-most-open-minded-daters/.

To cite a magazine article you find on the open Web, follow the author and title with information for the container: the title of the magazine, the publication date (day, month, year), and the URL. To cite a reader's comment on an article, see model 40, page 671.

12. Article in a monthly or bimonthly magazine

Wong, Kate. "Rise of the Human Predator." *Scientific American,* Apr. 2014, pp. 46-51.

Follow the magazine title with the month and the year of publication. If the date on the magazine spans two months, give both months: Jan.-Feb. 2016.

3 Books and government publications

Complete books

A complete, stand-alone book is self-contained, so the title of a book is followed by the names of other contributors (if any) and publication information. If you found the book in a library database or on the Web, provide the name of the database or Web site and a DOI or URL after the publication information.

13. Basic format for a complete book

To cite a book, give the author, the title, the publisher, and the date. When other information is present, give it between the author's name and the title, between the title and the publication information, or at the end of the entry, as in models 14–23.

a. Print book or book on an e-reader

Shteir, Rachel. *The Steal: A Cultural History of Shoplifting.* The Penguin Press, 2011.

See the next two pages for an explanation of this format and where to find the required information in a print book or an e-book with print publication information.

If an e-book has no print publication information, give the e-book publication instead. Your in-text citations will vary depending on whether you are citing a print or digital version: for a print version you will cite page numbers; for an e-book version you will cite chapters. See pages 635–36 and 638.

b. Database book

Levine, Daniel. *Bayard Rustin and the Civil Rights Movement.* Rutgers UP, 2000. *eBook Collection*, web.a.ebscohost.com/ehost/ebookviewer/ebook/e6967d23-394e-41d9-ab54-d292ebd6287b =2.

To cite a book that you find in a database, give any print publication information before information about the container—the name of the database and a DOI or URL. See the next two pages for an explanation of this format and where to find the required information in a database.

c. Web book

Cather, Willa. *One of Ours*. Alfred A. Knopf, 1922. *Bartleby.com*, 2000, www.bartleby.com/1006/1.html.

Providing print publication information for a book on the Web is not required, but it can be helpful to readers. This example gives the original publisher and publication date followed by information for the container: the title of the Web site and the URL. (The title of the

(text continues on p. 662)

Citing books: Print and database

Print book

Title page

like a man gone mad

Poems in a New Century

Samuel Hazo

Syracuse University Press

② Title and subtitle

① Author

③ Publisher

Copyright page

Copyright © 2010 by Syracuse University Press
Syracuse, New York 13244-5290

All Rights Reserved

④ Publication date

Database book

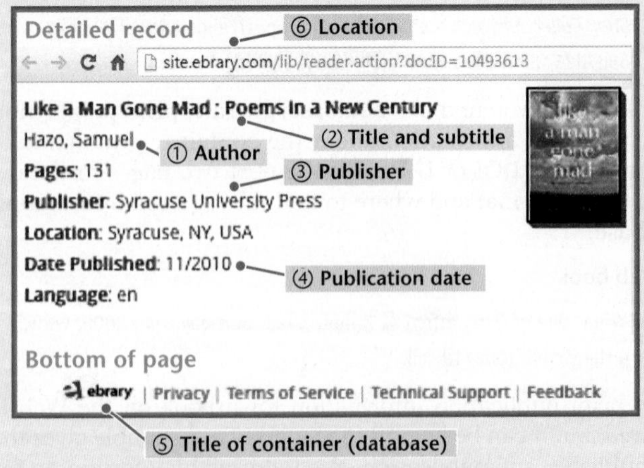

Works-cited entry: Print book

① Hazo, Samuel. ② *Like a Man Gone Mad: Poems in a New Century.* ③ Syracuse UP, ④ 2010.

Works-cited entry: Database book

① Hazo, Samuel. ② *Like a Man Gone Mad: Poems in a New Century.* ③ Syracuse UP, ④ 2010. ⑤ *Ebrary,* ⑥ site.ebrary.com/lib/reader.action?docID=10493613.

① **Author.** Give the full name—last name first, a comma, first name, and any middle name or initial. Omit *Dr., PhD,* or any other title. End the name with a period.

② **Title,** in italics. Give the full title and any subtitle, separating them with a colon. Capitalize all significant words of the title even if the book does not. End the title with a period.

③ **Publisher.** Give the name as it appears on the title page or copyright page, followed by a comma. Shorten "University Press" to UP and omit "Company," "Co.," and "Inc." from other publishers' names. If two publisher names are listed on the title or copyright page, determine their relationship: If they are both independent entities, list them both with a forward slash between the names (see model 19). If one is a division of the other (for instance, Scribner is a division of Simon & Schuster), cite only the division.

④ **Publication date.** If the date doesn't appear on the title page, look for it on the next page. End with a period.

⑤ **Title of container (database),** in italics. End with a comma.

⑥ **Location.** Give the URL without "http://," ending with a period. If the database record gives a DOI, provide it instead. (For more on DOIs, see p. 648.)

See pp. 659 and 662–64 for how to cite other types of books.

(continued from p. 659)

Web site and the name of the publisher are the same, so only the Web site is given.)

14. Second or subsequent edition

Bolinger, Dwight L. *Aspects of Language.* 3rd ed., Harcourt Brace Jovanovich, 1981.

Books are often revised and published in new editions. For any edition after the first, place the edition number after the title. Use the designation given in the source, such as Expanded ed., Updated ed., or 3rd ed., as in the example.

15. Book with an editor

Holland, Merlin, and Rupert Hart-Davis, editors. *The Complete Letters of Oscar Wilde.* Henry Holt, 2000.

Handle editors' names like authors' names (models 1–4), but add a comma and editor or editors after the last editor's name.

16. Book with an author and an editor

Mumford, Lewis. *The City in History.* Edited by Donald L. Miller, Pantheon, 1986.

When citing the work of the author, give the author's name first. After the title, give the editor's name (another contributor) preceded by Edited by.

When citing the work of the editor, use model 15 for a book with an editor, adding By and the author's name after the title:

Miller, Donald L., editor. *The City in History.* By Lewis Mumford, Mariner Books, 1968.

17. Book with a translator

Alighieri, Dante. *The Inferno.* Translated by John Ciardi, New American Library, 1971.

When citing the work of an author, shown above, give his or her name first, and give the translator's name (another contributor) after the title, preceded by Translated by.

When citing the work of the translator, give his or her name first, followed by a comma and translator. Follow the title with By and the author's name.

Ciardi, John, translator. *The Inferno.* By Dante Alighieri, New American Library, 1971.

When a book you cite by the author's name has a translator *and* an editor, give the translator's and the editor's names in the order used on the book's title page.

18. Anthology

Kennedy, X. J., and Dana Gioia, editors. *Literature: An Introduction to Fiction, Poetry, Drama, and Writing.* 13th ed., Pearson, 2016.

Cite an entire anthology only when citing the work of the editor or editors or when your instructor permits cross-referencing like that shown in model 28. Give the name of the editor or editors (followed by editor or editors) and then the title of the anthology.

19. Illustrated book or graphic narrative

Wilson, G. Willow. *Cairo.* Illustrated by M. K. Perker, Vertigo / DC Comics, 2005.

When citing the work of the writer of a graphic narrative or illustrated book, follow the example above: the author's name, the title, Illustrated by, and the illustrator's name (another contributor). This book's two publishers, Vertigo and DC Comics, are separated by a forward slash.

When citing the work of an illustrator, list his or her name first, followed by a comma and illustrator. After the title and By, list the author's name.

Williams, Garth, illustrator. *Charlotte's Web.* By E. B. White, Harper & Brothers, 1952.

20. Multivolume work

Lincoln, Abraham. *The Collected Works of Abraham Lincoln.* Edited by Roy P. Basler, vol. 5, Rutgers UP, 1953. 8 vols.

When the work you cite is one volume in a set of numbered volumes, give the volume number before the publication information (vol. 5 in the example). The total number of volumes at the end of the entry is optional (8 vols. in the example).

If you use two or more volumes of a multivolume work, give the work's total number of volumes before the publication information (8 vols. in the following example). Your in-text citation will indicate which volume you are citing (see p. 639).

Lincoln, Abraham. *The Collected Works of Abraham Lincoln.* Edited by Roy P. Basler, 8 vols., Rutgers UP, 1953.

21. Book in a series

Bergman, Ingmar. *The Seventh Seal.* Simon and Schuster, 1960. Modern Film Scripts Series 12.

When the work you cite is part of a series, you may give the name of the series, not italicized or in quotation marks, at the end of the entry.

MLA 47b

22. Book published before 1900

James, Henry. *The Bostonians.* London, 1886.

Although the city of publication is not required in most works-cited entries, MLA recommends giving the city rather than the publisher for books published before 1900 because such books are usually associated with the cities in which they were published.

23. Republished book

Achebe, Chinua. *Things Fall Apart.* 1958. Anchor Books, 1994.

Many books, especially classic literary works, are republished and reissued by publishers. If the original publication date of a book is important to your use of it, give the date after the title. Then provide the publication information for the source you are using.

24. Sacred works

The Bible: Authorized King James Version with Apocrypha. Edited by Robert Carroll and Stephen Prickett, Oxford UP, 2008.

The Koran. Translated by N. J. Dawood, rev. ed., Penguin, 2015.

When citing a sacred work, give the edition you consulted, beginning with the title unless you are citing the work of an editor or translator.

25. Book with a title in its title

Eco, Umberto. *Postscript to* The Name of the Rose. Translated by William Weaver, Harcourt Brace Jovanovich, 1983.

When a book's title contains another book title (here *The Name of the Rose*), do not italicize the second title. When a book's title contains a quotation or the title of a work normally placed in quotation marks, keep the quotation marks and italicize both titles: *Critical Response to Henry James's "The Beast in the Jungle."*

26. Book lacking publication information or pagination

Carle, Eric. *The Very Busy Spider.* Philomel Books, 1984, n. pag.

Some books are not paginated or do not list a publisher or date of publication. Although MLA style no longer requires you to indicate missing information, your instructor may ask you to do so for clarity. These abbreviations are conventional: n.p. if no publisher, n.d. if no publication date, and n. pag. if no page numbers.

Parts of books

Parts of books include selections from anthologies, articles and chapters in scholarly collections and reference works, and the like.

Works-cited entries for these short works include the author and title as well as information about the container in which they appear: the title, any other contributors, publication information, and page numbers, if available.

27. Selection from an anthology

Munro, Alice. "How I Met My Husband." *Literature: An Introduction to Fiction, Poetry, Drama, and Writing,* edited by X. J. Kennedy and Dana Gioia, 13th ed., Pearson, 2016, pp. 189-201.

This listing adds to the anthology entry in model 18: author of selection, title of selection (in quotation marks), and inclusive page numbers for the selection. If you wish, you may also supply the original date of publication for the work you are citing, after its title. See model 23.

If the work you cite comes from a collection of works by one author that has no editor, use the following form:

Hempel, Amy. "San Francisco." *The Collected Stories of Amy Hempel,* Scribner, 2006, pp. 27-28.

28. Two or more selections from the same anthology

Bradstreet, Anne. "The Author to Her Book." Kennedy and Gioia, pp. 657-58.

Kennedy, X. J., and Dana Gioia, editors. *Literature: An Introduction to Fiction, Poetry, Drama, and Writing.* 13th ed., Pearson, 2016.

Merwin, W. S. "For the Anniversary of My Death." Kennedy and Gioia, p. 828.

Stevens, Wallace. "Thirteen Ways of Looking at a Blackbird." Kennedy and Gioia, pp. 831-33.

When you are citing more than one selection from the same anthology, your instructor may allow you to avoid repetition by giving the anthology information in full (the Kennedy and Gioia entry) and then simply cross-referencing it in entries for the works you used. Thus the Bradstreet, Merwin, and Stevens examples replace full publication information with Kennedy and Gioia and the appropriate pages in that book. Note that each entry appears in its proper alphabetical place among other works cited.

29. Work from a collection of scholarly articles

Molloy, Francis C. "The Suburban Vision in John O'Hara's Short Stories." *Short Story Criticism: Excerpts from Criticism of the Works of Short Fiction Writers,* edited by David Segal, Gale, 1989, pp. 287-92. Originally published in *Critique: Studies in Modern Fiction,* vol. 25, no. 2, 1984, pp. 101-13.

Scholarly articles may be in collections like the one in the preceding example, *Short Story Criticism*. If the articles were written for the collection, you can follow model 27 for a selection from an anthology. However, if the articles were previously printed elsewhere—for instance, in scholarly journals—your instructor may ask you to provide the information for the earlier publication of articles you cite. Add Originally published in to the end of the entry and then give information for the earlier publication.

30. Article in a reference work

List an article in a reference work by the title if no author is given (models a and b) or by the author (model c). Then give the information for the container.

a. Print reference work

"Fortune." *Encyclopedia of Indo-European Culture,* edited by J. P. Malloy and D. Q. Adams, Fitzroy, 1997, pp. 211-12.

b. Web reference work

"Ming Dynasty." *Encyclopaedia Britannica,* 14 Dec. 2015, www.britannica.com/topic/Ming-dynasty-Chinese-history.

c. CD-ROM or DVD-ROM reference work

Nunberg, Geoffrey. "Usage in the Dictionary." *The American Heritage Dictionary of the English Language,* 4th ed., Houghton Mifflin, 2000.

Single-issue CD-ROMs may be encyclopedias, dictionaries, books, and other resources that are published just once. Cite such sources like print books.

31. Introduction, preface, foreword, or afterword

Quindlen, Anna. Foreword. *A Tree Grows In Brooklyn,* by Betty Smith, HarperCollins, 2011, pp. vii-xv.

An introduction, foreword, or afterword is often written by someone other than the book's author. When citing such a piece, give its name without quotation marks or italics, as with Foreword in the example. (If the piece has a title of its own, provide it, in quotation marks, between the name of the author and the title of the book.) Give the inclusive page numbers of the part you cite. (In the preceding example, the small Roman numerals refer to the front matter of the book, before page 1.)

When the author of a preface or introduction is the same as the author of the book, give only the last name after the title:

Gould, Stephen Jay. Prologue. *The Flamingo's Smile: Reflections in Natural History,* by Gould, W. W. Norton, 1985, pp. 13-20.

32. Published letter

Buttolph, Mrs. Laura E. Letter to Reverend and Mrs. C. C. Jones. 20 June 1857. *The Children of Pride: A True Story of Georgia and the Civil War,* edited by Robert Manson Myers, Yale UP, 1972, pp. 334-35.

List a published letter under the writer's name. Give it a descriptive label, specifying that the source is a letter and to whom it was addressed, and give the date on which it was written. Do not put this description in quotation marks or italics. Treat the rest of the information like a selection from an anthology (model 27, p. 665), giving the title of collection, the editor, publication information, and any page numbers.

Government publications

33. Government publication

a. Publication cited by author

Gray, Colin S. *Defense Planning for National Security: Navigation Aids for the Mystery Tour.* United States Army War College P, 2014.

United States, Dept. of Defense, Office of Civil Defense. *Fallout Protection: What to Know and Do about Nuclear Attack.* US Government Printing Office, 1961.

If a government publication lists a person as author or editor, treat the source as an authored or edited book (first example). If a publication does not list an author or editor, give the government and the agency as author (second example).

For a congressional publication, give the house and committee involved before the title. Then give the title (in italics) and information for the container: the title of the Web site, the date, and the URL.

United States, Congress, Senate, Committee on Veterans' Affairs. *Post-9/11 Veterans Educational Assistance Improvements Act of 2010.* US Government Printing Office, 2010, www.gpo.gov/fdsys/pkg/BILLS-111s3447.

If you like, after the URL you may include the number and session of Congress, the chamber (House of Representatives or Senate), and the type and number of the publication—for instance, 111th Congress, 2nd session, Senate Bill 3447.

b. Publication cited by title

"Autism Spectrum Disorder." *National Institute of Mental Health,* Sept. 2015, www.nimh.nih.gov/health/publications/autism-spectrum-disorder-qf-15-5511/index.shtml.

"A Comprehensive Approach to Bullying Prevention." *Wisconsin Dept. of Public Instruction,* 24 Feb. 2016, dpi.wi.gov/sspw/safe-schools/bullying-prevention.

MLA style recommends omitting a corporate author when it is the same as the publisher and omitting the publisher when it has the same name as its Web site. The preceding examples begin with the title and then give information for the container: the title of the Web site, the date, and the URL. (For more on corporate authors, see model 5, p. 651.)

4 Web sources and social media

Web sites and parts of Web sites

The following models encompass pages, essays, articles, stories, poems, plays, and other works that you find on larger Web sites. To cite journal, newspaper, and magazine articles that you find on the open Web, see, respectively, models 7c, 9c, and 11c (pp. 653, 656, 658). To cite books that you find on the open Web, see model 13c (p. 659). To cite a government document on a Web site, see model 33 (previous page). To cite a complete Web site, see model 35 (p. 670).

34. Page or work on a Web site

When you cite a page or work that you find on a Web site, treat the Web site as the container of the source. After the author and title, give the title of the Web site, in italics, any other contributors (such as an editor of the site), the publisher (if different from the site title), the publication date, and the location of the source (the URL).

a. Work with an author and a title

Murray, Amanda. "Invention Hot Spot: Birth of Hip-Hop in the Bronx, New York, in the 1970s." *Lemelson Center for the Study of Invention and Innovation,* Smithsonian Institution, 15 Oct. 2010, invention.si.edu/invention-hot-spot-birth-hip-hop-bronx-new-york-1970s.

See opposite for an explanation of this format and where to find the required information on a Web site.

Most works on Web sites are brief, and their titles should be placed in quotation marks. However, some works, such as books and plays, are longer, and their titles should be italicized. (See pp. 462 and 486–87 for titles to be quoted or italicized.) The work cited below is a collection of poems:

Wheatley, Phillis. *Poems on Various Subjects, Religious and Moral.* London, 1773. *Bartleby.com,* www.bartleby.com/150/.

Citing a page or work on a Web site

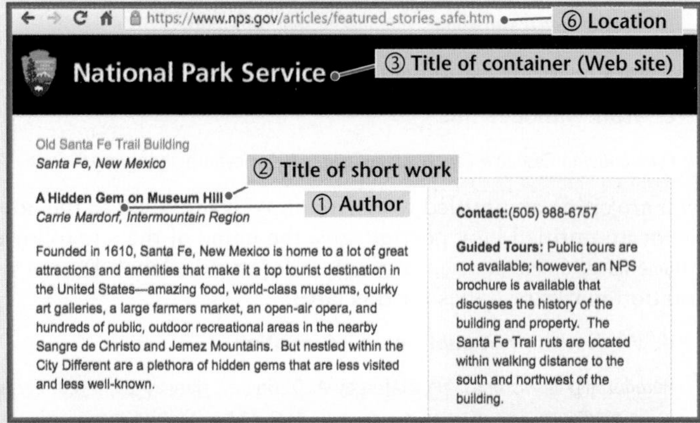

Bottom of page

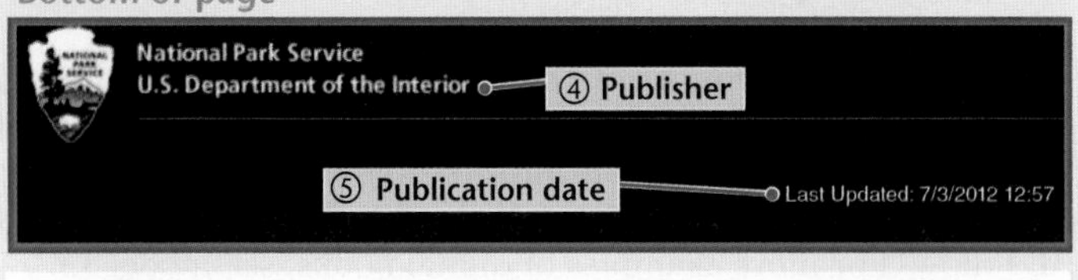

①Mardorf, Carrie. ②"A Hidden Gem on Museum Hill." ③*National Park Service,* ④US Dept. of the Interior, ⑤3 July 2012, ⑥www.nps.gov/articles/featured_stories_safe.htm.

① **Author.** Give the full name—last name first, a comma, first name, and any middle name or initial. Omit *Dr., PhD,* or any other title. End the name with a period. If no author is listed, begin with the title of the short work.

② **Title of the short work,** in quotation marks. End the title with a period inside the final quotation mark.

③ **Title of container (Web site),** in italics. End with a comma.

④ **Publisher,** followed by a comma. The publisher of a Web site may be at the top of the home page, at the bottom of the home page, or on a page that provides information about the site. If the site title and the publisher are the same, omit the publisher.

⑤ **Publication date.** For dates that include day and month, give the day first, then month, then year. Abbreviate all months except May, June, and July. End with a comma.

⑥ **Location.** Give the URL without "http://." End with a period.

b. Work without an author

"Eliminating Polio in Haiti." *Center for Global Development,* 2015, millionssaved.cgdev.org/case-studies/eliminating-polio-in-haiti.

If the work lacks an author, start with the title.

c. Work without a title

Cyberbullying Research Center. Home page. 2016, cyberbullying.org/.

If you are citing an untitled work from a Web site, such as the home page or an untitled blog posting, give the name of the site followed by Home page, Online posting, or another descriptive label. Do not use quotation marks or italics for this label.

d. Work with print publication information

Herodotus. *The Histories.* Translated by A. D. Godley, Harvard UP, 1920. *Perseus Digital Library,* Tufts U, Dept. of Classics, www.perseus.tufts.edu/hopper/text?doc=Perseus:text:1999.01.0126.

If the print information for a source is relevant to your research, give it after the title of the work. In this example, the name of the translator and the publication information identify a specific version of the work. The title of the Web site, the publisher, and the URL follow. For more examples of digital books, see model 13.

35. Entire Web site

a. Web site with an author or an editor

Crane, Gregory, editor. *The Perseus Digital Library.* Tufts U, Dept. of Classics, 1985-2016, www.perseus.tufts.edu/hopper/.

When citing an entire Web site—for instance, a scholarly project or a foundation site—include the name of the editor or author (if available), followed by the title of the site, the publisher, the publication date, and the URL.

b. Web site without an author or an editor

Center for Financial Security. U of Wisconsin, 2016, cfs.wisc.edu/.

If a Web site lacks an author or an editor (as many do), begin with the title of the site.

36. Wiki

"Podcast." *Wikipedia.* Wikimedia Foundation, 6 Apr. 2016, en.wikipedia.org/wiki/Podcast.

To cite an entry from a wiki, give the entry title, the site title, the publisher (if different from the title of the Web site), the publication date, and the URL.

37. Undated Web source

"Clean Cars 101." *Union of Concerned Scientists*, www.ucsusa.org/our-work/clean-vehicles/clean-cars-101#.Vwa-KfkrKM8. Accessed 7 Apr. 2016.

MLA style no longer requires access dates for all online sources. However, if the work you cite is undated, or if your instructor requires an access date, give it at the end of the entry preceded by Accessed.

Social Media

38. Post on a blog

Minogue, Kristin. "Diverse Forests Are Stronger against Deer." *Smithsonian Insider*, 8 Apr. 2014, insider.si.edu/2014/04/diverse-forests-resist-deer-better/2014.

Cite a blog post like a work on a Web site, giving the author, the title of the post, and information about the container. The example gives the title of the blog, the publication date, and the URL. It does not give the name of the publisher because the name is clear from the title of the blog.

Cite an entire blog as you would cite an entire Web site (see model 35).

39. Post on a social-networking site

Literacy Network. Status update. *Facebook*, 5 Apr. 2016, www.facebook.com/LiteracyNetwork/?fref=ts.

Give the name of the author (a person or an organization, as here), the type of post, the title of the site, the publisher (if different from the site title), the date of the post, and the URL.

40. Comment

Teka. Comment on "When a Feminist Pledges a Sorority." By Jessica Bennett, *The New York Times*, 9 Apr. 2016, www.nytimes.com/2016/04/10/fashion/sorority-ivy-league-feminists.

List the author's name or user name if the author uses a pseudonym (as here). Then give Comment on followed by the title of the article or post the comment responds to and the information for the container. This example includes the author of the article the comment responds to, the title of the site, the article's publication date, and the URL.

41. Tweet

Bittman, Mark. "Eating Less Meat Could Save up to $31 Trillion (and Many Lives) bit.ly/1UyYxyp." *Twitter*, 21 Mar. 2016, 2:21 p.m., twitter.com/bittman/status/712026468738404352?lang=en.

Give the author's name or user name if the author uses a pseudonym. Give the tweet in its entirety, using the author's capitalization, in quotation marks. Then give the information for the container: the name of the site (*Twitter*), the date and time of the tweet, and the URL.

42. Post to a discussion group

Williams, Frederick. "Circles as Primitive." *The Math Forum @ Drexel,* Drexel U, 28 Feb. 2012, mathforum.org/kb/thread.jspa?threadID=2583537.

If a discussion-group post does not have a title, say Online posting instead. Then give the information for the container: the title of the discussion group, the publisher, the date, and the URL of the discussion thread.

43. E-mail or text message

Green, Reginald. "Re: College Applications." Received by the author, 2 May 2016.

For an e-mail message, use the subject heading as the title, in quotation marks, with standard capitalization. Then name the recipient, whether yourself (the author) or someone else. Cite a text message like an e-mail message but without a subject title:

Soo, Makenna. Text message to the author. 16 Apr. 2016.

5 Visual, audio, and other media sources

44. Painting, photograph, or other work of visual art

a. Original artwork

Abbott, Berenice. *Soap Bubbles.* 1946, Museum of Modern Art, New York.

To cite a work of visual art that you see in person, such as in a museum, name the artist and give the title (in italics). Then give the date of creation and the name and location of the place where you saw the work. You may omit the city if the name of the place includes the city.

b. Reproduction of an artwork in a print publication

Graham, David. *Bob's Java Jive, Tacoma, Washington, 1989. Only in America: Some Unexpected Scenery,* Alfred A. Knopf, 1991, p. 93.

To cite a reproduction of a work of visual art, give the artist and title of the work followed by information for the container in which you found it. In the example, the container is a print book with title, publisher, publication date, and location (a page number).

c. Work of art on the Web

O'Keefe, Georgia. *It Was Red and Pink.* 1959, *Milwaukee Art Museum*, collection.mam.org/details.php?id=6725.

To cite a work of art that you view on the Web, give the name of the artist or creator, the title of the work, and the date of the work (if any). Then give information for the container: the title of the Web site, the publisher of the Web site (if different from the title), and the location of the work (here, a URL).

d. Artwork in a digital file

Girls on the playground. Personal photograph by the author, 10 Aug. 2015.

To cite an unpublished artwork in a digital file that you are reproducing, such as personal photograph or work of art, give a description of it, the photographer, and the date.

45. Advertisement

a. Advertisement without a title

Apple iPhone SE. Advertisement. *Vogue*, May 2016, p. 3.

To cite an advertisement without a title, start with the name of the company and/or product followed by Advertisement. Then give information for the container of the source, in this case a print magazine: title, date, and location (page number).

b. Advertisement with a title

Honey Maid. "This Is Wholesome." *YouTube*, 10 Mar. 2016, youtu.be/2xeanX6xnRU.

Many companies post titled advertisements on their Web sites and on *YouTube*. To cite such an ad, give the company's name and/or product followed by the title of the ad in quotation marks. Then give information for the container: the site where you viewed the ad, the date, and the URL.

46. Comic strip or cartoon

a. Titled comic strip

Johnston, Lynn. "For Better or Worse." *San Francisco Chronicle*, 22 Aug. 2014, p. E6.

Cite a titled comic strip with the artist's name, the title of the strip (in quotation marks), and the information for the container—here, the title of the newspaper, the date, and the page number.

b. Individual cartoon

Sipress, David. Cartoon. *The New Yorker*, 7 Apr. 2016, www.newyorker.com/cartoons/daily-cartoon/daily-cartoon-thursday-april-7th/.

To cite a cartoon that is not part of a comic strip, start with the name of the artist. If the cartoon has a title, give it in quotation marks. If it does not have a title, provide the description Cartoon (as in the example), without quotation marks or italics. Then give information for the container of the work—here, the title of the Web site, the date, and the URL.

47. Map, chart, or diagram

Unless the creator of an illustration is given on the source, list the illustration by its title. Put the title in quotation marks if it is contained in another publication or in italics if it is published independently. If the illustration does not have a title, provide a description in place of the title, without quotation marks or italics (for instance, Diagram). End with publication information for the source.

a. Print map, chart, or diagram

"The Sonoran Desert." *Sonoran Desert: An American Deserts Handbook*, by Rose Houk, Western National Parks Association, 2000, p. 12.

b. Web map, chart, or diagram

"Water Cycle Diagram." *Earthguide*, Scripps Institution of Oceanography, 2013, earthguide.ucsd.edu/earthguide/diagrams/watercycle/index.html.

48. Television episode or series

To cite a television series or episode, start with the title (first example) unless you are citing the work of a person or persons (second example). Give the names of contributors if they are important to your project. The models in this section show various contributors and their roles. To cite contributors to specific episodes, give the name(s) after the episode title (second example). To cite contributors to an entire series, give the names(s) after the series title (third and fourth examples).

a. Broadcast TV episode

"Sink or Swim." *Nurse Jackie*, season 6, episode 1, Showtime, 2014.

This example gives the episode title and information for the container: the series title, the season and episode numbers, the name of the network, and the date.

b. Web TV episode

Peretz, Jesse, director. "Sink or Swim." By Clyde Phillips. *Nurse Jackie*, season 6, episode 1, Showtime, 2014. *Netflix*, www.netflix.com/watch/80065552.

This example gives the director and title of the episode. The writer is given next because he wrote this episode, not the entire series. Container 1 includes the name of the series, the season, and the episode number. Container 2 gives the streaming service, *Netflix,* and the URL.

c. TV episode on DVD, Blu-ray, or videocassette

"Sink or Swim." *Nurse Jackie Complete Collection,* created by Liz Brixius, Linda Wallem, and Evan Dunsky, performance by Edie Falco, season 6, episode 1, Lion's Gate, 2016, disc 7.

This example gives the episode title followed by the information for the container, a DVD set. The creators of the series and the actor who played the central character are named, followed by the season and episode numbers and publication information about the DVD.

d. TV series

Nurse Jackie. Created by Liz Brixius, Linda Wallem, and Evan Dunsky, Showtime, 2009-15.

This example gives information on the series as a whole: the title, the creators, the network, and the years during which the series aired.

49. Radio program

To cite a radio program, start with the title of the program (first example) unless you are citing the work of a person or persons (second example). Then give information about the container: the title of the radio show, any contributors you wish to include (first example), and broadcast or Web publication information. (To cite a podcast, see model 53.)

a. Broadcast radio program

On the Media. Hosted by Brooke Gladstone and Bob Garfield, WNYC, New York, 5 Feb. 2016.

This example gives the name of the radio program, the main contributors, the station that produces the show, and the date.

b. Web radio program

McEvers, Kelly. "Opioid Epidemic Sparks HIV Outbreak in Tiny Indiana Town." *All Things Considered,* National Public Radio, 31 Mar. 2016, www.npr.org/2016/03/31/472577254/opioid-epidemic-sparks-hiv-outbreak-in-tiny-indiana-town.

Radio content streamed from a Web site may give the names of reporters and titles of stories. This example gives the name of the reporter, the title of the story, and information about the container: the name of the program, the publisher (because it is different from the title of the site), the date, and the URL. If instead of listening to the story you consulted the written transcript, add Transcript at the end of the entry, followed by a period.

50. Interview

This section provides models for interviews you heard or saw. See model 57 (p. 678) to cite an interview you conducted yourself.

a. Broadcast interview

Schumer, Amy. Interview by Terry Gross. *Fresh Air,* National Public Radio, WHYY, Philadelphia, 18 Apr. 2014.

For an interview broadcast on radio or television, begin with the name of the person interviewed, followed by a description (not italicized or in quotation marks) in place of a title, such as Interview by and the name of the interviewer. Then give information for the container: the title of the program and broadcast information.

b. Web interview

Gates, Henry Louis, Jr. Interview by Tavis Smiley. *Tavis Smiley,* Public Broadcasting Service, 31 Oct. 2013, pbs.org/video/2365708336/.

For a video or audio interview on the Web, follow the interviewer's name with information about the container: the title of the Web site, the publisher (if different from the site title), the date, and the URL.

51. Film or video

Start with the title (model a) unless you are citing the work of a person or a corporation (models b and c). Generally, list the director. You may also cite other contributors and their roles after the title (model b).

a. Film

Chi-Raq. Directed by Spike Lee, Amazon Studios, 2015.

For a film you see in a theater, end with the distributor and the date.

b. DVD, Blu-ray, or videocassette

Balanchine, George. *Serenade.* 1991. Directed by Hilary Bean, performance by the San Francisco Ballet, PBS Video, 1999.

For a DVD, Blu-ray disc, or videocassette, include the original release date after the title (as here) if it is relevant to your use of the source.

c. Video on the Web

CBS News. "1968 King Assassination Report." 4 Apr. 1968. *YouTube,* 3 Apr. 2008, youtube/cmOBbxgxKvo.

For a film or video on the Web, give a creator, if available, and a title or a description. Then give information for the container: the title of the Web site, the date (if available), and the URL. If the video's original publication date is significant, give it after the title, as here.

52. Sound recording

Sound recordings include music on vinyl LPs, CDs, the Web, and other devices. They also include spoken-word recordings.

a. Song

Springsteen, Bruce. "This Life." *Working on a Dream*, Columbia, 2009.

Start with the name of the artist and the title of the song. Treat the album like a container, giving the title, publisher, and date.

For a song you stream on the Web, treat the service like a second container:

Jackson, Michael. "Billie Jean." *Thriller*, MJJ Productions, 1982. *Spotify*, play.spotify.com/track/5ORmAhIMRTcisVlB6jShJl.

b. Album

Shocked, Michelle. *Short, Sharp, Shocked.* PolyGram Records, 1988.

Give the name of the artist and the title of the album. Then give information about the container: other contributors if relevant, the recording company (as in the example), and the date of release. For an album on the Web, add the name of the streaming service and a URL, as in the Jackson example above.

If you are citing a musical work identified by form, number, and key, see model 54.

c. Spoken word

Dunbar, Paul Laurence. "We Wear the Mask." Narrated by Rita Dove. *Poetry Out Loud,* Poetry Foundation / National Endowment for the Arts, 2014, www.poetryoutloud.org/poems-and-performance/listen-to-poetry.

Spoken-word performances include readings, recitations, monologues, and the like. This example, of a poem read aloud, gives the author of the poem, the title, the narrator, and the container information: the Web site, the publishers (separated by a slash), the date, and the URL.

53. Podcast

Sedaris, David. "Now We Are Five." *This American Life,* Chicago Public Media, 31 Jan. 2014, www.thisamericanlife.org/podcast/episode/517/day-at-the-beach?act=4.

This podcast from a radio program lists the author of a story on the program, the title of the story (in quotation marks), and information about the container: the title of the program, the publisher, the date of the broadcast, and the URL. If a podcast does not list an author or other creator, begin with the title.

54. Live performance

Beethoven, Ludwig van. Symphony no. 9 in D-minor. Performance by Ricardo Muti and the Chicago Symphony Orchestra, 8 May 2015, Symphony Center, Chicago.

The New Century. By Paul Rudnick, directed by Nicholas Martin, 6 May 2013, Mitzi E. Newhouse Theater, New York.

For a live performance, place the title first (second example) unless you are citing the work of an individual (first example). After the title, provide relevant information about contributors as well as the date of the performance, the performance venue, and the city (if it is not part of the venue's name).

If you are citing a work of classical music identified by form, number, and key (first example), do not use quotation marks or italics for the title.

55. Lecture, speech, address, or reading

Fontaine, Claire. "Economics and Education." 7 June 2014, Museum of Contemporary Art, North Miami. Address.

Give the speaker's name and the title of the talk (if any), the date of the presentation, the name of the venue, and the city (if it is not part of the venue's name). If the presentation occurred at a sponsored meeting, add the title of the meeting and the sponsor's name before the date. You can also give the type of presentation (Lecture, Speech, Address, Reading) if doing so will help readers understand what you are citing.

To cite a classroom lecture in a course you are taking, adapt the preceding format by giving a description in place of the title:

Cavanaugh, Carol. Class lecture on teaching mentors. Lesley U, 4 Apr. 2014. Lecture.

To cite a video of a lecture or other presentation that you view on the Web, see model 51b.

56. Video game, computer software, or app

Notch Development. *Minecraft: Pocket Edition*. Version 0.14.1, Mojang, 6 Apr. 2016, minecraft.net.

For a video game, computer program, or app, give the name of the developer or author, the title, the version, the publisher, the publication date, and the URL.

6 Other sources

57. Personal interview

Greene, Matthew. Personal interview. 7 May 2014.

Begin with the name of the person interviewed. For an interview you conducted, give a description of the interview—Personal interview, Telephone interview, or E-mail interview—and then give the date.

See also model 50 to cite a broadcast interview or a video of an interview on the Web.

58. Unpublished or personal letter

a. Unpublished letter

James, Jonathan E. Letter to his sister. 16 Apr. 1970. Jonathan E. James papers, South Dakota State Archive, Pierre.

For an unpublished letter in the collection of a library or archive, give the writer, a description in place of a title, and the date (if the letter is dated). Then give the information for the container: the title of the archive and the location.

See also model 32 to cite a published letter.

b. Personal letter

Murray, Elizabeth. Letter to the author. 6 Apr. 2016.

For a letter you received, give a description in place of the title and the date. To cite an e-mail message, see model 43.

59. Dissertation

McFaddin, Marie Oliver. *Adaptive Reuse: An Architectural Solution for Poverty and Homelessness.* Dissertation, U of Maryland, 2007. UMI, 2007.

Treat a published dissertation like a book, but after the title insert Dissertation, the name of the degree-granting institution, and the year.

60. Pamphlet or brochure

Understanding Childhood Obesity. Obesity Action Network, 2013.

Most pamphlets and brochures can be treated as books. In this example, the pamphlet has no listed author, so the title comes first. If your source has an author, give the name first, followed by the title and publication information.

Exercise 47.1 Writing works-cited entries

Prepare works-cited entries from the following information. Follow the MLA models given in this chapter unless your instructor specifies a different style. Arrange the finished entries in alphabetical order, not numbered.

1. An article titled "Who's Responsible for the Digital Divide?" in the March 2011 issue of the journal *Information Society*, volume 27, issue 2. The article appeared on pages 92–104. The authors are Dmitry Epstein, Erik C. Nisbet, and Tarleton Gillespie. You found the article in the online database *Academic Search Complete.* The DOI for the article is 10.1080/01972243.2011.548695.

2. A Web article titled "Who's Not Online and Why" on the Web site *PewResearch Internet Project.* The author of the article is Kathryn Zickuhr. The publisher of the site is the Pew Research Center. The article is dated September 25, 2013. The URL for the article is www.pewinternet.org/2013/09/25/whos-not-online-and-why/.
3. A Web article with no listed author on the Web site *Digital Divide Institute*. The publisher of the site is DigitalDivide.org. The title of the article is "Banking the Unbanked" and the date is January 24, 2014. The URL for the article is www.digitaldivide.org/#!dd-banking.
4. A print book titled *Technology and Social Inclusion: Rethinking the Digital Divide* by Mark Warschauer. The book was published in 2003 by MIT Press.
5. An article in the newspaper *The New York Times,* published on March 20, 2013, on page B1. The author is Jane L. Levere. The title is "Reaching Those on the Wrong Side of the Digital Divide." You found the source in the database *LexisNexis Academic*. The URL for the article is www.lexisnexis.com/lnacademic/HEADLINE(Reaching+those+wrong%2C+side+divide)%1B2013.
6. A government report you consulted online. The title of the report is "A Nation Online: Entering the Broadband Age." It was published in September 2004 on the Web site of the National Telecommunications and Information Administration, an agency of the US government that is also the author and publisher of the report. The URL for the report is www.ntia.doc.gov/report/2004/nation-online-entering-broadband-age.
7. An e-mail interview you conducted with Naomi Lee on April 23, 2014.
8. A blog post to the Web site *Code for America* by Jacob Solomon. The title is "People, Not Data." The post is dated January 6, 2014. The publisher of the site is Code for America Labs. The URL for the post is www.codeforamerica.org/blog/2014/01/06/people-not-data/.

MLA 47c

47c Using MLA paper format

The MLA's Web site (*style.mla.org*) provides guidelines for the format of a paper, with just a few elements. For guidelines on type fonts, headings, lists, illustrations, and other features that MLA style does not specify, see pages 108–16.

The samples opposite show the formats for the first page and a later page of a paper. For the format of the list of works cited, see page 644.

Margins Use one-inch margins on all sides of every page.

Spacing and indentions Double-space throughout. Indent the first lines of paragraphs one-half inch. (See opposite for treatment of poetry and long prose quotations.)

Paging Begin numbering on the first page, and number consecutively through the end (including the list of works cited). Use Arabic numerals (1, 2, 3) positioned in the upper right, about

First page of MLA paper

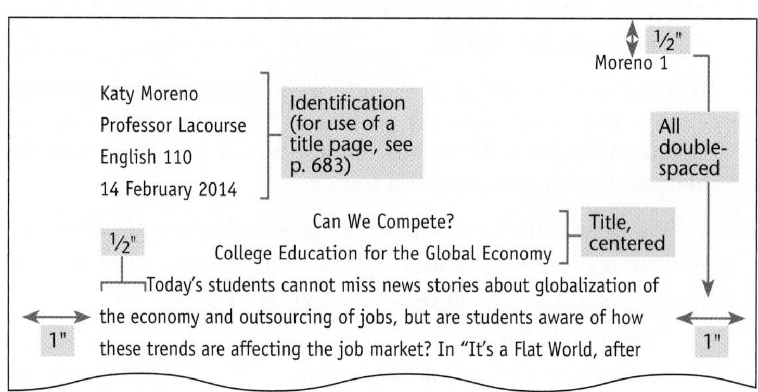

Later page of MLA paper

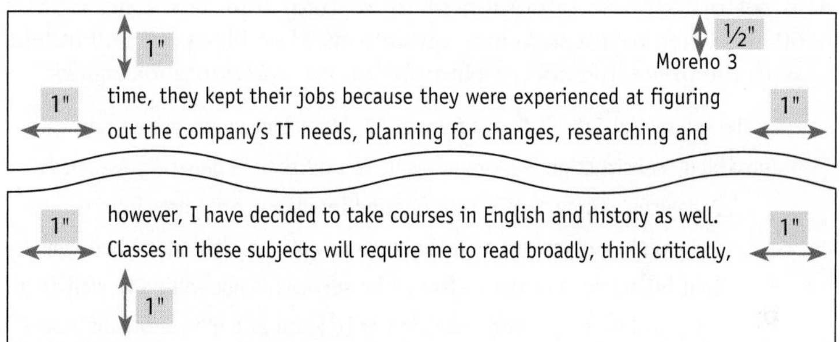

one-half inch from the top. Place your last name before the page number in case the pages later become separated.

Identification and title A title page is not required. If your instructor asks you to supply a title page, see page 683. Otherwise, follow the first sample above, providing your name, the date, and other information requested by your instructor. Place this identification an inch from the top of the page, aligned with the left margin and double-spaced.

Double-space again, and center the title. Do not highlight the title with italics, underlining, boldface, larger type, or quotation marks. Capitalize the words in the title according to the guidelines on page 481. Double-space the lines of the title and between the title and the text.

Poetry and long prose quotations Treat a single line of poetry like any other quotation, running it into your text and enclosing it in quotation marks. You may run in two or three lines of poetry as well, separating the lines with a slash surrounded by space.

An example of Robert Frost's incisiveness is in two lines from "Death of the Hired Man": "Home is the place where, when you have to go there / They have to take you in" (119-20).

Always set off from your text a poetry quotation of more than three lines. Use double spacing above and below the quotation and for the quotation itself. Indent the quotation one-half inch from the left margin. *Do not add quotation marks.*

In "The Author to Her Book," written in 1678, Anne Bradstreet characterizes her book as a child. In these lines from the poem, she captures a parent's and a writer's frustration with the imperfections of her offspring:

> I washed thy face, but more defects I saw,
> and rubbing off a spot, still made a flaw.
> I stretched thy joints to make thee even feet,
> Yet still thou run'st more hobbling than is meet. (13-16)

Also set off a prose quotation of more than four typed lines. (See p. 603 on when to use such long quotations.) Double-space and indent as with the preceding poetry example. *Do not add quotation marks.*

In the influential *Talley's Corner* from 1967, Elliot Liebow observes that "unskilled" construction work requires more skill than is generally assumed:

> A healthy, sturdy, active man of good intelligence requires from two to four weeks to break in on a construction job. . . . It frequently happens that his foreman or the craftsman he services is not willing to wait that long for him to get into condition or to learn at a glance the difference in size between a rough 2 × 8 and a finished 2 × 10. (62)

Do not use a paragraph indention for a quotation of a single complete paragraph or a part of a paragraph. If the quotation contains more than one paragraph, indent the first lines of the second and any subsequent paragraphs.

48 Two Research Papers in MLA Style

The following pages show the research papers of Justin Malik and Vanessa Haley, whose work we followed in Chapters 41–46. (Malik's paper begins on the facing page, Haley's on p. 710.) Both students followed the eighth edition of the *MLA Handbook* to document their sources and format their papers.

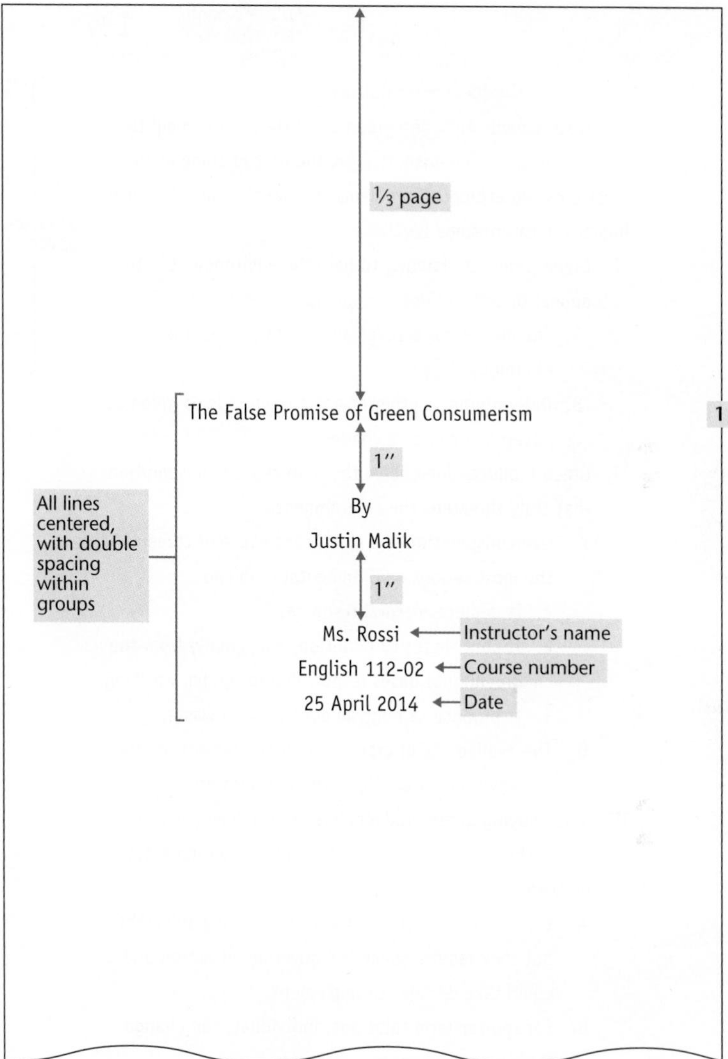

1 **Title page format.** If your instructor requires a title page, prepare it as shown above. Also use a title page if you are required to submit an outline with your paper.

If your instructor does not require a title page for your paper, place your name, the identifying information, and the date on the first page of the paper. See Vanessa Haley's paper, page 710, for this format.

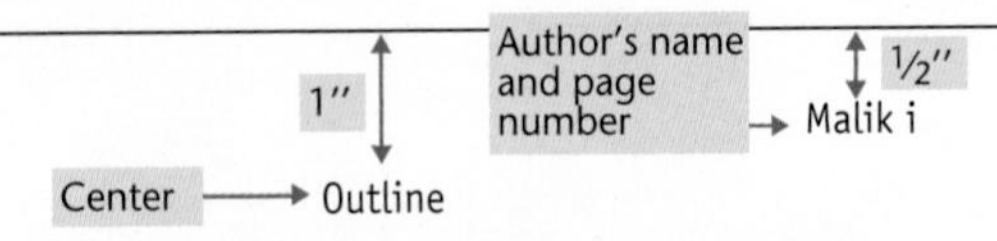

Center → Outline 2 3

Thesis statement: Although green consumerism can help the environment, consumerism itself is the root of some of the most pressing ecological problems. To make a real difference, humans must consume less.

Double-space

I. Green products claiming to help the environment both appeal to and confuse consumers.
   A. The market for ecologically sound products is enormous.
   B. Determining whether or not a product is as green as advertised can be a challenge.

II. Green products don't solve the high rate of consumption that truly threatens the environment.
   A. Overconsumption is a significant cause of three of the most serious environmental problems.
      1. It depletes natural resources.
      2. It contributes to pollution, particularly from the greenhouse gases responsible for global warming.
      3. It produces a huge amount of solid waste.
   B. The availability of greener products has not reduced the environmental effects of consumption.

III. Since buying green products does not reduce consumption, other solutions must be found for environmental problems.
   A. Experts have proposed many far-reaching solutions, but they require concerted government action and could take decades to implement.
   B. For shorter-term solutions, individuals can change their own behavior as consumers.
      1. Precycling may be the greenest behavior that individuals can adopt.

Malik ii

a. Precycling means avoiding purchase of products that use raw materials and excessive packaging.

b. More important, precycling means avoiding purchases of new products whenever possible.

2. For unavoidable purchases, individuals can buy green products and influence businesses to embrace ecological goals.

2 **Outline format.** If your instructor asks you to include your final outline, place it between the title page and the text and number the pages with small Roman numerals (i, ii). Follow the formatting annotations on the facing page.

3 **Outline content.** Malik includes his final thesis statement as part of his outline so that his instructor can see how the parts relate to the whole. Notice that each main division (numbered with Roman numerals) relates to the thesis statement and that all the subdivisions relate to their main division.

Malik casts his final outline in full sentences. Some instructors request topic outlines, in which ideas appear in phrases instead of in sentences and do not end with periods. (See p. 39 for this format.)

The writing situation: Research paper

- **Subject:** Green products and consumerism; student's choice for a research paper assigned in a first-year writing course
- **Purpose:** To explain a problem (environmental effects of human consumption) and propose a solution (reducing consumption and using green products)
- **Audience:** Classmates, instructor, others who are interested in the environment
- **Genre:** Research paper—writing that informs and often makes an argument, drawing on and synthesizing multiple sources from the writer's perspective
- **Sources:** Articles from scholarly and popular periodicals, books, government documents, and a personal interview (all cited in MLA style)

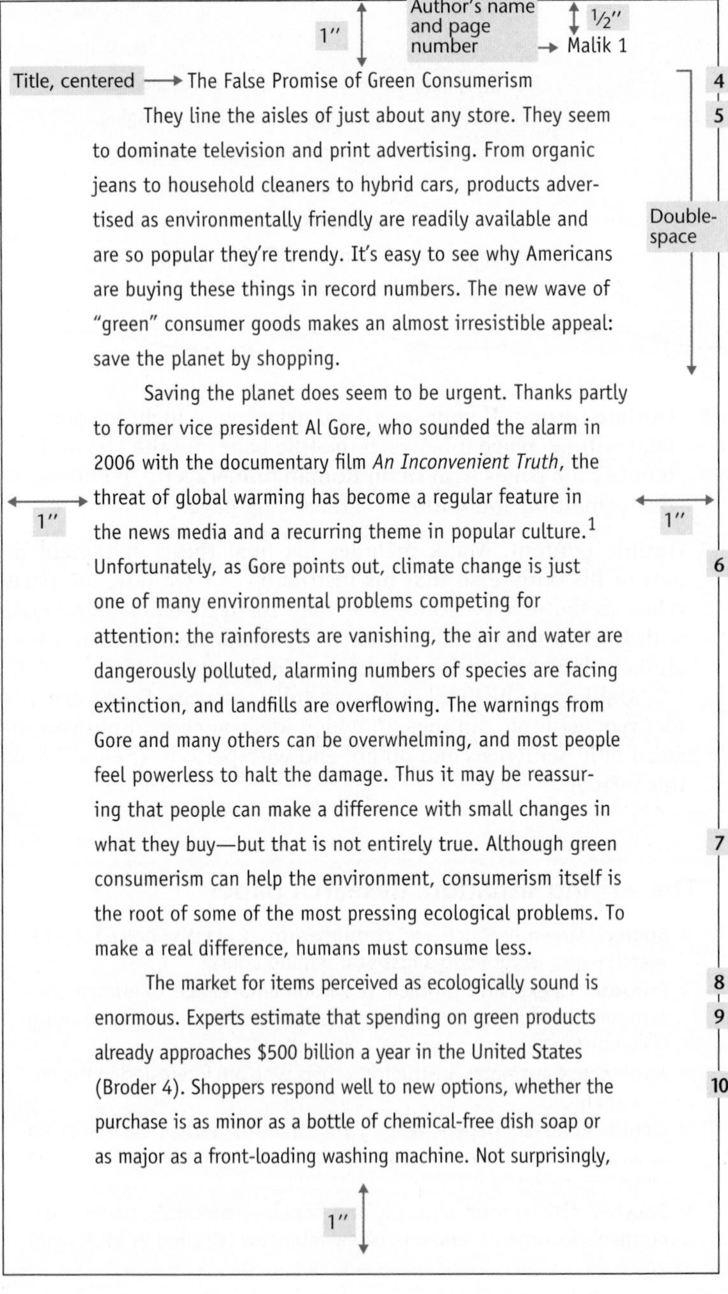

Malik 1

The False Promise of Green Consumerism 4

They line the aisles of just about any store. They seem 5
to dominate television and print advertising. From organic
jeans to household cleaners to hybrid cars, products advertised as environmentally friendly are readily available and
are so popular they're trendy. It's easy to see why Americans
are buying these things in record numbers. The new wave of
"green" consumer goods makes an almost irresistible appeal:
save the planet by shopping.

Saving the planet does seem to be urgent. Thanks partly
to former vice president Al Gore, who sounded the alarm in
2006 with the documentary film *An Inconvenient Truth*, the
threat of global warming has become a regular feature in
the news media and a recurring theme in popular culture.[1]
Unfortunately, as Gore points out, climate change is just 6
one of many environmental problems competing for
attention: the rainforests are vanishing, the air and water are
dangerously polluted, alarming numbers of species are facing
extinction, and landfills are overflowing. The warnings from
Gore and many others can be overwhelming, and most people
feel powerless to halt the damage. Thus it may be reassur-
ing that people can make a difference with small changes in
what they buy—but that is not entirely true. Although green 7
consumerism can help the environment, consumerism itself is
the root of some of the most pressing ecological problems. To
make a real difference, humans must consume less.

The market for items perceived as ecologically sound is 8
enormous. Experts estimate that spending on green products 9
already approaches $500 billion a year in the United States
(Broder 4). Shoppers respond well to new options, whether the 10
purchase is as minor as a bottle of chemical-free dish soap or
as major as a front-loading washing machine. Not surprisingly,

4 a **Title.** Malik's title clearly indicates the topic of his paper and previews his main idea. b **Paper format.** Because he provides a title page as requested by his instructor, Malik does not repeat his full name on the first page of the text. If Malik did not provide a title page, he would add the following to the upper left of this first page:

Justin Malik

Ms. Rossi

English 112-02

25 April 2014

(See Vanessa Haley's paper, p. 710, for an example of a research paper without a title page.) Follow the formatting annotations on the facing page for margins and spacing.

5 **Introduction.** Malik offers examples of the subject of his paper—green consumer products—and suggests a reason for their popularity. He delays presenting his thesis in order to establish some background about the severity of the environmental problems that the products address.

6 a **Omission of parenthetical citations.** Malik does not provide parenthetical citations for either mention of Gore's film *An Inconvenient Truth* because he names Gore in the text and the DVD has no reference numbers. b **Using an endnote for supplementary information.** Here Malik inserts a reference to a note at the end of the paper that gives examples of global warming as a recurring theme in popular culture (see p. 704). Malik signals the note with the raised numeral 1.

7 **Thesis statement.** Malik's introduction has led up to this statement, which asserts the claim that he will support in the paper. See page 626 for a note on thesis statements like Malik's that are expressed in two (or more) sentences.

8 **Relation to outline.** This paragraph begins part I of Malik's outline (see p. 684).

9 **Selecting supporting evidence.** Malik paraphrases and quotes two sources in this paragraph to support his point about the size of the market for green consumer products. The use of signal phrases and the placement of parenthetical citations clarify the sources of the information.

10 **Citation of a newspaper article in a database.**

Malik 2

companies are responding by offering as many new eco-products
as they can. The journalist Rebecca Harris reports in *Marketing*
Magazine that the recent "proliferation of green products" has
been a revolution for business. She cites a market research report 11
by TerraChoice: in the first decade of this century, the number of
new packaged goods labeled as green increased by approximately
75% each year, and now nearly five thousand consumer items
claim to be good for the environment. These products are offered 12
for sale at supermarkets and at stores like Walmart, Target, Home
Depot, Starbucks, and Pottery Barn. Clearly, green consumerism
has grown into a mainstream interest.

Determining whether or not a product is as green as
advertised can be a challenge. Claims vary: a product might be
labeled as organic, biodegradable, energy efficient, recycled,
carbon neutral, renewable, or just about anything that sounds
environmentally positive. However, none of these terms carries
a universally accepted meaning, and no enforceable labeling
regulations exist (Atkinson and Rosenthal 34-35). Some of the 13
new product options offer clear environmental benefits: for instance, LED lightbulbs last fifty times longer than regular bulbs
and draw about 15% of the electricity ("LED Lightbulbs" 25), 14
and paper made from recycled fibers saves many trees. But other 15
"green" products just as clearly do little or nothing to help the
environment: a disposable razor made with less plastic is still a
disposable razor, destined for a landfill after only a few uses.

Distinguishing truly green products from those that are 16
not so green merely scratches the surface of a much larger
issue. The products aren't the problem; it's humans' high rate
of consumption that poses the real threat to the environment. People seek what's newer and better—whether cars,
clothes, phones, computers, televisions, shoes, or gadgets—
and they all require resources to make, ship, and use them.

11 a **Mixing quotation and paraphrase.** In addition to quoting Harris, Malik paraphrases statistical information from the article that Harris had quoted in his original note. b **Citation of an article with no page numbers.** The database Malik used presented articles in HTML format and without page or other reference numbers. He already named the author (Harris) in the text, so he omits a parenthetical citation. c **Use of an indirect source.** Harris cited TerraChoice, and Malik uses the same information. TerraChoice is thus an indirect source. Such sources are appropriate only when the cited material is not available to consult. In this case, Malik could not find a copy of the original TerraChoice report, so use of the indirect source is appropriate.

12 **Common knowledge.** Malik already knew that major stores stock green products; in fact, he had purchased many of the products he names as examples throughout the paper. Thus he treats the information as common knowledge and does not cite a source. (See p. 617 for more on common knowledge.)

13 **Citation of a work with two authors.** Because Malik does not name the authors in the text, he gives both their last names in parentheses, separating them with and.

14 a **Anonymous source.** Malik cites a magazine article for which no author is named, so he uses the title for the citation. b **Citation of a paraphrase.** Because he does not give the title of the anonymous article in the text, Malik correctly gives the title in the citation. c **Placement of a parenthetical citation.** Malik used "LED Lightbulbs" only for the information on lightbulbs, so he places the parenthetical citation directly after the borrowed example.

15 **Common knowledge and personal experience.** Many sources mentioned the trees saved by recycled paper, so Malik treats the example as common knowledge and omits a source citation. Malik also omits a citation for the razor example, which came from his personal experience.

16 a **Relation to outline.** This paragraph begins part II of Malik's outline. See page 684. b **Transitional sentences.** The first two sentences of the paragraph shift the emphasis from green products (the previous section of the paper) to the environmental effects of consumption. c **Drawing conclusions.** Malik begins his discussion of the problem of consumption with his own conclusions about what he learned.

Malik 3

Political scientists Princen and his coauthors maintain that overconsumption is a leading force behind several ecological crises, warning that 17

> ever-increasing pressures on ecosystems, life-supporting environmental services, and critical natural cycles are driven not only by the sheer number of resource users . . . but also by the patterns of resource use themselves. (4)

Those patterns of resource use are disturbing. In just the last half century, gross world product (the global output of consumer goods) grew at five times the rate of population growth—a difference explained by a huge rise in consumption 18
per person. (See fig. 1.) Such growth might be good for the

19

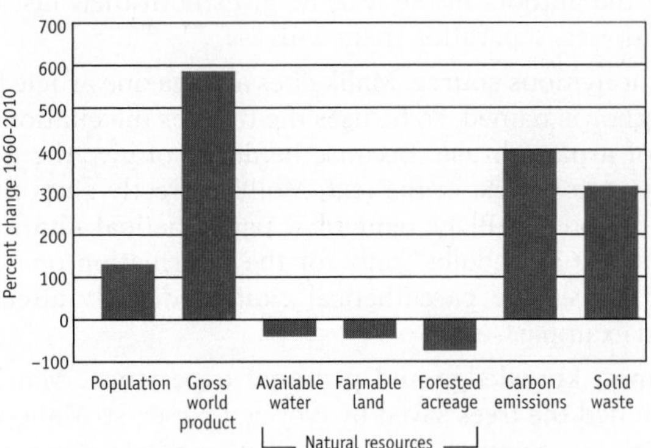

20

Fig. 1. Global population, consumption, and environmental impacts, 1960-2010. Data from United Nations Development Programme, *Human Development Report: Sustainability and Equity—A Better Future For All*, Palgrave, 2011, pp. 32, 37-38, 165; and from "Data Center," *Earth Policy Institute*, 16 Feb. 2014, www.earth-policy.org/?/data_center/C22/.

17 a **Citation of a work with more than two authors.** When a work has more than two authors and you are naming the authors in your text, you can give all their names or give just the first author's name followed by "and others" or "and his [*or* her] coauthors." When you are naming the authors in a parenthetical citation, use et al. (the Latin abbreviation for "and others") after the first author's name. See the DeGraaf citation on page 692. b **Format of a long quotation.** This quotation exceeds four typed lines, so Malik sets it off from his text without quotation marks, with double spacing throughout, and with an indention of one-half inch. c **Omission of an ellipsis mark.** Malik omits the first part of the quoted sentence, but he doesn't use an ellipsis mark because the small *e* in "ever" makes the omission clear. d **Use of an ellipsis mark.** Malik uses an ellipsis mark (three spaced periods) to show that he has omitted words from the quotation. e **Citation with a displayed quotation.** The parenthetical citation after the quotation falls *outside* the sentence period.

18 **Synthesis of sources.** Here and in the next several paragraphs, Malik integrates information from sources with his own conclusions about the significance of the data and ideas. Signal phrases and source citations clearly distinguish Malik's ideas from sources' information.

19 **Use of a figure.** Malik created a bar chart to show the relative increases in consumption and population and to illustrate the effects of both on the environment. He refers to the figure and elaborates on its meaning in the text.

20 a **Figure caption.** Malik captions the figure so that readers know how to interpret it. b **Citation of sources for data.** The caption includes complete information on the two sources for the data. If this were the only use of the sources, Malik would not have to repeat the information in his list of works cited. However, he cites both sources in his text as well, so his works-cited list includes entries for them.

Malik 4

economy, but it is bad for the environment. As fig. 1 shows,
it is accompanied by the depletion of natural resources, increases in the carbon emissions that cause global warming,
and increases in the amount of solid waste disposal.

The first negative effect of overconsumption, the depletion of resources, occurs because the manufacture and distribution of any consumer product depends on the use of water,
land, and raw materials such as wood, metal, and oil. Paul 21
Hawken, a respected environmentalist, explains that just in
the United States "[i]ndustry moves, mines, extracts, shovels,
burns, wastes, pumps, and disposes of *4 million pounds of*
material in order to provide one average . . . family's needs
for a year" (qtd. in DeGraaf et al. 78; emphasis added). The 22
United Nations Development Programme's 2011 *Human De-* 23
velopment Report warns that many regions in the world don't
have enough water, productive soil, or forests to meet the
basic needs of their populations (4-5). Additional data from
the Web site of the Earth Policy Institute confirm that as
manufacturing and per-person consumption continue to rise,
the resources needed for survival continue to decline ("Data 24
Center"). Thus heavy consumption poses a threat not only to
the environment but also to the well-being of the human race.

In addition to using up scarce natural resources, manufacturing and distributing products harm the earth by spewing
pollution into the water, soil, and air. The most worrisome
aspect of that pollution may be its link to climate change. Al
Gore explains the process as it is understood by most scien- 25
tists: the energy needed to power manufacturing and distribution comes primarily from burning fossil fuels, which releases
carbon dioxide and other greenhouse gases into the air; the
gases build up and trap heat in the earth's atmosphere; and
the rising average temperatures will raise sea levels, expand

21 a **Integrating source material.** Here and elsewhere, Malik establishes his source's credentials in a signal phrase and effectively integrates paraphrases and quotations into his own sentences. b **Editing a quotation with brackets.** By using brackets around the small *i,* Malik indicates that he changed the capitalization of the original source so that it would fit into his own sentence.

22 a **Citation of an indirect source.** With the use of `qtd. in`, Malik indicates correctly that he found the quotation by Hawken (an indirect source) in the book by DeGraaf et al. (a direct source). b **Indirect sources.** Indirect sources are appropriate only when the quoted material is not available to consult. Malik's source, DeGraaf et al., gave full bibliographic information for Hawken's book, and Malik should have gone directly to it. c **Adding emphasis to a quotation.** Malik italicizes important words in the quotation. He acknowledges this change in the parenthetical citation with `emphasis added`, separated from the page number by a semicolon. d **Punctuation with a parenthetical citation.** The period that ends a sentence containing a quotation comes after the citation.

23 a **Citation of a work with a corporate author.** The source Malik cites here does not name individual authors, so he lists the sponsoring organization as author. Naming the organization in the text avoids an awkwardly long parenthetical citation. b **Citation when the author is named in your text.** Because Malik names the United Nations Development Programme in his text, he does not repeat the name in the parenthetical citation that follows his paraphrase.

24 **Article cited by title.** The article cited here, "Data Center," is listed by its title in the works cited, so Malik gives the title in the text. The article comes from the Web site of Earth Policy Institute and lacks page or other identifying numbers.

25 a **Clarifying the boundaries of source material.** Much of this paragraph summarizes information from several places in Al Gore's film *An Inconvenient Truth,* surrounded by Malik's interpretation of its implications for his thesis. If Malik had had a parenthetical citation for Gore, he could have placed it at the end of the summary to show the extent of his borrowing from Gore. However, the movie DVD had no reference numbers to cite in parentheses, so Malik gives the summary in a single sentence and then, with "This view" on the next page, clearly indicates that the summary is finished.

Malik 5

deserts, and cause more frequent floods and hurricanes around the world. This view is reflected in the bar chart of fig. 1, which shows that carbon emissions, like the production of consumer goods in general, are rising at rates out of proportion with population growth. The more humans consume, the more they contribute to global warming. 26

As harmful as they are, gradual global warming and the depletion of resources can be difficult to comprehend or appreciate. A more immediate environmental effect of buying habits can be seen in the volumes of trash those habits create. A US government study found that in a single year (2012), US residents and organizations produced 251 million tons of municipal solid waste, equal to "4.38 pounds per person per day" ("Municipal Solid Waste Generation" 1). Nearly a third of that trash came just from the wrappers, cans, bottles, and boxes used for shipping consumer goods. (See fig. 2.) Yet 27

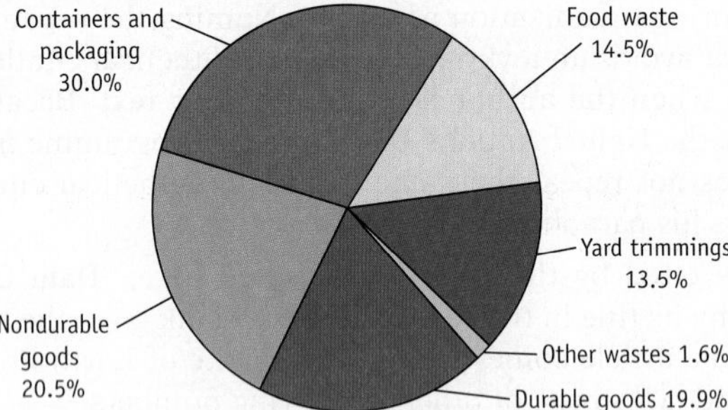

28

Fig. 2. Sources of municipal solid waste in the United States, 2012. Chart from "Municipal Solid Waste Generation, Recycling, and Disposal in the United States: Facts and Figures for 2012," *US Environmental Protection Agency*, Feb. 2014, www3.epa.gov/wastes/nonhaz/municipal/pubs/2012.pdf. 29

26 **Synthesis of sources.** Rather than leave it to his readers to interpret the information provided in his chart and the paragraphs surrounding it, Malik offers his own interpretation of what the information means in the context of his thesis.

27 **Revision of a draft.** In his first draft Malik sometimes strung his source information together without interpreting it. In revising he added comments of his own (in blue) to introduce the information in the context of his ideas:

> As harmful as they are, gradual global warming and the depletion of resources can be difficult to comprehend or appreciate. A more immediate environmental effect of buying habits can be seen in the volumes of trash those habits create. A US government study found that in a single year (2012), US residents and organizations produced 251 million tons of municipal solid waste, equal to "4.38 pounds per person per day" ("Municipal Solid Waste Generation" 1). Nearly a third of that trash came just from the wrappers, cans, bottles, and boxes used for shipping consumer goods. (See fig. 2.) Yet the mountains of trash left over from consumption are only a part of the problem. In industrial countries overall, 90% of waste comes not from what gets thrown out, but from the manufacturing processes of converting natural resources into consumer products (DeGraaf et al. 192). Nearly everything people buy creates waste in production, comes in packaging that gets discarded immediately, and ultimately ends up in landfills that are already overflowing.

28 **Use of a figure.** Malik uses a pie chart to show that containers and packaging account for the largest portion of solid waste produced in the United States. He refers to the figure in the preceding text.

29 a **Figure caption.** Malik captions the figure so that readers know how to interpret it. b **Citation of a source for a figure.** Malik provides a source note indicating where he obtained the figure. The note includes complete information for the source. If this were the only use of the source, Malik would not have to repeat the information in his list of works cited. However, he cites the source in his text as well, so his works-cited list includes an entry for it.

Malik 6

the mountains of trash left over from consumption are only
a part of the problem. In industrial countries overall, 90%
of waste comes not from what gets thrown out, but from the
manufacturing processes of converting natural resources into
consumer products (DeGraaf et al. 192). Nearly everything 30
people buy creates waste in production, comes in packaging
that gets discarded immediately, and ultimately ends up in
landfills that are already overflowing.

Unfortunately, the growing popularity of green products
has not reduced the environmental effects of consumption.
The journalist David Owen notes that as eco-friendly and 31
energy-efficient products have become more available, the
"reduced costs stimulate increased consumption" (80). The
author gives the example of home cooling: in the last fifty
years, air conditioners have become much more affordable and
energy efficient, but seven times more Americans now use them
on a regular basis, for a net gain in energy use. At the same
time, per-person waste production in the United States has
risen by nearly 20% ("Municipal Solid Waste Generation" 10). 32
Greener products may reduce our cost of consumption and even
reduce our guilt about consumption, but they do not reduce
consumption and its effects.

If buying green won't solve the problems caused by 33
overconsumption, what will? Politicians, environmentalists, 34
and economists have proposed an array of far-reaching ideas,
including creating a financial market for carbon credits and
offsets, aggressively taxing consumption and pollution, offering financial incentives for environmentally positive behaviors, and even abandoning market capitalism altogether (de
Blas).[2] However, all of these are "top-down" solutions that 35
require concerted government action. Gaining support for
any one of them, putting it into practice, and getting results

30 **Citation when the author is not named in your text.** Because Malik does not name DeGraaf et al. in his text, he provides the information in the parenthetical citation along with a page number.

31 a **Mixing quotation and paraphrase.** Malik quotes and paraphrases from Owen's article to give readers a good sense of the issue he raises. b **Editing a quotation.** Malik had the following long quotation by Owen, but he selected from it only the words that supported the point he was making.

Consumer behavior

Owen 80

"Efficiency improvements push down costs at every level—from the mining of raw materials to the fabrication and transportation of finished goods to the frequency and intensity of actual use—and reduced costs stimulate increased consumption. (Coincidentally or not, the growth of American refrigerator volume has been roughly paralleled by the growth of American body-mass index.) Efficiency-related increases in one category, furthermore, spill into others. Refrigerators are the fraternal twins of air conditioners, which use the same energy-hungry compressor technology to force heat to do something that nature doesn't want it to."

c **Punctuation with a quotation and citation.** The period falls after the citation, not inside the closing quotation mark.

32 **Drawing conclusions.** Malik ends his discussion of the environmental effects of consumption with his own conclusion about green products as a solution.

33 a **Relation to outline.** With this paragraph, Malik begins part III of his outline (see p. 684). b **Transitional question.** Malik uses a question to bridge the previous discussion and the next one.

34 a **Summary of sources.** Malik opted to summarize the more far-reaching solutions to overconsumption because he wanted to focus on individuals' actions. b **Using an endnote for citation of several sources.** Malik avoids a lengthy and obtrusive parenthetical citation by referring readers to endnote 2, which lists several sources that reinforce de Blas (see p. 706).

35 **Citation of an article without page numbers.** The de Blas article, which Malik found on the Web, has no page or other reference numbers, so the citation includes only the author's name.

Malik 7

could take decades. In the meantime, the environment would continue to deteriorate. Clearly, short-term solutions are also essential.

The most promising short-term solution is for individuals to change their own behavior as consumers. The greenest 36
behavior that individuals can adopt may be precycling, the term widely used for avoiding purchases of products that involve the use of raw materials. Precycling includes choosing eco-friendly products made of nontoxic or recycled materials (such as aluminum-free deodorants and fleece made from discarded soda bottles) and avoiding items wrapped in excessive packaging (such as kitchen tools strapped to cardboard and printer cartridges sealed in plastic clamshells). More important, though, precycling means not buying new things in the first place. Renting and borrowing, when possible, saves money and resources; so does keeping possessions in good repair and not replacing them until absolutely necessary. Good-quality used items, from clothing to furniture to electronics, can be obtained for free, or very cheaply, through online communities like *Craigslist* and *Freecycle*, from thrift stores and yard sales, or by trading with friends and relatives. When consumers choose used goods over new, they can help to reduce demand for manufactured products that waste energy and resources, and they can help to keep unwanted items out of the waste stream.

Avoiding unnecessary purchases brings personal benefits
as well. Brenda Lin explained in an e-mail interview that fru- 37
gal living not only saves money but also provides pleasure:

> You'd be amazed at what people throw out or give away: perfectly good computers, oriental rugs, barely used sports equipment, designer clothes, you name it. . . . It's a game for me to find what I need in other

36 **a** **Common knowledge.** In his reading Malik saw many references to the concept of precycling, so he treats the information in this paragraph as common knowledge and does not cite a source for it. (See p. 617 for more on common knowledge.) **b** **Defining terms.** Because readers might not be familiar with precycling, Malik defines the concept and expands on the definition with four examples. **c** **Omission of citations.** The precycling examples and suggestions in this paragraph are Malik's own and so do not require source citations.

37 **a** **Primary source: personal interview.** Malik tested his ideas by conducting an e-mail interview with the producer of a public-access television program about voluntary simplicity. He uses both a paraphrase and a quotation from the interview, with the subject's permission. **b** **Introducing borrowed material.** Malik paraphrases and quotes Lin as an expert, so he should have established her credentials. **c** **Editing a quotation with an ellipsis mark.** Malik uses an ellipsis mark (three spaced periods) and a period to show that he has omitted a full sentence from the quotation. **d** **Omission of a parenthetical citation.** Malik does not provide a parenthetical citation at the end of the quotation on the next page because the source (an interview) has no page or other reference numbers and the necessary information (Lin's name) appears in the text before the quotation. See page 690 for a long quotation with a parenthetical citation.

> people's trash or at Goodwill. You should see the shock on people's faces when I tell them where I got my stuff. I get almost as much enjoyment from that as from saving money and helping the environment at the same time.

Lin's experience relates to research on the personal and social consequences of consumerism by the sociologist Juliet
B. Schor. In one study, Schor found that the more people
buy, the less happy they tend to feel because of the stress
of working longer hours to afford their purchases (*Overspent* 38
11-12). Researching the opposite effect, Schor surveyed
thousands of Americans who had drastically reduced their
spending so that they would be less dependent on paid
work. For these people, she discovered, a deliberately lower
standard of living improved their quality of life by leaving
them more time to socialize, get involved with their communities, and pursue personal interests (*True Wealth* 126-27,
139). Reducing consumption, it turns out, does not have to
translate into sacrifice.

For unavoidable purchases like food and light bulbs,
buying green can make a difference by influencing corporate
decisions. Some ecologists and economists believe that as
more shoppers choose earth-friendly products over their
traditional counterparts—or boycott products that are
clearly harmful to the environment—more manufacturers and
retailers will look for ways to limit the environmental effects
of their industrial practices and the goods they sell (de Blas; 39
Gore). Indeed, as environmental business consultant Joel
Makower and his coauthors point out, Walmart, Coca-Cola,
Procter & Gamble, General Motors, and other major companies
have already taken up sustainability initiatives in response 40
to market pressure. In the process, the companies have

38 a **Citation of a work by an author of two or more works.** Malik draws on two books by Schor. To clarify which book he is citing, Malik gives a shortened version of the title in each of the parenthetical citations. b **Clarifying the boundaries of source material.** By mentioning Schor's name before he summarizes her findings and citing titles and page numbers for each summary, Malik indicates which ideas are Schor's and which are his own. c **Citation of an e-book in a database.** Malik found Schor's *True Wealth* in a database through his library's Web site. The database preserves the page numbers of the print edition, so Malik gives the appropriate numbers in his citation.

39 **Citation of more than one work.** Malik found the idea that consumer pressure can affect business behavior in two sources, so he cites both in parentheses, separating the citations with a semicolon. Both sources lacked page or other reference numbers, so neither citation includes a number.

40 **Defining terms.** *Sustainability initiatives* might be unfamiliar to readers, so Malik should have defined the term or avoided it. The term refers to actions taken to reduce resource use and pollution in order to preserve the environment.

Malik 9

discovered that environmentally minded practices tend
to raise profits and strengthen customer loyalty (8-11). 41
By giving industry solid, bottom-line reasons to embrace 42
ecological goals, consumer demand for earth-friendly products
can magnify the effects of individual action.

Careful shopping can help the environment, but green 43
doesn't necessarily mean "Go." All consumption depletes resources, increases the likelihood of global warming, and creates waste, so even eco-friendly products must be used in moderation. Individuals can play small roles in helping the environment—and help themselves at the same time—by not buying anything they don't really need, even if it seems environmentally sound. The sacrifice by each person in reducing his or her personal impact on the earth is a small price for preserving a livable planet for future generations.

41 **Citation when the author is named in the text.** Because Malik names Makower and coauthors in his text (previous page of the paper), he gives just the page number in the parenthetical citation.

42 **Drawing a conclusion.** Rather than leave it to readers to figure out the significance of the preceding paragraph, Malik offers his own conclusion.

43 **Conclusion.** In his final paragraph Malik summarizes the main points of his paper to remind readers of both the environmental problems caused by consumption and the benefits of consuming less.

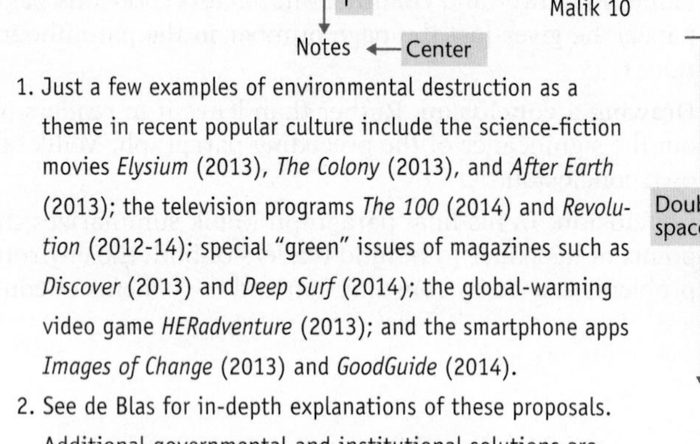

Malik 10

Notes

1. Just a few examples of environmental destruction as a theme in recent popular culture include the science-fiction movies *Elysium* (2013), *The Colony* (2013), and *After Earth* (2013); the television programs *The 100* (2014) and *Revolution* (2012-14); special "green" issues of magazines such as *Discover* (2013) and *Deep Surf* (2014); the global-warming video game *HERadventure* (2013); and the smartphone apps *Images of Change* (2013) and *GoodGuide* (2014).
2. See de Blas for in-depth explanations of these proposals. Additional governmental and institutional solutions are described in DeGraaf et al., in Gore, in Princen et al., and in United Nations Development Programme.

44 **Format of notes.** The heading Notes is centered one inch from the top of the page. (The heading would be singular—Note—if Malik had only one note.) Follow the annotations on the facing page for formatting.

45 **Endnotes for additional relevant information.** Malik uses endnotes for information and sources that are somewhat relevant to his thesis but not essential and that don't fit easily into the text. Note 1 provides several examples to support his comment that global warming has become a recurring theme in popular culture. Note 2 directs readers to a source for more information and cites several additional sources that would be obtrusive in a parenthetical citation. (See pp. 643–44 for more on supplementary notes.)

MLA 48

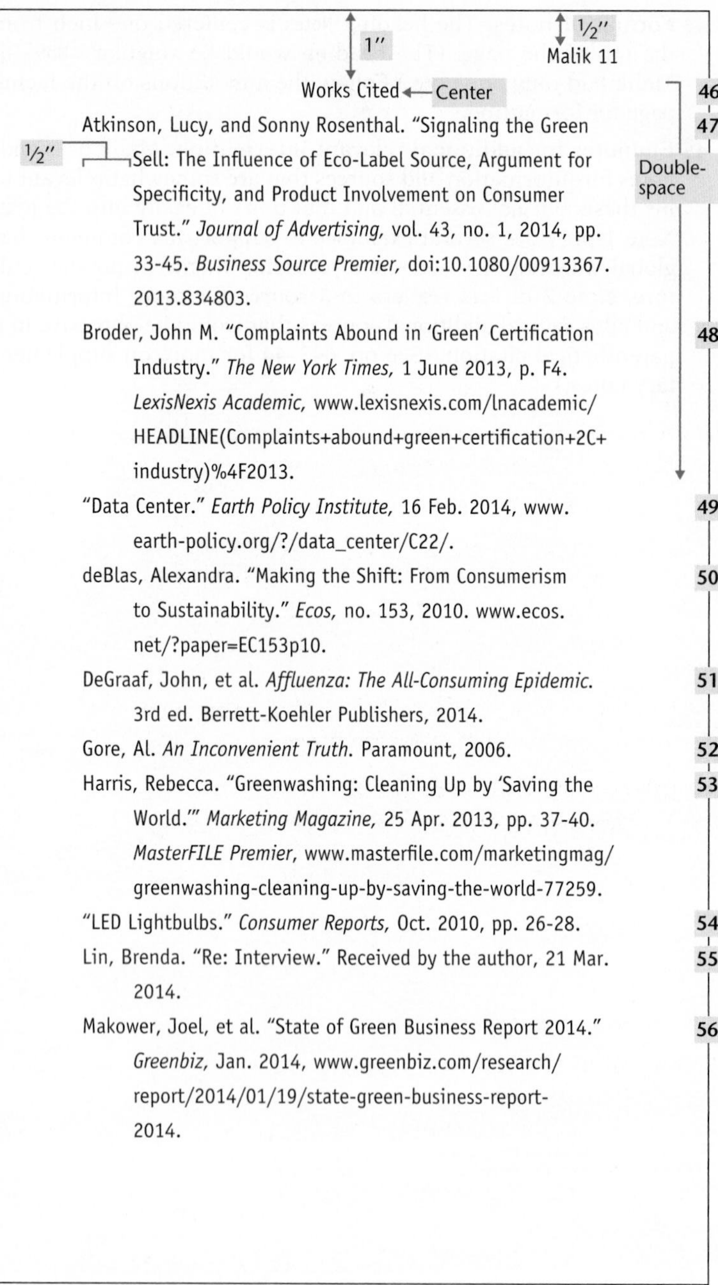

Malik 11

Works Cited 46

Atkinson, Lucy, and Sonny Rosenthal. "Signaling the Green Sell: The Influence of Eco-Label Source, Argument for Specificity, and Product Involvement on Consumer Trust." *Journal of Advertising,* vol. 43, no. 1, 2014, pp. 33-45. *Business Source Premier,* doi:10.1080/00913367.2013.834803. 47

Broder, John M. "Complaints Abound in 'Green' Certification Industry." *The New York Times,* 1 June 2013, p. F4. *LexisNexis Academic,* www.lexisnexis.com/lnacademic/HEADLINE(Complaints+abound+green+certification+2C+industry)%4F2013. 48

"Data Center." *Earth Policy Institute,* 16 Feb. 2014, www.earth-policy.org/?/data_center/C22/. 49

deBlas, Alexandra. "Making the Shift: From Consumerism to Sustainability." *Ecos,* no. 153, 2010. www.ecos.net/?paper=EC153p10. 50

DeGraaf, John, et al. *Affluenza: The All-Consuming Epidemic.* 3rd ed. Berrett-Koehler Publishers, 2014. 51

Gore, Al. *An Inconvenient Truth.* Paramount, 2006. 52

Harris, Rebecca. "Greenwashing: Cleaning Up by 'Saving the World.'" *Marketing Magazine,* 25 Apr. 2013, pp. 37-40. *MasterFILE Premier,* www.masterfile.com/marketingmag/greenwashing-cleaning-up-by-saving-the-world-77259. 53

"LED Lightbulbs." *Consumer Reports,* Oct. 2010, pp. 26-28. 54

Lin, Brenda. "Re: Interview." Received by the author, 21 Mar. 2014. 55

Makower, Joel, et al. "State of Green Business Report 2014." *Greenbiz,* Jan. 2014, www.greenbiz.com/research/report/2014/01/19/state-green-business-report-2014. 56

46 **Format of a list of works cited.** The heading Works Cited is centered at the top of the page. The entries are alphabetized by the last name of the first author or (for sources without authors) by the first main word of the title.

47 a **Source with two authors.** Malik reverses the first author's name and, after and, gives the second author's name in normal order. b **Article in a scholarly journal consulted in a database.** Here and in all other entries for database sources, Malik provides print publication information followed by the database title and either a DOI (as here) or a URL. c **Scholarly journal that numbers volumes and issues.** The volume and issue numbers for this source are given as vol. 43, no. 1.

48 **Newspaper article in a database.**

49 **Source with a corporate author.** Earth Policy Institute has three roles with this source: it is the corporate author, the title of its Web site, and the publisher of the site. MLA style recommends omitting a corporate author when it and the publisher are the same and omitting the publisher when it and its site title are the same. Thus Malik lists and alphabetizes this source by its title ("Data Center") and names Earth Policy Institute only in the site title. See the entry for United Nations Development Programme (next page) for a different treatment of a corporate author.

50 a **Article in a scholarly journal on the Web.** b **Scholarly journal that uses only issue numbers.** The issue number for this source is given as no. 153. c **Article with no page numbers.** Malik does not give page numbers because the article is unpaginated.

51 a **Source with more than two authors.** Malik reverses the first name and uses et al. ("and others") in place of the other authors' names. (See p. 651.) b **Third edition of a book.** The notation 3rd ed. follows the title.

52 **Film on DVD.** Malik cites Gore's documentary movie, giving the distributor and the release date.

53 **Magazine article in a database.**

54 a **Source with no listed author.** Malik lists and alphabetizes the source by its title. b **Article in a print monthly magazine.**

55 **Personal interview by e-mail.**

56 **Source with more than two authors.**

Malik 12

"Municipal Solid Waste Generation, Recycling, and Disposal in 57
the United States: Facts and Figures for 2012." *US Environmental Protection Agency,* Feb. 2014, www3.epa.gov/wastes/nonhaz/municipal/pubs/2012_msw_dat_tbls.pdf.

Owen, David. "The Efficiency Dilemma." *The New Yorker,* 20 58
Dec. 2010, pp. 78-85. *Points of View Reference Center,* www.ebscohost.com/points-of-view/article=AN159870231.

Princen, Thomas, et al. Introduction. *Confronting Consump-* 59
tion, edited by Princen et al., MIT P, 2002, pp. 1-20.

Schor, Juliet B. *The Overspent American: Upscaling, Downshift-* 60
ing, and the New Consumer. Basic Books, 1998.

---. *True Wealth: How and Why Millions of Americans Are Creat-* 61
ing a Time-Rich, Ecologically Light, Small-Scale, High-Satisfaction Economy. Penguin, 2011. *Ebrary,* site.ebrary.com/lib/reader.action?docID=10493613.

United Nations Development Programme. *Human Development* 62
Report: Sustainability and Equity—A Better Future for All. Palgrave, 2011.

57 **US government source on the Web.** As with "Data Center" (annotation 49), in this source the corporate author and publisher are the same, so Malik lists the source by its title. See the entry for United Nations Development Programme (next page) for a different treatment of a corporate author.

58 **Article in a weekly magazine in a database.** The database preserves the page numbers of the print magazine, so Malik gives them.

59 **a** **Selection from an anthology.** **b** **Introduction to a book.** This source is the untitled introduction to an anthology, so Malik inserts Introduction in place of a title. Since the book is also edited by the three authors, he gives only Princen's last name and et al. after edited by.

60 **Book with one author.**

61 **a** **Additional source by the same author.** Since the author of the previous entry is also Juliet B. Schor, in this entry Malik replaces the name with three hyphens followed by a period. **b** **E-book in a database.** Malik read Schor's book in a database, *Ebrary,* so he gives not only print publication information but also the database name and the URL.

62 **Book with a corporate author.** The source does not list an individual as author, so Malik names the organization as author. In contrast to "Data Center" (annotation 49) and "Municipal Solid Waste Generation" (annotation 57), in this source the author and publisher are different, so Malik names them both.

Haley 1

Format of heading and title when no title page is required (see also p. 680)

Vanessa Haley

Professor Moisan

English 101

6 February 2014

Annie Dillard's Healing Vision

Introduction of environmental theme

It is almost a commonplace these days that human arrogance is destroying the environment. Environmentalists, naturalists, and now the man or woman on the street seem to agree: the long-held belief that human beings are separate from nature, destined to rise above its laws and conquer it, has been ruinous.

Focus on issue to be resolved

Unfortunately, the defenders of nature tend to respond to this ruinous belief with harmful myths of their own: nature is pure and harmonious; humanity is corrupt and dangerous. Much writing about nature lacks a recognition that human beings and their civilization are as much a part of nature as trees and whales are, neither better nor worse. Yet without such a recognition, how can humans overcome the damaging sense of separation between themselves and the earth? How can humans develop realistic solutions to environmental problems that will work for humanity *and* the rest of nature?

The writing situation: Literary research paper

- **Subject:** The relationship of humans to nature in Annie Dillard's *Pilgrim at Tinker Creek*; student's choice for a research paper assigned in a literature course
- **Purpose:** To argue for an interpretation of a literary nonfiction book
- **Audience:** Classmates and instructor
- **Genre:** Literary research paper—writing that argues for interpretation of a literary work in the context of others' interpretations and/or information (see p. 137)
- **Sources:** Literary nonfiction work, scholarly articles and book, reviews (all cited in MLA style)

One nature writer who seems to recognize the naturalness of humanity is Annie Dillard. In her best-known work, *Pilgrim at Tinker Creek,* she is a solitary person encountering the natural world, and some critics fault her for turning her back on society. But in those encounters with nature, Dillard probes a spiritual as well as a physical identity between human beings and nature that could help to heal the rift between them.

Introduction of Dillard to resolve issue

Thesis statement

Dillard is not renowned for her sense of involvement with human society. Like Henry David Thoreau, with whom she is often compared, she retreats from rather than confronts human society. The critic Gary McIlroy points out that although Thoreau discusses society a great deal in *Walden*, he makes no attempt "to find a middle ground between it and his experiment in the woods" (113). Dillard has been similarly criticized. For instance, the writer Eudora Welty comments that

Acknowledgment of opposing critical view

> Annie Dillard is the only person in her book, substantially the only one in her world; I recall no outside human speech coming to break the long soliloquy of the author. Speaking of the universe very often, she is yet self-surrounded and, beyond that, book-surrounded. Her own book might have taken in more of human life without losing a bit of the wonder she was after. (37)

It is true, as Welty says, that in *Pilgrim* Dillard seems detached from human society. However, she actually was always close to it at Tinker Creek. In a later book, *Teaching a Stone to Talk*, she says of the neighborhood, "This is, mind you, suburbia. It is a five-minute walk in three directions to rows of houses. . . . There's a 55 mph highway at one end of the pond, and a nesting pair of wood ducks at the other" (qtd. in Suh).

First response to opposing view

Rather than hiding from humanity, Dillard seems to be trying to understand it through nature. In *Pilgrim* she recalls

Second response to opposing view

once seeing through a microscope "red blood cells whip, one by one, through the capillaries" of a goldfish (124). Now watching her own goldfish, Ellery Channing, she sees the blood in his body as a bond between fish and human being: "Those red blood cells are coursing in Ellery's tail now, too, in just that way, and through his mouth and eyes as well, and through mine" (125). Gary McIlroy observes that this blood, "a symbol of the sanctity of life, is a common bond between Dillard and the fish, between animal and human life in general, and between Dillard and other people" (115).

Secondary source's analysis of Dillard

For Dillard, the terror and unpredictability of death unify all life. The most sinister image in *Pilgrim*—one that haunts Dillard—is that of the frog and the water bug. Dillard reports walking along an embankment scaring frogs into the water when one frog refused to budge. As Dillard leaned over to investigate, the frog "slowly crumpled and began to sag. The spirit vanished from his eyes as if snuffed. His skin emptied and dropped; his very skull seemed to collapse and settle like a kicked tent" (6). The frog was the victim of a water bug that injects poisons to "dissolve the victim's muscles and bones and organs" (6). Such events lead Dillard to wonder about a creator who would make all life "power and beauty, grace tangled in a rapture with violence" (8). Human beings no less than frogs and water bugs are implicated in this tangle.

Combination of quotation and Haley's own analysis (next four paragraphs) interprets and synthesizes Dillard's ideas

Mixture of summary and quotation provides context and keeps quotations trim

Discussion of physical identity of all creatures: death and birth

Dillard is equally as disturbed by birth as by death. In a chapter of *Pilgrim* called "Fecundity," she focuses unsentimentally on the undeniable reproductive urge of entire species:

> I don't know what it is about fecundity that so appalls. I suppose it is the teeming evidence that birth and growth, which we value, are ubiquitous and blind, that life itself is so astonishingly cheap, that nature is as careless as it is bountiful, and that with extravagance

Comment on quotation advises reader what to look for

Quotations, including some long ones set off from the text, convey Dillard's voice as well as her ideas

Haley 4

> goes a crushing waste that will one day include our own cheap lives. (160)

The cheapness and brutality of life are problems Dillard wrestles with, wondering which is "amiss": the world, a "monster," or human beings, with their "excessive emotions" (177-78). No matter how hard she tries to leave human society, Dillard has no choice but to "bring human values to the creek" (179). The violent, seemingly pointless birth and death of all life are, spiritually,

Discussion of spiritual identity of all creatures

> two branches of the same creek, the creek that waters the world. . . . We could have planned things more mercifully, perhaps, but our plan would never get off the drawing board until we agreed to the very compromising terms that are the only ones that being offers. (180)

For Dillard, accepting the monstrousness as well as the beauty of "being" is the price all living things pay for freedom.

Haley's interpretation of Dillard's ideas

In "The Waters of Separation," the final chapter of *Pilgrim*, Dillard writes about a winged maple key, or seed. At this point in the book, the critic Sandra Humble Johnson notes, Dillard "has been humbled and emptied; she can no longer apply effort to her search for meaning in a parasitic world" (4). And then Dillard spies the maple key descending to earth and germination. "It rose, just before it would have touched a thistle, and hovered pirouetting in one spot, then twirled on and finally came to rest" (267). The key moved, says Dillard, "like a creature muscled and vigorous, or a creature spread thin to that other wind, the wind of the spirit . . . , a generous, unending breath" (268). Dillard vows to see the maple key in all of the earth and in herself. "If I am a maple key falling, at least I can twirl" (268).

Resolution of Dillard's concerns

Conclusion: ties together divergent critical views, environmental theme, and Dillard's work

According to the critic John Becker, "Annie Dillard does not walk out on ordinary life in order to bear witness against it"; instead, she uses the distance from other people "to make meaning out of the grotesque disjointedness of man and nature" (408). Gary McIlroy says, nonetheless, that Dillard "does not succeed in encompassing within her vision any but the most fragmentary consequences for society at large" (116). Possibly both are correct. In *Pilgrim at Tinker Creek*, Annie Dillard suggests a vision of identity among all living things that could inform humanity's efforts to thrive in harmony with its environment, but she does not make the leap to practicalities. She says, "We must somehow take a wider view [of life], look at the whole landscape, really see it, and describe what's going on here" (9). The description, and acting on it, may take generations. As we proceed, however, we may be guided by Dillard's efforts to mend the disjointedness, to see that human beings and maple keys alike twirl equally.

Haley 6

Works Cited

Becker, John E. "Science and the Sacred: From Walden to Tinker Creek." *Thought: A Review of Culture and Ideas*, vol. 62, 1987, pp. 400-13.

Dillard, Annie. *Pilgrim at Tinker Creek*. Harper's Magazine Press, 1974.

Johnson, Sandra Humble. *The Space Between: Literary Epiphany in the Work of Annie Dillard*. Kent State UP, 1992.

McIlroy, Gary. "*Pilgrim at Tinker Creek* and the Social Legacy of *Walden*." *South Atlantic Quarterly*, vol. 85, no. 2, 1996, pp. 111-16.

Suh, Grace. "Ideas Are Tough, Irony Is Easy." *Yale Herald*, 4 Oct. 1996, www.yaleherald.com/archive/xxii/10.4.96/ae/dillard.html.

Welty, Eudora. "Meditation on Seeing." *New York Times Book Review*, 24 Mar. 1974, pp. 36-37. *ProQuest Historical Newspapers*, www.proquestnews/99/03/28/dillard-tinker/24031974+36-37.

PART 10

Writing in the Academic Disciplines

49 Reading and Writing about Literature

By Sylvan Barnet

Chapter essentials

- Use the methods and evidence common in literary analysis (below).
- Understand your writing assignment (p. 726).
- Use the tools and language of literary analysis (p. 727).
- Use MLA style for citing sources and formatting papers (p. 728).
- Develop a thesis, gather evidence, and draft, revise, and edit your work (p. 728).
- Consider the distinctive approaches to writing about fiction, poetry, and drama (p. 733).

Visit MyWritingLab™ for more resources on reading and writing about literature.

Why read literature? Let's approach this question indirectly by asking why people *write* literature. A thousand years ago a Japanese writer, Lady Murasaki, offered an answer. Here is one of her characters talking about what motivates a writer:

> Again and again something in one's own life or in the life around one will seem so important that one cannot bear to let it pass into oblivion. There must never come a time, the writer feels, when people do not know about this.

When we read certain works—Murasaki's *The Tale of Genji* is one of them—we share this feeling; we are caught up in the writer's world, whether it is the Denmark of Shakespeare's *Hamlet* or the America of Toni Morrison's *Beloved.* We read literature because it gives us an experience that seems important, usually an experience that is both new and familiar. A common way of putting this is to say that reading broadens us and helps us understand our own experience.

49a Using the methods and evidence of literary analysis

When we read nonliterary writings, it may be enough to get the gist of the argument; in fact, we may have to work through many words to find the heart of the matter—say, three claims on behalf of capital punishment. But when we read a story, a poem, or a play, we must pay extremely close attention to what might be called the feel of the words. For instance, the word *woods* in Robert Frost's "Stopping by Woods on a Snowy Evening" has a rural, folksy quality that *forest* doesn't have, and many such small distinctions contribute to the poem's effect.

Literary authors are concerned with presenting human experience concretely, with *showing* rather than *telling.* Consider the following proverb and an unmemorable paraphrase of it.

A rolling stone gathers no moss.

If a rock is always moving around, vegetation won't have a chance to grow on it.

The familiar original offers a small but complete world: hard (stone) and soft (moss), inorganic and organic, at rest and in motion. The original is also shapely: each noun (*stone, moss*) has one syllable, and each word of motion (*rolling, gathers*) has two syllables, with the accent on the first of the two. Such relationships unify the proverb into a pleasing whole that stays in our minds.

1 Reading a work of literature

Reading literature critically involves interacting with a text. The techniques complement those for critically reading any text, so if you haven't read Chapter 7 on such reading, you should do so. Responding critically is a matter not of making negative judgments but of analyzing the parts, interpreting their meanings, seeing how the parts relate, and evaluating significance or quality.

CULTURE LANGUAGE All readers benefit from hearing literature—particularly poetry—read out loud, but the experience can be especially helpful if standard English is not your first language or dialect. Listening reveals the pronunciation, tone, and rhythm of the words and can illuminate structure and themes. The Academy of American Poets, at *poets.org*, offers hundreds of poems read by their authors and by others.

Previewing and responding

You can preview a literary text somewhat as you can preview any other text. You may gauge the length of the text to determine whether you can read it in one sitting, and you may read a biographical note to learn about the author. In a literary text, however, you won't find aids such as section headings or summaries that can make previewing other texts especially informative. You have to dive into the words themselves.

Do write while reading. If you own the book you are reading, don't hesitate to underline or highlight passages that especially interest you for one reason or another. Don't hesitate to annotate the margins, indicating your pleasures, displeasures, and uncertainties with remarks such as *Nice detail* or *Do we need this long description?* or *Not believable.* If you don't own the book, make these notes on separate sheets or on your computer.

An effective way to interact with a text is to keep a **reading journal.** A journal is not a diary in which you record your doings; instead, it is a place to develop and store your reflections on what you read, such as an answer to a question you may have posed in the margin of the text. You could make an entry in the form of a letter to the author or from one character to another. In many literature courses, students collaborate to develop their understanding of a literary work. In such a case, you may want to use your journal to reflect on what other students have said—for instance, why your opinion differs so much from someone else's.

You can keep a reading journal in a notebook or on your computer. Some readers prefer a two-column format like that illustrated on page 154, with summaries, paraphrases, and quotations from the text on the left and with their own responses to these passages on the right. Or you may prefer a less structured format like that illustrated on pages 722–23.

Reading a sample story

49a

Here is a very short story by Kate Chopin (1851–1904). (The last name is pronounced in the French way, something like "show pan.") Following the story are a student's annotations and journal entry on the story.

Kate Chopin

The Story of an Hour

Knowing that Mrs. Mallard was afflicted with a heart trouble, great care was taken to break to her as gently as possible the news of her husband's death.

It was her sister Josephine who told her, in broken sentences, veiled hints that revealed in half concealing. Her husband's friend Richards was there, too, near her. It was he who had been in the newspaper office when intelligence of the railroad disaster was received, with Brently Mallard's name leading the list of "killed." He had only taken the time to assure himself of its truth by a second telegram, and had hastened to forestall any less careful, less tender friend in bearing the sad message.

She did not hear the story as many women have heard the same, with a paralyzed inability to accept its significance. She wept at once with sudden, wild abandonment, in her sister's arms. When the storm of grief had spent itself she went away to her room alone. She would have no one follow her.

There stood, facing the open window, a comfortable, roomy armchair. Into this she sank, pressed down by a physical exhaustion that haunted her body and seemed to reach into her soul.

She could see in the open square before her house the tops of trees that were all aquiver with the new spring life. The delicious breath of rain was in the air. In the street below a peddler was crying his wares. The notes of a distant song which some one was singing reached her faintly, and countless sparrows were twittering in the eaves.

There were patches of blue sky showing here and there through the clouds that had met and piled one above the other in the west facing her window.

She sat with her head thrown back upon the cushion of the chair quite motionless, except when a sob came up into her throat and shook her, as a child who has cried itself to sleep continues to sob in its dreams.

She was young, with a fair, calm face, whose lines bespoke repression and even a certain strength. But now there was a dull stare in her eyes, whose gaze was fixed away off yonder on one of those patches of blue sky. It was not a glance of reflection, but rather indicated a suspension of intelligent thought.

There was something coming to her and she was waiting for it, fearfully. What was it? She did not know; it was too subtle and elusive to name. But she felt it creeping out of the sky, reaching toward her through the sounds, the scents, the color that filled the air.

Now her bosom rose and fell tumultuously. She was beginning to recognize this thing that was approaching to possess her, and she was striving to beat it back with her will—as powerless as her two white slender hands would have been.

When she abandoned herself a little whispered word escaped her slightly parted lips. She said it over and over under her breath: "Free, free, free!" The vacant stare and the look of terror that had followed it went from her eyes. They stayed keen and bright. Her pulses beat fast, and the coursing blood warmed and relaxed every inch of her body.

She did not stop to ask if it were not a monstrous joy that held her. A clear and exalted perception enabled her to dismiss the suggestion as trivial.

She knew that she would weep again when she saw the kind, tender hands folded in death; the face that had never looked save with love upon her, fixed and gray and dead. But she saw beyond that bitter moment a long procession of years to come that would belong to her absolutely. And she opened and spread her arms out to them in welcome.

There would be no one to live for her during those coming years; she would live for herself. There would be no powerful will bending her in the blind persistence with which men and women believe they have a right to impose a private will upon a fellow creature. A kind intention or a cruel intention made the act seem no less a crime as she looked upon it in that brief moment of illumination.

And yet she had loved him—sometimes. Often she had not. What did it matter! What could love, the unsolved mystery, count for in face of this possession of self-assertion which she suddenly recognized as the strongest impulse of her being.

"Free! Body and soul free!" she kept whispering.

Josephine was kneeling before the closed door with her lips to the keyhole, imploring for admission. "Louise, open the door! I beg; open the door—you will make yourself ill. What are you doing, Louise? For heaven's sake open the door."

"Go away. I am not making myself ill." No; she was drinking in the very elixir of life through that open window.

Her fancy was running riot along those days ahead of her. Spring days, and summer days, and all sorts of days that would be her own. She breathed a quick prayer that life might be long. It was only yesterday she had thought with a shudder that life might be long.

She arose at length and opened the door to her sister's importunities. There was a feverish triumph in her eyes, and she carried herself unwittingly like a goddess of Victory. She clasped her sister's waist and together they descended the stairs. Richards stood waiting for them at the bottom.

Some one was opening the front door with a latchkey. It was Brently Mallard who entered, a little travel-stained, composedly carrying his gripsack and umbrella. He had been far from the scene of accident, and did not even know there had been one. He stood amazed at Josephine's piercing cry; at Richards' quick motion to screen him from the view of his wife.

But Richards was too late.

When the doctors came they said she had died of heart disease—of joy that kills.

Following a student's work

In this chapter we'll follow the analysis and writing of a student, Janet Vong, to see one approach to Chopin's story. Vong first annotated the story while reading it. The opening five paragraphs, with her notes, appear below:

Knowing that Mrs. Mallard was afflicted with a heart trouble, great care was taken to break to her as gently as possible the news of her husband's death. *"heart disease" at end of story*

It was her sister Josephine who told her, in broken sentences, veiled hints that revealed in half concealing. Her husband's friend Richards was there, too, near her. It was he who had been in the newspaper office when intelligence of the railroad disaster was received, with Brently Mallard's name leading the list of "killed." He had only taken the time to assure himself of its truth by a second telegram, and had hastened to forestall any less careful, less tender friend in bearing the sad message. *Too hasty, it turns out*

Would men have heard differently? Is au. sexist? She did not hear the story as many women have heard the same, with a paralyzed inability to accept its significance. She wept at once with sudden, wild abandonment, in her sister's arms. When the storm of grief had spent itself she went away to her room alone. She would have no one follow her. *old-fashioned style*

There stood, facing the open window, a comfortable, roomy armchair. Into this she sank, pressed down by a physical exhaustion that haunted her body and seemed to reach into her soul.

She could see in the open square before her house the tops of trees that were all aquiver with the new spring life. The delicious breath of rain was in the air. In the street below a peddler was crying his wares. The notes of a distant song which some one was singing reached her faintly, and countless sparrows were twittering in the eaves. *Notices spring: odd in a story of death*

Writing in her journal, Vong then posed questions about Chopin's story—critical points, curiosities about characters, possible implications:

Title nothing special. What might be a better title?

Could a woman who loved her husband be so heartless? *Is* she heartless? *Did* she love him?

What are (were) Louise's feelings about her husband?

Did she want too much? *What* did she want?

Could this story happen today? Feminist interpretation?
Sister (Josephine)—a busybody?
Tricky ending—but maybe it could be true.
"And yet she had loved him—sometimes. Often she had not." Why does one love someone "sometimes"?
Irony: plot has reversal. Are characters ironic too?

Vong's journal entry illustrates brainstorming—the discovery technique of listing ideas (or questions) however they occur, without editing (see pp. 23–24). Another productive journal technique is focused freewriting—concentrating on a single issue (such as one of Vong's questions) and writing nonstop for a set amount of time, again without editing (p. 23).

2 Analyzing a work of literature

Like any discipline, the study of literature involves particular frameworks of analysis—particular ways of seeing literary works that help determine what elements are identified and how they are interpreted. Literary frameworks include historical or cultural criticism, which considers the effect of the author's context on a work; feminist or gender criticism, which focuses on the representation of gender in a work; and reader-response criticism, which stresses the effect of a work on its readers.

This chapter emphasizes so-called formalist criticism, which focuses on a literary work primarily as something to be understood in itself. This critical framework engages the reader immediately in the work of literature, without requiring extensive historical or cultural background, and it introduces the conventional elements of literature that all critical approaches discuss, even though they view the elements differently. The box on the next two pages lists these elements—plot, characters, setting, and so on—and offers questions about each one that can help you think constructively and imaginatively about what you read.

One significant attribute of a literary work is its meaning or themes, or what we can interpret to be its themes. Readers may well disagree over the persuasiveness of someone's argument, but they will rarely disagree over its meaning. With literature, however, disagreements over themes occur all the time because (as we have seen) literature *shows* rather than *tells*: it gives us concrete images of imagined human experiences, but it usually does not say how we ought to understand the images.

Further, readers bring to their reading not only different critical views, as noted earlier, but also different personal experiences. A woman who has recently lost her husband may interpret "The Story of an Hour" differently from most other readers. Or a story that bores a reader at age fifteen may deeply move him at twenty-five. The words on the page remain the same, but their meaning changes.

(continued on p. 726)

Questions for a literary analysis

See later boxes for specific questions on fiction (p. 734), poetry (p. 735), and drama (p. 738).

Plot

The relationships and patterns of events. Even a poem has a plot, such as a change in mood from bitterness to resignation.

What actions happen?

What conflicts occur?

How do the events connect to each other and to the whole?

Characters

The people the author creates, including the narrator of a story or the speaker of a poem.

Who are the principal people in the work?

How do they interact?

What do their actions, words, and thoughts reveal about their personalities and the personalities of others?

Do the characters stay the same, or do they change? Why?

Point of view

The perspective or attitude of the speaker in a poem or the voice who tells a story. The point of view may be **first person** (a participant, using *I*) or **third person** (an outsider, using *he, she, it, they*). A first-person narrator may be a major or a minor character in the narrative and may be **reliable** or **unreliable** (unable to report events wholly or accurately). A third-person narrator may be **omniscient** (knows what goes on in all characters' minds), **limited** (knows what goes on in the mind of only one or two characters), or **objective** (knows only what is external to the characters).

Who is the narrator (or the speaker of a poem)?

How does the narrator's point of view affect the narrative?

Tone

The narrator's or speaker's attitude, perceived through the words (for instance, joyful, bitter, or confident).

What tone (or tones) do you hear? If there is a change, how do you account for it?

Is there an ironic contrast between the narrator's tone (for instance, confidence) and what you take to be the author's attitude (for instance, pity for human overconfidence)?

Imagery

Word pictures or details involving the senses: sight, sound, touch, smell, taste.

What images does the writer use? What senses do they draw on?

What patterns are evident in the images (for instance, religious or commercial images)?

What is the significance of the imagery?

Symbolism

Concrete things standing for larger and more abstract ideas. For instance, the American flag may symbolize freedom, a tweeting bird may symbolize happiness, a dead flower may symbolize mortality.

What symbols does the author use? What do they seem to signify?

How does the symbolism relate to the other elements of the work, such as character or theme?

Setting

The place where the action happens.

What does the locale contribute to the work?

Are scene shifts significant?

Form

The shape or structure of the work.

What *is* the form? (For example, a story might divide sharply in the middle, moving from happiness to sorrow.)

What parts of the work does the form emphasize, and why?

Themes

The main ideas—conceptions of human experience suggested by the work as a whole. A theme is neither a plot (what happens) nor a subject (such as mourning or marriage). Rather it is what the author says with that plot about that subject.

Can you state each theme in a sentence? Avoid mentioning specific characters or actions; instead, write an observation applicable to humanity in general. For instance, you might state the following about Kate Chopin's "The Story of an Hour": *Happiness depends partly on freedom.*

Do certain words, passages of dialog or description, or situations seem to represent a theme most clearly?

How do the work's elements combine to develop each theme?

Appeal

The degree to which the work pleases you.

What do you especially like or dislike about the work?

Do you think your responses are unique, or would they be common to most readers? Why?

(continued from p. 723)

In writing about literature, we can offer only our *interpretation* of meaning rather than *the* meaning. Still, most people agree that there are limits to interpretation: it must be supported by evidence from the work that a reasonable reader will find at least plausible if not totally convincing. For instance, the student who says that in "The Story of an Hour" Mrs. Mallard does not die but merely falls into a deathlike trance goes beyond the permissible limits because the story offers no evidence for such an interpretation.

3 Using evidence in writing about literature

The evidence for a literary analysis always comes from at least one primary source (the work or works being discussed) and may come from secondary sources (critical and historical works). (See p. 549 for more on primary and secondary sources.) For example, if you were writing about Chopin's "The Story of an Hour," the primary material would be the story itself, and the secondary material (if you used it) might be critical studies of Chopin.

The bulk of your evidence in writing about literature will usually be quotations from the work, although you will occasionally summarize or paraphrase as well (see pp. 599–603). When using quotations, keep in mind the criteria in the box on page 604.

Your instructor will probably tell you if you are expected to consult secondary sources for an assignment. They can help you understand a writer's work, but your primary concern should always be the work itself, not what critics A, B, and C say about it. In general, then, quote or summarize secondary material sparingly. And always cite your sources.

49b Understanding writing assignments in literature

Two common assignments in writing about literature are described and illustrated in this chapter and in Chapter 48:

- **A literary analysis (no secondary sources):** Give your ideas about a work of literature—your interpretation of its meaning, significance, or representations. Generally, a literary analysis centers on an arguable thesis statement that you support with evidence from the work. See pages 732–33 and 739–41 for literary analyses of fiction and drama.
- **A literary research paper (with secondary sources):** Combine analysis of a literary work with research in secondary sources about the work. You might consider other scholars' interpretations of the work, biographical information about the author, or accounts of the context in which the author wrote the work. Generally, such a paper centers on an arguable thesis statement that you support with evidence from the text and from

secondary sources, which must be cited. For example, you might respond to what scholars have written about a character in a play by Tennessee Williams. See pages 710–15 and 736–37 for examples of literary research papers.

In addition, a literature instructor may ask you to write papers in the following genres:

- **A personal response or reaction paper:** Give your thoughts and feelings about a work of literature. For example, you might compare a novel's description of a city with your experience of the same city.
- **A book review:** Give a summary of a book and a judgment about the book's value. In a review of a novel, for example, you might discuss whether the plot is interesting, the characters are believable, and the writing style is enjoyable. You might also compare the work to other works by the author.
- **A theater review:** Give your reactions to and opinions about a theatrical performance. You might summarize the plot of the play, describe the characters, identify the prominent themes, evaluate the other elements (writing, performances, direction, stage setting), and recommend whether others should see the performance.

49c Using the tools and language of literary analysis

1 Writing tools

The fundamental tool for writing about literature is reading critically. Asking analytical questions such as those on pages 724–25 can help you focus your ideas. In addition, keeping a reading journal can help you develop your thoughts. Keep careful, well-organized notes on any research materials. Finally, discuss the work with others who have read it. They may offer reactions and insights that will help you shape your own ideas.

2 Language considerations

Use the present tense of verbs to describe both the action in a literary work (*Brently Mallard suddenly appears*) and the writing of an author (*Chopin briefly describes the view* or *In his essay he comments that . . .*). Use the past tense to describe events that actually occurred in the past (*Chopin was born in 1851*).

Some instructors discourage students from using the first-person *I* (as in *I felt sorry for the character*) in writing about literature. At least use *I* sparingly to avoid sounding egotistical. Rephrase sentences to avoid using *I* unnecessarily—for instance, *The character evokes the reader's sympathy.*

49d Citing sources and formatting papers in writing about literature

Unless your instructor specifies otherwise, use the documentation style of the Modern Language Association (MLA), detailed in Chapter 47. In this style, citations in the text of the paper refer to a list of works cited at the end. Sample papers illustrating this style appear in Chapter 48 as well as in this chapter.

Use MLA format for headings, margins, and other elements, as detailed on pages 680–82.

49e Drafting and revising a literary analysis

The process for writing a literary analysis is similar to that for any other kind of essay: once you've done the reading and thought about it, you need to focus your ideas, gather evidence, draft your paper, and revise it.

1 Conceiving a thesis

After reading, rereading, and making notes, you will probably be able to formulate a tentative thesis statement—an assertion of your main point, your argument. (For more on thesis statements, see pp. 28–33.) Clear the air by glancing over your notes and by jotting down a few especially promising ideas—brief statements of what you think your key points may be and their main support. One approach is to seek patterns in the work, such as recurring words, phrases, images, events, symbols, or other elements. (Go back to the work, if necessary, to expand the patterns your notes reveal.) Such patterns can help you see themes both in the work itself and in your ideas about it.

Considering Kate Chopin's "The Story of an Hour," Janet Vong at first explored the idea that Mrs. Mallard, the main character, was unrealistic and thus unconvincing. (See Vong's journal entry on pp. 722–23.) But the more Vong examined the story and her notes, the more she was impressed by a pattern of ironies, or reversals, that helped to make Mrs. Mallard believable. In her journal Vong explored the idea that the many small reversals paved the way for Mrs. Mallard's own reversal from grief to joy:

title? "Ironies in an Hour" (?) "An Hour of Irony" (?) "Kate Chopin's Irony" (?)
thesis: irony at end is prepared for
chief irony: Mrs. M. dies just as she is beginning to enjoy life
smaller ironies:

1. "sad message" brings her joy
2. Richards is "too late" at end
3. Richards is too early at start
4. "joy that kills"
5. death brings joy and life

From these notes Vong developed her thesis statement:

> The irony of the ending is believable partly because it is consistent with earlier ironies in the story.

This thesis statement asserts a specific idea that can be developed and convincingly argued with evidence from Chopin's story. A good thesis statement will neither assert a fact (*Mrs. Mallard dies soon after hearing that her husband has died*) nor overgeneralize (*The story is an insult to women*).

2 Gathering evidence

In writing about literature, you use mainly evidence gathered from the work itself: quotations and sometimes paraphrases and summaries that support your ideas about the work. You can see examples of quoting and paraphrasing in Janet Vong's final draft on pages 732–33. The box below offers guidelines for using quotations in literary analysis.

Guidelines for using quotations in literary analysis

- **Use quotations to support your assertions, not to pad the paper.** Quote at length only when necessary to your argument.
- **Specify how each quotation relates to your idea.** Introduce the quotation—for example, *At the outset Chopin conveys the sort of person Richards is: ". . ."* Sometimes, comment after the quotation. (See pages 603–05 for more on integrating quotations into your writing.)
- **Reproduce spelling, punctuation, capitalization, and all other features exactly as they appear in the source.** See page 472 for the use of brackets when you need to add something to a quotation, and see page 473 for the use of an ellipsis mark when you need to omit something from a quotation.
- **Document your sources.** See pages 623–24.

You may wonder how much you should summarize the plot of the work. A brief plot summary can be helpful to readers who are unfamiliar with the work. Sometimes plot elements place your ideas in the context of the work or remind readers where your quotations come from. Plot elements may even be used as evidence, as Vong uses the ironic ending of the Chopin story. But plot summary is not literary analysis, and summary alone is not sufficient evidence to support a thesis. Keep any plot summaries brief and to the point.

For a literary research paper, evidence will come from the work itself and from secondary sources such as scholarly works and critical appraisals. The thesis and principal ideas of the paper must still be your own, but you may supplement your reading of the work with the views of respected scholars or critics. Sometimes you may choose to build your own argument in part by disputing others' views. However you draw on secondary sources, remember that they must be clearly identified and documented, even when you use your own words.

Note You can find student essays on the Web that may lead you to other sources or may suggest ideas you hadn't considered. If you want to use another student's paper as a secondary source, you must evaluate it with special care because it will not have passed through a reviewing process, as an article in a scholarly journal does. (See pp. 583–93 on evaluating online sources.) You must also, of course, clearly identify and document the source: borrowing *any* other writer's ideas or words without credit is plagiarism. (See pp. 614–20.)

3 Writing a draft

Drafting your essay is your opportunity to develop your thesis or to discover it if you haven't already. The draft below was actually Janet Vong's second: she deleted some digressions from her first draft and added more evidence for her points. The numbers in parentheses refer to the pages from which she drew the quotations. (See pp. 634–41 on this form of documentation.) Ask your instructor whether you should always give such citations, especially for a short poem or story like Chopin's.

Ironies in an Hour

After we know how the story turns out, if we reread it we find irony at the very start, as is true of many other stories. Mrs. Mallard's friends assume, mistakenly, that Mrs. Mallard is deeply in love with her husband, Brently Mallard. They take great care to tell her gently of his death. The friends mean well, and in fact they *do* well. They bring her an hour of life, an hour of freedom. They think their news is sad. Mrs. Mallard at first expresses grief when she hears the news, but soon she finds joy in it. So Richards's "sad message" (549), though sad in Richards's eyes, is in fact a happy message.

Among the ironic details is the statement that when Mallard enters the house, Richards tries to conceal him from Mrs. Mallard, but Richards is "too late" (551). This is ironic because earlier Richards has "hastened" (549) to bring his sad message; if he had been too late at the start, Brently Mallard would have arrived at home first, and Mrs. Mallard's life would not end an hour later but would simply go on as before. Yet another irony at the end of the story is the diagnosis of the doctors. The doctors say she died of "heart disease—of joy that kills" (551). In one sense the doctors are right: Mrs. Mallard has experienced a great joy. But of course the doctors totally misunderstand the joy that kills her.

The central irony resides not in the well-intentioned but ironic actions of Richards, or in the unconsciously ironic words of the doctors, but in her own life. She "sometimes" (550) loved her husband, but in a way she has been dead. Now, his apparent death brings her new life. This new life comes to her at the season of the year when "the tops of trees . . . were all aquiver with the new spring life" (550). But, ironically, her new life will last only an hour. She looks forward to "summer days" (550), but she will not see even the end of this spring day. Her years of marriage were ironic. They brought her a sort of living death instead of joy. Her new life is ironic, too. It grows out of her moment of grief for her supposedly dead husband, and her vision of a new life is cut short.

4 Revising and editing

As in other writing, use at least two drafts to revise and edit, so that you can attend separately to the big structural issues and the smaller surface problems. See pages 53–54 and 62–63 for general revision and editing checklists. The additional checklist below can help you with a literary analysis.

Checklist for revising a literary analysis

- **Title:** Does the title of your essay give the title and author of the work you discuss and also an idea of your approach to the work?
- **Introduction:** Does the introductory paragraph name the author and the title so that readers know exactly what work you are discussing? (Avoid opening sentences such as "In this story. . . .") Does the introduction state and develop your thesis a bit so that readers know where they will be going?
- **Thesis:** Does the thesis state the interpretation you are arguing for?
- **Organization:** How effective is the organization? The essay should not dwindle or become anticlimactic; rather, it should build up.
- **Quotations:** What evidence does each quotation provide? Do quotations let readers hear the author's voice?
- **Analysis vs. summary:** Is the essay chiefly devoted to analysis, not to summary? Summarize the plot only briefly and only to further your own ideas. A summary is not an essay.
- **Verb tenses:** Have you used the present tense of verbs to describe both the author's work and the action in the work (for example, *Chopin shows* and *Mrs. Mallard dies*)?
- **Evaluation:** How well will readers understand your evaluation of the work and what it is based on? Give the reasons for your judgment of the work. It is not enough to express your likes or dislikes; readers need the support of specific evidence from the work.
- **Are all your sources documented in MLA style?**

Janet Vong's final draft follows, with annotations that highlight some of its features.

Literary analysis of fiction (no secondary sources)

Author's name and identification in MLA format (p. 680)

Janet Vong

Mr. Romano

English 102

20 February 2014

Paper title incorporating author and title of analyzed work

Ironies of Life in Kate Chopin's
"The Story of an Hour"

Introduction naming author/title

Thesis statement: student's interpretation

Kate Chopin's "The Story of an Hour"—which takes only a few minutes to read—has an ironic ending: Mrs. Mallard dies just when she is beginning to live. On first reading, the ending seems almost too ironic for belief. On rereading the story, however, one sees that the ending is believable partly because it is consistent with other ironies in the story.

Detailing of story's ironies, using quotations and some summary to emphasize the reversals

Irony appears at the very start of the story. Because Mrs. Mallard's friends and her sister assume, mistakenly, that she is deeply in love with her husband, Brently Mallard, they take great care to tell her gently of his death. They mean well, and in fact they *do* well, bringing her an hour of life, an hour of joyous freedom, but it is ironic that they think their news is sad. True, Mrs. Mallard at first expresses grief when she hears the news, but soon (unknown to the others) she finds joy. So Richards's "sad message" (549), though sad in Richards's eyes, is in fact a happy message.

In-text citations in MLA style

Among the small but significant ironic details is the statement near the end of the story that when Mallard enters the house, Richards tries to conceal him from Mrs. Mallard, but Richards is "too late" (551). Almost at the start of the story, in the second paragraph, Richards has "hastened" (549) to bring his sad news. But if Richards had arrived too late at the start, Brently Mallard would have arrived at home first, and Mrs. Mallard's life would not end an hour later but would simply go on as before. Yet

The writing situation: Literary analysis (short story)

- **Subject:** Irony in "The Story of an Hour," by Kate Chopin; student's choice for an assignment in a literature course
- **Purpose:** To argue for an interpretation of a short story
- **Audience:** Classmates and instructor
- **Genre:** Literary analysis—writing that argues for an interpretation of a literary work, in this case a short story
- **Source:** Selection from an anthology (cited in MLA style); no secondary sources

another irony at the end of the story is the diagnosis of the doctors. They say she died of "heart disease—of joy that kills" (551). In one sense they are right: Mrs. Mallard has for the last hour experienced a great joy. But of course the doctors totally misunderstand the joy that kills her. It is not joy at seeing her husband alive, but her realization that the great joy she experienced during the last hour is over.

All of these ironic details add richness to the story, but the central irony resides not in the well-intentioned but ironic actions of Richards, or in the unconsciously ironic words of the doctors, but in Mrs. Mallard's own life. She "sometimes" (550) loved her husband, but in a way she has been dead, a body subjected to her husband's will. Now, his apparent death brings her new life. Appropriately, this new life comes to her at the season of the year when "the tops of trees . . . were all aquiver with the new spring life" (550). But, ironically, her new life will last only an hour. She is "Free, free, free" (550)—but only until her husband walks through the doorway. She looks forward to "summer days" (550), but she will not see even the end of this spring day. If her years of marriage were ironic, bringing her a sort of living death instead of joy, her new life is ironic, too, not only because it grows out of her moment of grief for her supposedly dead husband, but also because her vision of "a long procession of years" (550) is cut short within an hour on a spring day.

[New page.]

Work cited in MLA style

Work Cited

Chopin, Kate. "The Story of an Hour." *Literature: An Introduction to Fiction, Poetry, and Drama,* edited by X. J. Kennedy and Dana Gioia, 12th ed., Longman, 2013, pp. 549-51.

49f Writing about fiction, poetry, and drama

A work of literature falls into a literary **genre**—fiction, poetry, or drama—depending on how it is structured. The different genres of literature require different approaches in writing.

1 Writing about fiction

The "Questions for a literary analysis" on pages 724–25 will help you think about any work of literature, including a story or novel, and find a topic to write on. The following questions provide additional prompts for thinking about fiction. For an example of writing about fiction, see Janet Vong's essay beginning on the previous page.

Questions for analyzing fiction

- **What happens in the story?** For yourself, summarize the plot (the gist of the happenings). Think about what your summary *leaves out*—what is in the story *besides* plot.
- **Is the story told in chronological order, or are there flashbacks or flashforwards?** On rereading, what foreshadowing (hints of what is to come) do you detect?
- **What conflicts does the work include?**
- **How does the writer develop characters?** Are the characters revealed by explicit comment or through action? With which character(s) do you sympathize? Are the characters plausible? What motivates them? What do minor characters contribute to the work?
- **Who tells the story?** Is the narrator a character, or does the narrator stand entirely outside the characters' world? What does the narrator's point of view contribute to the story's theme? (On narrative points of view, see p. 724.)
- **What is the setting?** What do the time and place of the action contribute to the work?
- **Are certain characters, settings, or actions symbolic?** Do they stand for something in addition to themselves?
- **What are the themes?** That is, what does the work add up to? Do the themes reinforce your values, or do they challenge them?
- **Is the title informative?** Did its meaning change for you after you read the work?

2 Writing about poetry

Two types of essays on poetry are especially common. One is an analysis of some aspect of the poem in relation to the whole—for instance, the changes in the speaker's tone or the functions of meter and rhyme. The second is an explication, a line-by-line (sometimes almost word-by-word) reading that seeks to make explicit everything that is implicit in the poem. Thus an explication of the first line of Robert Frost's "Stopping by Woods on a Snowy Evening" (the line goes "Whose woods these are I think I know") might call attention to the tentativeness of the line ("I think I know") and to the fact that the words are not in the normal order ("I think I know whose woods these are"). These features might support the explanation that the poet is introducing—very quietly—a note of the *un*usual, in preparation for the experience that follows. Although one might conceivably explicate a long poem, the method is so detailed that in practice writers usually confine it to short poems or to short passages from long poems.

The "Questions for a literary analysis" on pages 724–25 will help you think about any work of literature, including a poem, and find a topic to write on. The following questions provide additional ways to think about poetry.

Questions for analyzing poetry

- **What parts of the poem interest or puzzle you?** What words seem especially striking or unusual?
- **How can you describe the poem's *speaker* (sometimes called the *persona* or the *voice*)?** The speaker may be different from the author.
- **What tone or emotion do you detect**—for instance, anger, affection, sarcasm? Does the tone change during the poem?
- **What is the structure of the poem?** Are there stanzas (groups of lines separated by space)? If so, how does the thought relate to them?
- **What are the themes of the poem?** What is it about? Are the themes stated or implied?
- **What images do you find?** Look for evocations of sight, sound, taste, touch, or smell. Is there a surprising pattern of images—say, images of business in a poem about love? What does the poem suggest symbolically as well as literally? (Trust your responses. If you don't sense a symbolic overtone, move on. Don't hunt for symbols.)

Literary research paper on poetry

The sample paper beginning on the next page analyzes the short poem below by Agha Shahid Ali. The paper argues for a particular interpretation of the poem both by analyzing the poem and by drawing on secondary sources—that is, critical works *about* the poem. In the opening paragraph, for instance, the writer quotes a secondary source to establish how her interpretation differs from that of other readers. This quotation and the other uses of secondary sources are support for the writer's points, not padding.

Note In the paper, the in-text citations for Ali's poem give line numbers of the poem, whereas the citations for the secondary sources give page numbers of the sources. See pages 640 and 635–36, respectively, for these two forms of citation.

Agha Shahid Ali

Postcard from Kashmir

Kashmir shrinks into my mailbox,
my home a neat four by six inches.
I always loved neatness. Now I hold
the half-inch Himalayas in my hand.

This is home. And this the closest
I'll ever be to home. When I return,
the colors won't be so brilliant,
the Jhelum's waters so clean,
so ultramarine. My love
so overexposed.

And my memory will be a little
out of focus, in it
a giant negative, black
and white, still undeveloped.

Jessie Glenn

Professor Narracci

English 101

14 March 2014

Past and Future in
Agha Shahid Ali's "Postcard from Kashmir"

Introduction naming author/title and summarizing other interpretations

Most literary critics interpret Agha Shahid Ali's "Postcard from Kashmir" as a longing for a lost home, a poetic expression of the heartbreak of exile. For instance, Maimuna Dali Islam describes the speaker's futile effort "to capture his homeland" (262). However, such a reading of the poem seems too narrow. "Postcard from Kashmir" does evoke the experience of being displaced from a beloved home, but the speaker does not seem to feel an intense loss. Instead, he seems to reflect on his position of having more than one home.

Thesis statement: student's interpretation

Summary of poem

Ali's brief poem consists of three stanzas and divides into two parts. In the first half, the speaker examines a postcard he has received from his former home of Kashmir (lines 1-6). In the second half, the speaker looks forward, imagining how Kashmir will look the next time he sees it and assuming that the place will be different from the idealized view of the postcard and his memory (6-14). The geography is significant. Kashmir has been in the news for many years as the focus of territorial conflict, often violent, among the bordering nations of India, Pakistan, and China. Many residents of the region have been killed, and many have left the region. One of the exiles was Ali: he moved to the United States in 1976 and lived here until his death in 2001, but he also regularly visited his family in Kashmir (Benvenuto 261, 263).

Background information

In-text citations in MLA style

The writing situation: Literary research paper (poem)

- **Subject:** The meaning of home in "Postcard from Kashmir," by Agha Shahid Ali; student's choice for an assignment in a first-year writing course emphasizing literature
- **Purpose:** To argue for an interpretation of a poem
- **Audience:** Classmates and instructor
- **Genre:** Literary research paper—writing that argues for an interpretation of a literary work, in this case a poem, in the context of others' interpretations and/or information
- **Sources:** Poem, published interview with the poet, and critics' interpretations of the poem (all cited in MLA style)

In the context of Kashmir, the literary theorist Jahan Ramazani concludes that the poem "dramatizes the . . . condition" of losing one's homeland to political turmoil (12). Yet several lines in the poem suggest that the speaker is not mourning a loss but musing about having a sense of home both in Kashmir and in the United States. This sense is evident in the opening stanza: "Kashmir shrinks into my mailbox, / my home a neat four by six inches" (1-2), with "my mailbox" conveying his current residence as home and "my home" referring to Kashmir. The dual sense of home is even more evident in the lines "This is home. And this is the closest / I'll ever be to home" (5-6). Although Maimuna Dali Islam assumes that "This" in these lines refers to the Kashmir pictured on the postcard (262), it could also or instead refer to the home attached to the mailbox.

Critic's interpretation

First point supporting thesis

Quotations from poem

Critic's interpretation

The speaker also seems to perceive that his dual sense of home will continue into the future. The critics do not mention that the second half of the poem is written in the future tense. Beginning with "When I return" (6), the speaker makes it clear that he expects to find himself in Kashmir again, and he imagines how things will be, not how they were. Islam takes the image on the postcard as proof that "there is a place that can be captured in a snapshot" (263), but the speaker compares photography to memory, characterizing both as flawed and deceptive with terms such as "overexposed" (10) and "out of focus" (12). He acknowledges that the place won't be like the photograph: "the colors won't be so brilliant, / the Jhelum's waters so clean, / so ultramarine" (7-9). Kashmir still exists, but not as any photograph or memory has recorded it. And the speaker's relationship to his original home, his "love" (9), is changing with the place itself.

Second point supporting thesis

Quotation from secondary source

In "Postcard from Kashmir" the speaker reflects on home and displacement as he gazes into a representation of his past and considers the future. If the poem mourns a loss, as the critics suggest, it is a loss that has not happened yet, at least not completely. More convincingly, the poem captures a moment when the two homes and the past, present, and future all meet.

Conclusion restating critics' and student's interpretations

[New page.]

Works Cited

Ali, Agha Shahid. "Postcard from Kashmir." *The Half-Inch Himalayas*, Wesleyan UP, 1987, p. 1.

Benvenuto, Christine. "Agha Shahid Ali." *The Massachusetts Review*, vol. 43, no. 2, Summer 2002, pp. 261-63.

Works cited in MLA style

Islam, Maimuna Dali. "A Way in the World of an Asian American Existence: Agha Shahid Ali's Transimmigrant Spacing of North America and India and Kashmir." *Transnational Asian American Literature: Sites and Transits*, edited by Shirley Lim et al., Temple UP, 2006, pp. 257-73.

Ramazani, Jahan. *The Hybrid Muse: Postcolonial Poetry in English*. U of Chicago P, 2001.

3 Writing about drama

Because plays—even some one-act plays—are relatively long, analytic essays on drama usually focus on only one aspect of the play, such as the structure of the play, the function of a single scene, or a character's responsibility for his or her fate. The essay's introduction indicates what the topic is and why it is of some importance, and the introduction may also state the thesis. The conclusion often extends the analysis, showing how a study of the apparently small topic helps to illuminate the play as a whole.

The "Questions for a literary analysis" on pages 724–25 will help you think about any work of literature, including a play, and find a topic to write on. The questions in the following box provide additional prompts for thinking about drama.

Questions for analyzing drama

- **How does the plot (the sequence of happenings) unfold?** Does it seem plausible? If not, is the implausibility a fault? If there is more than one plot, are the plots parallel, or are they related by way of contrast?
- **Are certain happenings recurrent?** If so, how are they significant?
- **What kinds of conflict are in the play**—for instance, between two groups, two characters, or two aspects of a single character? How are the conflicts resolved? Is the resolution satisfying to you?
- **How does the author develop the characters?** How trustworthy are the characters when they describe themselves or others? Do some characters serve as **foils,** or contrasts, for other characters, thus helping to define the other characters? Do the characters change as the play proceeds? Are the characters' motivations convincing?
- **What do the author's stage directions add to your understanding and appreciation of the play?** If there are few stage directions, what do the speeches imply about the characters' manner, tone, and gestures?
- **What do you make of the setting, or location?** Does it help to reveal characters or themes?
- **Do certain costumes or properties strike you as symbolic?** See page 725 on symbolism.

Literary analysis of drama (no secondary sources)

The following essay on William Shakespeare's *Macbeth* focuses on the title character, examining the extent to which he is and is not a tragic hero. Although the writer bases the essay on his personal response to the play, he does not simply state a preference, as if saying he likes vanilla more than chocolate; instead, he argues a case and offers evidence from the play to support his claims.

Note The in-text citations in this essay include act, scene, and line numbers—MLA style for citations of verse plays (see p. 640).

Michael Spinter
Professor Nelson
English 211, sec. 4
8 October 2013

Shakespeare's Macbeth as Hero

When people imagine a tragic hero, they probably think of a fundamentally sympathetic person who is entangled in terrifying circumstances and who ultimately dies, leaving the world a diminished place. For instance, in Shakespeare's *Hamlet* the title character must avenge his father's murder, and in doing so he performs certain actions that verge on the wrongful, such as behaving cruelly to his beloved Ophelia and his mother and killing Rosencrantz and Guildenstern. But in the end Hamlet seems fundamentally a decent man and Denmark seems the poorer for his death.

Introduction defining *tragic hero* with example

The title character of Shakespeare's *Macbeth* is different. He kills or hires the killers of King Duncan and Duncan's grooms, kills Banquo, attempts to kill Banquo's son, and finally kills Lady Macduff and her children and servants. Other characters call him "devilish" (4.3.117), a "tyrant" (5.7.14), a "hell-hound" (5.8.3), and a "butcher" (5.8.69). Readers and spectators cannot deny the truth of these characterizations, and

In-text citations in MLA style referring to act, scene, and line of play

The writing situation: Literary analysis (play)

- **Subject:** The main character in William Shakespeare's *Macbeth* as tragic hero; student's choice in a literature course
- **Purpose:** To argue for an interpretation of a play
- **Audience:** Classmates and instructor
- **Genre:** Literary analysis—writing that argues for an interpretation of a literary work, in this case a play
- **Source:** Play (cited in MLA style); no secondary sources

Thesis statement: student's interpretation

yet Macbeth is more than a mere villain. He is a deeply interesting tragic hero who, despite his ruthlessness, appeals to the audience through his bravery, his victimization by others, his conscience, his isolation, and his eloquent speech.

First point supporting thesis

Macbeth is appealing because he is an impressive military figure. In the first extended description of Macbeth, the Captain speaks of "brave Macbeth—well he deserves that name" (1.2.16). The Captain tells how Macbeth valiantly fought on behalf of his king, and King Duncan exclaims, "O valiant cousin! Worthy gentleman!" (1.2.2). True, Macbeth sometimes cringes, such as when he denies responsibility for Banquo's death: "Thou canst not say I did it" (3.4.51). But throughout most of the play, he is a bold and courageous soldier.

Second point supporting thesis

Of course, Macbeth's ability as a soldier is not enough by itself to explain his appeal. He is at the same time a victim—a victim of his wife's ambition and a victim of the witches. Yes, he ought to see through his wife's schemes, and he ought to resist the witches, just as Banquo resists them, but surely Macbeth is partly tricked into crime. He is responsible, but others can imagine themselves falling as he does, and his status as a victim arouses sympathy.

Third point supporting thesis

Also contributing to a sense of Macbeth's humanity is the conscience he retains despite his terrible deeds. For instance, after he murders Duncan he cannot sleep at night. When he tells Lady Macbeth that he has heard a voice saying "Macbeth does murder sleep" (2.2.35), she ridicules him, but the voice is prophetic: he is doomed to sleepless nights. Macbeth's torment over his deed shows that he knows he has done wrong and that he still has some decent human feelings.

Fourth point supporting thesis

Macbeth eventually loses all of his allies, even his wife, and he then claims sympathy as a lonely, guilt-haunted figure. On this point, scene 2 of act 3 is especially significant. When Lady Macbeth asks Macbeth why he keeps to himself (line 8), he confides something of the mental stress that he is undergoing. But when she asks, "What's to be done?" (44), he cannot bring himself to tell her that he is plotting the deaths of Banquo and Fleance. Instead of further involving his wife, the only person with whom he might still have a human connection, Macbeth says, "Be innocent of the knowledge, dearest chuck . . ." (45). The word *chuck*, an affectionate form of *chick*, shows warmth and intimacy that are touching, but his refusal or his inability to confide in his wife and former partner in crime shows how fully isolated he is from all human contact. Readers and spectators cannot help feeling some sympathy for him.

Finally, Macbeth is appealing, rather than disgusting, because he speaks so eloquently. The greatness of his language compels rapt attention. Some speeches are very familiar, such as "My way of life / Is fall'n into the sear, the yellow leaf . . ." (5.3.23-24) and "Tomorrow and tomorrow and tomorrow / Creeps in this petty pace from day to day . . ." (5.5.19-20). But almost every speech Macbeth utters is equally memorable, from his first, "So foul and fair a day I have not seen" (1.3.38), to his last:

Fifth point supporting thesis

Before my body
I throw my warlike shield. Lay on, Macduff:
And damned be him that first cries, "Hold, enough!" (5.8.32-34)

If readers and spectators judge Macbeth only by what he does, of course they will see a foul murderer. But if they give due weight to his bravery, his role as a victim, his tormented conscience, his isolation, and especially his moving language, then they will not simply judge Macbeth. Rather, they will see that this villain is not merely awful but awesome.

Conclusion restating thesis

[New page.]

Work Cited

Shakespeare, William. *The Tragedy of Macbeth.* Edited by Sylvan Barnet, New American Library, 1987.

Work cited in MLA style

50 Writing in Other Humanities

Chapter essentials

- Use the methods and evidence common in the humanities (next page).
- Understand your writing assignment (next page).
- Use the tools and language of your discipline (p. 743).
- Use Chicago style for citing sources and formatting papers (pp. 744, 757).

Visit MyWritingLab™ for more resources on writing in other humanities.

The humanities include literature, the visual arts, music, film, dance, history, philosophy, and religion. The preceding chapter discusses the particular requirements of reading and writing about literature. This chapter concentrates on history. Although the arts, religion, and other humanities have their own concerns, they share many important goals and methods with literature and history.

50a Using the methods and evidence of the humanities

Writers in the humanities record and speculate about the growth, ideas, and emotions of human beings. Based on the evidence of written words, artworks, and other human traces and creations, humanities writers explain, interpret, analyze, and reconstruct the human experience.

The discipline of history focuses particularly on reconstructing the past. In Greek the word for history means "to inquire": historians inquire into the past to understand its events. Then they report, explain, analyze, and evaluate the events in their context, asking such questions as what happened before or after the events or how the events were related to then existing political and social structures.

Historians' reconstructions of the past—their conclusions about what happened and why—are always supported with reference to the written record. The evidence of history is mainly primary sources, such as eyewitness accounts and contemporary documents, letters, commercial records, and the like. For history papers, you might also be asked to support your conclusions with those in secondary sources.

In reading historical sources, you need to weigh and evaluate their evidence. If, for example, you find conflicting accounts of the same event, you need to consider the possible biases of the authors. In general, the more a historian's conclusions are supported by public records such as deeds, marriage licenses, and newspaper accounts, the more reliable the conclusions are likely to be.

50b Understanding writing assignments in the humanities

Writing assignments in the humanities often require traditional academic essays that follow the conventional pattern of introduction, thesis statement, supporting paragraphs, and conclusion. Humanities assignments generally use the genres of analysis, argument, and informing that are described on pages 134–36. An assignment may further refine the genre with one or more of the following words:

- **Explain:** For instance, show how a painter developed a particular technique or clarify a general's role in a historical battle.
- **Argue:** Assert and defend an opinion—for instance, about the meaning of a poem or the causes of a historical event.
- **Analyze:** Examine the elements of a philosophical argument or break down the causes of a historical event.
- **Interpret:** Infer the meaning of a film from its images or the significance of a historical event from contemporary accounts of it.

- **Synthesize:** Find a pattern in a composer's works or in a historical period.
- **Evaluate:** Judge the quality of an architect's design or a historian's conclusions.

See Chapters 7 and 9 for discussion of these words.

50c Using the tools and language of the humanities

The tools and language of the humanities vary according to the discipline. Many reference works can clarify specific tools you need and the language you should use. To find such works, consult a reference librarian.

1 Writing tools

A useful tool for the arts is to ask a series of questions to analyze and evaluate a work. (A list of such questions for reading literature appears on pp. 724–25.) In any humanities discipline, a journal—a log of questions, reactions, and insights—can help you discover and record your thoughts. (See pp. 148–49 and 543.)

In history the tools are those of any thorough and efficient researcher, as discussed in Chapters 41–43: a system for finding and tracking sources; a methodical examination of sources, including evaluating and synthesizing them; a system for gathering source information; and a separate system, such as a research journal, for tracking one's own evolving thoughts.

2 Language considerations

Historians strive for precision and logic. They do not guess about what happened or speculate about "what if." They avoid trying to influence readers' opinions with words having strongly negative or positive connotations, such as *stupid* or *brilliant*. Instead, historians show the evidence and draw conclusions from that. Generally, they avoid using *I* because it tends to draw attention away from the evidence and toward the writer.

Writing about history demands some attention to the tenses of verbs. To refer to events that occurred in the past, historians generally use the past tense, the present perfect tense, or the past perfect tense. They reserve the present tense only for statements about the present or statements of general truths. For example:

> Franklin Delano Roosevelt <u>died</u> in 1945. [Simple past.]
>
> He <u>had contracted</u> polio at age thirty-nine. [Past perfect.]
>
> Many historians <u>have praised</u> Roosevelt as President. [Present perfect.]

Some of his economic reforms persist today, such as Social Security and unemployment compensation. [Present.]

See pages 298–304 for more on verb tenses.

50d Citing sources in Chicago style

Writers in the humanities generally rely on one of the following guides for source-citation style:

The Chicago Manual of Style, 16th ed., 2010
A Manual for Writers of Research Papers, Theses, and Dissertations, by Kate L. Turabian, 8th ed., rev. Wayne C. Booth, Gregory G. Colomb, and Joseph M. Williams, 2013
MLA Handbook, 8th ed., 2016

The recommendations of the *MLA Handbook* are discussed and illustrated in Chapter 47. Unless your instructor specifies otherwise, use these recommendations for papers in English and foreign languages. In history, art history, and many other disciplines, however, writers rely on *The Chicago Manual of Style* or the student reference adapted from it, *A Manual for Writers.*

Both books detail two documentation styles. One, used mainly by scientists and social scientists, closely resembles the style of the American Psychological Association, covered in Chapter 51. The other style, used more in the humanities, calls for footnotes or endnotes and an optional bibliography. This style is described below.

1 Using Chicago notes and a bibliography

In the Chicago note style, a raised numeral in the text refers the reader to source information in an endnote or a footnote. In these notes, the first citation of each source contains all the information readers need to find the source. Thus your instructor may consider a bibliography optional because it provides much the same information. Ask your instructor whether you should use footnotes or endnotes and whether you should include a bibliography.

For both footnotes and endnotes, use single spacing for each note and double spacing between notes, as shown in the samples opposite. (This is the spacing recommended by *A Manual for Writers,* the student guide. For manuscripts that will be published, *The Chicago Manual* recommends double spacing throughout.) Separate footnotes from the text with a short line. Place endnotes directly after the text, beginning on a new page. For a bibliography at the end of the paper, use the format opposite. Arrange the sources alphabetically by the authors' last names.

The examples on page 746 illustrate the essentials of a note and a bibliography entry.

Chicago footnotes

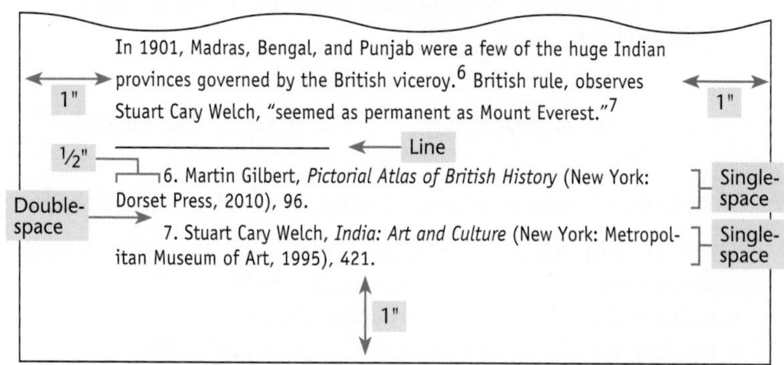

In 1901, Madras, Bengal, and Punjab were a few of the huge Indian provinces governed by the British viceroy.6 British rule, observes Stuart Cary Welch, "seemed as permanent as Mount Everest."7
1"
1"
Line
½"
6. Martin Gilbert, *Pictorial Atlas of British History* (New York: Dorset Press, 2010), 96.
Double-space
7. Stuart Cary Welch, *India: Art and Culture* (New York: Metropolitan Museum of Art, 1995), 421.
Single-space
Single-space
1"

Chicago endnotes

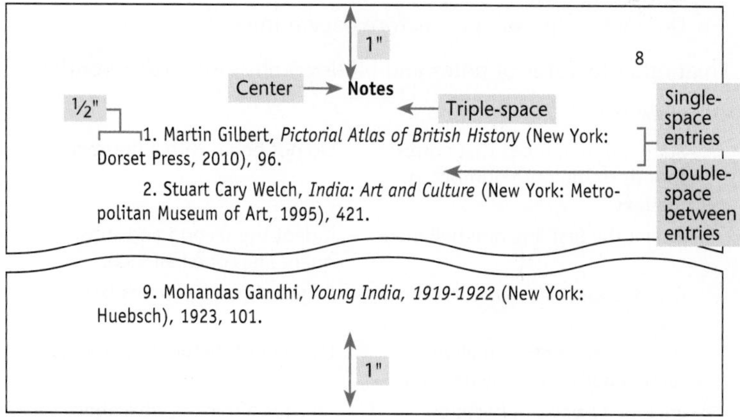

1"
8
Center
Notes
Triple-space
½"
1. Martin Gilbert, *Pictorial Atlas of British History* (New York: Dorset Press, 2010), 96.
2. Stuart Cary Welch, *India: Art and Culture* (New York: Metropolitan Museum of Art, 1995), 421.
Single-space entries
Double-space between entries
9. Mohandas Gandhi, *Young India, 1919-1922* (New York: Huebsch), 1923, 101.
1"

Chicago bibliography

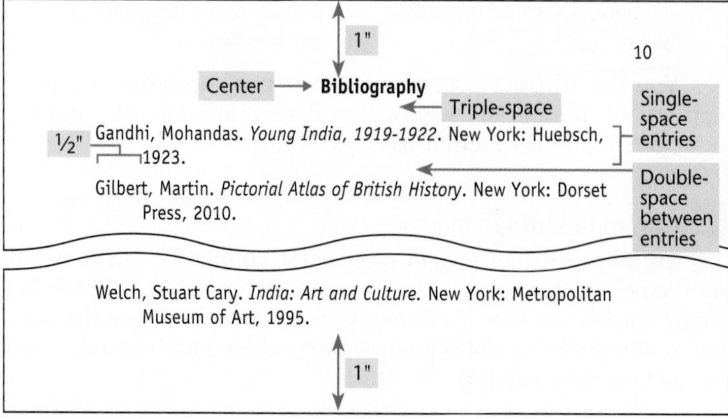

Note

6. Martin Gilbert, *Pictorial Atlas of British History* (New York: Dorset Press, 2010), 96.

Bibliography entry

Gilbert, Martin. *Pictorial Atlas of British History*. New York: Dorset Press, 2010.

Treat some features of notes and bibliography entries the same:

- Unless your instructor requests otherwise, single-space each note or entry, and double-space between them.
- Italicize the titles of books and periodicals.
- Enclose in quotation marks the titles of parts of books or articles in periodicals.
- Do not abbreviate publishers' names, but omit "Inc.," "Co.," and similar abbreviations.
- Do not use "p." or "pp." before page numbers.

Treat other features of notes and bibliography entries differently:

Note	Bibliography entry
Start with a number that corresponds to the note number in the text.	Do not begin with a number.
Indent the first line one-half inch.	Indent the second and subsequent lines one-half inch.
Give the author's name in normal order.	Begin with the author's last name.
Use commas between elements such as author's name and title.	Use periods between elements.
Enclose a book's publication information in parentheses, with no preceding punctuation.	Precede a book's publication information with a period, and don't use parentheses.
Include the specific page number(s) you borrowed from, omitting "p." or "pp."	Omit page numbers except for parts of books or articles in periodicals.

You can instruct your computer to position footnotes at the bottoms of appropriate pages. It will also automatically number notes and renumber them if you add or delete one or more.

2 Following Chicago models

An index of the Chicago models for common sources begins on the next page. The models themselves show notes and bibliography entries together for easy reference. Be sure to use the numbered note form for notes and the unnumbered bibliography form for bibliography entries.

Chicago notes and bibliography entries

Finding the right model for a source

1. **What type of source is it?** Locate the type in the index beginning below.

   Article, models 4–7
   Book or part of book, models 8–16
   Government publication, model 17
   Web or social media, models 18–21
   Visual, audio, other media, models 22–26
   Other, models 27–29

2. **What is the medium of the source?** From within each type of source, choose the right model for the medium. Common media:

   Print
   Web
   Database
   E-book
   Original artwork or reproduction
   Film
   DVD; Blu-ray; video
   LP; CD

3. **Who is the author?** Choose the right model for the number and type of author(s).

   How many authors? models 1–2
   No named author? model 3

(continued)

Chicago notes and bibliography entries

(continued)

Chic 50d

Note Chicago style generally recommends notes only, not bibliography entries, for personal communication such as e-mail, personal letters, and interviews you conduct yourself. Bibliography entries are shown here in case your instructor requires such entries.

Authors

1. One, two, or three authors

1. Carol Gilligan, *In a Different Voice: Psychological Theory and Women's Development* (Cambridge: Harvard University Press, 1982), 27.

Gilligan, Carol. *In a Different Voice: Psychological Theory and Women's Development*. Cambridge: Harvard University Press, 1982.

1. Dennis L. Wilcox, Phillip H. Ault, and Warren K. Agee, *Public Relations: Strategies and Tactics,* 10th ed. (New York: Pearson, 2011), 182.

Wilcox, Dennis L., Phillip H. Ault, and Warren K. Agee. *Public Relations: Strategies and Tactics*. 10th ed. New York: Pearson, 2011.

2. More than three authors

2. Geraldo Lopez et al., *China and the West* (Boston: Little, Brown, 2004), 461.

Lopez, Geraldo, Judith P. Salt, Anne Ming, and Henry Reisen. *China and the West*. Boston: Little, Brown, 2004.

The Latin abbreviation et al. in the note means "and others."

3. Author not named (anonymous)

3. *The Dorling Kindersley World Atlas* (London: Dorling Kindersley, 2013), 150-51.

The Dorling Kindersley World Atlas. London: Dorling Kindersley, 2013.

Articles in journals, newspapers, and magazines

4. Article in a scholarly journal

For journals that are paginated continuously through an annual volume, include at least the volume number—or, for greater clarity, add the issue number, if any, or the month or season of publication as in models a and b below. The month or season precedes the year of publication in parentheses. The issue number is required if the journal pages issues separately (no. 1 in models c and d).

a. Print journal article

4. Janet Lever, "Sex Differences in the Games Children Play," *Social Problems* 23 (Spring 1996): 482.

Lever, Janet. "Sex Differences in the Games Children Play." *Social Problems* 23 (Spring 1996): 478-87.

b. Database or Web journal article with DOI

4. Jonathan Dickens, "Social Policy Approaches to Intercountry Adoption," *International Social Work* 52 (September 2009): 600, doi:10.1177/0020872809337678.

Dickens, Jonathan. "Social Policy Approaches to Intercountry Adoption." *International Social Work* 52 (September 2009): 595-607. doi:10.1177/0020872809337678.

A DOI, or Digital Object Identifier, is a unique identifier that many publishers assign to journal articles and other documents. (See p. 767 for more on DOIs.) If the article you cite has a DOI, give it in the format shown in the source: preceded by doi, as above, or preceded by http://dx.doi.org/.

c. Database journal article without DOI

4. Nathan S. Atkinson, "Newsreels as Domestic Propaganda: Visual Rhetoric at the Dawn of the Cold War," *Rhetoric and Public Affairs* 14, no. 1 (Spring 2011): 72, Academic Search Complete (60502112).

Atkinson, Nathan S. "Newsreels as Domestic Propaganda: Visual Rhetoric at the Dawn of the Cold War." *Rhetoric and Public Affairs* 14, no. 1 (Spring 2011): 69-100. Academic Search Complete (60502112).

If no DOI is available for an article in a database, give the name of the database and the accession number. Notice that these and the next models include the issue number as well as the volume number because the journal pages each issue separately.

d. Web journal article without DOI

4. Rebecca Butler, "The Rise and Fall of Union Classification," *Theological Librarianship* 6, no. 1 (2013): 21, https://journal.atla.com/ojs/index.php/theolib/article/view/254.

Butler, Rebecca. "The Rise and Fall of Union Classification." *Theological Librarianship* 6, no. 1 (2013): 21-28. https://journal.atla.com/ojs/index.php/theolib/article/view/254.

If no DOI is available for an article you find on the open Web, give the URL.

5. Article in a newspaper

a. Print newspaper article

5. Annie Lowery, "Cities Advancing Inequality Fight," *New York Times,* April 7, 2014, national edition, A1.

Lowery, Annie. "Cities Advancing Inequality Fight." *New York Times,* April 7, 2014, national edition, A1.

b. Database newspaper article

5. Rob Stein, "Obesity May Stall Trend of Increasing Longevity," *Washington Post,* March 15, 2014, final edition, A2, LexisNexis Academic.

Stein, Rob. "Obesity May Stall Trend of Increasing Longevity." *Washington Post,* March 15, 2014, final edition, A2. LexisNexis Academic.

If an accession number is available, give it after the database name, as in model 6b below.

c. Web newspaper article

5. Marcia Dunn, "Vast Ocean Found beneath Ice of Saturn Moon," *Detroit News,* April 3, 2014, http://www.detroitnews.com/article/20140403/SCIENCE/304030081.

Dunn, Marcia. "Vast Ocean Found beneath Ice of Saturn Moon." *Detroit News,* April 3, 2014. http://www.detroitnews.com/article/20140403/SCIENCE/304030081.

6. Article in a magazine

a. Print magazine article

6. Jeffrey Toobin, "This Is My Jail," *New Yorker,* April 14, 2014, 28.

Toobin, Jeffrey. "This Is My Jail." *New Yorker,* April 14, 2014, 26-32.

b. Database magazine article

6. Colin Barras, "Right on Target," *New Scientist,* January 25, 2014, 42, Academic Search Complete (93983067).

Barras, Colin. "Right on Target." *New Scientist,* January 25, 2014, 40-43. Academic Search Complete (93983067).

If no accession number is available, give just the database name, as in model 5b.

c. Web magazine article

6. Laura Stampler, "These Cities Have the Most Open-Minded Daters," *Time*, April 14, 2014, http://time.com/61947/these-cities-have-the-most-open-minded-daters.

Stampler, Laura. "These Cities Have the Most Open-Minded Daters." *Time*, April 14, 2014. http://time.com/61947/these-cities-have-the-most-open-minded-daters.

7. Review

7. John Gregory Dunne, "The Secret of Danny Santiago," review of *Famous All over Town,* by Danny Santiago, *New York Review of Books,* August 16, 1994, 25.

Dunne, John Gregory. "The Secret of Danny Santiago." Review of *Famous All over Town,* by Danny Santiago. *New York Review of Books,* August 16, 1994, 17-27.

Books and government publications

8. Basic format for a book

a. Print book

8. Barbara Ehrenreich, *Dancing in the Streets: A History of Collective Joy* (New York: Henry Holt, 2006), 97-117.

Ehrenreich, Barbara. *Dancing in the Streets: A History of Collective Joy*. New York: Henry Holt, 2006.

b. Database book

8. Daniel Levine, *Bayard Rustin and the Civil Rights Movement* (New Brunswick: Rutgers University Press, 1999), 21-45, eBook Collection (44403).

Levine, Daniel. *Bayard Rustin and the Civil Rights Movement.* New Brunswick: Rutgers University Press, 1999. eBook Collection (44403).

c. E-book

8. Marilyn Booth, *May Her Likes Be Multiplied: Biography and Gender Politics in Egypt* (Oakland: University of California Press, 2001), Kindle edition.

Booth, Marilyn. *May Her Likes Be Multiplied: Biography and Gender Politics in Egypt.* Oakland: University of California Press, 2001. Kindle edition.

d. Web book

8. Jane Austen, *Emma*, ed. R. W. Chapman (1816; Oxford: Clarendon, 1926; Oxford Text Archive, 2014), chap. 1, http://ota.ahds.ac.uk/Austen/Emma.1519.

Austen, Jane. *Emma*. Edited by R. W. Chapman. 1816. Oxford: Clarendon, 1926. Oxford Text Archive, 2014. http://ota.ahds.ac.uk/Austen/Emma.1519.

Provide print publication information, if any.

9. Book with an editor

9. Patricia Rushton, ed., *Vietnam War Nurses: Personal Accounts of Eighteen Americans* (Jefferson, NC: McFarland, 2013), 70-72.

Rushton, Patricia, ed. *Vietnam War Nurses: Personal Accounts of Eighteen Americans*. Jefferson, NC: McFarland, 2013.

10. Book with an author and an editor

10. Lewis Mumford, *The City in History,* ed. Donald L. Miller (New York: Pantheon, 1986), 216-17.

Mumford, Lewis. *The City in History*. Edited by Donald L. Miller. New York: Pantheon, 1986.

11. Translation

11. Dante Alighieri, *The Inferno,* trans. John Ciardi (New York: New American Library, 1971), 51.

Alighieri, Dante. *The Inferno*. Translated by John Ciardi. New York: New American Library, 1971.

12. Later edition

12. Dwight L. Bolinger, *Aspects of Language,* 3rd ed. (New York: Harcourt Brace Jovanovich, 1981), 20.

Bolinger, Dwight L. *Aspects of Language*. 3rd ed. New York: Harcourt Brace Jovanovich, 1981.

13. Work in more than one volume

a. One volume without a title

13. Abraham Lincoln, *The Collected Works of Abraham Lincoln,* ed. Roy P. Basler (New Brunswick: Rutgers University Press, 1953), 5:426-28.

Lincoln, Abraham. *The Collected Works of Abraham Lincoln*. Edited by Roy P. Basler. Vol. 5. New Brunswick: Rutgers University Press, 1953.

b. One volume with a title

13. Linda B. Welkin, *The Age of Balanchine,* vol. 3 of *The History of Ballet* (New York: Columbia University Press, 1999), 56.

Welkin, Linda B. *The Age of Balanchine*. Vol. 3 of *The History of Ballet*. New York: Columbia University Press, 1999.

14. Selection from an anthology

14. Rosetta Brooks, "Streetwise," in *The New Urban Landscape,* ed. Richard Martin (New York: Rizzoli, 2005), 38-39.

Brooks, Rosetta. "Streetwise." In *The New Urban Landscape,* edited by Richard Martin, 37-60. New York: Rizzoli, 2005.

15. Work in a series

15. Ingmar Bergman, *The Seventh Seal,* Modern Film Scripts 12 (New York: Simon and Schuster, 1995), 27.

Bergman, Ingmar. *The Seventh Seal.* Modern Film Scripts 12. New York: Simon and Schuster, 1995.

16. Article in a reference work

As shown in the following examples, use the abbreviation s.v. (Latin *sub verbo,* "under the word") for reference works that are alphabetically arranged. Well-known works (model a) do not need publication information except for the edition number. Chicago style generally recommends notes only, not bibliography entries, for reference works; bibliography models are given here in case your instructor requires such entries.

a. Print reference work

16. *Merriam-Webster's Collegiate Dictionary,* 11th ed., s.v. "reckon."

Merriam-Webster's Collegiate Dictionary. 11th ed. S.v. "reckon."

b. Web reference work

16. *Wikipedia,* s.v. "Wuhan," last modified May 9, 2014, http://en.wikipedia.org/wiki/Wuhan.

Wikipedia. S.v. "Wuhan." Last modified May 9, 2014. http://en.wikipedia.org/wiki/Wuhan.

17. Government publication

17. House Comm. on Agriculture, Nutrition, and Forestry, *Food and Energy Act of 2008,* 110th Cong., 2nd Sess., H.R. Doc. No. 884, at 21-22 (2008).

House Comm. on Agriculture, Nutrition, and Forestry. *Food and Energy Act of 2008.* 110th Cong. 2nd Sess. H.R. Doc. No. 884 (2008).

17. Hawaii Department of Education, *Kauai District Schools, Profile 2013-14* (Honolulu, 2014), 38.

Hawaii Department of Education. *Kauai District Schools, Profile 2013-14.* Honolulu, 2014.

Web sites and social media

18. Page or work on a Web site

18. Justin W. Patchin, "Ban School, Open Facebook," Cyberbullying Research Center, accessed May 10, 2014, http://cyberbullying.us/021649.

Patchin, Justin W. "Ban School, Open Facebook." Cyberbullying Research Center. Accessed May 10, 2014. http://cyberbullying.us/021649.

For Web pages and works that are not dated or are likely to change, *The Chicago Manual* suggests giving the date of your access, as here, or a statement beginning with last modified (model 16).

19. Post on a blog or discussion group

19. Bettina Smith, "No Such Animal," *Smithsonian Collections Blog,* April 29, 2014, http://si-siris.blogspot.com.

Smith, Bettina. "No Such Animal." *Smithsonian Collections Blog.* April 29, 2014. http://si-siris.blogspot.com.

20. Comment

20. Tony Drees, April 15, 2014, comment on Nicholas Kristof, "Standing by Our Veterans," *On the Ground* (blog), *New York Times,* April 12, 2014, http://kristof.blogs.nytimes.com.

Kristof, Nicholas. *On the Ground* (blog). *New York Times.* http://kristof.blogs.nytimes.com.

In a note cite a reader's comment on a blog by the reader's name (Drees above). However, in the bibliography cite the entire blog by the blog author's name (Kristof above).

21. E-mail

21. Naomi Lee, "Re: Atlanta," e-mail message to author, May 16, 2014.

Lee, Naomi. "Re: Atlanta." E-mail message to author. May 16, 2014.

Video, audio, and other media sources

22. Work of art

a. Original artwork

22. John Singer Sargent, *In Switzerland,* 1908, Metropolitan Museum of Art, New York.

Sargent, John Singer. *In Switzerland.* 1908. Metropolitan Museum of Art, New York.

b. Print reproduction of an artwork

22. David Graham, *Bob's Java Jive, Tacoma, Washington, 1989,* photograph, in *Only in America: Some Unexpected Scenery* (New York: Knopf, 1991), 93.

Graham, David. *Bob's Java Jive, Tacoma, Washington, 1989.* Photograph. In *Only in America: Some Unexpected Scenery.* New York: Knopf, 1991.

c. Web reproduction of an artwork

22. Jackson Pollock, *Shimmering Substance,* 1946, Museum of Modern Art, New York, http://moma.org/collection/conservation/pollock/shimmering_substance.html.

Pollock, Jackson. *Shimmering Substance.* 1946. Museum of Modern Art, New York. http://moma.org/collection/conservation/pollock/shimmering_substance.html.

23. Film or video

a. Film, DVD, Blu-ray, or video recording

23. George Balanchine, *Serenade,* San Francisco Ballet, performed February 2, 2000 (New York: PBS Video, 2006), DVD.

Balanchine, George. *Serenade*. San Francisco Ballet. Performed February 2, 2000. New York: PBS Video, 2006. DVD.

b. Video on the Web

23. Leslie J. Stewart, *96 Ranch Rodeo and Barbecue* (1951); 16mm, from Library of Congress, *Buckaroos in Paradise: Ranching Culture in Northern Nevada, 1945-1982,* MPEG, http://memory.loc.gov/cgi-bin/query.

Stewart, Leslie J. *96 Ranch Rodeo and Barbecue*. 1951. 16 mm. From Library of Congress, *Buckaroos in Paradise: Ranching Culture in Northern Nevada, 1945-1982*. MPEG. http://memory.loc.gov/cgi-bin/query.

24. Published or broadcast interview

24. Dexter Filkins, interview by Terry Gross, *Fresh Air,* NPR, April 29, 2014.

Filkins, Dexter. Interview by Terry Gross. *Fresh Air*. NPR. April 29, 2014.

25. Sound recording

a. LP or CD

25. Philip Glass, *String Quartet no. 5,* with Kronos Quartet, recorded 1991, Nonesuch 79356-2, 1995, compact disc.

Glass, Philip. *String Quartet no. 5*. Kronos Quartet. Recorded 1991. Nonesuch 79356-2. 1995. Compact disc.

b. Web recording

25. Ronald W. Reagan, "State of the Union Address," January 26, 1982, Vincent Voice Library, Digital and Multimedia Center, Michigan State University, http://www.lib.msu.edu/vincent/presidents/reagan.html.

Reagan, Ronald W. "State of the Union Address." January 26, 1982. Vincent Voice Library. Digital and Multimedia Center, Michigan State University. http://www.lib.msu.edu/vincent/presidents/reagan .html.

26. Podcast

26. Stephanie Foo, "The Hounds of Blairsville," *This American Life,* podcast audio, April 11, 2014, http://www.thisamericanlife.org/radio-archives/episode/522/tarred-and-feathered?act=1.

Foo, Stephanie. "The Hounds of Blairsville." *This American Life*. Podcast audio. April 11, 2014. http://www.thisamericanlife.org/radio-archives/episode/522/tarred-and-feathered?act=1.

Other sources

27. Letter

a. Published letter

27. Mrs. Laura E. Buttolph to Rev. and Mrs. C. C. Jones, June 20, 1857, in *The Children of Pride: A True Story of Georgia and the Civil War,* ed. Robert Manson Myers (New Haven, CT: Yale University Press, 1972), 334.

Buttolph, Laura E. Mrs. Laura E. Buttolph to Rev. and Mrs. C. C. Jones, June 20, 1857. In *The Children of Pride: A True Story of Georgia and the Civil War,* edited by Robert Manson Myers. New Haven, CT: Yale University Press, 1972.

b. Personal letter

27. Ann E. Packer, letter to author, June 15, 2011.

Packer, Ann E. Letter to author. June 15, 2011.

28. Personal interview

28. Janelle White, interview by author, December 19, 2013.

White, Janelle. Interview by author. December 19, 2013.

Chic 50d

29. Work on CD-ROM or DVD-ROM

29. *The American Heritage Dictionary of the English Language,* 4th ed. (Boston: Houghton Mifflin, 2006), CD-ROM.

The American Heritage Dictionary of the English Language. 4th ed. Boston: Houghton Mifflin, 2006. CD-ROM.

Shortened notes

To streamline documentation, Chicago style recommends shortened notes for sources that are fully cited elsewhere, either in a bibliography or in previous notes. Ask your instructor whether your paper should include a bibliography and, if so, whether you may use shortened notes for first references to sources as well as for subsequent references.

A shortened note contains the author's last name, the work's title (minus any initial *A*, *An*, or *The*), and the page number. Reduce long titles to four or fewer key words.

Complete note

4. Janet Lever, "Sex Differences in the Games Children Play," *Social Problems* 23 (Spring 1996): 482.

Complete bibliography entry

Lever, Janet. "Sex Differences in the Games Children Play." *Social Problems* 23 (Spring 1996): 478-87.

Shortened note

12. Lever, "Sex Differences," 483.

You may use the Latin abbreviation ibid. (meaning "in the same place") to refer to the same source cited in the preceding note. Give a page number if it differs from that in the preceding note.

> 12. Lever, "Sex Differences," 483.
>
> 13. Gilligan, *In a Different Voice,* 92.
>
> 14. Ibid., 93.
>
> 15. Lever, "Sex Differences," 483.

Chicago style allows for in-text parenthetical citations when you cite one or more works repeatedly. In the following example, the raised number 2 refers to the source information in a note; the number in parentheses is a page number in the same source.

> British rule, observes Stuart Cary Welch, "seemed as permanent as Mount Everest."[2] Most Indians submitted, willingly or not, to British influence in every facet of life (42).

50e Formatting a paper in Chicago style

The following guidelines for paper format come mainly from Turabian's *Manual for Writers,* which offers more specific advice than *The Chicago Manual* on the format of students' papers. See pages 744–46 for the format of footnotes, endnotes, and a bibliography. And see pages 108–13 for advice on type fonts, lists, illustrations, and other elements of design.

Margins and spacing Use minimum one-inch margins on all pages of the body. Double-space your own text and between notes and bibliography entries; single-space displayed quotations (see the next page) and each note and bibliography entry.

First page of Chicago paper

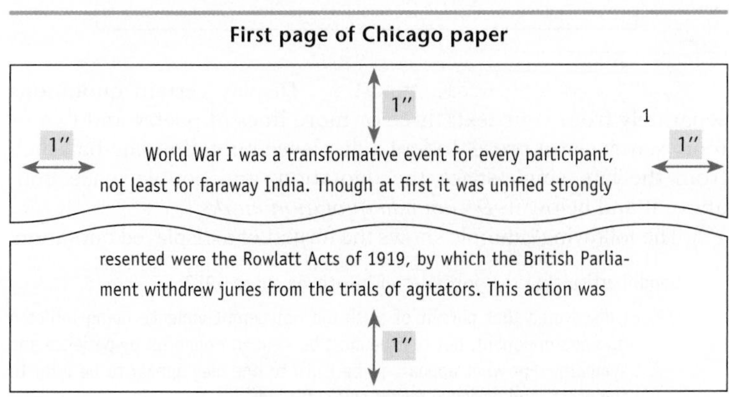

1″
1
1″
1″
World War I was a transformative event for every participant,
not least for faraway India. Though at first it was unified strongly
resented were the Rowlatt Acts of 1919, by which the British Parliament withdrew juries from the trials of agitators. This action was
1″

Paging Number pages consecutively from the first text page through the end (endnotes or bibliography). Use Arabic numerals (1, 2, 3) in the upper right corner of all pages.

Title page On an unnumbered title page provide the title of the paper, your name, the course title, your instructor's name, and the date.

Chicago title page

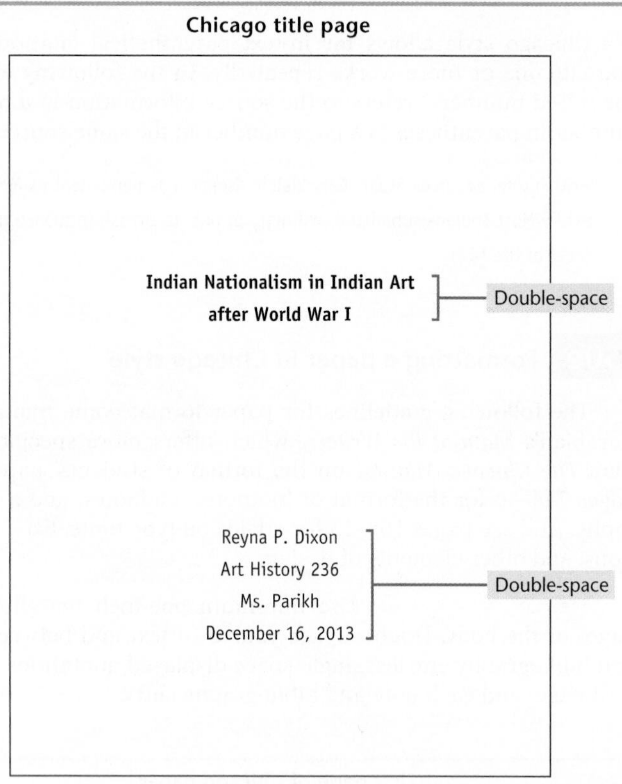

Indian Nationalism in Indian Art
after World War I
Double-space
Reyna P. Dixon
Art History 236
Ms. Parikh
December 16, 2013
Double-space

Poetry and long prose quotations Display certain quotations separately from your text: three or more lines of poetry and two or more sentences of prose. Indent a displayed quotation one-half inch from the left, single-space the quotation, and double-space both above it and below it. *Do not add quotation marks.*

The following example shows the format of a displayed quotation:

Gandhi articulated the principles of his movement in 1922:

> I discovered that pursuit of truth did not permit violence being inflicted on one's opponent, but that he must be weaned from error by patience and sympathy. For what appears to be truth to one may appear to be error to the other. And patience means self-suffering.[9]

51 Writing in the Social Sciences

Chapter essentials

- Use the methods and evidence common in the social sciences (below).
- Understand your writing assignment (next page).
- Use the tools and language of your discipline (next page).
- Use APA style for citing sources and formatting papers (pp. 761, 782).

Visit MyWritingLab™ for more resources on writing in the social sciences.

The social sciences—including anthropology, economics, education, management, political science, psychology, and sociology—focus on the study of human behavior. As the name implies, the social sciences examine the way human beings relate to themselves, to their environment, and to one another.

51a Using the methods and evidence of the social sciences

Researchers in the social sciences systematically pose a question, formulate a **hypothesis** (a generalization that can be tested), collect data, analyze those data, and draw conclusions to support, refine, or disprove their hypothesis. This is the scientific method developed in the natural sciences (see p. 793).

Social scientists gather data in several ways:

- **They interview subjects about their attitudes and behavior,** recording responses in writing or electronically. (See pp. 567–77 for guidelines on conducting an interview.)
- **They conduct broader surveys using questionnaires,** asking people about their attitudes and behavior. (See pp. 577–78 for guidelines on conducting a survey.)
- **They make firsthand observations of human behavior,** recording the observations in writing or electronically. (See p. 578 for guidelines on conducting an observation.)
- **They conduct controlled experiments,** structuring an environment in which to encourage and measure a specific behavior.

In their writing, social scientists explain their own research or analyze and evaluate others' research.

Social science research methods generate two kinds of data:

- ***Quantitative data* are numerical,** such as statistical evidence based on surveys, polls, tests, and experiments. When public-opinion pollsters announce that 47% of US citizens polled approve of the President's leadership, they are offering quantitative data gained from a survey. Social science writers present quantitative data in graphs, charts, and other illustrations that accompany their text.

- ***Qualitative data* are not numerical but more subjective:** they are based on interviews, firsthand observations, and inferences, taking into account the subjective nature of human experience. Examples include an anthropologist's description of the initiation rites in a culture she is studying or a psychologist's interpretation of interviews he conducted with a group of adolescents.

51b Understanding writing assignments in the social sciences

Depending on what social science courses you take, you may be asked to write in a variety of genres:

- **A research report:** Explain your own original research or your attempt to replicate the work of other researchers. A research report begins on page 784.
- **A summary or review of research:** Report on the available research literature on a subject, such as infants' perception of color.
- **A case analysis:** Explain the components of a phenomenon, such as a factory's closing.
- **A problem-solving analysis:** Explain the elements of a problem, such as unreported child abuse, and suggest ways to solve it.
- **A research paper:** Interpret and sometimes analyze and evaluate the writings of other social scientists about a subject, such as the effect of national appeals in advertising. An example appears in Chapter 48, pages 686–709.

Many social science disciplines have special requirements for the content and organization of each kind of assignment. The requirements appear in the style guides of the disciplines, listed on page 762. For instance, the American Psychological Association specifies the outline for research reports that is described on pages 782–83. Because of the differences among disciplines and even among different kinds of papers in the same discipline, you should always ask your instructor what he or she requires for an assignment.

51c Using the tools and language of the social sciences

The following guidelines for tools and language apply to most social sciences. However, the particular discipline you are writing in, or an instructor in a particular course, may have additional requirements. Reference works, available through your library, can clarify the disciplines' conventions. To use such works, consult a reference librarian.

1 Writing tools

Many social scientists rely on a **research journal** or **log,** in which they record their ideas throughout the research-writing process. Even if a research journal is not required in your courses, you may want to use one. As you formulate a hypothesis, you can record preliminary questions. Then when you are conducting research, you can use the journal to react to your findings, to record changes in your ideas, and to assess your progress. (See pp. 148–49 and 543 for more on journals.)

To avoid confusing your reflections on your findings with the evidence itself, keep records of actual data—notes from interviews, observations, surveys, and experiments—separately from the journal.

2 Language considerations

Each social science discipline has specialized terminology for concepts basic to the discipline. In sociology, for example, the words *mechanism, identity,* and *deviance* have specific meanings different from those of everyday usage. And *identity* means something different in sociology, where it applies to groups of people, than in psychology, where it applies to the individual. Social scientists also use precise terms to describe or interpret research. For instance, they say *The subject expressed a feeling of* rather than *The subject felt* because human feelings are not knowable for certain; or they say *These studies indicate* rather than *These studies prove* because conclusions are only tentative.

Just as social scientists strive for objectivity in their research, they also strive to demonstrate their objectivity through language in their writing. They avoid expressions such as *I think* in order to focus attention on what the evidence shows, not the researcher's opinions. For the same reason, they also generally use the passive voice of verbs to describe their methods and results, as in *The subjects' responses were recorded*. (However, many social scientists prefer *I* to *the researcher* when they refer to their own actions, as in *I recorded the subjects' responses.* Ask your instructor for his or her preferences.) Social scientists also avoid direct or indirect expression of their personal biases or emotions, either in discussions of other researchers' work or in descriptions of research subjects. Thus one social scientist does not call another's work *sloppy* or *immaculate* and does not refer to his or her own subjects as *drunks* or *innocent victims.* Instead, the writer uses neutral language and ties conclusions strictly to the data.

51d Citing sources in APA style

Some of the social sciences publish style guides that advise practitioners how to organize, document, and type papers in those fields. The following is a partial list:

American Anthropological Association, *AAA Style Guide,* 2009 (*www.aaanet.org/publications/style_guide.pdf*)
American Political Science Association, *Style Manual for Political Science,* 2006(*www.apsanet.org/media/PDFs/Publications/APSAStyleManual2006.pdf*)
American Psychological Association, *Publication Manual of the American Psychological Association,* 6th ed., 2010
American Sociological Association, *ASA Style Guide,* 4th ed., 2010
Linguistic Society of America, "LSA Style Sheet," published every December in *LSA Bulletin*
A Uniform System of Citation (law), 19th ed., 2010

By far the most widely used style is that of the American Psychological Association (APA), so we detail it here. Always ask your instructor in any class whether to use APA or another style.

Note The APA provides answers to frequently asked questions at *www.apastyle.org/learn/faqs.*

1 Using APA in-text citations

In APA documentation style, citations within the text refer the reader to a list of sources at the end of the text. An in-text citation contains the author's last name, the date of publication, and sometimes the page number from which material is borrowed.

Note When you cite the same source more than once in a paragraph, APA style does not require you to repeat the date beyond the first citation as long as it's clear what source you refer to. Do give the date in every citation if your source list includes more than one work by the same author(s).

APA
51d

1. Author not named in your text

One critic of Milgram's experiments questioned whether the researchers behaved morally toward their subjects (Baumrind, 1988).

When you do not name the author in your text, place in parentheses the author's last name, the date of the source, and sometimes the page number as explained below. Separate the elements with commas. Position the reference so that it is clear what material is being documented *and* so that the reference fits as smoothly as possible into your sentence structure. (See pp. 641–42 for guidelines.)

Unless none is available, the APA requires a page or other identifying number for a direct quotation and recommends an identifying number for a paraphrase:

In the view of one critic of Milgram's experiments (Baumrind, 1988), the subjects "should have been fully informed of the possible effects on them" (p. 34).

Use an appropriate abbreviation before the number—for instance, p. for *page* and para. for *paragraph.* The identifying number may fall by itself in parentheses, as in the preceding example, or it may fall with the author and date: (Baumrind, 1988, p. 34). See also model 11, page 765.

APA in-text citations

2. Author named in your text

Baumrind (1988) insisted that the subjects in Milgram's study "should have been fully informed of the possible effects on them" (p. 34).

When you use the author's name in the text, do not repeat it in parentheses. Place the date of the source in parentheses after the author's name. Place any page or paragraph reference either after the borrowed material (as in the example) or with the date: (1988, p. 34).

3. Work with two authors

Bunning and Ellis (2013) revealed significant communication differences between teachers and students.

One study (Bunning & Ellis, 2013) revealed significant communication differences between teachers and students.

When given in the text, two authors' names are connected by and. In a parenthetical citation, they are connected by an ampersand, &.

4. Work with three to five authors

Pepinsky, Dunn, Rentl, and Corson (2010) demonstrated the biases evident in gestures.

In the first citation of a work with three to five authors, name all the authors.

In the second and subsequent references to a work with three to five authors, generally give only the first author's name, followed by et al. (Latin abbreviation for "and others"):

In the work of Pepinsky et al. (2010), the loaded gestures included head shakes and eye contact.

However, two or more sources published in the same year could shorten to the same form—for instance, two references shortening to Pepinsky et al., 2010. In that case, cite the last names of as many authors as you need to distinguish the sources, and then give et al.: for instance, (Pepinsky, Dunn, et al., 2010) and (Pepinsky, Bradley, et al., 2010).

5. Work with six or more authors

One study (McCormack et al., 2012) explored children's day-to-day experience of living with a speech impairment.

For six or more authors, even in the first citation of the work, give only the first author's name, followed by et al. If two or more sources published in the same year shorten to the same form, give additional names as explained with model 4.

6. Work with a group author

The students' later work improved significantly (Lenschow Research, 2013).

For a work that lists an institution, agency, corporation, or other group as author, treat the name of the group as if it were one person's name. If the name is long and has a familiar abbreviation, you may use the abbreviation in the second and subsequent citations. For example, you might abbreviate American Psychological Association as APA.

7. Work with no author or an anonymous work

One article ("Leaping the Wall," 2013) examines Internet freedom and censorship in China.

For a work with no named author, use the first two or three words of the title in place of an author's name, excluding an initial *The, A,* or *An.* Italicize book and journal titles, place quotation marks around article titles, and capitalize the significant words in all titles cited in the text. (In the reference list, however, do not use quotation marks for article titles, and capitalize only the first word in all but periodical titles. See pp. 766–67.)

For a work that lists "Anonymous" as the author, use that word in the citation: (Anonymous, 2014).

8. One of two or more works by the same author(s)

At about age seven, most children begin to use appropriate gestures to reinforce their stories (Gardner, 1973a).

When you cite one of two or more works by the same author(s), the date will tell readers which source you mean—as long as your reference list includes only one source published by the author(s) in that year. If your reference list includes two or more works published by the same author(s) *in the same year,* the works should be lettered in the reference list (see p. 770). Then your text citation should include the appropriate letter with the date: 1973a above.

9. Two or more works by different authors

Two studies (Marconi & Hamblen, 1999; Torrence, 2011) found that monthly safety meetings can dramatically reduce workplace injuries.

List the sources in alphabetical order by their authors' names. Insert a semicolon between sources.

10. Indirect source

Supporting data appeared in a study by Wong (as cited in Gallivan, 2013).

The phrase as cited in indicates that the reference to Wong's study was found in Gallivan. Only Gallivan then appears in the list of references.

11. Electronic or Web source

Ferguson and Hawkins (2012) did not anticipate the "evident hostility" of the participants (para. 6).

Many electronic and Web sources can be cited like printed sources, with the author's last name, the publication date, and page numbers. Others are missing one or more pieces of information:

- **No page numbers:** When quoting or paraphrasing a source that numbers paragraphs instead of pages, provide the paragraph number preceded by para., as in the preceding example. If the source does not number pages or paragraphs but does include headings, list the heading under which the quotation appears and then (counting paragraphs yourself) the number of the paragraph in which the quotation appears—for example, (Endter & Decker, 2013, Method section, para. 3). When the source does not number pages or paragraphs or provide frequent headings, omit any reference number.
- **No author:** For a source with no listed author, follow model 7.
- **No date:** For a source that is undated, use n.d. ("no date") in place of the date.

2 Using an APA reference list

In APA style, the in-text citations refer readers to the list of sources at the end of the text. Title this list References and include in it the full publication information for every source you cited in your paper. Place the list at the end of the paper, and number its page(s) in sequence with the preceding pages.

The following sample shows the format of the first page of the APA reference list:

APA reference list

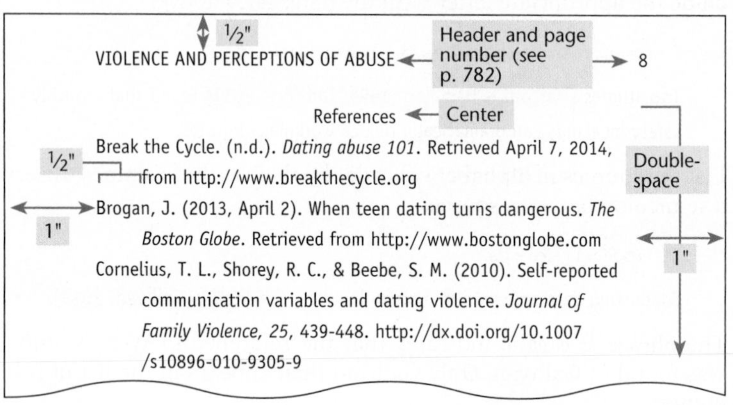
VIOLENCE AND PERCEPTIONS OF ABUSE 8

References

Break the Cycle. (n.d.). *Dating abuse 101*. Retrieved April 7, 2014, from http://www.breakthecycle.org

Brogan, J. (2013, April 2). When teen dating turns dangerous. *The Boston Globe*. Retrieved from http://www.bostonglobe.com

Cornelius, T. L., Shorey, R. C., & Beebe, S. M. (2010). Self-reported communication variables and dating violence. *Journal of Family Violence, 25*, 439-448. http://dx.doi.org/10.1007/s10896-010-9305-9

Arrangement Arrange sources alphabetically by the author's last name. If there is no author, alphabetize by the first main word of the title.

Spacing Double-space everything in the references unless your instructor requests single spacing. (If you do single-space the entries themselves, always double-space *between* them.)

Indention Begin each entry at the left margin, and indent the second and subsequent lines one-half inch. Your word processor can create this so-called hanging indent automatically.

Punctuation Separate the parts of the reference (author, date, title, and publication information) with a period and one space. Do not use a final period in references that conclude with a DOI or URL (see opposite).

Authors For works with up to seven authors, list all authors with last name first, separating names and parts of names with commas. Use initials for first and middle names even when names are listed fully on the source itself. Use an ampersand (&) before the last author's name. See model 3, page 769, for the treatment of eight or more authors.

Publication date Place the publication date in parentheses after the author's or authors' names, followed by a period. Generally, this date is the year only, though for some sources (such as magazine and newspaper articles) it includes the month and sometimes the day as well.

Titles In titles of books and articles, capitalize only the first word of the title, the first word of the subtitle, and proper nouns; all other words begin with small letters. In titles of journals, capitalize all significant words (see p. 481 for guidelines). Italicize the titles of books and journals. Do not italicize or use quotation marks around the titles of articles.

City and state of publication For sources that are not periodicals (such as books or government publications), give the city of publication, a comma, the two-letter postal abbreviation of the state, and a colon. Omit the state if the publisher is a university whose name includes the state name, such as University of Arizona.

Publisher's name Also for nonperiodical sources, give the publisher's name after the place of publication and a colon. Shorten names of many publishers (such as Morrow for William Morrow), and omit *Co.*, *Inc.*, and *Publishers*. However, give full names for associations, corporations, and university presses (such as Harvard University Press), and do not omit *Books* or *Press* from a publisher's name.

Page numbers Use the abbreviation p. or pp. before page numbers in books and in newspapers. Do *not* use the abbreviation for journals and magazines. For inclusive page numbers, include all figures: 667-668.

Digital Object Identifier (DOI) or retrieval statement At the end of each entry in the reference list, APA style requires a DOI for print and electronic sources (if one is available) or a retrieval statement for electronic sources.

- **DOI:** Many publishers assign a DOI to journal articles, books, and other documents. A DOI is a permanent URL that links to the text and functions as a unique identifier. When a DOI is available, include it in your citation of any print or electronic source. DOIs appear in one of two formats, as shown in model 7a (p. 771) and model 10 (p. 774). Use the format given in the source.
- **Retrieval statement:** If a DOI is not available for a source you found in a database or on the Web, provide a statement beginning with Retrieved from and then giving the URL of the periodical's or Web site's home page (model 7c, p. 771). You need not include the date you retrieved the source unless it is undated (model 22b, p. 777) or is likely to change (model 29, p. 779). If the source is difficult to find from the home page, you may give the complete URL. If you have questions about whether to include a home-page URL or a complete URL, ask your instructor.

Do not add a period after a DOI or a URL. Break a DOI or URL from one line to the next only before punctuation, such as a period or a slash, and do not hyphenate.

See the next two pages for an index to APA reference-list models. If you don't see a model for the kind of source you used, try to find one that comes close, and provide ample information so that readers can trace the source. Often you will have to combine models to cite a source accurately.

APA reference-list models

Finding the right model for a source

1. **What type of source is it?** Locate the type in the index beginning below.

   Article, models 7–13
   Complete book or part of book, models 14–20
   Government publication, model 21
   Report, model 22
   Dissertation, model 23
   Web or social media, models 24–30
   Visual, audio, other media, models 31–37

2. **What is the medium of the source?** From within each type of source, choose the right model for the medium. Common media:

   Print
   Web
   Database
   E-book
   Tweet
   Television; radio
   Film; video recording
   Computer software; app

3. **Who is the author?** Choose the right model for the number and type of author(s).

   How many authors? models 1–3
   Corporation, agency, or other group author? model 4
   No named author? model 5
   Author(s) of two or more of your sources? model 6

Authors

1. One author

Rodriguez, R. (1982). *A hunger of memory: The education of Richard Rodriguez.* Boston, MA: Godine.

The initial R. appears instead of the author's first name, even though the author's full first name appears on the source. In this book title, only the first words of the title and subtitle and the proper name are capitalized.

2. Two to seven authors

Nesselroade, J. R., & Baltes, P. B. (1999). *Longitudinal research in behavioral studies.* New York, NY: Academic Press.

With two to seven authors, separate authors' names with commas and use an ampersand (&) before the last author's name.

3. Eight or more authors

Wimple, P. B., Van Eijk, M., Potts, C. A., Hayes, J., Obergau, W. R., Smith, H., . . . Zimmer, S. (2001). *Case studies in moral decision making among adolescents.* San Francisco, CA: Jossey-Bass.

For a work by eight or more authors, list the first six authors' names, insert an ellipsis mark (three spaced periods), and then give the last author's name.

4. Group author

Lenschow Research. (2013). *Trends in secondary curriculum.* Baltimore, MD: Arrow Books.

For a work with a group author—such as a research group, a committee, a government agency, or a corporation—begin the entry with the group name. In the reference list, alphabetize the work as if the first main word (excluding any *The, A,* or *An*) were an author's last name.

5. Author not named (anonymous)

Merriam-Webster's collegiate dictionary (11th ed.). (2008). Springfield, MA: Merriam-Webster.

Resistance is not futile. (2014, April 5). *New Scientist, 221*(15), 5.

When no author is named, list the work under its title and alphabetize it by the first main word (excluding any *The, A, An*).

For a work whose author is actually given as "Anonymous," use that word in place of the author's name and alphabetize it as if it were a name:

Anonymous. (2014). *Teaching research, researching teaching.* New York, NY: Alpine Press.

6. Two or more works by the same author(s) published in the same year

APA 51d

Gardner, H. (1973a). *The arts and human development.* New York, NY: Wiley.

Gardner, H. (1973b). *The quest for mind: Piaget, Lévi-Strauss, and the structuralist movement.* New York, NY: Knopf.

When citing two or more works by exactly the same author(s), published in the same year, arrange them alphabetically by the first main word of the title and distinguish the sources by adding a letter to the date. Both the date and the letter are used in citing the source in your text (see p. 764).

When citing two or more works by exactly the same author(s) but *not* published in the same year, arrange the sources in order of their publication dates, earliest first.

Articles in journals, magazines, and newspapers

7. Article in a scholarly journal

Some journals number the pages of issues consecutively during a year, so that each issue after the first begins numbering where the previous issue left off—say, at page 132 or 416. For this kind of journal, give the volume number after the title (models a, b, c). Other journals as well as most magazines start each issue with page 1. For these journals and magazines, place the issue number in parentheses and not italicized immediately after the volume number (model 8).

a. Print, database, or Web journal article with a DOI

Hirsh, A. T., Gallegos, J. C., Gertz, K. J., Engel, J. M., & Jensen, M. P. (2010). Symptom burden in individuals with cerebral palsy. *Journal of Rehabilitation Research & Development, 47,* 860-876. doi:10.1682/JRRD.2010.03.0024

See the next two pages for an explanation of this format and the location of the required information on a source. The format is the same for any journal article that has a DOI—print, database, or Web.

Note DOIs appear in one of two formats, as shown above and in model 10 (p. 774). Use the format given in the source.

b. Print journal article without a DOI

Atkinson, N. S. (2011). Newsreels as domestic propaganda: Visual rhetoric at the dawn of the cold war. *Rhetoric and Public Affairs, 14,* 69-105.

If a print journal article does not have a DOI, simply end with the page numbers of the article.

c. Database or Web journal article without a DOI

Rosen, I. M., Maurer, D. M., & Darnall, C. R. (2008). Reducing tobacco use in adolescents. *American Family Physician, 77,* 483-490. Retrieved from http://www.aafp.org/online/en/home/publications/journals/afp.html

APA 51d

If a journal article you found in a database or on the Web does not have a DOI, use a search engine to find the home page of the journal and give the home-page URL, as above. Generally, do not give the name of a database in which you found an article because readers may not be able to find the source the same way you did. However, do give the database name if you cannot find the home page of the journal on the Web, as in this example:

Smith, E. M. (1926, March). Equal rights—internationally! *Life and Labor Bulletin, 4,* 1-2. Retrieved from Women and Social Movements in the United States, 1600-2000, database.

8. Article in a magazine

For magazine articles, give the month of publication as well as any day along with the year. If the magazine gives volume and issue numbers, list them after the title of the magazine. Italicize the volume number and place the issue number, not italicized, in parentheses.

a. Print magazine article

Newton-Small, J. (2013, February 18). Blood for oil. *Time, 181*(6), 22.

(continued on p. 774)

Citing journal articles: Print, database, or Web with DOI

Print journal article

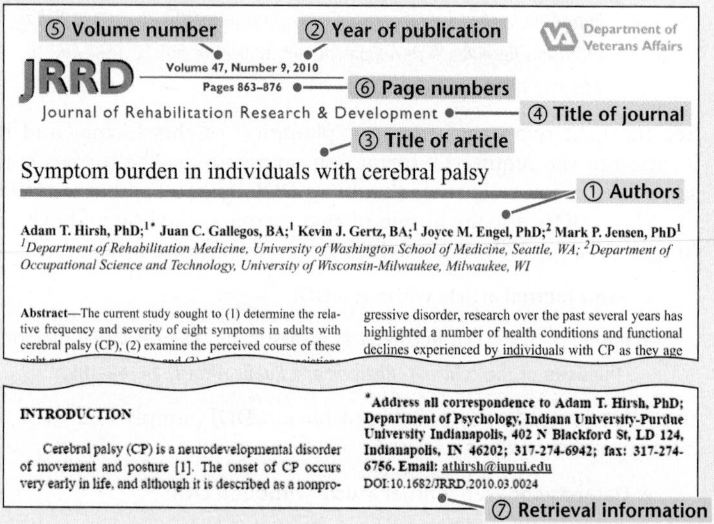

⑤ Volume number
② Year of publication
Department of Veterans Affairs
JRRD
Volume 47, Number 9, 2010
Pages 863–876
⑥ Page numbers
Journal of Rehabilitation Research & Development
④ Title of journal
③ Title of article
Symptom burden in individuals with cerebral palsy
① Authors
Adam T. Hirsh, PhD;[1*] Juan C. Gallegos, BA;[1] Kevin J. Gertz, BA;[1] Joyce M. Engel, PhD;[2] Mark P. Jensen, PhD[1]
[1]Department of Rehabilitation Medicine, University of Washington School of Medicine, Seattle, WA; [2]Department of Occupational Science and Technology, University of Wisconsin-Milwaukee, Milwaukee, WI
Abstract—The current study sought to (1) determine the relative frequency and severity of eight symptoms in adults with cerebral palsy (CP), (2) examine the perceived course of these
gressive disorder, research over the past several years has highlighted a number of health conditions and functional declines experienced by individuals with CP as they age
INTRODUCTION
Cerebral palsy (CP) is a neurodevelopmental disorder of movement and posture [1]. The onset of CP occurs very early in life, and although it is described as a nonpro-
*Address all correspondence to Adam T. Hirsh, PhD; Department of Psychology, Indiana University-Purdue University Indianapolis, 402 N Blackford St, LD 124, Indianapolis, IN 46202; 317-274-6942; fax: 317-274-6756. Email: athirsh@iupui.edu
DOI:10.1682/JRRD.2010.03.0024
⑦ Retrieval information

Database or Web journal article

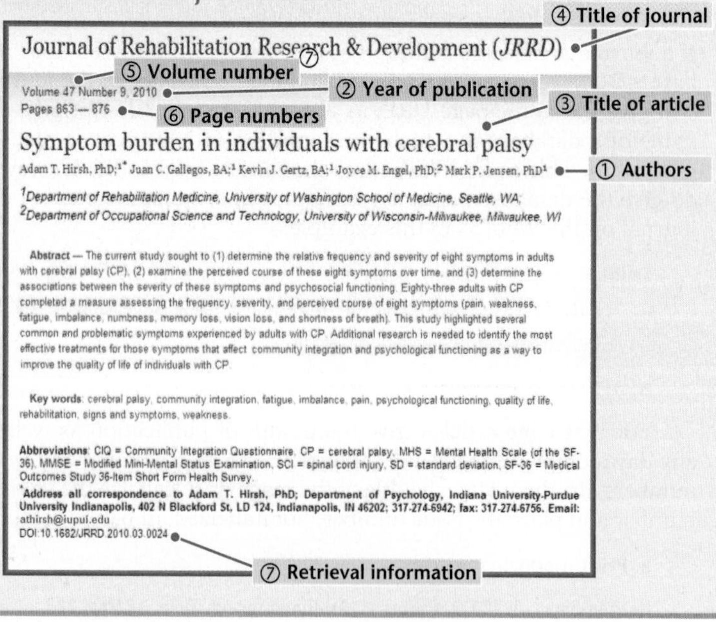

④ Title of journal
Journal of Rehabilitation Research & Development (JRRD)
⑤ Volume number
⑦
Volume 47 Number 9, 2010
② Year of publication
Pages 863 — 876
⑥ Page numbers
③ Title of article
Symptom burden in individuals with cerebral palsy
Adam T. Hirsh, PhD;[1*] Juan C. Gallegos, BA;[1] Kevin J. Gertz, BA;[1] Joyce M. Engel, PhD;[2] Mark P. Jensen, PhD[1]
① Authors
[1]Department of Rehabilitation Medicine, University of Washington School of Medicine, Seattle, WA;
[2]Department of Occupational Science and Technology, University of Wisconsin-Milwaukee, Milwaukee, WI
Abstract — The current study sought to (1) determine the relative frequency and severity of eight symptoms in adults with cerebral palsy (CP), (2) examine the perceived course of these eight symptoms over time, and (3) determine the associations between the severity of these symptoms and psychosocial functioning. Eighty-three adults with CP completed a measure assessing the frequency, severity, and perceived course of eight symptoms (pain, weakness, fatigue, imbalance, numbness, memory loss, vision loss, and shortness of breath). This study highlighted several common and problematic symptoms experienced by adults with CP. Additional research is needed to identify the most effective treatments for those symptoms that affect community integration and psychological functioning as a way to improve the quality of life of individuals with CP.
Key words: cerebral palsy, community integration, fatigue, imbalance, pain, psychological functioning, quality of life, rehabilitation, signs and symptoms, weakness.
Abbreviations: CIQ = Community Integration Questionnaire, CP = cerebral palsy, MHS = Mental Health Scale (of the SF-36), MMSE = Modified Mini-Mental Status Examination, SCI = spinal cord injury, SD = standard deviation, SF-36 = Medical Outcomes Study 36-Item Short Form Health Survey.
*Address all correspondence to Adam T. Hirsh, PhD; Department of Psychology, Indiana University-Purdue University Indianapolis, 402 N Blackford St, LD 124, Indianapolis, IN 46202; 317-274-6942; fax: 317-274-6756. Email: athirsh@iupui.edu
DOI:10.1682/JRRD.2010.03.0024
⑦ Retrieval information

References entry: Print, database, or Web journal article with DOI

① Hirsh, A. T., Gallegos, J. C., Gertz, K. J., Engel, J. M., & Jensen, M. P. ② (2010). ③ Symptom burden in individuals with cerebral palsy. ④ *Journal of Rehabilitation Research & Development,* ⑤ *47,* ⑥ 860-876. ⑦ doi:10.1682/JRRD.2010.03.0024

① **Authors.** Give each author's last name, first initial, and any middle initial. Separate names from initials with commas, and use & before the last author's name. Omit *Dr., PhD,* or any other title. See models 1–6 (pp. 769–70) for how to cite various numbers and kinds of authors.

② **Year of publication,** in parentheses and followed by a period.

③ **Title of article.** Give the full article title and any subtitle, separating them with a colon. Capitalize only the first words of the title and subtitle, and do not place the title in quotation marks.

④ **Title of journal,** in italics. Capitalize all significant words and end with a comma.

⑤ **Volume number,** italicized and followed by a comma. Include just the volume number when all the issues in each annual volume are paginated in one sequence. Include the issue number only when the issues are paginated separately.

⑥ **Inclusive page numbers of article,** without "pp." Do not omit any numerals.

⑦ **Retrieval information.** If the article has a DOI, give it using the format here or as shown in model 10. Do not end with a period. If the article does not have a DOI, see models 7b and 7c. (See p. 767 for more on DOIs and retrieval statements.)

(continued from p. 771)

b. Database or Web magazine article

Weir, K. (2014, March 22). Your cheating brain. *New Scientist, 221*(12), 35-37. Retrieved from http://www.newscientist.com

If a magazine article includes a DOI, give it after the page numbers. Otherwise, give the URL of the magazine's home page in a retrieval statement. If you do not find the home page, give the name of the database in which you found the article (see the Smith example on p. 771).

9. Article in a newspaper

For newspaper articles, give the month and day of publication along with the year. Use *The* in the newspaper name if the paper itself does.

a. Print newspaper article

Zimmer, C. (2014, May 4). Young blood may hold key to reversing aging. *The New York Times,* p. C1.

Precede the page number(s) with p. or pp.

b. Database or Web newspaper article

Angier, N. (2013, November 26). The changing american family. *The New York Times.* Retrieved from http://www.nytimes.com

Give the URL of the newspaper's home page in the retrieval statement. If you do not find the newspaper's home page, give the name of the database in which you found the article (see the Smith example on p. 771).

10. Review

Bond, M. (2008, December 18). Does genius breed success? [Review of the book *Outliers: The story of success,* by M. Gladwell]. *Nature, 456,* 785. http://dx.doi.org/10.1038/456874a

If a review has no title, use the bracketed information in its place, keeping the brackets.

11. Interview

Shaffir, S. (2013). It's our generation's responsibility to bring a genuine feeling of hope [Interview by H. Schenker]. *Palestine-Israeli Journal of Politics, Economics, and Culture, 18*(4). Retrieved from http://pij.org

List an interview under the interviewee's name and give the title, if any. If there is no title, or if the title does not indicate that the source is an interview, add a bracketed explanation, as above. End with publication information for the kind of source the interview appears in—here a journal on the Web, which requires retrieval information.

See model 32 (p. 780) to cite a recorded interview. See model 30 (p. 779) to cite an interview you conduct, which should be treated like a personal communication and cited only in the text.

12. Supplemental periodical content that appears only online

Anderson, J. L. (2014, May 2). Revolutionary relics [Supplemental material]. *The New Yorker.* Retrieved from www.newyorker.com

If you cite material from a periodical's Web site that is not included in the print version of the publication, add [Supplemental material] after the title and give the URL of the publication's home page.

13. Abstract of a journal article

Polletta, F. (2008). Just talk: Public deliberation after 9/11. *Journal of Public Deliberation, 4*(1). Abstract retrieved from http://services.bepress.com/jpd

When you cite the abstract of an article, give the full publication information for the article, followed by Abstract and information about where you found the abstract.

Books, government publications, and other independent works

14. Basic format for a book

a. Print book

Ehrenreich, B. (2007). *Dancing in the streets: A history of collective joy.* New York, NY: Holt.

Give the author's or authors' names, following models 1–4. Then give the complete title, including any subtitle. Italicize the title, and capitalize only the first words of the title and subtitle. End the entry with the city and state of publication and the publisher's name. (See p. 767 for how to treat these elements.)

b. Web or database book

Reuter, P. (Ed.). (2010). *Understanding the demand for illegal drugs.* Retrieved from http://books.nap.edu

For a book available on the Web or in an online library or database, replace any print publication information with a DOI if one is available (see model 7a) or with a retrieval statement, as above.

c. E-book

Waltz, M. (2013). *Autism: A social and medical history* [Kindle version]. Retrieved from http://www.amazon.com

For an e-book, give the format in brackets and a retrieval statement.

15. Book with an editor

Dohrenwend, B. S., & Dohrenwend, B. P. (Eds.). (1999). *Stressful life events: Their nature and effects*. New York, NY: Wiley.

List the names of the editors as if they were authors, but follow the last name with (Eds.).—or (Ed.). with only one editor. Note the periods inside and outside the final parenthesis.

16. Book with a translator

Trajan, P. D. (1927). *Psychology of animals* (H. Simone, Trans.). Washington, DC: Halperin.

17. Later edition

Bolinger, D. L. (1981). *Aspects of language* (3rd ed.). New York, NY: Harcourt Brace Jovanovich.

18. Work in more than one volume

Lincoln, A. (1953). *The collected works of Abraham Lincoln* (R. P. Basler, Ed.). (Vol. 5). New Brunswick, NJ: Rutgers University Press.

Lincoln, A. (1953). *The collected works of Abraham Lincoln* (R. P. Basler, Ed.). (Vols. 1-8). New Brunswick, NJ: Rutgers University Press.

APA 51d

The first entry cites a single volume (5) in the eight-volume set. The second entry cites all eight volumes. Use Vol. or Vols. in parentheses and follow the closing parenthesis with a period. In the absence of an editor's name, this description would follow the title directly: *The collected works of Abraham Lincoln* (Vol. 5).

19. Article or chapter in an edited book

Paykel, E. S. (1999). Life stress and psychiatric disorder: Applications of the clinical approach. In B. S. Dohrenwend & B. P. Dohrenwend (Eds.), *Stressful life events: Their nature and effects* (pp. 239-264). New York, NY: Wiley.

Give the publication date of the collection (1999 here) as the publication date of the article or chapter. After the article or chapter title and a period, say In and then provide the editors' names (in normal order), (Eds.) and a comma, the title of the collection, and the page numbers of the article in parentheses.

20. Article in a reference work

Wood, R. (1998). Community organization. In W. A. Swados, Jr. (Ed.), *Encyclopedia of religion and society*. Retrieved from http://hirr.hartsem.edu/ency/commorg.htm

If the entry you cite has no named author, begin with the title of the entry and then the date. Use a DOI instead of a URL if the source has one.

21. Government publication

a. Print publication

Hawaii. Department of Education. (2014). *Kauai district schools, profile 2013-14*. Honolulu, HI: Author.

Stiller, A. (2012). *Historic preservation and tax incentives*. Washington, DC: U.S. Department of the Interior.

If no person is named as the author, list the publication under the name of the sponsoring agency. When the agency is both the author and the publisher, use Author in place of the publisher's name, as in the first example.

For legal materials such as court decisions, laws, and testimony at hearings, the APA recommends formats that correspond to conventional legal citations. The following example of a congressional hearing includes the full title, the number of the Congress, the page number where the hearing transcript starts in the official publication, and the date of the hearing.

Medicare payment for outpatient physical and occupational therapy services: Hearing before the Committee on Ways and Means, House of Representatives, 110th Cong. 3 (2007).

b. Web publication

National Institute on Alcohol Abuse and Alcoholism. (2013, July). *Underage drinking* [Fact sheet]. Retrieved from http://pubs.niaaa.nih.gov/publications/UnderageDrinking/Underage_Fact.pdf

For a government publication on the Web, add a retrieval statement.

APA 51d

22. Report

a. Print report

Gerald, K. (2003). *Medico-moral problems in obstetric care* (Report No. NP-71). St. Louis, MO: Catholic Hospital Association.

Treat a printed report like a book, but provide any report number in parentheses after the title, with no punctuation between them.

b. Web report

Anderson, J. A., & Rainie, L. (2014, March 11). *Digital life in 2025*. Retrieved from Pew Research Internet Project website: http://www.pewinternet.org

For a report on the Web, give the name of the publisher in the retrieval statement if the publisher is not the author of the report. Generally, provide the URL of the Web site's home page.

If the work you cite is undated, use the abbreviation n.d. in place of the publication date and give the date of your access in the retrieval statement:

U.S. Census Bureau. (n.d.). *Men's marital status: 1950-2013.* Retrieved April 23, 2014, from https://www.census.gov/hhes/families/files/graphics/MS-1a.pdf

23. Dissertation

a. Dissertation in a commercial database

McFaddin, M. O. (2007). *Adaptive reuse: An architectural solution for poverty and homelessness* (Doctoral dissertation). Available from ProQuest Dissertations and Theses database. (ATT 1378764)

If a dissertation is from a commercial database, give the name of the database in the retrieval statement, followed by the accession or order number in parentheses.

b. Dissertation in an institutional database

Chang, J. K. (2003). *Therapeutic intervention in treatment of injuries to the hand and wrist* (Doctoral dissertation). Retrieved from http://medsci.archive.liasu.edu/61724

If a dissertation is from an institution's database, give the URL in the retrieval statement.

Web sources and social media

Specific types of Web sources are covered under their respective categories, such as articles in periodicals (models 7a, 7c, 8b, 9b), books (model 14b), and reports (model 22b). When citing URLs, APA recommends giving the home-page URL unless the source is difficult to find from the home page. In such a case, provide the complete URL.

24. Part or all of a Web site

American Psychological Association. (2014). Information for students with disabilities [Web page]. Retrieved from http://www.apa.org

To cite a page or document on a Web site, give the author (if any), the date (or n.d. if the page or site is undated), the title of the page or document, a description in brackets, and a retrieval statement.

Cite an entire Web site just in the text of your paper, giving the name of the site in your text and the URL in parentheses:

The Web site of the Cyberbullying Research Center provides information on the causes and nature of cyberbullying among teenagers (http://cyberbullying.us).

Although APA does not require you to include entire Web sites in your list of references, some instructors ask for such references. Then you can use the format shown in the first example, substituting the title of the Web site for the title of the Web page or document.

25. Post to a blog or discussion group

Kristof, N. (2014, March 22). Confronting the netherworld of child pornography [Blog post]. Retrieved from http://kristof.blogs.nytimes.com

Include postings to blogs and discussion groups in your list of references only if they are retrievable by others. (The source above is retrievable by a search of the home page URL.) Follow the message title with [Blog post], [Electronic mailing list message], or [Online forum comment]. Include the name of the blog or discussion group in the retrieval statement if it isn't part of the URL.

26. Blog comment

Peter. (2014, March 23). Re: Confronting the netherworld of child pornography [Blog comment]. Retrieved from http://kristof.blogs.nytimes.com

27. Post to a social-networking site

Environmental Defense Fund. (2014, May 1). Extreme weather = extreme consequences [Facebook status update]. Retrieved from https://www.facebook.com/EnvDefenseFund?fref=ts

28. Tweet

Bittman, M. [bittman]. (2014, April 1). Almost 90% of fast food workers say they've experienced wage theft: buff.ly/1i18eTb [Tweet]. Retrieved from http://twitter.com/bittman

29. Wiki

Clinical neuropsychology. (2013, November 12). Retrieved April 15, 2014, from Wikipedia: http://en.wikipedia.org/wiki/Clinical_neuropsychology

Give your date of retrieval for sources that are likely to change, such as this wiki.

30. E-mail or other personal communication (text citation)

At least one member of the research team has expressed reservations about the design of the study (L. Kogod, personal communication, February 6, 2014).

Personal e-mail, personal letters, interviews that you conduct yourself, and other communication that is not retrievable by others should be cited only in the text, not in the list of references.

APA 51d

Video, audio, and other media sources

31. Film or video recording

If you cite a film or video as a whole, begin with the producer's name as in the first example below. Otherwise, cite the name or names of the creator, director, or other contributor, followed by the function in parentheses. Add the medium in brackets after the title: [Motion picture] for film, [DVD], [Videocasette], or [Video file].

a. Motion picture or DVD

American Psychological Association (Producer). (2001). *Ethnocultural psychotherapy* [DVD]. Available from http://www.apa.org/videos

Tyrrell, C. (Director). (2010). *The Joneses* [Motion picture]. United States: Bjort Productions.

For a work in wide circulation (second example), give the country of origin and the studio that released the picture. For a work that is not widely circulated (first example), give the distributor's address or URL.

b. Video on the Web

CBS News (Producer). (1968, April 4). *1968 King assassination report* [Video file]. Retrieved from http://www.youtube.com/watch?v=cmOBbxgxKvo

In the retrieval statement, give the home-page URL unless the film or video you cite is difficult to locate from the home page. In that case, give the complete URL, as in the example.

32. Recorded interview

Ambar, S. (2014, April 1). Interview by T. Smiley [Video file]. Retrieved from http://www.pbs.org/wnet/tavissmiley

For an interview you view or listen to on the Web, give the name of the interviewee, the date, and the title of the interview, if any. Then give the interviewer's name if you wish, the type of file [Video file] or [Audio file], and a retrieval statement.

For an interview you see on television or hear in a podcast, adapt the preceding example using model 33b or 35.

33. Television series or episode

a. Television series

Rhimes, S. (Executive producer). (2014). *Grey's anatomy* [Television series]. New York, NY: ABC.

For a television series, begin with the producer's name and function. Add [Television series] after the title, and give either the city and name of the network or a Web retrieval statement.

b. Broadcast episode of television program

McKee, S. (Writer), & Wilson, C. (Director). (2014). Do you know? [Television series episode]. In S. Rhimes (Executive producer), *Grey's anatomy*. New York, NY: ABC.

For a TV episode, begin with the writer and then the director, identifying the function of each in parentheses, and add [Television series episode] after the episode title. Then provide the series information, beginning with In and the producer's name and function, giving the series title, and ending with the city and name of the network.

c. Web episode of a television program

Randall, T. (Writer & Director). (2012). How smart can we get? [Television series episode]. In J. Cort (Executive producer), *Nova*. Retrieved from http://www.pbs.org/wgbh/nova

Cite a TV episode you view on the Web as you would a broadcast episode, giving a retrieval statement rather than the city and name of the network.

34. Musical recording

Springsteen, B. (2002). Empty sky. On *The rising* [CD]. New York, NY: Columbia.

Begin with the name of the writer or composer. (If you cite another artist's recording of the work, provide this information after the title of the work—for example, [Recorded by E. Davila].) Give the medium in brackets ([CD], [LP], [mp3 file], and so on). Finish with the city, state, and name of the recording label or a retrieval statement.

35. Podcast

Glass, I. (Producer). (2014, April 11). The hounds of Blairsville [Audio podcast]. *This American life*. Retrieved from http://www.thisamericanlife.org

36. Visual

Southern Illinois University School of Medicine. (n.d.). Reporting child abuse and neglect [Diagram]. Retrieved from http://www.siumed.edu/oec/Year4/how_to_report_child_abuse.pdf

United Nations Population Fund (Cartographer). (2014). *Percent of population living on less than $1/day* [Demographic map]. Retrieved from http://www.unfpa.org

37. Video game, computer software, or app

Mojang. (2014). Minecraft: Pocket Edition (Version 0.8.1) [Mobile application software]. Retrieved May 7, 2014, from https://minecraft.net

For a video game, computer program, or app, give the following: the name of the developer or author, the date, the title, the version, a bracketed description of the program (such as [Video game], [Computer software], or [Mobile application software], as here), and a retrieval statement.

51e Formatting a paper in APA style

Use the following guidelines and samples to prepare a paper in APA format. Check with your instructor for any modifications to this format.

Note See pages 766–67 for the APA format of a reference list. And see pages 108–13 for guidelines on type fonts, lists, tables and figures, and other elements of design.

Margins Use one-inch margins on the top, bottom, and both sides.

Spacing and indentions Double-space everywhere. (The only exception is in tables and figures, where related data, labels, and other elements may be single-spaced.) Indent paragraphs and displayed quotations one-half inch.

Paging Begin numbering on the title page, and number consecutively through the end (including the reference list). Provide a header about one-half inch from the top of every page, as shown in the sample paper that begins on page 784. The header consists of the page number on the far right and your full or shortened title on the far left. Type the title in all-capital letters. On the title page only, precede the title with the label Running head and a colon. Omit this label on all other pages.

Title page Include the full title, your name, the course title, the instructor's name, and the date. (See p. 784.) Type the title on the top half of the page, followed by the identifying information, all centered horizontally and double-spaced.

Abstract Summarize (in a maximum of 120 words) your subject, research method, findings, and conclusions. (See p. 784.) Put the abstract on a page by itself.

Body Begin with a restatement of the paper's title, and organize the body into sections:

1. The introduction (not labeled) presents the problem you researched, your method, the relevant background (such as related studies), and the purpose of your research.)
2. A section labeled **Method** provides a detailed discussion of how you conducted your research, including a description of the research subjects, any materials or tools you used (such as questionnaires), and the procedure you followed. You may want

to break the discussion of methods into subsections labeled with headings, formatted as follows:

First-Level Heading

Second-Level Heading

Third-level heading. Run this heading into the text paragraph with a standard paragraph indention.

3. A section labeled **Results** summarizes the data you collected, explains how you analyzed them, and presents them in detail, often in tables, graphs, or charts. (See p. 786.)
4. A section labeled **Discussion** interprets the data and presents your conclusions. (See p. 787.) (When the discussion is brief, you may combine it with the previous section under the heading **Results and Discussion**.)
5. A section labeled **References**, beginning a new page, includes all your sources. (See pages 766–67 for an explanation and sample.)

Long quotations Run into your text all quotations of forty words or less, and enclose them in quotation marks. For quotations of more than forty words, set them off from your text by indenting all lines one-half inch, double-spacing throughout.

Echoing the opinions of other Europeans at the time, Freud (1961) had a poor view of Americans:

> The Americans are really too bad. . . . Competition is much more pungent with them, not succeeding means civil death to every one, and they have no private resources apart from their profession, no hobby, games, love or other interests of a cultured person. And success means money. (p. 86)

Do not use quotation marks around a quotation displayed in this way.

Illustrations Present data in tables, graphs, or charts, as appropriate. (See the sample on p. 789 for a clear table format to follow.) Begin each illustration on a separate page. Number each kind of illustration consecutively and separately from the other (Table 1, Table 2, etc., and Figure 1, Figure 2, etc.). Refer to all illustrations in your text—for instance, (see Figure 3). Generally, place illustrations immediately after the text references to them. (See pp. 110–16 for more on illustrations.)

APA 51f

51f Examining a sample research report

A sociology research report appears on the following pages. The student writer followed the organization described on the preceding pages both in establishing the background for her study and in explaining her own research. She also followed the APA style of source citation and document format.

The writing situation: Research report

- **Subject:** Violence and perceptions of abuse among college-age dating couples; student's choice for an assignment in a sociology course
- **Purpose:** To inform readers about the writer's own research and published research
- **Audience:** Classmates and instructor
- **Genre:** Research report—an explanation of the writer's research, with a formal structure of abstract, introduction (including discussion of prior research), methods, results, discussion of results, and references
- **Sources:** Student's survey data and published research (cited in APA style)

[Title page.]

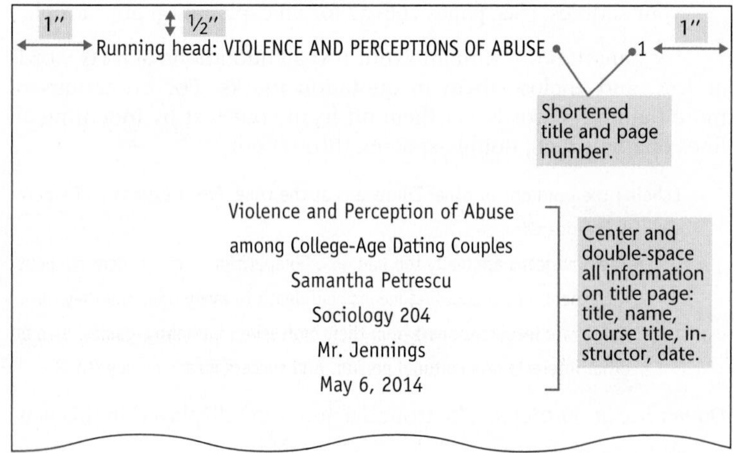

1″
½″
1″
Running head: VIOLENCE AND PERCEPTIONS OF ABUSE 1
Shortened title and page number.
Violence and Perception of Abuse
among College-Age Dating Couples
Samantha Petrescu
Sociology 204
Mr. Jennings
May 6, 2014
Center and double-space all information on title page: title, name, course title, instructor, date.

[New page.]

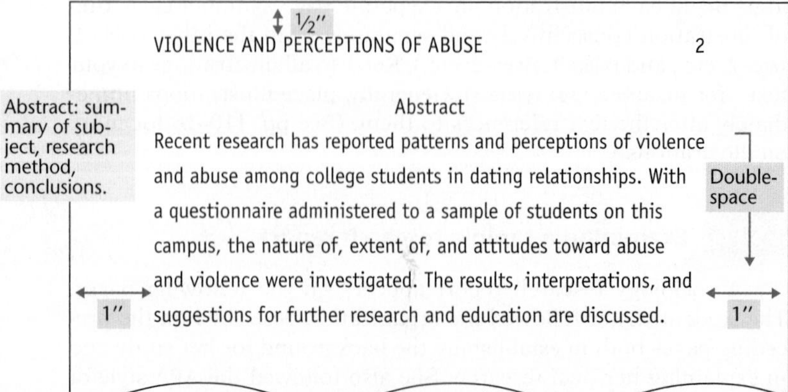

½″
VIOLENCE AND PERCEPTIONS OF ABUSE 2
Abstract: summary of subject, research method, conclusions.
Abstract
Recent research has reported patterns and perceptions of violence
and abuse among college students in dating relationships. With
a questionnaire administered to a sample of students on this
campus, the nature of, extent of, and attitudes toward abuse
and violence were investigated. The results, interpretations, and
suggestions for further research and education are discussed.
Double-space
1″
1″

APA 51f

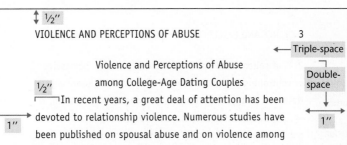

½″

VIOLENCE AND PERCEPTIONS OF ABUSE 3

Triple-space

Violence and Perceptions of Abuse
among College-Age Dating Couples

Double-space

½″

1″

1″

In recent years, a great deal of attention has been devoted to relationship violence. Numerous studies have been published on spousal abuse and on violence among teenage couples. The media have issued alarming news about teen relationship violence. For example, *The Boston Globe* reported that nearly 1.5 million high school students have been intentionally injured by a boyfriend or girlfriend and noted that mobile technologies have created new opportunities for abusers to intimidate their victims (Brogan, 2013). Violence among college-age dating couples has also been researched, as this study will discuss. With so much information about relationship violence available, it seems that rates of abuse would decrease each year. And yet published studies indicate that rates of relationship abuse have remained fairly consistent. This study confirms that trend on one college campus, and it suggests that perceptions of abuse in relationships need to change.

Introduction: presentation of the problem researched by the writer.

Citation form: author not named in the text.

Advocacy groups have defined dating violence as "a pattern of destructive behaviors used to exert power and control over a dating partner" (Break the Cycle, n.d.). These behaviors include both physical assault, from slapping to sexual coercion, and psychological abuse such as insults and threats. In an early study of dating behaviors, Makepeace (1981) reported that one-fifth of his respondents at Bemidji State University had at least one encounter with dating violence. He extended these percentages to students nationwide, suggesting "the existence of a major hidden social problem" (p. 100).

Definition of dating violence.

Citation form: undated source by group author not named in the text. No page number given because online source is unnumbered.

Citation form: page number given for quotation.

More recent research has extended Makepeace's findings. Kaura and Lohman (2007) found that 28.76% of respondents at Iowa State University had experienced premarital abuse. Similarly, a national poll revealed that

Review of published research.

Citation form: source with two authors, named in the text.

1″

Citation forms: source with group author and source with three authors, not named in the text.

27% of college students have been subjected to possessive or controlling behaviors from a dating partner (Knowledge Networks, 2011). Another study (Helweg-Larsen, Harding, & Kleinman, 2008) found that so-called date rape, while more publicized, was reported by many fewer respondents (less than 2%) than was other physical violence during courtship (20%). And although the media tend to focus on female victims, a number of researchers have shown that dating violence affects men and women at similar rates, both as recipients and as perpetrators (Cornelius, Shorey, & Beebe, 2010; Kaura & Lohman, 2007; Knowledge Networks, 2011; Miller, 2011).

Citation form: more than one source cited at once.

Recent research has also shown that students tend not to identify their own and others' behavior as violent or abusive even when it meets the experts' definition of dating violence. Kaura and Lohman (2007) discovered that when dating couples give examples of behavior that qualify as abusive or violent in relation to other couples, both the perpetrators and the victims in these relationships tend not to describe their interactions as abusive or violent. Miller (2011) discovered that more than 85% of students in violent dating relationships do not label the abuse as such, while Knowledge Networks (2011) found that 57% of college students in the United States say they do not know what abusive behavior looks like.

The purpose of the present study was to survey students on this campus to test whether the incidence of abusive relationships and attitudes toward abuse were similar to the patterns reported in published studies.

First- and second-level headings.

Method

Sample

"Method" section: discussion of how research was conducted.

I conducted a survey of 200 students (109 females, 91 males) enrolled in an introductory sociology course at a large state university in the northeastern United

States. Participants were primarily sophomores (67%) and juniors (18%), with an average age of 20. After I omitted from the analysis both incomplete questionnaires and responses from subjects who indicated they were married or not currently dating, the sample totaled 123 subjects.

The Questionnaire

A questionnaire exploring the personal dynamics of relationships was approved by the Institutional Review Board and distributed during class with informed consent forms. Questions were answered anonymously at home using a secure online survey system.

The questionnaire consisted of three sections. The first asked for basic demographic information such as gender, age, and relationship status. The second section required participants to assess aspects of their current dating relationships, such as levels of stress and frustration, communication between partners, and patterns of decision making. These variables were expected to influence the amount of violence in a relationship.

The third part of the survey was adapted from Straus's revised Conflict Tactics Scales (2006), an instrument designed to measure relationship conflict and how it ends, including in negotiation, psychological aggression, and physical assault. This section provided a list of 26 physically and psychologically abusive behaviors ranging from minor (yelling, slapping) to severe (punching, choking) and instructed subjects to identify those they had experienced with their dating partner. One question asked respondents to characterize their relationship as abusive or not. The last question asked respondents to rate their overall satisfaction with the relationship.

Results

The questionnaire revealed significant levels of psychological aggression among unmarried couples, consistent

"Results" section: summary and presentation of data.

with the published studies. Of the respondents who indicated they were dating, just over half (62 of 123 subjects) reported that they had experienced verbal abuse at least once, being either insulted or sworn at. Nearly 18% (22 of 123) had been shouted at by a romantic partner. In addition, almost 14% of respondents (17 of 123) had been threatened with some type of violence. (See Table 1.)

Reference to table.

Rates of physical assault were also consistent with the published research. More than 16% of the study subjects reported being pushed or shoved by a partner, more than 12% had been slapped, and almost 6% had been kicked, bitten, or punched by a partner. Nine respondents (7.3%) indicated that an object had been thrown at them. One subject reported being attacked with a deadly weapon. (See Table 1.)

Most participants in relationships that experts would characterize as violent did not say that they consider themselves victims of violence. Of the 33 respondents (27% of the total) who reported two or more aggressive or violent incidents with their romantic partners, less than a quarter (8 individuals) self-identified their relationships as abusive. Among the 123 study subjects as a whole, 108 (87.8%) stated they were mostly or completely satisfied with their current relationships; only 15 (12.2%) indicated they were dissatisfied.

"Discussion" section: interpretation of data and presentation of conclusions.

Discussion

Violence within premarital relationships has been widely acknowledged in the sociological research, and the present study confirms previous findings. On this campus, abuse and force occur among college couples, and like the subjects of published studies the perpetrators and victims of violence here often do not characterize their relationships as abusive. A high number of respondents indicated that they have been subjected to minor forms of abuse such

Table 1

Incidence of courtship violence

Type of violence	Number of students reporting	Percentage of sample
Psychological aggression		
Insulted or swore	62	50.4
Shouted	22	17.8
Threatened	17	13.8
Physical assault		
Pushed or shoved	20	16.3
Slapped	15	12.2
Kicked, bit, or punched	7	5.7
Threw something that could hurt	9	7.3
Used a knife or gun	1	0.8

Table on a page by itself.

Table presents data in a clear format.

as verbal aggression, yet most claimed to be satisfied with their relationships. Although the percentages of physical violence are relatively small, so was the sample. Extending the results to the entire campus population would mean significant numbers. For example, if the incidence of being kicked, bitten, or punched is typical at 6%, then 900 students of a 15,000-member student body might have experienced this type of violence.

If college-age relationships are significantly abusive and violent, what accounts for this pattern of interaction? The survey examined some variables that appeared to influence the relationships. Level of stress and frustration, both within the relationship and in the respondent's life, was one such variable. The communication level between partners, both the frequency of discussion and the frequency of agreement, was another. Gender was not a factor: male and female subjects both reported inflicting and receiving abuse, although females were subjected to more severe forms of violence.

As other studies have shown, participation in an abusive relationship can have lasting consequences. Kaura and Lohman (2007), among others, have shown that dating violence leads to mental health issues—especially anxiety and depression—for both men and women. Miller (2011) found that those who don't label abusive behavior as such are more likely to perpetuate it and to accept it as victims, while Prather, Dahlen, Nicholson, and Bullock-Yowell (2012) discovered that violence tends to become more severe as relationships become more serious. Cornelius et al. concluded that for young men and women alike, premarital violence is a problem of "highly maladaptive interactional patterns" similar to those that surface in abusive marriages (p. 445). Researchers at Cornell University found that those who experience abuse in young adult relationships are at increased

Citation form: source with four authors, named in the text.

Citation form: second mention of source with three to five authors shortened to "et al."

risk of entering into violent marriages (as cited in Brogan, 2013).

Citation form: indirect source.

Conclusion: summary and implications for further research.

These published studies suggest that a great deal is at stake for the participants in abusive relationships, not only in the present but for the future. This study extended research on this subject by contributing data on violence and abuse among college-age dating couples. The survey results provided an overview of the variables that may contribute to abusive relationships, the rates and types of dating abuse, and perceptions of abusive behaviors. The study found that rates of abuse are similar to those in published studies, as are the participants' attitudes toward abuse. If the courtship period sets the stage for later relationships, including marriage, and if attitudes of denial contribute to the perpetuation of abuse, then more attention should be given to educating young people to recognize and stop the behavior.

VIOLENCE AND PERCEPTIONS OF ABUSE 10

New page for reference list.

References

Page on a Web site with retrieval information.

Double-space

½"

Break the Cycle. (n.d.). Dating abuse 101 [Web page]. Retrieved April 7, 2014, from http://www.breakthecycle.org

Brogan, J. (2013, April 2). When teen dating turns dangerous. *The Boston Globe*. Retrieved from http://www.bostonglobe.com

Cornelius, T. L., Shorey, R. C., & Beebe, S. M. (2010). Self-reported communication variables and dating violence. *Journal of Family Violence, 25*, 439-448. http://dx.doi.org/10.1007/s10896-010-9305-9

Helweg-Larsen, M., Harding, H. G., & Kleinman, K. E. (2008). Risk perceptions of dating violence among college women. *Journal of Social and Clinical Psychology, 27,* 600-620. Retrieved from http://www.guilford.com

Kaura, S. A., & Lohman, B. J. (2007). Dating violence victimization, relationship satisfaction, mental health problems, and acceptability of violence: A comparison of men and women. *Journal of Family Violence, 22,* 367-381. doi:10.1007/s10896-007-9092-0

Knowledge Networks. (2011). *College dating violence and abuse poll*. Retrieved from http://www.loveisrespect.org/pdf/College_Dating_And_Abuse_Final_Study.pdf

Makepeace, J. M. (1981). Courtship violence among college students. *Family Relations, 30*(1), 97-102.

Miller, L. M. (2011). Physical abuse in a college setting: Perceptions and participation. *Journal of Family Violence, 26,* 71-80. doi:10.1007/s10896-010-9344-2

Prather, E., Dahlen, E. R., Nicholson, B. C., & Bullock-Yowell, E. B. (2012). Relational aggression in college students' relationships. *Journal of Aggression, Maltreatment, and Trauma, 21.* doi:10.1080/10926771.2012.693151

Straus, M. A. (2006). *Conflict Tactics Scales (CTS) sourcebook.* Torrance, CA: Western Psychological Services.

Online newspaper article with URL of home page.

Journal article with a Digital Object Identifier (DOI).

Journal article accessed through a database, with journal homepage URL

Report from the Web site of an organization.

Article in a print journal.

Book. ("Tactics Scales" is capitalized because it is part of a proper name.)

52 Writing in the Natural and Applied Sciences

Chapter essentials

- Use the methods and evidence common in the natural and applied sciences (below).
- Understand your writing assignment (next page).
- Use the tools and language of your discipline (next page).
- Use CSE style for citing sources and formatting papers (pp. 795, 802).

Visit MyWritingLab™ for more resources on writing in the natural and applied sciences.

The natural and applied sciences include biology, chemistry, physics, mathematics, engineering, computer science, and their branches. Their purpose is to understand natural and technological phenomena. (A *phenomenon* is a fact or event that can be known by the senses.) Scientists conduct experiments and write to explain the step-by-step processes in their methods of inquiry and discovery.

52a Using the methods and evidence of the sciences

Scientists investigate phenomena by the **scientific method,** a process of continual testing and refinement.

The scientific method

- **Observe carefully.** Accurately note all details of the phenomenon being researched.
- **Ask questions about the observations.**
- **Formulate a *hypothesis,*** or preliminary generalization, that explains the observed facts.
- **Test the hypothesis** with additional observation or controlled experiments.
- **If the hypothesis proves accurate, formulate a *theory,*** or unified model, that explains *why*.
- **If the hypothesis is disproved, revise it or start anew.**

Scientific evidence is almost always quantitative—that is, it consists of numerical data obtained from the measurement of phenomena. These data are called **empirical** (from a Greek word for "experience"); they result from observation and experience, generally in a controlled laboratory setting but also (as sometimes in astronomy or biology) in the natural world. Often the empirical evidence for scientific writing comes from library research into other people's reports of their investigations. Surveys of known data or existing literature are common in scientific writing.

52b Understanding writing assignments in the sciences

No matter what your assignment, you will be expected to document and explain your evidence carefully so that anyone reading can check your sources and replicate your research. It is important for your reader to know the context of your research—both the previous experimentation and research on your particular subject (acknowledged in the survey of the literature) and the physical conditions and other variables surrounding your own work.

Assignments in the natural and applied sciences include the following genres:

- **A laboratory report:** Explain the procedure and results of an experiment that you conducted. (See p. 803 for an example.)
- **A summary:** Distill a research article to its essence in brief, concise form. (Summary is discussed in detail on pp. 155–57.)
- **A critique:** Summarize and critically evaluate a scientific report.
- **A research report:** Explain the experimental research of other scientists and your own experiment's methods, findings, and conclusions.
- **A research proposal:** Review the relevant literature and explain your plan for further research.

52c Using the tools and language of the sciences

Tools and language concerns vary from discipline to discipline in the sciences. Consult your instructor for specifics about the field in which you are writing. You can also discover much about a discipline's tools and language in reference works available through your library. To use such works, consult a reference librarian.

1 Writing tools

In the sciences a **lab notebook** or **scientific journal** is almost indispensable for accurately recording the empirical data from observations and experiments. Use such a notebook or journal for these purposes:

- **Record observations** from reading, from class, or from the lab.
- **Ask questions and refine hypotheses.**
- **Record procedures.**
- **Record results.**

- **Keep an ongoing record of ideas and findings** and how they change as data accumulate.
- **Sequence and organize your material** as you compile your findings and write your report.

Make sure that your records of data are clearly separate from your reflections on the data so that you don't mistakenly confuse the two in drawing your conclusions.

2 Language considerations

Science writers prefer to use objective language that removes the writer as a character in the situation and events being explained, except as the impersonal agent of change, the experimenter. Although usage is evolving, scientists still rarely use *I* in their reports and evaluations, and they often resort to the passive voice of verbs, as in *The mixture was then subjected to centrifugal force.* This conscious objectivity focuses attention (including the writer's) on the empirical data and what they show. It discourages the writer from, say, ascribing motives and will to animals and plants. For instance, instead of asserting that the sea tortoise *developed* its hard shell *to protect* its body, a scientist would write only what could be observed: that the hard shell *covers and thus protects* the tortoise's body.

Science writers typically change verb tenses to distinguish between established information and their own research. For established information, such as that found in journals and other reliable sources, use the present tense: *Baroreceptors monitor blood pressure.* For your own and others' research, use the past tense: *The bacteria died within three hours. Marti reported some success.*

Each discipline in the natural and applied sciences has a specialized vocabulary that permits precise, accurate, and efficient communication. Some of these terms, such as *pressure* in physics, have different meanings in the common language and must be handled carefully in science writing. Others, such as *enthalpy* in chemistry, have no meanings in the common language and must simply be learned and used correctly.

52d Citing sources in CSE style

Within the natural and applied sciences, practitioners use one of two styles of documentation, varying slightly from discipline to discipline. Following are some of the style guides most often consulted:

American Chemical Society, *ACS Style Guide: A Manual for Authors and Editors*, 3rd ed., 2006

American Institute of Physics, *Style Manual for Guidance in the Preparation of Papers*, 4th ed., 1990 (*www.aip.org/pubservs/style/4thed/AIP_Style_4thed.pdf*)

American Medical Association Manual of Style, 10th ed., 2007
Council of Science Editors, *Scientific Style and Format: The CSE Manual for Authors, Editors, and Publishers,* 8th ed., 2014

The most thorough and widely used of these guides is the last one, *Scientific Style and Format*, which details both styles of scientific documentation: one using author and date and one using numbers. Both types of text citation refer to a list of references at the end of the paper (see the next page). Ask your instructor which style you should use.

1 Using CSE name-year text citations

In the CSE name-year style, parenthetical text citations provide the last name of the author being cited and the source's year of publication. At the end of the paper, a list of references, arranged alphabetically by authors' last names, provides complete information on each source.

The CSE name-year style closely resembles the APA name-year style detailed on pages 762–65. You can follow the APA examples for in-text citations, making several notable changes for CSE:

- **Do not use a comma to separate the author's name and the date:** (Baumrind 1968).
- **Separate two authors' names with and (not "&"):** (Pepinsky and DeStefano 1997).
- **For sources with three or more authors, use et al. (Latin abbreviation for "and others") after the first author's name:** (Singh et al. 2014).

2 Using CSE numbered text citations

In the CSE number style, raised numbers in the text refer to a numbered list of references at the end of the paper.

Two standard references[1, 2] use this term.

These forms of immunity have been extensively researched.[3]

Hepburn and Tatin[2] do not discuss this project.

Assignment of numbers The number for each source is based on the order in which you cite the source in the text: the first cited source is 1, the second is 2, and so on.

Reuse of numbers When you cite a source you have already cited and numbered, use the original number again (see the last example above, which reuses the number 2 from the first example).

This reuse is the key difference between the CSE numbered citations and numbered references to footnotes or endnotes. In the CSE style, each source has only one number, determined by the order in which the source is cited. With notes, in contrast, the numbering proceeds in sequence, so that each source has as many numbers as it has citations in the text.

Citation of two or more sources When you cite two or more sources at once, arrange their numbers in sequence and separate them with a comma and a space, as in the first example on the previous page.

3 Using a CSE reference list

For both the name-year and the number styles of in-text citation, provide a list, titled References, of all sources you have cited. Center this heading about an inch from the top of the page, and double-space beneath it.

The following examples show the differences and similarities between the name-year and number styles:

Name-year style

Hepburn PX, Tatin JM. 2005. Human physiology. New York (NY): Columbia University Press.

Number style

2. Hepburn PX, Tatin JM. Human physiology. New York (NY): Columbia University Press; 2005.

Spacing In both styles, single-space each entry and double-space between entries.

Arrangement In the name-year style, arrange entries alphabetically by authors' last names. In the number style, arrange entries in numerical order—that is, in order of their citation in the text.

Format In the name-year style, type all lines of entries at the left margin—do not indent. In the number style, begin the first line of each entry at the left margin and indent subsequent lines as shown above.

Authors In both styles, list each author's name with the last name first, followed by initials for first and middle names. Do not use a comma between an author's last name and initials, and do not use periods or spaces with the initials. Do use a comma to separate authors' names.

Placement of dates In the name-year style, the date follows the author's or authors' names. In the number style, the date follows the publication information (for a book) or the periodical title (for a journal, magazine, or newspaper).

Journal titles In both styles, do not italicize or underline journal titles. For titles of two or more words, abbreviate words of six or more letters (without periods) and omit most prepositions, articles, and conjunctions. Capitalize each word. For example, *Journal of Chemical and Biochemical Studies* becomes J Chem Biochem Stud, and *Hospital Practice* becomes Hosp Pract.

Book and article titles In both styles, do not italicize, underline, or use quotation marks around a book or an article title. Capitalize only the first word and any proper nouns.

Publication information for journal articles The name-year and number styles differ in the placement of the publication date (see the previous page). However, after the journal title both styles give the journal's volume number, any issue number in parentheses, a colon, and the inclusive page numbers of the article, run together without space: 28:329-30 or 62(2):26-40. See model 6 on page 800.

The following box indexes the CSE models. The models themselves include examples of both a name-year reference and a number reference for each type of source.

CSE reference-list models

Finding the right model for a source

1. **What type of source is it?** Locate the type in the index beginning below.

   Article, models 6–8
   Complete book or part of book, models 9–11
   Web or social media, models 12–14
   Other, models 15–18

2. **What is the medium of the source?** From within each type of source, choose the right model for the medium. Common media:

   Print
   Web
   Database
   Blog post
   Personal communication
   Audio or visual recording

3. **Who is the author?** Choose the right model for the number and type of author(s).

   How many authors? models 1–3
   No named author? model 4
   Author(s) of two or more of your sources? model 5

CSE
52d

Authors

1. One author

Gould SJ. 1987. Time's arrow, time's cycle. Cambridge (MA): Harvard University Press.

1. Gould SJ. Time's arrow, time's cycle. Cambridge (MA): Harvard University Press; 1987.

2. Two to ten authors

Hepburn PX, Tatin JM, Tatin JP. 2012. Human physiology. New York (NY): Columbia University Press.

2. Hepburn PX, Tatin JM, Tatin JP. Human physiology. New York (NY): Columbia University Press; 2012.

3. More than ten authors

Evans RW, Bowditch L, Dana KL, Drumond A, Wildovitch WP, Young SL, Mills P, Mills RR, Livak SR, Lisi OL, et al. 2011. Organ transplants: ethical issues. Ann Arbor (MI): University of Michigan Press.

3. Evans RW, Bowditch L, Dana KL, Drummond A, Wildovitch WP, Young SL, Mills P, Mills RR, Livak SR, Lisi OL, et al. Organ transplants: ethical issues. Ann Arbor (MI): University of Michigan Press; 2011.

CSE 52d

4. Author not named

Health care for children with diabetes. 2014. New York (NY): US Health Care.

4. Health care for children with diabetes. New York (NY): US Health Care; 2014.

5. Two or more cited works by the same author(s) published in the same year

Gardner H. 1973a. The arts and human development. New York (NY): Wiley.

Gardner H. 1973b. The quest for mind: Piaget, Lévi-Strauss, and the structuralist movement. New York (NY): Knopf.

(The number style does not require such forms.)

Articles in journals, newspapers, and magazines

6. Article in a journal

a. Print article

Campos JJ, Walle EA, Dahl A, Main A. 2011. Reconceptualizing emotion regulation. Emotion Rev. 3(1):26-35.

6. Campos JJ, Walle EA, Dahl A, Main A. Reconceptualizing emotion regulation. Emotion Rev. 2011;3(1):26-35.

b. Database or Web article

Grady GF. 2014. New research on immunizations. Today's Med. [accessed 2014 Dec 10];10(3):45-49. http://www.fmrt.org/todaysmedicine/Grady050389.pdf8. doi:10.1087/262534887.

6. Grady GF. New research on immunizations. Today's Med. 2014 [accessed 2014 Dec 10];10(3):45-49. http://www.fmrt.org/todaysmedicine/Grady050389.pdf8. doi:10.1087/262534887.

Give the date of your access after the journal title (first example) or after the publication date (second example). If the article has no page, paragraph, or other reference numbers, give your calculation of its length in brackets—for instance, [about 15 p.] or [20 paragraphs]. Conclude with the source's URL and the DOI (Digital Object Identifier) if one is available. (See p. 767 for more on DOIs.)

7. Article in a newspaper

Zimmer C. 2014 May 8. Antibiotic-resistant germs lying in wait everywhere. New York Times (National Ed.). Sect. C:1 (col. 1).

7. Zimmer C. Antibiotic-resistant germs lying in wait everywhere. New York Times (National Ed.). 2014 May 8;Sect. C:1 (col. 1).

8. Article in a magazine

Talbot M. 2013 Mar 18. About a boy. New Yorker. 56-65.

8. Talbot M. About a boy. New Yorker. 2013 Mar 18;56-65.

Books

9. Basic format for a book

a. Print book

Wilson EO. 2004. On human nature. Cambridge (MA): Harvard University Press.

9. Wilson EO. On human nature. Cambridge (MA): Harvard University Press; 2004.

b. Web book

Ruch BJ, Ruch DB. 2013. New research in medicine and homeopathy. New York (NY): Albert Einstein College of Medicine; [accessed 2014 Jan 25]. http://www.einstein.edu/medicine/books/ruch&ruch.pdf.

9. Ruch BJ, Ruch DB. New research in medicine and homeopathy. New York (NY): Albert Einstein College of Medicine; 2013 [accessed 2014 Jan 25]. http://www.einstein.edu/medicine/books/ruch&ruch.pdf.

10. Book with an editor

Jonson P, editor. 2014. Anatomy yearbook 2014. Los Angeles (CA): Anatco.

10. Jonson P, editor. Anatomy yearbook 2014. Los Angeles (CA): Anatco; 2014.

11. Selection from a book

Kriegel R, Laubenstein L, Muggia F. 2005. Kaposi's sarcoma. In: Ebbeson P, Biggar RS, Melbye M, editors. AIDS: a basic guide for clinicians. 2nd ed. Philadelphia (PA): Saunders. p. 100-126.

11. Kriegel R, Laubenstein L, Muggia F. Kaposi's sarcoma. In: Ebbeson P, Biggar RS, Melbye M, editors. AIDS: a basic guide for clinicians. 2nd ed. Philadelphia (PA): Saunders; 2005. p. 100-126.

Web sites and social media

12. Web site

American Medical Association. c1995-2014. Chicago (IL): American Medical Association; [accessed 2014 Nov 22]. http://ama-assn.org/ama.

12. American Medical Association. Chicago (IL): American Medical Association; c1995-2014 [accessed 2014 Nov 22]. http://ama-assn.org/ama.

If you are unable to determine the most recent update to a Web site, give the copyright date, typically found at the bottom of the home page, preceded by c: c1995-2014 in the preceding examples.

13. Blog post

Tenenbaum, LF. 2014 Apr 29. Zombies vs. Goldilocks: the insurrection [blog post]. Earth Right Now. [accessed 2014 May 19]. http://climate.nasa.gov/blog/1075.

13. Tenenbaum, LF. Zombies vs. Goldilocks: the insurrection [blog post]. Earth Right Now. 2014, Apr 29. [accessed 2014 May 19]. http://climate.nasa.gov/blog/1075.

CSE 52d

14. Personal communication (text citation)

One member of the research team has expressed reservation about the study design (personal communication from L. Kogod, 2014 Feb 6; unreferenced).

A personal letter or e-mail message should be cited in your text, not in your reference list. The format is the same for both the name-year and the number styles.

Other sources

15. Report written and published by the same organization

Warnock M. 2006. Report of the Committee on Fertilization. Waco (TX): Baylor University Department of Embryology. Report No.: BU/DE.4261.

15. Warnock M. Report of the Committee on Fertilization. Waco (TX): Baylor University Department of Embryology; 2006. Report No.: BU/DE.4261.

16. Report written and published by different organizations

Hackney, JD (Rancho Los Amigos Hospital, Downey, CA). 2012. Effect of atmospheric pollutants on human physiologic function. Washington (DC): Environmental Protection Agency (US). Report No.: R-801396.

16. Hackney, JD (Rancho Los Amigos Hospital, Downey, CA). Effect of atmospheric pollutants on human physiologic function. Washington (DC): Environmental Protection Agency (US); 2012. Report No.: R-801396.

17. Audio or visual recording

Cell mitosis [DVD–ROM]. 2014. White Plains (NY): Teaching Media.

17. Cell mitosis [DVD-ROM]. White Plains (NY): Teaching Media; 2014.

18. Document on CD-ROM or DVD-ROM

Reich WT, editor. c2013. Encyclopedia of bioethics [DVD-ROM]. New York (NY): Co-Health. 1 DVD.

18. Reich WT editor. Encyclopedia of bioethics [DVD-ROM]. New York (NY): Co-Health; c2013. 1 DVD.

52e Formatting a paper in CSE style

Scientific Style and Format is not specific about margins, spacing for headings, and other elements of paper format. Unless your instructor specifies otherwise, you can use the format of the APA (pp. 782–83). The CSE exception to this style is the list of references, which is described on pages 797–98.

The most troublesome aspects of manuscript preparation in the sciences are equations or formulas, tables, and figures. When typing equations or formulas, be careful to reproduce alignments, indentions, underlining, and characters accurately. If your word processor lacks special characters, leave space for them and write them in by hand.

Because you will be expected to share your data with your readers, most of your writing for the sciences is likely to require illustrations to present the data in concise, readable form. Tables usually summarize raw data (see p. 805 for an example), whereas figures (mainly charts, graphs, and diagrams) recast the data to show noteworthy comparisons or changes. Follow the guidelines on pages 108–13 for preparing tables and figures.

52f Examining a sample science paper

The following biology paper illustrates the CSE number style for documenting sources. On page 806, passages from the paper and a reformatted list of references show the name-year style. Except for the in-text citations and the references, the paper is formatted in APA style because CSE does not specify a format.

This paper illustrates the five major sections of a laboratory report:

1. **"Abstract"**: A summary of the report.
2. **"Introduction" or "Objective"**: A review of why the study was undertaken, a summary of the background of the study, and a statement of the problem being studied.
3. **"Method" or "Procedure"**: A detailed explanation of how the study was conducted, including any statistical analysis.
4. **"Results"**: An explanation of the major findings (including unexpected results) and a summary of the data presented in graphs and tables.
5. **"Discussion"**: An interpretation of the results and an explanation of how they relate to the goals of the experiment. This section also describes new hypotheses that might be tested as a result of the experiment. If the section is brief, it may be combined with the previous section in a single section labeled "Conclusions."

In addition, this lab report includes a list of references because the writer consulted other sources.

A laboratory report: CSE number style

[Title page.]

Exercise and Blood Pressure

Liz Garson

Biology 161

Ms. Traversa

December 13, 2013

[New page.]

Abstract

The transient elevation of blood pressure following exercise was demonstrated by pressure measurements of twenty human subjects before and after exercise.

[New page.]

Exercise and Blood Pressure

Introduction

The purpose of this experiment was to verify the changes in blood pressure that accompany exercise, as commonly reported.[1,2] A certain blood pressure is necessary for the blood to supply nutrients to the body tissues. Baroreceptors near the heart monitor pressure by determining the degree to which blood stretches the wall of the blood vessel.

The writing situation: Laboratory report

- **Subject:** The effect of exercise on blood pressure; student's choice for an assignment in a biology class
- **Purpose:** To inform readers about the student's research and published research
- **Audience:** Classmates and instructor
- **Genre:** Laboratory report—an explanation of an experiment conducted by the writer, with a formal structure consisting of abstract, introduction (including discussion of prior research), method (including procedure), results, discussion of results, and references
- **Sources:** Student's experimental data and published research (cited in CSE style)

[The introduction continues.]

During exercise, the metabolic needs of the muscles override the influence of the baroreceptors and result in an increase in blood pressure. This increase in blood pressure is observed uniformly (irrespective of sex or race), although men demonstrate a higher absolute systolic pressure than do women.[3] During strenuous exercise, blood pressure can rise to 40 percent above baseline.[1]

Method

The subjects for this experiment were twenty volunteers from laboratory classes, ten men and ten women. All pressure measurements were performed using a standard sphygmomanometer, which was tested for accuracy. To ensure consistency, the same sphygmomanometer was used to take all readings. In addition, all measurements were taken by the same person to avoid discrepancies in method or interpretation.

The first pressure reading was taken prior to exercise as the subject sat in a chair. This pressure was considered the baseline for each subject. All subsequent readings were interpreted relative to this baseline.

In the experiment, the subjects ran up and down stairs for fifteen minutes. Immediately after exercising, the subjects returned to the laboratory to have their pressure measured. Thirty minutes later, the pressure was measured for the final time.

Results

Table 1 contains the blood pressure measurements for the male and female subjects. With the exception of subjects 3 and 14, all subjects demonstrated the expected post-exercise increase in blood pressure, with a decline to baseline or near baseline thirty minutes after exercise. The data for subjects 3 and 14 were invalid because the subjects did not perform the experiment as directed.

[Table on a page by itself.]

Table 1. Blood pressure measurements for all subjects (mmHg)

Subject	Baseline[a]	Post-exercise	30-minute reading
Male			
1	110/75	135/80	115/75
2	125/80	140/90	135/85
3	125/70	125/70	125/70
4	130/85	170/100	140/90
5	120/80	125/95	120/80
6	115/70	135/80	125/75
7	125/70	150/80	130/70
8	130/80	145/85	130/80
9	140/75	180/85	155/80
10	110/85	135/95	115/80
Female			
11	110/60	140/85	115/60
12	130/75	180/85	130/75
13	125/80	140/90	130/80
14	90/60	90/60	90/60
15	115/65	145/70	125/65
16	100/50	130/65	110/50
17	120/80	140/80	130/80
18	110/70	135/80	120/75
19	120/80	140/90	130/80
20	110/80	145/90	120/80

[a]Normal blood pressure at rest: males, 110-130/60-90; females, 110-120/50-80.

Discussion

As expected, most of the subjects demonstrated an increase in blood pressure immediately after exercise and a decline to near baseline levels thirty minutes after exercise. The usual pressure increase was 20-40 mmHg for the systolic pressure and 5-10 mmHg for the diastolic pressure.

In the two cases in which blood pressure did not elevate with exercise (subjects 3 and 14), the subjects simply left the laboratory and returned fifteen minutes later without having exercised. The experimental design was flawed in not assigning someone to observe the subjects as they exercised.

[New page.]

References

1. Guyton AC. Textbook of medical physiology. Philadelphia (PA): Saunders; 2010.
2. Rowell LB. Blood pressure regulation during exercise. Ann Med. 2004;28:329-333.
3. Gleim GW, Stachenfeld NS. Gender differences in the systolic blood pressure response to exercise. Am Heart J. 2001;121:524-530.

A laboratory report: CSE name-year style

These excerpts from the preceding paper show documentation in CSE name-year style:

The purpose of this experiment was to verify the changes in blood pressure that accompany exercise, as commonly reported (Guyton 2010; Rowell 2004).

This increase in blood pressure is observed uniformly (irrespective of sex or race), although men demonstrate a higher absolute systolic pressure than do women (Gleim and Stachenfeld 2001). During strenuous exercise, blood pressure can rise to 40 percent above baseline (Guyton 2010).

References

Gleim GW, Stachenfeld NS. 2001. Gender differences in the systolic blood pressure response to exercise. Am Heart J. 121:524-530.

Guyton AC. 2010. Textbook of medical physiology. Philadelphia (PA): Saunders.

Rowell LB. 2004. Blood pressure regulation during exercise. Ann Med. 28:329-333.

Glossary of Usage

This glossary provides notes on words or phrases that often cause problems for writers. The recommendations for standard American English are based on current dictionaries and usage guides such as the ones listed on pp. 508–09. Items labeled **nonstandard** should be avoided in academic and business settings. Those labeled **colloquial** and **slang** occur in speech and in some informal writing but are best avoided in formal college and business writing. (Words and phrases labeled *colloquial* include those labeled by many dictionaries with the equivalent term *informal.*) See Chapters 37 and 38 for further discussion of word choice and for exercises in usage. See p. 508 for a description of dictionary labels. Also see pp. 527–28 for a list of commonly confused words that are pronounced the same or similarly.

The glossary is necessarily brief. Keep a dictionary handy for all your writing, and make a habit of referring to it whenever you doubt the appropriateness of a word or phrase.

a, an Use *a* before words beginning with consonant sounds, including those spelled with an initial pronounced *h* and those spelled with vowels that are sounded as consonants: *a historian, a one-o'clock class, a university.* Use *an* before words that begin with vowel sounds, including those spelled with an initial silent *h*: *an organism, an L, an honor.*

The article before an abbreviation depends on how the abbreviation is read: *She was once an AEC undersecretary* (*AEC* is read as three separate letters); *Many Americans opposed a SALT treaty* (*SALT* is read as one word, *salt*).

For the use of *a/an* versus *the,* see pp. 332–34.

accept, except *Accept* is a verb meaning "receive." *Except* is usually a preposition or conjunction meaning "but for" or "other than"; when it is used as a verb, it means "leave out." *I can accept all your suggestions except the last one. I'm sorry you excepted my last suggestion from your list.*

adverse, averse *Adverse* and *averse* both mean "opposed" or "hostile." But *averse* describes the subject's opposition to something, whereas *adverse* describes something opposed to the subject: *The President was averse to adverse criticism.*

advice, advise *Advice* is a noun, and *advise* is a verb: *Take my advice; do as I advise you.*

affect, effect Usually *affect* is a verb, meaning "to influence," and *effect* is a noun, meaning "result": *The drug did not affect his driving; in fact, it seemed to have no effect at all.* But *effect* occasionally is used as a verb meaning "to bring about": *Her efforts effected a change.* And *affect* is used in psychology as a noun meaning "feeling or emotion": *One can infer much about affect from behavior.*

aggravate *Aggravate* should not be used in its colloquial meaning of "irritate" or "exasperate" (for example, *We were aggravated by her constant arguing*). *Aggravate* means "make worse": *The President was irritated by the Senate's indecision because he feared any delay might aggravate the unrest in the Middle East.*

agree to, agree with *Agree to* means "consent to," and *agree with* means "be in accord with": *How can they agree to a treaty when they don't agree with each other about the terms?*

ain't Nonstandard for *am not, isn't,* or *aren't.*

all, all of Usually *all* is sufficient to modify a noun: *all my loving, all the things you are.* Before a pronoun or proper noun, *all of* is usually appropriate: *all of me, in all of France.*

all ready, already *All ready* means "completely prepared," and *already* means "by now" or "before now": *We were all ready to go to the movie, but it had already started.*

all right *All right* is always two words. *Alright* is a common error.

all together, altogether *All together* means "in unison" or "gathered in one place." *Altogether* means "entirely." *It's not altogether true that our family never spends vacations all together.*

allusion, illusion An *allusion* is an indirect reference, and an *illusion* is a deceptive appearance: *Paul's constant allusions to Shakespeare created the illusion that he was an intellectual.*

almost, most *Almost* means "nearly"; *most* means "the greater number (or part) of." In formal writing, *most* should not be used as a substitute for *almost*: *We see each other almost* [not *most*] *every day.*

a lot *A lot* is always two words, used informally to mean "many." *Alot* is a common misspelling.

among, between Use *among* for relationships involving more than two people or things. Use *between* for relationships involving only two or for comparing one thing to a group to which it belongs. *The four of them agreed among themselves that the choice was between New York and Los Angeles.*

amongst Although common in British English, in American English *amongst* is an overrefined substitute for *among.*

amount, number Use *amount* with a singular noun that names something not countable (a noncount noun): *The amount of food varies.* Use *number* with a plural noun that names more than one of something countable (a plural count noun): *The number of calories must stay the same.*

an, and *An* is an article (see *a, an*). *And* is a coordinating conjunction.

and etc. *Et cetera* (*etc.*) means "and the rest"; *and etc.* therefore is redundant. See also *et al., etc.*

and/or *And/or* indicates three options: one or the other or both (*The decision is made by the mayor and/or the council*). If you mean all three options, *and/or* is appropriate. Otherwise, use *and* if you mean both, *or* if you mean either.

and which, and who *And which* or *and who* is correct only when used to introduce a second clause beginning with the same relative pronoun:

Jill is my cousin who goes to school here and who calls me constantly. Otherwise, *and* is not needed: *WCAS is my favorite AM radio station, which* [not *and which*] *I listen to every morning.*

ante-, anti- The prefix *ante-* means "before" (*antedate, antebellum*); the prefix *anti-* means "against" (*antiwar, antinuclear*). Before a capital letter or *i, anti-* takes a hyphen: *anti-Freudian, anti-isolationist.*

anxious, eager *Anxious* means "nervous" or "worried" and is usually followed by *about. Eager* means "looking forward" and is usually followed by *to. I've been anxious about getting blisters. I'm eager* [not *anxious*] *to get new running shoes.*

anybody, any body; anyone, any one *Anybody* and *anyone* are indefinite pronouns; *any body* is a noun modified by *any*; *any one* is a pronoun or adjective modified by *any. How can anybody communicate with any body of government? Can anyone help Amy? She has more work than any one person can handle.*

any more, anymore *Any more* means "no more"; *anymore* means "now." Both are used in negative constructions: *He doesn't want any more. She doesn't live here anymore.*

anyplace Colloquial for *anywhere.*

anyways, anywheres Nonstandard for *anyway* and *anywhere.*

apt, liable, likely *Apt* and *likely* are interchangeable. Strictly speaking, though, *apt* means "having a tendency to": *Horace is apt to forget his lunch in the morning. Likely* means "probably going to": *Horace is leaving so early today that he's likely to catch the first bus.*

Liable normally means "in danger of" and should be confined to situations with undesirable consequences: *Horace is liable to trip over that hose.* Strictly, *liable* means "responsible" or "exposed to": *The owner will be liable for Horace's injuries.*

are, is Use *are* with a plural subject (*books are*), *is* with a singular subject (*book is*).

as *As* may be vague or ambiguous when it substitutes for *because, since,* or *while*: *As the researchers asked more questions, their money ran out.* (Does *as* mean "while" or "because"?) *As* should never be used as a substitute for *whether* or *who. I'm not sure whether* [not *as*] *we can make it. That's the man who* [not *as*] *gave me directions.*

as, like See *like, as.*

as, than In comparisons, *as* and *than* precede a subjective-case pronoun when the pronoun is a subject: *I love you more than he* [*loves you*]. *As* and *than* precede an objective-case pronoun when the pronoun is an object: *I love you as much as* [*I love*] *him.* (See also p. 278.)

assure, ensure, insure *Assure* means "to promise": *He assured us that we would miss the traffic. Ensure* and *insure* are often used interchangeably to mean "make certain," but some reserve *insure* for matters of legal and financial protection and use *ensure* for more general meanings: *We left early to ensure that we would miss the traffic. It's expensive to insure yourself against floods.*

as to A stuffy substitute for *about: The suspect was questioned about* [not *as to*] *her actions.*

at The use of *at* after *where* is wordy and should be avoided: *Where are you meeting him?* is preferable to *Where are you meeting him at?*

at this point in time Wordy for *now, at this point,* or *at this time.*

averse, adverse See *adverse, averse.*

awful, awfully Strictly speaking, *awful* means "awe-inspiring." As intensifiers meaning "very" or "extremely" (*He tried awfully hard*), *awful* and *awfully* should be avoided in formal speech or writing.

a while, awhile *Awhile* is an adverb; *a while* is an article and a noun. Thus *awhile* can modify a verb but cannot serve as the object of a preposition, and *a while* is just the opposite: *I will be gone awhile* [not *a while*]. *I will be gone for a while* [not *awhile*].

bad, badly In formal speech and writing, *bad* should be used only as an adjective; the adverb is *badly. He felt bad because his tooth ached badly.* In *He felt bad,* the verb *felt* is a linking verb and the adjective *bad* is a subject complement. (See also p. 326.)

being as, being that Colloquial for *because,* the preferable word in formal speech or writing: *Because* [not *Being as*] *the world is round, Columbus never did fall off the edge.*

beside, besides *Beside* is a preposition meaning "next to." *Besides* is a preposition meaning "except" or "in addition to" as well as an adverb meaning "in addition." *Besides, several other people besides you want to sit beside Dr. Christensen.*

better, had better *Had better* (meaning "ought to") is a verb modified by an adverb. The verb is necessary and should not be omitted: *You had better* [not just *better*] *go.*

between, among See *among, between.*

bring, take Use *bring* only for movement from a farther place to a nearer one and *take* for any other movement. *First, take these books to the library for renewal, then take them to Mr. Daniels. Bring them back to me when he's finished.*

bunch In formal speech and writing, *bunch* (as a noun) should be used only to refer to clusters of things growing or fastened together, such as bananas and grapes. Its use to mean a group of items or people is colloquial; *crowd* or *group* is preferable.

burst, bursted; bust, busted *Burst* is a standard verb form meaning "to fly apart suddenly." Its main forms are *burst, burst, burst;* the form *bursted* is nonstandard. The verb *bust* (*busted*) is slang.

but, hardly, scarcely These words are negative in their own right; using *not* with any of them produces a double negative (see p. 342). *We have but* [not *haven't got but*] *an hour before our plane leaves. I could hardly* [not *couldn't hardly*] *make out her face.*

but, however, yet Each of these words is adequate to express contrast. Don't combine them. *He had finished, yet* [not *but yet*] *he continued.*

but that, but what These wordy substitutes for *that* and *what* should be avoided: *I don't doubt that* [not *but that*] *you are right.*

calculate, figure, reckon As substitutes for *expect* or *imagine* (*I figure I'll go*), these words are colloquial.

can, may Strictly, *can* indicates capacity or ability, and *may* indicates permission: *If I may talk with you a moment, I believe I can solve your problem. May* also indicates possibility: *You may like what you hear.*

can't help but This idiom is common but redundant. Either *I can't help wishing* or the more formal *I cannot but wish* is preferable to *I can't help but wish.*

case, instance, line Expressions such as *in the case of, in the instance of,* and *along the lines of* are usually padding and should be avoided.

censor, censure To *censor* is to edit or remove from public view on moral or some other grounds; to *censure* is to give a formal scolding. *The lieutenant was censured by Major Taylor for censoring the letters her soldiers wrote home from boot camp.*

center around *Center on* is more logical than, and preferable to, *center around.*

climatic, climactic *Climatic* comes from *climate* and refers to weather: *Recent droughts may indicate a climatic change. Climactic* comes from *climax* and refers to a dramatic high point: *During the climactic duel between Hamlet and Laertes, Gertrude drinks poisoned wine.*

complement, compliment To *complement* something is to add to, complete, or reinforce it: *Her yellow blouse complemented her black hair.* To *compliment* something is to make a flattering remark about it: *He complimented her on her hair. Compliment* also functions as a noun: *She thanked him for the compliment.* The adjective *complimentary* can also mean "free": *complimentary tickets.*

compose, comprise *Compose* means "to make up": *The parts compose the whole. Comprise* means "to consist of": *The whole comprises the parts.* Thus, *The band comprises* [not *is comprised of*] *twelve musicians. Twelve musicians compose* [not *comprise*] *the band.*

conscience, conscious *Conscience* is a noun meaning "a sense of right and wrong"; *conscious* is an adjective meaning "aware" or "awake." *Though I was barely conscious, my conscience nagged me.*

contact Often used imprecisely as a verb instead of a more exact word such as *consult, talk with, telephone,* or *write to.*

continual, continuous *Continual* means "constantly recurring": *Most movies on television are continually interrupted by commercials. Continuous* means "unceasing": *Some cable channels present movies continuously without commercials.*

convince, persuade In the strictest sense, to *convince* someone means to change his or her opinion; to *persuade* someone means to move him or her to action. *Convince* is thus properly followed by *of* or *that,* whereas *persuade* is followed by *to*: *Once he had convinced Othello of Desdemona's infidelity, Iago easily persuaded him to kill her.*

could care less The expression is *could not* [*couldn't*] *care less. Could care less* indicates some care, the opposite of what is intended.

could of See *have, of.*

couple of Used colloquially to mean "a few" or "several."

credible, creditable, credulous *Credible* means "believable": *It's a strange story, but it seems credible to me. Creditable* means "deserving of credit" or "worthy": *Steve gave a creditable performance. Credulous* means "gullible": *The credulous Claire believed Tim's lies.* See also *incredible, incredulous.*

criteria The plural of *criterion* (meaning "standard for judgment"): *Our criteria are strict. The most important criterion is a sense of humor.*

data The plural of *datum* (meaning "fact"): *Out of all the data generated by these experiments, not one datum supports our hypothesis.* Usually, a more common term such as *fact, result,* or *figure* is preferred to *datum.* Though *data* is often used with a singular verb, many readers prefer the plural verb and it is always correct: *The data fail* [not *fails*] *to support the hypothesis.*

device, devise *Device* is the noun, and *devise* is the verb: *Can you devise some device for getting his attention?*

different from, different than *Different from* is preferred: *His purpose is different from mine.* But *different than* is widely accepted when a construction using *from* would be wordy: *I'm a different person now than I used to be* is preferable to *I'm a different person now from the person I used to be.*

differ from, differ with To *differ from* is to be unlike: *The twins differ from each other only in their hairstyles.* To *differ with* is to disagree with: *I have to differ with you on that point.*

discreet, discrete *Discreet* (noun form *discretion*) means "tactful": *What's a discreet way of telling Maud to be quiet? Discrete* (noun form *discreteness*) means "separate and distinct": *Within a computer's memory are millions of discrete bits of information.*

disinterested, uninterested *Disinterested* means "impartial": *We chose Pete, as a disinterested third party, to decide who was right. Uninterested* means "bored" or "lacking interest": *Unfortunately, Pete was completely uninterested in the question.*

don't *Don't* is the contraction for *do not,* not for *does not*: *I don't care, you don't care, and he doesn't* [not *don't*] *care.*

due to *Due* is an adjective or noun; thus *due to* is always acceptable as a subject complement: *His gray hairs were due to age.* Many object to *due to* as a preposition meaning "because of" (*Due to the holiday, class was canceled*). A rule of thumb is that *due to* is always correct after a form of the verb *be* but questionable otherwise.

due to the fact that Wordy for *because.*

each and every Wordy for *each* or *every.* Write *each one of us* or *every one of us,* not *each and every one of us.*

eager, anxious See *anxious, eager.*

effect See *affect, effect.*

elicit, illicit *Elicit* is a verb meaning "bring out" or "call forth." *Illicit* is an adjective meaning "unlawful." *The crime elicited an outcry against illicit drugs.*

emigrate, immigrate *Emigrate* means "to leave one place and move to another" (the Latin prefix *e-* means "out of": "migrate out of"): *The Chus emigrated from Korea. Immigrate* means "to move into a place where one was not born" (the Latin prefix *im-* means "into": "migrate into"): *They immigrated to the United States.*

ensure See *assure, ensure, insure.*

enthused Used colloquially as an adjective meaning "showing enthusiasm." The preferred adjective is *enthusiastic*: *The coach was enthusiastic* [not *enthused*] *about the team's prospects.*

especially, specially *Especially* means "particularly" or "more than other things"; *specially* means "for a specific reason." *I especially treasure my boots. They were made specially for me.*

et al., etc. Use *et al.*, the Latin abbreviation for "and other people," only in source citations: *Jones et al.* Avoid *etc.*, the Latin abbreviation for "and other things," in formal writing, and do not use it to refer to people or to substitute for precision, as in *The government provides health care, etc.* See also *and etc.*

everybody, every body; everyone, every one *Everybody* and *everyone* are indefinite pronouns: *Everybody* [or *Everyone*] *knows Tom steals. Every one* is a pronoun modified by *every*, and *every body* is a noun modified by *every*. Both refer to each thing or person of a specific group and are typically followed by *of*: *The game commissioner has stocked every body of fresh water in the state with fish, and now every one of our rivers is a potential trout stream.*

everyday, every day *Everyday* is an adjective meaning "used daily" or "common"; *every day* is a noun modified by *every*: *Everyday problems tend to arise every day.*

everywheres Nonstandard for *everywhere.*

except See *accept, except.*

except for the fact that Wordy for *except that.*

explicit, implicit *Explicit* means "stated outright": *I left explicit instructions. He explicitly consented. Implicit* means "implied, unstated": *We had an implicit understanding. I trust Megan implicitly.*

farther, further *Farther* refers to additional distance (*How much farther is it to the beach?*), and *further* refers to additional time, amount, or other abstract matters (*I don't want to discuss this any further*).

feel Avoid this word in place of *think* or *believe*: *She thinks* [not *feels*] *that the law should be changed.*

fewer, less *Fewer* refers to individual countable items (a plural count noun), *less* to general amounts (a noncount noun, always singular): *Skim milk has fewer calories than whole milk. We have less milk left than I thought.*

field The phrase *the field of* is wordy and generally unnecessary: *Margaret plans to specialize in* [not *in the field of*] *family medicine.*

figure See *calculate, figure, reckon.*

fixing to Avoid this colloquial substitute for "intend to": *The school intends* [not *is fixing*] *to build a new library.*

flaunt, flout *Flaunt* means "show off": *If you have style, flaunt it. Flout* means "scorn" or "defy": *Hester Prynne flouted convention and paid the price.*

flunk A colloquial substitute for *fail.*

former, latter *Former* refers to the first-named of two things, *latter* to the second-named: *I like both skiing and swimming, the former in the winter and the latter all year round.* To refer to the first- or last-named of three or more things, say *first* or *last*: *I like jogging, swimming, and hang gliding, but the last is inconvenient in the city.*

fun As an adjective, *fun* is colloquial and should be avoided in most writing: *It was a pleasurable* [not *fun*] *evening.*

further See *farther, further.*

get This common verb is used in many slang and colloquial expressions: *get lost, that really gets me, getting on. Get* is easy to overuse; watch out for it in expressions such as *it's getting better* (substitute *improving*) and *we got done* (substitute *finished*).

go As a substitute for *say* or *reply, go* is colloquial: *He says* [not *goes*], *"How do you do, madam?"*

good, well *Good* is an adjective, and *well* is nearly always an adverb: *Larry's a good dancer. He and Linda dance well together. Well* is properly used as an adjective only to refer to health: *You look well.* (*You look good,* in contrast, means "Your appearance is pleasing.")

good and Colloquial for "very": *I was very* [not *good and*] *tired.*

had better See *better, had better.*

had ought The *had* is unnecessary and should be omitted: *He ought* [not *had ought*] *to listen to his mother.*

half Either *half a* or *a half* is appropriate usage, but *a half a* is redundant: *Half a loaf* [not *A half a loaf*] *is better than none. I'd like a half- gallon* [not *a half a gallon*] *of mineral water, please.*

hanged, hung Though both are past-tense forms of *hang, hanged* is used to refer to executions and *hung* is used for all other meanings: *Tom Dooley was hanged* [not *hung*] *from a white oak tree. I hung* [not *hanged*] *the picture you gave me.*

hardly See *but, hardly, scarcely.*

have, of Use *have,* not *of,* after helping verbs such as *could, should, would, may, must,* and *might: You should have* [not *should of*] *told me.*

he, she; he/she Convention has allowed the use of *he* to mean "he or she": *After the infant learns to creep, he progresses to crawling.* However, many writers today consider this usage inaccurate and unfair because it seems to exclude females. The construction *he/she,* one substitute for *he,* is awkward and objectionable to most readers. The better choice is to make the pronoun plural, to rephrase, or, sparingly, to use *he or she.* For instance: *After infants learn to creep, they progress to crawling. After learning to creep, the infant progresses to crawling. After the infant learns to creep, he or she progresses to crawling.* (See also pp. 321–22 and 504–05.)

herself, himself See *myself, herself, himself, yourself.*

hisself Nonstandard for *himself.*

hopefully *Hopefully* means "with hope": *Freddy waited hopefully for a glimpse of Eliza.* The use of *hopefully* to mean "it is to be hoped," "I hope," or "let's hope" is now very common; but try to avoid it in writing because many readers continue to object strongly to the usage. *I hope* [not *Hopefully*] *the law will pass.*

idea, ideal An *idea* is a thought or conception. An *ideal* (noun) is a model of perfection or a goal. *Ideal* should not be used in place of *idea*: *The idea* [not *ideal*] *of the play is that our ideals often sustain us.*

if, whether For clarity, use *whether* rather than *if* when you are expressing an alternative: *If I laugh hard, people can't tell whether I'm crying.*

illicit See *elicit, illicit.*

illusion See *allusion, illusion.*

immigrate, emigrate See *emigrate, immigrate.*

impact Both the noun and the verb *impact* connote forceful or even violent collision. Avoid the increasingly common diluted meanings of *impact*: "an effect" (noun) or "to have an effect on" (verb). The diluted verb (*The budget cuts impacted social science research*) is bureaucratic jargon.

implicit See *explicit, implicit.*

imply, infer Writers or speakers *imply,* meaning "suggest": *Jim's letter implies he's having a good time.* Readers or listeners *infer,* meaning "conclude": *From Jim's letter I infer he's having a good time.*

in, into *In* indicates location or condition: *He was in the garage. She was in a coma. Into* indicates movement or a change in condition: *He went into the garage. She fell into a coma.* Generally avoid the slang sense of *into* meaning "interested in" or "involved in": *I am into Zen.*

in . . . A number of phrases beginning with *in* are needlessly wordy and should be avoided: *in the event that* (for *if*); *in the neighborhood of* (for *approximately* or *about*); *in this day and age* (for *now* or *nowadays*); *in spite of the fact that* (for *although* or *even though*); and *in view of the fact that* (for *because* or *considering that*). Certain other *in* phrases are nothing but padding and can be omitted entirely: *in nature, in number, in reality,* and *in a very real sense.* (See also pp. 520–21.)

incredible, incredulous *Incredible* means "unbelievable," while *incredulous* means "unbelieving": *When Nancy heard Dennis's incredible story, she was frankly incredulous.* See also *credible, creditable, credulous.*

individual, person, party *Individual* should refer to a single human being in contrast to a group or should stress uniqueness: *The US Constitution places strong emphasis on the rights of the individual.* For other meanings *person* is preferable: *What person* [not *individual*] *wouldn't want the security promised in that advertisement? Party* means "group" (*Can you seat a party of four for dinner?*) and should not be used to refer to an individual except in legal documents. See also *people, persons.*

infer See *imply, infer.*

in regards to Nonstandard for *in regard to, as regards,* or *regarding.* See also *regarding.*

inside of, outside of The *of* is unnecessary when *inside* and *outside* are used as prepositions: *Stay inside* [not *inside of*] *the house. The decision is outside* [not *outside of*] *my authority. Inside of* may refer colloquially to time, though in formal English *within* is preferred: *The law was passed within* [not *inside of*] *a year.*

instance See *case, instance, line.*

insure See *assure, ensure, insure.*

irregardless Nonstandard for *regardless.*

is, are See *are, is.*

is because See *reason is because.*

is when, is where These are faulty constructions in sentences that define: *Adolescence is a stage* [not *is when a person is*] *between childhood and adulthood. Socialism is a system in which* [not *is where*] *government owns the means of production.* (See also p. 375.)

its, it's *Its* is the pronoun *it* in the possessive case: *That plant is losing its leaves. It's* is a contraction for *it is* or *it has*: *It's* [*It is*] *likely to die. It's* [*It has*] *got a fungus.* Many people confuse *it's* and *its* because possessives are most often formed with *-'s*; but the possessive *its,* like *his* and *hers,* never takes an apostrophe.

-ize, -wise The suffix *-ize* changes a noun or an adjective into a verb: *revolutionize, immunize.* The suffix *-wise* changes a noun or adjective into an adverb: *clockwise, otherwise, likewise.* Avoid the two suffixes except in established words: *The two nations are ready to settle on* [not *finalize*] *an agreement. I'm highly sensitive* [not *sensitized*] *to that kind of criticism. Financially* [not *Moneywise*], *it's a good time to buy land.*

kind of, sort of, type of In formal speech and writing, avoid using *kind of* or *sort of* to mean "somewhat": *He was rather* [not *kind of*] *tall.*

Kind, sort, and *type* are singular and take singular modifiers and verbs: *This kind of dog is easily trained.* Agreement errors often occur when these singular nouns are combined with the plural adjectives *these* and *those*: *These kinds* [not *kind*] *of dogs are easily trained. Kind, sort,* and *type* should be followed by *of* but not by *a*: *I don't know what type of* [not *type* or *type of a*] *dog that is.*

Use *kind of, sort of,* or *type of* only when the word *kind, sort,* or *type* is important: *That was a strange* [not *strange sort of*] *statement.*

later, latter *Later* refers to time; *latter* refers to the second-named of two items. See also *former, latter.*

lay, lie *Lay* means "put" or "place" and takes a direct object: *We could lay the tablecloth in the sun.* Its main forms are *lay, laid, laid. Lie* means "recline" or "be situated" and does not take an object: *I lie awake at night. The town lies east of the river.* Its main forms are *lie, lay, lain.* (See also p. 288.)

leave, let *Leave* and *let* are interchangeable only when followed by *alone*; *leave me alone* is the same as *let me alone.* Otherwise, *leave* means "depart" and *let* means "allow": *Julia would not let Susan leave.*

less See *fewer, less.*

let See *leave, let.*

liable See *apt, liable, likely.*

lie, lay See *lay, lie.*

like, as In formal speech and writing, *like* should not introduce a full clause (with a subject and a verb) because it is a preposition. The preferred choice is *as* or *as if*: *The plan succeeded as* [not *like*] *we hoped. It seemed as if* [not *like*] *it might fail. Other plans like it have failed.*

When *as* serves as a preposition, the distinction between *as* and *like* depends on meaning. *As* suggests that the subject is equivalent or identical to the description: *She was hired as an engineer. Like* suggests resemblance but not identity: *People like her do well in such jobs.* See also *like, such as.*

like, such as Strictly, *such as* precedes an example that represents a larger subject, whereas *like* indicates that two subjects are comparable. *Steve has recordings of many great saxophonists such as Ben Webster and Lee Konitz. Steve wants to be a great jazz saxophonist like Ben Webster and Lee Konitz.*

Many writers prefer to keep *such* and *as* together: *Steve admires saxophonists such as* . . . rather than *Steve admires such saxophonists as*. . . .

likely See *apt, liable, likely.*

line See *case, instance, line.*

literally This word means "actually" or "just as the words say," and it should not be used to qualify or intensify expressions whose words are not to be taken at face value. The sentence *He was literally climbing the walls* describes a person behaving like an insect, not a person who is restless or anxious. For the latter meaning, *literally* should be omitted.

lose, loose *Lose* means "mislay": *Did you lose a brown glove? Loose* means "unrestrained" or "not tight": *Ann's canary got loose. Loose* can also function as a verb meaning "let loose": *They loose the dogs as soon as they spot the bear.*

lots, lots of Colloquial substitutes for *very many, a great many,* or *much.* Avoid *lots* and *lots of* in college or business writing. When you use either one informally, be careful to maintain subject-verb agreement: *There are* [not *is*] *lots of fish in the pond.*

may, can See *can, may.*

may be, maybe *May be* is a verb, and *maybe* is an adverb meaning "perhaps": *Tuesday may be a legal holiday. Maybe we won't have classes.*

may of See *have, of.*

media *Media* is the plural of *medium* and takes a plural verb: *All the news media are increasingly visual.* The singular verb is common, even in the media, but many readers prefer the plural verb and it is always correct.

might of See *have, of.*

moral, morale As a noun, *moral* means "ethical conclusion" or "lesson": *The moral of the story escapes me. Morale* means "spirit" or "state of mind": *Victory improved the team's morale.*

most, almost See *almost, most.*

must of See *have, of.*

myself, herself, himself, yourself, ourselves, themselves, yourselves Avoid using the *-self* pronouns in place of personal pronouns: *No one except me* [not *myself*] *saw the accident. Michiko and I* [not *myself*] *planned the ceremony.* The *-self* pronouns have two uses: they emphasize a noun or other pronoun (*Paul did the work himself; he himself said so*), or they indicate that the sentence subject also receives the action of the verb: *I drove myself to the hospital.*

nohow Nonstandard for *in no way* or *in any way.*

nothing like, nowhere near These colloquial substitutes for *not nearly* are best avoided in formal speech and writing: *That program is not nearly* [not *nowhere near*] *as expensive.*

nowheres Nonstandard for *nowhere.*

number See *amount, number.*

of, have See *have, of.*

off of *Of* is unnecessary. Use *off* or *from* rather than *off of*: *He jumped off* [or *from,* not *off of*] *the roof.*

OK, O.K., okay All three spellings are acceptable, but avoid this colloquial term in formal speech and writing.

on, upon In modern English, *upon* is usually just a stuffy way of saying *on.* Unless you need a formal effect, use *on*: *We decided on* [not *upon*] *a location for our next meeting.*

on account of Wordy for *because of.*

on the other hand This transitional expression of contrast should be preceded by its mate, *on the one hand*: *On the one hand, we hoped for snow. On the other hand, we worried that it would harm the animals.* However, the two combined can be unwieldy, and a simple *but, however, yet,* or *in contrast* often suffices: *We hoped for snow. Yet we worried that it would harm the animals.*

outside of See *inside of, outside of.*

owing to the fact that Wordy for *because.*

party See *individual, person, party.*

people, persons In formal usage, *people* refers to a general group: *We the people of the United States. . . . Persons* refers to a collection of individuals: *Will the person or persons who saw the accident please notify. . . .* Except when emphasizing individuals, prefer *people* to *persons.* See also *individual, person, party.*

per Except in technical writing, an English equivalent is usually preferable to the Latin *per*: *$10 an* [not *per*] *hour; sent by* [not *per*] *parcel post; requested in* [not *per* or *as per*] *your letter.*

percent (per cent), percentage Both of these terms refer to fractions of one hundred. *Percent* always follows a number (*40 percent of the voters*), and the word is often used instead of the symbol (%) in nontechnical writing. *Percentage* stands alone (*the percentage of votes*) or follows an adjective (*a high percentage*).

person See *individual, person, party.*

persons See *people, persons.*

persuade See *convince, persuade.*

phenomena The plural of *phenomenon* (meaning "perceivable fact" or "unusual occurrence"): *Many phenomena are not recorded. One phenomenon is attracting attention.*

plenty A colloquial substitute for *very*: *The reaction occurred very* [not *plenty*] *fast.*

plus *Plus* is standard as a preposition meaning *in addition to*: *His income plus mine is sufficient.* But *plus* is colloquial as a conjunctive adverb: *Our group is larger; moreover* [not *plus*], *we have more money.*

practicable, practical *Practicable* means "capable of being put into practice"; *practical* means "useful" or "sensible": *We figured out a practical new design for our kitchen, but it was too expensive to be practicable.*

precede, proceed The verb *precede* means "come before": *My name precedes yours in the alphabet.* The verb *proceed* means "move on": *We were told to proceed to the waiting room.*

prejudice, prejudiced *Prejudice* is a noun; *prejudiced* is an adjective. Do not drop the *-d* from *prejudiced*: *I knew that my parents were prejudiced* [not *prejudice*].

pretty Overworked as an adverb meaning "rather" or "somewhat": *He was somewhat* [not *pretty*] *irked at the suggestion.*

previous to, prior to Wordy for *before.*

principal, principle *Principal* is an adjective meaning "foremost" or "major," a noun meaning "chief official," or, in finance, a noun meaning "capital sum." *Principle* is a noun only, meaning "rule" or "axiom." *Her principal reasons for confessing were her principles of right and wrong.*

proceed, precede See *precede, proceed.*

provided, providing *Provided* may serve as a subordinating conjunction meaning "on the condition (that)"; *providing* may not. *The grocer will begin providing food for the soup kitchen provided* [not *providing*] *we find a suitable space.*

question of whether, question as to whether Wordy substitutes for *whether.*

raise, rise *Raise* means "lift" or "bring up" and takes a direct object: *The Kirks raise cattle.* Its main forms are *raise, raised, raised. Rise* means "get up" and does not take an object: *They must rise at dawn.* Its main forms are *rise, rose, risen.* (See also p. 288.)

real, really In formal speech and writing, *real* should not be used as an adverb; *really* is the adverb and *real* an adjective. *Popular reaction to the announcement was really* [not *real*] *enthusiastic.*

reason is because Although colloquially common, this expression should be avoided in formal speech and writing. Use a *that* clause after *reason is*: *The reason he is absent is that* [not *is because*] *he is sick.* Or: *He is absent because he is sick.*

reckon See *calculate, figure, reckon.*

regarding, in regard to, with regard to, relating to, relative to, with respect to, respecting Stuffy substitutes for *on, about,* or *concerning*: *Mr. McGee spoke about* [not *with regard to*] *the plans for the merger.*

respectful, respective *Respectful* means "full of (or showing) respect": *Be respectful of other people. Respective* means "separate": *The French and the Germans occupied their respective trenches.*

rise, raise See *raise, rise.*

scarcely See *but, hardly, scarcely.*

sensual, sensuous *Sensual* suggests sexuality; *sensuous* means "pleasing to the senses." *Stirred by the sensuous scent of meadow grass and flowers, Cheryl and Paul found their thoughts growing increasingly sensual.*

set, sit *Set* means "put" or "place" and takes a direct object: *He sets the pitcher down.* Its main forms are *set, set, set. Sit* means "be seated" and does not take an object: *She sits on the sofa.* Its main forms are *sit, sat, sat.* (See also p. 288.)

shall, will *Will* is the future-tense helping verb for all persons: *I will go, you will go, they will go.* The main use of *shall* is for first-person questions requesting an opinion or consent: *Shall I order a pizza? Shall we dance?* (Questions that merely inquire about the future use *will*: *When will I see you again?*) *Shall* can also be used for the first person when a formal effect is desired (*I shall expect you around three*), and it is occasionally used with the second or third person to express the speaker's determination (*You shall do as I say*).

should, would *Should* expresses obligation: *I should fix dinner. You should set the table. Jack should wash the dishes. Would* expresses a wish or hypothetical condition: *I would do it. Wouldn't you?* When the context is formal, however, *should* is sometimes used instead of *would* in the first person: *We should be delighted to accept.*

should of See *have, of.*

since *Since* mainly relates to time: *I've been waiting since noon.* But *since* is also often used to mean "because": *Since you ask, I'll tell you.* Revise sentences in which the word could have either meaning, such as *Since I studied physics, I have been planning to major in engineering.*

sit, set See *set, sit.*

situation Often unnecessary, as in *The situation is that we have to get some help* (revise to *We have to get some help*) or *The team was faced with a punting situation* (revise to *The team was faced with punting* or *The team had to punt*).

so Avoid using *so* alone as a vague intensifier: *He was so late. So* needs to be followed by *that* and a clause that states a result: *He was so late that I left without him.*

some *Some* is colloquial as an adverb meaning "somewhat" or "to some extent" and as an adjective meaning "remarkable": *We'll have to hurry somewhat* [not *some*] *to get there in time. Those are remarkable* [not *some*] *photographs.*

somebody, some body; someone, some one *Somebody* and *someone* are indefinite pronouns; *some body* is a noun modified by *some*; and *some one* is a pronoun or an adjective modified by *some. Somebody ought to invent a shampoo that will give hair some body. Someone told Janine she should choose some one plan and stick with it.*

someplace Informal for *somewhere.*

sometime, sometimes, some time *Sometime* means "at an indefinite time in the future": *Why don't you come up and see me sometime? Some-*

times means "now and then": *I still see my old friend Joe sometimes. Some time* means "a span of time": *I need some time to make the payments.*

somewheres Nonstandard for *somewhere.*

sort of, sort of a See *kind of, sort of, type of.*

specially See *especially, specially.*

such Avoid using *such* as a vague intensifier: *It was such a cold winter. Such* should be followed by *that* and a clause that states a result: *It was such a cold winter that Napoleon's troops had to turn back.*

such as See *like, such as.*

supposed to, used to In both of these expressions, the *-d* is essential: *I used to* [not *use to*] *think so. He's supposed to* [not *suppose to*] *meet us.*

sure Colloquial when used as an adverb meaning *surely*: *James Madison sure was right about the need for the Bill of Rights.* If you merely want to be emphatic, use *certainly*: *Madison certainly was right.* If your goal is to convince a possibly reluctant reader, use *surely*: *Madison surely was right. Surely Madison was right.*

sure and, sure to; try and, try to *Sure to* and *try to* are the correct forms: *Be sure to* [not *sure and*] *vote. Try to* [not *Try and*] *vote early to avoid a line.*

take, bring See *bring, take.*

than, as See *as, than.*

than, then *Than* is a conjunction used in comparisons, *then* an adverb indicating time: *Holmes knew then that Moriarty was wilier than he had thought.*

that, which *That* always introduces an essential clause: *We should use the lettuce that Susan bought* (*that Susan bought* limits *lettuce* to a particular lettuce). *Which* can introduce both essential and nonessential clauses, but many writers reserve *which* only for nonessential clauses: *The leftover lettuce, which is in the refrigerator, would make a good salad* (*which is in the refrigerator* simply provides more information about the lettuce we already know of). Essential clauses (with *that* or *which*) are not set off by commas; nonessential clauses (with *which*) are. (See also pp. 427–28.)

that, who, which Use *that* to refer to most animals and to things: *The animals that escaped included a zebra. The rocket that failed cost millions.* Use *who* to refer to people and to animals with names: *Dorothy is the girl who visits Oz. Her dog, Toto, who accompanies her, gives her courage.* Use *which* only to refer to animals and things: *The river, which runs more than a thousand miles, empties into the Indian Ocean.* (See also p. 356.)

their, there, they're *Their* is the possessive form of *they*: *Give them their money. There* indicates place (*I saw her standing there*) or functions to postpone the sentence subject (*There is a hole behind you*). *They're* is a contraction for *they are*: *They're going fast.*

theirselves Nonstandard for *themselves.*

them In standard American English, *them* does not serve as an adjective: *Those* [not *Them*] *people want to know.*

then, than See *than, then.*

these kind, these sort, these type, those kind See *kind of, sort of, type of.*

this, these *This* is singular: *this car* or *This is the reason I left. These* is plural: *these cars* or *These are not valid reasons.*

this here, these here, that there, them there Nonstandard for *this, these, that,* and *those.*

thru A colloquial spelling of *through* that should be avoided in all academic and business writing.

thusly A mistaken form of *thus.*

till, until, 'til *Till* and *until* have the same meaning; either is acceptable. *'Til,* a contraction of *until,* is an old form that has been replaced by *till.*

time period Since a *period* is an interval of time, the expression is redundant: *They did not see each other for a long time* [not *time period*]. *Six accidents occurred in a three-week period* [not *time period*].

to, too, two *To* is a preposition; *too* is an adverb meaning "also" or "excessively"; and *two* is a number. *I too have been to Europe two times.*

too Avoid using *too* as a vague intensifier: *Monkeys are too mean.* When you do use *too,* explain the consequences of the excessive quality: *Monkeys are too mean to make good pets.*

toward, towards Both are acceptable, though *toward* is preferred. Use one or the other consistently.

try and, try to See *sure and, sure to*; *try and, try to.*

type of See *kind of, sort of, type of.* Don't use *type* without *of*: *It was a family type of* [not *type*] *restaurant.* Or, better: *It was a family restaurant.*

uninterested See *disinterested, uninterested.*

unique *Unique* means "the only one of its kind" and so cannot sensibly be modified with words such as *very* or *most*: *That was a unique* [not *a very unique* or *the most unique*] *movie.*

until See *till, until, 'til.*

upon, on See *on, upon.*

usage, use *Usage* refers to conventions, most often those of a language: *Is "hadn't ought" proper usage? Usage* is often misused in place of the noun *use*: *Wise use* [not *usage*] *of insulation can save fuel.*

use, utilize *Utilize* can be used to mean "make good use of": *Many teachers utilize computers for instruction.* But for all other senses of "place in service" or "employ," prefer *use.*

used to See *supposed to, used to.*

wait for, wait on In formal speech and writing, *wait for* means "await" (*I'm waiting for Paul*), and *wait on* means "serve" (*The owner of the store herself waited on us*).

ways Colloquial as a substitute for *way*: *We have only a little way* [not *ways*] *to go.*

well See *good, well.*

whether, if See *if, whether.*

which, that See *that, which.*

which, who, that See *that, who, which.*

who, whom *Who* is the subject of a sentence or clause (*We don't know who will come*). *Whom* is the object of a verb or preposition (*We do not know whom we invited*). (See also pp. 279–80.)

who's, whose *Who's* is the contraction of *who is* or *who has*: *Who's* [*Who is*] *at the door? Jim is the only one who's* [*who has*] *passed. Whose* is the possessive form of *who*: *Whose book is that?*

will, shall See *shall, will.*

wise See *-ize, -wise.*

with regard to, with respect to See *regarding.*

would See *should, would.*

would be Often used instead of *is* or *are* to soften statements needlessly: *One example is* [not *would be*] *gun-control laws. Would* can combine with other verbs for the same unassertive effect: *would ask, would seem, would suggest,* and so on.

would have Avoid this construction in place of *had* in clauses that begin with *if* and state a condition contrary to fact: *If the tree had* [not *would have*] *withstood the fire, it would have been the oldest in the state.* (See also p. 306.)

would of See *have, of.*

you In all but very formal writing, *you* is generally appropriate as long as it means "you, the reader." In all writing, avoid indefinite uses of *you,* such as *In one ancient tribe your first loyalty was to your parents.* (See also p. 355.)

your, you're *Your* is the possessive form of *you*: *Your dinner is ready. You're* is the contraction of *you are*: *You're bound to be late.*

yourself See *myself, herself, himself, yourself.*

Glossary of Terms

This glossary defines terms of grammar, rhetoric, literary analysis, research, and other aspects of writing. Page numbers in parentheses refer you to sections of the text where the terms are explained more fully.

absolute phrase A phrase consisting of a noun or pronoun plus the *-ing* or *-ed* form of a verb (a participle): *Our accommodations arranged, we set out on our journey. They will hire a local person, other things being equal.* An absolute phrase modifies a whole clause or sentence (rather than a single word), and it is not joined to the rest of the sentence by a connector. (See p. 262.)

abstract and concrete Two kinds of language. **Abstract** words refer to ideas, qualities, attitudes, and conditions that can't be perceived with the senses: *beauty, guilty, victory.* **Concrete** words refer to objects, persons, places, or conditions that can be perceived with the senses: *Abilene, scratchy, toolbox.* See also *general and specific.* (See p. 833.)

acronym A pronounceable word formed from the initial letter or letters of each word in an organization's title: for example, NATO (North Atlantic Treaty Organization).

active voice See *verb voice.*

adjectival A term sometimes used to describe any word or word group, other than an adjective, that is used to modify a noun. Common adjectivals include nouns (*wagon train, railroad ties*), phrases (*fool on the hill*), and clauses (*the man that I used to be*).

adjective A word used to modify a noun (*beautiful morning*) or a pronoun (*ordinary one*). (See Chapter 16.) Nouns, some verb forms, phrases, and clauses may also serve as adjectives: *book sale*; *a used book*; *sale of old books*; *the sale, which occurs annually.* (See *clauses, prepositional phrases,* and *verbals and verbal phrases.*)

Adjectives come in several classes:

- A **descriptive adjective** names some quality of a noun: *beautiful morning, dark horse.*
- A **limiting adjective** narrows the scope of a noun. It may be a **possessive** (*my, their*); a **demonstrative adjective** (*this train, these days*); an **interrogative adjective** (*what time? whose body?*); or a number (*two boys*).
- A **proper adjective** is derived from a proper noun: *French language, Machiavellian scheme.*

Adjectives can also be classified according to position:

- An **attributive adjective** appears next to the noun it modifies: *full moon.*
- A **predicate adjective** is connected to its noun by a linking verb: *The moon is full.* See also *complement.*

adjective clause See *adjective.*

adjective phrase See *adjective.*

adverb A word used to modify a verb (*warmly greet*), an adjective (*only three people*), another adverb (*quite seriously*), or a whole sentence (*Fortunately, she is employed*). (See Chapter 16.) Some verb forms, phrases, and clauses may also serve as adverbs: *easy to stop, drove by a farm, plowed the fields when the earth thawed.* (See *clause, prepositional phrase,* and *verbals and verbal phrases.*)

adverb clause See *adverb.*

adverbial A term sometimes used to describe any word or word group, other than an adverb, that is used to modify a verb, an adjective, another adverb, or a whole sentence. Common adverbials include nouns (*This little piggy stayed home*), phrases (*This little piggy went to market*), and clauses (*This little piggy went wherever he wanted*).

adverbial conjunction See *conjunctive adverb.*

adverb phrase See *adverb.*

agreement The correspondence of one word to another in person, number, or gender. A verb must agree with its subject (*The chef orders egg sandwiches*), a pronoun must agree with its antecedent (*The chef surveys her breakfast*), and a demonstrative adjective must agree with its noun (*She likes these kinds of sandwiches*). (See Chapter 15.)

Logical agreement requires consistency in number between other related words, usually nouns: *The students brought their books* [not *book*]. (See p. 359.)

analogy A comparison between members of different classes, such as a nursery school and a barnyard or a molecule and a pair of dancers. Usually, the purpose is to explain something unfamiliar to readers through something familiar. (See p. 96.)

analysis The separation of a subject into its elements. Sometimes called **division**, analysis is fundamental to critical thinking, reading, and writing (pp. 158–59, 167–68) and is a useful tool for developing essays (p. 26) and paragraphs (p. 94).

antecedent The word to which a pronoun refers: *Jonah, who is not yet ten, has already chosen the college he will attend* (*Jonah* is the antecedent of the pronouns *who* and *he*). (See pp. 319–23.)

APA style The style of documentation recommended by the American Psychological Association and used in many of the social sciences. (For discussion and examples, see pp. 761–82.)

appeals Attempts to engage and persuade readers. An **emotional appeal** touches readers' feelings, beliefs, and values. An **ethical appeal** presents the writer as competent, sincere, and fair. A **rational appeal** engages readers' powers of reasoning. (See pp. 214–16.)

appositive A word or phrase appearing next to a noun or pronoun that renames or identifies it and is equivalent to it: *My brother Michael, the best horn player in town, won the state competition* (*Michael* identifies which brother is being referred to; *the best horn player in town* renames *Michael*). (See pp. 266–67.)

argument Writing whose primary purpose is to convince readers of an idea or persuade them to act. (See Chapters 8–9.)

article The word *a, an,* or *the.* Articles are sometimes called **determiners** because they always signal that a noun follows. (See pp. 332–34 for when to use *a/an* versus *the.* See p. 807 for when to use *a* versus *an.*)

assertion See *claim.*

assumption A stated or unstated belief or opinion. Uncovering assumptions is part of critical thinking, reading, and writing (see pp. 159, 169–71). In argument, assumptions connect claims and evidence (see p. 189).

audience The intended readers of a piece of writing. Knowledge of the audience's needs and expectations helps a writer shape writing so that it is clear, interesting, and convincing. (See pp. 11–14.)

auxiliary verb See *helping verb.*

balanced sentence A sentence consisting of two clauses with parallel constructions: *Do as I say, not as I do. Befriend all animals; exploit none.* Their balance makes such sentences highly emphatic. (See p. 387.)

belief A conviction based on morality, values, or faith. Statements of belief may serve as assumptions or even as evidence, but they are not arguable and so cannot serve as the thesis in an argument. (See p. 183.)

blog A Web site, often created and maintained by a person or small group of people, with dated entries of commentary or descriptions of events.

body In a piece of writing, the large central part where ideas supporting the thesis are presented and developed. See also *conclusion* and *introduction.*

brainstorming A technique for generating ideas about a subject: concentrating on the subject for a fixed time (say, fifteen minutes), you list every idea and detail that comes to mind. (See pp. 23–24.)

cardinal number The type of number that shows amount: *two, sixty, ninety-seven.* Contrast *ordinal number* (such as *second, ninety-seventh*).

case The form of a noun or pronoun that indicates its function in the sentence. Most pronouns have three cases:

- The **subjective case** (*I, she*) for the subject of a verb or for a subject complement.
- The **objective case** (*me, her*) for the object of a verb, verbal, or preposition.
- The **possessive case** to indicate ownership, used either as an adjective (*my, her*) or as a noun (*mine, hers*).

(See p. 275 for a list of the forms of personal and relative pronouns.)

Nouns use the subjective form (*dog, America*) for all cases except the possessive (*dog's, America's*).

cause-and-effect analysis The determination of why something happened or what its consequences were or will be. (See pp. 26 and 97.)

characters The people in a literary work, including the narrator of a story or the speaker of a poem. (See p. 724.)

Chicago style A style of documentation recommended by *The Chicago Manual of Style* and used in history, art, and some other humanities. (For discussion and examples, see pp. 744–57.)

chronological organization The arrangement of events as they occurred in time, usually from first to last. (See pp. 41, 80.)

citation In research writing, the way of acknowledging material borrowed from sources. Most citation systems use a number or brief parenthetical reference in the text to signal that material is borrowed and to direct the reader to information on the source at the end of the work. (See pp. 634–79 for MLA style, pp. 744–57 for Chicago style, pp. 761–82 for APA style, and pp. 799–802 for CSE style.)

claim A positive statement or assertion that requires support. Claims are the backbone of any argument. (See pp. 182–84.)

classification The sorting of many elements into groups based on their similarities. (See pp. 26 and 94–95.)

clause A group of related words containing a subject and a predicate. A **main (independent) clause** can stand by itself as a sentence. A **subordinate (dependent) clause** serves as a single part of speech and so cannot stand by itself as a sentence.

Main clause	We can go to the movies.
Subordinate clause	We can go if Julie gets back on time.

A subordinate clause may function as an adjective (*The car that hit Fred was speeding*), an adverb (*The car hit Fred when it ran a red light*), or a noun (*Whoever was driving should be arrested*). (See p. 263.)

clichés See *trite expressions.*

climactic organization The arrangement of material in order of increasing drama or interest, leading to a climax. (See pp. 42, 82.)

clustering A technique for generating ideas about a subject: drawing and writing, you branch outward from a center point (the subject) to pursue the implications of ideas. (See pp. 24–25.)

coherence The quality of an effective essay or paragraph that helps readers see relations among ideas and move easily from one idea to the next. (See pp. 43, 77–87.)

collaborative learning Students working together in groups to help each other become better writers and readers. (See pp. 56–57.)

collective noun See *noun.*

colloquial language The words and expressions of everyday speech. Colloquial language can enliven informal writing but is generally inappropriate in formal academic or business writing. See also *formal and informal.* (See p. 501.)

comma splice A sentence error in which two main clauses are separated by a comma with no coordinating conjunction. (See Chapter 18.)

Comma splice	The book was long, it contained useful data.
Revised	The book was long; it contained useful data.
Revised	The book was long, and it contained useful data.

common noun See *noun.*

comparative See *comparison.*

comparison The form of an adverb or adjective that shows its degree of quality or amount.

- The **positive degree** is the simple, uncompared form: *gross, shyly.*
- The **comparative degree** compares the thing modified to at least one other thing: *grosser, more shyly.*
- The **superlative degree** indicates that the thing modified exceeds all other things to which it is being compared: *grossest, most shyly.*

The comparative and superlative degrees are formed either with the endings *-er/-est* or with the words *more/most, less/least.* (See pp. 327–29.)

comparison and contrast The identification of similarities (comparison) and differences (contrast) between two or more subjects. (See pp. 26, 95.)

complement A word or word group that completes the sense of a subject, an object, or a verb. (See pp. 253–54.)

- A **subject complement** follows a linking verb and renames or describes the subject. It may be an adjective, noun, or pronoun. *I am a lion tamer, but I am not yet experienced* (the noun *lion tamer* and the adjective *experienced* complement the subject *I*). Adjective complements are also called **predicate adjectives.** Noun complements are also called **predicate nouns** or **predicate nominatives.**
- An **object complement** follows and modifies or refers to a direct object. The complement may be an adjective or a noun. *If you elect me president, I'll keep the students satisfied* (the noun *president* complements the direct object *me,* and the adjective *satisfied* complements the direct object *students*).
- A **verb complement** is a direct or indirect object of a verb. It may be a noun or pronoun. *Don't give the chimp that peanut* (*chimp* is the indirect object and *peanut* is the direct object of the verb *give*; both objects are verb complements).

complete predicate See *predicate.*

complete subject See *subject.*

complex sentence See *sentence.*

compound construction Two or more words or word groups serving the same function, such as a **compound subject** (*Harriet and Peter poled their barge down the river*), **compound predicate** (*The scout watched and waited*) or parts of a predicate (*She grew tired and hungry*), and **compound sentence** (*He smiled, and I laughed*). (See p. 272.) **Compound words** include nouns (*featherbrain, strip-mining*) and adjectives (*two-year-old, downtrodden*).

compound-complex sentence See *sentence.*

compound predicate See *compound construction.*

compound sentence See *sentence.*

compound subject See *compound construction.*

conciseness Use of the fewest and freshest words to express meaning clearly and achieve the desired effect with readers. (See Chapter 39.)

conclusion The closing of an essay, tying off the writer's thoughts and leaving readers with a sense of completion. (See pp. 105–06 for suggestions.)

A *conclusion* is also the result of deductive reasoning. See *deductive reasoning* and *syllogism.*

concrete See *abstract and concrete.*

conditional statement A statement expressing a condition contrary to fact and using the subjunctive mood of the verb: *If she were mayor, the unions would cooperate.* See also *mood.*

conjugation A list of the forms of a verb showing tense, voice, mood, person, and number. The conjugation of the verb *know* in present tense, active voice, indicative mood is *I know, you know, he/she/it knows, we know, you know, they know.* (See p. 299 for a fuller conjugation.)

conjunction A word that links and relates parts of a sentence.

- **Coordinating conjunctions** (*and, but, or, nor, for, so, yet*) connect words or word groups of equal grammatical rank: *The lights went out, but the doctors and nurses kept caring for patients.* (See p. 268.)
- **Correlative conjunctions** or correlatives (such as *either . . . or, not only . . . but also*) are two or more connecting words that work together: *He was certain that either his parents or his brother would help him.* (See pp. 268–69.)
- **Subordinating conjunctions** (*after, although, as if, because, if, when,* and so on) begin subordinate clauses and link them to main clauses: *The seven dwarfs whistle while they work.* (See pp. 263–64.)

conjunctive adverb (adverbial conjunction) An adverb (such as *besides, consequently, however, indeed,* or *therefore*) that relates two main clauses in a sentence: *We had hoped to own a house by now; however, housing costs have risen too fast.* (See p. 269.) The error known as a comma splice results when two main clauses related by a conjunctive adverb are separated only by a comma. (See pp. 348–49.)

connector (connective) Any word or phrase that links words, phrases, clauses, or sentences. Common connectors include coordinating, correlative, and subordinating conjunctions; conjunctive adverbs; and prepositions.

connotation An association called up by a word, beyond its dictionary definition. Contrast *denotation.* (See p. 510.)

construction Any group of grammatically related words, such as a phrase, a clause, or a sentence.

contraction A condensation of an expression, with an apostrophe replacing the missing letters: for example, *doesn't* (for *does not*), *we'll* (for *we will*). (See pp. 455–56.)

contrast See *comparison and contrast.*

coordinate adjectives Two or more adjectives that equally modify the same noun or pronoun: *The camera panned the vast, empty desert.* (See pp. 433–34.)

coordinating conjunction See *conjunction.*

coordination The linking of words, phrases, or clauses that are of equal importance, usually with a coordinating conjunction: *He and I laughed, but she was not amused.* Contrast *subordination.* (See pp. 392–93.)

correlative conjunction (correlative) See *conjunction.*

count noun See *noun.*

critical thinking, reading, and writing Looking beneath the surface of words and images to discern meaning and relationships and to build knowledge. (See Chapter 7.)

CSE style Either of two styles of documenting sources recommended by the Council of Science Editors and frequently used in the natural and applied sciences and in mathematics. (For discussion and examples, see pp. 799–802.)

cumulative (loose) sentence A sentence in which modifiers follow the subject and verb: *Ducks waddled by, their tails swaying and their quacks rising to heaven.* Contrast *periodic sentence.* (See p. 385.)

dangling modifier A modifier that does not sensibly describe anything in its sentence. (See pp. 370–72.)

Dangling Having arrived late, the concert was underway.

Revised Having arrived late, we found that the concert was underway.

data In argument, a term used for *evidence.* See *evidence.*

database A collection and organization of information (data). A database may be printed, but the term is most often used for electronic sources.

declension A list of the forms of a noun or pronoun, showing inflections for person (for pronouns), number, and case. See p. 275 for a declension of the personal and relative pronouns.

deductive reasoning Applying a generalization to specific circumstances in order to reach a conclusion. See also *syllogism.* Contrast *inductive reasoning.* (See pp. 210–12.)

definition Specifying the characteristics of something to establish what it is and is not. (See pp. 26, 93, 184.)

degree See *comparison.*

demonstrative adjective See *adjective.*

demonstrative pronoun See *pronoun.*

denotation The main or dictionary definition of a word. Contrast *connotation.* (See p. 510.)

dependent clause See *clause.*

derivational suffix See *suffix.*

description Detailing the sensory qualities of a thing, person, place, or feeling. (See pp. 26 and 91.)

descriptive adjective See *adjective.*

descriptor See *keyword(s).*

determiner A word that marks and precedes a noun: for example, *a, an, the, my, your.* See also *article.* (See pp. 332–35 for the uses of determiners before nouns.)

dialect A variety of a language used by a specific group or in a specific region. A dialect may be distinguished by its pronunciation, vocabulary, and grammar. (See pp. 498–99.)

diction The choice and use of words. (See Chapters 37–39.)

dictionary form See *plain form.*

Digital Object Identifier (DOI) A unique identifying label assigned to journal articles, books, and other publications. (See p. 767.)

direct address A construction in which a word or phrase indicates the person or group spoken to: *Have you finished, John? Farmers, unite.*

direct object See *object.*

direct question A sentence asking a question and concluding with a question mark: *Do they know we are watching?* Contrast *indirect question.*

direct quotation (direct discourse) See *quotation.*

discussion list A mailing list of subscribers who use e-mail to converse on a particular subject.

division See *analysis.*

documentation In research writing, supplying citations that legitimate the use of borrowed material and support claims about its origins. Contrast *plagiarism.* (See pp. 623–24.)

document design The control of a document's elements to achieve the flow, spacing, grouping, emphasis, and standardization that are appropriate for the writing situation. (See Chapter 5.)

domain The part of a Web address (or URL) that gives the organization sponsoring the site.

double negative A generally nonstandard form consisting of two negative words used in the same construction so that they effectively cancel each other: *I don't have no money.* Rephrase as *I have no money* or *I don't have any money.* (See p. 329.)

double possessive A possessive using both the ending *-'s* and the preposition *of*: *That is a favorite expression of Mark's.*

double talk (doublespeak) Language intended to confuse or to be misunderstood. (See p. 502.)

drafting The stage of the writing process when ideas are expressed in connected sentences and paragraphs. (See pp. 47–49.)

editing A distinct step in revising a written work, focusing on clarity, tone, and correctness. Compare *revising.* (See pp. 61–63.)

ellipsis The omission of a word or words from a quotation, indicated by the three spaced periods of an **ellipsis mark**: *"that all . . . are created equal."*

elliptical clause A clause omitting a word or words whose meaning is understood from the rest of the clause: *David likes Minneapolis better than* [*he likes*] *Chicago.* (See p. 265.)

emotional appeal See *appeals.*

emphasis The manipulation of words, sentences, and paragraphs to stress important ideas. (See Chapter 23.)

essay A nonfiction composition of multiple paragraphs, focused on a single subject and with a central idea or thesis.

essential element A word or word group that is necessary to the meaning of a sentence because it limits the thing it refers to: removing it would leave the meaning unclear or too general. Also called a **restrictive element**, an essential element is not set off by punctuation: *The keys to the* *car are on the table. That man who called about the apartment said he'd try to call again tonight.* Contrast *nonessential element.* (See pp. 427, 440.)

ethical appeal See *appeals.*

etymology The history of a word's meanings and forms.

euphemism A presumably inoffensive word or phrase that a writer or speaker substitutes for a word deemed possibly offensive or too blunt—for example, *passed away* for "died." (See p. 502.)

evaluation A judgment of the quality, value, currency, bias, or other aspects of a work. (See pp. 162, 171, 580–93.)

evidence The facts, examples, expert opinions, and other information that support the claims in an argument. (See pp. 185–88, 213–14.)

expletive A sentence that postpones the subject by beginning with *there* or *it* and a form of the verb *be*: *It is impossible to get a ticket. There should be more seats available.* (See p. 271.)

exposition Writing whose primary purpose is to explain something about a subject.

fallacies Errors in reasoning. Some fallacies evade the issue of the argument; others oversimplify the argument. (See pp. 193–98.)

faulty predication A sentence error in which the meanings of subject and predicate conflict, so that the subject is said to be or do something illogical: *The installation of air bags takes up space in a car's steering wheel and dashboard.* (See pp. 375–76.)

figurative language (figures of speech) Expressions that suggest meanings different from their literal meanings in order to achieve special effects. (See pp. 515–17.) Some common figures:

- **Hyperbole**, deliberate exaggeration: *The bag weighed a ton.*
- **Metaphor**, an implied comparison between two unlike things: *The wind stabbed through our clothes.*
- **Personification**, the attribution of human qualities to a thing or idea: *The water beckoned seductively.*
- **Simile**, an explicit comparison, using *like* or *as,* between two unlike things: *The sky glowered like an angry parent.*

A **mixed metaphor** is a confusing or ludicrous combination of incompatible figures: *The wind stabbed through our clothes and shook our bones.*

finite verb Any verb that makes an assertion or expresses a state of being and can stand as the main verb of a sentence or clause: *The moose eats the leaves.* Contrast *verbal,* which is formed from a finite verb but is unable to stand alone as the main verb of a sentence: *We watched the moose eating the leaves.*

first person See *person.*

foil A character in a literary work who contrasts with another character and thus helps to define that other character. (See p. 738.)

formal and informal Levels of usage achieved through word choice and sentence structure. More informal writing, as in a letter to an acquaintance or a personal essay, resembles some speech in its colloquial language, contractions, and short, fairly simple sentences. More formal writing, as in academic papers and business reports, avoids these attributes of speech and tends to rely on longer and more complicated sentences.

format The arrangement and spacing of elements in a document. See also *document design.*

fragment See *sentence fragment.*

freewriting A technique for generating ideas: in a fixed amount of time (say, fifteen minutes), you write continuously without stopping to reread. (See pp. 22–23.)

Terms

function word A word, such as an article, conjunction, or preposition, that serves primarily to clarify the roles of and relations between other words in a sentence: *We chased the goat for an hour but finally caught it.* Contrast *lexical word.*

fused sentence (run-on sentence) A sentence error in which two main clauses are joined with no punctuation or connecting word between them. (See p. 346.)

Fused I heard his lecture it was dull.

Revised I heard his lecture; it was dull.

future perfect tense See *tense.*

future tense See *tense.*

gender The classification of nouns or pronouns as masculine (*he, boy, handyman*), feminine (*she, woman, actress*), or neuter (*it, typewriter, dog*).

general and specific Terms designating the relative number of instances or objects included in a group signified by a word. The following list moves from most **general** (including the most objects) to most **specific** (including the fewest objects): *vehicle, four-wheeled vehicle, automobile, sedan, Ford Taurus, blue Ford Taurus, my sister's blue Ford Taurus named Hank.* See also *abstract and concrete.* (See p. 824.)

generalization A claim inferred from evidence. See also *inductive reasoning.*

generic *he* *He* used to mean *he or she.* For ways to avoid *he* when you intend either or both genders, see pp. 321–22 and 505.

generic noun A noun that refers to a typical member of a group rather than to a specific person or thing: *Any person may come. A student needs good work habits.* A singular generic noun takes a singular pronoun (*he, she,* or *it*). (See pp. 321–22.)

genitive case Another term for possessive case. See *case.*

genre A type of writing, such as case study, research report, essay, or poem. (See pp. 15–16 and 134–38.)

gerund A verbal that ends in *-ing* and functions as a noun: *Working is all right for killing time* (*working* is the subject of *is*; *killing* is the object of *for*). See also *verbals and verbal phrases.* (See p. 260.)

gerund phrase A word group consisting of a gerund plus any modifiers or objects. See also *verbals and verbal phrases.*

grammar A description of how a language works.

grounds A term used for *evidence* in argument. See *evidence.*

helping verb (auxiliary verb) A verb used with another verb to convey time, obligation, and other meanings: *You should write a letter. You have written other letters.* The **modals** include *can, could, may, might, must, ought, shall, should, will, would.* The other helping verbs are forms of *be, have,* and *do.* (See pp. 284–85, 290–94.)

homonyms Words that are pronounced the same but have different spellings and meanings, such as *heard/herd* and *to/too/two.* (See pp. 527–28 for a list.)

hyperbole See *figurative language.*

idiom An expression that is peculiar to a language and that may not make sense if taken literally: for example, *bide your time,* and *by and large.* See p. 514 for a list of idioms involving prepositions, such as *agree with them* and *agree to the contract.*

illustration or support Examples or reasons that develop an idea. (See pp. 26 and 92.)

imagery A word or phrase that draws on the sense of sight, hearing, touch, taste, or smell to describe an object or feeling, as in *she wrapped the shaking child in her spindly arms, thundering waves beat the beach,* or *his smooth skin suggested a life lived indoors.*

imperative See *mood.*

indefinite pronoun See *pronoun.*

independent clause See *clause.*

indicative See *mood.*

indirect object See *object.*

indirect question A sentence reporting a question, usually in a subordinate clause, and ending with a period: *The student asked when the paper was due.* Contrast *direct question.*

indirect quotation (indirect discourse) See *quotation.*

inductive reasoning Inferring a generalization from specific evidence. Contrast *deductive reasoning.* (See p. 209.)

infinitive A verbal formed from the plain form of the verb plus the **infinitive marker** *to*: *to swim, to write.* Infinitives and infinitive phrases may function as nouns, adjectives, or adverbs. See also *verbals and verbal phrases.* (See p. 260.)

infinitive marker See *infinitive.*

infinitive phrase A word group consisting of an infinitive plus any subject, objects, or modifiers. See also *verbals and verbal phrases.*

inflection The variation in the form of a word that indicates its function in a particular context. See *declension,* the inflection of nouns and pronouns; *conjugation,* the inflection of verbs; and *comparison,* the inflection of adjectives and adverbs.

inflectional suffix See *suffix.*

informal See *formal and informal.*

intensifier A modifier that adds emphasis to the word(s) it modifies: for example, *very slow, so angry.*

intensive pronoun See *pronoun.*

interjection A word standing by itself or inserted in a construction to exclaim or command attention: *Hey! Ouch! What the heck happened?*

interpretation The determination of meaning or significance—for instance, in a work such as a poem or photograph or in the literature on some issue such as job discrimination. (See pp. 159, 169.)

interrogative Functioning as or involving a question.

interrogative adjective See *adjective.*

interrogative pronoun See *pronoun.*

intransitive verb A verb that does not take a direct object: *The woman laughed.* (See p. 252.)

introduction The opening of an essay, a transition for readers between their world and the writer's. The introduction often contains a statement of the writer's thesis. (See pp. 101–04 for suggestions.)

invention The discovery and exploration of ideas, usually occurring most intensively in the early stages of the writing process. (See pp. 17–27 for invention techniques.)

inversion A reversal of the usual word order in a sentence, as when a verb precedes its subject or an object precedes its verb: *Down swooped the hawk. Our aims we stated clearly.*

irony The use of words to suggest a meaning different from what the words say literally: *What a happy face!* (said to someone scowling miserably); *With that kind of planning, prices are sure to go down* (written with the expectation that prices will rise).

irregular verb A verb that forms its past tense and past participle in some other way than by the addition of *-d* or *-ed* to the plain form: for example, *go, went, gone*; *give, gave, given.* Contrast *regular verb.* (See pp. 286–87 for a list of irregular verbs.)

jargon In one sense, jargon is the specialized language of any group, such as doctors or baseball players. In another sense, jargon is vague, pretentious, wordy, and ultimately unclear writing such as that found in some academic, business, and government publications. (See p. 502.)

journal A personal record of observations, reactions, ideas, and other thoughts. Besides providing a private place to think in writing, a journal is useful for making notes about reading, discovering ideas for essays, and keeping track of research.

journalist's questions A set of questions useful for probing a subject to discover ideas about it. (See p. 25.)

keyword(s) A word or words that define a subject, used for searching the Web and databases such as periodical indexes. (See p. 558.)

lexical word A word, such as a noun, verb, or modifier, that carries part of the meaning of language. Contrast *function word.*

linking verb A verb that relates a subject to its complement: *Julie is a Democrat. He looks harmless. The boy became a man.* Common linking verbs are the forms of *be*; the verbs relating to the senses, such as *look* and *smell*; and the verbs *become, appear,* and *seem.* (See p. 253.)

listserv See *discussion list.*

logical agreement See *agreement.*

logical fallacies See *fallacies.*

main clause See *clause.*

main verb The part of a verb phrase that carries the principal meaning: *had been walking, could happen, was chilled.* See also *verb phrase.*

mass noun Another term for noncount noun. See *noun.*

mechanics The use of capital letters, italics or underlining, abbreviations, numbers, and divided words. (See Chapters 33–36.)

metaphor See *figurative language.*

misplaced modifier A modifier so far from the term it modifies or so close to another term it could modify that its relation to the rest of the sentence is unclear. (See Chapter 21.)

> **Misplaced** The boys played with firecrackers that they bought illegally in the field.
>
> **Revised** The boys played in the field with firecrackers that they bought illegally.

A **squinting modifier** could modify the words on either side of it: *The plan we considered seriously worries me.*

mixed construction A sentence containing two or more parts that do not fit together in grammar or in meaning. (See pp. 373–76.)

mixed metaphor See *figurative language.*

MLA style The style of documenting sources recommended by the Modern Language Association and used in many of the humanities, including English. (For explanation and examples, see Chapter 47.)

modal See *helping verb.*

modifier Any word or word group that limits or qualifies the meaning of another word or word group. Modifiers include adjectives and adverbs as well as words, phrases, and clauses that act as adjectives and adverbs.

mood The form of a verb that shows how the speaker or writer views the action. (See pp. 305–06.)

- The **indicative mood**, the most common, is used to make statements or ask questions: *The play will be performed Saturday. Did you get the tickets?*
- The **imperative mood** gives a command: *Please get good seats.*
- The **subjunctive mood** expresses a wish, a condition contrary to fact, a recommendation, or a request: *I wish George were coming with us. Did you suggest that he join us?*

narration Recounting a sequence of events, usually in the order of their occurrence. (See pp. 26 and 91.) Literary narration tells a story. (See Chapter 49.)

narrator The speaker in a poem or the voice who tells a story. (See pp. 724, 734, 735.)

nominal A noun, a pronoun, or a word or word group used as a noun: *Joan and I talked. The rich owe a debt to the poor* (adjectives acting as subject and object). *Baby-sitting can be exhausting* (gerund acting as subject). *I like to play with children* (infinitive phrase acting as object).

nominative Another term for subjective case. See *case*.

noncount noun See *noun*.

nonessential element A word or word group that does not limit the term or construction it refers to and thus is not essential to the meaning of the sentence. Also called a **nonrestrictive element**, a nonessential element is set off by punctuation, usually commas: *The new apartment building, in shades of tan and gray, will house fifty people* (nonessential adjective phrase). *Sleep, which we all need, occupies a third of our lives* (nonessential adjective clause). *His wife, Patricia, is a chemist* (nonessential appositive). Contrast *essential element*. (See p. 427.)

nonfinite verb See *verbals and verbal phrases*.

nonrestrictive element See *nonessential element*.

nonstandard Words and grammatical forms not conforming to standard American English. (See pp. 498–99.)

noun A word that names a person, place, thing, quality, or idea: *Maggie, Alabama, clarinet, satisfaction, socialism*. Nouns normally form the possessive case by adding *-'s* (*Maggie's*) and the plural by adding *-s* or *-es* (*clarinets, messes*), although there are exceptions (*men, women, children*). The forms of nouns depend partly on where they fit in certain overlapping groups:

- **Common nouns** name general classes and are not capitalized: *book, government, music*.
- **Proper nouns** name specific people, places, and things and are capitalized: *Susan, Athens, Fenway Park*.
- **Count nouns** name things considered countable in English (they form plurals): *ounce/ounces, camera/cameras, person/people*.
- **Noncount nouns** name things not considered countable in English (they don't form plurals): *chaos, fortitude, silver, earth, information*.
- **Collective nouns** are singular in form but name groups: *team, class, family*.

noun clause A word group containing a subject and a verb and functioning as a subject, object, or complement: *Everyone wondered how the door opened. Whoever opened it had left.*

number The form of a noun, pronoun, demonstrative adjective, or verb that indicates whether it is singular or plural: *woman, women; I, we; this, these; runs, run*.

object A noun, pronoun, or word group that receives the action of or is influenced by a transitive verb, a verbal, or a preposition.

- A **direct object** receives the action of a verb or verbal and frequently follows it in a sentence: *We sat watching the stars. Emily caught whatever it was you had.* (See p. 252.)
- An **indirect object** tells for or to whom something is done: *I lent Stan my car. Reiner bought us all champagne.* (See p. 253.)

- An **object of a preposition** usually follows a preposition and is linked by it to the rest of the sentence: *They are going to Rhode Island for the blues festival.* (See p. 257.)

object complement See *complement.*

objective See *case.*

opinion A conclusion based on facts; an arguable, potentially changeable claim. Claims of opinion form the backbone of any argument. (See p. 182.)

ordinal number The type of number that shows order: *first, eleventh, twenty-fifth.* Contrast *cardinal number* (such as *one, twenty-five*).

paragraph Generally, a group of sentences set off by a beginning indention and developing a single idea. That idea is often stated in a **topic sentence.** (See Chapter 4.)

parallelism Similarity of grammatical form between two or more coordinated elements: *Rising prices and declining incomes left many people in bad debt and worse despair.* (See Chapter 25.)

paraphrase The restatement of source material in one's own words and sentence structures, useful for borrowing the original author's line of reasoning but not his or her exact words. Paraphrases must always be acknowledged in source citations. (See pp. 600–03.)

parenthetical citation In the text of a paper, a brief reference, enclosed in parentheses, indicating that material is borrowed and directing the reader to the source of the material. See also *citation.*

parenthetical expression A word or construction that interrupts a sentence and is not part of its main structure, called *parenthetical* because it could (or does) appear in parentheses: *Childe Hassam (1859–1935) was an American painter. The new restaurant, incidentally, is terrible.* (See pp. 471–72.)

participial phrase A word group consisting of a participle plus any objects or modifiers. See also *verbals and verbal phrases.*

participle A verbal showing continuing or completed action, used as an adjective or part of a verb phrase but never as the main verb of a sentence or clause. (See p. 259.)

- A **present participle** ends in *-ing*: *My heart is breaking* (part of verb phrase). *I like to watch the rolling waves* (adjective).
- A **past participle** most commonly ends in *-d, -ed, -n,* or *-en* (*wished, shown, given*) but sometimes changes the spelling of the verb (*sung, done, slept*): *Jeff has broken his own record* (part of verb phrase). *The closed door beckoned* (adjective).

See also *verbals and verbal phrases.*

particle A preposition or adverb in a two-word verb: *look up, catch on.* (See p. 297.)

parts of speech The classes into which words are commonly grouped according to their form, function, and meaning: nouns, pronouns, verbs, adjectives, adverbs, conjunctions, prepositions, and interjections. See separate entries for each part of speech.

passive voice See *verb voice.*

past participle See *participle.*

past perfect tense See *tense.*

past tense See *tense.*

patterns of development Ways of thinking that can help you develop and organize ideas in essays and paragraphs. (See pp. 25–26 and 91–99.)

perfect tenses See *tense.*

periodic sentence A suspenseful sentence in which modifiers precede the main clause, which falls at the end: *Postponing decisions about family while striving to establish themselves in careers, many young adults are falsely accused of greed.* Contrast *cumulative sentence.* (See pp. 384–85.)

person The form of a verb or pronoun that indicates whether the subject is speaking, spoken to, or spoken about. In English only personal pronouns and verbs change form to indicate difference in person. In the **first person**, the subject is speaking: *I am* [or *We are*] *planning a party.* In the **second person**, the subject is being spoken to: *Are you coming?* In the **third person**, the subject is being spoken about: *She was* [or *They were*] *going.*

personal pronoun See *pronoun.*

personification See *figurative language.*

phrase A group of related words that lacks a subject or a predicate or both and that acts as a single part of speech. See *absolute phrase, prepositional phrase, verbals and verbal phrases,* and *verb phrase.*

plagiarism The presentation of someone else's ideas or words as if they were one's own. Whether careless or deliberate, plagiarism is a serious and often punishable offense. (See pp. 614–20.)

plain case Another term for the subjective case of nouns. See *case.*

plain form The dictionary form of a verb: *make, run, swivel.* See also *verb forms.*

plot The pattern of events in a work of literature. (See p. 724.)

plural More than one. See *number.*

point of view The perspective or attitude of the narrator or speaker in a work of literature. See also *person.* (See p. 724.)

positive degree See *comparison.*

possessive See *case.*

predicate The part of a sentence that makes an assertion about the subject. A predicate must contain a finite verb and may contain modifiers, objects of the verb, and complements. The **simple predicate** consists of the verb and its helping verbs: *A wiser person would have made a different decision.* The **complete predicate** includes the simple predicate and any modifiers, objects, and complements: *A wiser person would have made a different decision.* See also *intransitive verb, linking verb,* and *transitive verb.* (See pp. 247, 251–54.)

predicate adjective See *complement.*

predicate noun (predicate nominative) See *complement.*

prefix A letter or group of letters (such as *sub, in, dis, pre*) that can be added at the beginning of a root or word to create a new word: *sub* + *marine* = *submarine; dis* + *grace* = *disgrace.* Contrast *suffix.*

premise Generally, a claim or assumption basic to an argument. In a deductive syllogism, one premise applied to another leads logically to a conclusion. See also *syllogism.* (See pp. 210–12.)

preposition A word that forms a noun or pronoun (plus any modifiers) into a prepositional phrase: *about love, down the steep stairs.* The common prepositions include these as well as *after, before, by, for, from, in, on, to,* and many others. (See p. 257.)

prepositional phrase A word group consisting of a preposition and its object, plus any modifiers. A prepositional phrase usually functions as an adjective (*The boy in green stood up*) or as an adverb (*He walked to the speaker's platform*). (See pp. 257–58.)

present participle See *participle.*

present perfect tense See *tense.*

present tense See *tense.*

pretentious writing Writing that is more elaborate than the situation requires, usually full of fancy phrases and showy words. (See pp. 502–03.)

primary source Firsthand information, such as an eyewitness account of events; a diary, speech, record, letter or other historical document; a work of literature or art; a report of a survey or experiment; and one's own interview, observation, or correspondence. Contrast *secondary source.* (See p. 549.)

principal clause A main or independent clause. See *clause.*

principal parts The plain form, past-tense form, and past participle of a verb. See *verb forms.* (See pp. 282–84.)

problem-solution organization The arrangement of material to state and explain a problem and then to propose and explain a solution. (See pp. 42, 81.)

process analysis The explanation of how something works or how to do something. (See pp. 26, 98.)

progressive tense See *tense.*

pronoun A word used in place of a noun. There are eight types of pronouns:

- **Personal pronouns** refer to a specific individual or to individuals: *I, you, he, she, it, we, they.* (See p. 275.)
- **Indefinite pronouns**, such as *everybody* and *some,* do not refer to specific nouns (*Everybody speaks*). (See p. 315.)
- **Relative pronouns**—*who, whoever, which, that*—relate groups of words to nouns or pronouns (*The book that won is a novel*). (See pp. 264, 275.)
- **Interrogative pronouns**—*who, whom, whose, which, what*—introduce questions (*Who will contribute?*).
- **Intensive pronouns**—personal pronouns plus *-self* or *-selves*—emphasize a noun or other pronoun (*He himself asked that question*). (See pp. 817–18.)

- **Reflexive pronouns** have the same form as intensive pronouns. They indicate that the sentence subject also receives the action of the verb (*They injured themselves*). (See pp. 817–18.)
- **Demonstrative pronouns** such as *this, that,* and *such* identify or point to nouns (*This is the problem*).
- **Reciprocal pronouns**—*each other* and *one another*—are used as objects of verbs when the subjects are plural (*They loved each other*).

proofreading Reading and correcting a final draft for misspellings, typographical errors, and other mistakes. (See pp. 66–67.)

proper adjective See *adjective.*

proper noun See *noun.*

purpose For a writer, the chief reason for communicating something about a subject to a particular audience. Purposes are both general (usually explanation or persuasion) and specific (taking into account the subject and desired outcome). (See pp. 9–11.)

quotation Repetition of what someone has written or spoken. In **direct quotation (direct discourse)**, the person's words are duplicated exactly and enclosed in quotation marks: *Polonius told his son, Laertes, "Neither a borrower nor a lender be."* An **indirect quotation (indirect discourse)** reports what someone said or wrote but not in the exact words and not in quotation marks: *Polonius advised his son, Laertes, not to borrow or lend.*

rational appeal See *appeals.*

reciprocal pronoun See *pronoun.*

reflexive pronoun See *pronoun.*

regional language Expressions common to the people in a particular geographical area. (See p. 501.)

regular verb A verb that forms its past tense and past participle by adding *-d* or *-ed* to the plain form: *love, loved, loved; open, opened, opened.* Contrast *irregular verb.* (See p. 285.)

relative clause A subordinate clause beginning with a relative pronoun such as *who* or *that* and functioning as an adjective.

relative pronoun See *pronoun.*

restrictive element See *essential element.*

revising The stage of the writing process in which one considers and improves the meaning and underlying structure of a draft. Compare *editing.* (See pp. 51–55.)

rhetoric The principles for finding and arranging ideas and for using language in speech or writing to achieve the writer's purpose in addressing his or her audience.

rhetorical question A question asked for effect, with no answer expected. The person asking the question either intends to provide the answer or assumes it is obvious: *If we let one factory pollute the river, what does that say to other factories that want to dump wastes there?*

run-on sentence See *fused sentence.*

sans serif See *serifs.*

secondary source A source reporting or analyzing information in other sources, such as a critic's view of a work of art, a historian's report on eyewitness accounts, or a sociologist's summary of others' studies. Contrast *primary source.* (See p. 549.)

second person See *person.*

sentence A complete unit of thought, consisting of at least a subject and a predicate that are not introduced by a subordinating word. Sentences can be classed by structure in four ways. A **simple sentence** contains one main clause: *I'm leaving.* A **compound sentence** contains at least two main clauses: *I'd like to stay, but I'm leaving.* A **complex sentence** contains one main clause and at least one subordinate clause: *If you let me go now, you'll be sorry.* A **compound-complex sentence** contains at least two main clauses and at least one subordinate clause: *I'm leaving because you want me to, but I'd rather stay.* (See pp. 272–73.)

sentence fragment A sentence error in which a group of words is set off as a sentence even though it begins with a subordinating word or lacks a subject or a predicate or both. (See Chapter 17.)

Fragment	She lost the race. Because she was injured. [*Because,* a subordinating conjunction, makes the underlined clause subordinate.]
Revised	She lost the race because she was injured.
Fragment	He could not light a fire. Thus could not warm the room. [The underlined word group lacks a subject.]
Revised	He could not light a fire. Thus he could not warm the room.

sentence modifier An adverb or a word or word group acting as an adverb that modifies the idea of the whole sentence in which it appears rather than any specific word: *In fact, people will always complain.*

series A sequence of three or more items of equal importance: *The children are named John, Hallie, and Nancy.* The items in a series are separated with commas. (See p. 433.)

serifs Small lines on the characters in type fonts, such as those at the bottom of this A. **Sans serif** type, such as Arial, does not have serifs. (See p. 108.)

setting The place where the action of a literary work happens. (See p. 725.)

sexist language Language expressing narrow ideas about men's and women's roles, positions, capabilities, or value. (See pp. 504–05.)

signal phrase Words that indicate who is being quoted: *"In the future," said Andy Warhol, "everyone will be world-famous for fifteen minutes."* (For punctuating signal phrases, see p. 436. For using signal phrases to integrate quotations, see pp. 610–11.)

simile See *figurative language.*

simple predicate See *predicate.*

simple sentence See *sentence.*

simple subject See *subject.*

simple tense See *tense.*

singular One. See *number.*

slang Expressions used by the members of a group to create bonds and sometimes exclude others. Most slang is too vague, short-lived, and narrowly understood to be used in any but very informal writing. (See pp. 500–01.)

spatial organization In a description of a person, place, or thing, the arrangement of details as they would be scanned by a viewer—for instance, from top to bottom or near to far. (See pp. 41 and 79–80.)

specific See *general and specific.*

split infinitive The often awkward interruption of an infinitive and its marker *to* by an adverb: *Management decided to immediately introduce the new product.* (See p. 367.)

squinting modifier See *misplaced modifier.*

standard American English The dialect of English used and expected by educated writers and readers in colleges and universities, businesses, and professions. (See pp. 141, 498–99.)

subject In grammar, the part of a sentence that names something and about which an assertion is made in the predicate. The **simple subject** consists of the noun alone: *The quick brown fox jumps over the lazy dog.* The **complete subject** includes the simple subject and its modifiers: *The quick brown fox jumps over the lazy dog.* (See pp. 247–48.)

subject complement See *complement.*

subjective See *case.*

subjunctive See *mood.*

subordinate clause See *clause.*

subordinating conjunction See *conjunction.*

subordination The use of grammatical constructions to de-emphasize one element in a sentence by making it dependent on rather than equal to another element: *Although I left six messages, the doctor failed to call.* Contrast *coordination.* (See pp. 394–97.)

substantive A word or word group used as a noun.

suffix A **derivational suffix** is a letter or group of letters that can be added to the end of a root word to make a new word, often a different part of speech: *child, childish; shrewd, shrewdly; visual, visualize.* An **inflectional suffix** adapts a word to different grammatical relations: *boy, boys; fast, faster; tack, tacked.*

summary A condensation and restatement of source material in one's own words and sentence structures, useful in reading for comprehending the material (see pp. 155–57) and in research writing for presenting the gist of the original author's idea (pp. 599–600). Summaries appearing in a paper must always be acknowledged in source citations.

superlative See *comparison.*

syllogism A form of deductive reasoning in which two premises stating generalizations or assumptions together lead to a conclusion. *Premise:*

Hot stoves can burn me. Premise: This stove is hot. Conclusion: This stove can burn me. See also *deductive reasoning.* (See pp. 210–12.)

symbolism The use of a concrete thing to suggest something larger and more abstract, as a red rose may symbolize passion. (See p. 725.)

synonyms Words with approximately but not exactly the same meanings, such as *snicker, giggle,* and *chortle.*

syntax In sentences, the grammatical relations among words and the ways those relations are indicated.

synthesis Drawing one's own conclusions about the elements within a work (such as images or symbols in a poem) or entire works (entire poems, stories, or plays). Synthesis is an essential skill in critical thinking and reading (pp. 161–62, 171), in academic writing (pp. 173–74), and in research writing (pp. 593–95).

tag question A question attached to the end of a statement and consisting of a pronoun, a helping verb, and sometimes the word *not*: *It isn't raining, is it? It is sunny, isn't it?*

tense The form of a verb that expresses the time of its action, usually indicated by the verb's inflection and by helping verbs.

- The **simple tenses** are the **present** (*I race, you go*), the **past** (*I raced, you went*), and the **future**, formed with the helping verb *will* (*I will race, you will go*).
- The **perfect tenses**, formed with the helping verbs *have* and *had,* indicate completed action. They are the **present perfect** (*I have raced, you have gone*), the **past perfect** (*I had raced, you had gone*), and the **future perfect** (*I will have raced, you will have gone*).
- The **progressive tenses**, formed with the helping verb *be* plus the present participle, indicate continuing action. They include the **present progressive** (*I am racing, you are going*), the **past progressive** (*I was racing, you were going*), and the **future progressive** (*I will be racing, you will be going*).

(See p. 299 for a list of tenses with examples.)

theme The main idea of a work of literature. (See p. 725.)

thesis The central, controlling idea of an essay, to which all assertions and details relate. (See p. 28.)

thesis statement A sentence or more that asserts the central, controlling idea of an essay and perhaps previews the essay's organization. (See pp. 28–33.)

third person See *person.*

tone The sense of a writer's attitudes toward self, subject, and readers revealed by words and sentence structures as well as by content. (See pp. 14, 190, 724.)

topic The subject of an essay or paragraph.

topic sentence See *paragraph.*

transitional expression A word or phrase, such as *thus* or *for example,* that links sentences and shows the relations between them. (See pp. 85–86 for a list.) The error known as a comma splice occurs when two main clauses related by a transitional expression are separated only by a comma. (See pp. 348–49.)

transitive verb A verb that requires a direct object to complete its meaning. (See p. 253.)

trite expressions (clichés) Stale expressions that make writing dull and suggest that the writer is careless or lazy. (See p. 517.)

two-word verb A verb plus a preposition or adverb that affects the meaning of the verb: *jump off, put away, help out.* (See pp. 297–98.)

unity The quality of an effective essay or paragraph in which all parts relate to the central idea and to each other. (See pp. 43 and 73–76.)

URL (uniform resource locator) An address for a Web site or document.

variety Among connected sentences, changes in length, structure, and word order that help readers see the importance and complexity of ideas. (See Chapter 26.)

verb A word or group of words indicating the action or state of being of a subject. The inflection of a verb and the use of helping verbs with it indicate its tense, mood, voice, number, and sometimes person. See separate listings for each aspect and for *predicate.* (See Chapter 14.)

verbals and verbal phrases **Verbals** are verb forms used as adjectives (*swimming children*), adverbs (*designed to succeed*), or nouns (*addicted to running*). The verbals in the preceding examples are a participle, an infinitive, and a gerund, respectively. (See separate entries for each type.) Verbal phrases consist of verbals plus objects or modifiers: *Swimming fast, the children reached the raft. Willem tried to unlatch the gate. Running in the park is his only recreation.* (See pp. 259–61.)

A verbal is a **nonfinite verb**: it cannot serve as the only verb in the predicate of a sentence. For that, it requires a helping verb.

verb forms Verbs have five distinctive forms. The first three are the verb's **principal parts**:

- The **plain form** is the dictionary form: *live, swim.*
- The **past-tense form** adds *-d* or *-ed* to the plain form if the verb is regular: *live, lived.* If the verb is irregular, the plain form changes in some other way, such as *swim, swam.*
- The **past participle** is the same as the past-tense form for regular verbs. For irregular verbs, the past participle may differ (*swum*).
- The **present participle** adds *-ing* to the plain form: *living, swimming.*
- The -s **form** adds *-s* or *-es* to the plain form: *lives, swims.*

verb phrase A verb consisting of a helping verb and a main verb: *has started, will have been invited.* A verb phrase can serve as the predicate of a clause: *The movie has started.*

verb voice The form of a verb that tells whether the sentence subject performs the action or is acted upon. In the active voice the subject acts: *We made the decision.* In the passive voice the subject is acted upon: *The decision was made by us.* (See pp. 307–09.)

voice The sense of oneself projected in one's writing through selection of information, role played in relation to readers, and tone. (See pp. 13–14.)

warrant A term used for *assumption* in argument. See *assumption.*

wiki A Web site that can be contributed to or modified by anyone who registers to use the site.

word order The arrangement of words in a sentence, which plays a part in determining the grammatical relation among words in English.

writing process The activities involved in producing a finished piece of writing. The overlapping stages of the process—developing or planning, drafting, and revising—vary among writers and even for the same writer in different writing situations. (See Chapters 1–3.)

writing situation The unique combination of writer, subject, audience, purpose, and other elements that defines an assignment or occasion and helps direct the writer's choices. (See pp. 4–6.)

Credits

Text

Ali, Agha Shahid. "Postcard from Kashmir" from *The Half-Inch Himalayas.* © by Agha Shahid Ali. Reprinted by permission of Wesleyan University Press.

Catton, Bruce. "A Study in Contrasts" by Bruce Catton, 1956. Copyright © 1956 United States Capitol Historical Society. Reprinted with permission.

Borelli, Deneen. "Global Warming Statists Threaten Our Liberty." Published by Project 21, a program of The National Center for Public Policy Research.

Dyson, Freeman J. From *Disturbing the Universe* by Freeman J. Dyson. Copyright © 1979. Reprinted by permission of Basic Books, a member of The Perseus Books Group.

Hazo, Samuel. *Like a Man Gone Mad: Poems in a New Century* (Syracuse: Syracuse University Press, 2010), iv © Syracuse University Press. Reprinted with permission from the publisher.

McCardell, John M. "Let Them Drink at 18, With a Learner's Permit" from the *New York Times*, May 28, 2012. © John M. McCardell.

Ornstein, Robert, From "A Letter to the Director" by Robert Ornstein, *Human Nature*, August 1978.

Sowell, Thomas. "Student Loans" from *Is Reality Optional? and Other Essays* by Thomas Sowell, 1993. Reprinted by permission of Thomas Sowell and Creators Syndicate, Inc.

Staples, Brent. Excerpt from "Black Men and Public Space" by Brent Staples. *Harper's,* December 1986. Copyright © 1986 by Brent Staples. Reprinted by permission of the author.

Photos and Illustrations

109: Everett Collection. **115 left:** Image reprinted courtesy of BISSELL Homecare, Inc. **115 right:** Courtesy of Electrolux. **119:** Bill Aron/PhotoEdit. **128:** Bill Aron/PhotoEdit. **165:** Courtesy of the Ad Council/Teach.org. **169:** Courtesy of Steve Simon. **170:** UNFPA, The United Nations Population Fund. **178:** Courtesy of the Ad Council/Teach.org. **205:** Courtesy of the Ad Council. **508 top and bottom**: By permission. From *Merriam-Webster's Collegiate® Dictionary,* 11th Edition © 2014 by Merriam-Webster, Inc. (*www.Merriam-Webster.com*). **562 top, middle, bottom:** Images courtesy *www.linccweb.org*. **566 top and bottom:** © 2014 EBSCO Publishing, Inc. All rights reserved. **567:** © 2014 EBSCO Pub-lishing, Inc. All rights reserved. **585 top:** © *Vegetarian Times*. Reprinted with Permission. **585 bottom:** Tim Jackson, "Live Better By Consuming Less? Is there a "Double Dividend" in Sustainable Consumption?", *Journal of Industrial Ecology,* Volume 9, February 8, 2008, 19-36. Copyright © 2008 John Wiley & Sons, Ltd. **587:** © Center for Climate and Energy Solutions (C2ES). All rights reserved. Reprinted by permission. **592:** Courtesy of the American Anthropological Association (*www.aaanet.org*). **650:** © 2014 EBSCO Publishing, Inc. All rights reserved. **654:** *LexisNexis Academic* screen shot reprinted with the permission of LexisNexis, a division of Reed Elsevier Inc.

Index

A

B

D

G

H

N

Q

S

V

Useful Lists and Summaries

Editing Symbols

Boldface numbers and letters refer to chapters and sections of the handbook.

ab	Faulty abbreviation, 35
ad	Misused adjective or adverb, 16
agr	Error in agreement, 15
ap	Apostrophe needed or misused, 30
appr	Inappropriate language, 37
arg	Faulty argument, 8–9
awk	Awkward construction
case	Error in case form, 13
cap	Use capital letter, 33
cit	Missing source citation or error in form of citation, 44–45
coh	Coherence lacking, 2c-4, 4c
con	Be more concise, 39
coord	Coordination needed or faulty, 24a
cs	Comma splice, 18a–b
d	Ineffective diction (word choice), 37–39
des	Ineffective or incorrect document format, 5
det	Error in use of determiner, 16h
dev	Inadequate development, 2, 4d
div	Incorrect word division, 40d
dm	Dangling modifier, 21h
eff	Ineffective sentence(s), 23–26
emph	Emphasis lacking or faulty, 23
exact	Inexact language, 39
fp	Faulty predication, 22b
frag	Sentence fragment, 17
fs	Fused sentence, 18
gram	Error in grammar, 12–16
hyph	Error in use of hyphen, 40d
inc	Incomplete construction, 22c–e
ital	Italicize or underline, 34
k	Awkward construction
lc	Use lowercase (small) letter, 33f
log	Faulty logic, 8g, 9d
mech	Error in mechanics, 33–36
mixed	Mixed construction, 22a–b
mm	Misplaced modifier, 21a–g
mng	Meaning unclear
no cap	Unnecessary capital letter, 33f
no ^,	Comma not needed, 28j
no ¶	No new paragraph needed, 4
num	Error in use of numbers, 36

p	Error in punctuation, 27–32
. ? !	Period, question mark, exclamation point, 27
^,	Comma, 28
;	Semicolon, 29
ˇ'	Apostrophe, 30
" "	Quotation marks, 31
: — ( ) [ ] . . . /	Colon, dash, parentheses, brackets, ellipsis mark, slash, 32
par, ¶	Start new paragraph, 4
¶ *coh*	Paragraph not coherent, 4c
¶ *dev*	Paragraph not developed, 4d
¶ *un*	Paragraph not unified, 4b
pass	Ineffective passive voice, 14k
pn agr	Error in pronoun-antecedent agreement, 15b
ref	Error in pronoun reference, 19
rep	Unnecessary repetition, 39c
rev	Revise or proofread, 3
shift	Inconsistency, 20
sp	Misspelled word, 40
sub	Subordination needed or faulty, 24b
t	Error in verb tense, 14g–h
t seq	Error in tense sequence, 14h
trans	Transition needed, 4a, 4c-6
und	Underline or italicize, 34
usage	See Glossary of Usage, p. 845
var	Vary sentence structure, 26
vb	Error in verb form, 14a–f
vb agr	Error in subject-verb agreement, 15a
w	Wordy, 39
ww	Wrong word, 38b
//	Faulty parallelism, 25
#	Separate with a space
⁀	Close up the space
ℊ	Delete
the (triple underline)	Capitalize, 33
The (slash through T)	Use a small letter, 33
teh (transposition mark)	Transpose letters or words
X	Obvious error
^	Something missing, 22e
??	Document illegible or meaning unclear

CULTURE LANGUAGE Guide

Throughout this handbook, the symbol CULTURE LANGUAGE signals topics for students whose first language or dialect is not standard American English. These topics can be tricky because they arise from rules in standard English that are quite different in other languages and dialects. Many of the topics involve significant cultural assumptions as well.

Whatever your language background, as a college student you are learning the culture of US higher education and the language that is used and shaped by that culture. The process is challenging, even for native speakers of standard American English. It requires not just writing clearly and correctly but also mastering conventions of developing, presenting, and supporting ideas. The challenge is greater if, in addition, you are trying to learn standard American English and are accustomed to other conventions. Several habits can help you succeed:

- **Read.** Besides course assignments, read newspapers, magazines, and books in English. The more you read, the more fluently and accurately you'll write.
- **Write.** Keep a journal in which you practice writing in English every day.
- **Talk and listen.** Take advantage of opportunities to hear and use English.
- **Ask questions.** Your instructors, tutors in the writing lab, and fellow students can clarify assignments and help you identify and solve writing problems.
- **Don't try for perfection.** No one writes perfectly, and the effort to do so can prevent you from expressing yourself fluently. View mistakes not as failures but as opportunities to learn.
- **Revise first; then edit.** Focus on each essay's ideas, support, and organization before attending to grammar and vocabulary. See the revision and editing checklists on pages 53–54 and 62–63.
- **Set editing priorities.** Concentrate first on any errors that interfere with clarity, such as problems with word order or subject-verb agreement.

The following index leads you to text discussions of writing topics that you may need help with. The pages marked * provide exercises for self-testing.